SYSTEMS ANALYSIS AND DESIGN OF REAL-TIME MANAGEMENT INFORMATION SYSTEMS

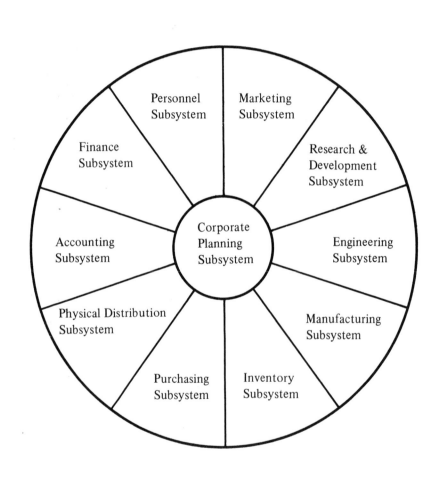

ROBERT J. THIERAUF, Ph.D., C.P.A.

Professor of Management

Chairman, Department of Management
and Information Systems

D.J. O'Conor Memorial Professor
in Business Administration

Xavier University
Cincinnati, Ohio

SYSTEMS ANALYSIS AND DESIGN OF REAL-TIME MANAGEMENT INFORMATION SYSTEMS

PRENTICE-HALL, INC., Englewood Cliffs, New Jersey

Library of Congress Cataloging in Publication Data

Thierauf, Robert J
    Systems analysis and design of real-time management information systems.

    Bibliography: p.
    Includes index.
    1. Management information systems. 2. System analysis. I. Title.
T58.6.T49   658.4'03   74-28368
ISBN 0-13-881219-5

Printed in the United States of America

10 9 8 7 6 5

Prentice-Hall International, Inc., *London*
Prentice-Hall of Australia, Pty. Ltd., *Sydney*
Prentice-Hall of Canada, Ltd., *Toronto*
Prentice-Hall of India Private Limited, *New Delhi*
Prentice-Hall of Japan, Inc., *Tokyo*

CONTENTS

PREFACE

The outpouring of publications on real-time management information systems (MIS) has been unusually large. For the most part, the quality of these publications has left much to be desired. Only recently has worthwhile material on the subject been available. The direction taken in this book is to further the "how-to" knowledge of the academician and the practitioner in the analysis and design of real-time management information systems, particularly those operating in an operations research (OR) or quantitative environment. From this viewpoint, the book is a definitive work on real-time MIS, thereby adding another dimension to the growing body of information available about management information systems.

For the information systems student or journeyman, the purpose of the book is to broaden his expertise in designing real-time management information systems. Rather than talk in general terms, as most books do, about a firm's major subsystems, the text presents a complete real-time management information system in some detail for a progressive manufacturing firm. Subsystems are analyzed, designed, and evaluated for corporate planning, marketing, research and development, engineering, manufacturing, inventory, purchasing, physical distribution, accounting, finance, and personnel functions. Likewise, appropriate management science models are identified and related to each functional area of the firm. Because the book is not burdened with rigorous mathematics, the systems practitioner or student who has little or no knowledge of higher mathematics will experience no difficulty in comprehending the subject matter. The net result of this "nuts and bolts" approach is a comprehensive look at a complete real-time management information system unavailable in any other publication to date.

The text is suitable for an undergraduate or graduate business course covering the fundamentals of information system analysis and design or the fundamentals of management information systems. The material can be used for any time period, i.e., one quarter, two quarters, or one semester. Likewise, the text is designed for use in the field by the management information system specialist who wishes to broaden his perception of integrated and real-time management information systems in a manufacturing firm.

The structure of this book follows a logical sequence for treating comprehensive real-time management information systems. The major areas covered are as follows:

Part I, Introduction to Real-Time Management Information Systems. Chapter 1 briefly surveys various management information systems developed over the years, particularly integrated MIS. The essential characteristics of real-time management information systems are discussed in Chapter 2.

Part II, Feasibility Study Through Systems Implementation of Real-Time Management Information Systems. Chapter 3 concentrates on systems analysis to provide a comprehensive look at a present integrated management information system. In Chapter 4, design considerations for real-time MIS are discussed, with emphasis on designing MIS modules. Equipment selection and systems implementation in a real-time MIS environment are treated in Chapters 5 and 6, respectively.

Part III, Systems Analysis and Design of Real-Time MIS Subsystems. The major subsystems of a complete real-time management information system operating in a manufacturing firm, called the Consumer Products Corporation, are presented in Chapter 7. Chapters 8 through 17 give a thorough analysis (systems analysis) of these MIS subsystems: corporate planning, marketing, research and development, engineering, manufacturing, inventory, purchasing, physical distribution, accounting, finance, and personnel. After exploring real-time MIS design considerations (data base elements, operations research models, and detailed design modules), real-time MIS subsystems and their appropriate modules are designed for the Consumer Products Corporation (systems design).

Part IV, The Future of Management Information Systems. The future thrust of management information systems toward data management and data communications systems is the subject of Chapter 18. Information systems that extend beyond the firm are also explored.

For an undertaking of this magnitude, I want to thank those who read the original manuscript and contributed helpful suggestions. I am deeply indebted to the following individuals and their firms (currently undertaking the implementation of some aspect of real-time management information systems): William F. Carpenter, Procter and Gamble; Richard Curless, Cincinnati Milacron; Michael C. Drewes, Regional Computer Center, Cincinnati; Michael J. Free, Western Electric Company; Thomas R. Gilligan, Cincinnati Bell, Inc.; James Goughenour, Cooper Industries; Edward Hammann, General Electric, Evendale; Richard Hughenburg, Stearns and Foster; Donna Krabbe, Office of Solid Waste Programs, Environmental Protection Agency; G. A. Lasson, Industrial Nucleonics Corporation; David R. Meade, Management Horizon Corporation; F. W. Sweet, Merrell-National Laboratories; William Thiel, Cincinnati Milacron; David Tietsort, Champion International; Claude von den Broeck, Procter and Gamble; and Jacqueline Wyatt, Management Information Division, Department of Public Welfare, State of Ohio. I am also grateful to Michael Hendren of the Honeywell Information Systems, Neil G. Segars of the UNIVAC Division (Sperry Rand Corporation), and Frank B. Smith of the International Business Machines Corporation as well as Charles H. Kriebel of the Carnegie-Mellon University and Daniel J. Couger of the University of Arizona for their constructive comments. Finally, I would like to thank the following professors at Xavier University who offered their assistance: Daniel Geeding, John Niehaus, and J. Michael Thierauf.

ROBERT J. THIERAUF

SYSTEMS ANALYSIS AND DESIGN OF REAL-TIME MANAGEMENT INFORMATION SYSTEMS

part one

INTRODUCTION TO REAL-TIME MANAGEMENT INFORMATION SYSTEMS

SYSTEMS PRIOR TO REAL-TIME MANAGEMENT INFORMATION SYSTEMS

1

An in-depth examination of any business system reveals some type of management information being generated. In a sole proprietorship or a small partnership, the management information system is very simple, with the bulk of the information transmitted orally. As the organization becomes larger and more complex, the information system is more formal and its output probably consists of written records and written reports, manually prepared. The next higher system level may utilize calculators, bookkeeping machines, and punched card equipment to process information for controlling the business. In a still larger firm, a computer or computers of varying speeds and types are employed for handling the desired information. In a very large firm, a large-scale computer system, possibly assisted by other computers, is connected to remote field offices, plants, and headquarters by data communication equipment. At this high level of computer sophistication, the information system operating cost is high, running into the millions of dollars annually.

Within this chapter, the need for computer information systems, the under-

3

lying concepts of information systems, and appropriate information system developments prior to real-time management information systems (MIS) are explored. Emphasis will be placed on custodial accounting, responsibility reporting, integrated data processing, and integrated management information systems. This orderly study of information systems evolution serves to place current and future MIS developments in their proper perspective.

RELATIONSHIP OF SYSTEM TO INFORMATION

Before discussing the need for information systems, it would be helpful to review the meanings of some basic terms—*data, information,* and *system.* The term *data* (plural of datum) is defined as unstructured facts, forming the necessary inputs to an information system. On the other hand, *information* is defined as selected data that represent output from a system and are meaningful to the user of that output. In simple terms, then, the function of the system is the transformation of data to information. As noted in Figure 1-1, a *system* is defined as an ordered set of methods, procedures, and resources designed to facilitate the achievement of an objective or objectives. This very general and simplistic definition also applies to management information systems.

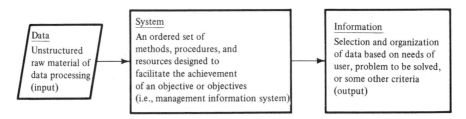

FIGURE 1-1. An effective system (i.e., management information system) stores, organizes, and retrieves the required data to produce meaningful information.

SIGNIFICANCE OF INFORMATION

Information, the logical output of an information system (Figure 1-1), is of vital importance to the managers of a firm to achieve short-, intermediate-, and long-range goals. Management needs a fairly accurate measurement of its sales and cost factors for various time periods. It must maximize its income through higher selling prices and/or larger inventory turnover, and minimize costs of products and services. In short, management wants a combination of selling prices, turnover, costs, and profit per unit that will provide the highest return on invested capital. Given adequate information on these essential facts, management can rely more on deductive and analytical methods than on guesses and intuitive judgment, which it must employ when many of the relevant facts are missing. Many wrong decisions have been the result of insufficient or inadequately processed information.

There is a growing awareness that accurate and timely information is a vital resource of the firm and that an effective information system is a means of providing the needed information. Many top managers are finding that information is a source of competitive power. It gives them the ability to out-maneuver their rivals at critical times, especially when introducing new products. If the data processing system does not have the information necessary for management to handle its operations effectively, an "out-of-control" condition may result and the firm may never recover. An examination of firms that have experienced difficult times over the years will verify this point.

THE NEED FOR INFORMATION SYSTEMS

The need for effective information systems is of paramount concern to the firm now, as well as in the future. Because the firm does not operate in a vacuum, it must coordinate its operations with the business universe. Of prime importance is information about markets in which the firm operates, current knowledge of its customers and competitors, availability of capital, capabilities of available personnel, and knowledge concerning sources of supply. Increasing prices of purchased materials, rising labor costs, and foreign competition signal the need for an information system that describes the firm's economic environment and coordinates the external environment with the internal factors to provide meaningful management information (Figure 1-2).

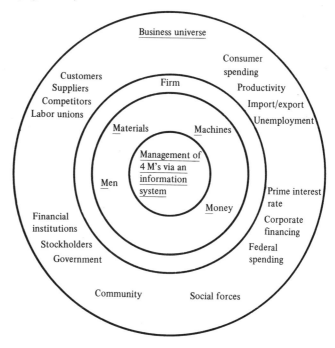

FIGURE 1-2. The relationship of the internal and external factors to the firm's information system.

The information system, in addition to recognizing trends external to the firm, must treat changes that have occurred and will yet occur in the internal business environment. Advancements in the behavioral sciences, continuing developments in management science, and increasing utilization of paperless computer output terminals must be reflected in the design of the information system. Interdepartmental approaches have transcended the traditional, functional lines of business in complex systems. Still other system technology developments have occurred regarding methods, procedures, computer equipment, and data communications equipment. By no means is this listing of internal factors complete, but it does serve to exemplify what is causing the firm's information system to change.

The changes taking place within and outside the firm generally do not stand alone; each advancement tends to effect and overlap another development. As a result, there is a need for management information systems capable of integrating these advances with the needs and capabilities of the firm. It is a generally accepted notion that more frequent and more accurate information leads to better decisions, thereby enhancing operational efficiency.

BASIC COMPUTER DATA PROCESSING SYSTEMS

Management information systems, like many other data processing systems, can be characterized as two basic types:

> batch processing
> real-time processing

Under the first approach, transactions are accumulated into batches and the batches are processed periodically. The transactions in a batch may be in sequential or random order (explained below). Using the on-line real-time processing approach (often abbreviated OLRT), records are stored on line and updated as the transactions occur. The term *on line* refers to the fact that input/output devices, data files, and comparable equipment are connected to a computer in such a way that a transaction may be entered at once or information may be retrieved relatively quickly at any time. The concept of *real time* means that information may be retrieved in sufficient time to control the operating environment. When comparison is made between these two basic computer data processing systems in an MIS environment, the requirements for processing on-line data in real time are found to be considerably different from those used in a batch processing mode.

Peripheral file storage devices attached to computer systems can be of two types:

> sequential access
> direct (random) access

In sequential access files, the data are stored in some predetermined order. Before a record can be read, all preceding records must first be read, as in magnetic tape files. When operating with direct or random access file equipment, it is possible to locate and read any record without having to read others first. On-line computer devices that have this latter ability are magnetic drums, magnetic disks, magnetic strips, and magnetic cards.

BATCH PROCESSING

The batch processing approach to MIS is characterized by the periodic processing of transactions accumulated into batches over a period of time. Normally the accumulated transactions must be sorted into a desired order, and there must generally be a sufficient number of transactions accumulated before it is economically feasible to process the data further. Batch processing is normally associated with records that are maintained on punched cards, magnetic tape, magnetic disk, or bulk core.

Sequential Access Files

In a sequential access system, the entire master file is read and written each time transactions are processed against the master file. This updating procedure requires sorting all input data (i.e., transactions) in the same sequence that is in the master file (Figure 1-3). Batch processing with sequential access file storage is ideally suited for payroll and accounts-payable applications. It usually costs less (per transaction) to process batches than to process each transaction, as it occurs,

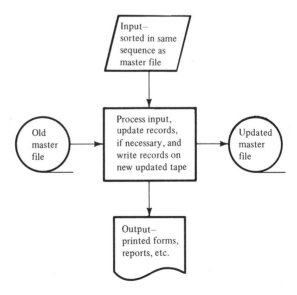

FIGURE 1-3. Batch processing with sequential access file storage—magnetic tape.

immediately on line. However, for other processing that requires timely information for immediate decisions, the real-time processing approach may be justified.

Direct (Random) Access Files

Batch processing is not limited to sequential access files. In a MIS environment, the batch approach can also use direct, or random access file devices, depicted in Figure 1-4. The most common form of random access storage is the magnetic disk, which allows the direct updating of the desired record. For applications involving few transactions relative to the size of the master file, the direct access file approach is widely used. An added advantage of the direct access over the sequential access file approach is that there is no need to sort the input data into a specific sequence. Also, sequential access updating means that new records are created; after updating, both old and new records exist. In direct access, the old record is updated and rewritten to disk.

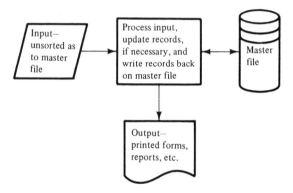

FIGURE 1-4. Batch processing with direct (random) access file storage—magnetic disk.

BATCH PROCESSING MODE

The batch processing mode for management information systems may consist of:

local batch
remote batch

Local batch processing means that data, accumulated into batches on the premises of the firm, are sent directly to the computer center for processing, and reports or other types of printed documents are returned. With remote batch processing, data are sent over a data transmission system to the data center for the desired processing. Reports are returned to the remote site via the same system. Remote batch represents an intermediate stage of data processing, combining remote data transmission with batch processing.

Local Batch

Local batch processing was illustrated in Figures 1-3 and 1-4. The outstanding feature of sequential batch processing (Figure 1-3) is that a new updated master file is written each time data are changed. In contrast, direct (random) access batch processing (Figure 1-4) does not require the computer to write an entire new file. Only those records that are affected by the current transaction being processed are updated while all others are ignored. Neither of these local batch processing methods utilizes data communications equipment because input data are processed on the firm's premises.

Remote Batch

Remote batch processing combines data transmission with batch processing and is used to process data created at points distant from the main computer installation. Based upon a predetermined schedule, data are transferred over the data communications channel to the main computer site in one of two ways: (1) onto a machine-processable medium, such as magnetic tape or disk, for future processing (off line) or (2) into the computer itself for processing (on line). The transfer of output information involves basically the same steps, but in the opposite direction—that is, from the main computer complex to the outlying data processing locations.

When remote batch is used in an *off-line mode,* there are neither enough transactions to warrant a permanent communication with the main computer nor a continuing need for an immediate response. All data are first captured on some machine-processable medium before computer processing at the firm's central facility is initiated. The chief advantage of this off-line approach is the comparatively low data communications cost. The flowchart for off-line remote batch processing is depicted in Figure 1-5.

The other approach to remote batch is an *on-line mode* whereby accumulated data are transferred to and from the computer with little manual intervention. It is also possible to maintain a permanent communication link with the central computer to eliminate the need for establishing a manual connection (via telephone) when a group of data is to be transferred. This type of remote batch is used when there is a large number of transactions to be transferred and/or a large number of locations for transferring data. The flowchart for on-line remote batch processing is illustrated in Figure 1-6. It should be noted that the telephone is optional, depending upon the mode of operation, and that transferred information is stored on secondary storage devices, such as magnetic disk, drum, or tape, for subsequent processing.

REAL-TIME PROCESSING

Of the two basic computer data processing systems, the trend continues toward more real-time processing for management information systems. Transactions and inquiries into the system are processed as they occur, generally in event-occurrence order with respect to each other. Data stored on-line in direct access

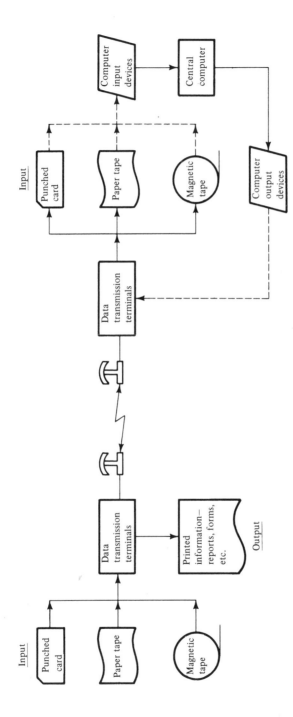

FIGURE 1-5. The transfer of data (input) to and the receipt of information (output) from the central computer facility in an off-line remote batch processing mode.

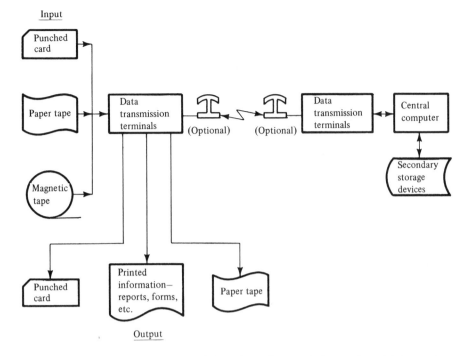

Input

Output

FIGURE 1-6. The transfer of data (input) to and the receipt of information (output) from the central computer facility in an on-line remote batch processing mode.

files are always up to date to reflect the current operating status of the firm, whether it concerns marketing, manufacturing, finance, accounting, personnel, engineering, or some other functional area. However, it should be noted that magnetic tapes are essential for logging messages, taking snapshots before and after master file records in case of data base recovery, and to back-up programs and files periodically in a real-time system.

Direct (Random) Access Files

In an on-line real-time system, transactions and inquiries are processed as they occur. Each transaction originating point has an input/output (I/O) terminal connected to the computer. The terminal is used to send transactions to and to receive responses from the central computer complex. All information is stored in direct access file devices that are available at all times for immediate interrogation (Figure 1-7). Present applications include accounts receivable, airline reservation systems, bank deposit and withdrawal accounting, hotel accounting and reservations systems, law enforcement intelligence systems, patient hospital records, savings and loan deposit accounting, and stock market information.

REAL-TIME PROCESSING MODE

The OLRT processing mode found in management information systems may consist of:

time-sharing
real-time

11

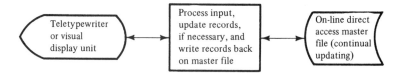

FIGURE 1-7. Real-time processing with direct access file storage.

A time-sharing system is a type of real-time system in that it is a special purpose on-line system designed to serve the problem-solving needs of many users. On the other hand, a real-time management information system can be designed to fulfill the data processing requirements for one firm as opposed to many organizations "sharing" a time-sharing system. The operating environmental characteristics of both systems, then, are quite similar.

Time-Sharing

Time-sharing systems utilize remote keyboard terminals for program development and testing as well as for entering data into and retrieving information from the system. As illustrated in Figure 1-8, secondary storage devices of varying types (direct and sequential) are employed. To service a large number of users, the amount of time available to each incoming program is allocated and controlled by the operating system. The computer controls the input terminals in such a manner

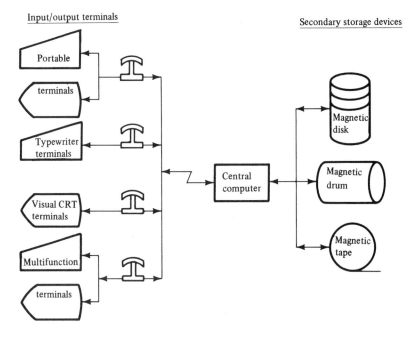

FIGURE 1-8. Time-sharing with input/output terminals plus direct (random) access and sequential access file storage.

that each user feels he has sole access to the computer while, in reality, the computer is servicing many different programs at the same time.

An important advantage of time-sharing, like real-time, is its "conversational mode"—that is, its ability to analyze each line of the program for syntax as the program is being entered. As errors are detected by the computer, they are typed or displayed on the user's terminal for corrective action. In the same manner, data entered via input/output terminals are tested for accuracy or sense before further processing occurs. If errors are detected, they are typed or displayed for appropriate action before processing proceeds.

Real-Time

Real-time systems, especially when they are an integral part of advanced management information systems, must be capable of processing information within short time intervals. There must be a fast conversion (or turnaround) of input to output that has the ability to affect the operation(s) of the current environment.

Real-time systems vary in their capabilities. Most maintain a continuous connection between the many geographically dispersed terminals (commonly called dedicated terminals) and the central computer facility, shown in Figure 1-9. Generally, an input transaction from an on-site or an outlying location triggers

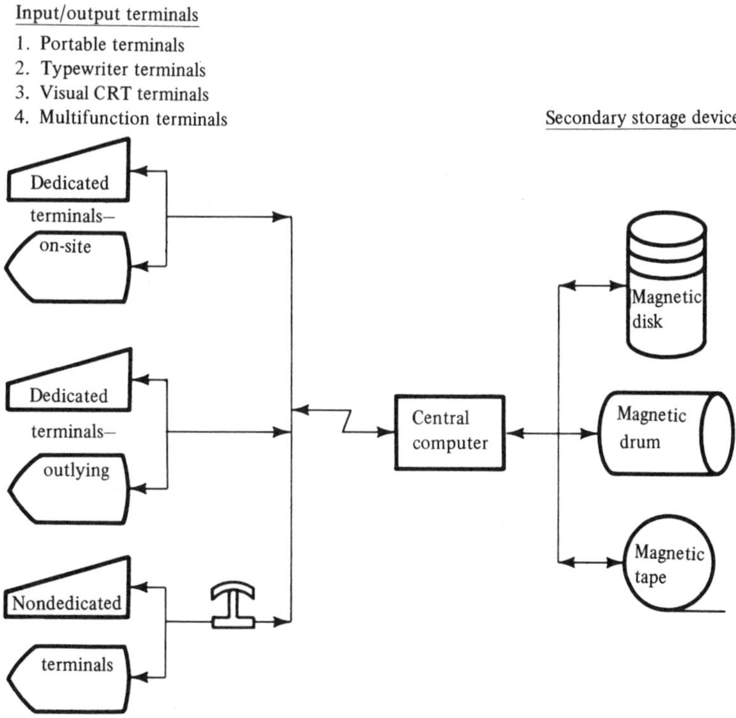

FIGURE 1-9. Real-time processing with input/output terminals, and direct (random) access and sequential access file storage.

immediate processing of the data, with the "answer" being returned in seconds if deemed necessary. Not only is the central computer capable of updating data files (on secondary devices, such as magnetic disks) from input transactions, but it can also route output to another terminal location either immediately or at a near future time.

BASIC COMPUTER DATA PROCESSING SUBSYSTEMS

Going beyond the basic computer data processing systems delineated above for possible approaches to MIS, it is common to dissect a system into a series of related subsystems. As shown in Figure 1-10 (extension of Figure 1-2), a group of basic

FIGURE 1-10. The relationship of the business universe (external factors) to the firm's MIS subsystems (internal functions).

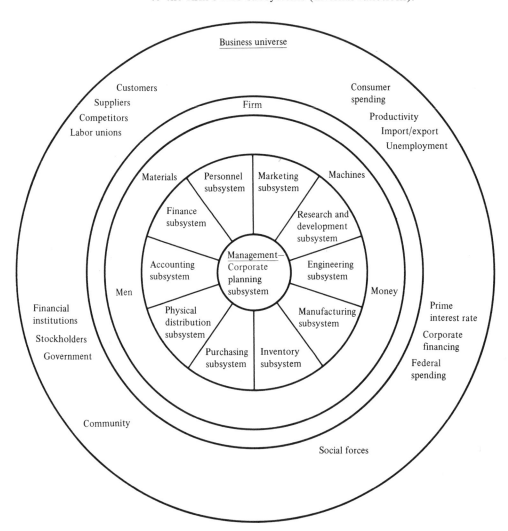

subsystems comprises a management information system, the focal point of which is corporate planning. All other subsystems are secondary to this major function. In addition, there is a hierarchy of subsystems; that is, the parts that form a major system may themselves be systems, and their parts may be systems, and so forth. Thus, each component (activity or function) is called a subsystem which, in turn, interacts with other components (subsystems) to accomplish the firm's objectives.

HIERARCHY OF SUBSYSTEMS

A hierarchy of subsystems for a typical manufacturing firm is illustrated in Figure 1-11. Each of the firm's major functions generates information to assist other subsystems while carrying out its own function. Implied in the activities of these major subsystems are organizational objectives that complement one another. Moving down to the intermediate subsystem for accounting, we have another level of subsystems that interact with each other, represented by connecting lines. (A comparable manufacturing breakdown for this level might include production plans, routings, schedules, inventories, engineering information, quality reports, and manufacturing management reports.) The lowest level for the accounting subsystem, called the minor subsystem, is shown only for payroll. Again, there is an interdependency among the functions to be performed. A system, then, involves relationships among subsystems on a higher, lower, or equal level for the many functions operating within a firm.

Because subsystem interdependencies are not restricted to activities revolving around one function and one level, many subsystems are related to other subsystems on a higher or lower level. Although this is not shown in Figure 1-11, these relationships become quite complex. For example, payroll and personnel functions are frequently integrated into a management information system. In such a system, payroll, formerly performed separately in each plant, is consolidated at one location. By the same token, related functions, such as payroll and personnel, which worked cooperatively but separately from one another, are consolidated by the creation of a single on-line computer file to serve both. Integration of the new employee file allows the firm to prepare payroll checks, test the consequence of payroll changes as labor union negotiations progress, project the number of new employees for the coming year after evaluating the current personnel status, prepare the required governmental reports on the employees, and answer similar requests. In essence, a system can involve relationships among subsystems of both similar and dissimilar functions. These relationships can have either a direct or an indirect bearing on the behavior and performance of other subsystems. Furthermore, they can, and generally do, affect the performance of the overall system.

UNDERLYING CONCEPTS OF COMPUTER DATA PROCESSING SYSTEMS

Now that the basics of computer data processing systems have been explored, it will be helpful to investigate their underlying concepts. An understanding will help the reader obtain an overview of the various approaches to past, present, and future

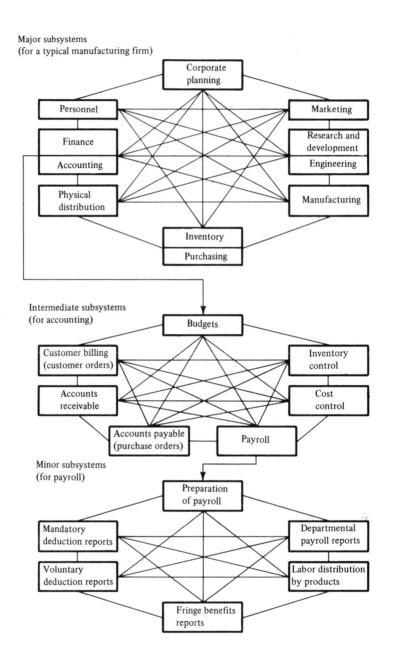

Major subsystems
(for a typical manufacturing firm)

Intermediate subsystems
(for accounting)

Minor subsystems
(for payroll)

FIGURE 1-11. Major, intermediate (accounting), and minor (payroll) sub-systems for a typical manufacturing firm.

16

management information systems. Although many basic concepts have been developed, this discussion will center around the more important ones. These include:

the total systems concept
the management information systems concept
the modular systems concept

As time passes, advanced data processing concepts will supplement the current listing.

THE TOTAL SYSTEMS CONCEPT

The total systems concept of data processing encompasses important interrelationships among the following:

1. the objectives of the firm
2. the organization structure itself
3. the information system
4. the decision-making process

FIGURE 1-12. Important relationships that are an integral part of the total systems concept.

Logically, one cannot design an effective information system without considering the decisions that must be made and where these decisions are located within the framework of the firm. When these important factors are combined in a manner that encompasses and enhances the objectives of the firm, the end result is the "total systems concept." Figure 1-12 illustrates these four interrelationships.

This concept includes being guided by sound policies that are integrated into the many subsystems. Mechanization with advanced equipment is systems-oriented rather than isolated and problem-oriented; thus patchwork is avoided. Furthermore, the total systems concept is oriented toward putting methods and procedures into action as economically as possible, giving timely and correct information to the right personnel, and protecting the integrity of the information by effective internal control. In other words, the total systems concept provides the right information to the right people at the right time in the right format and at the lowest possible cost.

Inputs and Outputs—Automatically Coordinated

The total systems concept, when carried to a high degree of application, tends to be utopian. In this highly idealized state, all the firm's inputs and outputs are automatically coordinated. Markets would be automatically gauged, incoming orders would result in the proper allocations of labor and materials, production and inventories would be appropriately adjusted, and finances would reflect current operations. Management would have to be concerned only with exceptions, reported instantaneously by terminal devices that provide feedback for making the appropriate adjustments. In essence, an elaborate self-adjusting mathematical model would be necessary to oversee such a system. Although such a total systems concept has been unattainable by business in the past, a few scattered applications are tending in this direction; in particular, airline reservation systems and gasoline refinery control systems.

Extension Beyond the Firm

The total systems concept need not be restricted to the confines of the firm. When it encompasses other firms, all important business data are communicated back and forth between suppliers, manufacturers, wholesalers, retailers, customers, and, in some cases, competitors. This total system is much larger than that of one firm at which company boundaries are not too meaningful. Even though this approach has not been implemented, future system designers should consider such possibilities as their ultimate goals. This highest degree of sophistication for the total systems concept involves having all the inputs and outputs for a series of firms automatically coordinated. The demand response of customers will be instantaneously relayed back to raw material suppliers who will forward the goods to the manufacturers for further processing. The completed products, in turn, will be shipped via the proper distribution channels so that sellers will have the right product available at the proper time and place for their customers.

Total Systems Concept Defined

Having presented various ways of viewing the total systems concept, it is rather difficult to state a precise definition with which all data processing personnel will agree. However, the following general definition encompasses the essentials. The *total systems concept* is an approach to data processing that views a firm (and possibly a group of firms) as a single unit. It is composed of many interrelated and interdependent subsystems that function effectively and efficiently together so that accurate and timely information can be produced for management decision making. This leads to the overall optimization of the firm's short-, intermediate-, and long-term objectives and profits at all times.

THE MANAGEMENT INFORMATION SYSTEMS CONCEPT

A most important current systems design concept is one referring to "management information systems," sometimes called management information and control systems (so called because of their output—information and control reports). Although it is possible to have noncomputerized management information systems, this book stresses the computer as an essential part of a MIS. External and internal information is channeled into a single, centralized computer system. In this manner, output will be relevant and effective for management decisions.

Common Data Files

Basically, a computerized management information system captures originating data as close to their source as possible, feeds the data directly or at a later time into the computer system, and permits the system to utilize common data files (a data bank such as magnetic tapes, or a data base, such as magnetic disks) that can service several different outputs (Figure 1-13). In this type of environment, a single piece of information is entered into the data processing system only once. From then on, it is available to serve all processing requirements until its usefulness is exhausted. Under these ideal conditions, adequate and correct information can be presented to managers in a coordinated rather than a segmented manner. Likewise, the information provided is timely. The output of a management information system is report-oriented—an orderly flow of timely information for meeting specific management needs.

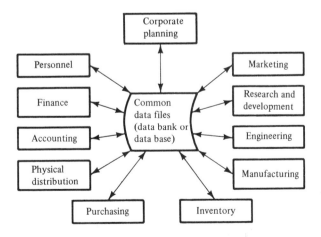

FIGURE 1-13. Common data files (a data bank or a data base)—an essential part of a management information system.

Control Reports

Control reports produced by this system include those necessary to service the basic business functions of the firm. Among these are sales forecasting, shipping and warehousing, finished goods replenishment, production control, materials management, manufacturing cost control, personnel skills and manning control, and management incentives. Other reports include short- and long-range financial and operating budgets, monthly financial and operating statements, and various historical data for short- or long-range planning. Sales and order entry statistics, including sales quotas, salesmen's compensation, and shipping orders, are additional examples of output that provide input to many other subsystems.

An essential part of any management information system is feedback that shows what has happened to the financial plan to date, or what would happen if hypothetical changes were made in the plan. Control reports, then, are concerned with monitoring actual results through feedback in order to determine whether the firm's functions are proceeding according to plans and standards.

Management Information Systems Concept Defined

A management information system can be defined as a collection of subsystems and related program parts or modules that are interconnected to fulfill the information requirements necessary to plan, organize, direct, and control business operations. It is a system for producing and delivering timely information that will support management in accomplishing its specific tasks in an enterprise. Among the many benefits of such a system to the firm are:

more timely information
greater facility to carry out managerial functions
improved decision making
more effective use of manpower and facilities
prompt communication
very little need to re-create data
elimination of peak period volume reports
prompt correction of out-of-control conditions (management by exception)

In addition, an advanced management information system should be computer-based, integrated with all subsystems, accessible through a common data bank or data base, utilize I/O (input-output) terminals on-site and at remote locations, timely through use of communications capability, and interactive between the user and the information available.

For a management information system to qualify as excellent in terms of speed, it should be capable of sending the information to the user within the operational time span in order to aid him in making the right decision or in taking the appropriate action. To qualify as excellent in content, the data should be relevant to the user's needs in terms of the problem under study. Using the criterion of cost, the management information system should compare favorably with alternative methods available and with the benefits mentioned above. These qualifications only highlight the essential considerations for converting to such a system.

THE MODULAR SYSTEMS CONCEPT

As a means of obtaining systems design objectives now and in the future, EDP (electronic data processing or computer) personnel have found it necessary to formulate the "modular systems concept." Under this concept, separate but detailed information system modules are identified. For example, the finance function (major module) can be subdivided into three intermediate modules (cash management, capital budgeting, and sources of funds) which can be further divided into minor and basic modules, as shown in Figure 1-14. The modular systems concept can be defined as a method of breaking down a system and its programs into their lowest-level component parts so that modules can be logically grouped for implementation and ease of making changes.

The advantage of this approach at a very low level is the ability to develop a system, and applications within it, in an orderly and planned fashion. Just as important is the capability to alter individual program modules without the need to reconstruct the entire program and related methods and procedures. This modular-

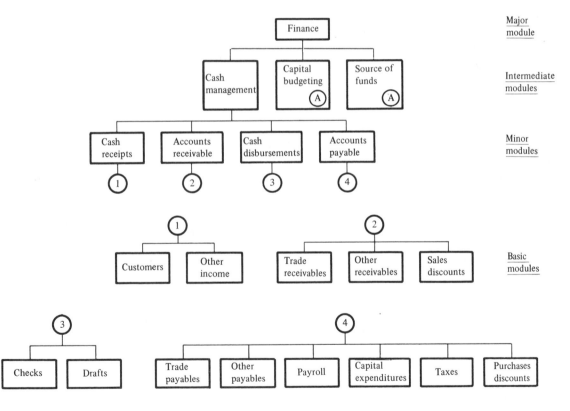

Ⓐ Similar type breakdowns are applicable to these intermediate modules.

FIGURE 1-14. The modular systems concept applied to a firm's finance function.

ity or building block approach allows programming personnel to test each subsection (containing several modules) of the final program separately. It should be noted that the modular concept is compatible with many of the programming (procedure-oriented) languages being offered today.

Modular Programs

The more progressive firms in the field are writing several hundred or even a thousand or more independent computer program modules that are capable of utilizing a common data base. To generate a specific application program, the desired modules are tied together by master control blocks which are written by the programmer for each application. These modules can be integrated into any kind of management information system or storage and retrieval system. Thus, program structuring and data structuring must be flexible, complete, and consistent to permit the use of the modular systems concept.

To utilize this concept effectively, business applications must specify the interacting functions between modules. Otherwise, many program modules will be developed and available but not used in the firm's applications. An important characteristic for this systems concept is to integrate the modules as they are developed. For instance, it would be advisable to integrate the modules required for the various computer programs in corporate planning, especially budgets, with accounting and finance before developing other program modules for marketing, research and development, engineering, manufacturing, inventory, purchasing, physical distribution, and personnel. However, once program modules have been written for all areas of the firm, the task of making major changes in programs will be minimized by modular programming. Only the individual program modules requiring correction need be changed. New program modules can be tested before being inserted into the required program(s).

SYSTEM DEVELOPMENTS DURING THREE COMPUTER DECADES

The current direction of real-time management information systems in business and industry can best be understood by reviewing past approaches to data processing systems. Prior to the first decade of computer use, custodial accounting systems were widely used to produce usable information. Basically, the accent was on producing historical data.

FIRST COMPUTER DECADE (1952-1961)

Attempts to achieve a companywide total system were largely unsuccessful during the first decade of computers. However, the concept came to be an accepted goal for data processing systems of the future. The total systems concept was finally shelved as being completely unrealistic and unobtainable when consideration was given to the hardware and software as well as to the systems design capabilities of the time. In its place, more manageable systems such as responsibility reporting systems and integrated data processing systems were developed.

SECOND COMPUTER DECADE (1962-1971)

In the second computer decade, the integrated data processing systems concept was replaced by integrated management information systems. Toward the end of the decade, real-time management information systems came to the forefront (explained in Chapter Two and thereafter). This change brought the total systems concept back into the limelight. The reason for this is that a real-time MIS approach is a starting point for future advanced systems that encompass the basic tenets of the total systems concept.

THIRD COMPUTER DECADE (1972-1981)

Within the third computer decade, real-time management information systems are expected to achieve their full potential. Their replacement will be a data base management information system, the name of which has been shortened to a "data-managed system."[1] Basically, this advanced management information system has a broader viewpoint of managerial decisions (explained in Chapter Eighteen). Instead of being concerned with lower and middle levels of managerial decision, the data-managed system will accent all levels—from the highest to the lowest—in order to maximize all the available resources within the firm. This systems approach will depend upon sophisticated mathematical modeling of operations research to optimize the firm's overall results. Considerable research and development as well as hard work must be undertaken before the data-managed system can be operational and capable of achieving its goals. The implementation of this advanced MIS system will put the data processing systems designer much closer to realizing the total systems concept. In essence, all input and output will be automatically coordinated by a series of interrelated mathematical models for the firm. The data-managed system can also be extended to several firms whose operations are interrelated.

DATA PROCESSING SYSTEMS PRIOR TO REAL-TIME MIS

Data processing systems prior to real-time management information systems have been backward-looking; that is, they have concentrated on producing various types of historical reports. For the most part, they were not designed to produce relevant information for controlling current operations or future operating conditions. These systems centered around the following:

custodial accounting systems
responsibility reporting systems
integrated data processing systems
integrated management information systems

Each of these systems will be explored along with their respective deficiencies.

[1]P. D. Walker and S. D. Catalano, "Where Do We Go from Here with MIS?" *Computer Decisions,* September, 1969, p. 36.

CUSTODIAL ACCOUNTING SYSTEMS

Information systems, prior to the introduction of computers, were concerned generally with the historical facts of the firm; in particular, the balance sheet and the income statement. There was very little concern for control of operations day by day or hour by hour. The accent was centered on what had occurred and not on what might be done to control current operations. This orientation led to what is now termed "custodial accounting."

The designers of custodial accounting systems were not concerned about the basic needs of management; that is, obtaining feedback of critical information to compare actual performance with a predetermined plan or standard. However, the blame for this "backward-looking" approach should not be placed entirely on the systems designers. In most cases, managers were not trained to utilize such information. Consequently, they did not ask that timely management reports be provided.

Deficiencies of Custodial Accounting

For custodial accounting systems, manual methods, bookkeeping equipment, and punched card equipment were used to process the batched data. The major subsystems were treated as separate entities where record keeping was concerned. There was no attempt to integrate records that might serve several functions at the same time. Not only was there a proliferation of excess records in the firm, but it also generally took a long time to produce historical reports. By the time data were assimilated, it was much too late for meaningful analysis. In total, the custodial accounting system approach had more bad points than good points. It is no wonder that systems designers initially became overly enthusiastic about the total systems concept.

The important characteristics of custodial accounting systems, as well as other approaches to business data processing systems, are summarized in Figure 1-17.

RESPONSIBILITY REPORTING SYSTEMS

An outgrowth of custodial accounting was the preparation of reports on the basis of responsibility assignments. Thus responsibility reporting system accumulates historical data for specific time intervals according to the various activities and levels of responsibility. The basis for determining responsibility is the firm's organization structure. Responsibility reporting is concerned with those activities that are directly controllable and accountable by the individual. A typical set of reports in a responsibility reporting system (manufacturing firm) is found in Figure 1-15.

Under responsibility reporting, each manager, regardless of his level, has the right to participate in the preparation of the budget by which he is evaluated monthly. Although noncontrollable costs are included in the reports distributed, the manager is only held accountable for unfavorable deviations of controllable costs from the predetermined plans or the budget. The budget is constructed from

Organization Structure—
Individual responsible and accountable   Responsibility reports

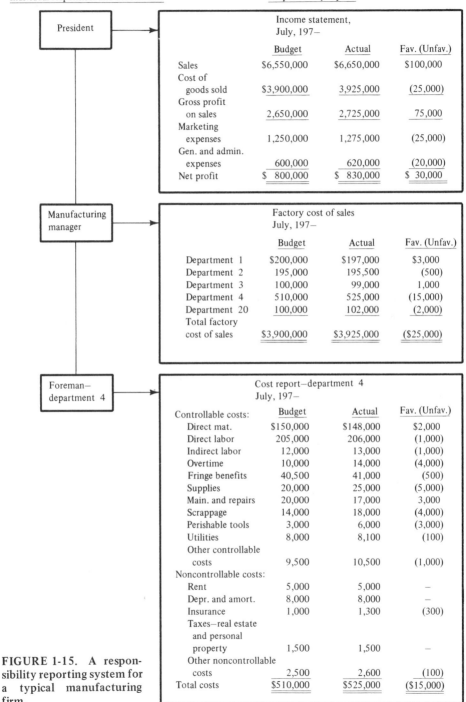

President	Income statement, July, 197—		
	Budget	Actual	Fav. (Unfav.)
Sales	$6,550,000	$6,650,000	$100,000
Cost of goods sold	$3,900,000	3,925,000	(25,000)
Gross profit on sales	2,650,000	2,725,000	75,000
Marketing expenses	1,250,000	1,275,000	(25,000)
Gen. and admin. expenses	600,000	620,000	(20,000)
Net profit	$ 800,000	$ 830,000	$ 30,000

Manufacturing manager	Factory cost of sales July, 197—		
	Budget	Actual	Fav. (Unfav.)
Department 1	$200,000	$197,000	$3,000
Department 2	195,000	195,500	(500)
Department 3	100,000	99,000	1,000
Department 4	510,000	525,000	(15,000)
Department 20	100,000	102,000	(2,000)
Total factory cost of sales	$3,900,000	$3,925,000	($25,000)

Foreman— department 4	Cost report—department 4 July, 197—		
Controllable costs:	Budget	Actual	Fav. (Unfav.)
Direct mat.	$150,000	$148,000	$2,000
Direct labor	205,000	206,000	(1,000)
Indirect labor	12,000	13,000	(1,000)
Overtime	10,000	14,000	(4,000)
Fringe benefits	40,500	41,000	(500)
Supplies	20,000	25,000	(5,000)
Main. and repairs	20,000	17,000	3,000
Scrappage	14,000	18,000	(4,000)
Perishable tools	3,000	6,000	(3,000)
Utilities	8,000	8,100	(100)
Other controllable costs	9,500	10,500	(1,000)
Noncontrollable costs:			
Rent	5,000	5,000	—
Depr. and amort.	8,000	8,000	—
Insurance	1,000	1,300	(300)
Taxes—real estate and personal property	1,500	1,500	—
Other noncontrollable costs	2,500	2,600	(100)
Total costs	$510,000	$525,000	($15,000)

FIGURE 1-15. A responsibility reporting system for a typical manufacturing firm.

the top level of management to the lowest level, that of a foreman, department head, or supervisor. Only in this manner can the individual be held responsible and accountable for costs that he controls directly.

More Timely Reports

The adoption of this type of reporting system required too much time when manual methods and bookkeeping machines were used. Even with punched card equipment, the problem of preparing detailed cards, handling the cards manually, and running off the reports was a time-consuming task. The utilization of a batch processing computer system to perform the required manipulation of data and storage of prior data expedited the preparation of the reports (Figure 1-15). Instead of waiting weeks under an older accounting system, management had reports in hand within a week after the close of a period. With the operations relatively fresh in their minds, they were able to review results sooner.

Improvements of Responsibility Reporting Over Custodial Accounting

The responsibility reporting system was an improvement over the custodial accounting system in several ways. There were more detailed reports and they were on a more timely basis. Also, the various levels of managerial reports show not only what has happened but also who is responsible for unfavorable as well as favorable deviations from the established plans.

INTEGRATED DATA PROCESSING SYSTEMS

An examination of the responsibility reporting approach indicates that it centered primarily around the accounting function. Initial accounting applications were discrete and were processed individually. There were several reasons for this approach. First, computers were regarded as large accounting machines that represented only a further mechanization of the data processing function by the accounting section. For example, first payroll was designed and programmed, followed by accounts receivable, then inventory, and so forth. Second, this piecemeal approach was the result of following the organizational boundaries that have traditionally existed in the firm. Third, these early installations were justified not on the basis of giving management more information and control over their entire operations, but on the basis of the computer's ability to perform accounting jobs faster and more economically. Because of the stress on accounting applications, the electronic data processing system generally became a part of the accounting department within its existing framework.

As time passed, systems designers recognized that operations go considerably beyond the accounting aspects. They saw the great need for a system that integrates all subsystems of the firm's operations that can be logically interrelated. The system must integrate men, machines, money, materials, and management in conformity with the firm's objectives, policies, methods, and procedures. The net result is a unified system, commonly known as an "integrated data processing system."

In addition to a network of related subsystems developed according to an integrated scheme for carrying out the firm's major functions, integrated data processing systems have other distinguishing characteristics, such as single data entry for multiple uses and responsiveness to changes or increased flexibility.

Single Data Entry for Multiple Uses

Data entered into the system transcends organizational boundaries—that is, data stored in a machine-processable form—can be used by many functional areas of the firm. Records that are kept for one purpose may actually have several other uses. Related elements in different processing activities are combined into common coordinated procedures and work flows. This is made possible by having the whole business system interrelated. For example, bills of materials which are prepared by the engineering department can be utilized as is or manipulated by manufacturing, purchasing, accounting, and other appropriate departments. The manufacturing section can determine material requirements from the bills of materials which, in turn, can be the basis for ordering from vendors, initiating production orders, and pricing the final products.

Responsiveness to Changes—Flexibility

An integrated information system does not require a computer. However, a computer can facilitate meeting the essential requirements of such a system. This is particularly true because a computerized system can respond to external influences and conditions as well as to internal requirements. Activities, methods, procedures, responsibilities, and similar items are continually changing. It is easier to effect changes with computer systems because many of these can be programmed without the need for retraining personnel with new equipment and procedures. Thus, flexibility is generally an important part of an integrated data processing system.

Deficiencies of Integrated Data Processing Systems

The integration of many data processing activities reduced the duplication of data and files as well as improving the coordination of the firm's major functions with one another. However, the integration of major functional activities does not, in itself, guarantee optimum results. Although historical output reports were prepared for various operating levels, output for controlling current operations was needed. In essence, reports that could better facilitate the managerial functions were lacking in integrated data processing systems.

INTEGRATED MANAGEMENT INFORMATION SYSTEMS

Several of the deficiencies of integrated data processing systems were remedied by improving upon its basic concepts. Among the improvements was the preparation of output reports for all management levels of past operations so that the system could take over routine decision making. The net result of this system upgrading was an "integrated management information system."

Reports to Assist Management

Formerly, the primary interest of a data processing system was developing financial statements. When an integrated MIS is installed, its major purpose is the production of reports that will assist management. The periodic financial reports are secondary, representing a by-product of the information processed to assist in controlling current operations. From this standpoint, data processing records can serve several uses, thereby reducing costs of obtaining essential managerial reports.

Performance of Routine Decision Making

A true integrated management information system involves more than a mechanical linking together of various functions of the firm. It aids management by taking over routine decision making. If a manager can define his decision criteria, they can be computerized. Thus, management can concentrate its efforts on those areas that are not routine.

Major Characteristics of Integrated MIS

An integrated management information system is a network of related subsystems, integrated to perform the functional activities of a firm. Its essentials include producing meaningful output for management and taking over routine decision making. Activities that are common to all departments are stored in a data file or data bank. Transactions that affect more than one functional area are captured but once and processed in a manner appropriate for all users of the information. It is, thereby, a considerable improvement over prior systems.

Integrated MIS Illustrated

The introduction of a customer order creates an open order file that forms the basis for preparing invoices and for updating the accounts-receivable file at a later time. The customer order also affects the raw material orders, manpower scheduling, production scheduling, finished goods inventory, shipping orders, sales commissions, and marketing forecasts. Incoming orders, through their effect on inventory levels, may trigger an automatic computer reordering subroutine through the issuance of a purchase order. (The reorder quantity is based on reorder levels and quantities determined by mathematical formulas designed as part of the system.) The purchase orders, in turn, create a liability, requiring payment to vendors. In such a system, the operations aspects of order entry, billing, accounts receivable, inventory control, purchasing, and accounts payable are interwoven. This approach is illustrated in Figure 1-16.

In addition to illustrating the foregoing parts of this integrated management information system, Figure 1-16 shows data input (from major business functions) being sent to a computer system on some predetermined periodic basis. Inputs in previous periods have resulted in master magnetic tape files of data relating to customers, employees, inventories, and all other business phases accumulated from previous processing cycles. As current data are processed by the computer system, the appropriate master magnetic tape files are updated. From these, documents, forms, and reports are prepared automatically. The kinds and number of control and information reports generated from the basic data are dictated by the needs of management and the capabilities of the equipment.

Although the preceding discussion has centered around sequential access files, integrated MIS can also employ random access files. The reader is reminded that random access files were not illustrated in Figure 1-16.

Deficiencies of Integrated MIS and Prior Systems

Even though the integrated management information system rectified the problem of being accounting-oriented and is an information system that provides feedback in the form of reports through its various subsystems, it is still deficient in one important respect. Data must be accumulated for a period of time before processing is feasible. Whether sequential or random access files are utilized, there is still the problem of time lag. For this reason all prior systems, whether they are custodial accounting, responsibility reporting, integrated data processing, or integrated management information systems, are called "backward-looking control systems." The methods, procedures, and equipment look to past history before reports are produced for feedback. What is needed is a "forward-looking control system"—one that looks to the present and future. Such an approach to data processing is found in a "real-time management information system."

The foregoing data processing systems prior to real-time management information systems are summarized in Figure 1-17. Their important characteristics are set forth for comparative purposes.

SUMMARY

Several different approaches to data processing systems have been designed by systems analysts for managerial use. Before the dawn of the computer age, management was fact-minded rather than information-oriented; accounting-oriented in terms of reports rather than toward information for controlling all of the firm's basic business functions. It dealt with today's problems in the light of yesterday's results. This approach, represented by the custodial accounting system, was appropriate for the times. The structure of the firm and its markets was static and changes came gradually. As a result, today's problems were not too different from yesterday's. With the arrival of the computer, management found it could produce many accounting reports for a more comprehensive approach. This led to the development of a responsibility reporting system that was capable of producing accounting-oriented reports for all levels of management.

These accounting-oriented approaches satisfied management during the first generation of computers. The dynamics of the ever-changing business world, the

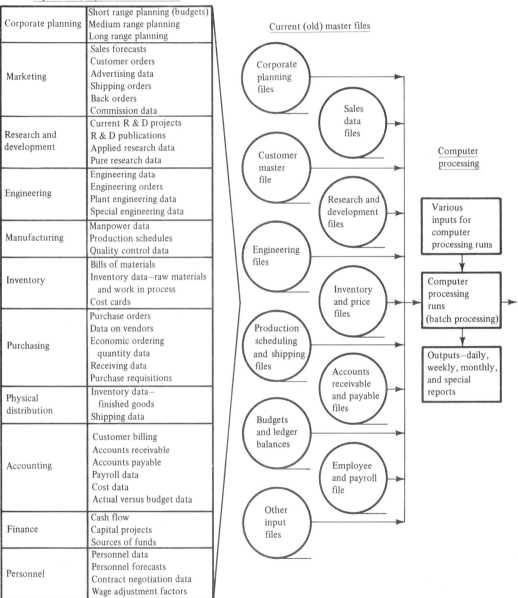

Inputs from major business functions

Corporate planning	Short range planning (budgets) Medium range planning Long range planning
Marketing	Sales forecasts Customer orders Advertising data Shipping orders Back orders Commission data
Research and development	Current R & D projects R & D publications Applied research data Pure research data
Engineering	Engineering data Engineering orders Plant engineering data Special engineering data
Manufacturing	Manpower data Production schedules Quality control data
Inventory	Bills of materials Inventory data—raw materials and work in process Cost cards
Purchasing	Purchase orders Data on vendors Economic ordering quantity data Receiving data Purchase requisitions
Physical distribution	Inventory data— finished goods Shipping data
Accounting	Customer billing Accounts receivable Accounts payable Payroll data Cost data Actual versus budget data
Finance	Cash flow Capital projects Sources of funds
Personnel	Personnel data Personnel forecasts Contract negotiation data Wage adjustment factors

Current (old) master files

Corporate planning files

Sales data files

Customer master file

Research and development files

Engineering files

Inventory and price files

Production scheduling and shipping files

Accounts receivable and payable files

Budgets and ledger balances

Employee and payroll file

Other input files

Computer processing

Various inputs for computer processing runs

Computer processing runs (batch processing)

Outputs—daily, weekly, monthly, and special reports

FIGURE 1-16. Integrated management information system for a typical manufacturing firm—data stored on magnetic tapes can be used for more than one report.

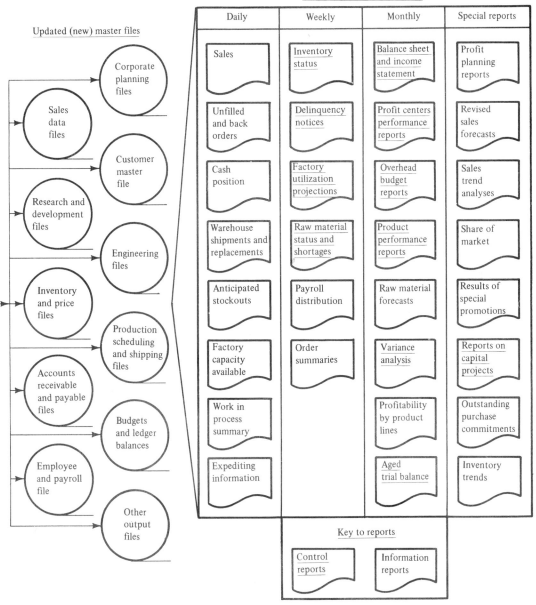

Updated (new) master files

Outputs—management reports

Daily	Weekly	Monthly	Special reports
Sales	Inventory status	Balance sheet and income statement	Profit planning reports
Unfilled and back orders	Delinquency notices	Profit centers performance reports	Revised sales forecasts
Cash position	Factory utilization projections	Overhead budget reports	Sales trend analyses
Warehouse shipments and replacements	Raw material status and shortages	Product performance reports	Share of market
Anticipated stockouts	Payroll distribution	Raw material forecasts	Results of special promotions
Factory capacity available	Order summaries	Variance analysis	Reports on capital projects
Work in process summary		Profitability by product lines	Outstanding purchase commitments
Expediting information		Aged trial balance	Inventory trends

Corporate planning files

Sales data files

Customer master file

Research and development files

Engineering files

Inventory and price files

Production scheduling and shipping files

Accounts receivable and payable files

Budgets and ledger balances

Employee and payroll file

Other output files

Key to reports

Control reports

Information reports

31

Important Characteristics of Data Processing Systems	Custodial Accounting System	Responsibility Reporting System	Integrated Data Processing System	Integrated Management Information System
Type of System	Backward-looking control system and subsystems	→	→	→
Reports Prepared	Historical output reports for the firm	Historical output reports on a responsibility reporting basis	Historical output reports to various operating levels	Output reports directed to all levels of management for past operations
Exception Reporting	Very few accounting exception reports	Accounting exception reports	Accounting and other exception reports	Management exception reports
Information Orientation	Output-oriented	→	→	→
Processing Mode	Batch processing	→	→	→
Data Elements	Primarily accounting data	Common files →	Common files	Common data bank
Type of Files	Sequential access file storage	→	→	Sequential and random access file storage
Mathematical Models	—	—	—	Limited use of standard operations research models

→ Denotes continued use and improvement.

FIGURE 1-17. Important characteristics of data processing systems prior to real-time management information systems.

volume and complexity of producing needed managerial information, and the recognition of the computer's potential by personnel in the data processing field provided the initial thrust for better systems. Simultaneously, management began to realize that the information potential of the computer had not been fully exploited. Based on these initial developments, integrated data processing systems were developed and were further refined into integrated management information systems. These systems and prior ones were backward-looking and generally batch-processing oriented. The next systems development, currently in vogue, is the real-time management information system. the subject matter for most of the book.

QUESTIONS

1. Define the following terms:
   a. information
   b. system
   c. subsystem
   d. data bank
   e. total systems concept
   f. MIS concept
   g. modular systems concept
   h. management by exception

2. a. What are the two basic types of computer systems? Explain.

   b. What types of files are employed for each basic type?

3. Differentiate between real-time processing and time-sharing.

4. Explain what is meant by a hierarchy of subsystems within any data processing system.

5. a. Distinguish between a custodial accounting system and a responsibility reporting system.

   b. How does a responsibility reporting system effect better control over a custodial accounting system for a typical firm?

6. a. What are the essential differences between an integrated data processing system and an integrated management information system?

   b. In what ways is integrated MIS better than integrated DP from a management point of view?

7. a. What is meant by a backward-looking control system?

   b. What systems are of this type?

8. a. How much influence did the total systems concept have on integrated management information systems? Explain.

   b. How much influence did the modular systems concept have on integrated management information systems? Explain.

9. What caused the development of management information systems? Explain.

REFERENCES

Boutell, W. S., *Computer-Oriented Business Systems.* Englewood Cliffs, N.J.: Prentice-Hall, Inc., 1973, Chapter 14.

Brooker, W. M. A. "The Total Systems Myth," *Systems and Procedures Journal,* July-August, 1965.

Caruth, D. L., "How Will Total Systems Affect the Corporation?" *Datamation,* February, 1969.

Karp, W., "Management in the Computer Age," *Data Management,* December, 1970.

Martin, J., *Design of Real-Time Computer Systems.* Englewood Cliffs, N.J.: Prentice-Hall, Inc., 1967, Chaps. 1, 2, 3.

O'Haren, P., "Total Systems: Operating Objective or Planning Structure," *Journal of Systems Management,* November, 1970.

Prince, T. R., *Information for Management Planning and Control.* Homewood, Ill.: Richard D. Irwin, Inc., 1970, Chapter 5.

Rothstein, M. F., *Guide to the Design of Real-Time Systems.* New York: John Wiley & Sons, Inc., 1970, Chapter 1.

Sage, D. M., "Information Systems: A Brief Look Into History," *Datamation,* November, 1968.

Smith, A. W., "Toward A Systems Theory of the Firm," *Journal of Systems Management,* February, 1971.

Swanson, E. B., "Management Information Systems: Appreciation and Involvement," *Management Science,* October, 1974.

Walker, P. D., and Catalano, S. D., "Where Do We Go from Here With MIS?" *Computer Decisions,* September, 1969.

Withington, F. G., "Five Generations of Computers," *Harvard Business Review,* July-August, 1974.

REAL-TIME
MANAGEMENT INFORMATION SYSTEMS

2

Real-time management information systems, rapidly becoming "paperless" business systems, are currently the most sophisticated computer systems available that respond to managerial needs. The evolution of this systems technology is in response to managerial needs for specific information at a particular time. In place of hard copy output, display terminals are being used. Some examples are airline reservation systems, on-line banking systems, on-line cash registers, on-line machine tools, and real-time data entry systems.

The progress of important on-line real-time systems from the development of the SAGE and SABRE systems to the present mode is detailed within this chapter. Basically, the chapter discusses the essential characteristics of a real-time management information system, in particular, the common data base. These essential elements form the basis for defining the subject matter of the book. In addition, the principal mathematical models of operations research are detailed in the chapter's Appendix.

SAGE AND SABRE SYSTEMS

The SAGE and SABRE systems, forerunners of real-time management information systems, enabled users to assess their environment with an effectiveness previously not possible. By supplying facts "on-line" (as they were born) and in "real-time" (promptly enough to affect the occurrence of environmental events as they took place), SABRE and SAGE gave users information that was ample and relevant for past, present, and future operating conditions.

SAGE

SAGE (Semi-Automatic Ground Environment) actually means the semi-automatic control of the basic national defense environment in which the Air Defense Command operates. The system was designed to protect the United States against surprise air attacks. It performs its job with a network of radar-fed computers that continuously analyze air space around the country. All airborne objects approaching the United States are tracked instantly so that appropriate defensive actions, if any, can be initiated. M.I.T.'s Lincoln Laboratories, working with IBM and Burroughs, took seven years to develop SAGE to the point where the first of its sixteen centers was completed in 1958. The System Development Corporation of Santa Monica, California, spent no fewer than 1,800 man-years writing SAGE's original programs.

One important lesson learned from SAGE, aside from the fact that it puts the information on-line in real time, is how to manage both man and machine. SAGE matches the two easily, allowing the computer to help rather than take over. The computer, when it discovers something suspicious in our airspace, notifies human monitors, who check with FAA and other authorities. If necessary, the monitors notify the weapons director, who decides whether to send interceptor planes or missiles. Although the computer itself can decide what and how many to send up and from what base, the weapons director usually asks the SAGE system for several alternatives, from which he picks the best. Once a plane has taken off, the computer can guide it to its interception and back. All the human pilot need do is to take off, turn on his automatic pilot and gunsight, and land his craft. Also, the pilot can and does override the computer, if necessary.

SAGE has taught the data processing industry more about computer simulation than any other previous installation. Although no real attack has ever occurred, the SAGE staff keeps improving its ability by simulating attacks in real time. In the command and control room, the generals sit in a semicircle facing a huge luminous screen on which the computer displays the game in progress. They command the computer to deliver relevant information, to make calculations, and to compute alternative courses. Finally, they analyze their mistakes in order to improve future performance.

SABRE

SABRE (originally spelled SABER for Semi-Automatic Business Environment Research), diagrammed in Figure 2-1, is American Airlines' $30-million real-time

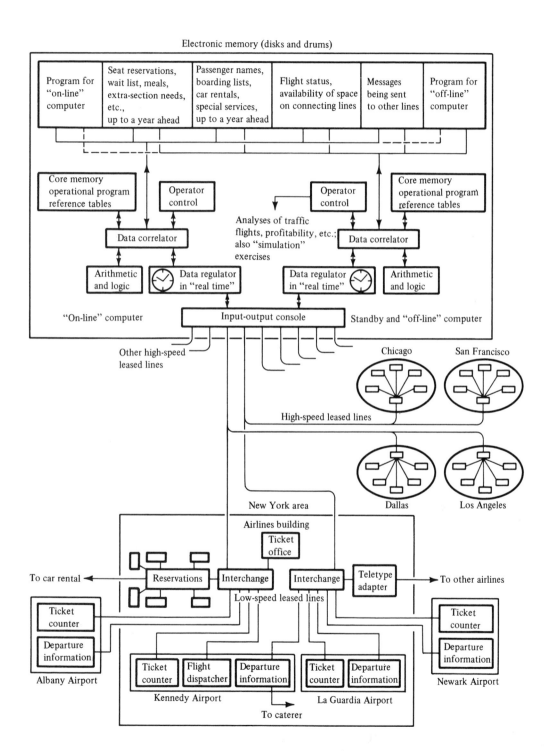

FIGURE 2-1. American Airlines SABRE (real-time) system.

seat-reservation system. Without SAGE, however, the SABRE system would not have been developed as soon as it was. IBM, while it was still working on SAGE, collaborated with American Airlines to research seat inventory problems. As a result, more than eighty different steps or actions are involved in making a reservation via the SABRE system; the specifications for its programs fill five thick volumes and the system contains more than a million instructions. For IBM, as well as for American Airlines, the time was well spent, because priceless knowledge about real-time systems was acquired.

The most important and difficult management problem in running an airline is not flying the planes, but handling the inventory of seats. The problem worsens as traffic increases. Not only has the cost of handling each customer's request for space risen faster than revenues, but the difficulty in keeping up the occupancy rate or "load factor" has increased. Unless a certain percentage of its seats are occupied by flight time, the plane flies at a loss; and the difference between profit and loss is very small—often no more than the difference between a load factor of 50 and 55 percent. But making money is not a simple matter of selling a few more seats on each flight. Approximately 40 percent of American Airlines' traffic is on flights that are technically sold out twenty-four hours before departure, although actually they are rarely sold out. For various reasons, including "no-shows," planes are fortunate to depart 50 percent full. Raising that load percentage makes an enormous difference in the company's final profit. If anybody cancels a seat anywhere on the system, the company ideally should be able to offer it a second later to someone else anywhere on the system. This ability, among other things, is what SABRE is capable of providing.

SABRE Mode of Operation

The original SABRE system (Figure 2-1), which became operational in 1964 and which has since been revamped, is interrogated by many user terminals scattered throughout the country. The sales agent asks for space on a particular flight and date by depressing the proper keys on a typewriter terminal. If a certain light on the terminal flashes, the agent knows space is available as of that instant, and he has a priority over anyone else at any one of the other sales centers on line. (If another light flashes, the flight is sold out.) By pressing an "X" button, he reserves the seat. But the transaction is not closed until the agent types a list of data about the customer. As these data are punched or typed, they are transmitted by regular leased telephone lines to a nearby *interchange* (buffer). This holds incoming data for a matter of microseconds until a complete message is ready for transmission to the SABRE center in Westchester County, New York.

Meanwhile back at SABRE's headquarters, the *input/output console* "polls" each interchange station for messages on a split-second basis. The data travel from interchange to console over special high-speed AT&T lines. The console then routes it to one of the two IBM 7090 computers that is on line while the standby, ready to cut in instantly if needed, goes about special problems fed in by the local operator. At the *data regulator,* incoming bits and characters are checked for sense and accuracy, and then assembled into six-character (thirty-six bit) words for computer use.

The rest of the boxes shown in Figure 2-1 are schematic elements of the original computer operation. The *data correlator* pulls together all the computer operations and sets one element working for another as necessary. The *arithmetic and logic section* provides any computation required before or after information passes into the memory units. The *core memory* holds the programs that direct the entire operation. The data on the passenger are routed to the disk and drum storage of the *electronic memory,* available for split-second retrieval. Here also are recorded the logical consequences of the reservation action steps.

The SABRE system has now been redesigned and rewritten for newer IBM hardware. The company has installed CRT (cathode ray tube) input/output units to replace teleprinters at agent stations. At the hub of the SABRE system (now in Tulsa, Oklahoma) are IBM large-scale computers. Similar improvements have been effected in SABRE's operating software. Also, American Airlines has developed An Analytical Information Management System.[1]

CHARACTERISTICS OF REAL-TIME
MANAGEMENT INFORMATION SYSTEMS

The SAGE and SABRE systems provided the necessary thrust for continuing developments of on-line real-time systems. The net result of these innovations is today's real-time MIS, whose characteristics are depicted in Figure 2-2. Each of these will be explained subsequently. In addition, these characteristics are used in developing a real-time management information system for a typical manufacturing firm, called the Consumer Products Corporation (the subject matter for Chapters Seven through Seventeen).

1. ESTABLISHMENT OF REAL-TIME MIS OBJECTIVES

To initiate the installation of a real-time MIS, there must be weaknesses in the present data processing system, desire to replace the present system, or some other valid reason. Whatever rationale is given, an executive committee from top management must be established which, in turn, must select and give direction to a MIS committee. The executive committee must establish challenging standards of performance for the MIS committee to achieve. Basically, the function of both committees is to determine desirable real-time MIS objectives (short-range to long-range) as well as other important related matters.

Typical objectives for initiating a real-time MIS include more timely decision information, improved service to customers, and greater utilization of mathematical models for more man/machine interaction. The selection of many desired objectives usually results in the need for an advanced computer system more costly than the present one. No matter what objectives are established through the joint effort of the executive committee and the MIS committee, they become the basis for evalu-

---

[1]Janet M. Taplin, "AAIMS: American Airlines Answers the What Ifs," *Infosystems,* February, 1973.

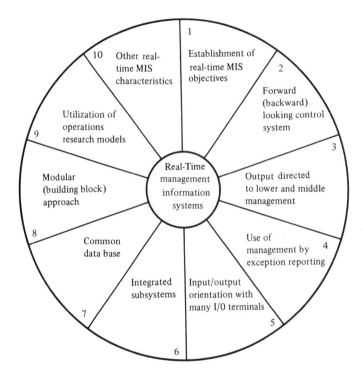

FIGURE 2-2. Essential characteristics of real-time management information systems.

ating factors involved in the feasibility or nonfeasibility of implementing a real-time MIS. More will be said about the committees and their relationships to objectives in the next chapter.

2. FORWARD- AND BACKWARD-LOOKING CONTROL SYSTEM

An essential characteristic of a real-time MIS is that it is a forward-looking control system—that is, it maintains data files on line that are available to the central processing unit when needed for controlling present and future operations. The firm's data elements are updated as events occur and can be interrogated from remote I/O terminals. Company personnel receive responses from the system in time to satisfy their own real-time environmental requirements. Response time may range from a fraction of a second to minutes, hours, and days, depending on the attendant circumstances.

To illustrate the forward-looking concept, suppose the production planning department has developed a computerized on-line daily scheduler. Because all variable manufacturing data are entered as they occur, the on-line data base for this function as well as others is always up to date. Before the start of each day, the computerized scheduler simulates the activities of the factory for that day. Knowing what has occurred during the previous day—that is, which jobs are backed up or behind schedule and where production bottlenecks are occurring—this manufacturing simulation model can determine what will happen as the day begins, and thereby alert the foremen and plant supervisor about critical areas that need immediate attention. A response, then, has been fed back in sufficient time to control the upcoming manufacturing activities.

Real-time MIS is not only forward-looking but also looks to the past for reporting historical information, which is of great importance for external reporting, in particular, to the firm's stockholders and various governmental taxing agencies. To design an advanced MIS system without the backward-looking aspects can be detrimental to the firm.

3. OUTPUT DIRECTED TO LOWER AND MIDDLE MANAGEMENT

Designing a structured data base for accommodating the various levels of management is a formidable task for the systems designers. Currently, they are concentrating on satisfying the needs of lower and middle management for organizing, directing, and controlling the firm's activities around established operational plans. Sample outputs found in real-time MIS for a typical manufacturing firm are found in Figure 2-3.

Because the output of a real-time MIS is directed toward lower and middle management, it is beneficial to relate the managerial levels to the following types of information:

> operational
> tactical
> strategic

Generally, lower management is concerned with operational information while tactical and strategic information are applicable to middle and top management respectively. The type of information-supplied has to do with the relative position of the manager in the company's hierarchy and the activities with which the information is concerned—the internal environment of the organization and the external environment in which the firm operates. It is a generally recognized fact that internal information should be increasingly summarized as the level of management for which it is prepared rises in the hierarchical structure, with top management receiving the most comprehensive reports. The rationale for this is that internal data are control-oriented, and the lower echelons of management are the most control-oriented; top management, however, is more planning-oriented.

Information concerning the external environment of the firm should be summarized exactly opposite to that of the internal environment. That is, because the upper levels of management are more planning-oriented and because planning necessitates more information concerning the organization's external environment, information concerning the external environment should be increasingly summarized and selective as the position of the receiver decreases in the managerial hierarchy.

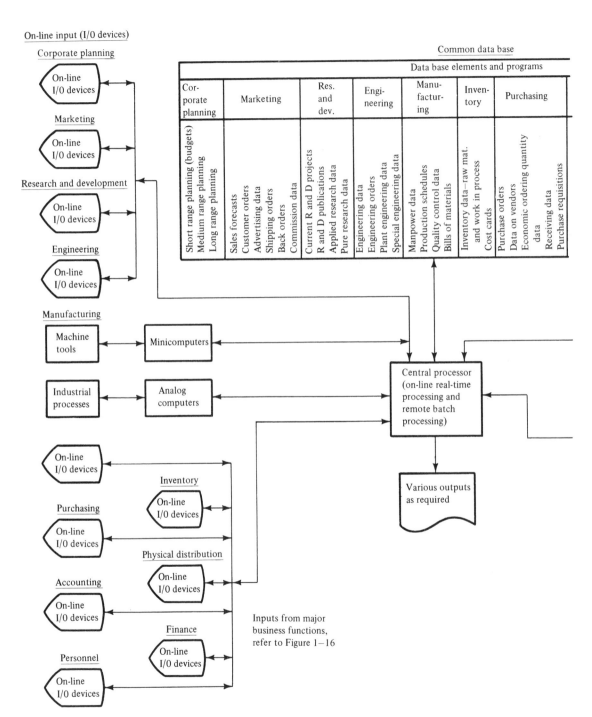

FIGURE 2-3. Real-time management information system for a typical manufacturing firm—data base elements stored on line can be used for more than one report.

Physical distribution	Accounting	Finance	Personnel
Inventory data—finished goods / Shipping data	Customer billing / Accounts receivable / Accounts payable / Payroll data / Cost data / Actual versus budget data	Cash flow / Capital projects / Source of funds	Personnel data / Personnel forecasts / Contract negotiation data / Wage adjustment factors

Input/output

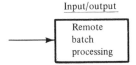

Remote
batch
processing

Input/output

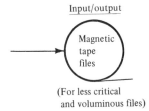

Magnetic
tape
files

(For less critical
and voluminous files)

Outputs—management
reports, refer to
Figure 1–16

On-line output—typed or visual (I/0 devices)

Corporate planning
Budget data
Short range planning data
Medium range planning data
Long range planning data

Marketing
Customer order status
Back order status
Finished products available
    for sale

Research and development
Research references for
    review
Graphic displays
Pure and applied reasearch
    results

Engineering
Plotted engineering data
Results of mathematical
    calculations
New engineering designs

Manufacturing
Production order status
Inventory levels on
    specific items
Production control data

Purchasing
Purchase order status
Results of vendor
    comparison

Finance
Cash flow status
Capital projects data
Cost of capital data

Personnel
New personnel needs
Payroll forecasts
Available personnel
    within to fill new
    job openings

Inventory
Shipments received
    over quantities
    ordered
Location of stock items
Items available
    in stock

Physical distribution
Routing information
Data on location of
    goods to be shipped
Shipping schedule
    data

Accounting
Net profit to date
Expense accounts
    exceeding budget
Accounts receivable
    status on individual
    accounts
Credit check
Accounts payable
    by vendors
Overdue invoices

Thus, time spent in planning and controlling for lower, middle, and top management complement one another in a MIS environment, as indicated in Figure 2-4.

Operational Information

Operational information, being at the lowest level, is concerned with structured and repetitive activities that are measurable in achieving specific results. It allows line managers, such as plant foremen and department heads, to measure performance against predetermined results, including standards and budgeted figures. Similarly, operational information allows lower management to comment on how operating standards and policies can be improved to assist day by day operations. The feedback of essential information from this low level keeps higher levels of management aware of unfavorable as well as favorable results. Illustrated in Figure 2-5 is operational information employed to control the major subsystems of a typical manufacturing firm.

Tactical Information

Tactical information that covers relatively short time periods (not greater than twelve months) is used by middle management to implement strategic plans at functional levels. As with operational information, tactical operational data are used by a large number of people. Examples are a functional budget report comparing actual to estimated amounts, a production report that evaluates assembly operations, and a vendor performance evaluation report that rates overall vendor performance. Typical tactical information generated in a manufacturing firm is shown in Figure 2-6.

Strategic Information

Strategic information is used primarily by top management and their staff to cover a long time span—generally one to five years. This type of information is used for planning purposes and for analysis of problem areas to discover the underlying reasons for specific problems or situations. In many cases, the objective of strategic information is to find answers to the question *why* rather than *what* or *where*. Examples are found in Figure 2-7.

Before strategic information can be forthcoming, planning must be undertaken. Strategic planning concerns itself with the establishment of objectives and policies that will govern the acquisition, use, and disposition of the resources needed to achieve those objectives. It is normally conducted at the highest level of management and a very broad level of detail. Primarily, it requires large amounts of information derived from or relating to areas of knowledge outside the organization. Finally, strategic planning is original and covers the entire spectrum of the organization's activities.

4. USE OF MANAGEMENT BY EXCEPTION REPORTING

The "management by exception" principle is an integral part of real-time MIS in that only extraordinary events—favorable or unfavorable—are brought to the

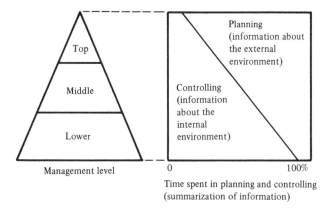

FIGURE 2-4. The relationship of the managerial levels to time spent on planning and controlling, and to the summarization of information.

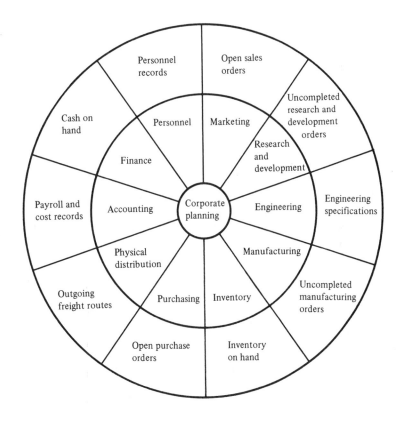

FIGURE 2-5. Operational information needed to control the major subsystems of a typical manufacturing firm.

45

FIGURE 2-6. Tactical information needed to implement strategic plans for the major subsystems of a typical manufacturing firm.

attention of those responsible and accountable. Often, exceptions to established plans, procedures, or standards are referred to the next higher level of command. Viewing the principle from this perspective, a manager gives his attention only to those matters which deviate from an established level and thereby require some type of action. The management by exception principle also insures that normal events are processed without necessitating management's attention. Company personnel at each level of lower and middle management work within established ranges of authority and responsibility. The exception principle, then, is designed to serve several purposes:

It specifies areas of direction and supervision, the contents of which can be processed according to normal routine

It identifies the unique problem or the unusual event requiring higher decision

It establishes a system for handling problems on a higher level when those problems cannot be solved on the level on which they occur

In order to make the exception principle function in a real-time MIS, there are problems of relative balance in job assignment and in the managerial direction at each specific level of organization. First, there is the matter of balance with respect to the functions that constitute a job—the selection of those functions which fit and those which do not fit. Collectively, the functions should be structured so that authority actually fits responsibility and accountability. Second, balance is dependent upon the priority of functions which comprise the job. A ranking of order is required to determine which of the functions has to be discharged first, which comes second, and so forth. Without this priority of orders, the manager would be flooded with information, some of which is not necessary. Relativity of job balance

FIGURE 2-7. Strategic information needed to plan, organize, direct, and control the major subsystems of a typical manufacturing firm.

that makes the management by exception principle feasible revolves around authority, responsibility, and accountability.

The management by exception principle can be illustrated by referring to the sales function in Figure 2-8. From the existing on-line data files or data base, records of sales and sales orders for the past several years are available. It takes a relatively simple computer program to compute averages and ranges of past sales for comparison with current figures. Comparison of actual sales against expected sales patterns and control limits leads to identification of control and out-of-control conditions. Where an out-of-control condition appears, it can be reported to management either as a visual display or as a printout accompanied by a sales control chart (showing where the upper or lower control limits have been violated). This management exception routine can apply to all products and product lines where detailed control is necessary for marketing management.

5. INPUT/OUTPUT ORIENTATION WITH MANY I/O TERMINALS

A real-time MIS environment requires a number of on-line input/output devices that are located throughout the firm's operations. Typewriters and visual

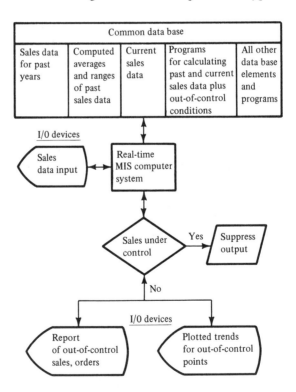

FIGURE 2-8. Real-time MIS and the management by exception principle illustrated for comparison of past and current sales and sales orders.

display devices are capable of sending as well as receiving information that relates to any of the basic business operations (Figure 2-3). They may be many miles away from one another, but are linked through a data communication network for producing forward-looking information.

The real-time system, for example, may be so designed that input data from an I/O device will trigger a production order when inventory reaches a predetermined level. The number of units to be produced will be based upon an economic order quantity (mathematical model). The computer program will scan the present production schedules of the many plants scattered throughout the country and determine which plant will produce the order, based on its capabilities and previous production commitments. Likewise, the computer program will indicate to which warehouse the end products will be shipped, based upon proximity to the factory and level of present inventory. During this process, the computer files are updated to reflect these changing conditions. Feedback to the various activities via I/O terminals is concerned with present and future operating conditions.

6. INTEGRATED SUBSYSTEMS

Subsystems operating in a real-time mode are integrated so that they can function as a unified system. Information is processed according to functional needs rather than along departmental lines. Data acquired from one source are often used in many subsystems to reduce duplication. Basically, the subsystems are designed to focus on the total corporate perspective.

The manager responsible for choosing among alternatives, allocating specific resources to meet the firm's objectives, and directing certain aspects of a complex organization must be able to mesh his operations (subsystem) with other related functional activities (subsystems). Such a manager needs accurate, consistent, and timely data to make decisions. If the integrated subsystem approach is not used, wasted motion and higher costs occur because each subsystem must treat the same data without taking advantage of processing accomplished by other subsystems. Integrated subsystems thus integrate all related data and functions into a comprehensive information and control system that keeps management informed about activities of concern to them.

The concept of integrated subsystems is illustrated in Figure 2-9. On-site or remote terminals which allow two-way communication with the computer are found at various locations of the firm. In the first or lowest level, data are fed into the central computer from an I/O device and routed back to the same or another I/O device within the same subsystem (for example, marketing). For the second level, data flows into the central computer from one subsystem (marketing) and the information is retrieved by another subsystem (manufacturing). The third or last level revolves around introducing external data into the central computer facility for use by all subsystems. Thus, I/O terminal devices are positioned at the various levels of data generation to bring together knowledge that can be used by all subsystems in integrating company activities. This approach yields a system capable of developing organization-wide strategies for managerial action.

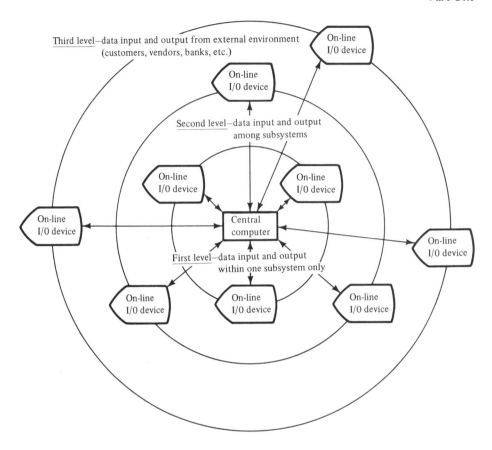

FIGURE 2-9. Concept of integrated subsystems operating on three separate levels in a real-time MIS environment.

7. COMMON DATA BASE

Data accumulated from the many detailed on-line transactions are commonly referred to as the data base elements or the organization's common data base. In addition to having all data collected in one place (basically secondary on-line storage), a firm's data base must be data- or functional-oriented rather than oriented on a departmental basis, as mentioned previously. For example, the inventory data base may be used by a number of functions, such as manufacturing, production control, inventory control, purchasing, and finance. In another example, a data base element is an employee skill number that can assist in preparing weekly payroll, referencing personnel records, filling new job openings, preparing contract negotiations, and the like. Thus, a data base for a firm refers to data elements in a common storage medium that form the foundation for all information provided to company personnel.

Structure of Data Base

An important problem confronting the systems designer in structuring the data base concerns not how many levels there should be for data base elements but rather the method of structuring the common data base—horizontally, vertically, or both. In Figure 2-10, the lower levels reflect the need to maintain the detailed business transactions. All the details of transactions occurring at the lowest level in the firm must be maintained much as they have been with prior data processing systems. At the lower or operating management level, this detail is necessary for completing the product and/or service being undertaken. For example, operating management needs to know the on-hand quantity of an inventory item, or the location of a shop order, or the balance of a customer's account. On the next (middle management) level, less detail is necessary and summarization and interpretation of the detailed transactions are required. At top management, there is need for another subset of the overall data base. The needs for each management level, then, differ in its requirements from the common data base.

The question can now be raised: will the real-time MIS be best served by three separate data bases (horizontal structure—Figure 2-10a), one single data base (vertical structure—Figure 2-10b), or a combination of both (horizontal and vertical structure—Figure 2-10c)? With the horizontal approach, there is going to be some duplication of the data elements maintained on line because data within the same level may be duplicated in part at the next level in order to meet higher-order managerial information requirements. However, there is little duplication of data base elements within the same level because data are retrievable by all functions. Under the vertical approach, there is a problem of redundancy by all major functions because data stored for one function are not retrievable by another function. On the other hand, data are available for use by all management levels for that function. The problem of duplication, then, is apparent in the horizontal and vertical approaches.

The best approach to structuring the data base is found in Figure 2-11 (or Figure 2-10c). The combined approach integrates the data base for all management levels and allows retrieval of information on the same level. It is a decision-oriented data base that can be used, for example, to identify potential market demands, indicate improvements in operating costs, and show profit profiles of alternative investment plans. As illustrated in Figure 2-11, the business operations structure of each level is equated horizontally and vertically with the data base which, in turn, is equated again in both directions with the information structure. In three dimensions, a matrix could be formed in which the plane of each structure level would intersect with each of the other levels.

Before the firm's data base can be structured in a combined horizontal/vertical manner, it is first necessary to identify the information requirements of management—that is, which data base elements are required. Second, the data base elements must be fully identified: specifically, where they are located, how they are obtained, how large they are, and what their specific contents are. The last requirement dictates that relationships among the data base elements be known clearly so

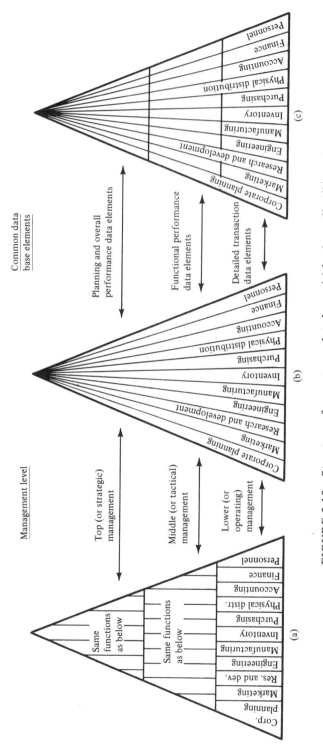

FIGURE 2-10. Structure of a common data base—(a) horizontally, (b) vertically, and (c) combination of both.

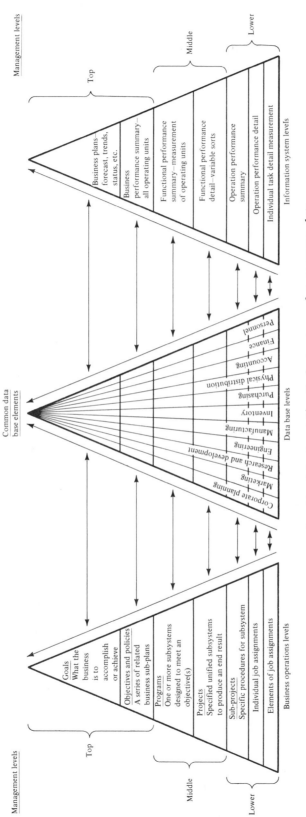

FIGURE 2-11. Combined horizontal/vertical structure of a common data base that relates business operations levels to information system levels.

that many different information requests can be served with a minimum of programming. The data elements should be related to as many different outputs as possible; in particular, those needed for timely managerial reports. In order to extract the desired information as is or with modification from the data base, multipurpose retrieval programs are needed to provide a close interaction between the computer and the individual.

Data Base Management System

Today, numerous generalized data base management systems are available to the user. They are called data management systems,[2] file management systems,[3] and generalized information retrieval systems. For instance, a data base management system may be designed to allow selective retrieval of information and to produce managerial reports with a minimum of time and effort. Generally, the system establishes, for a given data base, a dictionary containing all the information necessary to define not only the file or files comprising the data base but also each field within the data base. When the dictionary is written, a search name which can be referenced is assigned to each field, whereby the system gains flexibility and can be used for a different data base by simply creating a new dictionary.

A typical dictionary method for building a common data base consists of a hierarchy of data. As shown in Figure 2-12, the data set contains records A and B, where record A is composed of segments 1 and 2. Segment 1 includes independent elements a, b, and c as well as groups i and ii. Element group i consists of three elements (d, e, and f) while element group ii consists also of three elements (g, h, and i). Although not shown, record B might be divided into segments and broken down further by element groups and independent elements. Also, segment 2 of record A would probably include several elements and groups.

Advantages of the Data Base

The data base that is founded on a single-record concept has many advantages and is a logical way to handle the information explosion that has overwhelmed the business world. All information about a company's operation is contained in one readily accessible file, which is so arranged that duplication and redundancy are minimized. Information concerning ongoing business activity is captured, validated, and entered only once into its proper location on the data base. Each department then utilizes the same central on-line file or common data base in satisfying its total information needs.

Because of the single-record concept, total file space is reduced. Duplicate files previously maintained by various functional organizational units can be eliminated. As a corollary, there should be a reduction in manual effort required in these same functional areas—effort previously necessary to provide the inputs for the multiple files.

[2]S. Lawrence Prendergast, "Selecting a Data Management System," *Computer Decisions,* August, 1972.

[3]Donald S. Steig, "File Management Systems Revisited," *Datamation,* October, 1972.

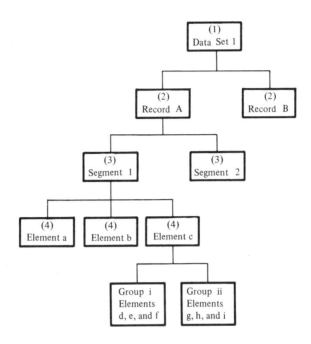

FIGURE 2-12. A typical dictionary for building a common data base—
(1) data set, (2) record, (3) segment, and (4) independent or
group element.

Having a central data base for all information about a business supports
real-time inquiry capability for any functional area that must determine the current
status or history of any item contained in the total system. Summary information,
on an exception basis, can be extracted for managerial needs. The data base provides consistent and timely status and historic information to all users. However, it
should be noted that only the most critical data are stored on line. Less critical and
more voluminous files are maintained on magnetic tape and other less expensive
media.

8. MODULAR (BUILDING BLOCK) APPROACH

The modular or building block approach to real-time management information systems results in a fluid state. Specifically, the data and modules are not
permanent and relationships are not fixed; they are adaptable to new situations.
Not only are the data base elements being continually updated, but the modules are
being expanded and contracted to meet ever-changing system requirements. The
system modules for data capture and information dissemination must be flexible
enough to accommodate new external and internal environment factors. Each input
module must have the ability to take source transactions and "explode" them into
other related transactions for other applications. This feature allows transactions to

be "recycled," thereby allowing one module "to talk to other modules" on line in real time. The result of the modular approach is meaningful and timely output that can be specified by the user.

The modular approach to systems design and programming is related to the various real-time MIS subsystems as well as to the common data base. For example, a standard cost module which is an integral part of the accounting subsystem is concerned with past and current operating data and therefore forms an important segment of the data base. The existence of on-line cost data elements provides the opportunity to develop other subsystems for the projection or simulation of future events. Complex portions of future annual budgets can be developed; the cost effect of proposed changes in product components can be simulated at various volume and mix levels; and monthly profit forecasts with comparison to actual variance factors can be developed.

The foregoing application of the modular approach to cost should not stop here. The cost module should be integrated further with other subsystem modules. This can be accomplished by building in "open ends" to other planned MIS modules as well as interfacing with the present system modules. The integration of related cost data and data processing requirements improves accuracy, reduces significantly the effort required to secure results, and improves the timing of output data.

Another example of the building block approach is illustrated in Figure 2-13. The basic modules of the finance function are the lowest level in the data base. These are summarized in the minor modules, which, in turn, are brought together to form the intermediate module or the cash management module. This module plus capital budgeting and source of funds modules complete the major module, finance. Thus, each file of unit finance data within the data base is a building block. The finance modules are coordinated with others of the data base in order to keep data duplication to a minimum. The structure of the on-line finance files requires constant coordination with other related functions and their data requirements. This is a major function of the data base administrator.

9. UTILIZATION OF OPERATIONS RESEARCH MODELS

A successful real-time MIS should be built on the foundation of operations research. To try any other approach for meshing together the many subsystems of the firm is difficult. For example, suppose a sales department wants a large on-hand inventory of assorted products so that it can promise immediate delivery to customers. The production department, however, wants an inventory that can be produced in large lots at a low unit cost. Similarly, the purchasing department wants to purchase raw materials and supplies in large quantities to procure goods at high unit price-break levels, resulting in purchases having the lowest possible unit price. However, the finance department demands that inventories be kept small in order to avoid the large investment in physical assets, thereby reducing the cost of storage, record keeping, and maintenance. Needless to say, the inventory problem is extraordinarily complex. The most logical method of solving this problem is from an operations research (OR) viewpoint.

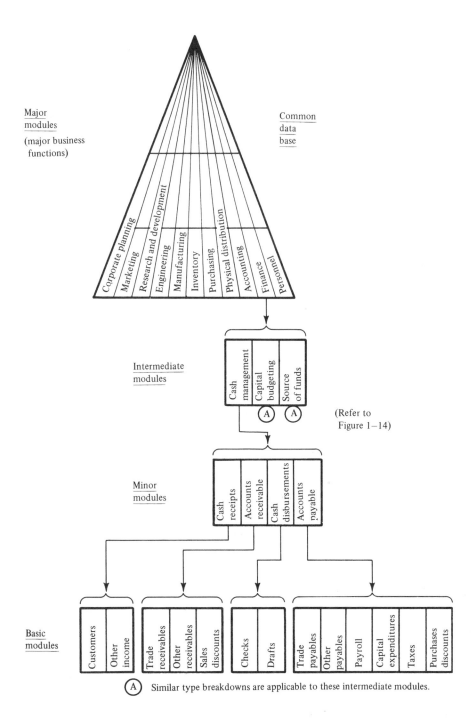

Major modules

(major business functions)

Common data base

Corporate planning
Marketing
Research and development
Engineering
Manufacturing
Inventory
Purchasing
Physical distribution
Accounting
Finance
Personnel

Intermediate modules

Cash management
Capital budgeting
Source of funds

(A) (A)

(Refer to Figure 1–14)

Minor modules

Cash receipts
Accounts receivable
Cash disbursements
Accounts payable

Basic modules

Customers
Other income

Trade receivables
Other receivables
Sales discounts

Checks
Drafts

Trade payables
Other payables
Payroll
Capital expenditures
Taxes
Purchases discounts

(A) Similar type breakdowns are applicable to these intermediate modules.

FIGURE 2-13. Data base modules for the finance function—in particular, cash management.

The requirements for an OR model that optimizes inventory is obviously very stringent. Often, the real world is far too complex to be described completely with a series of equations, objectives are too poorly defined and diffused to be captured precisely, or similar complicating factors exist. It is therefore necessary to develop mathematical models that *approximate* the real world in order to make them computationally feasible in a real-time MIS environment. Linear relationships, for example, may be employed in place of more complex nonlinear relationships that, in fact, more closely reflect reality. Or a single fixed value may be used in place of several estimated values. In reality, some accuracy must be sacrificed in order to gain computational efficiency.

The scope and detail of an OR model govern the number of variables included in it. In turn, this affects the complexity and computational requirements of the model. A preferred approach to a complex model, such as inventory, is to develop its essential parts first. In order to integrate, at a later date, the separate parts into a working whole, an aggregate OR model that sets constraints and/or adjusts the objective functions of the model's segments should be developed. A hierarchy of linked models ultimately allows a convergence toward maximization of overall organizational objectives.

Classification of OR Models

Operations research models that are capable of being successfully implemented in a real-time MIS environment are numerous and varied. They are categorized as follows:

allocation	replacement
assignment	routing
competition	search
decision theory	sequencing
dynamic programming	simulation
inventory	transportation
optimization	combined OR methods
queuing	heuristic methods

An introduction to each of these quantitative models is presented in the chapter's Appendix. The reader should not be too influenced by the name of the model; he should keep an open mind as to functional areas where it can be applied. The major functional areas (subsystems of a typical manufacturing firm) and OR models that correspond to the above classification are presented in Figure 2-14.

The real payoff from operations research comes from integrating the mathematical models into the real-time management information system (Figure 2-15). Data for OR models come directly from inputs and/or the data base under the control of computer programs. The interworkings of one function with another focus on the utilization of common data base elements. For example, sales are forecasted by the quantitative technique of exponential smoothing. The sales fore-

Major Business Functions–Subsystems	Operations Research Models (Major Classification per Figure 2-15)
Corporate Planning	Budgeting models (allocation) Operational gaming models (competition) Corporate planning models (combined OR methods) Venture analysis (combined OR methods) Corporate simulation (simulation)
Marketing	Linear programming (allocation) Venture analysis (combined OR methods) Game theory (competition) Decision trees (decision theory) Markov chains (decision theory) Dynamic programming (dynamic programming) Pricing models (optimization) Exponential smoothing (search) Input/output analysis (search) Marketing simulation (simulation)
Research and Development	R & D models (assignment) PERT[a]/Cost (sequencing) R & D simulation (simulation)
Engineering	Linear programming (allocation) Nonlinear programming (allocation) Value engineering (optimization) Plant expansion models (replacement) PERT/LOB[b] (sequencing) Production design simulation (simulation)
Manufacturing	Linear programming (allocation) Bayesian statistics (decision theory) Dynamic allocation (dynamic programming) Waiting line theory (queuing) PERT/Time, PERT/Cost, and PERT/LOB (sequencing) Manufacturing simulation (simulation) Monte Carlo simulation (simulation)
Inventory	Dynamic inventory models (dynamic programming) EOQ[c] models (inventory) Inventory control models (inventory) Inventory simulation (simulation)
Purchasing	Linear programming (allocation) Vendor performance models (heuristic methods)
Physical Distribution	Linear programming (allocation) Service level models (heuristic methods) Logistics models (routing) Physical distribution simulation (simulation) Transportation models (transportation)
Accounting	Linear programming (allocation) Discriminant analysis (decision theory) Cost accounting models (inventory) Cost estimating models (optimization)

[a]Program Evaluation and Review Technique. [c]Economic order quantity.
[b]Line of balance.

FIGURE 2-14. Major business functions and operations research models in a real-time MIS environment.

Major Business Functions— Subsystems	Operations Research Models (Major Classification per Figure 2-15)
Finance	Dynamic finance models (dynamic programming) Optimization models (optimization) Facilities planning (replacement) Cash flow models (simulation) Financial simulation (simulation)
Personnel	Company/union game models (competition) Markov chains (decision theory) Skills models (search)

FIGURE 2-14.   (Cont.)

cast is then input to determine the number of finished goods to be manufactured. This process continues to the actual ordering of raw materials and issuing of factory orders on an economic order basis (another OR technique). Other integrated activities that can employ operations research models include scheduling and dispatching of manufacturing orders, controlling assembly and subassembly operations, and shipping finished goods to customers or distributors.

10. OTHER REAL-TIME MIS CHARACTERISTICS

The foregoing characteristics of real-time management information systems are defined briefly in Figure 2-16. Although they form the basis for defining real-time MIS, there are several other important characteristics. Generally, there are several types of control devices employed which will be enumerated in Chapter Five. The wide offering of input/output devices allows management to select those devices that best serve its needs. As a result, I/O devices that provide the desired on-line response encourage more management involvement.

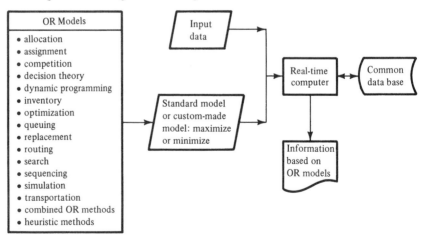

FIGURE 2-15. The appropriate OR model (standard or custom-made) is combined with input data and/or the common data base in a real-time MIS environment for producing meaningful information.

A real-time MIS computer is capable of handling remote batch processing for applications that are not ideal candidates for real-time processing. In effect, it can handle remote input/output devices as well as remote batch processing. The question of what processing approach is best can be answered by examining the activity under investigation.

Of all the operations system developments to date, real-time management information systems come the closest to the total systems concept. By way of review, the total systems concept views the firm as a single entity, composed of various interrelated subsystems working together to provide timely and accurate information for management decision making, thereby leading to optimization of company objectives. Many of the essential characteristics of this concept are found in Figure 2-16.

Having defined the essential characteristics of real-time management information systems, a comparison with integrated MIS is depicted in Figure 2-17. An examination of their basic differences indicates the superiority of a real-time MIS operating mode.

1. *Establishment of real-time MIS objectives*—providing more timely information and improved customer service.
2. *Forward- and backward-looking control system*—controlling present and future operations through real-time computer responses as well as through the issuing of periodic informational and special reports.
3. *Output directed to lower and middle management*—reporting trends and controlling activities needing the attention of lower and middle management.
4. *Use of management by exception reporting*—continuous monitoring of internal and external exceptions that need to be brought to the attention of the appropriate manager or employee.
5. *Input/output-orientation with many I/O terminals*—immediate recording of input data, and a real-time response, for controlling the operating environment.
6. *Integrated subsystems*—processing data once for use by all subsystems along functional rather than departmental lines.
7. *Common data base*—historical and current data operating as a system of files that are logically divided by functions with the least amount of redundancy.
8. *Modular (building block) approach*—building open-ended modules that start with the lowest level so that they can be linked together to form a system.
9. *Utilization of operations research models*—decision models utilizing common data elements to answer "what if" questions in a man/machine interaction mode.
10. *Other real-time MIS characteristics*—management-oriented I/O control devices, more management involvement, fast on-line response, remote batch processing, and close to the total systems concept.

FIGURE 2-16. **Essential characteristics of real-time management information systems defined.**

Important Characteristics of Management Information Systems	Integrated Management Information System	Real-Time Management Information System
Type of System	Backward-looking control system and integrated subsystems	Forward- and backward-looking control system and integrated subsystems
Reports Prepared	Output reports directed to all levels of management for past operations	Output reports directed mainly to lower and middle management for past, current, and future operations
Exception Reporting	Past activities contained in management exception reports	Current plans and objectives used for management exception reports
Information Orientation	Output-oriented	Input/output-oriented with I/O terminals
Processing Mode	Batch processing	On-line real-time processing and remote batch processing
Data Elements	Common data bank	Common data base
Modularity	Very little modularity of systems design	Use of modular design approach
Type of Files	Sequential and random access file storage	Accent on random access on-line file storage
Mathematical Models	Limited use of standard operations research models	Great use of standard and some complex operations research models

FIGURE 2-17. Comparison of important characteristics for integrated and real-time management information systems.

REAL-TIME MANAGEMENT INFORMATION SYSTEM DEFINED

In terms of basic characteristics, the following definition is proposed:

A real-time management information system is a group of integrated subsystems that is modularly structured on a forward- and backward-looking basis to accomplish company objectives wherein informational data are recorded, manipulated, and retrieved from a common data base via I/O terminals in order to plan, organize, direct, and control quantitative (and qualitative) managerial and operational activities in sufficient time to affect their respective operations.

The inclusion of the word "quantitative" means that the results of operations research should be applied to the managerial and operational activities (problems) at hand.

Deficiencies of Real-Time Management Information Systems

Although the real-time MIS does respond to the managerial needs of the first two (lower and middle) levels, it falls short of providing the information desired by top-level executives for their wide range of activities. Their principal task revolves around strategic planning that is a review of long-run studies made by staff personnel. A real-time MIS system does not provide long-range information; however, it does respond with the immediate feedback from present operations which is essential to modify future plans.

The structure of a real-time management information system is not compatible with the full requirements of top management; the data base required for top-level management needs must be restructured to accommodate them. For example, detailed information is needed for past, current, and future sales/cost performance that can be related to a financial simulation model which will produce an optimum mix of resources for producing a desired level of profits and investment return.

The major deficiencies of real-time MIS can be overcome by progressing to the next level of management information systems. Future MIS or data-managed systems that provide top management with appropriate information, particularly on long-range planning, is discussed at some length in Chapter Eighteen.

SUMMARY

The state of computer systems has progressed in terms of both hardware and software for the implementation of real-time MIS. Real-time MIS has been shown to be a forward-looking control system that maintains data base elements on line and is available to the central processing unit when needed. The firm's modular data base is always updated as events occur and can be interrogated from remote I/O terminals. With source data being entered as they happen, the real-time approach reduces repetitive recording, makes data available to all integrated subsystems needing them, and reduces conflicting reports that arise from varying coding or interpretations and unsynchronized timing. As a result, all departments work with the same information, thereby making it possible to tie their decisions with those of other functions. Also, information stored on line can be obtained upon request from a number of locations at a distance from the main computer system. The computer's ability to interact on line with people on a timely basis is its greatest asset. Management can be made aware of trends, exceptions, and results of recent decisions in order to initiate corrective action that meets predetermined business plans. Environmental feedback alerts the manager as to how the total business is operating—favorably or unfavorably—in relation to internal and external conditions.

A real-time management information system is defined as "a group of integrated subsystems that is modularly structured on a forward- and backward-looking basis to accomplish company objectives wherein informational data are recorded, manipulated, and retrieved from a common data base via I/O terminals in order to plan, organize, direct, and control quantitative (also qualitative) managerial and operational activities in sufficient time to affect their respective operations." It should be noted that operations research models are an integral part of real-time MIS, being included under the word "quantitative."

Managers with the aid of business system analysts (well-versed in data processing and operations research) can utilize Bayesian statistics, decision trees, game theory, PERT networks, and similar quantitative models to minimize the risk of doing business in a real-time MIS environment. They are able to do this on the basis of up-to-date information retrieved from the computer's data base. The end result is that important information is displayed by terminal devices. The potential of the computer, then, is more fully realized now for effective management than it has been in the past. Today's managers can utilize the computer as effectively as yesterday's managers used the telephone.

QUESTIONS

1. Explain why the SAGE and SABRE systems were the forerunners of real-time management information systems.

2. How important is it to set objectives for a real-time MIS?

3. a. Distinguish between a backward-looking control system and a forward-looking control system.

   b. What type is a real-time management information system?

4. Why is output from real-time MIS directed basically toward lower and middle management?

5. What part does the management by exception principle play in a real-time management information system?

6. Name and explain the various levels of informational data operating in the various integrated subsystems of real-time MIS.

7. a. What is the best method for structuring the data base in a real-time MIS environment? Why?

   b. What is the relationship of the data base structure to the modular (building block) approach in a real-time management information system?

8. What are the advantages of an on-line data base in real-time versus off-line files in batch processing?

9. What categories of OR models are well-suited for a real-time MIS operating mode? Explain.

10. What are the essential differences between a integrated management information system and a real-time management information system?

REFERENCES

Anderson, D. R., "Viewing MIS from the Top," *Journal of Systems Management,* July, 1973.

Argyris, C., "Management Information Systems: The Challenge to Rationality and Emotionality," *Management Science,* February, 1971.

Boulden, J. B., and Buffa, E. S., "Computer Models: On-Line Real-Time Systems," *Harvard Business Review,* July-August, 1970.

Brandenburg, W. H., "Dynamic System Design for Airlines," *Datamation,* March, 1969.

Brown, W. F., and Hawkins, D. H., "Remote Access Computing: The Executive's Responsibility," *Journal of Systems Management,* June, 1972.

Burch, J. G., and Strater, F. R., "Tailoring the Information System," *Journal of Systems Management,* February, 1973.

Burdeau, H. B., "Environmental Approach to MIS," *Journal of Systems Management,* April, 1974.

Cuozzo, D. E., and Kurtz, J. F., "Building a Base for Data Base: A Management Perspective," *Datamation,* October, 1973.

Dearden, J., McFarlan, F. W., and Zani, W. M., *Managing Computer-Based Information Systems.* Homewood, Ill.: Richard D. Irwin, Inc., 1971, Chapter 6.

Dearden, J., "Myth of Real-Time Management Information," *Harvard Business Review,* May-June, 1966.

———, "MIS Is a Mirage," *Harvard Business Review,* January-February, 1972.

Emery, J. E., "Decision Models," *Datamation,* Part I, September 1, 1970 and Part II, September 15, 1970.

Field, R., "MIS Comes Percolating Up the Organization," *Computer Decisions,* May, 1972.

Flynn, R. L., "A Brief History of Data Base Management," *Datamation,* August, 1974.

Frey, J. P., "Managing Data Is the Key to MIS," *Computer Decisions,* January, 1971.

Gosden, J. A., "The Making of a Management Information Data Base," *Computer Decisions,* May, 1972.

Hanold, T., "An Executive View of MIS," *Datamation,* November, 1972.

Head, R. V., *Manager's Guide to Management Information Systems.* Englewood Cliffs, N.J.: Prentice-Hall, Inc., 1973.

———, "The Elusive MIS," *Datamation,* September 1, 1970.

———, "Management Information Systems: A Critical Appraisal," *Datamation,* May, 1967.

Lohara, C. S., "A New Approach to Management Information Systems," *Journal of Systems Management,* Part I, July, 1971, and Part II, August, 1971.

Mancinelli, T. B., "Management Information Systems: The Trouble with Them," *Computers and Automation,* July, 1972.

Olle, T. W., "MIS: Data Bases," *Datamation,* November 15, 1970.

Pan, G. S., "The Characterization of Data Management Systems," *Data Management,* June, 1971.

Price, G. F., "The Ten Commandments of Data Bases," *Data Management,* May, 1972.

Rothstein, M. F., *Guide to the Design of Real-Time Systems.* New York: John Wiley & Sons, Inc., 1970, Chapter 1.

Schubert, R. F., "Basic Concepts in Data Base Management Systems," *Datamation,* July, 1972.

Shults, E. C., and Bruun, R. J., "The Hard Road to MIS Success," *Infosystems,* May, 1974.

Seese, D. A., "Initiating a Total Information System," *Journal of Systems Management,* April, 1970.

Spiro, B. E., "What's a Management Information System," *Datamation,* July, 1972.

Taplin, J. M., "AAIMS: American Airlines Answers the What Ifs," *Infosystems,* February, 1973.

Urban, G. L., "Building Models for Decision Makers," *Interfaces,* Vol. 4, No. 3, May, 1974.

Vandell, R. F., "Management Evolution in the Quantitative World," *Harvard Business Review,* January-February, 1970.

OPERATIONS RESEARCH MODELS
Appendix to Chapter Two

OPERATIONS RESEARCH DEFINED

Operations research can best be defined in terms of its basic characteristics as follows:

> Operations research utilizes the planned approach [updated scientific method] and an interdisciplinary team in order to represent complex functional relationships as mathematical models for the purpose of providing a quantitative basis for decision making and uncovering new problems for quantitative analysis.[1]

This lengthy but all-inclusive definition of OR is concerned basically with the construction and application of mathematical models (based upon probability theory, statistics, and higher mathematics) for solving recurring business problems

[1] Robert J. Thierauf and Robert C. Klekamp, *Decision Making Through Operations Research* (New York: John Wiley & Sons, Inc., 1975), p. 15.

that can be best handled by computers. To try to solve these problems with manual methods would be costly and time-consuming. In many cases, conditions are likely to change before application can be effected.

In view of these difficulties with manual methods, a model of the real world is constructed to reflect the essential characteristics of the actual situation. When the model is constructed, the variables in the problem must be identified. A variable which obtains its value from some other element or variable is dependent. On the other hand, an independent variable is one whose value is determinable without reference to other elements or variables. Once these two broad categories are set forth explicitly in the problem, the relationship of these variables to one another or the effect each has on the others is defined. This relationship is necessary in defining an appropriate measure of effectiveness, such as maximizing profits or minimizing costs. With the pertinent variables stated in mathematical notation and in equation form, the manipulative facility of mathematics now makes it an easy job for the computer.

MATHEMATICAL FOUNDATION OF OPERATIONS RESEARCH

Operations research utilizes several areas of mathematics, including probability theory and statistics. Because probability theory is an integral part of many mathematical models, understanding its essentials is necessary for operations research. Probability is quite useful in the reduction of risk and uncertainty in many business situations. Similarly, a knowledge of statistics is helpful in predicting the future with a minimum amount of information available. Statistical techniques include inference, point and interval estimation, testing of hypotheses, control charts, linear and multiple regression, correlation, and analysis of variances. All these methods are very useful for dealing with uncertainty, errors, sampling, estimation, and prediction.

Higher mathematics also provides a foundation for solving standard OR problems. Matrix algebra, vectors, determinants, differentiation, integration, partial derivatives, Lagrange multiplier, and differential equations are essential in developing reliable OR models. Often, calculus methods are necessary to solve basic OR models because other mathematical approaches fail to solve them or to give satisfactory proofs of them. In addition, calculus methods provide a means for selecting the best solution without having to search through every alternative course of action, a problem characteristic of the many OR techniques that follow.

OVERVIEW OF OR MODELS

The successful marriage of the computer with mathematical models has produced a rapid growth in the number of quantitative techniques for solving business problems. The number is still increasing as more techniques are developed for new business applications. Problems that have been successfully solved are not restricted to one functional area of the firm, but often involve the entire firm. The principal

OR models that have been used to solve business problems encompass the following:

> allocation
> assignment
> competition
> decision theory
> dynamic programming
> inventory
> optimization
> queuing
> replacement
> routing
> search
> sequencing
> simulation
> transportation
> combined OR methods

The foregoing models are applicable to well-structured problems. Operations researchers have also developed *heuristic methods*—capable of solving poorly structured problems. A problem is said to be well-structured if the relationships between the variables and the objective function are known in the problem and if computational procedures exist for determining the values of the variables that optimize the objective. A problem is said to be poorly structured when it does not satisfy these conditions.

No attempt will be made to describe each quantitative area in great detail. Rather, an introduction will be given below.

Allocation

Allocation, sometimes called resource allocation, is applicable to problems dealing with limited resources. When there are a number of activities to be performed, alternative ways of doing them, and limited resources or facilities for performing each activity in the most effective way, there is an allocation problem. The approach to such a problem is to combine activities and resources so that overall efficiency is maximized; that is, profit is maximized or cost is minimized. This is known as "mathematical programming." When the constraints and the objective function (maximize profits or minimize costs) are expressed as linear equations, this is known as "linear programming." Production/distribution, production mix, and blending problems are examples of this category. If any of the constraints or the objective function are nonlinear, however, this is called "nonlinear programming." Other types of mathematical programming techniques include integer, quadratic, convex, stochastic, decision, and parametric programming. They differ in the kinds of data which they handle and the kind of assumptions that are made.

Assignment

Assignment problems involve the assignment of a number of jobs to the same number of resources (personnel). The desired assignment is one that will result in the greatest overall benefit to the firm. This problem type becomes more complex if some of the jobs require more than one resource and if the resources can be used for more than one job. Typical problems are those of scheduling jobs on machines or assigning tasks to people for minimum overall cost or time.

Competition

Competition models are used by business to develop advertising strategies, pricing policies, and timing for the introduction of new products. Statistical decision theory (probability) is an essential part of game theory to evaluate strategies. Because each competitor has many possible alternative courses of action, the problem is to determine the best method for making specific choices during the game.

Decision Theory

The essential characteristic of decision theory is that the consequences of courses of action are not known with certainty. In these instances, probabilities are used. Decision theory is used in competitive-type problems such as bidding, pricing, and some marketing problems. Pricing policies are also examples of this application. The effect of raising or lowering prices, probabilities of increasing or losing a share of the market, probable competitive reaction, and effect on profits can be tested in this manner.

Dynamic Programming

Dynamic programming is a relatively recent approach to problem solving in which decisions have to be made sequentially. Instead of optimizing each decision as it occurs, dynamic programming takes into account the effect of current decisions on future periods and adjusts every decision to yield the best overall performance. Models of this type are especially suitable for processes that extend over a number of time periods. The method consists of a search for the optimal combination of decisions to be made in all periods, and requires the manipulation of large amounts of information. Hence, the computer is almost always indispensable. Examples are truck-routing problems, production-line problems, and the replacement of machines or facilities.

Inventory

Inventory models are concerned basically with two decisions—how much to order at one time and when to order to keep total costs at a minimum. Carrying costs, ordering costs, and out-of-stock costs of inventory are determined so that a cost effectiveness model can be employed to find an appropriate balance between costs and shortages. Lowest cost decision rules for inventory can be obtained by algebra, calculus, probability theory, and simulation. The appropriate OR inventory technique to use will depend upon the attendant circumstances.

Optimization

Optimization is associated with the maxima and minima procedures of calculus. Briefly, when a characteristic can be represented by an equation in one variable that plots as a smooth continuous curve, the maximum and minimum values of the curve can be found by setting the first derivative to zero for locating horizontal or flat spots on the curve. Then, the mathematical sign of the second derivative at these points is examined (negative for maxima and positive for minima) for proving the problem. Where two parameters are involved such that x and y determine variable z (visualize a surface instead of a curve), maxima and minima can be found by using partial derivatives in a process similar to that employed for a one-variable case. Other OR problems require the use of differential equations, partial integration, Lagrange multiplier, or some combination of advanced calculus methods for their solutions.

Queuing

Queuing models, sometimes referred to as waiting-line theory, is concerned with uniform or random arrivals at a servicing or processing facility of limited capacity. The objective of this model is to determine the optimum number of personnel or facilities necessary to service arriving customers when considering the cost of service and the cost of waiting or congestion. Waiting lines are applicable not only to customers, shop personnel, trucks, and airplanes, but also to problems such as inventory. Items in stock can be considered as an idle service facility waiting for customers. The demand for stock is comparable to an arrival for service, and the depletion of stock can be compared to a queue of customers. Queuing theory makes great use of probability theory, calculus, and the Monte Carlo method of simulation.

Replacement

Replacement problems are generally of two types: those involving items that degenerate over a period of time and those that fail after a certain amount of time. The first group consists of the firm's fixed assets, such as machines and equipment, while the second type are inexpensive items, such as vacuum tubes and tires. Solutions to high-cost item problems are obtained by the use of calculus and specialized programming methods. Indifference (breakeven) analysis provides another method for solving equipment, selection, and replacement problems. Statistical sampling and probability theory are used to replace low-cost items as they fail or at specified intervals.

Routing

Routing models are concerned with selecting a route from a point of origin, through each city (intermediate point) on a trip, and back to the starting point in the shortest distance in terms of time or cost. The routing model has been applied to production such that the number of models or items produced is analogous to cities. Change-over production costs correspond to the cost of travel between cities.

Major Business Functions (Subsystems)	Allocation	Assignment	Competition	Decision Theory	Dynamic Programming	Inventory	Optimization
Corporate Planning	Analyze wage, salary, and dividend policies	Assign firm resources to growth areas	Assess corporate policies, competition	Analyze long-range planning policies	Assess multistage corporate strategies	Assess the work force, assets, etc.	Optimize the resources of the firm
Marketing	Determine distribution handling	Assign salesmen on an optimum basis	Assess effects of price changes	Analyze timing of new products	Evaluate long-term marketing trends	Analyze warehousing needs	Determine optimum selling prices
Research and Development	Allocate manpower funds to projects	Determine allocation of funds to research projects	Evaluate alternative R & D designs	Assess life expectancy of new products	Determine reliability to be designed into products	Determine size of staff and the reserve of projects	Determine areas for R & D projects
Engineering	Allocate engineering projects	Assign engineers to projects	Select the better engineering projects	Control long-range engineering projects	Assess multistage engineering projects	Determine purchasing assignments	Optimize resources for engineering products
Manufacturing	Determine best allocation of production facilities	Schedule job shop operations	Assess production changes	Analyze for stabilization of production and employment	Determine optimum production sequences	Schedule operations, considering current stock levels	Determine the need for new machines
Inventory	Allocate proper space for inventory	Assign optimal number of personnel to inventory	Assess one product versus another	Analyze future inventory movements	Determine multistage inventory policies	Utilize economic order quantity policies	Optimize for lowest inventory cost
Purchasing	Assess in-house manufacture versus outside purchase	Assign buyers in an optimal manner	Assess competitive vendor behavior	Analyze projected long-range prices	Assess multistage buying policies	Develop optimum buying practices	Determine optimum buying periods
Physical Distribution	Determine location and sizes of warehouses, retail outlets, etc.	Space allocation for stock accessability	Assess distribution policy	Determine company-owned stores versus franchises	Plan alternative distribution policy	Determine multilevel inventory system	Determine optimum warehousing size
Accounting	Allocate overhead and expenses on a logical basis	Schedule assignment of accounting jobs	Assess accounts-receivable policies	Analyze bad debts in the long run	Assess multilevel accounting policies	Analyze periodic inventory reports	Optimize net profits for the firm
Finance	Determine need for funds	Assign optimum credit policies	Select from competing sources of funds	Evaluate long-run investments	Assess long-range dividend policies	Assess investment in inventory	Optimize credit policies
Personnel	Select personnel to reduce labor turnover	Assign proper skills to jobs	Measure employee performance	Determine feasibility of accelerating automation	Assess recruiting policies	Evaluate causes for absenteeism	Optimize incentive schemes

FIGURE 2A-1. Major classification of operations research models.

Queuing	Replacement	Routing	Search	Sequencing	Simulation	Transportation
Staff service functions	Rotate or replace company personnel	Determine best routing of company products	Determine business strategies	Control integrated programs	Simulate, using corporate planning models	Analyze transportation costs for firm
Staff and assign priorities to projects	Replace or rotate sales personnel	Determine accounts to be handled by salesmen	Locate customers and/or competitors	Analyze sales strategies	Simulate allocation of advertising budget	Determine policy on freight out
Schedule sales calls	Replace analytical testing equipment	Route R & D projects in an optimum manner	Search for R & D data	Analyze and control R & D projects	Simulate basic and applied R & D projects	Determine effectiveness of R & D activities
Schedule engineering work	Replace engineering equipment	Analyze activities that may delay engineering projects	Retrieve and process engineering projects	Establish and control engineering projects	Simulate engineering projects	Evaluate movement of engineering projects
Schedule equipment and machinery maintenance	Replace old equipment with new	Route production orders in an optimum manner	Retrieve production information	Establish production schedules	Simulate the production process	Determine the best movement of in-plant goods
Analyze stockouts as queues	Consider two-bin inventory policy	Determine best route for inventory stock	Analyze for best physical placement of inventory	Establish sequence of inventory usage	Simulate for lowest cost inventory levels	Determine lowest cost handling procedures for inventory
Schedule to interview salesmen	Assess replacement policies	Determine best routing of incoming goods	Retrieve data on vendor performance	Control flow of purchased parts	Develop rules for buying under varying prices	Determine lowest incoming freight costs
Schedule outgoing traffic	Replace costly warehouses	Analyze for best logistics and supply system	Search and analyze physical distribution data	Determine physical distribution schedules	Simulate physical distribution system	Determine low-cost distribution channels
Schedule accounting functions	Evaluate present data processing equipment	Determine best routing of in-plant accounting data	Retrieve on-line data for credit check	Evaluate projects utilizing network analysis	Simulate sales and costs in budget analysis	Evaluate incoming freight costs
Schedule cash flow	Evaluate capital projects	Determine best method of obtaining funds	Retrieve important financial information	Determine long-range capital requirements	Simulate operations for cash needs	Allocate funds to projects on a timely basis
Evaluate queues of personnel and equipment	Assess personnel replacement policies	Route new employees through plant for indoctrination	Search in-plant for needed skills	Allocate personnel to network projects	Simulate for future personnel needs	Transport workers to work centers

Search

Search theory makes use of prior experience and information in order to narrow down the areas that have the attributes of the desired objective. It has been applied to problems dealing with the storage and retrieval of information and the search pattern of customers in stores, as well as to other problem areas such as exploration and quality control systems.

Transportation

The transportation problem is concerned with the most efficient shipping schedule for materials or products that must be moved from one location to another. There are often excess products at the origins and deficiencies at the destination points. What is required to solve the problem is a calculation of the minimum cost or time requirement. The whole field of physical distribution, in which transportation is the only or the major cost element, lends itself to this situation. Linear programming, the stepping stone method, and similar quantitative techniques can be employed to solve this kind of problem.

Combined OR Methods

Combined OR methods for well-structured problems indicate one of the future directions that operations research will take for solving complex problems. Several of the foregoing techniques are combined to produce a new OR tool for managers. For example, a production control problem usually includes some combination of inventory allocation and waiting-line models. Although the usual procedure for solving combined processes consists of solving them one at a time in some logical sequence, operations researchers must initially combine the models (where there are interrelationships) for an optimal solution.

Heuristic Methods

Heuristic methods denote learning or self-adapting systems for poorly structured problems. A *heuristic* is any rule for selecting an element from a set. The selected element may or may not have any desirable mathematical properties. Examples of heuristics are: "first-in, first-out" rule of inventory, shortest operation in job shop scheduling, and seniority rules in personnel management. In essence, rules of thumb are used to explore the most likely paths and to make educated guesses in reaching a conclusion. This replaces checking all the alternatives to find the best one—a characteristic of most approaches for well-structured problems. Heuristic programming is very promising for the future of operations research.

Alternative Way of Viewing OR Models

Most managers normally do not view problems in terms of their basic forms. Rather, they think more in terms of their content: the area of business in which these problems arise and are to be solved. The wide range of OR problems that have been successfully solved by major business functions are summarized in Figure 2A-1. The classification is by no means complete, but is a representative sample of OR models that have been applied to the firm's major functional areas.

EVALUATION OF OPERATIONS RESEARCH

OR models provide management with solutions for many of its problems. Operations research gives the manager an opportunity to consider additional courses of action that were not available under older methods. Instead of looking at the problem, say from a two-dimensional viewpoint, a third dimension is added. This permits the manager to supplement his subjective feelings—hunch, intuition, and judgment—with the objective findings of the OR model for a better managerial decision. Not only does the quality of the managerial decision-making process improve, but he is also freed from spending so much time on current problems—their formulation and solution. His time is available for investigating new problems and those poorly structured problems that have been ignored.

part two

FEASIBILITY STUDY THROUGH SYSTEMS IMPLEMENTATION OF REAL-TIME MANAGEMENT INFORMATION SYSTEMS

SYSTEMS ANALYSIS OF REAL-TIME MANAGEMENT INFORMATION SYSTEMS

3

The implementation of a real-time management information system is not a simple task. In order to install the new system effectively, a detailed and carefully devised plan must be initiated by management and followed by all personnel. The large outlays for equipment, programming, conversion, and related activities require systematic procedures for implementation. Otherwise, vast sums of money can be wasted.

The purpose of this chapter and succeeding ones in this section is to explore the steps of a feasibility study through systems implementation for a real-time MIS project in which the present system is an integrated management information system (batch-processing-oriented). The feasibility study encompasses three major steps:

1. the exploratory survey, including systems analysis
2. basic systems design
3. equipment selection

The initial step of the feasibility study is discussed in this chapter. Basically, the function of this important phase is to determine whether or not a real-time MIS is more beneficial to the firm than its present system. The feasibility or nonfeasibility of applying real-time equipment and procedures needs to be established for the firm. Systems analysis, a thorough and comprehensive review of the present system, is an integral part of the exploratory survey. This analysis allows the MIS task force to make a valid comparison among the many feasible systems alternatives. The chapter concludes with a discussion of the exploratory survey report to top management.

SYSTEMS PLANNING FOR REAL-TIME MIS

Analyzing, designing, and implementing a real-time MIS is a difficult and costly undertaking. The complex relationships that exist in such a system demand that a highly systematic and analytic approach to systems planning be established. Systems planning for real-time MIS must decide what must be done, how to do it, and when to do it. There are important relationships among and feedback from these three objectives. For example, at any given time, we are generally constrained in what we decide to do by limitations in capabilities and/or resources. Often, we simply do those things that we know how to do and ignore other important areas without weighing alternatives for best results.

In planning for a real-time MIS environment, a patchwork approach to systems development must be avoided. The patchwork approach can result in the development of unrelated and incompatible subsystems. Thoughtful systems planning centers around a single total system that provides coherence of architecture design, methods, standards, operating procedures, and other commonalities important for economy in development, implementation, and operation. The overall system should be structured as a set of integrated subsystems flexible enough to accommodate expansion or contraction of company activities.

Real-time MIS planning is not restricted to implementation of the current project. It also includes establishing long-range plans that must be updated continuously. Periodic reviews of the installed system determine its continuing relevance to the business environment.

REAL-TIME MIS EXPLORATORY SURVEY

The real-time MIS exploratory survey is the first major step of the feasibility study. It includes the appointment of selected committees and comprises several phases of investigation:

1. preliminary
2. overall
3. detailed
4. concluding

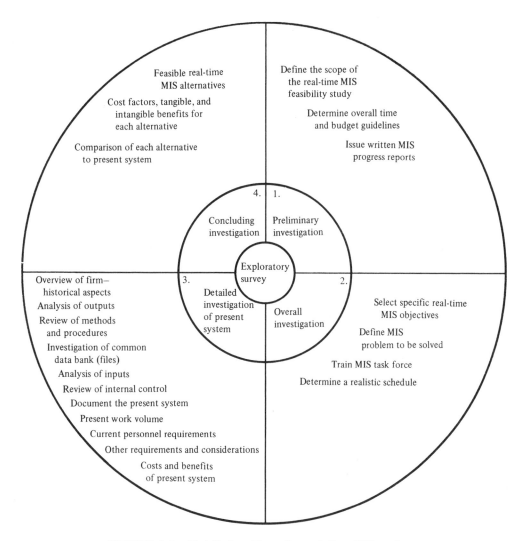

FIGURE 3-1. Detailed outline of a real-time MIS exploratory survey, including systems analysis—the first step of the feasibility study.

A detailed outline of an exploratory survey is found in Figure 3-1. These basic steps constitute a framework for the initial step of the feasibility study. They also serve as a basis for preparing a real-time MIS exploratory survey report to top management.

After a period of preliminary investigation or orientation (first phase), the real-time MIS exploratory survey pursues an overall investigation (second phase) of the current system in operation. This phase allows the MIS task force to comprehend the full scope of its undertaking. The detailed investigation (third phase) consists of the analysis of the present system, frequently referred to as *systems analysis.* In the concluding investigation (fourth phase), the MIS committee reaches one of two pivotal conclusions. One option is that the present integrated MIS appears better than any one of the new real-time MIS's conceived. The other option is that at least one of the new systems conceived appears to be superior to the present system. In this case, the feasibility study proceeds to the next step, basic systems design. In the first instance, however, the MIS group may examine additional systems or study new equipment developments that have come on the market since the analysis was initiated. If the exploratory survey still indicates a negative answer, the real-time MIS feasibility study will stop to await new developments.

The importance of doing a thorough exploratory survey cannot be over-emphasized. It is vital to the future well-being of the firm that this time-consuming first step be done accurately and conscientiously. A half-hearted attempt will often lead the firm to a premature conclusion about a new system. Only after installation do the facts come to light, often resulting in major data processing problems and/or higher data processing costs. A careful and systematic approach to the real-time MIS exploratory study is a must for installing a successful system. There are no legitimate shortcuts.

ORGANIZATION FOR REAL-TIME MIS

The establishment of two groups, the executive steering committee and the MIS task force, is a sound basis for organizing a real-time MIS project. The task force, made up of personnel involved in the problem under study, report to the executive steering committee, which is composed of those responsible executives whose departments and functions are affected by the study. The committee's basic functions are to direct the MIS task force and to report the progress of the systems project to all concerned personnel, including the board of directors.

The two groups serve to filter the systems project and help prevent errors. Their organization also helps to pinpoint all the relationships sought between processes and departments, that enter into a successful real-time MIS project. The foregoing groups also help to smooth the way for MIS personnel by enlisting the cooperation of operating personnel and by boosting the chance of acceptance of the task force's role.

Top management has come to realize the full significance of the often repeated statement, "management must learn to control the computer or the computer will control it." There are numerous case histories which disclose major failings in information systems simply because top management did not involve itself. Quite often, managers fear that information systems are too complicated and too technical for them to understand. When not significantly involved, management cannot possibly be aware of the direction that the computer technicians are taking in placing priorities and emphasis on applications. Furthermore, it is almost a foregone conclusion that without direct management influence, the applications will be slanted toward programmers' interpretation of management needs, and not by the actual needs of management and operating personnel.

Top management must get involved and face the problems to be studied in the real-time MIS project through the executive steering committee—and it must do this at the beginning of the project rather than at a later time.

SELECTION OF EXECUTIVE STEERING COMMITTEE

The purpose of establishing an executive steering committee, as indicated earlier, is to give direction to the MIS task force. The executive committee often includes several of the following: chairman of the board, president, executive vice-president, and vice-presidents—marketing, manufacturing, purchasing, finance, engineering, personnel, and research and development. This committee not only oversees what the MIS task force is doing, but also increases their chance of success because of its high status.

The executive committee's initial task is to issue a written statement that a MIS task force has been formed to study the feasibility of implementing a real-time management information system. The statement should clearly indicate that adjustments in personnel and jobs may be required to make the change. Some employees may have to be retrained and reassigned new data processing jobs, some of which may be higher or lower than the present ones. It should be emphasized that no one will be fired or asked to resign. This first memo to all employees should indicate that periodic written statements will be issued regarding the progress of the feasibility study. The failure to issue a memorandum of this type will cause alarm because of the fear of data processing equipment replacing people. The firm's grapevine can have a field day with this type of news.

SELECTION OF MIS TASK FORCE

A task concurrent with the preparation of the first written memorandum from the executive steering committee is the selection of the MIS task force, sometimes called the MIS committee or study group. The number of participants will depend on several factors, the following being the most important: the firm's size, the number of divisions and departments, the degree of centralization, the number of business functions, budget constraints, and time considerations.

Because a real-time MIS cuts across the entire organizational structure, a member from each of the firm's functional areas should be selected. If at all possible, each person selected should have several years of experience in his respective area, be objective in his thinking, and be capable of creative thinking. Also, he should be familiar with the major problems of his functional area. Generally, the individual who has the background and holds a responsible position in the firm has not had the opportunity to keep up with the latest developments in data processing technology. Therefore, it is necessary to have persons with real-time computer and programming experience on the MIS task force. This may mean going to the outside for qualified systems personnel and/or consultants if the firm lacks the technical knowledge. Whether the individuals selected are from inside or outside the firm, the task force will function best when knowledgeable personnel are present.

It is recommended that at least one person within the firm devote full time to the feasibility study in order to head the group and direct the study to maintain its momentum. Other members may work full or part time, depending upon their work assignments.

ORGANIZATION OF MIS TASK FORCE

The leader of the MIS task force should hold a rank comparable to that of a vice-president, because he will probably manage the new system once it is operational. A survey of many firms indicates a positive correlation between the study's success and the MIS manager's rank. A rank high on the executive ladder, so the individual has immediate access to top management, means the systems project has a much better chance than if his rank is one of lower or middle management.

Depending upon the size of the undertaking, the MIS group can range from five persons up to a dozen or more from inside or outside the firm. It is advisable to keep the number as small as possible to avoid problems associated with large groups. Although all members will not be working on the study continuously, they will be engaged as needed. Usually, the task force should be split into two or three smaller groups, sometimes called study or task groups. This will allow each group to investigate and report on one aspect of the study. Much time can be saved by this group study approach.

AUTHORITY DELEGATED TO MIS TASK FORCE

Authority must be clearly delegated to the task force. All those with whom the group comes into contact must fully comprehend the need for their help and complete cooperation. Without the authority officially delegated to the group, many managers might not participate constructively because they question the validity of newer data processing equipment, they do not understand the new system changes, or for some other reason. The authority delegated by top management may have to be used at times to overcome resistance. In these cases, the study group must use tact and diplomacy—otherwise, the consequential resentment may be detrimental to the entire study.

Systems work that cuts across the entire firm needs the active participation and cooperation of all management levels to be completed successfully. In addition, because they have the authority and the corresponding responsibility for a systems project, MIS personnel will be held accountable for their actions.

TOP MANAGEMENT BACKING OF MIS TASK FORCE

The MIS task force is constantly in touch with top-level executives and acquires prestige from this association. Systems personnel are often given important titles to insure that all relevant data from the various departments will be made available when needed. This means that the MIS group has moved out of the middle management level to a higher organizational position. The support of top management is important because the cost of the study alone, disregarding programming, testing, and conversion costs, is very high. Its support can represent the difference between success and failure.

1. PRELIMINARY INVESTIGATION—EXPLORATORY SURVEY

To initiate a real-time MIS study plan, there must be a reason. The present integrated MIS may have some weaknesses such as a lack of reports for controlling present and future operations, bottlenecks in the batch processing operation, or untimely system outputs. Whatever reasons are given by top management, there should be a preliminary investigation of the real-time MIS exploratory survey. Preliminary investigation centers around the activities of the executive steering committee. It consists of defining the scope of the feasibility study, determining overall time and budget constraints, and issuing written MIS progress reports, each of which is discussed below.

DEFINE THE SCOPE OF THE REAL-TIME MIS FEASIBILITY STUDY

The question of what will be included in the real-time MIS exploratory survey of the feasibility study is up to the executive committee. This top-level group might ask the MIS committee to direct its activities initially to production, marketing, finance, or other functions of the firm. Or the scope of the study might include all functional areas, in which case it is better to implement the system in manageable pieces, considering both the vertical and horizontal aspects of real-time MIS. From a horizontal structure approach, a marketing information subsystem may be implemented first, followed by a production control subsystem, and so forth. The vertical structure approach attempts to satisfy the informational needs of managers at different levels. The scope of the feasibility study may even be somewhere between these two approaches.

The scope of the study can be approached from another viewpoint. Management might want the task force to investigate those opportunity and cost areas critical to the firm, areas in which successful action is essential for business survival, in which profit opportunities are greatest, or in which the greatest costs are incurred.

The scope of the feasibility study must be clearly defined. Otherwise, analysis may extend to areas not of prime interest in developing a real-time MIS. Limiting the field of analysis at this beginning stage reduces the time required to analyze existing procedures and indicates those areas requiring extended analysis. In addition, it will assist in revealing functional areas where a real-time system is not feasible or would be too costly.

Redirection of the depth of analysis and areas of study can occur when the information being obtained by the MIS task force brings to light previously undisclosed problems. The MIS group will sometimes ask to enlarge or contract the area under investigation after a thorough investigation of all the facts. This can happen when the problem is defined precisely or may be redefined at a later stage in the exploratory survey. Thus, the executive steering committee is most concerned at this time with the overall scope; more attention will be given to the details of problem definition later.

DETERMINE OVERALL TIME AND BUDGET GUIDELINES

The executive steering committee develops general time and budget guidelines in conjunction with the MIS task force manager. The work required for the implementation of a real-time management information system is based on the scope of the systems project. Obviously, the more comprehensive the feasibility study is, the higher will be the cost. Also, the less time permitted to get the system operating, the more personnel and money will be required. This important factor (time) is often overlooked in planning a complex system.

A starting point can be a schedule developed from the initial estimate of available funds and/or a date by which management wants the project completed. There is a strong possibility that the guidelines developed will not meet the time limitation or that the estimated budget will be exceeded. In such cases, the executive steering committee must agree to modify the time and/or the budget guidelines until there is agreement between the budget and a feasible schedule. In subsequent steps of the exploratory survey, time and budget guidelines will be detailed and will be shown to form an important part of the feasibility study.

Research on installed MIS highlight several pitfalls to avoid, one of which is that firms, almost universally, indicate that construction of a MIS will take longer and cost more money than was originally budgeted.

ISSUE WRITTEN MIS PROGRESS REPORTS

One of the best ways for the executive steering committee to insure a successful feasibility study (as mentioned previously) is to issue written memorandums to all company employees. Generally, in the first memo, it is wise to include a statement on the broad scope of the study and the objectives to be accomplished by it. The names of the executive and MIS committees should also be included. Subsequent memos issued by the executive committee should be written in a manner not only detailing the progress of the project but also enhancing the stature of systems personnel. These memos should make it quite clear that top management wants effective results from the feasibility study undertaken by the MIS task force.

The MIS study manager should meet with the firm's departmental managers after the issuance of the first MIS memorandum. He should outline the work required of these managers in analyzing, designing, and implementing a real-time MIS. He should also acquaint the departmental managers with the names of those departmental personnel who will be responsible for making information available to the assigned analysts. The MIS manager, then, is the liaison man for his study team.

2. OVERALL INVESTIGATION— EXPLORATORY SURVEY

The first major tasks of the MIS task force, working in conjunction with the executive steering committee, center around the second phase of the exploratory survey—overall investigation. This consists of selecting desired objectives, defining the problem in specific terms, training the study group for specific tasks, and determining a realistic time schedule for the real-time MIS feasibility study.

SELECT SPECIFIC REAL-TIME MIS OBJECTIVES

The formulation of objectives is the joint effort of the executive steering committee and the MIS task force. Not only do clearly stated objectives force top management to think seriously about the firm's future, but they also bring to light problems that might otherwise have been overlooked. They provide a framework for both groups in which to operate. The constraints and limitations under which the project must function are clearly indicated. Experience has shown that a feasibility study goes much more smoothly when a formal statement of objectives has been clearly delineated.

The objectives desired by management can take many directions, as depicted in Figure 3-2. Objectives can center around a costs savings approach, in which case consideration should be given to both tangible and intangible benefits for evaluation to be complete and realistic. Other objectives can emphasize better and more timely information for management decisions. Actually, this approach is aimed at cost reduction as well as at faster service for customers. Ideally, a real-time MIS should be able to meet as many objectives as possible and, simultaneously, reduce costs for the firm.

Utilization of faster data processing equipment to speed the flow of data handled by the firm is representative of additional objectives desired by both groups. It allows the firm to schedule production more effectively and to notify customers of any shipping changes or delays. It also speeds billing procedures. The accurate and uniform handling of data is made available without the problems of human intervention. All these benefits improve customer relations and enhance the firm's competitive position.

Top management might also consider other objectives, such as elimination of conflicting and overlapping services within the firm and the employment of checks and balances as the data are processed to eliminate the need for manual checking. This would be part of internal control for the new system.

Another desirable objective is improved operations through greater use of operations research models. The utilization of mathematical models can reduce both the amount of inventory and production costs. Operations research has been successfully employed to increase managerial efficiency, to effect better utilization of plant personnel and equipment, and to improve employee and public relations. Major exceptions can be extracted and reported to responsible persons for immedi-

Better information to meet the firm's long-range planning needs.

Increased efficiency in the firm's operations.

Reduction in data processing costs to the firm.

More timely information for management decisions.

Improved information to meet the planning and controlling needs for daily operations.

Improved customer service and relations.

Increased flow of data for meaningful information.

Uniform and accurate handling of data with a minimum of human intervention.

Elimination of conflicting and overlapping services within the firm.

Improved operations through greater utilization of operations research.

Improved employee and public relations.

Increased managerial development and efficiency.

Reduction in collection of duplicate items of data.

Efficient utilization of personnel and equipment.

Increased overall net income from operations.

Reduction in data recording and manipulation errors.

FIGURE 3-2. Selection of desired objectives for a real-time MIS project.

ate action. Important OR applications have been detailed in the Appendix to Chapter Two.

Although the foregoing objectives revolve around using the real-time computer as a tool, the executive steering committee must demand that output be oriented toward the user. Never should the strict technical requirements of the hardware be favored if, by doing so, service to company personnel is impaired. Research has shown that problems involving people are much more extensive and more deeply rooted than those involving technical systems during a systems change. New methods and procedures can fail miserably if it becomes apparent that the computer is being favored to the detriment of user needs. Within the overall context, objectives that consider the human element must be incorporated into the man/machine operating mode of the real-time system.

The preceding list is only a cross-section of desirable objectives. In the final analysis, selection of real-time MIS objectives is primarily the responsibility of top-level executives. Generally, objectives are unlikely to be sufficiently demanding if not prescribed by the executive steering committee. It should be remembered that objectives can always be changed if, at a later date, they are found to be unrealistic.

DEFINE MIS PROBLEM TO BE SOLVED

As previously noted, the scope of the feasibility study has been stated in general terms by the executive steering committee. Once the objectives have been agreed upon by both groups, the MIS task force defines the problem more precisely. It is the job of the study team to specify the functional areas (subsystems) which will be explored in greater detail. The team must also make sure that the scope of the feasibility study is compatible with the objectives. If the objectives and the scope of the study conflict, a conference of the two committees should be called to resolve the problem.

Having defined the problem as accurately as possible within the scope of the study, preferably stated in writing, the study team should have little doubt as to the areas to be covered by the investigation. A written memorandum by the MIS group ensures the accomplishment of the original intentions and reduces the chances of going off on a tangent. A carefully laid-out plan, backed by the executive steering committee, indicates where the study will cut across organizational lines and where authority is needed for changes in systems, methods, procedures, forms, reports, or organization for the areas to be investigated.

TRAIN MIS TASK FORCE

Generally, the management information system task force includes members who are knowledgeable about the operations of the firm's functional areas and others who are data processing experts. Each member has only some of the knowledge necessary to carry a real-time MIS feasibility study to a successful conclusion. For this reason, both groups must receive additional training. Personnel from the functional areas should attend intensive data processing courses (ranging from one week to several weeks) given by computer manufacturers, consulting firms, or software firms. Meanwhile, computer personnel and outside consultants will spend time reviewing the present operations. This is usually the minimum amount of training the study group should have before it begins the investigation.

As stated in previous sections, it is advisable to go beyond the minimum training requirements indicated above. In order for the systems group to contribute most effectively to management's needs and desires, it must have a detailed knowledge of the overall company objectives and plans. Plans must be interpretable in terms of information system needs.

DETERMINE A REALISTIC SCHEDULE

The final step in the overall investigation of the exploratory survey is the preparation of a time schedule for the entire systems study. Generally, a MIS study takes place over a long period of time, up to several years. Experience has shown that there is a tendency to underestimate the time needed for the feasibility study as well as for all succeeding steps. The time factor is of secondary importance. If time becomes the most important consideration, an optimum decision for the firm's data processing needs in a real-time MIS operating mode will probably not be made.

When developing a time schedule, the MIS committee must determine the amount of work involved in each step of the systems change and the personnel and skills resources that will be needed. Likewise, consideration must be given to the following areas: training, programming, program testing, delivery of equipment, physical requirements and installation of the equipment, development of files, delivery of new forms and supplies, and conversion activities.

Major Parts of a Systems Project

An overview of the time, stated in percentage, needed for the various steps in a feasibility study and systems implementation is given in Figure 3-3. These percentages are not absolute values, but only a general guide for a typical MIS project of several years' duration. (As pointed out previously, research on the development of an effective management information system can take several years.) Depending on the complexity of the systems project, the Gantt chart, PERT/time, or PERT/cost can be used to control the activities. It should be recognized that the steps in Figure 3-3 have been grouped and that many subactivities are related to each one.

I.	Feasibility Study:	
	A. Exploratory survey, including systems analysis	12%
	B. Basic systems design	15
	C. Equipment selection	10
II.	Systems Implementation:	
	A. Preparatory work of new system:	
	1. Training all personnel	8
	2. Flowcharting, including decision tables	10
	3. Programming, desk checking, and systems testing	10
	4. Program compiling and testing	20
	B. Operation of new system:	
	1. Parallel operations for checking new system	5
	2. Final conversion to new system	10
		100

FIGURE 3-3.   Major steps of a systems project, stated in percentage of total time (based on past research).

The essentials of a systems project are illustrated in Figure 3-4. The relationships of the major parts in a real-time MIS project to the short-, intermediate-, and long-range plans is also depicted. As the figure indicates, the systems project is continuous. Examination of new system approaches or extensive "patching" of the present system may signal the necessity for a new feasibility study.

An examination of the time allocation in Figure 3-3 reveals that the feasibility study comprises more than one-third of the total time for a systems change. This may seem excessive but reduction of the time spent on the study generally leads to poor results.

The first step of systems implementation is the training of personnel, particularly programmers. Programmers cannot be sent to the manufacturer's programming school until the final step of the feasibility study, when the equipment is selected.

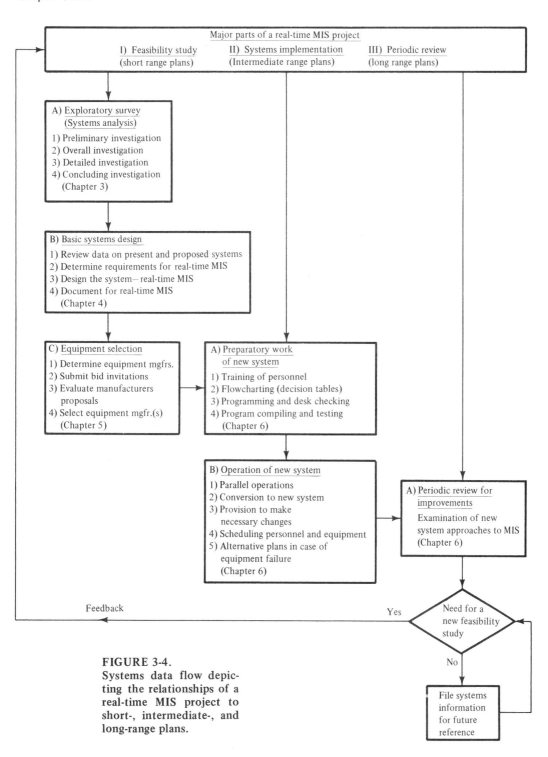

FIGURE 3-4.
Systems data flow depicting the relationships of a real-time MIS project to short-, intermediate-, and long-range plans.

Likewise, the equipment cannot be chosen until the firm has decided upon the basic systems design which forms the basis for the equipment bids. Thus, there is a logical sequence. Failure to follow this ordered pattern is likely to lead to chaos.

The period required for systems implementation comprises about two-thirds of the total time required for a systems change. It is unfortunate that many members of the executive steering committee feel that the real work has been completed when the feasibility study is over. Actually, it has just begun. This attitude often explains the hurry to get the equipment installed and running during the systems implementation phase, particularly when the rental on the equipment starts and management sees no production for the large cash outlays. The end results in such instances are incomplete, inefficient, and ill-conceived programs that are a disappointment to everyone involved in the project.

The study group should not only prepare a realistic time table but also be able to report at any time whether the study is ahead of, behind, or on schedule. The manager of the MIS task force should issue reports periodically to the executive steering committee on the status of the project. Information critical to the study, such as problem areas and delays, should be included in the reports. The use of the exception principle in progress reports is needed to control the project.

3. DETAILED INVESTIGATION OF PRESENT SYSTEM—
SYSTEMS ANALYSIS

During the entire exploratory survey, the executive steering committee and the MIS task force are in constant communication with each other. If functional areas included in the original scope of the study are found to be poor candidates during any phase or are found during the study to be incapable of meeting the firm's desired objectives, the two groups must meet to resolve the problem.

The detailed investigation of the present system, commonly referred to as systems analysis, involves collecting, organizing, and evaluating facts about the present system and the environment in which it operates. Enough information should be assembled that a qualified person could design the system without visiting any of the firm's operating departments. Generally, the study groups devote full time to this undertaking because it is so time-consuming. An intense review should be made of existing methods and procedures, data flow, outputs, files, inputs, and internal control in order to fully understand the present system and its problems. No area should be excluded if it has any bearing on the desired objectives and the problem definition.

Each functional area reviewed, commonly referred to as a subsystem project, requires the assignment of a leader. The overall project should be subdivided into specific tasks, each with a separate responsibility assignment and time schedule. The first phase of each task is to review the area in depth. The second phase involves documentation.

In order to perform a thorough analysis of the present system, it is necessary to have accurate information about the operating areas. To assure such input, operations personnel must become involved almost from the beginning. In fact, it is almost impossible to develop a sound existing-systems framework without assistance from the various departments. If operations people are not involved, there is also a risk that current-system specifications will not be complete.

OBJECTIVE OF SYSTEMS ANALYSIS

The objective of systems analysis is to understand the mechanics of the present system in terms of equipment, personnel, demands on the system, operating conditions, and related problems. Systems analysis serves as a basis for designing and installing a real-time system; basic design is concerned with systems development. The new systems design must be based on the facts obtained in the analysis stage and within the framework of the study. The systems implementation stage builds upon the systems analysis and basic systems-design phases by devising programs, methods, and procedures; recruiting and training qualified personnel; selecting and installing the equipment; and putting the new system into operation. Even though systems analysis, basic systems design, equipment selection, and systems implementation are discussed separately, they are intimately related because each has some affect on the others. Isolating these phases generally results in a mediocre system.

CONTENT OF SYSTEMS ANALYSIS

The essential elements of systems analysis that are preparatory for documentation are detailed in Figure 3-5. Overview of the firm, obtained through a review of the firm's history, is followed by:

> analysis of outputs
> review of methods and procedures
> investigation of common data bank (files)
> analysis of inputs
> review of internal control.

The foregoing analyses provide a sound basis for documentation of the current system. Reviewing the present work volume, analyzing current personnel requirements, and preparing a schedule of present-system costs and benefits are also considered part of systems analysis. Generally, these areas are analyzed by standard methods.

METHODS OF SYSTEMS ANALYSIS

The systems analysts of the MIS task force use several tools to obtain the necessary data during this study phase. Among these are interviews; company systems and procedures manuals; and forms, documents, and reports.

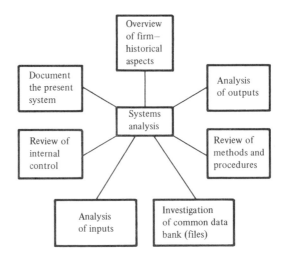

FIGURE 3-5. Essential elements in a detailed investigation of the present system, commonly referred to as systems analysis, that are preparatory for documentation.

Interviews

Generally, the best way to understand what is transpiring is to talk directly with the individuals responsible for getting the job done. The analyst should study the activities as presented by the person in charge of the department. Attention should also be given to the subordinates' work in order to confirm the supervisor's statements.

For a successful interview, the analyst should be formally introduced to all supervisory personnel. This approach immediately establishes the idea that the study is an official undertaking of the firm, backed by the executive steering committee and the board of directors. The interview should be friendly and informal. The analyst should take notes as he asks the supervisor his or her ideas on how the system can be improved. It is important to ask the supervisors' opinions in order to make them feel that they have contributed to the study. This feeling of participation will make the system changes easier later. The supervisor should be assured that any changes to be made will be discussed with him or her before implementation.

Company Systems and Procedures Manual

Another tool the task force uses is the firm's systems and procedures manual. Other names are sometimes used, but whatever the name, the manual contains descriptions of all procedures currently in use. Reference is made to inputs, outputs, and files employed in specific procedures. This will be helpful in documenting current operations later. Caution is necessary when using the manual, however. Quite often, conditions have changed since the material was written. Also, procedures listed are occasionally different from those actually in use, without management's knowledge. When the procedures manual is nonexistent or out of date, the analysts will have to spend more time during interviews to obtain the needed information.

Forms, Documents, and Reports

Most procedure manuals contain actual copies of forms, documents, and reports used. If not, samples can be obtained during the interview period. The caution mentioned previously concerning the procedure manual applies here as well. Often, changes made on documents and forms seem so insignificant that no one takes time to insert the new ones into the manual. Only after many changes is the difference apparent. A review of all samples forms may reveal a need to combine, eliminate, or design new ones.

OVERVIEW OF FIRM—HISTORICAL ASPECTS

A logical starting point in analyzing the present system is an overview, or brief history, of the firm. The historical facts should identify the milestones that have influenced the direction of the firm. Attention should be paid to the industry, the firm's markets, distribution channels, competitors, organizational structure, future trends, objectives, policies, government and union regulations affecting the firm. An historical review of the firm's organization chart will identify the growth of the various levels of management as well as the development in the various areas and departments of the firm. Not only must historical data be analyzed, but current and future plans must also be examined to understand the goals of the firm and their corresponding implications. The team should investigate what system changes have occurred in the past. These would include both successful and unsuccessful operations.

ANALYSIS OF OUTPUTS

The outputs produced by many departments of the firm become the inputs for other areas. For this reason, the firm's outputs or reports should be carefully scrutinized by the MIS task force to determine how well these meet the firm's needs. The questions of what information is needed and why, who needs it, and when and where it is needed must be answered. Additional questions concerning the sequence of the data, how often a form is used, and how long it is kept on file must be investigated. Reports, retained from earlier days, often have little relevance to current operations.

All reports for internal use should be timely, accurate, complete, concise, and useful; standardization of forms should be considered; and the cost of their preparation should not exceed their value to the firm. Reports for all areas of the firm should be carefully scrutinized. The study teams should not necessarily accept the present forms as ideal or even usable for the new system. New reports should be

determined objectively. In this manner, problems associated with the current outputs will be eliminated.

REVIEW OF METHODS AND PROCEDURES

A method prescribes the way an action is undertaken. A procedure specifies
what action is required, who is required to act, and under what condition the action
is to be undertaken. A procedure is larger in scope than a method.

A procedures review is an intensive survey of the methods by which each job
is accomplished, the tools utilized, and the actual location of operations. Its basic
objectives are to eliminate unnecessary tasks and to perceive improvement opportunities in the present system. Both tasks can be accomplished simultaneously. The
study group will often recommend immediate improvements in certain areas although the actual installation of the real-time MIS may be years away. This provides immediate cost reduction and increased efficiency within the respective
departments.

INVESTIGATION OF COMMON DATA BANK (FILES)

The task force should investigate the common data bank and other files
maintained by each department, their number and size, where they are located,
who uses them, and the number of times per given time interval they are referenced.
This information may be contained in the procedures manual. Information on
common data files should be an important consideration when designing a new
system. Both static and dynamic files are reviewed on the basis of the storage media
that best suits them: magnetic drum, magnetic disk, magnetic tape, laser, punched
card, microfilm, or some other type. The size of the files can also have an effect on
the equipment selected. Files can be the focal point in deciding what equipment to
select for a real-time MIS project.

A review of the on-line and off-line files maintained will reveal information
about data not contained in the firm's outputs. It is always better to have too much
on file than too little. This is particularly true when specialized studies are periodically undertaken. Gathering and retaining all potentially useful data has some merit.
However, the related cost of retrieving and processing the data is to be considered.
Files of information held for a long time may be difficult to store inexpensively and
may require a high processing cost when reports are prepared. Maintenance of large
data files over extended periods is a function of their ultimate value in terms of
future reports, storage costs, and legal requirements.

ANALYSIS OF INPUTS

Detailed analysis of present inputs, basic to the manipulation of data, is
important. Source documents are used to capture the originating data for any data
processing system. The systems analyst should be aware of the various sources from

which data are initially obtained, remembering that outputs for one area may serve as inputs for other areas.

Data processing personnel must understand such considerations as the nature of the form, what it contains, who prepared it, where the form is initiated, where it is completed, and the distribution of it. If the systems analysts answer these questions adequately, they will be able to determine how these inputs fit into the framework of the present system.

REVIEW OF INTERNAL CONTROL

A detailed investigation of the present system is not complete until internal control is reviewed; many systems analysts fail to spend adequate time on this item. Locating the control points helps the computer analyst visualize the essential parts and framework of a system. An examination of the present system for effective internal control may indicate weaknesses that should not be duplicated in the real-time MIS project. The utilization of advanced methods, procedures, and equipment permits greater control over the data than is available with the present system.

DOCUMENT THE PRESENT SYSTEM

As outputs, methods, procedures, files, reports, and internal control are reviewed and analyzed, the normal procedure is to document the present system. Documentation can take several forms which include:

system flowcharts
flow process charts
document flowcharts
decision tables
SOP (Study Organization Plan)
TAG (Time-Automated Grid)

The first four document techniques have been used extensively but the latter two are of rather recent origin. SOP and TAG are combination systems analysis and design techniques.

System Flowcharts

System flowcharts, sometimes referred to as procedural flowcharts, show the sequence of major activities that normally comprise a complete operation. They are generally prepared to help all company personnel, particularly the systems analyst, understand some specific data processing operation, as well as get an overview of the operation itself (See Figure 4-3, pp. 127-128). Before a system flowchart can be drawn, the data processing area under study must be clearly defined. Questions relating to the type and number of inputs (source documents), exceptions, transactions, files, reports, and similar items must be answered. Other questions refer to the relationship of the area under study to other functional parts of the system, the timeliness of data, and the sources of various data. Answers to these questions provide the necessary information for the system flowchart.

From the first overall flowchart, additional flowcharts can be drawn to show each major operation broken down into its sub-procedures. The detailed procedures can be related to each other and to the entire system by the flow of information among them.

The flowcharting of present operations not only organizes the facts for the MIS task force but also helps disclose gaps and duplication in the data gathered. It allows a thorough comprehension of the numerous details and related problems in the present operation. It should be noted that flowcharting, like other documentation techniques, need not be undertaken separately, but generally is combined with the other procedures of systems analysis.

Flow Process Charts

Flow process charts depict the sequence of operations by functions and individuals, as illustrated in Figure 3-6. Details are clearly shown so that they can be questioned and analyzed to determine better methods of operation. Operations are represented symbolically and a reminder of who, what, where, when, why, and how are listed so they can be considered during the investigation and analysis. Operational time, recommended action, and summary space are also provided on the chart. In addition to use as systems analysis documentation, the chart serves as a work simplification technique.

Document Flowcharts

Document flowcharts, like system flowcharts, are suitable for tracing the origin of input data through each phase of processing and communication, into files, and finally, out of files for desired outputs—many in the form of reports. They show the way various forms, documents, or reports move from person to person or from department to department. This is extremely helpful in understanding and obtaining an overview of paper flow for a specific function within the firm. Although no special flowcharting symbols are needed, the departments or individuals involved are usually identified on the top of the sheet. An example of this flowcharting technique for raw material purchases is found in Figure 3-7.

Decision Tables

Decision tables are similar to flowcharts in their use and construction. They can be used either independently or to complement flowcharts. A decision table, as shown later in Figure 3-15, shows conditions and actions in a simple and orderly manner. By presenting logical alternative courses of action under various operating conditions, a decision table enables one to think through a problem and present its

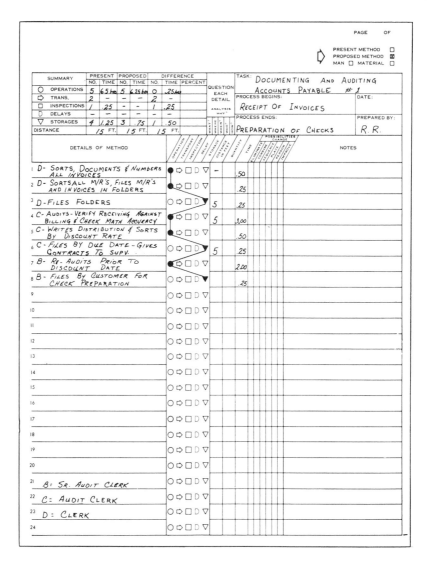

FIGURE 3-6. A flow process chart serves as documentation for systems analysis.

solution concisely. It allows a computer problem to be divided into its logical segments and provides a multilevel structure in the problem's analysis. At the highest level, decision tables can be used for an overall system by referring to lower-level tables.

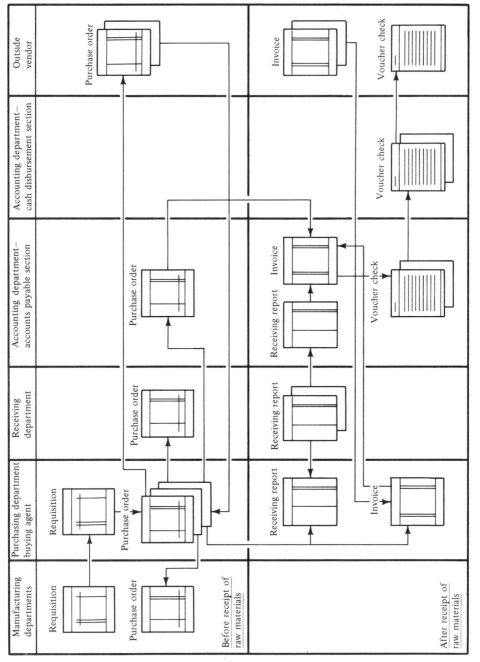

FIGURE 3-7. A document flowchart, such as this raw material purchases example, serves as documentation for systems analysis.

SOP (Study Organization Plan)

The Study Organization Plan,[1] developed by IBM in the early 1970's, is a formalized guide for systems analysis and design. It is an organized plan, divided into three phases:

1. understand the present business (Figure 3-8)
2. determine systems requirements
3. design the new system

The first phase covers techniques for gathering data and produces a report entitled "Present Business Description." Phase two is concerned with analysis of business activities in terms of inputs, outputs, and resources, resulting in another report entitled "Systems Requirements Specification." Phase three considers design alternatives, equipment configurations, and the economic impact of the system on the business. Its results are organized into a report entitled "New System Plan."

A recommended approach to SOP is to compile information that forms a hierarchy of detail. This approach permits systems personnel concerned with different levels of detail to deal selectively with the level in which they are interested.

TAG (Time Automated Grid)

The Time Automated Grid[2] is a technique for systems analysis based on a series of IBM-developed programs. It is intended to aid the systems analyst in the design of large-scale systems. Data to be analyzed are recorded on special input/output analysis forms that describe the characteristics of the inputs, outputs, or files to be analyzed, including length, format, and sequence as well as frequency, volume, and processing priority. Use of TAG begins with a description of system outputs. Once these have been prepared, TAG works backward to determine what inputs are necessary and at what periods of time. When both inputs and outputs have been defined, the next step of the program is to produce file and system flow descriptions. File contents and data flow are both based on time—the time at which data elements enter the system and the time within which they are required to produce output.

PRESENT WORK VOLUME

Many firms require their departmental managers to keep an accurate tabulation on the volume of inputs processed, files maintained, and outputs prepared within their respective departments. Other firms go a step further and compute an average cost for these items. Time can be saved if data on past and present work

[1]T. B. Glans, B. Grad, D. Holstein, W. E. Meyers, and R. N. Schmidt's *Management Systems* (New York: Holt, Rinehart and Winston, Inc., 1968) is an extensive description of SOP by its developers, augmented with case study illustrations.

[2]A description of TAG is contained in *IBM Sales and Systems Guide* Y20-0358-0. Contact: IBM Technical Publications Department, 112 East Post Road, White Plains, New York 10601.

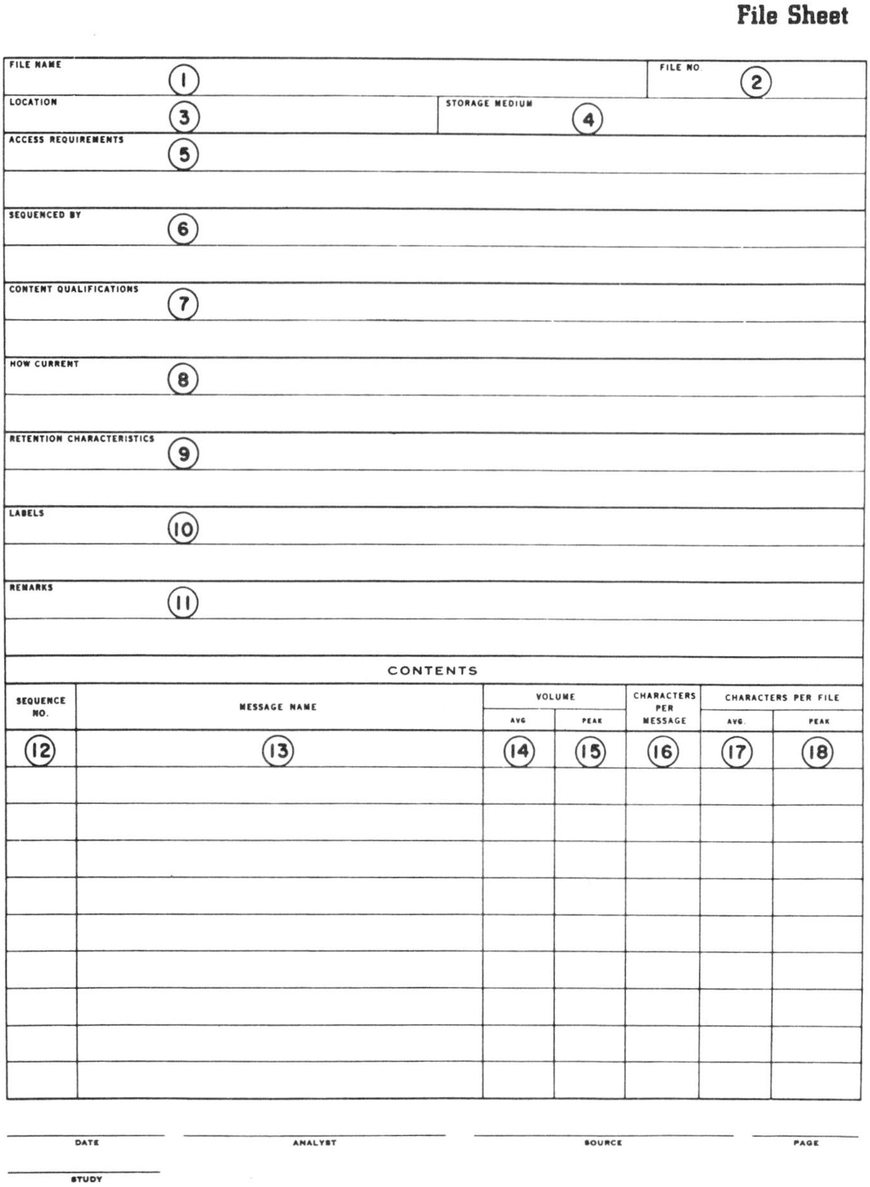

FILE NAME (1)			FILE NO (2)
LOCATION (3)	STORAGE MEDIUM (4)		
ACCESS REQUIREMENTS (5)			
SEQUENCED BY (6)			
CONTENT QUALIFICATIONS (7)			
HOW CURRENT (8)			
RETENTION CHARACTERISTICS (9)			
LABELS (10)			
REMARKS (11)			

CONTENTS

SEQUENCE NO.	MESSAGE NAME	VOLUME		CHARACTERS PER MESSAGE	CHARACTERS PER FILE	
		AVG	PEAK		AVG.	PEAK
(12)	(13)	(14)	(15)	(16)	(17)	(18)

DATE   ANALYST   SOURCE   PAGE

STUDY

FIGURE 3-8. An example of IBM's SOP File Sheet which contains information relating to one file. (Courtesy International Business Machines Corporation.)

volume are available. Otherwise, these data must be recompiled. It is important for the study group to determine not only reliable figures for average and peak days, but the work load at month's end as well. In addition, accurate figures from the past five years are necessary to ascertain growth or reduction in volumes. These data will be used to determine the present cost of operations and the projected savings and costs for a real-time MIS project.

Careful analysis of work volumes can be beneficial to the entire feasibility study. When work volumes are small and the processing procedures are complicated, the feasibility of applying real-time equipment is unlikely. On the other hand, when large volumes of work require routine and straightforward processing, the likelihood of employing real-time capabilities is very high. Work volume analysis is also helpful to the task force in determining whether a particular work station is a control point, a storage area, or a terminal point. These observations can indicate needs for visual display, storage, or special processing capabilities in the basic systems design.

An examination of existing on-line and off-line files may serve as a guide for their eventual reorganization. Separate files may contain a certain amount of common data. Each time the common data are changed, all files must be changed. An example of this problem is found with inventory magnetic tape files (batch processing mode) in which separate magnetic tape inventory files that vary in content are maintained for the marketing, manufacturing, and accounting departments respectively. This redundancy can be overcome by a real-time MIS which has one inventory file available for on-line processing. A comparable redundancy problem exists for the firm's outputs or reports.

CURRENT PERSONNEL REQUIREMENTS

Current personnel requirements should be broken down by type, skill, and related cost. The efficiency of personnel working with and without equipment should be measured and analyzed. Most of these data can be obtained from personnel records and departmental statements and interviews. A resume of the firm's personnel resources can be utilized to appraise the costs and benefits of the present system. Information about local available data processing specialists is needed if the skills of current personnel resources are limited. Information about employee turnover, fringe benefits, and management attitudes toward the firm's personnel and labor unions should be collected and considered for any new data processing system. Every effort should be made to understand any element of the firm that can make or break the systems project.

OTHER REQUIREMENTS AND CONSIDERATIONS

The major areas that should be analyzed in depth for a detailed investigation of the present system have been covered in the foregoing material. This has included the effect of exceptions and errors on the present system. Other requirements and considerations include the effect seasonal or other cyclical characteristics have on the present system, the firm's current financial resources and production facilities (including plant inventories), and their future trends. Information about the firm's financial status should be obtained from the financial statements. Data concerning land, buildings, equipment, and tools representing the firm's production facilities, as well as plans for new facilities and related equipment, should also be included in the study. Physical inventories as to total investment, number of items, and turnover should be ascertained. The data processing equipment currently in use, including communications facilities, is of special interest to the study team. Equipment utilization charts and tables should be reviewed for measuring the equipment's efficiency and effectiveness.

Work Simplification

Once the inputs, methods and procedures of processing data, and the outputs have been clearly delineated and documented, the task force is in a position to make recommendations regarding the present system. Recommendations may include eliminating outright duplication, unnecessary reports, and useless activities; combining operations to reduce paper handling; and improving layout and methods. Other recommendations may be to revise and redesign forms and to reduce the number of procedural steps for an activity. Improvements of this type are commonly referred to as *work simplification.*

The question of whether or not to make improvements in the present system at this time is one that must be answered by the executive steering committee in conjunction with the MIS task force. Generally, the time factor is the basis for answering the question. Because the actual implementation of the real-time systems project is considerably more than a year away, it is highly recommended that reports with improvement suggestions be issued to specific departments. For these reports to be effective, they must have the tacit approval of top management. Although this undertaking will lengthen the time of the feasibility study, it will provide a foundation for a friendly relationship between the departmental managers and the task group and will smooth the path for the new system installation. These work-simplification reports can also establish the task force as a knowledgeable and competent group in everyone's eyes. If the group does a poor job on this phase of the study, top management has the option of strengthening the group or cancelling the entire feasibility study.

COSTS AND BENEFITS OF PRESENT SYSTEM

One of the major reasons for reviewing the present operation is to determine its costs. Costs should be analyzed by department because this is the most common basis for reporting and provides an excellent means of comparing costs to a new system. Typical departmental costs, determined by the firm's accounting section, are found in Figure 3-9.

Tangible Versus Intangible Factors

Existing costs are not the only ones determined. Current-system benefits must be presented for later comparison with each proposed alternative. These benefits include the present level of service to customers, the value of reports, return on investment and profit, ability of the present system to grow with the firm, and inventory turnover. Many of these benefits can be measured precisely, but others

Salaries and wages
Payroll taxes
Fringe benefits (such as life insurance, hospital care, and pensions)
Equipment rental and/or depreciation of equipment
Repairs and maintenance of equipment
Facilities rental
Training costs
File maintenance costs
Personal property taxes on equipment
Insurance on equipment
Forms and supplies
Utilities
Outside processing costs by service bureaus and computer utilities
Other departmental costs

FIGURE 3-9. Feasibility study—sample listing of a firm's departmental costs.

are intangible and require subjective evaluation. Costs and tangible benefits are compared first for final evaluation of the present system and the proposed alternatives. If the selected alternative system meets the firm's established return on investment, there is no problem. However, if the proposed alternative falls below the acceptable level for the investment, the intangible factors become critical to the investment decision.

Five-Year Cost Study

The usual cost projections for the present system in a feasibility study is for a five-year period, starting with implementation of the new system. The rationale is that if a computer is selected, it will not be processing on a daily basis for about a year from the day of equipment selection (the final step of the feasibility study). Also, the equipment must be capable of handling the firm's work load over periods of from three to about five years. Thus, a five-year cost projection that starts with the completion of the feasibility study is a realistic approach for both the present and the new systems. Attempting to go beyond five years is undesirable because of the guesswork and assumptions that must be made about newer equipment. Although some studies include a longer period of time, the results tend to be much too unreliable.

4. CONCLUDING INVESTIGATION—EXPLORATORY SURVEY

The final phase before the exploratory survey report to the executive steering committee is prepared is the concluding investigation by the MIS task force. Because each functional area of the present system that is germane to the study has been carefully analyzed, a set of feasible processing alternatives must be developed in order to select the best one. No alternative will be developed to the same extent that the present system was studied. Such an effort would increase the time and manpower requirements of the study beyond its intended scope and budget.

FEASIBLE REAL-TIME MIS ALTERNATIVES

Proposed system specifications must be clearly defined before feasible system alternatives can be developed. These specifications, which pertain to each functional area of the feasibility study, are determined from the desired objectives initially determined in the study. Likewise, consideration is given to the strengths and the shortcomings of the existing system. Required real-time MIS specifications, which must be clearly defined and conform to the study's objectives, are:

1. Outputs to be produced, with great emphasis on real-time managerial reports that utilize the "exception principle."
2. Common data base to be maintained with on-line processing capabilities via I/O terminals.
3. Input data from original source documents for processing by the real-time system.
4. Methods and procedures that show the relationship of inputs and outputs to the common data base.
5. Work volumes and timing considerations for present and future periods, including peak periods.

One starting point for compiling the above specifications is the outputs. After they have been determined, it is then possible to infer what inputs and on-line and off-line files are required and what methods and procedures must be employed. Although it is possible to start with the inputs, the output-to-input procedure is recommended because the outputs are related directly to the firm's objectives, the study's most important consideration. The future work loads of the real-time MIS must be defined for the inputs, the data base, and the outputs in terms of average and peak loads, cycles, and trends.

Flexible System Requirements

The requirements of the new system may appear at first to be fixed. A closer examination, however, often reveals that these specifications have flexibility. For example, the objectives set forth in the study state that certain file data must be updated once a day. Perhaps the best data processing solution is to incorporate the data into the common data base that is updated as actual transactions occur. This approach is within the constraints as initially set forth and introduces a new way of maintaining files. The important point is that alternative methods are available in data processing areas which may have the outward appearances of being fixed. With this approach in mind, it is possible to design a number of different systems with varying features, costs, and benefits. In many cases, more data processing systems will be investigated and analyzed when flexible system requirements are considered.

Reduction in the number of personnel, lower salaries and wages.

Lower payroll taxes and fringe benefits with fewer people.

Sale or elimination of some equipment—depreciation and/or rental—no longer applicable.

Reduction in repairs, maintenance, insurance, and personal property taxes.

Lower space rental and utilities.

Elimination or reduction in outside processing costs.

FIGURE 3-10.   Feasibility study—estimated savings.

Consultant's Role in Feasible Systems Alternatives

A clear understanding of the new system requirements is the starting point for developing feasible systems alternatives. This phase is by far the most important and difficult undertaking of the study to date. An outside consultant's experience is of great value to the study group. His knowledge of many installations can help immeasurably to reduce the number of possible solutions for the firm. Too often, a study group goes off on a tangent about a specific systems approach which should have been discarded as unfeasible. The outside consultant can make certain that the study group does not waste time on trivial matters. Also, he can point out the shortcomings of a certain approach which may have been strongly advocated by other individuals. He can act with the head of the study group to resolve conflicts that might otherwise tend to divide the team. The consultant's objectivity in judging the merits and weaknesses of a new system can enhance the firm's chances of selecting an optimum system. The key to developing promising system alternatives and selecting the optimum one is to employ fully the talents and experience of the MIS task force.

COST FACTORS, TANGIBLE AND INTANGIBLE BENEFITS FOR EACH ALTERNATIVE

After developing feasible real-time MIS alternatives, the next step is to determine the estimated savings and incremental costs for each alternative. Estimated savings (sometimes referred to as cost displacement) are enumerated in Figure 3-10. Incremental costs are segregated into two categories: one-time costs and additional operating costs. These are listed in Figure 3-11. The difference between the estimated savings, and estimated one-time costs and additional operating costs, represents the estimated net savings (losses) to the firm before federal income taxes.

Accurate figures for a five-year period are of great importance, which indicates a need for accounting department assistance. Often the best way to increase the accuracy of the figures compiled by the study group is to have the outside consultant assist the group and review the data. His knowledge of current data processing equipment and ready access to equipment rental and purchase costs (per manuals maintained by his firm) will save time in this phase of the study. His

Estimated One-Time Costs:

Feasibility study (includes exploratory survey, systems analysis, basic systems design, and equipment selection).

Training of programming and operating personnel.

Documentation of all feasibility study applications.

Programming of these applications.

Program assembly and testing of programs for new system.

Common data base conversion.

Site preparation (includes construction costs, remodeling, air conditioning, and power requirements).

Additional computer time (in excess of hours alloted free of charge).

Parallel operations (the old and the new system operate concurrently—duplication of personnel and equipment for a given time period).

Conversion activities (from existing system to new system).

Other equipment and supplies (includes forms-handling equipment, files, magnetic disks, and magnetic tapes).

Estimated Additional Operating Costs:

Data processing equipment (computer and related equipment)—monthly rental and/or depreciation.

Maintenance of equipment (if not included above).

Program maintenance (programmers).

Wages and salaries of data processing personnel (direct supervision, equipment operation, and other data processing jobs), payroll taxes, and fringe benefits.

Forms and supplies (for new data processing equipment).

Miscellaneous additional costs (includes insurance, repairs, maintenance, and personal property taxes on equipment purchased; power costs; etc.).

FIGURE 3-11.   Feasibility study—estimated one-time costs and estimated additional operating costs.

exposure to other similar cost studies will add creditability to the final figures in the real-time MIS exploratory survey report to top management.

Cost Factors

It is not desirable to base the estimates of savings and incremental costs on the present data processing work load. Rather, the feasibility study group should review the operating work volume compiled during the investigation. The trend of growth or cutback in the firm's work load should be analyzed and projected for the next five years. These data can then be utilized to project savings and costs, as shown per the analysis in Figure 3-12. In this feasibility study for alternative 3, consideration has been given to higher future costs. Salaries and wages are generally increased by 5 percent. Cost reduction through work simplification in the present system has been incorporated in the analysis.

Because the projected savings and costs factors in a feasibility study are for five years (starting with systems implementation), the difference between the two

	Years from Start of Systems Implementation					Five Years Total
	1	2	3	4	5	
Estimated Savings:						
Reduction in personnel (including payroll taxes and fringe benefits)	$120,200	$400,500	$440,300	$490,500	$540,500	$1,992,000
Sale of equipment	120,000					120,000
Rental (space) savings	25,000	51,000	54,500	58,000	61,800	250,300
Elimination of rental equipment	2,050	4,380	4,690	5,000	5,300	21,420
Other savings	3,000	3,060	3,210	3,370	3,540	16,180
Total Estimated Savings	$270,250	$458,940	$502,700	$556,870	$611,140	$2,399,900
Estimated One-Time Costs:						
Feasibility study (for this year and prior year)	$ 95,000					$ 95,000
Training	50,000					50,000
Systems and programming	255,500					255,500
Data base conversion	272,500					272,500
Other conversion activities	75,500					75,500
Site preparation	55,400					55,400
Other one-time costs	22,300					22,300
Total Estimated One-Time Costs	$826,200					$ 826,200
Estimated Additional Operating Costs:						
Data processing equipment rental (include maintenance)	$110,000	$120,800	$127,400	$134,100	$141,000	$ 633,300
Additional personnel for new system (includes payroll taxes and fringe benefits)	34,000	60,700	62,300	63,400	64,600	285,000
Program maintenance	20,000	30,700	32,200	33,800	36,000	152,700
Forms and supplies	10,000	21,500	23,000	24,500	26,000	105,000
Other additional operating costs	4,400	12,400	12,800	13,200	17,600	60,400
Total Estimated Additional Operating Costs	$178,400	$246,100	$257,700	$269,000	$285,200	$1,236,400
Net Savings (losses) before Federal Income Taxes	($734,350)	$212,840	$245,000	$287,870	$325,940	$ 337,300

FIGURE 3-12. Feasibility study—real-time MIS alternative 3 of net savings (losses) for a five-year period (rental basis). Consumer Products Corporation.

sums, after taking into account federal income taxes, should be discounted back to the present time. The purpose of the discounted cash flow is to bring the time value of money into the presentation. This is shown in Figure 3-13 for systems alternative 3. Notice that the net savings after federal income taxes of $175,396 over the five-year period (anticipated life of the system), when discounted, shows a negative present value for this alternative of $27,229. With a discounted 20 percent esti-mated return on investment for this alternative, this one should not be chosen (the firm's cutoff point for capital investments is 20 percent). Even though the revised discounted rate of return is approximately 16 percent (based on present value fac-tors), additional benefits should be considered.

Year	Net Savings (Losses) Before Federal Income Taxes (Per Figure 3-12)	Federal Income Tax @ 48% Rate	Net Savings (Losses) After Federal Income Taxes	At 20% Present Value of $1	At 20% Present Value of Net Savings (Losses)
1	($734,350)	($352,488)	($381,862)	.833	($318,091)
2	212,840	102,163	110,677	.694	76,810
3	245,000	117,600	127,400	.579	73,765
4	287,870	138,178	149,692	.482	72,152
5	325,940	156,451	169,489	.402	68,135
Totals	$337,300	$161,904	$175,396		($ 27,229)

FIGURE 3-13. Feasibility study—real-time MIS alternative 3 dis-counted cash flow based on 20 percent return after federal income taxes (rental basis). Consumer Prod-ucts Corporation.

Tangible Benefits

In addition to the approximate 16-percent return on investment, important tangible benefits may be available to justify the real-time MIS project. Among these are reduced investment in the amount of inventory carried, less spoilage and ob-solescence of inventory, lower purchasing costs through automatic reordering, lower insurance costs and taxes on inventory, fewer warehouses needed, lower transportation costs, and lower interest charges on money needed to finance inven-tories. More effective inventory control can have a pronounced effect on this large balance sheet item. Similarly, a more accurate projection of the firm's cash position will reduce its needs for short-term financing. Other large asset items should be evaluated to determine whether or not tangible savings are available through more effective control. All these values discounted to the present should be added to Figure 3-13. If the present value of net savings for a systems alternative is still negative, and it usually is, after adding these tangible benefits, the intangible bene-fits must be explored.

Intangible Benefits

A number of intangible benefits, or qualitative factors, will be uncovered by studying the potential contributions of the new real-time MIS system to the firm's activities and problems. A list of these factors is found in Figure 3-14. Even though qualitative factors are nonquantifiable initially, their ultimate impact is in quantitative terms, reflected in the firm's financial statements.

An analysis of Figure 3-14 indicates that the intangible benefits of the real-time system ultimately offer two major benefits—increased revenues and decreased operating costs—to the firm. Better customer service and relations should enable the firm to increase sales to its present customers and to many potential ones who are looking for these characteristics in its vendors. A real-time MIS environment affects the firm not only externally but also internally in terms of faster and more frequent reporting of results. In addition to accuracy, speed, and flexibility, real-time processing equipment allows management more time to plan and organize activities and, in turn, direct and control according to the original plan.

Improved customer service by using better techniques to anticipate customer requirements, resulting in fewer lost sales, less overtime in the plant for rush orders, and similar considerations.

Better decision-making ability in the areas of marketing, research and development, engineering, manufacturing, inventory, purchasing, physical distribution, finance, accounting, personnel, and corporate planning through more timely and informative reports via I/O terminals.

More effective utilization of management's time for planning, organizing, directing, and controlling because of the availability of timely data and information.

Ability to handle more customers faster with more automatic data processing equipment.

Closer control over capital investments and expenses through comparisons with budgets or forecasts.

Improved scheduling and production control, resulting in more efficient employment of men and machines.

Greater accuracy, speed, and reliability in information handling and data processing operations.

Better control of credit through more frequent aging of accounts receivable and analysis of credit data.

Reversal of trend to higher hiring and training costs arising from the difficulties in filling clerical jobs.

Help prevent a competitor(s) from gaining an eventual economic advantage over the firm.

Ability to utilize the many quantitative techniques of operations research.

Improved promotional efforts to attract new customers and retain present ones.

Greater ability to handle increased work loads at small additional costs.

Enhanced stature in the business community as a progressive and forward-looking firm.

FIGURE 3-14.   Feasibility study—intangible benefits with a real-time management information system.

COMPARISON OF EACH ALTERNATIVE TO PRESENT SYSTEM

Once a thorough analysis of the important factors has been completed, the MIS task force will be in a position to compare the systems alternatives. There are two approaches to evaluating alternatives that can be employed for a definitive conclusion to the feasibility study: identifying and listing the relevant costs and benefits (tangible and intangible) and utilizing operations research simulation techniques.

Decision Table to Evaluate Systems Alternatives

The first approach can take the form of a decision table, shown in Figure 3-15. A decision table is helpful in resolving a complex management decision because it assembles all factors for every feasible systems alternative. A complete summary of all factors pertinent to making the important decision should be a part of the decision table for it to be a fully effective management tool.

The conditions in the upper part of the figure represent tangible and intangible benefits, while the lower part shows the possible courses of action. Each systems alternative represents a set of actions corresponding to a certain set of conditions. In this case, systems alternative 3 indicates the highest return for real-time MIS in comparison with the other alternatives. Its intangible benefits must be reevaluated for a final decision.

Simulation to Evaluate Systems Alternatives

The other approach to estimating overall performance of a proposed alternative through increased revenues or reduced costs is to utilize simulation. A simulation computer program uses past experience plus future forecasts to determine the step-by-step events that are likely to occur. The inputs can be simulated under the conditions of the proposed system. Processing orders under simulated conditions will give the task force a realistic estimate on the performance of each systems alternative. System simulating methods, such as GPSS (General Purpose System Simulator) and SCERT (System and Computer Evaluation and Review Technique), can monitor, for example, what happens as each order is received, how long the order waits before being processed, how much more time the order takes when errors are found, how often inventory is available or not available for the order, how many back orders result, and how much time is needed to process the entire order. Data on revenue and costs can also be compiled for the study.

REAL-TIME MIS EXPLORATORY SURVEY REPORT TO MANAGEMENT

At the conclusion of the foregoing studies, ample information should have been accumulated to make an objective, final recommendation to top management. The real-time MIS exploratory survey report, authored by the MIS task force, should be

Decision Table	Table Name: Feasibility Study—Real-Time MIS Exploratory Survey									Page 1 of 1		
	Chart No: FS-ES-1					Prepared by: R. J. Thierauf				Date: 7/25/7-		
	Condition	\multicolumn{12}{c}{*Rule Number*}
		1	*2*	*3*	*4*	*5*	*6*	*7*	*8*	*9*	*10*	*11*	*12*
Tangible Benefits:													
Meets return on investment criteria—20% after taxes*		N	N	N	N	N							
Lower order processing costs		Y	Y	Y	Y	Y							
Lower investment in inventory		Y	Y	Y	Y	Y							
Less future cash requirements		N	Y	Y	Y	N							
Intangible Benefits:													
Improved customer service		N	Y	Y	Y	Y							
Improved promotional efforts		Y	Y	Y	Y	Y							
Ability to handle more customers faster		N	N	Y	Y	Y							
Better decision making ability		Y	Y	Y	Y	Y							
More effective utilization of management's time		Y	Y	Y	Y	Y							
Improved scheduling and production control		Y	Y	Y	Y	Y							
Closer control over capital investments and expenses		Y	Y	Y	Y	Y							
Better control of credit		N	N	Y	Y	Y							
Ability to handle more volume at lower costs		Y	Y	Y	Y	Y							
More accuracy and reliability of data		Y	Y	Y	Y	Y							
Greater utilization of operations research techniques		Y	Y	Y	Y	Y							
Action													
Utilizes a real-time management information system		X	X	X	X	X							
Utilizes remote batch processing		—	—	X	X	X							
Minor changes of inputs and outputs		X	—	—	—	—							
Substantial changes of inputs and outputs		—	X	X	X	X							
Need for a common data base		X	X	X	X	X							
Moderate revision of methods and procedures		X	X	—	—	—							
Complete revision of methods and procedures		—	—	X	X	X							
Employ an additional consultant for study		—	—	X	X	X							
Recruit new data processing personnel		—	X	X	X	X							
Reevaluate intangible benefits		—	—	X	X	—							

*Other Information: *1-14%; 2-15%; 3-16%; 4-15%; 5-13%*

FIGURE 3-15. Feasibility study—decision table for appraising feasible real-time MIS alternatives.

a signed report to the executive steering committee. It should be financially oriented, because large sums of money are involved. Generally, the approval for one of the recommended alternatives must come from the board of directors or top management.

In preparing the survey report, the task force should be aware that a computer-oriented system is in a far better position than other systems to absorb growth in volume with a slight increase in operating costs. Comparable data processing principles should also be embodied in the report. In both their study and their recommendations, they should not attempt to alter the present system to meet the capabilities of the proposed equipment; rather, the equipment should meet the needs of the system that has been developed in their investigation.

RECOMMEND A REAL-TIME MANAGEMENT INFORMATION SYSTEM FROM THE ALTERNATIVES

As we have seen, the weighing of quantitative and qualitative factors, with emphasis on the firm's future growth patterns and related problems (and with particular consideration given to important intangible benefits), results in the feasibility or nonfeasibility of applying real-time equipment and techniques. Now a comprehensive report must be prepared that states this recommendation. A suggested listing for the final exploratory survey report is depicted in Figure 3-16. The report gives management an opportunity to examine the data and appraise their validity and merit. It also provides management with a sound basis for constructive criticism of the systems project.

1. Outline of the study, in which the objectives are stated and the problem is clearly defined.
2. Overview of the existing system, pointing out its weaknesses and problems.
3. Adequate description of the recommended systems alternative, indicating its tangible and intangible benefits to the firm, its superiority in eliminating or reducing the deficiencies of the present system, and its general impact on the firm.
4. Financial data on the recommended systems alternative, similar to that found in Figures 3-12 and 3-13.
5. Reference to other feasible systems alternatives which were investigated, giving reasons for their final rejection. A decision table, similar to Figure 3-15, should be included.
6. Financial data on systems alternatives that were not selected, similar to that found in Figures 3-12 and 3-13.
7. Schedule of funds required for specific periods of time during systems implementation.
8. List of additional personnel needed to implement the new system and personnel requirements during conversion.
9. Accurate time schedule for the remainder of the real-time MIS systems project.
10. Other special factors and considerations.

FIGURE 3-16.   Suggested listing for a real-time MIS exploratory survey report to top management.

In the example, an examination of Figure 3-15 indicates that alternatives 3 and 4 are best. Now the question is which one of these alternatives should be implemented. On the surface, both have about the same benefits except that alternative 3 gives a higher return on investment. A closer inspection, however, reveals that only alternative 4 utilizes optical character recognition equipment. Conversion today will mean no or minimal conversion costs in the future for OCR equipment. With this added advantage, the MIS task force feels the future cost savings justify accepting a lower return. Therefore, its recommendation to top management has been finally resolved.

NONFEASIBILITY OF APPLYING REAL-TIME MIS

A considerable expenditure of time, effort, and costs on the real-time MIS exploratory survey can result in a decision not to adopt such a system. This may happen for a number of reasons. For example, the scope of the study may have been restricted—it may have dealt only with areas that did not lend themselves to the use of real-time equipment. Frequently a study group decides to wait for future developments in hardware and software. This is clearly an erroneous decision because a firm's competitors will probably be moving ahead. Still another reason for not adopting a real-time MIS system may involve simply the high costs of either conducting the exploratory survey or the expense of implementing a new system, or both. These unfavorable situations can be avoided by using outside consultants or knowledgeable personnel within the firm. With their guidance, appropriate areas for study will be chosen and expert advice on study procedures can be utilized.

SUMMARY

In this chapter the necessary parts of a feasibility study to investigate the possibility of implementing a real-time MIS in a firm have been explored. The first and most important part in this type of study is the exploratory survey, which ultimately determines the basis of the study—what will be covered, who will be involved, when it will be done, and how it will be accomplished during the preliminary and overall investigation phases. The study team, then, concentrates on the detailed investigation of the present system, a lengthy process known as systems analysis. Next is the development of alternative solutions as compared to the present system. In the final phase, an optimum solution is obtained after an exhaustive analysis of all proposals. Application of these phases ensures top management that the best real-time MIS exploratory survey report will be compiled under the existing conditions.

QUESTIONS

1. What is meant by a real-time MIS feasibility study?

2. a. Why is it that the growth of a data processing system will lag behind the corresponding growth of the firm?

    b. What affect does this have on the real-time MIS feasibility study?

3. a. What are the steps involved in the exploratory survey of a real-time MIS feasibility study?

b. What are the steps involved in a real-time MIS systems project?

4. Why is it necessary to establish an executive steering committee before initiating a feasibility study?

5. Explain the relationship among the following:

a. the scope of the feasibility study

b. the selection of desired objectives

c. the definition of the problem

6. If you were assembling an ideal MIS task force for a real-time MIS project in a typical manufacturing firm, who would be the members?

7. What part of the detailed investigation of the present system is most important from a management point of view?

8. What problems can the firm expect when it has decided to convert to a real-time management information system from an integrated management information system (batch processing)?

9. What are the problems associated with calculating net savings after federal income taxes for feasible real-time MIS alternatives?

10. What questions must the systems analyst answer if he is going to improve the present system?

11. Why have a real-time MIS exploratory survey report? Why not save this expense and procure the necessary equipment for the new system?

12. What are the essential contents of a real-time MIS exploratory survey report to top management?

13. Many firms have found that, initially, real-time MIS benefits are over-estimated and costs are underestimated. What are the major factors contributing to this condition and how may they be overcome?

REFERENCES

Brookfield, K. L., "The Role of the Systems Man in Study Teams," *Journal of Systems Management,* October, 1971.

Brown, W. F., Bibaud, R. E., and Hodgkins, G. L., "Planning for the Future Computer Complex," *Computer Decisions,* January, 1973.

Cleland, D. I., and King, W. P., *Systems Analysis and Project Management.* New York: McGraw-Hill Book Co., 1968.

Congdon, F. P., "Advance Planning for the Systems Function," *Journal of Systems Management,* August, 1970.

Couger, J. D., "Evolution of Business System Analysis Techniques," *Computer Surveys,* Vol. 5, No. 3, September, 1973.

Gibson, C. F., and Nolan, R. L., "Managing the Four Stages of EDP Growth," *Harvard Business Review,* January-February, 1974.

Hartley, H. J., "Twelve Hurdles to Clear Before You Take on Systems Analysis," *Journal of Systems Management,* June, 1969.

Hartman, W., Matthes, H., and Proeme, A., *Management Information Systems Handbook.* New York: McGraw-Hill Book Co., 1968, Vols. 3 and 4.

Head, R. V., "Automated System Analysis," *Datamation,* August 15, 1971.

Holmes, R. W., "Twelve Areas to Investigate for Better MIS," *Financial Executive,* July, 1970.

Haas, I. R., "Can Systems Analysis Solve Social Problems?", *Datamation,* June, 1974.

Hoslett, J. W., "Design Table for Engaging a Consultant," *Journal of Systems Management,* July, 1971.

Jones, P. A., Jr., "The Computer: A Cost-Benefit Analysis," *Management Accounting,* July, 1971.

Kennedy, D. W., "What a President Needs to Know About MIS," *Financial Executive,* December, 1970.

Knutsen, K. E., and Nolan, R. L., "Assessing Computer Costs and Benefits," *Journal of Systems Management,* February, 1974.

Lande, H. F., "Planning-Data Systems," *IBM Systems Journal,* No. 2, 1973.

Lias, E. J., "On-Line Vs. Batch Costs," *Datamation,* December 1974.

Long, M. I., and Bruun, R. J., "MIS Implications for Top Management," *Infosystems,* October 1974.

McFarlan, F. W., "Problems in Planning the Information System," *Harvard Business Review,* March-April, 1971.

McMillan, C., and Gonzalez, R. F., *Systems Analysis, A Computer Approach to Decision Models.* Homewood, Ill.: Richard D. Irwin, Inc., 1973.

Moore, M. R., "Achieving Full Value from Your EDP Operations," *Journal of Systems Management,* February, 1970.

Rea, R. C., "Selection Criteria for an Accounting Computer," *The Journal of Accounting,* August, 1974.

Ross, J. E., *Management by Information Systems.* Englewood Cliffs, N.J.: Prentice-Hall, Inc., 1970, Chap. 9.

Rothstein, M. F., *Guide to the Design of Real-Time Systems.* New York: John Wiley & Sons, Inc., 1970, Chaps. 3 and 4.

Schefer, E. A., "Management Control of the Corporate Computer Activity," *Data Management,* September, 1972.

Schroeder, W. J., "If You Can't Plan It, You Can't Do It," *Journal of Systems Management,* April, 1969.

Schwartz, M. H., "MIS Planning," *Datamation,* September 1, 1970.

Scotise, P. G., "What Top Management Expects of EDP," *Business Automation,* February 1, 1971.

Seebach, R. W., "Planning a Management Information System," *Automation,* August, 1973.

Sollenberger, H. M., "Business of Planning MIS Development," *Managerial Planning,* July-August 1974.

Thies, J. B., "Computer Modeling and Simulation: A Management Tool for Systems Definition and Analysis," *Financial Executive,* September, 1970.

Thompson, L. A., "Effective Planning and Control of the Systems Effort," *Journal of Systems Management,* July, 1969.

Vancil, R. F., "What Kind of Management Control Do You Need?," *Harvard Business Review,* March-April, 1973.

Wofsey, M. W., *Management of Automatic Data Processing.* Washington, D.C.: Thompson Book Co., 1968, Chap. 1.

Zani, W., "Real-Time Information Systems: A Comparative Economic Analysis," *Management Science,* February, 1970.

SYSTEMS DESIGN OF REAL-TIME MANAGEMENT INFORMATION SYSTEMS

4

While systems analysis is an intensive study of the present facts, systems design, the next step, is the creation of a new system. Once a decision has been made to implement a real-time management information system, the details of the system must be specified. Imagination and creativity are necessary for this phase, for without these qualitites some of the basic weaknesses of the existing system may be duplicated unconsciously by the MIS task force. The fundamentals of basic systems design, the second step of a real-time MIS feasibility study, are covered in this chapter.

Systems design for real-time MIS involves the creation and development of new inputs, a common data base, off-line files, methods, procedures, and outputs for processing business data in conformity with the firm's objectives. In essence, the job of the systems designer is an arduous task that requires special design skills and talents.

IMAGINATIVE SYSTEMS DESIGN

Even though a basic systems alternative has been established in the real-time MIS exploratory survey report, there are innumerable approaches available to the systems designer within the selected framework. These can be utilized to fit the particular circumstances and can be adapted from past experience as well as from a broad knowledge of approaches that have been successful in other installations. The almost infinite variety of alternative designs makes the task a challenging one.

The participants of the exploratory survey report to management generally undertake the design of the recommended real-time MIS alternative. If systems designers are not part of the group, they should be hired. Likewise, if additional personnel are needed to represent the various departments affected by the systems project, they should be recruited and made an integral part of the MIS task group. This is necessary because participation and cooperation of all functional areas, represented by departmental personnel, is the key to implementing the new system successfully. It is much easier at this stage to accommodate their constructive suggestions on system design than to redesign at a later date.

CREATIVITY

Creative thinking is somewhat akin to the planned approach (updated scientific method) of operations research. Emphasis is on new and untried approaches to systems design. The unusual approach and the exploration of generally unfamiliar methods and procedures can often aid the systems designer in devising innovations for a proposed system. Too often, time for creative thinking is unduly restricted because of the ever-pressing demand for immediate results. This is typically the fault of top managers who do not understand the importance of this creative phase in relation to the overall quality of the resultant systems design.

Good systems design requires a good analytical mind that can reduce a complex situation to its essential elements. In addition to being able to think logically and be highly imaginative in his design approaches, the systems designer must be capable of communicating these ideas clearly. In essence, he must operate effectively in two worlds—the conceptual one of imaginative systems design and the real one of effective real-time management information systems.

Departmental representatives and systems designers can complement one another effectively. A departmental representative, who knows answers to the proverbial questions of who, what, when, where, how, and why, should be imaginative enough to recommend improvements over the present system. Likewise, he should be objective in his thinking and be able to accept changes set forth by the MIS study group. Not only does he act as a sounding board for systems designers, but he can also aid in the gathering of facts that may be needed for the new system design. Thus, both creativity and objectivity are also required on his part.

BRAINSTORMING

Brainstorming is an attempt to solve a problem by the unrestrained expression of ideas within a group. The accent is on quantity, rather than quality, and although most of the suggestions are ultimately rejected, lack of criticism and unrestricted free association frequently produces novel, creative, and fresh approaches to a planning force. In designing a real-time MIS system, the brainstorming technique is often successful in giving birth to new ideas, which the systems designer can modify for workable solutions to the problem under study.

CHARACTERISTICS OF A WELL-DESIGNED SYSTEM

Before examining the essential steps involved in basic systems design, it is helpful to review the characteristics of any well-designed system whether a real-time MIS or otherwise. Basically, characteristics associated with effective system operations encompass:

> acceptability
> decision-making ability
> economy
> flexibility
> reliability
> simplicity

ACCEPTABILITY

Success of a new system pivots on its acceptance or nonacceptance by company personnel. If operating personnel are convinced that it will not benefit them, that it is a poor system, that it does not follow established company policies, or some other legitimate reason, the new system is in serious trouble. To overcome this resistance, their participation is essential, particularly during the design and implementation phases, for in reality, they consitute the organization that must use and live with the newly designed system.

DECISION-MAKING ABILITY

The output of an effective system produces pertinent and timely information at the lowest possible cost for making decisions. In its attempt to meet the informational needs and requirements of business and its managers, the system must be able to utilize techniques that can allocate available resources most effectively. This means that a good system is designed to make decisions as efficiently and automatically as possible. Decisions that cannot be made automatically as a result of the nature of the system must be relegated to the appropriate level of management or nonmanagement personnel, thereby making the firm's objectives obtainable.

ECONOMY

For economic operations, data should be captured or created in machine language as near to the source as possible and allowed to flow through the system automatically from that point on. Activities that must be performed in sequence should be located as closely together as possible, both organizationally and physically. Eliminating duplicate information files, reducing the provision for every possible contingency, and eliminating small empires in the firm's functional areas are other examples of economically improving the firm's basis of operation.

The question of system cost versus the potential savings must be considered. No information or service should be produced that is not justified by its cost to the firm. It is often expensive to develop one functional area of the overall system that has greater capacity than its integrated and related parts. In essence, there is need for a proper balancing of the subsystems and their related parts to effect economy of operation. For example, it makes no sense to develop elaborate order processing methods and procedures for fast customer service in the office if the plant operations are not geared on a comparable basis for providing prompt service.

In deciding whether to centralize or decentralize the performance of the firm's functions, the economy of specialized operations and the elimination of duplicate functions must be compared with the reduction of communications and paperwork costs under decentralized conditions. Also, the reduction in time cycles, the increased flexibility, and the greater unity of control and responsibility possible under decentralized operation must be considered.

FLEXIBILITY

To be effective, the system must be flexible—capable of adapting to changing environmental conditions. There will always be variations of products, manufacturing processes, and accounting procedures, to name a few. Managers must be prepared to adjust their operations to changing conditions. Without this ability, the firm may lose customer goodwill as well as encounter problems with its own personnel. Thus, a well-designed system should be able to withstand change by providing for ease of expansion and for added output of production capacity. Basically, the modular approach to systems design can be employed to bring about a flexible system.

RELIABILITY

Reliability of the system refers to consistency of operations. In other words, are data input, processing methods and procedures, and output information consistent over an extended period of operation? The degree of reliability can range from a constant and predictable mode of operation to a complete breakdown of the system. Although most systems do not operate at these extremes continuously, they do operate somewhere between them. A high degree of reliability can be designed into the system by providing for good internal control—that is, numerous control points where variances from established norms and practices can be detected and corrected before processing continues. Control functions should be allocated to organizational units that are independent of the functions to be controlled. In all cases, controls should be incorporated into the system at the design phase.

SIMPLICITY

The trademark of any effective system is simplicity. Simplicity can be affected by providing a straight-line flow from one step to the next, avoiding needless backtracking. Input data should be recorded at their source, or as close to it as possible, to reduce or eliminate the need for recopying. Functions should be assigned to organizational units in a way that will reduce the need for coordination, communication, and paperwork. Each organization group should have the authority and responsibility for its area and be held accountable for its performance to one superior only.

SYSTEMS DESIGN APPROACHES TO REAL-TIME MIS

There is still a certain amount of controversy over the proper approach to designing a real-time MIS. One school of thought feels that the work involved in understanding the present system is a waste of time and tends to make the systems designer think too much in terms of the old system. Followers of this theory advocate developing an ideal system that doesn't take the present system into account. The opposite extreme advocates so much reliance on the present system in systems design that only marginal improvements are made in the new system. In this case very little creative thought is apt to be employed, resulting in a duplication of the existing system, except for use of more advanced data processing equipment.

The first viewpoint fails to take into account the exceptions and peculiar problems of specific areas which may not be apparent unless some time is spent in examining the present system. These realities can make the best-designed system an undesirable one for any firm. The other approach is too conservative and lacks the creativity that is needed for an effective new systems design.

PREFERRED SYSTEMS DESIGN APPROACH

The best systems design approach takes the desirable aspects of both schools of thought. Basically, it involves a thorough comprehension of the existing system with all its exceptions and problems. By considering data of the present system where necessary and at the same time not allowing them to be the controlling and overriding factors, the systems designer can employ his imagination and creativity to the fullest extent in designing a new system.

An important reason for using this combined approach in designing a real-time MIS is that details are of greater importance in designing a real-time system than in designing a batch-type system. First, a real-time system combines various types of operating equipment which must be closely coordinated with other equipment. Second, even minor errors and omissions can result in an unworkable system in a closely knit operational environment. Finally, the writing and testing of programs that are programmed separately must work together for handling the firm's data processing needs. Thus, there is a great need for meshing together the many functional areas whose detailed operations are generally complex. Only by a close analysis of exceptions and problems of the present system can these considerations be handled correctly in the design of the new system.

BASIC SYSTEMS DESIGN OF REAL-TIME MIS

Basic systems design is the most creative step in developing an operational real-time MIS environment. It involves reviewing data on the present system and that contained in the real-time MIS exploratory survey report—in particular, the new system recommendation. To determine the requirements for designing and documenting a real-time management information system, the following areas must be thoroughly analyzed: policies (consistent with company objectives), outputs, methods, procedures, a common data base, off-line files, inputs, a common data representation, human factors, internal control, real-time controls, and system performance.

The preceding steps—namely, (1) *reviewing data* on present and proposed system, (2) *determining requirements* for real-time MIS, (3) *designing* the real-time management information system, and (4) *documenting* for real-time MIS—are summarized in Figure 4-1. They form the basic material for the remainder of the chapter.

STARTING POINT FOR SYSTEMS DESIGN

A logical starting point for basic systems design may be one of the following: an activity that dominates the entire system; an area that will be the most costly for the new system; the most inefficient area of the existing system; or an area that will reap many intangible benefits (such as better customer service and improved managerial reporting). Based upon the area or activity selected, each important element must be analyzed and alternative ways of data handling must be developed. As indicated previously, considerable creativity is involved in the planning of feasible new subsystems within the framework of the selected systems alternative.

DESIGN SYSTEM IN GENERAL TERMS

The systems designer should design a new system that is capable of utilizing equipment from most equipment manufacturers. To design a system with only one manufacturer in mind is restrictive, reduces the potential of the system, and often limits the ultimate success of the systems project. Equipment is important at this stage, but only in terms of classes and types. (The selection of a particular model is discussed in the next chapter.)

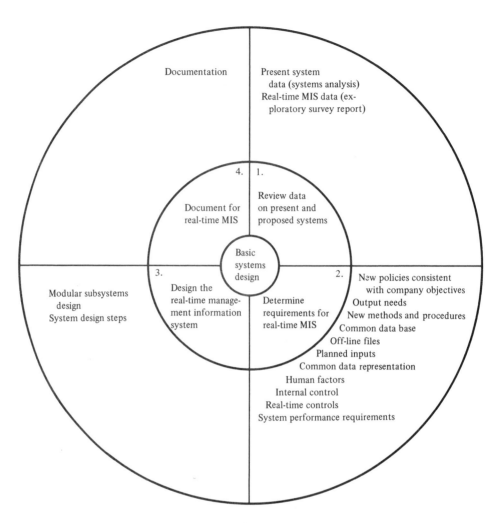

Documentation

Present system
  data (systems analysis)
Real-time MIS data (ex-
  ploratory survey report)

4.   1.

Document for
real-time MIS

Review data
on present and
proposed systems

Basic
systems
design

3.

Design the
real-time manage-
ment information
system

2.

Determine
requirements for
real-time MIS

New policies consistent
  with company objectives
  Output needs
New methods and procedures
Common data base
Off-line files
Planned inputs
Common data representation
Human factors
Internal control
Real-time controls
System performance requirements

Modular subsystems
  design
System design steps

FIGURE 4-1. Detailed outline of basic systems design for real-time
MIS—the second step of the feasibility study.

1. REVIEW DATA ON PRESENT AND PROPOSED SYSTEMS

A necessary requirement for effective systems design, as we have seen, is a
review of the present system and the proposed system. The best way to acquire
knowledge about the present operating system is to review the information accumulated during the systems analysis phase and that contained in the exploratory
survey report to top management. Similarly, information on the proposed real-time
MIS can be obtained from the latter source. Both areas are investigated below.

Present System Data (Systems Analysis)

Generally, many weeks have elapsed since the data have been compiled on the
present system. The purpose of the review is to recall pertinent facts about the

124

An evaluation of tangible and intangible benefits indicates too few for the present system, but will be increased within a real-time MIS operating mode.

Examination of how well the present system is practicing management by exception through feedback reporting.

The present uneven handling of exceptions will be eliminated.

Unnecessary inputs, reports, records, files, and forms of the present system will be eliminated with the new system.

Present duplication of operations, functions, and efforts will be avoided in order to achieve standardization among comparable data in the new system.

Excessive internal control will be eliminated, and the lack of control procedures in the existing system will be remedied.

Unnecessary refinement in the quality of data and superfluous data on reports will be eliminated.

The flow of work will be reviewed by the systems designer. Present peaks and valleys of data flow can be overcome by eliminating systems bottlenecks, establishing new cutoffs, and rescheduling certain operations in the new system.

Excessive steps in the present methods and procedures will be reduced in the new system.

Waiting time between data processing steps will be reduced or eliminated.

Present system's inability to handle the firm's growth on a one-shift basis will be eliminated.

Overall, the systems designer will evaluate how well or how badly the firm has met its objectives when considering the deficiencies and weaknesses of the present system.

FIGURE 4-2. Basic systems design—review present system's weaknesses in order to eliminate them in a real-time MIS operating mode.

system—in particular, its problems, shortcomings, and exceptions. A detailed listing of what should be evaluated in the review and avoided in the new system is contained in Figure 4-2. Notice the preponderance of the word "eliminate." Too often, the weaknesses of the old system are also present in the new one because this phase of systems design was performed superficially or entirely discarded.

An examination of Figure 4-2 indicates that the systems designer has certain questions in mind for determining the deficiencies and shortcomings of the present system. Basically, they are:

1. Can inputs, files, outputs, methods, and procedures be improved so as to accomplish the firm's objectives to the highest degree possible?
2. Are all operations necessary, or do some result in duplicate or overlapping operations, files, and the like?
3. Is there a faster, simpler, and/or more economical way of processing the data?
4. Are data recorded in a manner that is compatible with their final use?

5. Is it possible to reduce the work volume by modifying or changing policies, the organization structure, files, departmental functions, or other
   established firm practices?
6. Can the system be improved through work simplification?

These may not be new or revealing to the reader, but are necessary for an in-depth
review. The systems designer will discard many subsystems as a result of the above
questions and the comments in Figure 4-2 in order to devise more efficient ones.

Real-Time MIS Data (Exploratory Survey Report)

An intensive review of data in which the tangible and intangible benefits are
explicity enumerated will assist the systems designer in obtaining an overview of
what the new system is all about. All pertinent factors, such as the kind of changes
to be made in the organization structure and special factors to be considered, must
be studied.

The real-time MIS exploratory survey report contains a basic framework of
the new system. The overall system is defined and the related subsystems are stated
in general terms. Subsystems are flowcharted for each area of the study, also in
general terms, to depict the relationships among the many areas. An example of an
overall flowchart is illustrated in Figure 4-3 for a manufacturing firm. Its related
subsystems, as shown, are sales forecasting, finished goods, materials planning, inventory control, production scheduling, production dispatching, data collection,
and operations evaluation.

Even though system flowcharts are prepared for each major functional area,
the most meaningful ones to the systems designer are those that depict how the
various subsystems are interconnected, because the outputs from one subsystem
become the inputs for another. In the example, the output from sales forecasting
and finished goods inventory becomes the input for materials planning which, in
turn, produces output for inventory control (automatic purchasing). This succession of input-output activities continues through production scheduling, production
dispatching, data collection, and finally to operations evaluation, which employs
the management by exception concept. Only exception items when compared to
the current production schedule, budgets, standards, and comparable items need be
brought to the attention of management, no matter what level is associated with
the activity. An evaluation of Figure 4-3 indicates that management desires operational information as soon as it occurs to assist in keeping all operations under
control in accordance with the original plans. Thus, a review of all data, such as
flowcharts, decision tables, quantitative factors, and qualitative factors, provides a
sound basis for determining the requirements of the real-time management information system.

2. DETERMINE REQUIREMENTS FOR REAL-TIME MIS

Specifying requirements for a real-time management information system is a
difficult undertaking, even for the most experienced systems designers. A logical

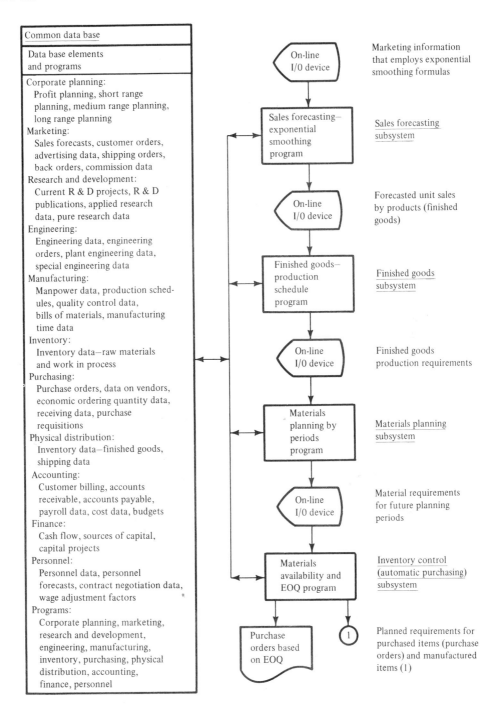

FIGURE 4-3. Basic systems design—an overall system flowchart of a real-time MIS operating in a manufacturing firm.

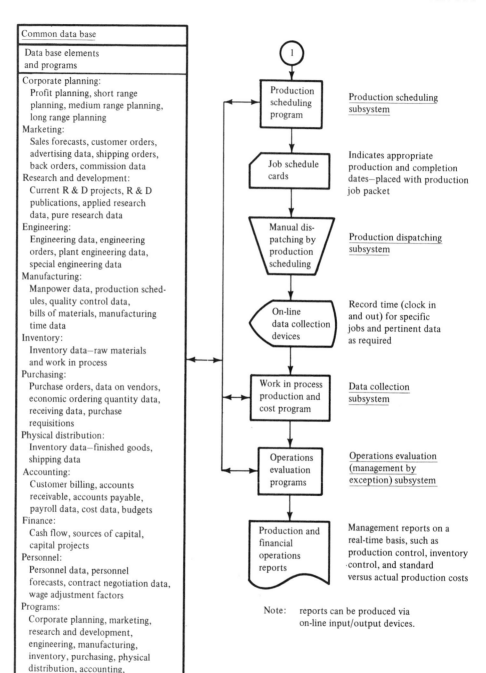

Common data base

Data base elements
and programs

Corporate planning:
  Profit planning, short range
  planning, medium range planning,
  long range planning
Marketing:
  Sales forecasts, customer orders,
  advertising data, shipping orders,
  back orders, commission data
Research and development:
  Current R & D projects, R & D
  publications, applied research
  data, pure research data
Engineering:
  Engineering data, engineering
  orders, plant engineering data,
  special engineering data
Manufacturing:
  Manpower data, production schedules, quality control data,
  bills of materials, manufacturing
  time data
Inventory:
  Inventory data—raw materials
  and work in process
Purchasing:
  Purchase orders, data on vendors,
  economic ordering quantity data,
  receiving data, purchase
  requisitions
Physical distribution:
  Inventory data—finished goods,
  shipping data
Accounting:
  Customer billing, accounts
  receivable, accounts payable,
  payroll data, cost data, budgets
Finance:
  Cash flow, sources of capital,
  capital projects
Personnel:
  Personnel data, personnel
  forecasts, contract negotiation data,
  wage adjustment factors
Programs:
  Corporate planning, marketing,
  research and development,
  engineering, manufacturing,
  inventory, purchasing, physical
  distribution, accounting,
  finance, personnel

Production
scheduling
program
Production scheduling
subsystem

Job schedule
cards
Indicates appropriate
production and completion
dates—placed with production
job packet

Manual dis-
patching by
production
scheduling
Production dispatching
subsystem

On-line
data collection
devices
Record time (clock in
and out) for specific
jobs and pertinent data
as required

Work in process
production and
cost program
Data collection
subsystem

Operations
evaluation
programs
Operations evaluation
(management by
exception) subsystem

Production and
financial
operations
reports
Management reports on a
real-time basis, such as
production control, inventory
control, and standard
versus actual production costs

Note: reports can be produced via
         on-line input/output devices.

FIGURE 4-3 (cont.)

starting point differs from one installation to another. No matter what area or activity is initially investigated, however, prime consideration is given to the firm's policy and output needs, which are an integral part of the new system's tangible and intangible benefits. Determination of the weaknesses of the present system is necessary for the creation of detail subsystems that start with outputs. These outputs are related to alternative methods, procedures, and data files from which they are derived. Finally, all activities are directed back to inputs that are compatible with the new systems design.

Because the systems designer specifies the new system requirements in more detail than contained in the real-time MIS exploratory survey report, it is possible that modifications to the initial design must be undertaken. If the changes are minor, chances that they will affect the system's benefits are slight. On the other hand, if the revised design calls for major modifications, it is quite possible that the original savings and costs, as well as other factors contained in the study, are erroneous. This situation calls for immediate action on the part of the MIS task force. There may also be important factors discovered at a later date which affect the feasibility of applying newer data processing equipment and procedures to a specific systems alternative; it may be necessary to reevaluate the contents of the real-time MIS exploratory survey report for a final decision. If the analysis is thorough, a reexamination of all data compiled will be unlikely. However, if the report is deficient in critical areas of investigation, the GIGO (garbage-in, garbage-out) principle will surface.

New Policies Consistent with Company Objectives

The systems designer is often forced into a corner when he must meet the constraints of the firm's policies currently in effect. A close scrutiny of the data on the new system will highlight those policies which are candidates for change; any need for further policy changes will become apparent as the systems design work progresses. Any approved policy changes by management should be consistent with the company's objectives as set forth in the final systems report.

Some questions must be asked relating to company policies. Can they be made more uniform in order to reduce the number of exceptions in the system? Sales commission rates, for example, are often too complex for any system, as are many pricing and discount policies. Basically, these complicated rate structures come into existence over the years to stimulate trade in special market segments. With the passage of time, the original reasoning given no longer applies, although the higher processing costs still remain. The problem can be resolved by determining whether or not customer dissatisfaction will result from simplification of the exceptions. If it does, the question of whether or not it will outweigh the data processing savings must be resolved.

Another possible policy adjustment is a reduction in the work volume. A good example concerns the expensing of low-value purchased materials initially rather than charging them to an inventory account and expensing them as they are withdrawn for production. Many firms have found that the cost of maintaining inventory records on these items—in terms of pricing, making the entries for withdrawal, and charging them to jobs—is greater than their actual value. Another example is accounts payable, where a firm's policy is to investigate overshipments and overcharges. The manpower needed to straighten out these discrepancies costs more than what may be lost, because errors on both sides tend to balance out over a period of time.

Output Needs

Output needs cover more than just reports that are generated on demand, by exception, and on schedule. They include listings, summaries, documents, magnetic tapes, magnetic disks, magnetic drums, cathode ray tube displays, responses from I/O terminals, etc. Many of these outputs provide the link between the data processing system itself and its ultimate users, which include the firm's customers and vendors plus the firm's personnel at all levels. The systems designer must develop systems output that meet the users' requirements; otherwise, output will probably not be available or in the desired format when needed. Information users or departmental managers and representatives, working with the systems analysts, will specify the format, detail desired, the degree of accuracy wanted, and the desired frequency of reports. The systems analyst may be able to improve on the output requirements of the user thanks to the real-time system.

During the detailed investigation phase or systems analysis, sample forms, documents, and reports were collected. These should be reviewed jointly by the systems designer and the departmental representatives. Two or more people will be in a better position to appraise the validity of the present output and its relationship to the output needs of the new system. A review method is to bring all output samples together and sort them in appropriate categories. With this method, duplication of outputs should be apparent upon close examination. Experience of many firms indicates that from 10 to 30 percent of all output records do not serve any valid purpose because they are either now-useless carryovers from earlier days or a duplication of other reports.

If the above analysis is restricted to the present reports, questions should be raised regarding their validity. (Appropriate questions are found in Figure 4-4.) A discussion of their merits will result in keeping some as they are, eliminating others, and combining data from other reports. (In general, consolidation of reports that have slightly different purposes into one report results in a standardization of the report's format.) Theoretically, the results of analyzing the present reports should coincide with the user's requirements as described above. However, there will be differences that must be reconciled in light of the proposed real-time MIS system and users' wants before the systems designer can finalize the output needs.

When specifying the outputs in a real-time MIS enviornment, consideration must be given to the management by exception principle. The integration of this important concept permits unusual events or knowledge to rise above the standard or ordinary ones and be referred to a higher level of management authority. This principle also insures that events under control are processed in the normal manner and that company personnel can work within established ranges of authority and responsibility. Thus, only extraordinary events which do not fit into regular operations will be brought to the attention of the next higher level of command.

Is the report necessary to plan, organize, direct, or control the activities of the firm?

Is the management by exception concept incorporated in real-time and non-real-time reports?

What would be the effect if operating personnel received more or less information than presently?

How would work be affected if the report were received less frequently or not at all?

Is all information contained in the report utilized?

How often is all or part of the information contained in the report utilized after its original use?

Can data on this report be obtained from another source?

How long is the report kept before it is discarded?

Is the report concise and easy to understand?

How many people refer to it?

Can the departments (functional subsystems) function without the report?

Are there other reports prepared from pertinent data on the report?

Does utilization of the data justify the preparation cost of the report?

Is the report flexible enough to meet changes in the firm's operating conditions?

Is the report passed to someone higher or lower in the organization structure?

When and where is the report filed?

FIGURE 4-4.   Basic systems design—questions to test the validity of a report in a real-time MIS operating mode.

Once the systems designer has clearly defined the legitimate output needs for a specific area, he is in a position to devise the methods, procedures, common data base, off-line files, and inputs that will produce the outputs. Basic design alternatives should be considered and evaluated for the best output. Here is where the true creative talents of the systems designer is needed. He must keep in mind that anything wanted as output must be planned and captured initially during the input phase. Actually, inputs, data files, methods, and procedures limit the type of output. A real-time management information system cannot supply the output needs unless it has read and stored the necessary input data either on line or off line. Even though input data have been captured and stored away, they must have the desired format for minimal processing.

New Methods and Procedures

Now that output requirements for the new system have been defined, the systems designer's attention is focused on new methods and procedures to produce these output needs. Consideration at this time must also be given to the on-line and off-line files as well as inputs, because it is difficult to isolate methods and procedures from system requirements. This phase requires intensive periods of creativity from the systems analyst. It is essentially a process of thinking logically and involves developing many systems design alternatives for a specific area. The new methods and procedures are tested for practicability, efficiency, and low cost. Attention must be given to those designs that meet as closely as possible the study's objectives. Once the many possibilities have been reduced to reasonable alternatives, say for one of the firm's functional subsystems, the alternative methods and procedures are examined thoroughly for the best one under the existing conditions. Included in these inventive steps is recognition that each functional area or activity is not isolated, but rather a part of the entire system. Thus, each related part must be considered in the final evaluation of the area under study. This requirement for compatibility of methods and procedures is exemplified in Figure 4-3. The addition of this dimension to the system designer's job increases the magnitude of his task.

In order for the systems analyst to perform the best job in designing new procedures, basic questions must be asked. These are set forth in Figure 4-5 and are comparable to the ones developed for testing the validity of a report. The validity of any procedure can be evaluated by these questions.

Can the procedure be improved to realize more fully the firm's objectives?

Are all steps in the procedure necessary?

Is it possible to simplify the procedure through modification of existing company policies, departmental structures, practices of other departments, or similar considerations?

Is there too much handling of the document in the procedure?

Does the procedure route the document through too many of the firm's personnel and departments?

Can the procedure be performed in a faster and a more economical manner?

Does the procedure make a contribution to the quality or flow of the work?

Is the cost of the procedure greater than its value to the firm?

Are all of the forms used in the procedure necessary? Can the forms be combined?

Does duplication of work exist in the procedure?

Are the steps in a logical sequence for the greatest efficiency in the procedure?

Are there parts of the procedure that functionally belong to another activity?

Is the procedure really essential to the firm's operations?

What would happen if one or more steps in the procedure were eliminated?

FIGURE 4-5.   Basic systems design—considerations for new procedures in a real-time MIS operating mode.

Probably the best method to determine how efficient are the new methods and procedures is to create an information flow from the input point to the final output stage. Any one of the documentation techniques of the prior chapter can be utilized. Which one(s) is (are) best depends on the area under investigation. In the final analysis, preference for flowcharting techniques is based upon the needs and wants of the systems designer.

Common Data Base Structure (On-Line Files)

Many system design approaches prior to real-time MIS utilized files structured for individual applications. Because of this individualistic approach, there was a great deal of redundancy—that is, the same data were carried in a number of files. Common keys which provided a means of referencing file data, such as employee number, were mandatory because they were the only method of cross-referencing two or more files. The redundancy information, however, extended far beyond the mandatory keys and included employee's name, department number, and the like, as depicted in Figure 4-6 (a).

The duplication of information in a variety of files is costly because excessive amounts of secondary storage capacity must be provided and a greater amount of magnetic tape, disk, or drum manipulation is required. A much more critical aspect, however, lies in the updating of the multitude of files. It is not difficult to conceive of one file being updated while the status of the same record on a second file, a third file, or other files remains unchanged due to an oversight or error in systems design, computer operation, or documentation. To overcome these problems, a real-time MIS utilizes the approach illustrated in Figure 4-6 (b)—the "single-record concept." Basically under this concept, all relevant information which formerly appeared in multiple data processing files now appear in one file of the firm's common data base.

(a)

Payroll File			
Employee No.	Name	Dept.	Payroll Data
Earnings File			
Employee No.	Name	Dept.	Earnings Data
Personnel File			
Employee No.	Name	Dept.	Personnel Data

(b)

Common Data Base					
Employee No.	Name	Dept.	Payroll Data	Earnings Data	Personnel Data

FIGURE 4-6. (a) Redundant data files with past system approaches versus (b) a common data base approach in a real-time MIS environment.

Basic to the design of a real-time management information system is the approach taken to structure the common data base. It is no longer possible to structure a data base by determining what management information needs are in general terms (one extreme) or by including every possible element of information that could be relevant to management's needs now and in the future (the other extreme). The first approach is much too general while the second one is impractical owing to the very large size of the resultant data base. Furthermore, mass random access storage, although relatively inexpensive today, is still a significant cost of any real-time MIS operating environment. Thus, the systems designer is forced to be selective in what he includes in the data base, resulting in compromises throughout the systems design phase.

Before the size of the common data base can be determined, a number of file design problems should be considered. Generally, the systems designer should know as much as possible about the various subsystems of the real-time MIS and the data to be considered in building the common data base—types of data files, number of data items, and number of characters per item. Also, he must consider the number of different application programs that are to be developed. The systems designer, then, must balance available on-line storage space against cost and other critical factors when structuring a common data base in a real-time MIS operating mode.

To assist the systems designer in structuring the common data base properly, several important questions are detailed in Figure 4-7. Of all the questions, the second one is probably the most difficult to answer—that is, the determination of what data to retain on line and for how long.

> What is the scope of the data base? What subsystems or application areas should be included in the design?
>
> What data should be retained and for how long? What priorities are applicable to these data in terms of response time required from the system?
>
> How should the various types of data be organized?
>
> What security controls are required to protect sensitive data?
>
> What storage medium should be selected? Is high-speed, direct-access memory required or are magnetic disks, drums, or other storage media suitable alternatives?
>
> What is the optimum method for entering data into and selecting data from the storage medium? What controls are required for these data to insure accuracy?
>
> What allowances can be made for growth of records or data sets?

FIGURE 4-7.   **Basic systems design—questions to assist in structuring a common data base in a real-time MIS operating mode.**

Another way of viewing the questions in Figure 4-7 for data base design is set forth in the seven requirements listed below. Observing these requirements assures economies in systems design and operation. Common data base requirements are that

1. It should permit the establishment of a single area for common information.
2. It should allow important information to be recorded on magnetic disk, drum, or laser while secondary records are maintained on magnetic tape or another low-cost storage medium.

3. It should guarantee accuracy of updating by an automatic maintenance feature for all segments of the data file.
4. It should allow variable-length records in order to conserve space.
5. It should provide for expanding or reducing the file.
6. It should allow for security of files or segments of files.
7. It must provide for some type of lockout feature so that certain files or areas of files or even records cannot be accessed during updating.

The design of the data base will dictate, or in some situations be constrained by, the type of storage devices to be used, the data management system chosen to manipulate information in the data base, the degree of security that must be built into the system to protect the data by the types of required responses to management inquiries, and other important considerations. No matter what constraints are placed on the systems designers, the data base elements should be integrated as illustrated in Figure 4-6 (b). However, where data are too long for one record, related elements should be capable of being referenced for appropriate information with a minimum of time, as depicted in Figure 4-8.

The preferred method of structuring the common data base, then, is the single-record concept, in which utilization of mass memory on-line devices improves the accessibility of information for computer users. Because the data base contains

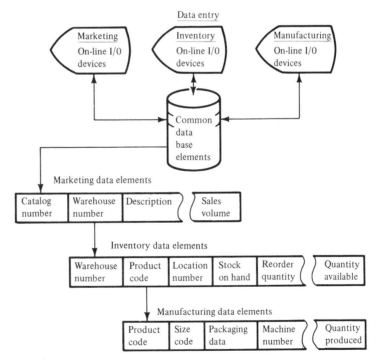

FIGURE 4-8.   Common data base whose data elements—marketing, inventory, and manufacturing—are integrated in a real-time MIS operating mode.

much of the information needed throughout the entire systems cycle—from the receipt of a customer order to the issuance of an invoice—the number of points at which information is entered into the system is minimized. This approach tends to reduce bottlenecks in the processing of data.

Conceptually, the common data base of a real-time MIS is a group of coordinated files of basic data elements in which duplication of data, if any, is kept to a minimum. Each file of individual data within the common data base is a building block or module, thereby permitting constant coordination of functions and data as related to each record. The data base, then, is a store of up-to-date, accessible unit data that is comprehensive enough to serve as a basis for preparation of any required information or report.

Off-Line Files

In a real-time MIS environment, all information need not be resident in one or more on-line files. In addition to data stored on line in magnetic disk, drum, laser storage, or comparable file devices, there is need for off-line files, such as magnetic tapes. These data files can be interrelated with on-line files to permit the automatic updating and retrieval of information. Thus, data that need to be referenced periodically, say weekly or less frequently, are poor candidates for on-line storage.

The systems designer should remember that more data should be provided for off-line files than is required for present output needs. Efficient systems design dictates keeping storage data at a minimum. However, this should be consistent with the ability to meet and satisfy output needs now and in the future as well as those that arise unexpectedly. If output requirements are specified in detail as they should be, the problem of what files to maintain and the appropriate information to be stored is no problem. A problem occurs when output requirements are so inadequately specified that it is difficult to design organized off-line files to meet the system needs.

The designing of more files than are needed for the requirements under study

> What should off-line files contain? Describe the type and kind of records and estimate the amount of each.
>
> How should the off-line files be referenced—by subject, by organization, by geography, by time, and so forth?
>
> How should the the information contained in the off-line files be structured—by subject or by organization?
>
> What indexing will be necessary for off-line files?
>
> What will be the annual rate of growth for these off-line files?
>
> Will any portion of the off-line files be restricted? What portion and to whom?
>
> What methods will be employed to prevent theft, destruction, or unlawful disclosure of off-line files?
>
> Will any unrestricted portion of the off-line files be vital and irreplaceable?

FIGURE 4-9. Basic systems design—questions to test the validity of off-line files in a real-time MIS operating mode.

assures that many future report requests can be fulfilled. As noted above, extreme caution must be used in such cases. There is generally a high cost for constructing and maintaining files of questionable value to the firm. The cost of this added information versus value received is the real issue in question. The systems designer should refer to the basic questions found in Figure 4-9 to evaluate off-line files. He obviously does not want to duplicate present file deficiencies and difficulties in the new system.

Planned Inputs

Inputs must be planned carefully by the systems designer because much time and cost is involved in converting data to information. They must be examined and evaluated from many viewpoints. Inputs may be handled in a more efficient manner on an individual or group basis. It might be possible to capture the data initially in a machine-processable form. The accuracy requirements of input data may call for editing and verifying methods. In some cases, inputs can be processed on a random sequence basis, while in others, there is need for a particular sequence before processing. The element of time constraints on the inputs and variations in input volume are valid considerations in the design of a new system.

Specific questions can be asked regarding how data are to be extracted from the source document. Will certain data be read directly into the computer by means of optical character recognition equipment? Will most data be keyed directly into the on-line processing system by input/output terminals located throughout the firm? Will data be keypunched and key-verified for a remote batching operation? Or will input data be considered in light of the above plus other pertinent questions? These questions can be answered by referring to the outputs, methods, procedures, and data files of the system designed. The inputs should be compatible as much as possible with their final use and interrelating parts of the data processing system. Otherwise, a less than optimum system will result.

Another approach to data input design is the provision for retention of raw data. This provides a basis for preparing future reports and answering questions not presently formulated. Here, caution must be exercised because of the high cost of retrieving and processing the data for meaningful output. Also, large amounts of raw input data must be stored, resulting in high storage costs. The criterion used for storage of file information is applicable to inputs—that is, the potential value from the stored data should be greater than the related cost of storing, retrieving, and processing the data.

Common Data Representation

One of the fundamentals of efficient processing is to capture data automatically in a common data processing language as a by-product of a previous phase. This means that captured data are in an acceptable format for subsequent handling on data processing equipment and are capable of being processed without human intervention. In handling large amounts of data, only a common language will permit their processing in a fast and accurate manner. Common data processing languages are print code (optical and magnetic ink), card code (80 or 96 columns), and channel code (punched paper tape and magnetic tape).

Most large data processing installations make use of more than one code. This is encouraged where the various codes are handled by data processing equipment and have no need for manual intervention. However, this should not be carried to the extreme. For example, the use of different channel codes is not recommended because it may be necessary to devise costly procedures for further processing. The best method is to design a system in which a language will be common to all its parts.

Human Factors

An extremely important design consideration for a real-time management information system (or any other system) is the human factor in coding and data representation. For example, research indicates that although a machine can read documents numbered "A4B" as easily as those coded "AB4," a human being cannot. Systems designers must consider the human element as well as procedures, data, and machines before finalizing any design. When trade-offs are deemed necessary, the human element should be given preference over the equipment.

Error rates with various coding schemes increase as the number of characters in the data code increases. It is suggested that longer codes be divided into smaller units of three or four characters, such as 123-456 instead of 123456, to increase the readability of coding. Characters used in the coding scheme should be those in common use; special symbols should be avoided. Also, wherever a number of data entry errors has occurred in the past, they should be studied to see if there is a systematic pattern. Factors that contribute to their occurrence should be considered in designing data codes.

In view of the problems associated with coding and data schemes, the systems designers should always examine their impact on company personnel when constructing work norms, procedures, and measurements, for individual or group effort. What may be perfectly logical and rational for them may be just the reverse for operations personnel who must utilize new methods and procedures.

A system, then, should be designed to interface with anyone who may come into contact with its results. This applies equally to the needs of employees and customers. If employees can understand what the system produces, what the system requires of them, and if, at the same time, the system is helpful to them, the end result can only be improved operating efficiency for the company. If the customer can easily understand and handle his bills, then improved customer relations will result. In the final analysis, less time and money will be spent dealing with customer inquiries and similar matters.

Internal Control

No systems design job is complete without adequate provision for internal control. The systems analyst should make certain that his final design allows no one person full responsibility over an entire operation. This should be apparent in such areas as cash and payroll because one person with complete responsibility can defraud the firm without too much difficulty. Control points must be built into the system. Checks at control points insure that what has been processed agrees with predetermined totals. Controls of this type insure accuracy during processing, resulting in reliable output.

Design of a new data processing system encompasses one or more of the following controls, which are outlined in Figure 4-10:

> MIS department
> input
> programmed
> output
> real-time (specified in the next section)
> hardware
> security

The successful incorporation of these controls will keep auditing procedures to a minimum. Sufficient safeguards, built into the system, are necessary to handle fraud and inaccuracies. Additional information on controls is necessary and can be found in a basic data processing textbook.[1]

Real-Time Controls

Controls attributed to a two-way directional flow of information in a real-time environment create many new problems not found in batch processing systems. For example, how can confidential data be made accessible to only authorized personnel? What happens to data in the system when the computer is down for repairs? How can accuracy be assured with on-line real-time processing? Generally, controls will be dictated by such factors as requirements of the system, the equipment itself, and security specifications. The areas set forth below are not all-inclusive, but are representative of the control requirements found in a real-time MIS. They include on-line processing controls, data protection controls, and diagnostic controls.

On-Line Processing Controls. These are necessary because messages from and to the input/output terminal devices can be lost or garbled. It is also possible that the terminal will go out of order during transmission or receipt of data. To guard against working with incorrect data under these conditions, the system should provide program routines for checking on messages. They are: message identification, message transmission control, and message parity check.

Message identification is used to identify each message received by the computer. Message number, terminal identification, date, and message code are the usual information sent to permit the data to be directed to the correct program for processing. If a message is received with an incorrect identification, it should be

[1]Robert•J. Thierauf, *Data Processing for Business and Management,* ed. Daniel W. Geeding (New York: John Wiley & Sons, Inc., 1973), Chapter 16.

MIS Department Controls
  Organization
  Methods and Procedures

Input Controls
  Verification Methods:
    Key verification, visual verification, self-checking numbers, and tabular
    listings
  Input Control Totals:
    Batch controls, hash totals, and record count totals
  External Labels

Programmed Controls
  Validation Checks and Tests:
    Sequence checks, character mode tests, self-checking digit tests, limit
    checks, code validity tests, blank transmission tests, alterations tests,
    and check points
  Computer Control Totals:
    Batch controls, hash totals, record count totals, balancing controls,
    cross-footing balance checks, zero balancing, and proof figures
  Internal Labels
  Error Routines

Output Controls
  Output Control Totals:
    Batch control totals, output hash totals, and record count totals
  Control By Exception
  Control Over Operator Intervention

Real-Time Controls
  On-line Processing Controls:
    Message identification, message transmission control, and message
    parity check
  Data Protection Controls:
    Supervisory protection programs, lockwords, and authority lists
  Diagnostic Controls

Hardware Controls
  Parity checks, duplicate circuitry, echo checks, dual heads, overflow
  check, and sign check

Security Controls
  Program control, equipment log, records control, tape rings, and preventive maintenance

**FIGURE 4-10.   Listing of controls used in designing internal control
                  for a real-time MIS.**

routed to an error routine for corrective action or rejection from the system. In
general, rejection necessitates retransmission of the entire data.

Message transmission control requires that all messages transmitted are in fact
received. One method is to assign a number to each message and periodically have
the computer check for missing numbers and out-of-sequence messages. Unac-
counted message numbers are printed for investigation. Another method is the
confirmation of all messages received, whether from the computer or the input/
output terminal.

Message parity check verifies the accuracy of the message sent. Because it originates at the sending terminal, a check digit is added to the end of the message, representing the number of bits in the message. In a similar manner, the receiving terminal compiles a check digit on the number of bits received in the message. If both check digits are equal, a correctly received signal is sent to the terminal or computer. If there is a difference, most systems will ask for a retransmission of the data.

Data Protection Controls. Data protection controls provide answers to many on-line real-time questions, such as: What happens when two separate transactions are trying to update concurrently the same record? What assurance is there that program segments read into the computer's memory will not be accidentally read in over data currently being processed? The software for data protection controls include supervisory protection programs and data security, lockwords and authority lists.

Supervisory protection programs, like IBM's "exclusive control," solves the problem of concurrent updating and the resulting loss of data. It permits only one data transmission to update an on-line record at a time. Basically, this software requires that each data set request permission of the supervisory program for updating a specific item. If the record is available, the proper machine instructions are executed. At no time during this updating process will the supervisory program allow other transactions access to this particular data record. Other manufacturers have comparable routines.

Lockwords and authority lists are a means of preventing unauthorized access to the on-line system. Lockwords (passwords) made up of several characters of a data file must be matched by the sender before access is granted to the file. The password may become common knowledge after a period of time, and so must be changed periodically. Another type of security is an authority list. In this case, the lockword identifies the sender. When reference is made to the authority list stored in the computer system, it indicates what type of data the sender is permitted to receive. Whether the first or second method of data security is employed, a control routine should be established within the on-line system. Its function is to count the number of trys in sending a message. If the number of unsuccessful trys have exceeded a certain number, say three or four, it is possible that some unauthorized person is tampering with a terminal device. It should be noted that these methods do not exhaust the list of data security controls, but are the more popular ones.

Diagnostic Controls. One of the possible difficulties in a real-time system is a malfunction of the equipment or a programming error that occurs during the system's operations. It is best to keep the system operating if the trouble can be circumvented; this can be accomplished if diagnostic programs are used to detect and isolate error conditions for proper corrective action. Once a problem has been determined, however, it is up to the supervisory program to make the necessary adjustments. It can restart the program in question, reexecute the faulty instruction, switch control to an error routine, initiate a switchover to another system, shut down part of the system, or halt the system. The first three methods are used to overcome software problems, while the latter three are necessary to control hardware malfunctions.

Diagnostic programs, in a real-time MIS operating mode, are dependent upon the system's design and equipment. They are a must when a terminal breaks down. While one diagnostic program checks the communication network and establishes that there is a problem, another checks each line until the down terminal(s) is (are) located. Having determined the problem, terminal control is returned to the supervisory program, which can close down the line for repairs and route all output messages to another terminal.

When the system must halt because of a breakdown of a major piece of equipment, emergency procedures must be set up to handle the work until the malfunctioning equipment has been repaired. Restart procedures must also be devised which include the use of a checkpoint record. This record, usually a magnetic disk or tape file, is a complete log of all messages and pertinent data processed up to a certain point in time. When a restart is necessitated, the checkpoint record restores the system to a time when this record was written. Every terminal is advised about the number of the last message that has been properly processed. All subsequent messages must be resent in order for the system to operate on a current basis.

System Performance Requirements

Determining system performance requirements involves ascertaining the number of transactions that the real-time computer must accept, process, and return to the I/O terminal operator. It is not sufficient to design a system that can process forty transactions per hour from an input/output terminal if these forty transactions represent the volume expected shortly after the system is operative and will be increasing subsequently. Transaction volume must be projected not only for normal, future processing loads but also for peak periods (the time interval during which the largest number of transactions will be processed). An analysis of project volumes plus a statistical sample of transactions can be used to determine the number of peak periods and the extent of overlapping of peak periods. If the new system is developed that cannot handle normal and peak loads in the future, it is not a feasible system. The most economical system that meets this benchmark volume of peak loads is the one that the firm should implement.

An important performance capability of a real-time management information system is its ability to reduce time delays. The prompt acceptance of input data whenever they are entered into the system from various terminal locations reduces the time span from input through processing to output. Receiving inputs and returning processed outputs on this basis necessitates the acceptance of transactions by the real-time computer, whose time and rate of entry is controlled by the terminal operator.

The best method for developing system performance requirements is to employ the following set of logical procedures:

1. define and list all transaction types
2. determine normal and peak periods for all transactions
3. project all normal and peak periods
4. determine the overall level of throughput for normal and peak periods

Regarding the first procedure, new transactions that come into being because the system is on line in real time must be added to the list of existing transactions. Otherwise, the volume of transactions for normal and peak periods is not determinable.

The second procedure is concerned with the highest utilization of one or more system components for a varying period of time. It is during peak periods that delays generally occur. These delays cause an increase in the time required to process a transaction before sending information back to its destination. The delays are caused by transactions entering the system at a more rapid rate than they can be processed. The system designer's job is to insure that such delays will be minimal— that is, as infrequent as possible.

Once the normal and peak transaction processing loads have been determined, the third procedure calls for projecting these volumes into the future as defined by the real-time MIS exploratory survey report. Actually, this procedure is evaluated along with the overall level of throughput, the fourth procedure. The performance requirements are often specified as x number of transactions per second, minute, or hour with a certain response or turnaround time. For example, the system is required to process 600 transactions per hour or 10 transactions per minute. If the response time of the real-time system is 20 transactions per minute, the system is capable of handling the throughput. Although the ability to handle the present volume is ample, consideration must be given to process future peak loads. If they fall into a range of 13 to 14 transactions per minute for normal loads and 15 to 16 transactions per minute for peak loads, the real-time system is still capable of providing the desired throughput response for all anticipated volume levels.

3. DESIGN THE REAL-TIME MANAGEMENT INFORMATION SYSTEM

Determining the above requirements is performed concurrently with designing the new system. After all, a system is nothing more than a total of all its parts. The design of a system involves making decisions about each of its parts—outputs desired, on-line and off-line files to be maintained, planned inputs, and data processing methods and procedures that link input with output. An integral part of systems design work is answering the many questions set forth in the preceding sections so that no one item is left unexplored.

For a realistic and feasible approach to the design of a real-time management information system, it is absolutely necessary to partition the total job into manageable segments. These segments are then tailored for each particular level of operation and for each specific managerial activity. This is not to say, however, that each of these segments is incompatible with all of the other segments. Just the opposite is true. By providing the system with a conceptually and technically sound blueprint as a basis for action, and by employing imaginative, intelligent, experienced design techniques, a consistent whole can be synthesized from each of the segments. Thus, real-time MIS is viewed as a dynamic system consisting of a number of subsystems which are in constant motion and interaction. The introduction of change in one subsystem will result in interaction with other subsystems.

Modular Subsystems Design

The design of the real-time management information system and its related subsystems should be approached from the outset with modularity, or the building block concept, in mind. This involves identifying all the major subsystems or major modules of the firm (in terms of the foregoing system requirements). At this point, all the major modules are identified in functional block diagrams. Because they are the highest-level functions, they represent a beginning point for a functional breakdown of a real-time MIS. Each of these functions is broken down into related functional parts, applying the process iteratively from the top down. The resulting analysis is represented by a tree diagram, wherein major functions at the top are successively broken into separate data processing functions in the lower branches of the tree. As illustrated in Figure 4-11, the major module (accounting) is broken down into seven intermediate modules (customer billing, accounts receivable, accounts payable, payroll, cost control, inventory control, and budgets). The intermediate module (payroll) is divided into six minor modules (gross pay, mandatory deductions, voluntary deductions, net pay, labor cost distribution, and fringe benefits). These minor modules, in turn, are subdivided into basic modules. Although not shown in the figure, it is necessary to break down further the other intermediate modules.

As the subdividing process occurs for a major module, two important phenomena are observed:

1. the branches begin to terminate (i.e., they do not lend themselves to further breakdown)
2. some of the functions turn up in more than one place (they are duplicate modules)

When the process is complete, a thorough functional analysis is obtained even though the system has not been fully designed. An analyst can often find alternative ways to break a function down into its component parts. He will spend a great deal of time changing his mind and filling in details which he considered unimportant on an earlier pass. But time spent here is worthwhile, because this step forms the heart of the design of the real-time management information system.

When the functional analysis is complete, the systems designer creates a system structure for the functional modules which will operate within whatever hardware constraints are imposed. This modular approach allows the bringing together of individual modules which are capable of standing alone. The net result is that the

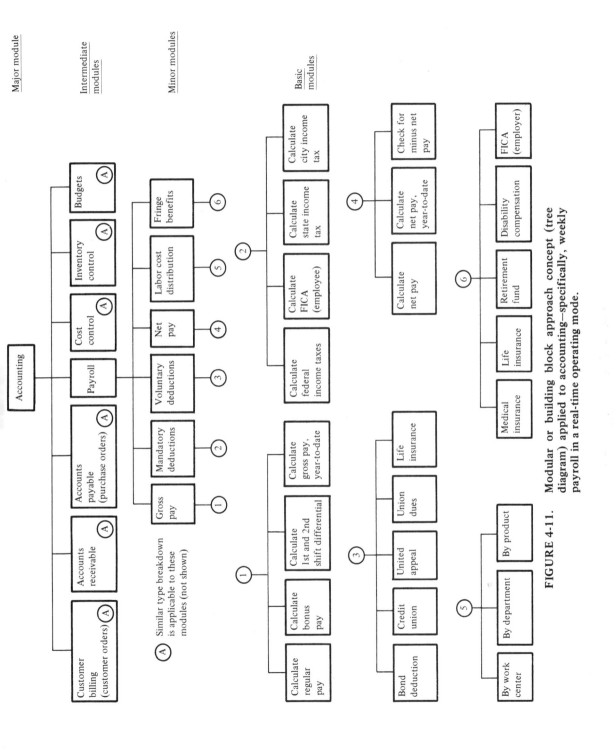

FIGURE 4-11. Modular or building block approach concept (tree diagram) applied to accounting—specifically, weekly payroll in a real-time operating mode.

Major module

Intermediate modules

Minor modules

Basic modules

Accounting

Customer billing (customer orders) (A) · Accounts receivable (A) · Accounts payable (purchase orders) (A) · Payroll · Cost control (A) · Inventory control (A) · Budgets (A)

(A) Similar type breakdown is applicable to these modules (not shown)

Gross pay (1) · Mandatory deductions (2) · Voluntary deductions (3) · Net pay (4) · Labor cost distribution (5) · Fringe benefits (6)

(1) Calculate regular pay · Calculate bonus pay · Calculate 1st and 2nd shift differential · Calculate gross pay, year-to-date

(2) Calculate federal income taxes · Calculate FICA (employee) · Calculate state income tax · Calculate city income tax

(3) Bond deduction · Credit union · United appeal · Union dues · Life insurance

(4) Calculate net pay · Calculate net pay, year-to-date · Check for minus net pay

(5) By work center · By department · By product

(6) Medical insurance · Life insurance · Retirement fund · Disability compensation · FICA (employer)

145

complexity of an overall system is reduced, because many of the duplicated modules are eliminated. Also, this approach facilitates any modification or updating of the system that may be necessary during succeeding stages of system design as well as in the future.

An alternative approach to the tree diagram illustrated in Figure 4-11 is the tabular approach, found in Figure 4-12. The advantage of the tabular form over the tree diagram is that it is a condensed form whereby duplicate modules can be readily identified. Referring to Figure 4-12, the intermediate modules—payroll and cost control—have the same minor module; namely, labor cost distribution. As a result, their basic modules are the same. When the time comes to program these areas,

Accounting—Major Module

Intermediate modules	Minor modules	Basic modules
Customer billing (Customer orders)	(A)	
Accounts receivable	(A)	
Accounts payable (Purchase orders)	(A)	
Payroll	Gross pay Mandatory deductions Voluntary deductions Net pay Labor cost distribution Fringe benefits	Refer to Figure 4–11 By work center By department By product

Cost control	Material costs
	  distribution
	
	Labor cost
	  distribution
	
	Overhead cost
	  distribution
	
	Cost exceptions
		By work center
		By department
		By product
		By work center
		By department
		By product
		By work center
		By department
		By product
		By work center
		By department
		By product

Inventory control	(A)	
Budgets	(A)	

(A) Similar type breakdown is applicable to these modules (not shown).

FIGURE 4-12.   Modular or building block concept (tabular form) applied to accounting—specifically, payroll and cost control in a real-time MIS operating mode.

the module needs to be programmed only once. If the remaining modules as well as other modules were completed in Figure 4-12 for the firm's many subsystems, the labor cost distribution module might appear one or more times, thereby indicating other duplicate modules. Thus, a breakdown of all basic modules is recommended at the systems design phase in order to keep overall work and duplicated modules at a minimum. By going down to the lowest level of the modular pyramid, the systems designer is forced to organize logically the data base elements and the source of raw information that must be analyzed and presented for viewing in a real-time MIS operating environment.

No matter what approach is employed in the detailed design of the modular subsystems, it is necessary to prepare final system flowcharts for the recommended new system. These flowcharts are drawn without specifying the equipment to be ordered. Accuracy, simplicity, and ease of understanding are the essential components, because nontechnical personnel will be reviewing and evaluating them. An example of a system flowchart is found in Figure 4-13 for a real-time raw material inventory updating procedure. This is an extension of the overall flowchart illustrated in Figure 4-3 for a real-time management information system.

Inspection of Figure 4-13 indicates that current transactions are updated as they occur. These include raw materials receipts from vendors, in-plant transfers to finished goods inventory, physical inventory count changes (physical inventory counting is performed on a rotating basis for counting raw materials once a month), and miscellaneous adjustments—based on spoilage, scrappage, obsolescence, shrinkage, and the like. Automatic purchasing of raw materials is performed on line. Also, automated outputs signal excess inventory and certain inventory errors of on-line activities. In essence, this approach to raw materials inventory allows inquiry into the system at any time for updated information and produces outputs for appropriate action.

In summary, a modular design approach is a process of breaking down the system into its lowest component parts and examining them for duplication. This functional approach serves as a basis for designing subsystems from the lowest to the highest level. This approach is also extremely helpful in integrating MIS modules on the same level as well as on a related basis—that is, integrating comparable modules, such as accounting and finance, before taking on other modules.

Systems Design Steps

The various steps involved in systems design are set forth in Figure 4-14. The initial step involves determining real-time MIS requirements. By way of review, these include: new policies consistent with company objectives, output needs, new methods and procedures, a common data base structure, off-line files, planned inputs, common data representation, human factors, and internal control. These requirements plus real-time controls and system performance are used to devise design alternatives in a modular or building block environment, the second step. The third step centers around preparing rough flowcharts that depict the modular relationships detailed above. The purpose of the flowcharts is to appraise the merits of the modular systems alternatives and to provide a basis for review with

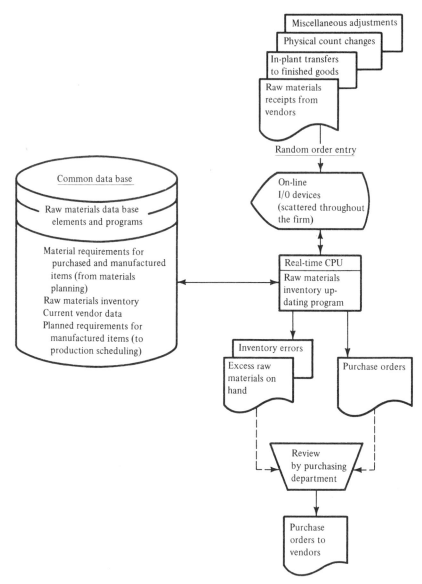

FIGURE 4-13.   Basic systems design—system flowchart for a raw
                 materials inventory updating run in a real-time MIS
                 operating mode.

appropriate company personnel, the fourth step. In essence, these steps have been
delineated in prior sections.

In the fifth step, the more promising alternatives are selected with the aid of
designated personnel. Their tangible and intangible benefits are compared with the
real-time MIS exploratory survey report to check their validity, the sixth step. For
the next two steps, alternative systems designs along with their tangible and in-

1. Determine the following requirements for real-time MIS: new policies consistent with company objectives, output needs, new methods and procedures, common data base structure, off-line files, planned inputs, common data representation, human factors, and internal control.

2. Devise many systems design alternatives through a modular or building block approach, including detailed inputs, methods, procedures, data files, and outputs. Give special consideration to real-time controls, system performance requirements, and other parts of the system as well.

3. Prepare rough flowcharts showing the modular relationships for the various alternatives in (2).

4. Review systems design alternatives with appropriate personnel.

5. Select the more promising alternatives with the aid of properly designated personnel.

6. Compare the tangible and intangible benefits of the promising alternatives with the real-time MIS exploratory survey report. Cost factors, volume, and requirements for equipment and personnel should be carefully analyzed to check the report's validity.

7. Consider alternative systems designs which incorporate alternative functional modules, equipment, and techniques that were not covered in the exploratory survey phase. (Promising system approaches that were not investigated initially often come to light during the creative design phase.)

8. Determine the tangible and intangible benefits for these new alternatives in (7).

9. Select the final systems design with the assistance of the firm's operating personnel that best meets the study's requirements from among all the promising alternatives.

10. Prepare final system flowcharts and/or decision tables for the recommended systems design and relate them to all other parts of the real-time MIS, thereby forming the basis for bid invitations to equipment manufacturers.

FIGURE 4-14. **Basic systems design—steps for one of the firm's functional areas (subsystems) in a real-time MIS operating mode.**

tangible benefits are considered which were not covered in the exploratory survey phase, but which have come to light during the creative design phase. The final systems design is selected per the ninth step with the assistance of the firm's operating personnel that best meets the study's requirements from among all of the promising real-time MIS alternatives. The foregoing approach permits a comprehensive review of all promising systems alternatives.

Once the final design has been resolved by the study group based on the existing tangible and intangible benefits, any significant deviations from the findings of the real-time MIS exploratory survey report must be reported to the executive steering committee. It is the function of these top managers to make a final decision on whether or not to apply the recommended system under new conditions. This is why the feasibility study is a continuing one even though the task force has endorsed a proposed system in the exploratory report. (The feasibility study is formally concluded with equipment selection, the subject matter for the next chapter.)

4. DOCUMENT FOR REAL-TIME MIS

Documentation for real-time MIS is the tenth and final step in Figure 4-14. As explained in Chapter 3, it can take several forms. These include system flow-charts, flow process charts, document flowcharts, decision tables, SOP (Study Organization Plan), and TAG (Time Automated Grid).

Detailed documentation is necessary for (1) submitting bid invitations to equipment manufacturers and (2) preparing program flowcharts. In regard to the first item, documentation is needed for the following: data origination and communications, planned inputs, common data base, off-line files, methods and procedures, output needs, and special requirements of the system. Also included in the bid invitation are system flowcharts depicting the interrelationships of the various parts to the entire system and those showing each area under study. Examples are found in Figures 4-3 and 4-13, respectively.

In order to prepare program flowcharts for coding at a later date, it is necessary to develop the appropriate logic. Although block diagrams or program flow-charts can be prepared for a detailed documentation of the new system, decision tables are preferred at this point for several reasons. They are easy to construct and give a more compact presentation than do program flowcharts, which are accompanied by a written narrative. Decision tables are easy to modify and update. They show more clearly than flowcharts the effects of system changes upon the logic of the overall system. The more complex the logic is, the more appealing are decision tables to the systems designer. Thus, they show conditions (if) and actions (then) in clear and logical manner, which facilitates programming during systems implementation.

Simulate the Systems Design

An alternative method to the preceding approach of systems design is the utilization of the computer to simulate the desired system. The general procedure of applying a systems model in a batch processing mode is to represent the given system parametrically, run the model, analyze the results, and determine in what direction future improvements can be made to the system. In general, an iterative procedure is carried out wherein the model and its parameters are changed and experimentation is repeated (Figure 4-15). The procedure of changing the model and its parameters to evolve the simulated system within its given constraints can be performed in a multitude of ways. A simulation run is usually analyzed to find further improvements possible for the simulated, evolving system. Often this means that parameters of the simulated system and sometimes the structure of the model must be changed. Thus, the model is run many times.

The systems simulation effort in a batch processing mode may be accomplished through the use of a simulation language, such as GPSS or SIMSCRIPT, or a systems simulation package, such as CASE, SAM, and SCERT.[2] In many cases, the

---

[2]Jeffrey N. Bairstow, "A Review of Systems Evaluation Packages," *Computer Decisions,* June 1970. This article describes CASE, SAM, and SCERT.

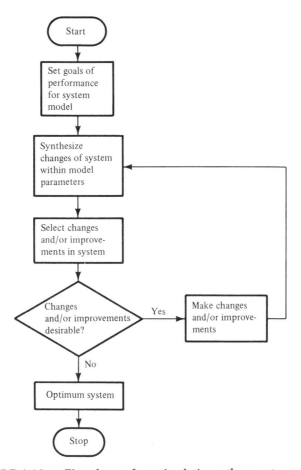

FIGURE 4-15. Flowchart for simulating the systems design.

simulation languages are free and are standard software for equipment manufacturers. On the other hand, the packages are either sold or leased to users. SCERT, CASE, and SAM are discussed below.

SCERT. The System and Computer Evaluation and Review Technique[3] package was the first to appear on the market. It is essentially an algorithmic simulator that has some discrete features for the simulation of time-dependent systems. Input to the system consists of a series of definitions of the files to be processed, the system to be employed, and the types of runs to be considered. Output from the simulator is a series of some sixteen or so reports, most of which can be suppressed by the analyst.

The operation of this system simulator has five phases. In phase one, SCERT introduces the processing requirements by accepting the environment, file, and system definitions. A model is built for each run, the input is validated, and diag-

[3]For more information on SCERT, contact Comress, 2 Research Court, Rockville, Md. 20850.

nostics, if any, are issued. In the second phase, SCERT builds models of the hardware and software from their definitions and the appropriate parts of the SCERT factor library. Phase three is referred to as a presimulation phase in which the system merges the work load and hardware-software models. The actual simulation takes place during phase four, in which each run is exploded into its maximum iterations. In time-sharing simulations, where the processing is random, SCERT enters a second stage in which it determines the effects of queuing and the results of combining real-time and batch processing in one work load. If the system being simulated has either multiprogramming or multiprocessing capabilities, SCERT has a third stage in which a critical path technique is used to determine priorities and contentions. Finally, in phase five, all data generated during the simulation runs are collected and output in a series of reports is produced.

CASE. The Computer-Aided System Evaluation[4] package is a statistical simulator that is written in FORTRAN. Like SCERT, it utilizes a fill-in-the-form technique for the input definitions of the work load and the hardware and operating system software to be used. In defining the work load, CASE has some ability to accept simple or detailed descriptions of the programs, depending on the level of detail that is known about each program. Different languages may be specified for each program in the work load. File blocking factors, device assignments, and file allocations may be specified exactly or may be left for the simulator to decide during the simulation run. Similarly, in the configuration definition, the system simulator allows the user considerable generality if he so desires. As with SCERT, CASE uses a library of hardware and software factors from which the program selects the necessary parameters to run the simulation.

The execution of CASE is an iterative process that involves frequent analysis and modification of the input data by an analyst. The simulation is event-oriented, rather like the event-oriented general-purpose simulation language, SIMSCRIPT. Statistics are kept on a time-period by time-period basis. The resulting reports may be printed out in two groups—the analyst reports and the management reports. At the end of each run, the analyst reports, such as the unit utilization report and the concurrent processing summary, show the analyst where he might make the changes necessary to achieve the study's objective. The simulation is repeated with the modified configuration or programs until the analyst is satisfied. After the final run, a number of management reports are generated for the final system's performance.

SAM. The System Analysis Machine[5] package differs from SCERT and CASE in that the input to the simulator is not by file and configuration definitions, but by a simple language that can be used to describe the hardware environment and the logic of the programs to be studied. As with the other simulators, SAM also has a model library for available hardware and software systems. Modules for this

[4]For more information on CASE, contact Computer Learning and Systems Corporation, 5530 Wisconsin Avenue, Chevy Chase, Md. 20015.

[5]For more information on SAM, contact Applied Data Research, Inc., Route 206 Center, Princeton, N.J. 08540.

library can be entered by the customer once they have been defined using the SAM language. Once a module has been entered, an executed macro-instruction will extract the module whenever it is needed.

Program data are supplied to SAM from flowcharts that describe both the programs and the operating system to be studied. The SAM language is used to code the flowchart descriptions. The flowcharts can encompass any level of detail required so that the resulting models may be precise or approximate.

Difficulties with System Simulators. The foregoing system simulators do have important drawbacks if they are operated in a batch processing mode. First, batch processing of a simulated system is a time-consuming process. The performance of the analyst as well as the evolution of the system may be degraded because the modeler may conceive of an idea or the effect of a parameter change, and then lose his train of thought as a result of waiting for computer turnaround. Second, it is difficult to work with large, complex systems like real-time management information systems that cut across the entire firm.

The better approach to system simulation in a batch processing mode is to allow the systems analyst to be placed on line with the simulator. In this way he can observe and control the simulation while it occurs. In such a situation, the simulator issues periodic reports as it progresses and if an interesting or questionable trend is noticed during simulation, he can request any of the following: a slowdown in the speed of simulation, more detailed reports, reprints of previously issued reports, and even a backtrace or replay of a certain simulated period. The analyst can also change certain parameters to observe their effects. If he wishes to change the model in structure, he can make the change on line and then resimulate up to the previous point in simulated time. Thus, the analyst is given a chance to observe the nature of the evolving system while obtaining more efficient use of his time.

SUMMARY

The design of a real-time MIS goes hand in hand with the creative ability of the systems designer. A fundamental of basic systems design is to devise a large number of alternatives with varying inputs, methods, procedures, and outputs that are compatible with the common data base and off-line files. The systems designer relies upon his experience and inventive ability to develop promising systems alternatives incorporating these important components. Each alternative is analyzed by a representative group within the firm to determine its benefits and impact on the firm. The most promising real-time MIS alternative is then chosen and documented with system flowcharts and decision tables. The basis for selection is the successful accomplishment of the firm's objectives and attainment of quantitative and qualitative factors set forth in the real-time MIS exploratory survey report.

Numerous questions must be answered by the systems designer before applying the modular subsystems design approach. These are enumerated in the chapter for determining the most suitable requirements of the new system. Any activity that touches the new system directly or indirectly is thoroughly investigated by these probing questions; their answers are utilized to develop the desired system. Intensive investigation, hard work, and imaginative talents of the systems designer plus the constructive criticism and cooperation of the firm's personnel are the key to designing promising new systems.

QUESTIONS

1. Define basic systems design. How does this differ from systems analysis?

2. How important are creativity and brainstorming in designing a real-time MIS?

3. What important factors must be taken into consideration in the design of an efficient and economical common data base?

4. Enumerate the essential components for designing a real-time management information system.

5. What are the questions a systems designer must ask himself when designing a system in a real-time MIS operating environment?

6. a. Why should the systems designer consider reporting requirements first when designing a real-time MIS?

   b. What is the relationship between reporting requirements and the structure of the common data base in real-time MIS?

7. What important factors must be taken into consideration when designing an efficient and economical common data base?

8. a. How important is the human factor in the design of real-time MIS?

   b. How important is internal control in the design of real-time MIS?

9. What is meant by system performance requirements in a real-time MIS environment?

10. What are the typical steps a systems designer should follow when designing a real-time MIS?

11. What is meant by the modular subsystems design approach? Explain thoroughly.

12. How important is documentation of the new system?

13. If a better system is determined during the basis systems design phase, what may have caused this to happen?

14. a. What are the advantages of using system simulators in systems design work?

   b. What are the problems associated with system simulators, such as SCERT and CASE?

REFERENCES

Axelrod, J. N. "14 Rules for Building an MIS," *Journal of Advertising Research,* June, 1970.

Babb, M., "Data Base Controls Computer Operations," *Journal of Systems Management,* February, 1971.

Balk, W. L., "The Human Dilemmas of MIS," *Journal of Systems Mangement,* August, 1971.

Benson, L. A., "Predict Your Business Future with Simulation Models," *Computer Decisions,* July, 1971.

Bruum, R., "Balancing People and Systems," *Infosystems,* September, 1974.

Burgstaller, H. A., and Forsyth, J. D., "The Key-Result Approach to Designing Management Information Systems," *Management Adviser,* May-June, 1973.

Cahill, J. J., "A Dictionary/Directory Method for Building a Common MIS Data Base," *Journal of Systems Management,* November, 1970.

Curtice, R. M., "Some Tools for Data Base Development," *Datamation,* July, 1974.

Fischer, H. A., "System Design Via On-Line Simulation," *Software Age,* February, 1970.

Flynn, R. L., "A Brief History of Data Base Management," *Datamation,* August, 1974.

Hartman, W., Matthes, H., and Proeme, A., *Management Information Systems Handbook.* New York: McGraw-Hill Book Co., 1968, Vols. 3 and 4.

Head, R. V., "Management Information System Structure," *Data Management,* September, 1971.

Holland, S. A., "The Remote Inquiry of Data Bases," *Datamation,* November 15, 1970.

Lyon, J. K., *An Introduction to Data Base Design.* New York: John Wiley & Sons, Inc., 1971.

Mandel, B. J., "Building Better MIS," *Financial Executive,* August, 1970.

Martin, J., *Design of Real-Time Computer Systems.* Englewood Cliffs, N.J.: Prentice-Hall, Inc., 1967.

Matthews, D. Q., *The Design of the Mangement Information System.* New York: Auerbach Publishers, 1971.

McKeever, J. M., "Building a Computer-Based MIS," *Journal of Systems Management,* February, 1970.

Mellichamp, J. M., "MIS: Which Way to Go," *Journal of Systems Management,* July, 1973.

Milano, J. V., "Modular Method of Structuring MIS," *Data Management,* February, 1970.

Murdick, R. G., and Ross, J. E., *Information Systems for Modern Management.* Englewood Cliffs, N.J.: Prentice-Hall, Inc., 1971, Chaps. 13 and 14.

Nolan, R. L., "Computer Data Bases: The Future Is Now," *Harvard Business Review,* September-October, 1973.

Pomerantz, A. G., "Predict Your System's Fortune: Use Simulation's Crystal Ball," *Computer Decisions,* June, 1970.

Prendergast, L. L., "Selecting a Data Management System," *Computer Decisions,* August, 1972.

Price, S. F., "The Ten Commandments of Data Base," *Data Management,* May, 1972.

Romberg, B. W., "Data Bases: There Really Is a Better Way to Manage Your Files," *Infosystems,* May, 1973.

Rothstein, M. F., *Guide to the Design of Real-Time Systems.* New York: John Wiley & Sons, Inc., 1970, Chap. 2.

Schubert, R. F., "Directions in Data Base Technology," *Datamation,* September, 1974.

———, "Basic Concepts in Data Base Management Systems," *Datamation,* July, 1972.

Shipman, F. W., "Designing M.I.S. for Managers," *Journal of Systems Management,* July 1969.

Sibley, E. H., and Merten, A. G., "Implementation of a Generalized Data Base Management System Within an Organization," *Management Informatics,* Vol. 2 (1973), No. 1.

Sterling, T. D., "Guidelines for Humanizing Computerized Information Systems: A Report from Stanley House," *Communications of ACM,* November, 1974.

Stimler, S., *Real-Time Data-Processing Systems.* New York: McGraw-Hill Book Co., 1969.

Vancil, R. F., "What Kind of Management Control Do You Need?" *Harvard Business Review,* March-April, 1973.

Wearing, M. L., "Upgrade Documentation With a Data Dictionary," *Computer Decisions,* August, 1973.

Wilkinson, J. W., "Classifying Information Systems," *Journal of Systems Management,* April, 1973.

Wofsey, M. W., *Management of Automatic Data Processing.* Washington, D.C.: Thompson Book Co., 1968, Chap. IV.

Yourdon, E., *Design of On-Line Computer Systems.* Englewood Cliffs, N.J.: Prentice-Hall, Inc., 1972.

Zani, W. M., "Blueprint for MIS," *Harvard Business Review,* November-December, 1970.

EQUIPMENT SELECTION FOR REAL-TIME MANAGEMENT INFORMATION SYSTEMS

5

Once the first two steps of the feasibility study (the real-time MIS exploratory survey report and the basic systems design) are completed, the MIS task force is ready to undertake the last major step, which is equipment selection. The final selection of the most suitable equipment may require some systems modification, which will necessitate modification of the original exploratory survey report at some time during this step. It is possible for these modifications to be major, but generally they are not. The feasibility or nonfeasibility of applying newer data processing equipment is not completely established until the order(s) is (are) placed with the respective manufacturer(s).

Initially, the chapter presents the important equipment specifications that are essential to any real-time system—namely, a communications network, terminal devices, auxiliary storage devices, and a central processing unit(s). This is followed by an illustration that typifies hardware and software requirements deemed necessary in a real-time MIS operating environment. Finally, the significant factors involved in selecting appropriate data processing equipment are discussed.

157

EQUIPMENT SPECIFICATIONS

The real-time MIS feasibility study effort, up to this point, has been directed toward the analysis of the present system and the basic systems design of the new system. By way of review, requirements for the real-time MIS have been determined—in particular, new policies (consistent with company objectives), output needs, new methods and procedures, a common data base, off-line files, planned inputs, common data representation, human factors, internal control (including real-time controls), and new system performance specifications. These requirements formed the basis for designing the new system on a modular subsystem basis.

The emphasis at this point in the feasibility study will be on the specifications of equipment to be used in the newly designed system. Specifically, the systems analysts will state in general terms the hardware requirements that are essential to a real-time system. These include:

a communications network
terminal and control devices
auxiliary storage devices
central processing unit(s)
other CPU peripherals (i.e., tape drives, card readers, printers, etc.)

COMMUNICATIONS NETWORK

Input/output terminals are able to send data to or request information from the real-time MIS only after they have been connected to the central computer by means of a communications network. Depending on the time requirements of company personnel, computer access can be on a "permanent" (leased lines) or an "as required" (dial-up arrangement) basis. The terminal specifications are necessary for determining the type (*simplex* allows one-way transmission of data; *half-duplex* carries data in both directions, but permits the transmission of data in only one direction at a time; and *full-duplex* has the ability to transmit data in both directions simultaneously) and the speed (*narrow-band* transmits data more slowly than that needed for voice transmission; *voice-band* transmits data at the level of voice transmission; and *broad-band* transmits data much faster than the level of voice transmission) of the lines. Because each terminal has a certain rated speed, the lines required to transfer data from the terminal to the centralized computer is determinable. Thus, the systems analyst must develop a network of lines which will transfer information to and from company personnel within the required time limits and at a low cost.

The type of equipment needed to connect the transmission lines to the main real-time computer is a study by itself. There are many kinds of units available, each with differing characteristics. Knowledge of the lines required for the real-time system is a prerequisite to the specification of the number and types of line control units that are needed. Each unit has a capacity as to the number of lines it can handle as well as the maximum speed of any line. In essence, a study should be made of the functions that available units can handle for lowest costs.

The two major components involved in the transfer of data in a real-time MIS environment are communication channels and terminals. The interconnection of these channels and terminals with a computer(s) forms a network whose purpose is to receive, process, and transfer information. As illustrated in Figure 5-1, there are several different types of lines that can be employed in a communications network for a real-time system. Lines (1) and (2) are examples of point-to-point transmission—that is, any connection between two terminals or between a terminal and a computer. Line (3) is a multipoint line which contains more than one terminal station on one communication line. Note that the connection between T-A and T-B is a point-to-point connection. Line (4) consists of three lines (multipoint) entering a line concentrator.

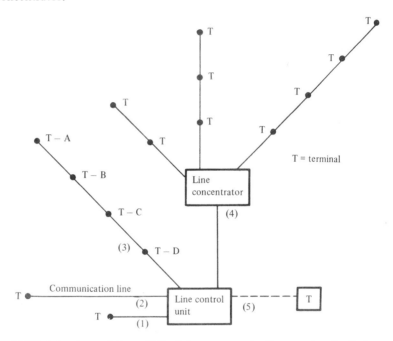

FIGURE 5-1.   A real-time MIS data communications network that utilizes several different types of lines.

A line concentrator is a hardware device that accepts data from many low-speed, low-activity stations and transfers the data to the computer at much higher speeds. It is also capable of receiving data from the computer at a faster rate than it sends to the terminals by storing the data temporarily in its own buffer memory. The purpose of this device is to make the communication process more efficient between the terminals and the computer(s) and to reduce overall communication network costs.

The last line (5) is a dial-up line that is employed in connection with the telephone. When a telephone connection is made, the terminal is connected directly to the computer. After the data transmission is completed, the terminal is disconnected from the computer. This data communications approach is used for terminals with limited data transmission requirements. It allows for keeping line costs to a minimum, because the user is charged only for the duration of the connection, which is not the case with lines (1) through (4).

The line control unit depicted in Figure 5-1 can be utilized as a simple data exchange unit or a multiplexor. Operating in a simple data exchange mode, it allows changing data transmission from one direction to another, say for half-duplex lines. As a multiplexor, it can be connected to a computer for handling simplex, half-duplex, and full-duplex lines or can be a stand-alone unit, working as a special-purpose computer. The maximum rate at which lines are able to transfer data to and from the computer is dependent upon the service provided—that is, narrow-band, voice-band, broad-band, or some other service. For a balanced approach, the speed at which a terminal device is able to transmit (send or receive) information should be equal to the speed of the line.

Referring again to line (2) in Figure 5-1, information may pass through several types of data communications equipment before it reaches its final destination. The required equipment is illustrated in Figure 5-2. It should be noted that the same equipment is required for any of the multipoint lines in Figure 5-1.

In Figure 5-2, unit 1 can be almost any type of input device or I/O device, as illustrated. It is the originating point of data or the transferring point of information. The terminal control unit, or unit 2, accepts and stores input data (reverse the procedure for forwarding output information) temporarily by means of a buffering device so that its speed is compatible with the communication facility. The data set (modulator—unit 3) converts bits into signals which can be transmitted over communication lines (unit 4). The data set (demodulator—unit 5) receives signals over the communication facility and converts the signals into bits. Unit 6—the line control unit—controls and coordinates the flow of information to and from the computer.

As pointed out above, unit 6 serves as a data exchange or a multiplexor for the control of information to and from the various terminals. Polling is a common technique employed to coordinate and control on-line flows of data. Basically, the system interrogates each station on each line and asks if there are data to be transferred to the computer for input terminals, and if the terminal is able to receive information for the output terminals. It should be noted that polling and/or the transferring of data can take place simultaneously on each communication line.

TERMINAL AND CONTROL DEVICES

Currently, there is a wide range of terminal and control devices for real-time MIS. Real-time terminals accept keyed or punched data as input to the computer and/or produce printed, displayed, punched, or audio messages as output from the computer. Below, the first four devices are commonly employed in processing data through a system and the last four have become associated with extracting higher-level information:

portable terminals
typewriter terminals

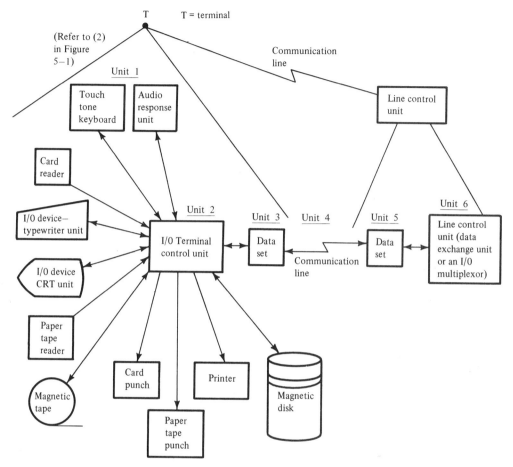

FIGURE 5-2. Data communications equipment needed for the transfer of data to and from remote locations for real-time MIS processing.

visual display terminals
multifunction terminals
picturephones
large screen display systems
computer graphic devices
management control centers

Portable Terminals

A portable terminal allows the user to travel to the problem itself and solve it right on the spot. For example, it allows one to take a physical inventory at some remote location and report the items after they have been counted for an immediate comparison to the perpetual inventory maintained on line.

Some units rent for as low as $20 per month. For example, the IBM 2721

Portable Audio Terminal (Figure 5-3) allows the user to enter alphabetic and numerical data into a System/360 (model 25 and up) or System/370 from any standard telephone. The unit, priced at $600 (numeric code only), communicates to the computer through an IBM 7770 Audio Response Unit (Figure 5-4).

In manufacturing applications, the 2721 Terminal allows workers to enter information on jobs in progress and tracks the status of jobs as they move from one department to another. Inventory clerks can use the unit to determine the nearest warehouse stocking a particular part. Other uses include the checking of critical delivery dates at the customer's office by industrial salesman, solving engineering problems, and customer credit verification. In operation, touch-tone signals are communicated to the 7770, which then converts these signals to 8-bit bytes. Pro-

FIGURE 5-3.
IBM 2721 Portable Audio Terminal. (Courtesy International Business Machines Corporation.)

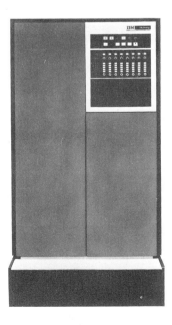

FIGURE 5-4. IBM 7770 Audio Response Unit. (Courtesy International Business Machines Corporation.

gramming must be written to translate these signals into a meaningful code for the computer. Unauthorized access to computer data can be prevented by assigning each terminal a special identification code number.

A recent addition to the category of portable computer terminals is the combination CRT/keyboard terminal (Figure 5-5). With this particular model, two operating modes can be selected by a front-panel push-button: local mode, which provides page transmission that allows local editing; and on-line mode, which transmits character by character, as does a teletypewriter. In either mode, the user can select half- or full-duplex channels. When the screen is full, the top line is deleted and the information remaining on display is shifted upward to allow new characters to be entered on the bottom of the display, just as a teletypewriter rolls up paper.

FIGURE 5-5.
Portable   CRT/keyboard
terminal. (Courtesy Ben-
dix, Inc.)

Another portable computer terminal is the PortaCom, illustrated in Figure 5-6. The PortaCom terminal produces full-page computer printout with carbon copies. Teletype-compatible, it needs only a standard power outlet and a telephone to being operating. The unit weighs 26 pounds, making it light enough to be hand-carried, and leases for about $80 per month.

Typewriter Terminals

A typewriter terminal for real-time processing, operating at 10 characters per second, is depicted in Figure 5-7. Teletype terminals are also widely used for time sharing and can produce punched paper tape as a by-product.

Faster typewriter terminals include the GE TermiNet 300 Teleprinter (Figure 5-8) and the NCR 260 Thermal Printer (Figure 5-9). Both units can print at a speed of 30 characters per second as well as at slower rates (10 to 15 characters per second). In the Thermal Printer, contact from a depressed typewriter key transmits current through an array of "heat flash" elements in a controlled shape formed by any of 21 or less contact spots. The proper combination of spots is brought into direct contact with heat-sensitive paper, which instantly forms the desired image.

FIGURE 5-6.
PortaCom portable data
communications terminal.
(Courtesy Data Products
Corporation.)

FIGURE 5-7. Teletype Model 38
ASR set. (Courtesy Teletype Corporation.)

FIGURE 5-8. GE TermiNet 300 Teleprinter. (Courtesy General Electric Corporation.)

Visual Display Terminals

Visual display units (CRT terminals) in a real-time MIS environment have gained in popularity because of their speed and flexibility—that is, their capability to display printed and graphic information at a much faster speed than typing information. Their major disadvantages are slightly higher costs and lack of hard copy in most cases.

The hardware of a visual display terminal consists of a keyboard, a signal generator-interpreter, a buffer, and a visual display screen. An inexpensive CRT data terminal is shown in Figure 5-10. The Bunker-Ramo 2210 CRT unit leases for $39 per month including maintenance. In a typical installation, a complete work station can be outfitted for on-line processing at approximately $55 per month. The unit's keyboard contains all alpha and numeric characters plus a selection of programmable function keys. A more expensive CRT display station, costing several hundred dollars per month, is illustrated in Figure 5-11.

For any CRT terminal, the keyboard is the means of inquiry for data which are stored on line by the computer system. Coded signals are generated and transmitted by data sets and communication channels to the computer system. Once the computer has interpreted the signals and retrieved the requested information, the

FIGURE 5-9.
(a) The NCR 260 Data Terminal prints up to 30 characters per second. (Courtesy National Cash Register Company.)

(b) The NCR 260 is a thermal printer which prints a legible dot pattern on paper with a special coating. (Courtesy National Cash Register Company.)

FIGURE 5-10.
Bunker-Ramo 2210 computer CRT terminal. (Courtesy The Bunker Ramo Corporation.)

FIGURE 5-11.
**IBM 3270 Display Station
with alphanumeric key-
board. (Courtesy Interna-
tional Business Machines
Corporation.)**

data are transmitted again, using data sets, back over the communication channel to
the visual display terminal in the form of coded signals. The signals, in turn, are
interpreted and displayed on the TV-type screen. Data that are displayed can be
printed if the visual display unit is equipped with an attached printer or integrated
within the CRT terminal, as shown in Figure 5-12. Real-time applications for display stations are numerous. Among these are credit check, accounts receivable,
production scheduling, inventory, shipping information, sales data, administration
data, stock prices, and similar business data. The number of applications is as wide
as the CRT terminals being marketed. The feasibility study must determine what
mixture of CRT units best serve the firm, because their capabilities and prices vary
from manufacturer to manufacturer.

Multifunction Terminals

The foregoing terminals may not be sufficiently flexible enough for all real-
time MIS applications. In such cases, there are a few devices that combine reasonably fast printing and card reading with the use of typewriter and paper tape
input/output. Shown in Figure 5-13 is a UNIVAC DCT 2000 remote input/output
batch terminal, which consists of a card reader, card punch, and a printer. As
indicated in its name, it is capable of remote batch processing. Even though these
input/output devices are slow when compared with similar computer equipment,
their speeds approach the limit of the standard voice-band grade channels. For all
practical purposes, multifunction terminals give the user some of the same facilities

FIGURE 5-12. Photophysics '45' CRT Data Terminal with hard copy
output. (Courtesy Photophysics.)

FIGURE 5-13. UNIVAC DCT 2000 Multifunction Remote Input/
Output Batch Terminal. (Courtesy UNIVAC Division
of the Sperry Rand Corporation.)

that a local small computer would be capable of providing without the initial cost outlay and support expenses that would be incurred.

Picturephones

The picturephone allows the participants in a telephone conversation to see each other while they talk and to transmit pictures of documents being discussed. But more importantly, it is capable of interrogating the common data base and displaying desired information to the user (Figure 5-14). On-line computer programs are used continually to update data for reference by the picturephone system, in particular, up-to-the-minute sales, inventory, and production figures. Thus, data ready for real-time access is not restricted to one area of the firm, but is applicable to most areas. Access to confidential data is controlled by appending a security code to the end of the user's identification number. This number is punched out on a "card dialer" which, when inserted into a telephone, identifies the user to the system.

Selecting Picturephone Information. Once the user is connected via the picturephone with the real-time management information system, his identification code determines the data to which he has access. The input keyboard of the standard touch-tone telephone contains keys for the numbers zero to 9 and for two-system control symbols used to define data desired. To access information on a subject, such as sales for a particular product produced by a certain division of the firm, the sales manager first selects the general category of "financial information."

FIGURE 5-14. Operating managers access data with picturephone. (Courtesy American Telephone and Telegraph.)

The display then produces a list of various financial data available, such as sales to date and production costs to date. Desiring further sales information, he would key in the number that appeared on the display beside the selected category. From a listing of divisions, the specific division would be chosen by depressing the desired key on the touch-tone keyboard. Then the individual is presented a listing of products for the division under study. Having depressed the proper key for the particular product under investigation, the manager would see important statistics about this one product, such as sales to date and units sold this year versus last year.

If the MIS has been programmed to retain past data, the viewer would continue to depress the control keys after studying the current information, whereby the previous day's data on the same topic would be presented. Several days of past information can be carried for topics to be indexed. In the sales example cited above, the sales manager could trace the sales fluctuations of a product by accessing past data.

Large-Screen Display Systems

Many of the problems with small-screen display units are overcome by large-screen display units that are capable of showing information from a remotely located real-time computer system. One such system is the Management Information Display System (MIDS), which utilizes laser technology. It has a 5-foot-square screen for viewing critical data (Figure 5-15a). Each point on the 512 by 512-point display matrix may be independently energized to form a high brightness, three-color, alphanumeric or graphical image (Figure 5-15b). The display format is determined by the user's applications and formats may be quickly changed using the system's internal processor.

Communication between the operator, display system, and remote computer is provided by a tabletop inquiry unit. This typewriter-sized unit enables an operator to select, enter, modify, and delete information on the system's 5-foot-square rear projection screen. A special control allows the operator to select any point on the screen and transfer the location of this point to the remote computer as the start point for updating or other action. This type of display combines the flexibility and performance of a cathode ray tube display with the convenience of a large viewing format in a real-time MIS environment.

Computer Graphic Devices

For the more forward-thinking managers, business decisions about sales, pricing, inventory, and production can be resolved by employing computer graphics. The CRT screen is linked to a real-time system so that when the individual indicates changes to the screen image with a light pen on the screen, the computer revises the lines or curves immediately (Figure 5-16). In reality, the manager tests his intuitive judgment by simple analysis of quantitative data and develops confidence in his decision, knowing that he has considered many feasible alternatives and has selected the optimum one. Thus, the "what if" questions have been answered through simulation techniques that are integrally related to computer graphics.

(a)

FIGURE 5-15. Management Information Display System (MIDS) with 5' x 5' rear projection screen (a) and a 512- by 512-point display matrix (b). (Courtesy Texas Instruments, Inc.)

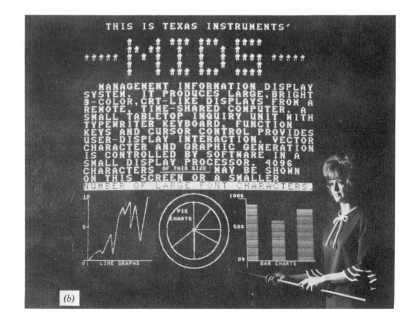

(b)

Computer graphics have been used for some time by engineers and designers to analyze and design complex shapes (Figure 5-16). However, what is relatively new is the ability of computer programs to analyze business problems for managers. For example, consider a problem involving inventory spanning five equal time periods where the choice is between overtime and plant expansion for one of two different products. In a graphic aids system, when the executive touches the screen with his pen, the graph will change in response to his order, and the problem will begin to be solved. Touching a specific area with the pen signals the computer to react and allows instructions to be sent to a subroutine program. It, in turn, performs new computations relative to the chosen area of interest and produces a revised display—i.e., a decision—that is a result of the joint efforts of man, program, and computer.

FIGURE 5-16.
Manager using a CRT display console in a real-time MIS environment. (Courtesy International Business Machines Corporation.)

To operate a computer graphics system, the user need not have a strong background in mathematics. The rationale is that all the complex mathematical derivations have been reduced to several simple identities embedded in the computer program. The purpose of these identities is to anticipate and verify intuitive guesses which are expected to be forthcoming from the businessman. Because the graphic display is a mirror image of the mathematical analysis performed by the computer, it is sufficient that the businessman see and work only from the display. Thus, the real-time MIS operating mode of computer graphics does not replace executive judgment, but rather enhances it by providing immediate quantitative answers to the manager's intuitive questions about the operation(s) of his specific area of business. Equally important, it allows him to test his judgment and satisfy himself that he had considered all the possible alternatives before pursuing a course of action.

Management Control Centers

A conviction that time is one of the firm's most important resources has made a substantial impact on management. Although most firms have a backlog of attractive investment opportunities, lack of money, for the most part, has been the excuse offered for not undertaking all of them. Actually, the manager is often bogged down in too much paperwork. To remedy this difficult situation, equipment manufacturers have developed large display devices that are capable of showing current operating and financial information (Figure 5-17). Whether this decision-making environment is called a "management control center" or a "decision room" is purely academic.[1] Its importance lies in its ability to call up a wide variety of management information. Instead of searching manual files and cluttering up the office with paperwork, executives can obtain the required information immediately. They can, for example, obtain sales figures for any time period together with comparable figures for previous periods. Current production schedules, the number of pending orders, status of back orders, amounts of accounts receivable and payable, profit analysis by periods and products, equipment utilization, and divisional performance factors are additional information that is available. By no means do the foregoing exhaust the possible applications for a management control center.

Benefits of Management Control Center. The benefits from a management control center are many for real-time (and future) management information systems. Data will always be current, accurate, and in a form well-suited for fast evaluation. Graphs, charts, indexes, and the like on the large display screen will keep the information to a minimum, thereby increasing management's understanding. Pages and pages of tabular information can be condensed into one projected display picture. Exception reporting will reduce the amount of data for possible viewing. The use of computer-generated displays will further reduce the need for paper reporting. The speed and simplification of reporting will allow the executive considerable time for performing the tasks for which he was employed.

Although current applications for a management control center are numerous, they can be characterized as operatonal and tactical applications, designed to meet the needs of lower and middle management, respectively, for the short run. This pertains to the real-time management information systems that are currently in use. What is needed are applications at the highest level (strategic) that utilize the real potential of a computer. For example, planning and evaluating new products over their life cycle, allocating available factory capacity in the most efficient manner throughout the firm, and setting long-range plans and objectives for the firm are areas in which answers are invaluable to top management. This is basically the approach that will be forthcoming from future management information systems (Chapter 18).

Combines Operations Research with Data Processing. Before strategic and tactical applications can be commonplace when utilizing the output from a manage-

---

[1]Francis E. Wylie, "Decision Rooms for Executive Warriors," *Finance Magazine,* October, 1972.

FIGURE 5-17. Management control center with executive armchair control panel (closeup) reduces the need for paper reports. (Courtesy Information Management International.)

ment control center, senior system analysts who possess both operations research and data processing skills are needed. They provide the required link between top and middle management and the computer system. These trained business analysts will be capable of programming sophisticated mathematical models and debugging them on input/output terminal devices. Once the program is operational, both management and the business analyst can sit down and simulate the actual operations in the management control center. The executive can request new output information based on changes in the parameters and constraints of the problem. Within the wide range of capabilities for a specific computer model, management will have answers that were heretofore unobtainable.

I/O Terminal and Control Devices. I/O terminal and control devices that enable personnel to send and receive messages can be as close or distant as desired from the main computer system. A management control center (Figure 5-18) is generally located near the central computer. On the other hand, input/output terminal devices can be connected to the computer via a communications network (Figure 5-19). An analyst from the task force who is assigned the job of specifying terminal requirements must choose the appropriate type of I/O devices and the location of each. To accomplish this task, he must analyze the requirement for the new system accumulated during the basic systems design phase.

In making the terminal selection, the systems analyst is concerned with reviewing the following information concerning the new real-time MIS environment:

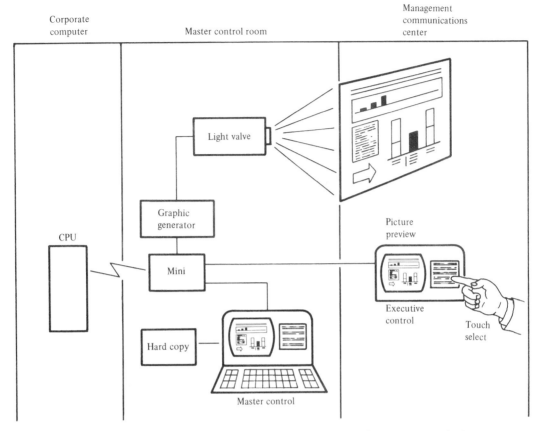

FIGURE 5-18. Computer-controlled display (CompuChrome) for a management control center in a real-time MIS processing mode. (Courtesy Information Management International Corporation.)

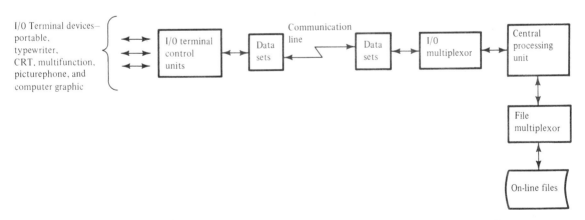

FIGURE 5-19. I/O terminal devices used in a real-time MIS processing mode (remote operations).

175

the data entering and the information being extracted from the system

the locations from which messages are received and the locations to which they are sent

the number of transactions that are sent and received at each location

the information that is added to or deleted from on-line files during various stages of the flow and where they take place

how soon the information must arrive to be useful, at what intervals is the information to be transmitted, how much delay is permissible, and what is the penalty for delay

the reliability requirements in respect to the accuracy of the transmitted data or system failure

An extensive study of the foregoing factors provides the necessary information for deciding on the type of terminal devices needed. Likewise, the analyst is able to determine the location of these units by analyzing the tasks that will be performed by operating personnel working in a real-time mode. If volume is high, several terminals of varying types may be required at a specific location. Thus, the results of this analysis plus the information regarding the location and type of terminals is utilized to determine the makeup of the data communications network.

AUXILIARY STORAGE DEVICES

For the newly designed system to process input data and answer questions on a real-time or timely basis, stored data will have to be immediately accessible to the computer. For this mode of operation, the common data base must be on-line. What particular information must be available on an immediate demand basis should have been answered previously when determining the requirements for the common data base structure. Generally, important data required by the system should be stored on line in auxiliary or secondary storage while less important data should be housed in other low-cost storage mediums.

Data which must be stored on line must be thoroughly evaluated by the analyst. He must determine the following:

the amount of space needed for storing the data in auxiliary storage

the time required to find and retrieve a record of information

the time needed to transfer the proper record from the terminal device to the main computer memory as well as from the computer to the device after the record has been processed

An intensive review and analysis of these factors is necessary to evaluate on-line storage capacity.

When establishing the size of the common data base per the first item above, consideration must be given to the current auxiliary storage devices available. Capacities, speeds, and transfer rates are set forth in Figure 5-20 for typical secondary storage devices. It should be noted that many other on-line storage devices are available.

The most important criterion from the standpoint of a real-time MIS is the rate at which data can be transferred to affect the functioning of the environment in real time. Referring to the second and third foregoing specifications, typical times for reading and writing a record between disk storage and primary storage (core) are set forth in Figure 5-21. To these times—120 milliseconds for reading a record and 45 milliseconds for writing a record—must be added processing time of the central processing unit, say 20 milliseconds. The total processing time for this type of on-line transaction is 185 milliseconds, which should be adjusted for other factors that are pertinent to the situation. Thus, total time may well exceed the 185 milliseconds.

Type of Random Access Storage Device	Capacity	Average Access Time (milliseconds)	Transfer Rate
1. Laser mass memory—690-212	one trillion bits	150	four billion bit per second
2. Magnetic disk—IBM 3330 (8 - drive unit)	800 million bytes	30	800,000 bytes per second
3. Magnetic drum—IBM 2301	4,100,000 bytes or 8,200,000 digits	4-8.75	1,200,000 bytes per second or 2,400,000 digits per second
4. Magnetic card—NCR 653-101 CRAM	145+ million bytes or 290+ packed decimal digits	125	83,125 bytes per second
5. Magnetic strip—IBM 2321 Data Cell	400 million bytes or 800 million packed decimal digits	300	55,000 bytes per second

FIGURE 5-20. Capacities, access times, and transfer rates of typical random access storage devices.

Read a Record		Write a Record	
Access motion time	90 milliseconds	Rotational delay	35 milliseconds
Rotational delay	25 milliseconds	Write the record	5 milliseconds
Read the data record	5 milliseconds	Write check	5 milliseconds
Total	120 milliseconds	Total	45 milliseconds

FIGURE 5-21. Typical times for reading and writing a record from disk storage into primary storage (core).

CENTRAL PROCESSING UNIT(S)

The purpose of having on-line input/output components is to communicate with the computer—namely, the central processing unit. Because of the differential in internal operating speeds of the computer and the various auxiliary units, new design techniques have been introduced over the past several years for real-time systems. The important data processing innovations that affect the central processing unit are:

1. simplex systems
2. duplex systems
3. multiprocessing systems
4. multiprogramming systems

Simplex Systems

Before discussing advanced approaches needed in a real-time MIS environment, it is helpful to examine less complex basic hardware configurations. The simplex system, displayed in Figure 5-22, provides no standby equipment in case of equipment failure or during routine maintenance. From a hardware standpoint, it is the least expensive. Likewise, it tends to be easier and cheaper to program because there are no complex routines necessary for controlling the central processing unit. Significant savings can be realized through the utilization of such a system, providing that the user is willing or able to lower system performance with an extensive manual backup system. System operations that have stringent time requirements, say no message can be delayed more than a few minutes, are not likely candidates for the simplex system.

Another configuration is the simplex system with an input-output multiplexor attached, shown in Figure 5-23. The I/O multiplexor acts as an interface between the terminal devices and the central processing unit. The advantages of this configuration include added modularity—that is, changes can be made in the multiplexor to effect different scan rates, changes in priority, and like items without

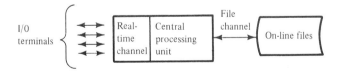

FIGURE 5-22. Simplex system.

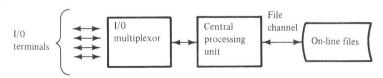

FIGURE 5-23. Simplex system with an input/output multiplexor.

disturbing the CPU (central processing unit) programs. In addition, memory allocations within the central processing unit are simpler because the I/O and queue
functions are controlled by the multiplexor.

In Figure 5-24, specialization of computer hardware is carried a step further
than that found in Figure 5-23. The file multiplexor acts as an interface between
the central processing unit and the on-line files. This configuration relieves the CPU
of communicating directly with both I/O terminals and accessing system files. As
with the preceding configuration, there is added programming for another piece of
equipment as well as further complicating hardware reliability and testing procedures.

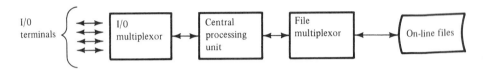

**FIGURE 5-24. Simplex system with input/output and file multi-
                plexors.**

Duplex Systems

In any type of simplex system, there is only one computer system. However,
in a duplex system, there is a second computer system with real-time capabilities
that can be switched over if the primary system fails or is taken off line for any
reason (Figure 5-25). Most duplexed systems use one of the computer systems for
batch processing until a malfunction occurs in the other system. When the on-line
processing system malfunctions, the procedure is to reroute the flow of information
by either automatic or manual switching to the other system. Programming considerations are extremely important because of both the complexity of control and
the monitor and switchover programs.

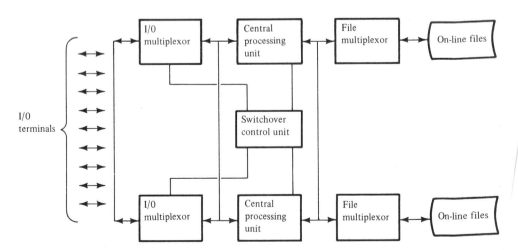

FIGURE 5-25. Duplex (or dual) system.

In addition to duplex systems, there are dual systems which are on line in parallel. They perform the same basic functions except that output is generated by one computer only. Checking is carried on continually in which results are compared between the two systems. The dual system is planned such that any variation in the results of computations performed by both computer systems receives immediate attention. Action can be initiated on an automatic or manual basis.

Multiprocessing Systems

In a multiprocessing system environment, two or more computer systems are each doing more than one job (Figure 5-26). Multiple processors share the same memory and operating system. The operating system is not duplicated as it is in a duplex system thereby resulting in a more efficient and less expensive utilization of memory. Standby in this system may be on a slightly "degraded" basis—that is, when one system goes off the air, another one in the network may pick up the load. Because the computer picking up the load must also continue to perform its own tasks, a lengthened system response time may result. The advantage of the multiprocessing system is standby reliability at a lower cost than for a duplex system. However, there are disadvantages. Among these are a possible lower level of service when one system is down and the difficulty of performing reliability analysis because of the complexities of such a system. Also, the planning, development, and testing of programs as well as control programs is more sophisticated than with duplex systems.

Multiprogramming Systems

The multiprogramming concept is found in a real-time computer environment, but just as important is its application to a batch processing computer mode of operation. The major objective of a multiprogramming system is to optimize the use of the total available computer resources. These resources include the core memory, the central processing unit, and the input/output devices in the system. To achieve this, jobs will not be organized into the type of sequential job streams used in a normal batch facility. Instead, priorities will be set, and even hierarchies of priorities, to allow a job mix that most fully utilizes these facilities.

There are basically two types of multiprogramming systems. In the IBM System/360 and System/370, for example, there is multiprogramming with a fixed number of tasks (MFT) and multiprogramming with a variable number of tasks (MVT).

Fixed Number of Tasks. Multiprogramming with a fixed number of tasks involves a set number of fixed-sized core partitions. These are dedicated to the processing of one job only. Quite often, the partition size will be much larger than the program size. In such a system, some core memory space is wasted—for example, suppose a system has fixed partitions of 100K each; running a 50K program in one 100K partition would require only half the partition space, the other half would be wasted.

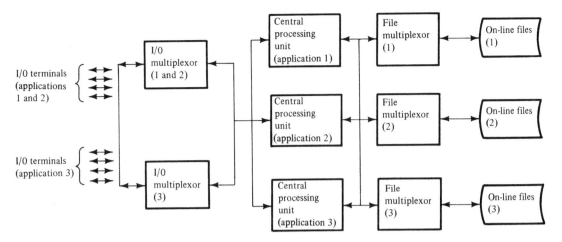

FIGURE 5-26. Multiprocessing system.

The users in a MFT system are responsible for determining the core memory partitions to be used by each program, the input/output device allocations, and various other functions. Because of this, the MFT system has a smaller portion of its core area dedicated to supervisory or operating system functions and can, therefore, offer the user control over a somewhat greater portion of his core memory space than would a system with a variable number of tasks.

Variable Number of Tasks. A multiprogramming system with a variable number of tasks can optimize the use of the total resource available in a more efficient manner. Logic is provided to enable the system to direct the processing sequence according to the pattern it selects and to communicate with the system operator to indicate the input/output pattern that it is currently running. To accomplish this, the MVT system employs dynamic core assignment techniques. The system selects the jobs it will run from the job queues that are in readily accessible storage, such as disk files. Depending on the pattern of optimum resources that the system selects, a multiprogramming job in process could consist of several tasks running concurrently. Each job step might consist of one or more tasks running concurrently.

In preparing programs for multiprogramming operations, two essential factors are involved. One is the segmenting of programs so that they can fit into partitions in the memory. The second is the insertion of linkages to tie together segments of the programs in the proper sequences. Batch programs are often bigger than the partition size, so they must be broken into segments such that no segment is larger than the partition in which it will reside. These segments are then processed in a predetermined order, and each will follow or overlay its predecessor in the same partitions. Thus, the complexity of a multiprogramming environment can be extremely difficult on data processing personnel.

Operating Systems

In order to maintain the proper sequence of operations for the many interrelated components of a real-time system, an operating system (generally called

181

OS—operating system—or AOS—advanced operating system) is necessary, the nucleus of which resides in a reserved portion of main storage. In a real-time MIS environment, the operating system must have the capabilities to:

> receive messages from a control unit, such as a multiplexor, at varying arrival rates with wide variations of message types
>
> provide storage for these messages as well as their data records for processing
>
> communicate with the various components of the system in order to permit processing of transactions and the transfer of processed messages to the appropriate remote locations
>
> maintain an awareness of the attached devices and their malfunctions

In essence, the operating system polices real-time computer operations as they occur.

Specifying the correct operating system is a difficult task, because operating systems vary from simple to very complex ones. The systems analyst must evaluate the various operating systems that are best suited for the real-time MIS environment and select the one requiring the least amount of internal storage and/or fastest possible response time. If system requirements cannot be met by manufacturer-supplied operating system, it may be necessary to modify the vendor-supplied operating system or to develop one. This is a costly and risky operation and should be avoided if at all possible.

Virtual Memory Systems

Virtual memory systems can be best understood by relating them to the more familiar real memory systems. In both memory systems, a program exists in program space, that is, a number of locations of computer memory has been allocated to the program. This space contains the program instructions, constants, data areas, and, perhaps, some unused space. Program space always exists in some hardware component. The two types of program space (hardware components) are main memory (central storage of the computer) and auxiliary memory (typically a drum or a disk). Instructions being executed by the central processor and the data referenced by these instructions must reside in main memory. Auxiliary memory is used to hold programs and portions of the operating system which are not candidates for immediate processing. A program in auxiliary memory must be called into main memory before it can be processed. A program in main memory may be temporarily suspended and paged (rolled out) to auxiliary memory while awaiting further processing.

Although the foregoing depicts the similarities of virtual and real memory systems, their major difference lies in the method used to allocate and control program space. In a real memory system, the program space for a given program occupies a contiguous set of locations in main memory. This entire program space must occupy main memory while the program is being processed. Dedicated areas must be established for segments and overlays of programs too large for main memory. On the other hand, in a virtual memory system, the program space for a given program occupies a noncontiguous set of locations in both main memory and in auxiliary memory. Large portions of the program reside only in auxiliary memory even when the program is being executed. Those portions of the program residing in main memory at a given moment generally include only those regions that contain the instructions currently being processed and the data referenced by those instructions. Hence, the term *virtual memory* refers to the entire program space (or address space) that is potentially available to an individual program.

As indicated previously, a multiprogramming operating system is designed to increase system throughput by optimizing the use of system resources. The key to this optimization process is to process a number of user programs concurrently. In general, the more programs that are being processed concurrently in main memory, the higher is the probability that all system resources are being used effectively. Virtual memory improves overall system throughput by improving memory utilization, thereby increasing the number of programs that can simultaneously occupy main memory. With the increased power and complexity of today's operating systems, it has become increasingly necessary to share the resources of the system among multiple users concurrently. VMOS (Virtual Memory Operating System) accomplishes this while also realizing the performance achievable from both the hardware and the hardware/software complex. The most valuable of all resources, the human element, is furnished with a unified command language and a commonality of data structures that allow the individual to interface with interactive and background language processors, service and utility programs, and to participate in the variety of information processing forms with a minimum of competition and concern which is so important in a real-time MIS environment.

REAL-TIME MIS SPECIFICATIONS ILLUSTRATION

Prior to examining the various steps involved in equipment selection, it would be helpful to present the hardware and software requirements deemed necessary for a typical real-time management information system. Not only will this approach bring to light important design considerations that are required for implementing real-time MIS, but it will also pinpoint the level of detail that must be specified.

HARDWARE

The hardware configuration will consist of a central computer in Dallas and terminals at all plant locations and warehouses which are to be tied together through a network of communication lines and multiplexors (Figure 5-27). The central computer must have real-time, multiprogramming capabilities which allow simultaneous operation of send/receive transmission modules, real-time data update and response modules, and non-real-time processing. Also in Dallas will be the necessary data sets (modems) and the multiplexing unit to handle transmission on the three lines feeding into the central computer.

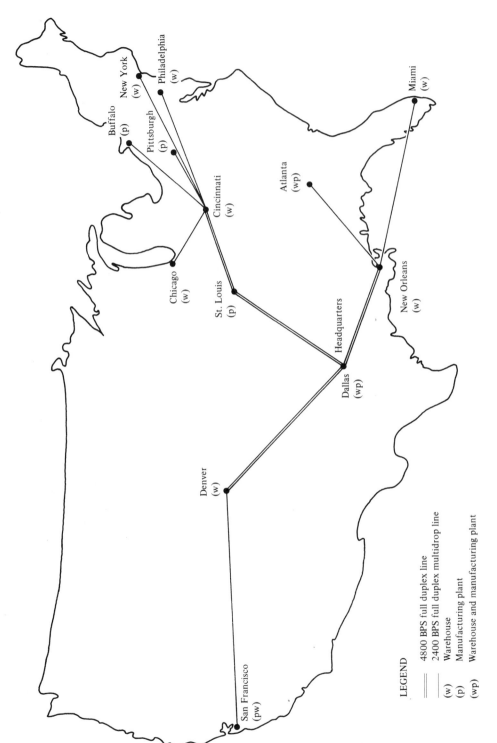

FIGURE 5-27. A typical data communications network in a real-time MIS operating environment.

LEGEND

━━━ 4800 BPS full duplex line

═══ 2400 BPS full duplex multidrop line

(w)   Warehouse

(p)   Manufacturing plant

(wp) Warehouse and manufacturing plant

184

The initial lines to the multiplexing units in Denver, New Orleans, and St. Louis (and this line on to Cincinnati) are to be 4800 BPS (bits per second) full-duplex leased lines. Leased lines have been chosen because the system operates approximately twenty hours a day. Although some warehouses may operate a single shift, some manufacturing plants operate two eight-hour shifts. To this sixteen-hour operation must be added three hours for changes in time zones as well as time for communication needed before and after each shift. These total requirements necessitate the need for almost around-the-clock network operations. At this degree of usage, public lines and exchanges would be more expensive and less efficient. Full-duplex lines make it possible to send and receive on the same line at the same time, shortening response time and increasing efficiency. A line that transmits at 4800 BPS gives the best transmission rate to cover long distances and utilizes the capabilities of the multiplexing units. To use a slower line would reduce the data rate that the multiplexors are capable of handling.

The purpose in specifying the multiplexors is to make it possible to transmit more than one message at a time, thus making possible the use of three single lines into the central multiplexor which deciphers and separates the messages. The speed of multiplexor send/receive capabilities is also much greater than that of I/O terminals.

Between each multiplexor and remote locations will be multidrop lines which are full-duplex 2400 BPS lines. This permits the simultaneous sending and receiving to different terminals on one line at a speed closely approximating the capacity of I/O terminals. A remote location would be a warehouse, plant, or combination of the two. If the geographical locations are the same, all the I/O terminals of one location would be on a single multidrop line. There is also a multidrop line connected directly to the central multiplexor that handles the terminals for the Dallas plant and warehouse.

A typical remote location would have a low-speed printer terminal for receiving large-quantity output (such as schedules and accounting reports), teletype-writers for inquiry and answer, and employee badge readers to collect employee time. This capability is also available at each remote location for one or several calls from the public network to be connected to this line. This makes it possible for area salesmen or sales offices to connect a portable CRT unit on line for inquiry and data entry. All of the terminals are to be buffered devices in order to minimize the time each uses the line.

SOFTWARE

The heart of this complete real-time MIS network will be the software of the central computer in Dallas. There are to be four basic divisions of software in the system (whose interaction is extremely important), which are:

1. supervisory software—schedules the processing done by the computer operating system or advanced operating system;
2. real-time control program—contains the input/output modules to handle

transmission inquiries and responses. Also, it makes the decisions about which real-time processing module is needed to act upon the message just received;

3. processing modules—evaluate the message, formulate a response, and control any file processing necessary;

4. non-real-time programs—include any batch processing runs or simulation programs.

To understand the relationships that exist among these various types of software, it is helpful to examine how a message is received and processed, remembering that the supervisor or supervisory software schedules everything that is done. Every several milliseconds, the supervisor will give control to the real-time control program (RTCP). Through a complex process that involves both the supervisor and the actual hardware, the RTCP determines if a message has been received. If not, the supervisor transfers control to another program and then returns after several milliseconds to check again. When there is a message, the RTCP determines what real-time processing module will be needed to process it. It passes this information back to the supervisor. The supervisor then calls the processing module in from auxiliary storage. After the module is in memory, control is passed to it for processing. This may involve retrieval and/or updating of data base files and the formulation of a response to be sent back to the terminal (when appropriate). If a response is to be made, the supervisor gives control back to the RTCP, which then follows another complex procedure to send the response on to the proper terminal. The supervisor then restarts this entire process to check for another incoming message.

It may happen that the time between incoming messages is shorter than the time needed for processing and response. This can occur because just like non-real-time programs, the real-time modules can also be interrupted so that the RTCP can check for incoming messages. When this condition occurs, incoming messages start building up in a queue file. A queue file is the technique for passing messages from the RTCP to the processing module. The RTCP also starts building a list of modules to be called in to process the queue; this list is a communication link between the RTCP and the supervisor. Similarly, there is a queue file that is used in sending response messages from the process modules to the RTCP.

It is easy to see from this real-time MIS operating environment several important points regarding software. First, the modular concept of programming is essential to this type of processing. There is not enough space to keep all of the processing routines resident within the computer's memory. Each must be called in from auxiliary storage as needed.

Second, apparent efficiency of the system will fluctuate in inverse proportion to the number of terminal messages. This means that as messages tend to stack up, processing on a particular message may take longer. This does not, however, mean that the utilization of the computer's capabilities is less efficient. It is at these times that the computer approaches its overall maximum efficiency. At peak load time, the system may be asked to perform more than the equipment is capable of handling. Just how much the apparent efficiency suffers is a prime consideration when selecting the entire hardware network.

Third, it is necessary to provide a speedy method of backup. For this purpose, the data base files are copied at the end of each day. Each incoming message is recorded on magnetic tape by the RTCP as it is received. In case of a system failure, the files are restored to the status at the beginning of the day. Then a non-real-time program is used to scan the tape and determine the modules to be used in processing each message that affects the status of the data base files. To attempt to re-create the day's activity through the real-time system would take a great deal more time. For this reason, the technique of capturing the activity on a faster medium (tape) has been employed.

Many more considerations must be made than those discussed here for hardware and software. However, this overview is a representative sampling. The degree of complexity gives a good indication as to why the selection of hardware and software is a difficult undertaking. Thus, the need for equipment selection— including software—as an integral part of a real-time MIS feasibility study, is paramount, the next matter for discussion in the chapter.

EQUIPMENT SELECTION

Equipment selection should be undertaken by the MIS task force upon the completion of the basic systems design and equipment specification phases. Its basic steps, set forth in Figure 5-28, include:

1. determining equipment manufacturers
2. submitting bid invitations to manufacturers
3. evaluating **manufacturers'** proposals
4. selecting equipment manufacturer(s)

The equipment selection approach taken by the study group is important for a successful conclusion to the real-time MIS feasibility study. There are two basic methods of selecting equipment. Only one is recommended.

The recommended approach is to submit to each manufacturer information compiled to date per the feasibility study in which the specific areas of the real-time MIS are outlined. General information on the company, its future processing plans, and list of new system specifications, should be forwarded to the competing manufacturers. The particulars of these specifications will be covered in subsequent sections.

The second approach is basically illogical because it disregards information compiled by the feasibility study group and requests that the equipment manufacturers start from scratch. Briefly, the manufacturers bring in their own systems personnel who study the present system and devise a new one tailored to their own equipment. The operations will be timed and cost savings will be calculated on this basis. Generally, different approaches by equipment manufacturers result, thereby making a final evaluation virtually impossible when they are placed on a common basis. Most manufacturers direct their proposals to highlight the specific features of their own equipment over that of their competition.

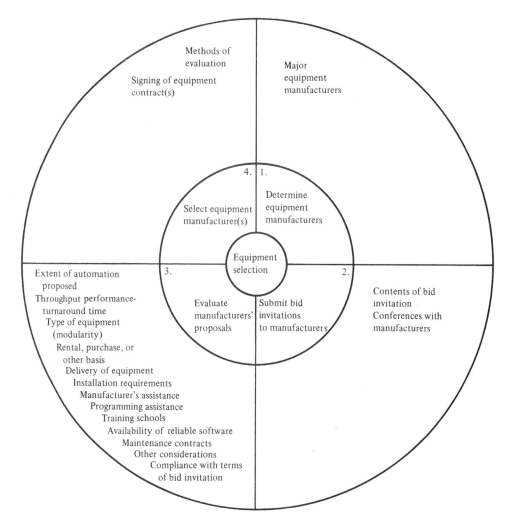

FIGURE 5-28. Detailed outline of equipment selection for real-time MIS—the third step of the feasibility study.

The problem of time is another important consideration, because each manufacturer must conduct a lengthy systems review on the firm's premises. For example, if five manufacturers are involved and each spends a month to review the present system, this means about one-half year of lost time plus continuous disruptions to current operations. After department heads, supervisors, and operating personnel have been through the same set of questions five times, their attitude toward a real-time MIS or any type system is, needless to say, negative. In a similar manner, their morale has reached an all-time low. Even after all this effort by a manufacturer, one month is still not ample time to learn a firm's system in sufficient detail, especially when it comes to exceptions and problem areas. Because of the manufacturer's inability to gather all the pertinent facts in the time allotted, its recommendation can be poor, and an impractical system is often advocated. Thus, this second approach should be discarded.

1. DETERMINE EQUIPMENT MANUFACTURERS

Most firms undertaking a real-time MIS project have specific computer equipment under consideration based on the exploratory survey report. Because most of them have computer and related peripheral equipment salesmen calling on them at various times, they have had previous contact with most of the manufacturers. The representatives of the various equipment manufacturers should be contacted and invited to an orientation meeting on the proposed system. During the course of the meeting, they should be instructed about the applications to be covered, general problems that will be encountered, approximate volumes—present and future—and other pertinent data. Each manufacturer should indicate in writing whether he wishes to receive a bid invitation. The reasons for this approach should be obvious. There is no need to prepare a packet of specifications, flowcharts, decision tables, and comparable material if the manufacturer has no interest in bidding.

2. SUBMIT BID INVITATIONS TO MANUFACTURERS

Once letters of intent to bid are on file from equipment manufacturers, the company submits bid invitations to the interested equipment suppliers. The preferred approach, when sending bid invitations, is to mail the same set of data to all competing manufacturers. This permits bids to be placed on an unbiased basis and informs the manufacturers what requirements they must meet, keeps the number of questions to a minimum, and is a valid basis for comparison of real-time equipment. The manufacturers will probably need additional information and assistance from the prospective customer as they progress with the preparation of their proposals. Generally, one person from the MIS task force will perform this consultative function for a specific manufacturer.

Utilizing this approach, the respective manufacturers should have ample information to familiarize themselves with the company and its peculiar data processing problems. The recommendations made in their proposals should show clearly how the equipment will meet the customer's needs. Specifications lacking clear definition from the beginning will result in proposals with standard approaches that are applicable to any and all potential customers, making all the firm's preliminary work a waste of time. It is of utmost importance that data submitted to manufacturers be as complete and self-explanatory as possible, especially in view of the complexities involved in a real-time management information system.

Contents of Bid Invitation

Much of the material needed for the bid invitation can be taken directly from the data contained in the exploratory survey report and developed during the basic systems design and equipment specification phases. The contents of the bid invitation include these areas:

1. general company information
2. future data processing plans
3. list of new system specifications
4. new system flowcharts and decision tables
5. list of equipment specifications (in general terms)
6. data to be forwarded by each manufacturer

The detail for each major topic is shown in Figure 5-29.

In Sections 1 and 2, the narrative should be brief so that attention can be focused on the remaining parts of the bid invitation. Data that are necessary for a thorough study are contained in Sections 3, 4, and 5, forming the basis for the manufacturer's proposal. Section 3 is composed of five essential parts: planned inputs, methods and procedures for handling data, data files to be maintained (common data base), output needs, and other requirements and considerations for the new system. Material developed for this section is found in the preceding chapter. If proper documentation was undertaken for basic systems design, the time to complete this area will be at a minimum because much of the material can be used in its present form.

New system flowcharts and decision tables are contained in Section 4 of Figure 5-29. System flowcharts are needed for each functional area under study and to show the interrelationships among the areas. Decision tables should be an integral part of the bid invitation. This will enable the manufacturer to have a complete understanding of the programming effort envisioned and help determine the hardware that is needed under the existing conditions. Finally, this section of the bid invitation should contain a flowchart that depicts the overall aspects of the new system. This allows the equipment manufacturer to obtain an overview of the system and its subsystems.

Section 5 contains a listing of equipment specifications in general terms. Competing manufacturers must have a basic understanding of the data communications network, I/O terminal devices, auxiliary storage devices, the central processing unit, and other CPU peripherals. The inclusion of this section not only details present owned equipment that is compatible with a real-time MIS operating environment, but also helps assure greater compatibility of bids from each competing equipment manufacturer.

In the final section, data to be included in each manufacturer's proposal are listed. Specifying in advance what the proposals should contain insures that comparable information for a final evaluation will be forthcoming.

1. *General Company Information*
    Description of the company and its activities.
    Overview of present data processing equipment and applications.
    Unusual data processing exceptions and problems.
    Other important general information.

2. *Future Data Processing Plans*
   Listing of areas encompased by the new system.
   Target date for installation of new system.
   Deadline date for submitting proposals.
   Equipment decision date by the company.
   Criteria to be employed in analyzing and comparing manufacturers' proposals.

3. *List of New System Specifications*
   a. Planned Inputs:
      Where data originate within the system.
      Name and content of input data, such as documents and forms.
      Hourly rates of input data.
      Volume of inputs, including high and low points.
   b. Methods and Procedures for Handling Data:
      Transmission of local and distant data from I/O terminal devices.
      Types of transactions handled.
      Computations and logical decisions required.
      New data generation within the system.
      Control points to test accuracy of data and eliminate processing of fraudulent
         data.
   c. Data Files to be Maintained:
      Where data are to be stored—on-line in a common data base and off-line.
      Name and contents of files to be maintained.
      Methods and procedures for updating files.
      Size of files to be maintained.
   d. Output Needs:
      Name and content of output, such as reports and summaries.
      Timely distribution of output data.
      Hourly rates of output data.
      Volume of outputs, including high and low points.
   e. Other Requirements and Considerations:
      Changes in policies to conform to new system.
      Compatibility of common data processing language.
      Limitations in relation to the human factor.
      Special internal control considerations—in particular, real-time controls.
      System performance—ability to handle the company's future growth,
         including peak loads.
      Lease or cost of equipment not to exceed a stated figure.
      Additional special requirements and considerations.

4. *New System Flowcharts and Decision Tables*
   Brief description of the systems approach for each functional area under
      study.
   System flowcharts and/or decision tables for each area.
   System flowcharts that show the interrelationships of the various areas for the
      new system.
   A flowchart that gives an overview of the new system.

5. *List of Equipment Specifications (in General Terms)*
   A communications network to handle the new system.
   Various types of input and output terminal devices.
   Auxiliary storage devices, such as magnetic disk, drum, and laser.
   Specific requirements of the central processing unit, such as duplexing,
      multiprocessing, and multiprogramming capabilities.
   Other CPU peripherals, such as tape drives, card readers, and printers.

**FIGURE 5-29. Contents of a real-time MIS bid invitation to an
equipment manufacturer.**

6. *Data to be Forwarded by Each Manufacturer*
   a. Processing time for each area on the equipment.
   b. Proposed Computer Hardware:
      Capabilities and technical features of basic and peripheral equipment,
         in particular, the data communication network, terminal devices, auxiliary
         storage devices, and the central processing unit.
      Expansion capabilities (modularity).
      Purchase price and monthly rental figures on an one-, two-, and three-shift
         basis for basic and peripheral equipment.
      Alternative purchase and lease option plan (third-party leasing).
      Estimated delivery and installation date.
      Number of disk packs, magnetic tapes, etc. required and their costs.
      Equipment cancellation terms.
   c. Site Preparation and Installation Requirements:
      Amount of space needed.
      Electrical power, air conditioning, and humidity control requirements.
      Flooring requirements and enclosure of equipment.
   d. Extent of Manufacturer's Assistance:
      Cost of manufacturer's personnel to assist in the installation and for how
         long.
      Availability and location of programming classes.
      Possibility of on-site training classes.
      Availability of higher-level programming languages, programming aids,
         and program libraries.
      Nearest testing facilities and on what shifts.
      Amount of equipment time for compiling and testing programs without
         charge.
   e. Maintenance service to be provided.
   f. Equipment support for emergency processing.
   g. Other pertinent information.

FIGURE 5-29. (Cont.)

Conferences with Manufacturers

Even though bid invitations specify the numerous details of the new system, legitimate questions will be raised by the various equipment firms. Many of the questions center around those areas which may have need of modification, which may sometimes be necessary to take advantage of the equipment's special features. The result may be favorable benefits to the firm in terms of cost savings. Conferences between the manufacturer and the potential customer, then, can prove beneficial to both parties. However, caution is necessary on the part of the study group during this period because salesmen may use this time to sell the firm and the final proposal, making the final evaluation of the manufacturers' proposals not objective, but subjective.

3. EVALUATE MANUFACTURERS' PROPOSALS

The manufacturers should be given a reasonable amount of time to prepare their proposals. In most cases, approximately two to three months is adequate. When the real-time MIS proposals are completed, several copies are mailed to the customer for review and are then followed by an oral presentation by the manufacturer's representative(s). At this meeting, the salesman will stress the important points of the proposal and answer questions. After this procedure has been followed by all competing manufacturers, the MIS task force should be prepared to evaluate the various proposals.

There are many criteria for evaluating a manufacturer's proposal. Among these are: extent of automation proposed, evaluation of throughput performance—turnaround time, type of equipment, method of acquiring equipment, delivery of equipment, installation requirements, manufacturer's assistance, programming assistance, training schools, availability of reliable software, maintenance contracts, and other considerations. Finally, the proposals are evaluated in terms of how well they have complied with the bid invitation. Only after an intensive analysis of the facts can the study group intelligently select the manufacturer(s) for basic and peripheral equipment.

Extent of Automation Proposed

A logical starting point for evaluation of the various proposals is the extent of automation proposed. Is the proposal a restatement of the present system, except for newer generation equipment? Is it an entirely new approach, utilizing the latest equipment? Or is it an approach somewhere between these two? Does the proposal extend beyond the functional areas contained in the bid invitation? Does it concentrate only on selected areas or does it cover the areas as requested? These are the type of questions that must be asked to determine how much automation is being proposed for the costs involved. This approach gives the MIS study group an overview of what is being advocated by each competitor.

Throughput Performance—Turnaround Time

Having acquired a good understanding of how much automation has been proposed, the study team should then make a thorough analysis of the equipment time required to process the data. This is a most critical area of evaluation because processing times, as stated, are generally much too low. The problem is not the hardware. No equipment manufacturer is going to give false information about speeds, capacity, and similar hardware considerations. The real reason for these incorrect speeds is that programming is not apt to be perfect. Seldom does a program utilize the computer's components in an optimum manner. Inefficient programming and compilers cause higher processing times than do jobs which are input- or output-bound. On-line system failures, reruns, error stops, input and output units out of paper, paper jams, temporary malfunctions of the computer's components, and similar problems often cause much higher times. In view of these difficulties, most experienced computer personnel add a certain percent to the manufacturer's time estimates. The percentage factor will depend on the type of equipment and its utilization as well as the type of supervisory system and control programs that are employed.

If time permits, there should be an independent evaluation of the manufacturer's times. This can be accomplished by utilizing benchmark problems and test problems. The benchmark problem approach consists of selecting a representative job to be performed by the new system; the results of this test are evaluated on how well the equipment meets the specified application. The test problem approach is aimed at measuring the functional capabilities of the equipment. The results of the equipment tests can be compared and cost performance can be evaluated. An alternative approach to testing equipment is the use of simulation and mathematical modeling techniques. In evaluating computer times, the final criterion for measuring system performance is throughput (the amount of data that can be processed within a specific period of time) and turnaround time.

Type of Equipment (Modularity)

The manufacturer must specify not only the make, model number, and quantity of basic and related peripheral equipment but also their capabilities, operating characteristics, and technical features. Data on internal memory size, operating speeds, storage capacity, and hardware controls are a part of the manufacturer's proposal on computers and related equipment. Supplies to implement the system are normally included in the proposal.

Modularity is an important consideration when evaluating real-time equipment. Computer modularity makes it possible to expand the present system in terms of building blocks by adding more main frame storage, enlarging secondary storage capacity, increasing the speeds of input/output devices, and similar additions. When the company has grown beyond the capabilities of the present model, the next size or larger model can be installed without having to devise a new system and reprogram. Compatibility of machines makes this possible. Thus, the new computer system must have the capability of being upgraded and added to, rather than having to be completely replaced. By and large, present-generation equipment incorporates this modularity concept.

Rental, Purchase, or Other Basis

Many financing plans are available to the firm acquiring equipment. These include rental, outright purchase, option to buy, and third-party leasing (lease-back arrangements). Rental contracts, a most common method of acquiring equipment, state the specific monthly rate and number of hours for operating on a one-, two-, or three-shift basis (rate adjustment may be made for excessive downtime). The terms of the contract, including renewal, cancellation, and manufacturer's policy on overtime rental, are subject to careful evaluation by the MIS study team. The policy of overtime rental can be a significant factor in the cost of a real-time computer because some manufacturers base usage on 176 hours per month while others are much higher. The rates on a second-shift rental also vary among manufacturers and can have a substantial impact on the final decision.

The decision to purchase must take into account these two important factors: obsolescence and availability of capital funds. Most firms that purchase equipment do so just after a new generation of computers has been announced. The rationale should be obvious. The newer line will be on the market for the next several years, reducing the problem of immediate obsolescence. Once another generation is announced, the problem of disposal can be significant, because the firm will get a better trade-in on a new system with the current manufacturer versus another one. Thus the study group may be limited in its selection of the best equipment for the proposed system because of the financial factors involved.

The decision to purchase or lease is sometimes resolved by the number of shifts. An evaluation of two- or three-shift operation gives a much higher return on investment, resulting in a buy decision. The MIS study group should compare the return for this capital investment with other potential ones. After all, the firm is well-advised to spend its available capital funds for automating its factories, replacing old plants with new ones, and investing in comparable projects that provide a higher return.

Many rental contracts have an "option to buy" clause whereby part of the rental is applied toward the equipment. Terms of any purchase option include the initial deposit, percent of rental payments applied toward the equipment purchases, and option expiration date. This approach allows a firm to evaluate objectively the new system before investing in hardware.

Another method of acquiring equipment is third-party leasing. The lease company buys the equipment from the manufacturer and then leases it back to the user. Experience has shown that many firms are better off with the third-party lease-back arrangement. In the final analysis, the equipment decision must be based upon the attendant circumstances as evaluated objectively by the MIS study group.

Delivery of Equipment

The manufacturer should specify a definite delivery date along with ample time to check out the equipment on the user's premises. Delivery dates vary from manufacturer to manufacturer, depending on the type of hardware and the order date. Many manufacturers experience a virtual flood of orders when a newer generation of equipment is announced, resulting in long delivery dates for some computer models. Occasionally, a competing manufacturer will be dropped from the evaluation process because of an abnormally remote delivery date.

The time to check out the equipment can range from two weeks to several months, depending upon the degree of on-line and data communication sophistication. A tentative date for turning the system over to the firm should be stated in writing. A penalty clause for failure to meet the quoted dates, which could cause the user financial loss, may be agreed upon and written into the final equipment contract.

Installation Requirements

Installation requirements must be stated by the manufacturer so that the customer can prepare his premises. The dimensions and weight of each piece of equipment is specified along with the necessary power and wiring requirements. The latter refers to false-floor, under-floor, or overhead wiring necessary to connect the computer units together. Most basic hardware of real-time MIS requires air conditioning and humidity control.

Other requirements include room for files, supplies, repair parts, and testing equipment. Space must be allocated for all personnel involved in the system— namely, department heads, systems analysts, systems designers, programmers, operators, and technicians. In general, a location close to where data originate and are used is preferred for the new equipment.

Manufacturer's Assistance

In the manufacturer's proposal, the amount of assistance that can be expected during systems implementation is clearly defined. Otherwise, needless disputes might develop which are detrimental to both parties. Potential areas of assistance offered by all major equipment manufacturers include: programmers, analysts, and engineers to implement the new system; training schools for the client's managers, programmers, and operators; software packages to simplify programming; and equipment for program testing prior to the installation. Referring to the last item, each manufacturer normally furnishes free equipment time for compiling and testing programs before installation on the client's premises. The time (shift) available and the location should be set forth in the proposal.

Programming Assistance

Some equipment manufacturers will furnish experienced programmers and systems personnel for a certain period of time. Care should be taken that the manufacturer's personnel do not take charge of the programming effort. Because programming and related systems work is a continuous job, the firm's personnel will have the task of maintaining the operation.

Not long ago, several manufacturers separated equipment pricing from the various services they offer. Charges for data processing education and systems engineering services are now billed separately to the user. Prior to this unbundling, the longstanding practice had been to charge customers a single price for equipment and all connected services. Based on the current arrangement, it behooves the customer to have the amount of free programming assistance spelled out in the contract. Otherwise, the firm will be spending more for systems implementation that was included in the real-time MIS exploratory survey report.

Training Schools

Training programs are provided by most manufacturers for their customers. With the present method of unbundling for the most part, in which prices are stated separately for machines and related services, the training is no longer free. Classroom courses and seminars in which the level of training varies are classified into the following categories: detailed instruction on programming the equipment; training of personnel for operating the computer and related peripheral equipment; instructing company personnel to perform preventive and machine maintenance if no service contract is signed on purchased equipment; and seminar training for executives, departmental managers, and staff personnel. On occasion, classes will be held on the user's premises if the equipment installation is large enough to justify it. The extent of training needed depends upon the complexity of the new system. When evaluating this area in the final analysis, quality and cost factors must be evaluated for each competing manufacturer.

Availability of Reliable Software

An important evaluation item is the availability of reliable software to support the hardware in an on-line, real-time MIS environment. Software includes the following areas:

operating systems for real-time processing and batch processing

programming languages for on-line (real-time) and remote batch processing

program packages for sort and merge routines, reading and writing on magnetic drums, and others

compilers for developing final machine language programs

executive routines to aid the computer operator during program debugging and supervisory programs to handle successive programs during production runs

monitor or dump routines for tracing execution of program instructions during program testing

packaged routines, such as linear programming and random number generator, for handling specialized OR problems

specialized simulation languages, such as GPSS and SIMCRIPT, for solving problems that lend themselves to simulation

The availability of software cuts the user's time and expense, because it allows the programmer to work at a reasonable high level of programming efficiency. The task of duplicating software packages that are utilized by many hundreds and even thousands of users is eliminated. Software support for an early delivery of new-generation equipment is an important consideration because it will be needed prior to installation of the machine. If the past is any indicator of the future, hardware has often preceded software by many months for a new generation of equipment; this has led to many embarrassing situations and penalties for equipment manufacturers.

Maintenance Contracts

The maintenance required to keep the equipment in good operating condition is provided free under a rental contract. Equipment rental normally includes machine engineers and servicing personnel plus parts and supplies for maintenance on the various shifts or a certain number of hours per month as specified in the contract. Time for preventive maintenance is generally scheduled so that regular computer operations will not be interrupted. On the other hand, outright purchase of the equipment allows two methods for servicing the equipment. The firm can train its own personnel by sending them to the manufacturer's school for maintenance training or it can enter into a separate contract with the manufacturer. Either approach should be investigated by the MIS study group.

For smaller equipment installations, the maintenance function will be performed from the manufacturer's sales office. The distance from the user, competence of the manufacturer's personnel, and their availability are important evaluation factors. For larger machine systems, the manufacturer may assign maintenance personnel to one or more systems. This is a plus factor in case of a machine malfunction during normal operating time. The evaluation group is advised to inquire about the quality of maintenance for each competing firm.

Other Considerations

Other items of a bid may be of importance in addition to those set forth in Figure 5-29. If the firm is planning a forthcoming merger, can the new system handle an additional load within a short period of time? The problem of programming checks and controls not built into the hardware may add considerable time to production runs. An extremely important factor is the adequacy of fallback and recovery procedures that can process data on an emergency basis if a major systems breakdown occurs. Questions concerning overtime personnel costs in terms of who will pay and similar considerations must be explored if they are applicable in selecting a specific equipment manufacturer.

Compliance with Terms of Bid Invitation

One last important consideration must be investigated. It revolves around how well each manufacturer has complied with the terms of the bid invitation. This involves completeness, clarity, and responsiveness. Does each proposal cover all points set forth in the bid invitation? Is the proposal clear in every respect? Are all estimates of time and cost for peak, medium, and low work loads accurate? Does the proposal reflect a proper understanding of the bid? Failure to fullfull any one of these points indicates a weakness on the part of the manufacturer that may be indicative of potential problems in the future. Final equipment evaluation, then, should include compliance with the original bid terms.

4. SELECT EQUIPMENT MANUFACTURER(S)

Selection of the equipment manufacturer(s) is a difficult task for the MIS study team. The selection process is much easier if the equipment proposed is identical for all practical purposes. In such cases, the choice is normally based on the lowest-cost equipment. However, this approach is generally not followed for real-time MIS because most manufacturers have certain unique real-time equipment features, and this results in slightly different approaches to the customer's proposed system. In order to resolve this dilemma among the various competitors, various methods have been developed for evaluating and selecting equipment.

Methods of Evaluation

One method of evaluation is utilization of a decision table, shown in Figure 5-30. A decision table for a final evaluation not only defines the important criteria in compact notation but also permits an objective evaluation, because the values will thus have been determined before receipt of the manufacturers' proposals. In the illustration, the highest possible score is one hundred points for each of the five competing manufacturers. A value of ten points is deducted for each *no* answer of a major criterion, while a value of five points is subtracted for each *no* answer of a minor criterion. The major criteria represent factors that have long-run effects on the firm in terms of profits and return on investment. Thus, the deduction of ten points indicates greater importance attached to this particular criterion. Values for another firm might be different from those found in Figure 5-30. For the hypothetical study, this is a realistic approach in making the final decision for a real-time MIS.

An alternative evaluation method consists of assigning different weighting factors to each criterion. Each manufacturer is given a score for each weighting

Decision Table	Table Name: Criteria to Select Equipment Manufacturer											Page 1 of 1		
	Chart No: FS—SEM—1			Prepared by: R. J. Thierauf								Date: 8/30/7—		

Condition	Rule Number											
	1	2	3	4	5	6	7	8	9	10	11	12
Major Criteria:												
Low-cost throughput performance	Y	Y	Y	Y	N							
Modularity of equipment	Y	Y	Y	N	Y							
Monthly rental within amount set forth in the exploratory survey report	N	Y	Y	Y	N							
Dependable and efficient software for proposed equipment	Y	Y	Y	N	Y							
Equipment backup in local area	N	Y	N	Y	Y							
Availability of operating personnel	Y	Y	Y	Y	Y							
Minor Criteria:												
High degree of automation proposed	Y	Y	Y	N	Y							
Availability of equipment when needed	Y	Y	N	Y	Y							
Capable of meeting installation requirements	Y	Y	Y	Y	Y							
Adequate programming assistance available	N	N	N	Y	N							
Good quality training offered	Y	Y	Y	Y	N							
Available equipment for compiling and testing program initially	N	Y	Y	Y	N							
Adequate equipment maintenance	Y	N	Y	Y	Y							
Compliance with terms of bid invitation	Y	Y	Y	N	Y							
Action												
Subtract 10 points for each major criteria no (N) answer	X	—	X	X	X							
Subtract 5 points for each minor criteria no (N) answer	X	X	X	X	X							

Other Information:
Total points = 100 (6 major criteria X 10 pts.) + (8 minor criteria X 5 pts.) = 100
Competitor's total points:
1-70; 2-90; 3-80; 4-70; 5-65

FIGURE 5-30. Criteria to select equipment manufacturer in a real-time MIS feasibility study.

factor. In most cases, the score is lower than the absolute value of the weighting factor. The values are summed for all criteria which represent the total points for each manufacturer. As with the decision table illustration, the competitor with the highest score is selected.

Another method is evaluating equipment superiority in terms of its performance per dollar. Caution is needed here, for the scoring method can put too much emphasis on the machine's characteristics without regard for the supporting parts, which may be just as important in the final analysis. All aspects of the machine's performance must be included, including various hardware speeds, reliability of the equipment, efficient software, and similar considerations.

The factors to consider in equipment selection are many, as depicted in Figure 5-30. In certain cases, some criteria are more important than others. Many of these are closely related to the hardware or software, while others encompass the operating environment of the new system. Still other criteria revolve around the human factor. No matter what factors are deemed critical in the evaluation process, the method must be objective for selection of one manufacturer(s) over the others. The MIS study team will be in a better position when presenting its final recommendation to the executive steering committee if a logical and methodical basis is used. In the final analysis, the purpose of spending so much time, effort, and expense on the feasibility study is to obtain the best real-time equipment for the firm.

Signing of Equipment Contract(s)

The signing of the equipment contract by a top-level executive, who has been the guiding force for both groups (executive steering committee and MIS task force) brings the real-time MIS feasibility study to a formal close. The exploratory survey report, basic systems design, and equipment selection, the major steps of the feasibility study, represent approximately one-third of the total time expended on a systems project. In the period just ahead—systems implementation—not only will more time be involved than in the feasibility study, but there will also be more involvement of the firm's resources in terms of its operations and personnel. The problem of how to coordinate and control the activities during this interim period is a challenging task even for the most seasoned data processing manager and his subordinates.

SUMMARY

The final step of the feasibility study revolves around equipment selection—in particular, that hardware (a communications network, terminal devices, auxiliary storage devices, a central processing unit, and other CPU peripherals) which is essential to real-time processing. Bid requests or invitations which describe the important aspects of the new system provide the basis for receiving proposals from manufacturers. Proposals are, then, compared for selected criteria which have specific numerical values assigned to them. All things being equal, the manufacturer who has the highest score is awarded the contract. The ultimate responsibility for determining equipment, however, is not that of the manufacturer, but the user. The same is true for the advanced planning that is necessary to install the equipment.

QUESTIONS

1. Why is equipment selection the final phase of the feasibility study?

2. a.   How important are terminal devices, large-screen display devices, and management control centers in a real-time MIS environment?

b.   What effect do real-time MIS control devices have on the utilization of OR models?

3. a.   Differentiate between simplex systems and duplex systems.

b.   Differentiate between multiprocessing systems and multiprogramming systems.

4. What real-time hardware should the systems analyst specify in general terms when preparing the bid invitation? Why?

5. What are the steps involved in determining what data processing equipment the firm should procure for a real-time management information system?

6. Are there any problems associated with having various computer manufacturers draw up the real-time MIS specifications for a firm and having them submit bids on this basis?

7. What are the most important factors to consider when selecting real-time computer equipment?

REFERENCES

Becker, H. B., "Information Network Design Can Be Simplified Step by Step," *Computer Decisions,* October, 1972.

Bradley, W. P., "Is Virtual Memory for Real," *Infosystems,* September, 1973.

Brewster, R. L., "Designing Optimum Data Networks," *Data Processing Magazine,* January, 1971.

Brocato, L. J., "Getting the Best Computer System for Your Money," *Computer Decisions,* September, 1971.

Carne, E. B., "Telecommunications: Its Impact on Business," *Harvard Business Review,* July-August, 1972.

Cotton, J. R., "Voice Response—Speaks for Itself," *Data Processing Magazine,* May, 1971.

Dors, P. H., "So You've Got to Get a New One," *Datamation,* September, 1973.

Elksberg, D. J., "Going Remote Batch," *Computer Decisions,* May, 1974.

Emery, J. C., "Problems and Promises of Regional Computing," *Datamation,* August, 1973.

Epstein, J., "Managing Communication Costs Rationally," *Management Adviser,* July-August, 1971.

Farbman, D. S., "A Team Approach to Hardware Analysis," *Computer Decisions,* November, 1974.

Ford, K. W., "About Communications Processors . . . ,"*Infosystems,* February, 1973.

Frank, H. and Hopewell, L., "Network Reliability," *Datamation,* August, 1974.

Ingerman, D., "Simulating Communications Systems," *Datamation,* October, 1974.

Laska, R. M., "Portable Terminals: You Can Take It With You When You Go," *Computer Decisions,* September, 1970.

Long, M. I., and Bruun, R. J., "MIS Implications for Top Management," *Infosystems,* October, 1974.

Martin, J., *Future Developments in Telecommunications.* Englewood Cliffs, N.J.: Prentice-Hall, Inc., 1971.

Menkhaus, E. J., "Terminals: Pipeline to Computer Power," *Business Automation,* May, 1970.

Miller, I. M., "Computer Graphics for Decision Making," *Harvard Business Review,* November-December, 1969.

Murdick, R. G., and Ross, J. E., *Information Systems for Modern Management.* Englewood Cliffs, N.J.: Prentice-Hall, Inc., 1971, Chap. 15.

Norman, J. L., "Network Errors," *Datamation,* October 1, 1971.

O'Brien, B. V., "Balance Your Terminal System," *Computer Decisions,* September, 1973.

Orlicky, J. A., "Computer Selection," *Computers and Automation,* September, 1968.

Poliski, I., "Mission Control at the First," *Business Automation,* March, 1970.

Pollard, J. E., "Putting the Computer Into the Telephone Exchange," *Computer Decisions,* June, 1970.

Pryke, J. T. M., "A Front-End Primer for IBM Users," *Datamation,* April, 1973.

Quinlan, R. V., "Linking the Computer to the Terminals," *Journal of Systems Management,* May, 1974.

Ringe, R. D., "The ABC's of Leasing," *Infosystem,* August, 1974.

Rothstein, M. F., *Guide to the Design of Real-Time Systems.* New York: John Wiley & Sons, Inc., 1970, Chap. 5, 6, and 7.

Sanders, R. W., "The Wideband Route to Multiplexing," *Computer Decisions,* January, 1971.

Schroer, B. J., "Interactive Computer Graphics," *Journal of Systems Management,* May, 1972.

Showalter, A. K., "Display Systems," *Datamation,* November 15, 1971.

Speers, G. S., "Monitoring/Control by Distributed Computing," *Datamation,* July, 1973.

Staff Report, "An Introduction to the Intelligent Terminal," *Computer Decisions,* January, 1974.

Staff Report, "Modems and Multiplexors," *Computer Decisions,* October, 1973.

Stenger, R. J., "Telecommunications Techniques," *Journal of Systems Management,* April, 1973.

Theis, D. J., "Communications Processors," *Datamation,* August, 1972.

Timmreck, "Computer Selection Methodology," *Computing Surveys,* Vol. 5, No. 4, December, 1973.

Widner, W.R., "The Management Communications Center," *Journal of Systems Management,* September, 1969.

Workman, W. E., "The Picturephone Puts Data at Management's Fingertips," *Computer Decisions,* October, 1970.

Wylie, F. E., "Decision Rooms for Executive Warriors," *Finance Magazine,* October, 1972.

SYSTEMS IMPLEMENTATION OF REAL-TIME MANAGEMENT INFORMATION SYSTEMS

6

Once the problem of what equipment to acquire for a real-time management information system has been resolved, the feasibility study has been officially concluded. Even though a substantial amount of time and money was expended on the feasibility study (systems analysis, systems design, and equipment selection), considerably more of both will be spent on systems implementation. In reality, long hours for data processing and non-data-processing personnel are just beginning and extreme patience is required. Otherwise, the best-planned feasibility study can be upset by those personnel who fail to cooperate in executing the plans devised.

In this chapter, the detailed steps involved in systems implementation are discussed, providing a logical framework for getting a real-time MIS underway. The employment of parallel operational procedures for checking the new system with the old are discussed before we treat the problem of converting the various subsystems and their related modules to daily operations. Discussion of the need for periodic review of the new system for possible improvements and common problems encountered in a systems project, such as a real-time MIS, concludes the chapter.

203

SYSTEMS IMPLEMENTATION

The task of systems implementation for a comprehensive real-time MIS is a major undertaking because it cuts across the entire organization structure. This results in a great need for implementation planning. A logical starting point for this type of planning involves knowledge of the following areas: personnel needs, programming, equipment selected, physical requirements, and conversion activities. An understanding of these areas establishes the specific tasks that need to be undertaken and the relationships among them. Also needed is a knowledge of the problems and the exceptions. This background permits the detailed planning of the various tasks that must be incorporated into a schedule having specific deadlines. The scheduling method should follow the natural flow of work to be undertaken. The usual questions of who, what, where, when, how, and why must be answered in developing the schedule. Implementation planning should include provisions for reviewing completed and uncompleted tasks so that the entire systems project will be under control.

The major steps for systems implementation can be summarized as:

1. preparatory work for real-time MIS
2. operation of real-time MIS
3. periodic review for improvements to real-time MIS

These basic elements and their related subcomponents are detailed in Figure 6-1.

1. PREPARATORY WORK FOR REAL-TIME MIS

Certain preparatory work must be accomplished before the real-time MIS can operate on a day-to-day basis. This includes preparing a detailed time and activity schedule, selecting and training qualified personnel, realigning personnel, altering the premises, testing and accepting new equipment, programming numerous production runs, testing programs, systems testing and finally, file conversion. The three basic steps of the feasibility study (systems analysis, systems design, and equipment selection) provide a starting point for completing these preparatory phases. System flowcharts, decision tables, and the manufacturer's proposal constitute the major material necessary to get the work started. Even though the data have been compiled and documented properly, the time and manpower requirements for the systems project are just beginning. Thus, it is necessary that the MIS manager be alert to keep costs within the confines of the exploratory survey report.

Scheduling the Installation

Installation work should be scheduled in sufficient detail so that each important milestone can be controlled. Even though uncertainty may exist for certain activities, accurate times should be developed as nearly as possible. Generally, the data set forth in the manufacturer's proposal can be used as a starting point in

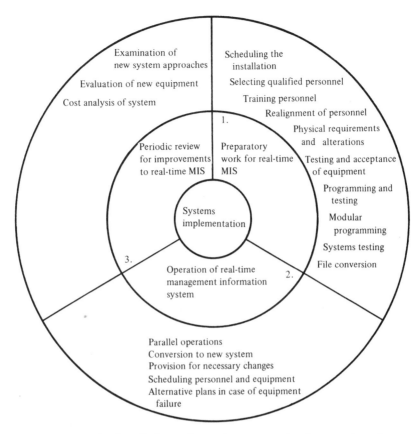

FIGURE 6-1. Detailed outline of systems implementation for a real-time management information system.

scheduling. (The user must consider lengthening the delivery time because it is possible for equipment manufacturers to experience difficulty.)

The scheduler must determine appropriate starting dates for each activity to find out whether or not data processing personnel have ample time to complete all the necessary tasks before the equipment is delivered. It is possible that overtime and additional personnel may be required to meet the equipment delivery date. The ability today to foresee a future problem is a great help to the data processing group in controlling the project.

PERT. One way of scheduling work is through the use of the PERT system. PERT, a refinement of the Critical Path Method, is illustrated in Figure 6-2 for an entire real-time MIS project. Although four years are indicated in the illustration, experience to date has indicated that considerably more time is needed for such a comprehensive undertaking. Hopefully in the future, less time will be required. For illustrative purposes only, a four-year period is utilized.

The circled numbers in Figure 6-2 are events which represent the completion of activities. Events have no time associated with them while activities, depicted as arrows, do. The time within the triangles represent expected time (te) which is

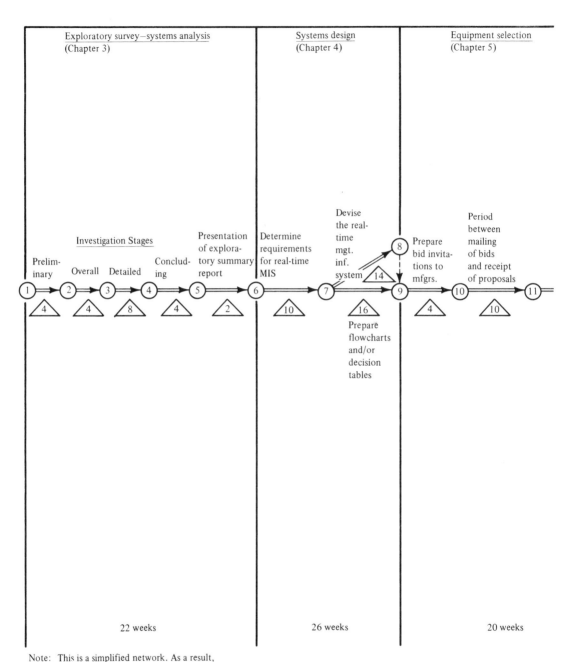

Exploratory survey—systems analysis
(Chapter 3)

Systems design
(Chapter 4)

Equipment selection
(Chapter 5)

Investigation Stages

Presentation
of explora-
tory summary
report

Determine
requirements
for real-time
MIS

Devise
the real-
time
mgt.
inf.
system

Prepare
bid invita-
tions to
mfgrs.

Period
between
mailing
of bids
and receipt
of proposals

Prelim-
inary

Overall   Detailed

Conclud-
ing

Prepare
flowcharts
and/or
decision
tables

22 weeks

26 weeks

20 weeks

Note: This is a simplified network. As a result,
      there are some overlapping activities not
      shown. In a more detailed network, these
      would be drawn as such.

Critical path equals 222 weeks
Arrows represent activities (shown as expected time in triangles)
Circles represent events (numbered from 1 to 50)

206

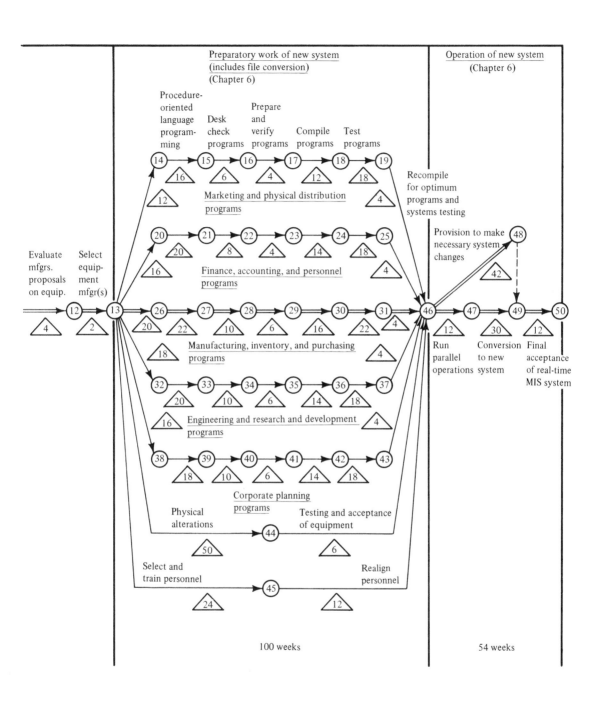

FIGURE 6-2. Simplified PERT network for a real-time MIS project.

calculated by the formula, $t_e = \dfrac{a + 4m + b}{6}$ where a equals the most optimistic time, m equals the most likely time, and b equals the most pessimistic time. The values developed from the formula have proven to be more accurate than those calculated by other methods.

Earliest expected times and latest expected times can be calculated, but are not shown in the example. The difference between these two times represent slack or extra time available for each activity within the project. In those cases in which the earliest and latest times are equal, the event is on the critical path. Dummy arrows (dotted lines) used in the PERT network do not represent activities, but rather connect related events in the network.

The double lines represent the longest time path through the PERT network and the critical path. Any delays in starting or completing times on this path will delay the end completion date. This calls for careful scrutiny of the critical path as the project progresses. It also means that initial consideration should be given to working personnel overtime or reallocating qualified personnel to the critical activities. Those activities which are not involved with the critical path (heavy lines) have slack time for their completion even though it is not shown. If they should exceed their expected time, it is possible these activities may be on the critical path. In essence, all noncritical activities have the potential of becoming critical ones if not carefully supervised.

In Figure 6-2, there are more than fifty events. Many of the important activities have been grouped for the sake of simplicity. For example, each computer program should be a separate and distinct activity. The programming phase alone might constitute well over one hundred activities. A computer is recommended for controlling such a large PERT network. In addition to determining the necessary level of detail, it is helpful to state the specific calendar days—earliest and latest expected times—throughout the network. This gives the MIS manager an overview of where the systems project stands—favorable or unfavorable—for its many activities.

Selecting Qualified Personnel

The placement of the equipment order and scheduling its installation indicates the need for selecting qualified personnel for systems implementation and normal operations. The head of the MIS task group is given the authority and responsibility for staffing the organization. Members of the task force and those who have worked closely with the group are logical candidates. However, even though they have worked (full time or part time) on the feasibility study and have accumulated a wealth of information and experience, the entire undertaking is a temporary one. Perhaps some study personnel plan to return to their respective departments because they are not interested in implementing the new system, the challenge is too difficult, or some other reason. Even the ones who qualify for key data processing positions should recognize that different operating conditions will be faced in their jobs versus those faced as a member of a study group. No matter what personnel are selected from within or from outside the data processing group, top mangement must reassure them that the firm's commitment to the real-time MIS is long range.

An additional and important source of personnel are those employees involved in existing data processing operations. There are many advantages to staffing from within. Knowledge of present methods and procedures is helpful in understanding the specialized tasks that must be accomplished with the new system. This understanding of procedural exceptions and problem areas can be of great importance in complying with difficult system changes. The departmental managers know these people and what can be expected from them. For the most part, they are desirable employees and want training, because it increases their professional status and pay. Thus, management's interest in them should increase their loyalty in return.

If the many jobs in a real-time MIS environment cannot be filled from within by qualified personnel, the MIS manager has no alternative but to go outside the firm. This includes hiring trained personnel with prior data processing experience and people with formal training in data processing. Applicants need to be tested and interviewed for their ability to handle positions for which they are being considered. In addition to hiring from the outside, many firms have procured the services of software and consulting firms for assistance in systems implementation.

Training Personnel

Considering the sources of qualified personnel to implement the new system, training of personnel will still be necessary. All equipment manufacturers provide training courses for their customers. These courses vary in length from several hours to several weeks, depending upon the subject matter and its depth. Courses on computer programming and the operation of various input/output devices are offered periodically at most sales-customer service offices by equipment manufacturers. Colleges, data processing schools, and associations also offer courses on the fundamentals of the MIS and its related areas.

By no means is training limited to those who will operate the new system, however. Management must have a good grasp of what real-time MIS is and how it can be applied effectively to the firm—otherwise, there will be a gap between management and the system technicans that will make realization of the full potential of newer methods and equipment unlikely. It is suggested that management keep abreast of this fast-changing field by formal training as well as by reading current literature.

Formal training is not complete without on-the-job exposure. The best method of acquiring real-time MIS knowledge is to have formal training supplemented by on-the-job training. For example, an ideal situation is to have programmers attend the manufacturer's school for two to three days a week on the firm's premises while the other time is used for programming specific real-time programs and their related modules on the job. This can be undertaken when the installation is large enough to warrant on-site training for the firm's personnel. Instead of using standard programming problems, those company programs which are simple and straightforward can be utilized during training. This approach allows the data processing manager to observe and evaluate his personnel, determine the validity of his implementation schedule, and obtain a general feel of the new system and its potential problem areas.

Realignment of Personnel

The increasing number of studies on employee displacement following the installation of past management information systems indicates that very few or no employees have to be discharged. This is in contrast to the situation that results when automation is implemented in the factory and a sizeable number of employees are replaced by machines. The chief reason for the low discharge rate is the high turnover rate for clerical sections in which personnel are being replaced by the computer. If the firm anticipates too many people in routine jobs when planning for future personnel requirements, normal attrition will eventually take care of excess personnel at this level.

Clerks and machine operators who perform routine tasks are generally no real problem. Lower-level supervisors and assistants to department heads, who are young for the most part, are quite capable of being retrained for new jobs that have not existed before. They are flexible enough to make the change with few problems. Their knowledge of the firm's operations plus the challenge of a new position have contributed greatly to many new systems. On the other hand, department heads and higher-level supervisors are generally older and less flexible; not only may their respective departments or supervisory areas disappear, but there will be fewer available positions for them because there will be fewer clerical jobs to supervise. Some of the tasks performed by these middle-level persons will be relegated to a computer. For example, automatic purchasing, production scheduling, and inventory control, among others, will be the normal output of a new system.

Those who are nearing retirement age can be requested to ask for an early retirement. However, there will be quite a few who must face a demotion in job title, although not in pay (for to cut both title and pay would be a serious blow to their morale). For all levels affected by the new system, management should make every attempt to consider employees' interests in relocation. Concern for the individual should be manifest at all time during this difficult period.

The realignment of personnel occurs once the parallel operations begins. During this sytems implementation step, both the new and old systems are running in parallel so that the new system can be checked out thoroughly. Personnel realignment begins on a massive scale once the firm is immersed in converting the many functional areas. Generally, long hours will be required of all personnel for the conversion. The data processing newsletter should praise the efforts of all those involved in conversion and reemphasize that the organization has a challenging job for all employees.

Physical Requirements and Alterations

The actual installation of the equipment may require more, less, or the same amount of space. However, requirements for conversion activities generally take more space because dual operations of the new and old systems must take place within the same general area. Alterations may be needed to handle new inputs, the common data base, off-line files, and outputs as well as many I/O terminal devices. New methods and procedures may require physical modifications to many departments. New departments will replace old ones, while other departments will have need of extensive modifications. Others will no longer be needed, providing space for new departmental requirements.

The physical requirements and alterations necessary should be an integral part of the systems implementation schedule. Although the MIS manager will not personnally supervise the new equipment installation and its physical environment alterations, he is, nevertheless, accountable in the final analysis. It is best to determine as early as possible the layout of the new system to permit the location of physical changes which may take a while to install. Too often in the past, the physical aspects of a new system have been ignored because prior system changes have gone smoothly without any need for large modifications.

Testing and Acceptance of Equipment

No matter what type of new equipment is being employed, the manufacturer's field service engineers must test it thoroughly before its acceptance by the user. Only the manufacturer has the necessary diagnostic routines for this testing. A common method is to utilize field service programs which are capable of testing the various pieces of hardware in the system. This method can be supplemented with a company computer program which has proved to be thoroughly operational at another location. Finally, long periods of operation without excessive downtime is an indicaton that the component parts are reliable for compiling and debugging programs.

Quite often, the first models of a new line require more testing than those which have been in the field for a long period, for even though new engineering designs may be sound, they may give field service problems. Electrical and mechanical components may also need changing. Generally, special programs developed by the manufacturer are used to test the subsections of any system that incorporate new design concepts. Other special programs can be written by the user to determine the reliability of the new equipment. This may be one of the major programs that will be a part of the regular production runs. If the equipment fails to meet its stated specifications, the user is in a better position knowing about its deficiency now than at a later date.

Programming and Testing

The major task of any data processing system, in particular, a real-time MIS system, is programming and testing computer programs. This point was highlighted earlier (See Figure 3-3). For a typical real-time MIS project of several years' duration, major systems implementation phases consist of (1) training personnel, (2) flowcharting, including decision tables, (3) programming and desk checking, (4) and program compiling and testing plus systems testing. The time factors for each area are 8, 10, 10, and 20 percent, respectively, totaling approximately one-half of the total project time. Referring to Figure 6-2 (a further elaboration of Figure 3-3), the preparatory work for the system totals about 2 years (100 weeks) out of an approximate four-year undertaking (222 weeks). (As indicated previously, a four-year period is used here for illustrative purposes only because most MIS projects have taken a much longer time in the past.) Although much time is allocated to other implementation areas, the task of programming and testing is of such a magnitude that it must be supervised effectively in order to obtain best results.

The detailed steps involved in developing a computer routine will not be discussed, except for the modular approach to programming. An overview of the important steps involved in developing an operational computer program are set forth in Figure 6-3. The listing indicates the numerous steps involved in programming and testing. It is also indicative of the formidable task in systems implementation.

1. The problem is clearly defined in terms of system flowcharts, decision tables, and description of the run (inputs, outputs, common data base elements, off-line files, logic, internal control, and other important considerations for coding).

2. The program flowcharts (block diagrams) and/or decision tables are utilized for detailed programming.

3. Procedure-oriented and specialized programming languages that lend themselves to the modular programming concept are employed for the entire programming effort.

4. The flowcharts, decision tables, and coded program are desk-checked for logical and clerical programming errors.

5. Program cards are prepared and verified to keep manual errors at a minimum.

6. A compiler is used to compile the source program.

7. Errors, as indicated on the initial compiler printout, are corrected by the preparation of new program source statements.

8. The program is recompiled producing a corrected printout as well as a magnetic tape or a magnetic disk to store the machine language output (i.e., the object program).

9. Testing of the object program necessitates a sample transaction deck which is representative of the data to be input for the program being tested.

10. Logical and clerical programming errors are corrected as testing takes place.

11. An optimum program, recompiled after all programming errors have been remedied during detailed testing, is utilized for systems testing.

12. Parallel operations are run for the new and old systems in order to detect errors that have not appeared in step (11).

13. Conversion to daily operations from the old system to the new sytem is undertaken.

14. Finally, documentation of the computer program is essential for review and control purposes. This step should be an integral part of all the prior steps.

FIGURE 6-3. Detailed steps involved in developing an operational computer program.

For the most part, programming and testing efforts become more difficult when installing a real-time MIS. Even though the conversion is from one computer to another, there are basic differences between a batch processing and a real-time processing system. Many programs must be started from scratch because there is no counterpart available in the previous system for emulating, simulating, or revising present programs. The fourteen steps enumerated will add time to the systems implementation phase. However, the next change from a real-time MIS to a data-managed system, for example, should not be as difficult.

As with any project, programming supervision is essential to meet the new installation deadlines. Too often, programmers take the most difficult route first instead of taking one that is relatively simple and straightforward. Invariably, they try their talents in utilizing the new features of the machine's hardware—in particular, the large number of index registers. This high level of sophistication can be undertaken at a later date when time is available to increase the program's through-put performance. Programmers must be content to get the system on the air and leave intricate programming until later time if they are not fully understood. Only in this manner can the systems implementation schedule be met.

Modular Programming

To make the job of programming and testing easier, a modular approach should be employed. Modular programming refers to the technique in which the logical parts of a problem are divided into a series of individual routines so that each routine may be programmed independently.[1] This enables complex problems to be divided into many sections. Access to the individual routines is controlled by a single routine, commonly known as the "mainline program" in a batch processing mode. The mainline routine makes all decisions that govern the flow of data to the proper processing routines, depicted from an overview approach in Figure 6-4.

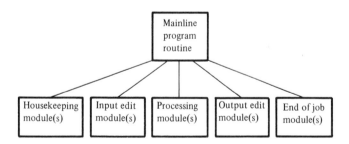

FIGURE 6-4. An overview of modular programming in a batch processing mode.

The success of modular programming hinges largely on the adherence to this sequence—modular analysis precedes modular design which precedes modular programming. The design of a system must be approached at the outset with modularity in mind, for the probability of successfully breaking a monolithic system into modules *after* the design is finished is very small.

In a modular programming approach, a program consists of several modules,

[1]Alan Cohen, "Modular Programs: Defining the Module," *Datamation,* January, 1972, and Maxine Iritz, "Modular Programming Makes Systems Satisfy User Needs," *Computer Decisions,* July, 1972.

each of which is generally limited to 50 to 200 machine language instructions or 2 to 6 pages of coding, with no module exceeding 4K storage locations. A program module is defined as a closed subroutine to which control is passed by a calling program (mainline program routine) and which returns control to the calling program when it completes its processing. Decisions may be made in a module that will cause a change in the flow of the system, but the module will not actually execute the branching. It will communicate the decision to the calling program which executes the branching. The creation of a modular design is relatively easy, because a computer problem consists of functional data processing modules. The specification of the actual processing in the modules is a function of the relationship between data elements and results from the analysis. The only functions that are actually programmed are the data processing functions at the bottom ends of the branches, because they are the building blocks of which the higher-level functions are made.

The placement of often-used functions within an overlay structure is an important element of the modular structural design. For example, consider the three-level structure below.

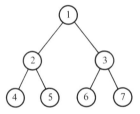

There will be one module from each level in memory at a single instant overlaying a previously called module. Hence, the execution of 5 requires that 1 and 2 be in memory. If 5 were a generalized function which must also be used by 6, the situation would not be feasible, whereas if 1 is the generalized module, it is available to all other modules. Execution of the modular system requires at least one module that is not on the above analysis tree. It is the mainline program routine mentioned earlier. Most of the fundamental system flow logic is in this control module, which controls the execution of the functional modules.

To illustrate the modular programming concept (batch processing mode), a typical weekly payroll program is broken down into eleven modules in Figure 6-5. These individual modules are separate tasks that vary in size and complexity. For example, the highest-level module (Process weekly employee payroll file) represents the solution to the weekly payroll program. The next and succeeding levels solve one of the tasks to be performed in order to process the program. Within this sample programming project, four programmers handle several modules within the same program. Each programmer is responsible for coding and testing his own modules, while the lead programmer supervises and is responsible for final program testing, as shown in Figure 6-6.

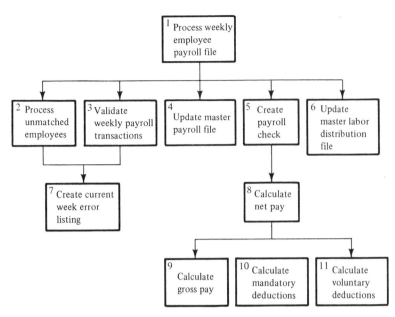

FIGURE 6-5. Major programming modules for a typical weekly payroll program.

So far we have described only one approach to modular programming—that in which every transference of control is made in a mainline program. However, for a real-time MIS environment, a more important type exists. In real time, for the sake of speed and efficiency, each module controls the program flow by ordering a RTCP (real-time control program) to call in another module. The RTCP is not a mainline program because its function is that of a housekeeper and it does not control the logical system flow. We have then a type of modular programming in which the flow continues on a smooth path through a chain of modules rather than going in and out of the mainline control program.

The benefits of a modular design is that it accommodates changes that occur after the systems design phase—coding, testing, learning, operating, and maintaining the system. Given that both fundamental system logic changes and specific procedural changes invariably occur throughout the system in terms of the application itself, the effect on the data base, the nature of the module interfaces, etc., modularity enhances the identification of these changes and therefore the control of the evolution of the system. The modular design approach, then, helps the programming staff to build a real-time MIS operating environment, together with the necessary batch functions, that is efficient and capable of being maintained.

Systems Testing

Before parallel operation is undertaken, it is recommended that systems testing be employed, inasmuch as programming testing is rather limited. Systems testing involves utilizing old files so that the system can be tested with past data

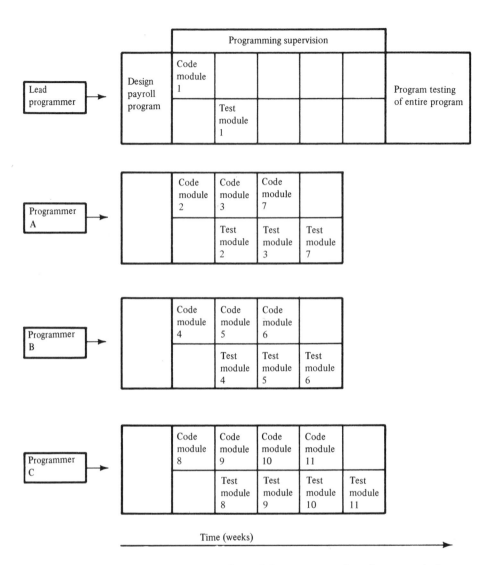

FIGURE 6-6. Organization of modular programming for a typical weekly payroll program, based upon Figure 6-5.

(primary objective). Such an approach introduces "realism," because testing is done with previous live data. Normal transactions and exceptions are tested against the computer program for reliability. Testing under real-world conditions should lessen the problems encountered with parallel operations. Depending on the type of system, this phase could be short or somewhat lengthy.

Systems testing is concerned with training the company employees in the operation of the new sytem as well as maintaining it (secondary objective). Employees must learn to operate what is being turned over to them. This can be accomplished by formal classroom sessions, seminars, on-the-job training, and computer-assisted instruction. Operating manuals for training, operating, and maintaining the system are necessary for efficient systems testing.

216

File Conversion

Because there are large files of information that must be converted from one medium to another, this phase should be started long before programming and testing is completed. The cost and related problems of file conversion are significant whether they involve on-line files (common data base) or off-line files. Present manual files are likely to be inaccurate and incomplete where deviations from the accepted format are common. In a similar manner, present punched card files tend also to be inaccurate and incomplete. Both files suffer from the shortcomings of inexperienced and, at times, indifferent personnel whose jobs are to maintain them. Computer-generated files tend to be more accurate and consistent. The formats of the present computer files are generally unacceptable for the new system.

Besides the need to provide a compatible format, there are several other reasons for file conversion. The files may require character translation that is acceptable to the character set of the new computer system. Data from punched cards, magnetic tape, and comparable storage mediums will have to be placed on magnetic disk, magnetic drum, and/or other mass storage files in order to construct an on-line common data base. Also, the rearrangement of certain data fields for more efficient programming may be desired. A new format that takes advantage of packed decimal fields may be necessary for conversion.

In order for the conversion to be as accurate as possible, file conversion programs must be thoroughly tested. Adequate controls, such as record counts and control totals, should be required output of the conversion program. The existing computer files should be kept for a period of time until sufficient files are accumulated for backup. This is necessary in case the files must be reconstructed from scratch when a "bug" is discovered at a later date in the conversion routine.

2. OPERATION OF REAL-TIME MIS

Completion of optimum computer programs and their systems testing (along with file conversion), as shown in step (11) in Figure 6-3, is shown as event 46 in Figure 6-2. Even though these programs have solved representative systems test data, there is no way to duplicate the actual flow of work with all its timing considerations and exceptions. The best way to prove the new system's reliability is to run parallel operations with the existing system.

Parallel Operations

Parallel operations consist of feeding both systems the same input data and comparing data files and output results. This is depicted as step (12) in Figure 6-3. Despite the fact that the best test data possible was used during the preparatory work phase, related conditions and combinations of conditions are likely to occur that were not envisioned. Last-minute changes to computer programs are necessary to accommodate these new conditions. Activity 46-48 represents this condition in Figure 6-2.

For a real-time MIS project, the process of running dual operations for both new and old systems is more difficult than for a batch processing system. The problem is that the new system has no true counterpart in the old system. One procedure for testing the new real-time system is to have several remote input/ output terminals connected on line and to have them operated by supervisory personnel who are backed up by other personal operating on the old system. The outputs are checked for compatibility and appropriate corrections are made to the on-line computer programs. Once this segment of the new system has proven satisfactory, the entire terminal network can be placed into operation for this one area. Additional sections of the system can be added by testing in this manner until all programs are operational.

During parallel operations, mistakes found are often not those of the new system, but the result of the old system. These differences should be reconciled as far as it is feasible economically. Those responsible for comparing the two systems should establish clearly that the remaining deficiencies are caused by the old system. A poor detail checking job at this point can cause undue harm later when complaints are received from customers, top management, salesmen, departments, and other parties. Again, it is the responsibility of the MIS manager and his assistants to satisfy themselves that adequate time for dual operations has been undertaken for each functional area changed.

The MIS group must keep the entire firm posted on parallel operations and conversion activities. This can be accomplished via the series of bulletins which started at the inception of the feasibility study. Departmental personnel should be informed when they are to start on systems implementation and what specific activities will be required of them. Department heads should be informed before the actual date of conversion activities so that anticipated problems can be worked out before they occur. Ample time should be spent instructing personnel on parallel operations or conversion activities to prevent wasted motion and time and eventually a cost that will exceed the original study figures by a wide margin. Activities must be organized, directed, and controlled around the original plan of the real-time MIS feasibility study.

Conversion to New System

After on-and off-line files have been converted and the new system's reliability has been proven for a functional area, daily processing can be shifted from the existing system to the new one. This is step (13) in Figure 6-3. A cutoff point is established so that all data files and other data requirements can be updated to the cutover point. All transactions initiated after this time are processed on the new system. Data processing personnel should be present to assist and answer any questions that might develop. Consideration may have to be given to operating the old system a short time longer to permit checking and balancing the total results of both systems. Differences must be reconciled. If necessary, appropriate changes should be made to the new system and its computer programs. The old system can be dropped as soon as the data processing group is satisfied with the new system's performance. It should be remembered that it is impossible to return to the old system if significant errors appear later in the new system. The operation of the existing system provides an alternate route in case of system failure during conversion.

Provision for Necessary Changes

Before any parallel or conversion activities can start, operating procedures must be clearly spelled out for personnel in the functional areas undergoing changes as specified per the final step (14) in Figure 6-3. This applies to both programming and operational procedures. Information on input, data files, methods, procedures, output, and internal control must be set forth in clear, concise, and understandable terms for the average reader. Written operating procedures must be supplemented by oral communication during the many training periods on the systems change. Having qualified data processing personnel in the conversion area to communicate and coordinate new developments as they occur is a must. Likewise, revisions to operating procedures should be issued as quickly as possible.

Once the new system has been completely converted, the data processing section should spend several days checking with all supervisory personnel about their respective areas. As with every new installation, the need for minor adjustments can be expected; the system as initially designed should be flexible enough to accommodate these changes. Channels of communication should be open between the data processing group and all supervisory personnel so that necessary changes can be initiated as conditions change. Thus, the proper machinery for making changes must be implemented, thereby bringing the sytems project to a formal close.

Scheduling Personnel and Equipment

Scheduling data processing operations of a real-time system for the first time is a difficult task for the MIS manager. As he becomes more familiar with the new system, the job becomes more routine. The objectives of scheduling both personnel and equipment are depicted in Figure 6-7.

> Maximize utilization of personnel and equipment, in particular, I/O terminal devices to further the objectives of the firm.
>
> Produce timely reports and meet deadlines for output desired.
>
> Increase productivity of personnel by including time for training and on-the-job training.
>
> Facilitate the planning of proposed new applications or modifications of existing applications for new and/or existing equipment.
>
> Reduce conflicts of several jobs waiting for a specific piece of equipment. (Conflicts may result in delays of important outputs or unnecessary overtime.)

FIGURE 6-7. Objectives of scheduling personnel and equipment.

Many times, before the systems project is complete, there is a great need to schedule the new equipment. Some programs will be operational while others will be in various stages of compiling and testing. Because production runs tend to push aside new-program testing, it is the task of the MIS manager to assign ample time for all individuals involved. This generally means second shift for those working on programs. Once all programs are implemented, scheduling becomes more exacting.

Schedules should be set up by the head of data processing in conjunction with the departmental managers of the operational units that are serviced by the equipment. The master schedule for next month should provide sufficient computer time to handle all required processing. Daily schedules should be prepared in accordance with the master schedule and should include time necessary for reruns, program testing, special nonrecurring reports, operations research programs, and other necessary runs. In all cases, the schedules should be as realistic as possible because it is more difficult to schedule a real-time system than a batch processing system.

The time to assign remote batch programs under normal operating conditions in real time is a problem because the number of interruptions that will occur is generally unknown. One approach to this problem is to assign a time block each day for operation of remote input/output devices. If this arrangement is not feasible, the MIS manager must look to past experience. When total random and sequential demands are not high, the machine will have sufficient capacity to complete all scheduled work even though batch processing runs will be stretched out by random system inquiries.

The practice of attaching recording clocks to keep track of the machine time in executing and awaiting instructions is quite common. It allows the data processing section to study the efficiency of each program and identify problem areas. The time clock is helpful in determining how the equipment's cost is to be charged to the firm's functional areas for statement purposes. However, for a real-time system, this is of no real value because executive programs are running continuously whether or not demands are being made for service. In essence, the total time for a real-time system has no real meaning. However, information can be accumulated internally by determining the input source and allocating this cost to the respective areas on the monthly departmental statements.

Just as the equipment must be scheduled for its maximum utilization, so must the personnel who operate the equipment. It is also imperative that personnel who enter input data and handle output data be included in the data processing schedule. Otherwise, data will not be available when the equipment needs it for processing. It is essential that each person follow the methods and procedures set forth by the data processing group. Noncompliance with established norms will have an adverse effect on the entire system. Effective supervision of personnel enhances compliance with established procedures and scheduled deadlines.

Alternative Plans in Case of Equipment Failure

Alternative processing plans must be employed in case of equipment failure. Priorities must be given to those jobs that are critical to the firm, such as billing, payroll, and inventory. These jobs can be performed manually until the equipment is functioning again. For obvious reasons, the preferred method is duplexing some or all of the system.

Duplexing, as explained in the last chapter, is the use of a redundant unit for the same purpose as the original one. If one malfunctions, the other is available. Although this approach increases equipment costs, it aids in transaction processing in that increased output is possible because both units can be used for regular processing and functions can be divided between the units. Thus, duplexing can resolve the problem of fallback in case of a system breakdown.

Documentation of alternative plans is the responsibility of the data processing section. It should be a part of the company's systems and procedures manual, which should state explicitly what the critical jobs are, how they are to be handled in case of equipment failure (use duplexing, manual methods, or some other approach), where compatible equipment is located (includes service bureaus), who will be responsible for each area during downtime, and what deadlines must be met during the emergency.

3. PERIODIC REVIEW FOR IMPROVEMENTS TO REAL-TIME MIS

Just after the system is installed, the MIS manager and staff should review the tangible and intangible system benefits set forth in the real-time MIS exploratory survey report. The purpose of such a review is to verify that these benefits are, in fact, being achieved. Discussions with managers of operating areas being serviced will determine how well the new system is performing. Tangible benefits, such as clerical reduction and lower inventory, and intangible benefits of improved customer service and more managerial information are open for constructive criticism. Typical comments will be along the following lines: certain areas have been improved significantly, some are about the same, and others are not as good as before. The task of the data processing section, then, is to make the necessary adjustments to accomplish the quantitative and qualitative goals of the feasibility study. It may take from several months up to one year to effect the changes, which include reprogramming the most frequently used programs for greater efficiency.

As time passes, the work load of the present data processing system increases. Factors that were not previously problems can become significant. Can the equipment run longer hours, or should additional equipment be obtained? Can modification of methods and procedures be made to reduce processing time and cost? Can noncritical processing be shifted to another time? How does the time differential affect the manning of a real-time system that is operating within the continental limits of the United States? Answers to these questions must be evaluated by the data processing section through a periodic review of the existing system. The ultimate aim of such an investigation is system improvements. It may be necessary to undertake a feasibility study periodically in order to evolve an optimum system for the firm's continually changing conditions.

Examination of New System Approaches

The data processing section should examine new system approaches that may lead to operational improvements. The reasons should be obvious. Systems projects such as the real-time MIS are so complex that it is almost impossible to complete them in the most efficient manner (for functional areas) the first time around. The efficiency of any large computer program is always open to question. Programming should be closely examined, along with the inputs, the common data base, off-line files, methods, procedures, and outputs that are related to the program. Questions such as whether or not the input cutoff can be set earlier through rescheduling of personnel, and whether or not there is a need to redesign certain inputs, forms, and documents are typical ones for new input approaches that eventually affect programming. Can the regular work be separated initially from the exceptions items so that each can be expedited faster and handled more accurately? Regarding output, are the present reports and outputs adequate in view of the firm's growth, technological improvements, and increasing complexities of business? Numerous questions can also be explored in areas that are related directly or indirectly to programming.

New system approaches should not be restricted to current applications, but should include new areas reflecting changed conditions within and outside the firm. The areas that previously processed a low volume of data may have experienced a phenomenal growth, making them suitable for real-time processing. A promising area for review in a real-time MIS is the storing of data on line—can meaningful managerial reports be prepared at a small additional cost because data are available at all times for processing? Also, operations research models for improving the firm's quantitative basis for decision making may be capable of utilizing the data stored on line. The ability to access large volumes of current data as well as to compile statistics on the data changes occurring within the system provide new system approaches. An examination of these may necessitate a new feasibility study when numerous changes are contemplated. This permits the implementation of a better system versus "patching" an existing system which may not lead to an optimum one.

Evaluation of New Equipment

Periodic review of the existing system for improvements includes keeping abreast of the latest developments in equipment. This refers not only to real-time computers but also to all related equipment. Even though the firm utilizes a computer with real-time capabilities, there is a constant parade of newer equipment that can make the present computer obsolete. Also, the newer equipment may be lower in price. New design concepts and circuitry permit the introduction of minicomputers, OCR equipment as input to a real-time MIS system, faster data communication equipment, and many other developments. Hardware innovations will not be restricted to the firm; equipment to handle supplier-manufacturer-distributor-retailer processing activities will be common in the future. The ultimate total system is the linking of all computer systems in the country for an electronic money system.

Cost Analysis of System

New equipment developments are fast changing the cost of data processing because of the addition of many newer models whose capabilities and performance are better than previous models. Later computer models of the same generation and different generations of computers have proven this to be true. Even though internal hardware speeds are faster with increased miniaturization of circuitry and components, many computer programs are input and/or output bound, which means the new speeds of the central processor may be of no assistance in speeding up their operations. Thus, the real criterion of lower data processing costs centers around throughput performance and turnaround time.

Estimated savings less estimated one-time costs and additional operating costs were computed for the estimated life of the new system in the exploratory survey report. Periodically, the MIS manager needs to compare these estimated figures with the actual amounts and evaluate the results with the firm's vice-president in charge of finance. The study's figures could be different from the actual results by a wide or narrow margin. Unfavorable deviations need assessment for possible courses of action to remedy the situation. It should be noted that fewer large differences are likely to occur when the MIS manager knows that there will be a series of reviews—that is, a comparison of the budgeted figures to actual amounts. Those data processing personnel who experience unfavorable results must be held accountable. For the most part, original estimates are stated realistically, but other factors have come into the picture that have distorted final results.

MAJOR STEPS INVOLVED IN A REAL-TIME MIS PROJECT

The major steps involved in the feasibility study through systems implementation of a real-time MIS, to review the subject matter for Chapters Three through Six, are illustrated in Figure 6-8. As noted previously, the feasibility study encompasses approximately one-third of the total time of the systems project, while systems implementation takes about two-thirds. By and large, a real-time MIS project takes several years to complete for a small firm while larger firms may take considerably longer. The completion of such a large undertaking generally signals the need to start the process over again because of the dynamics of the real world. Changing products and markets, internationalization of business, more government regulation, and greater concern for the environment, among other things, signal the need for a new feasibility study.

COMMON PROBLEMS ENCOUNTERED IN A SYSTEMS PROJECT

Tensions can run high within the computer section when serious problems are confronting this group. Problem areas cover a wide range as set forth in Figure 6-9. An examination of this listing indicates that many of them can be attributed to the

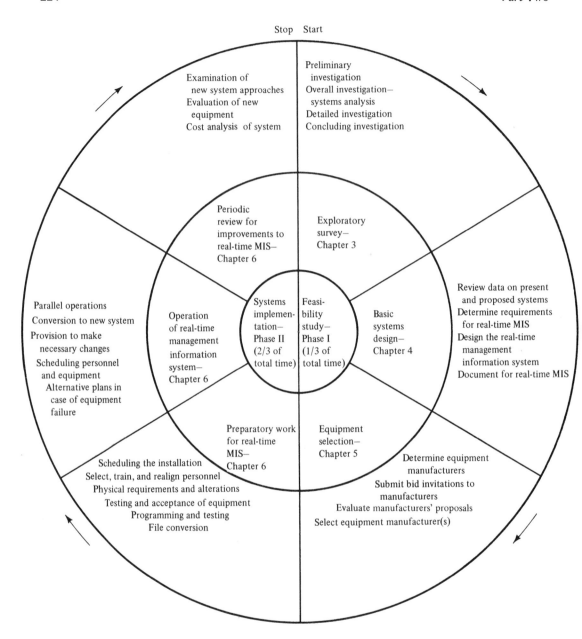

FIGURE 6-8. Summary of steps involved in the feasibility study through systems implementation of a real-time MIS.

indifference of top management. For this reason, top managers must set specific objectives that are focused on major business problems when implementing a real-time MIS.

Failure to set realistic objectives based upon the existing conditions.
   Installation of data processing equipment requires goals, objectives, and schedules like any other business undertaking.

Lack of top management participation in the systems project.
   This usually results in superimposing a new system on the present one without significant changes.

Inadequate attention to the psychological factors of company personnel.
   The natural resistance to change and the impact of new equipment on personnel must be taken into consideration.

Failure to evaluate available equipment properly.
   Hardware must be tailored to meet the needs of the system rather than vice versa.

Breakdown in communications between the needs of the operating subsystems and the systems personnel.
   Frequent and constructive meetings between the two groups should alleviate this difficulty.

Underutilization of equipment capability due to poor systems design and inadequately trained technical staff.
   Theoretical knowledge alone does not qualify one to cope with designing and programming a sophisticated real-time MIS.

Inadequate monitoring of progress on the systems project.
   A well-conceived plan provides adequate means of controlling the activities of the systems project.

Poor problem definition of individual computer programs.
   Poor logic and incomplete definition of inputs, common data base, off-line files, outputs, etc. cause difficulty during the flowcharting and programming phases.

Inadequate documentation as the systems project progresses.
   This can set the project back many months if there is a high rate of personnel turnover.

Poor supervision of conversion activities—in particular, data files conversion.
   This may mean costly reworking to correct deficiencies or starting anew.

Inaccurate cost estimates in the exploratory survey report.
   Major causes of inaccuracy is an underestimation of time to program the various applications, convert from present system to new system, and process the programs on the equipment.

Poor selection of data processing personnel to implement the new system.
   Marginal data processing personnel should not be allowed to manage and program a complex system.

No conception by top management of what is involved in the installation of a computer system.
   Top management should undergo some technical training to communicate effectively with the systems group.

Failure to incorporate adequate internal control in the new system and computer programs.
   This could make possible defrauding the firm's assets as well as the accumulation of incorrect values during the data processing flow.

Lack of operating personnel participation on problem areas and exception items.

   FIGURE 6-9. Common problems experienced when undertaking a systems project, such as a real-time MIS.

This results in a new systems design that does not reflect actual operating conditions.

By-passing parallel operations in the hope that no problems will be encountered.

The odds against this happening are extremely high.

Crashing a systems project.

A crash program often produces serious long-term effects and can adversely affect the firm's daily operations.

FIGURE 6-9 (cont.)

SUMMARY

Systems implementation begins after the formal signing of the equipment contract. Although the real-time MIS feasibility study consists of three steps—exploratory survey including systems analysis, basic systems design, and equipment selection—systems implementation involves two steps—preparatory work and operation of new system with a provision for periodic review of system improvements. Typically, systems implementation takes twice as much time as the feasibility study. The number of operating personnel outside the data processing group is substantially increased for the former phase. Also, the firm will experience high costs during the systems conversion phase.

Programming and testing, the mainstays of the preparatory work phase, are time-consuming and costly. Advanced programming techniques and programming languages should be utilized to assist in developing computer programs and reducing programming costs. Once a program has reached the operational stage, parallel operations should be initiated to check for abnormal conditions that might have not been present during systems testing. This phase culminates in conversion of all activities for daily operations in a real-time MIS operating environment. Consideration must be given to alternative plans in case of unforeseen difficulties during conversion as well as at a later date. Otherwise, the firm could be out of business temporarily.

Periodic review of the system, which involves examination of new system approaches, new equipment, and cost factors, should follow the installation. Often an evaluation of the existing system may signal the need for a new feasibility study, which means, in essence, that the systems project cycle must start again. This permits making system changes that are necessary to accommodate environmental factors as well as the introduction of more advanced hardware and software.

QUESTIONS

1. a. What kinds of personnel problems accompany the change from a batch processing system to a real-time system?
   b. How can they be overcome?

2. Once the equipment order has been signed, what type of training problems are likely to occur? Explain.

3. Describe the kind of operating procedures that should be a part of efficient real-time MIS processing.

4. a.   What programming difficulties can be experienced by the data processing section during the preparatory work phase?

b.   Explain how each can be resolved.

5. When installing a real-time computer system, what physical facilities are necessary?

6. How important are parallel operations in a real-time MIS environment? Explain.

7. Why should the firm review periodically its real-time MIS for improvements?

REFERENCES

Bell, T. E., Boehm, B. W., and Watson, R. A., "How to Get Started on Performance Improvement," *Computer Decisions,* March, 1973.

Black, D. L., "Controlling A Computer System," *Datamation,* April, 1974.

Bookman, P. G., Brotman, B. A., and Schmitt, K. L., "Use Measurement Engineering for Better System Performance," *Computer Decisions,* April, 1972.

Bures, J. P., "Time-Framing a PERT Chart," *Management Accounting,* October, 1974.

Chapin, N., House, R., McDaniel, N., and Wachtel, R., "Structured Programming Simplified," *Computer Decisions,* June, 1974.

Cohen, A., "Modular Programs: Defining the Module," *Datamation,* January, 1972.

Dearden, J., and Nolan, R. L., "How to Control the Computer Resource," *Harvard Business Review,* November-December, 1973.

Iritz, M., "Modular Programming Makes Systems Satisfy User Needs," *Computer Decisions,* July, 1972.

Maynard, J., *Modular Programming,* Princeton: Auerbach, 1972.

Metzger, P. H., *Managing a Programming Project.* Englewood Cliffs, N.J.: Prentice-Hall, Inc., 1973.

Murdick, R. G., "MIS Development Procedures," *Journal of Systems Management,* December, 1970.

Murdick, R. G., and Ross, J. E., *Information Systems for Modern Management.* Englewood Cliffs, N.J.: Prentice-Hall, Inc., 1971, Chap. 15.

Reid, H. V., "Problems in Managing the Data Processing Department," *Journal of Systems Management,* May, 1970.

Rhodes, J., "Tackle Software with Modular Programming," *Computer Decisions,* October, 1973.

Rothstein, M. F., *Guide to the Design of Real-Time Systems,* New York: John Wiley & Sons, Inc., 1970, Chap. 10.

Sewald, M. D., Rauch, M. E., Radiek, L., and Wertz, L., "A Pragmatic Approach to Systems Measurement," *Computer Decisions,* July, 1971.

Thorne, J. F., "Critical Factors in the Implementation of Real-Time Systems," *Data Management,* January, 1972.

VonderNoot, T. J., "Systems Testing . . . a Taboo Subject?," *Datamation,* November 15, 1971.

part three

SYSTEMS ANALYSIS AND DESIGN OF REAL-TIME MIS SUBSYSTEMS

MAJOR SUBSYSTEMS OF A REAL-TIME MANAGEMENT INFORMATION SYSTEM— CONSUMER PRODUCTS CORPORATION

7

Now that the fundamentals of systems analysis, design, and equipment selection have been presented for real-time management information systems, Part Three of this book concentrates on the overall and detailed design aspects. Basically, the Consumer Products Corporation—a typical manufacturing firm—is utilized throughout Chapters Seven through Seventeen to exemplify what comprises the essentials of a real-time MIS environment. In this chapter, the overall aspects are examined; the detailed design of each major subsystem is analyzed in subsequent chapters. In addition to detailing subsystems for real-time MIS, the prior system, an integrated MIS, is presented for comparison. This approach assists the reader in identifying basic differences that exist between an integrated MIS and a real-time MIS operating mode.

Initially, this chapter presents a brief background on the Consumer Products Corporation before concentrating on the firm's major subsystems as a whole. At periodic intervals throughout the discussion of subsystems, system flowcharts are developed. Their purpose is to tie together the various subsystems. Specifically, the subsystems examined in a real-time MIS environment for the Consumer Products Corporation encompass:

corporate planning
marketing
research and development
engineering
manufacturing
inventory
purchasing
physical distribution
accounting
finance
personnel

This logical breakdown of subsystems, then, is the structure for the remainder of the book, except for the last chapter.

CONSUMER PRODUCTS CORPORATION

The Consumer Products Corporation is a medium-size firm manufacturing products for the consumer market. The firm's sales are currently $95 million per annum and are projected to be about $120 to $125 million in five years. Its product line consists of about fifty products which can be categorized into seven basic product groups. Variations of these basic products are for specific customers whose requirements differ owing to the markets they serve. For large orders, products are shipped directly to retailers from the firm's manufacturing plants. All other orders are shipped from the firm's warehouses to the many retailers. Experience has shown that 20 percent of the firm's dollar volume represents direct shipments from the plants and 80 percent represents shipments through the firm's warehouses.

Corporate headquarters are located in St. Louis, as depicted in Figure 7-1. In addition, the locations of the firm's plants and warehouses are illustrated. Manufacturing plants are found in Minneapolis, Philadelphia, and Los Angeles, and twelve warehouses are distributed around the country. Wherever a manufacturing plant is located, a warehouse is attached as illustrated. The present employment level for the firm's entire operation is approximately 3500 employees.

The firm is organized around the major subsystems as set forth previously. As shown in the organization chart (Figure 7-2), the president and chief executive officer reports to the board of directors and is assisted by the corporate planning group. The executive vice-president, in turn, reports to the president. In a similar manner, nine vice-presidents (marketing, research and development and engineering, manufacturing, purchasing and inventory, physical distribution, accounting, finance, personnel, and management information system) report to the executive

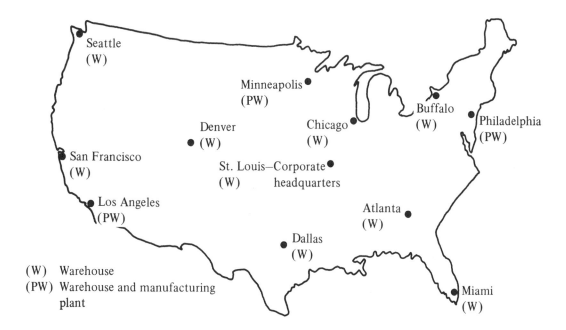

FIGURE 7-1. Three manufacturing plants and twelve warehouses of the Consmer Products Corporation.

vice-president. Various corporate headquarters managers, plant managers, and warehouse managers report to their respective vice-presidents.

The Consumer Products Corporation has progressed through a series of data processing systems limited by the constraints of available equipment. Many years ago, manual systems were augmented by adding machines and calculators. Punched card equipment and tabulating machines provided expanded system capabilities. As electronic computers became available, the data processing system was adapted to utilize these machines, making the translation of data into information much faster. Also, the computer provided capacity for the development of new applications. Presently, the firm uses an integrated management information system (batch-processing-oriented) which is being converted to a real-time MIS. The problem encountered with integrated MIS was that information (for management and non-management purposes) was not sufficiently timely to effect changes in the current operating environment. Too often, information was received too late by corporate headquarters to effect the necessary control over manufacturing and warehousing operations. Thus, the batch processing mode of integrated MIS (whereby data are collected for a period of time before being processed and summarized) did not facilitate optimal day-to-day decision making.

Because of this problem with the integrated MIS, it became apparent that a company-wide information system had to be developed. What is needed is a forward looking control system that promotes control over present and future opera-

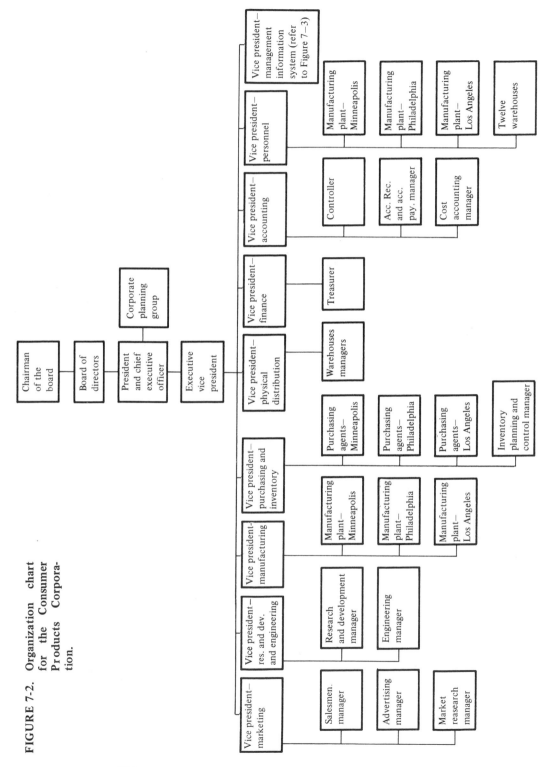

FIGURE 7-2. Organization chart for the Consumer Products Corporation.

tions. Because a real-time management information system is capable of accomplishing such a goal, the MIS vice-president initiated a feasibility study. The study disclosed the feasibility of a real-time MIS after giving consideration to tangible benefits and, more importantly, intangible benefits. Specifically, the more important reasons for implementing real-time MIS center around:

improved coordination and control of the overall firm

better customer service and improved selling efficiency

more timely and improved management information analysis and reporting

better opportunity to match demand with production

on-line information available from a common data base for management analysis of the firm's operations and prospective operations

DATA PROCESSING ORGANIZATION STRUCTURE

The data processing organization chart in a real-time MIS environment is illustrated in Figure 7-3 for the Consumer Products Corporation. The systems and programming manager and the EDP (Electronic Data Processing) operations manager report directly to the vice-president of the management information system. On the systems side of real-time MIS, systems analyst, operations research, and programming supervisors report to the systems and programming manager. Generally, the systems and programming positions are unchanged from the prior system, with the exception that program development and testing can take place in a man/machine mode by utilizing one of the many on-line I/O devices. From an operational viewpoint, the I/O terminals supervisor, the data collection supervisor, the computer supervisor, and the internal auditor (from the accounting department) report to the EDP operations manager. Unlike systems and programming, several organizational changes from the previous systems are applicable to the operations area. The I/O terminals supervisor controls on-line teletypewriter and CRT units at corporate headquarters, the plants, and the warehouses. In a similar manner, the data collection supervisor controls collection devices located in the plants and warehouses. The computer supervisor controls the computer's operators, data entry personnel, and servicemen. Thus, the real-time capabilities of the new system involve additional and more advanced equipment which must be supervised for effective control.

Although the specific positions and levels of systems work are clearly set forth (Figure 7-3), the systems project cannot be delegated completely to analysts who are asked to find "the answer." The firm's management must work closely with systems designers and operations research personnel to create an awareness of value systems and premises used in planning and decision making. Top management must exert leadership and operating managers must actively cooperate with computer specialists in order to form an effective team to implement the new MIS. Only when the firm's managers get involved, cooperate with data processing specialists, and relate their problems to the computer's real-time capabilities, can objec-

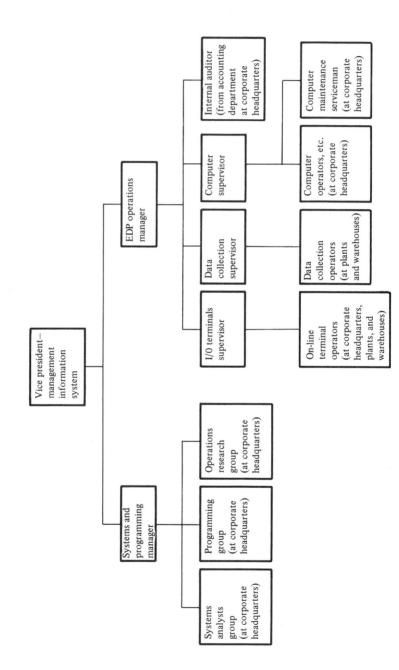

FIGURE 7-3.   Data processing organization in a real-time MIS environment for the Consumer Products Corporation.

tives be fully realized for the Consumer Products Corporation. Similarly, the firm's systems designers need to communicate and work with the operating people on the detailed methods and procedures of the new system. This is necessary in order to determine how exceptions and problems are to be handled. Also, cooperation is needed to evaluate realistically the decision-making process at all levels and the necessary information flow for that process. Systems analysts, operations researchers, and programmers must work with people above or below them as well as on the same level for effective results because the firm's managers and operating personnel generally will accept only methods and procedures that they fully comprehend.

DATA COMMUNICATIONS NETWORK

The data communications network for implementing a real-time MIS operating environment was determined during the equipment selection phase of the feasibility study. It is a full duplex system that links all of the firm's plants and warehouses to the corporate headquarters in St. Louis (Figure 7-4). The full duplex communication channels have the ability to transmit information in both directions simultaneously. In addition, all communication lines from and to corporate headquarters are full dedicated lines—that is, it is not necessary to telephone in order to reserve a communication line from the plants and warehouses to corporate head-

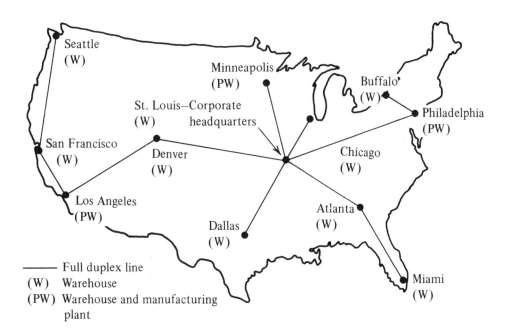

FIGURE 7-4. A data communications network for the Consumer
Products Corporation.

quarters or vice versa. This approach for relaying information back and forth simplifies the data communications network.

A further refinement of Figure 7-4 is found in the next illustration (Figure 7-5). The various I/O devices—teletypewriter and CRT units—at each plant or warehouse are first attached to a multistation control unit which, in turn, is connected via full duplex lines to the corporate CPU. In a similar manner, I/O devices at the plant level are hard-wired for entry into the plant or manufacturing division CPU which, in turn, can transmit information to the corporate CPU. This direct tie-in of all I/O devices and division CPU's with corporate headquarters permits the firm's corporate data base to be updated as needed in order to realize the real-time capabilities of the entire computerized system. Thus, a real-time MIS operating mode is possible within this data communications system (Figure 7-5).

OVERVIEW OF MAJOR SUBSYSTEMS

From an overview standpoint, the Consumer Products Corporation can be described as a "materials flow company." This concept for the three manufacturing plants is illustrated in Figure 7-6, shown as a double-line arrow on the outer rim of the system flowchart. Purchased materials and manufactured materials for stock flow into the various stages of the production process; as they do, the materials take on a variety of forms and shapes until they become finished goods. Next, the finished products flow through the distribution system either directly via direct shipments or indirectly through company-owned warehouses until they reach the customer. Thus, in this materials-flow concept, several of the major subsystems are involved.

Coupled with materials flow is their corresponding information flow (Figure 7-6). Materials-flow information is a most important factor in coordinating the diversified activities of the three manufacturing plants and twelve warehouses with corporate headquarters. It must be comprehensive, thereby integrating decision making throughout the entire materials-flow process—from purchased materials to shipment of finished goods. With this integrated flow of essential information, management and operating personnel can make adjustments swiftly and effectively in response to the ever-changing business environment. The materials-flow approach, then, is an essential part of the real-time MIS for the Consumer Products Corporation (or any firm, for that matter).

The information flow is not restricted to the materials area only. In fact, there may well be more information being generated for activities that are not related directly to the materials-flow process (Figure 7-6). Many subparts of the corporate planning, marketing, research and development, engineering, accounting, and finance subsystems are not related directly to the manufacture of the final product. No matter what the source or need of information is, the overall real-time information system must be "open-ended." This approach provides flexibility such that activities can be linked with one another at minimum cost and effort. But more importantly, the open-ended approach allows for changing the direction and speed of information flow in response to management and operating personnel needs. More will be said about the information flow for each subsystem in the following sections.

MAJOR SUBSYSTEMS IN A REAL-TIME
MIS ENVIRONMENT

The eleven subsystems to be presented in the forthcoming chapters represent an ultimate goal of the Consumer Products Corporation and may not be economically feasible to implement at one time. Firms such as Pillsbury[1] and Westinghouse[2] have made great strides in implementing several subsystems in a real-time MIS operating mode. However, these manufacturing firms have found that costs incurred can be higher than anticipated. Thus, the MIS group within a firm, including the Consumer Products Corporation, should choose those subsystems for implementation which can be economically justified. This approach, because it does not attempt a complete one-time change-over, results in a more orderly implementation. (It should be noted that a real-time MIS can be applied to other than just manufacturing firms.)

The major real-time MIS subsystems for the Consumer Products Corporation share up-to-date common data base elements (Figure 7-7) which are available to the central processing unit when needed. Data can be changed (i.e., added or deleted) as desired. In a similar manner, they can be retrieved in a variety of forms, manipulated or operated upon before presentation, and combined with elements from other data files. Also, data base information can be displayed in graphic form, selected so that only certain data meeting specified criteria will be issued, and transmitted in a computer-compatible format. The firm's data base is capable of being interrogated by any remote I/O device that is connected on line with the computer system.

With the ability to make inquiries of on-line files from any input/output device, the computer is capable of interacting with company personnel on a timely basis with essential information. It is possible to process data on a forward-looking or a real-time basis which results in feeding back information almost instantaneously. The various levels of operating management and their subordinates can be made aware of trends, exceptions, and results of recent transactions in order to initiate corrective action to meet predetermined plans. Feedback can alert company personnel about the internal and external factors affecting the firm's individual actions and overall performance.

In addition to the foregoing characteristics for the firm's major subsystems, integrated subsystems are linked directly or indirectly to one another. The quarterly sales forecast (marketing subsystem), based on external and internal factors, affects the quantity of finished goods to be produced (physical distribution sub-

[1]Terrance Hanold, "An Executive View of MIS," *Datamation,* November, 1972.
[2]William F. Workman, "The Picturephone Puts Data at Management's Fingertips," *Computer Decisions,* October, 1970.

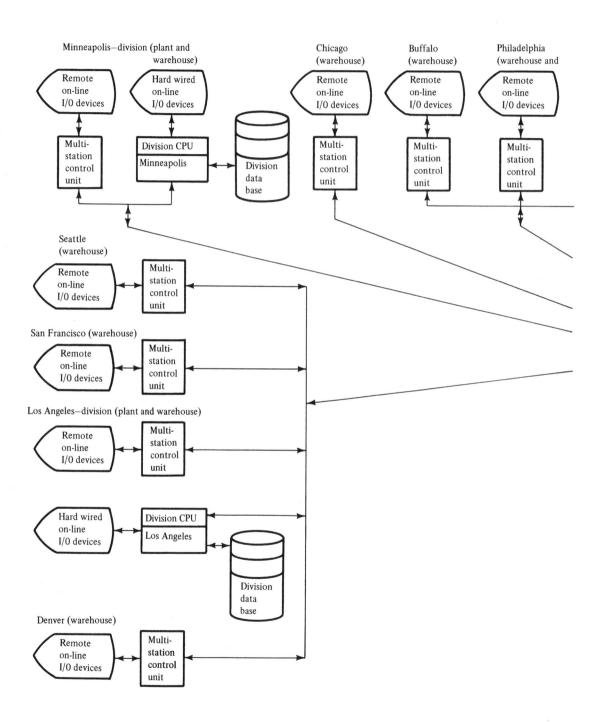

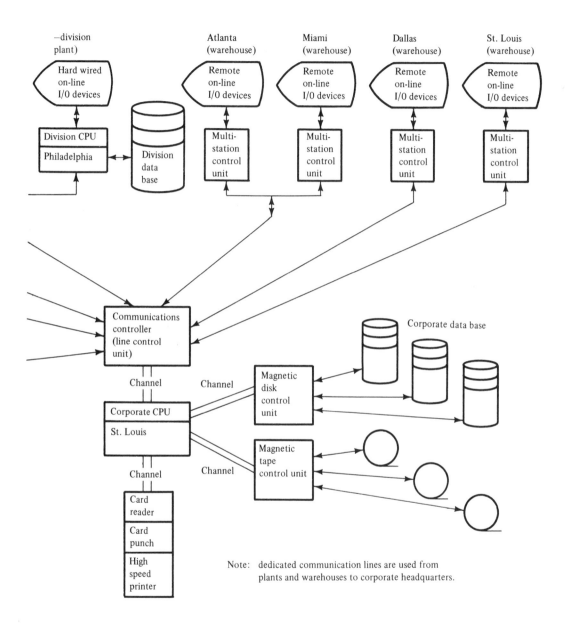

FIGURE 7-5. A data communication network system of the Consumer Products Corporation in a real-time MIS environment.

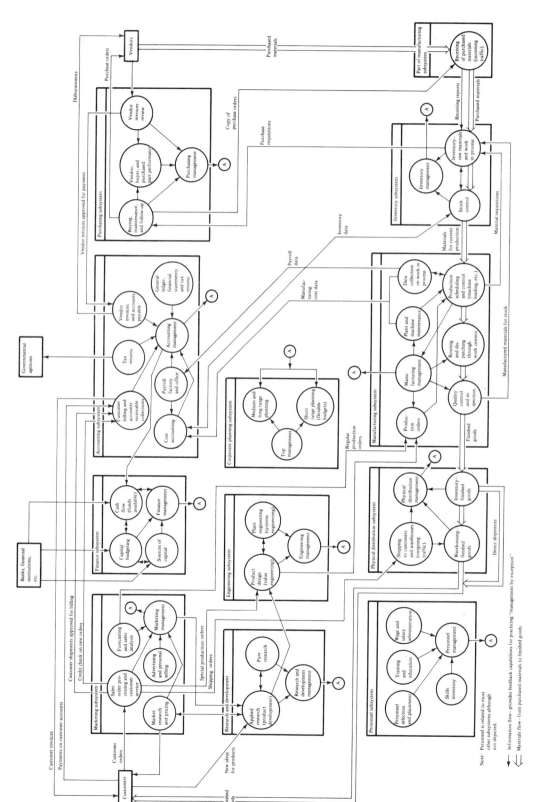

FIGURE 7-6. System flowchart depicting the major subsystems for the Consumer Products Corporation—a typical manufacturing firm.

Note: Personnel is related to most other subsystems although not depicted.

→ Information flow— provides feedback capabilities for practicing "management by exception"

⟹ Materials flow—from purchased materials to finished goods

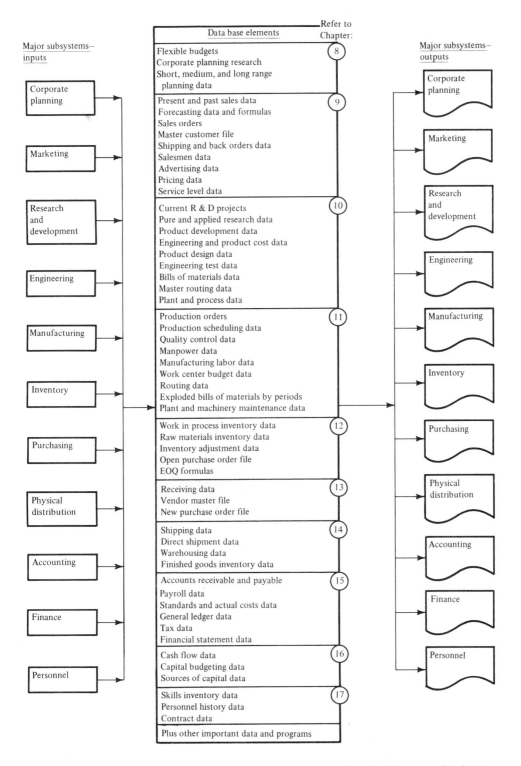

FIGURE 7-7. Common data base elements for the Consumer Products Corporation operating in a real-time MIS environment (Chapters Eight through Seventeen).

system) which, in turn, affects materials to be purchased from outside suppliers (purchasing subsystem) and to be manufactured within the firm (manufacturing subsystem) by future planning periods. Goods purchased or manufactured are procured on an optimum basis by using the economic order quantity (EOQ) formula and are eventually handled by the inventory section (inventory subsystem). Both are requisitioned to meet the manufacturing plan in accordance with the schedule of master operations (manufacturing subsystem). The operational or shop status of the final product, material, labor, and similar items is used for operations evaluation control at the manufacturing level. In some cases, operating information is significant enough for review by middle and top management. If this happens, feedback at this level of importance may make it necessary to review future plans (corporate planning subsystem). Also, it may be necessary to revise future sales forecasts. Finally, finished goods are shipped directly to the customers or through company-operated warehouses. This foregoing flow of information from one subsystem to another—in particular, from external and internal environmental factors through shipped goods to customers or company-owned warehouses—is depicted in Figure 7-8. It should be noted that this integration of information flow, although not shown per se in Figure 7-6, is an important part of this illustration. More will be said about the detailed aspects of this integrated subsystem approach in the next sections as well as in subsequent chapters.

CORPORATE PLANNING SUBSYSTEM

Before day-to-day activities can operate in an efficient manner, the corporate planning subsystem for the Consumer Products Corporation must give direction to the firm's subsystems. This integrated approach requires the following modules (Figure 7-6) in order to obtain the firm's goals and objectives:

1. long-range corporate planning
2. medium-range corporate planning
3. short-range corporate planning (flexible budgets)

The essentials for this central subsystem are set forth in Chapter Eight.

The questions that can be asked of the corporate planning subsystem for the various planning levels are innumerable. For example:

> What affect will a newly developed product have on sales five years hence (long-range)?
> What would happen to profits if certain products are redesigned and advertised quite extensively (medium-range)?
> What affect will the level of sales and production have on the current year's profit (short-range)?

No matter what type of system is employed, answers to these typical questions cannot be secured with absolute certainty. When the time factor is shortened, it is less difficult to predict the future, especially in the area of short-range corporate planning.

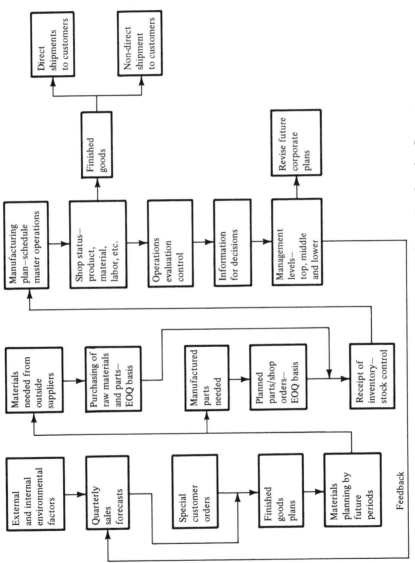

FIGURE 7-8. The integrated flow of information for the Consumer Products Corporation from the external and internal environmental phase to actual day-to-day operations whereby output from one subsystem becomes input to another subsystem.

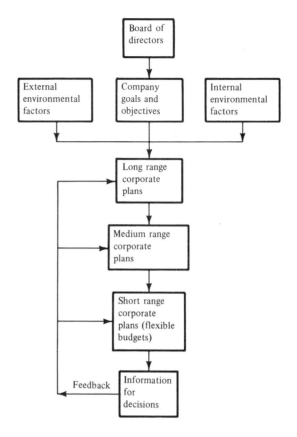

FIGURE 7-9. Type of plans—an essential part of the corporate planning subsystem (Consumer Products Corporation).

Long-range corporate plans, being the starting point for an overall planning subsystem as shown in Figure 7-9, reflect company goals and objectives as set forth by the firm's board of directors. They take into account the many external and internal environmental factors surrounding the firm and are translated into more current plans—namely, those of a short- and medium-range nature. By and large, the focal point of short-range plans are flexible budgets; that is, budgets designed to relate a certain level of sales to a corresponding level of production. Current output of flexible budgets provides the necessary feedback for making adjustments to the same or higher levels of plans, depending on the nature of the information.

MARKETING SUBSYSTEM

The firm's marketing subsystem consists of several modules. The more important ones are depicted in Figure 7-6 and are as follows:

1. forecasting and sales analysis
2. sales order processing and customer service
3. advertising and personal selling
4. market research and pricing

These major components are covered in Chapter Nine. Basically, quarterly sales forecasting was treated previously on an integrated subsystem basis. Similarily, sales order processing is treated below.

Common sales order processing problems are encountered when designing a management information system. Real-time MIS should be designed to answer these questions:

> Can this order be accepted?
> Does the firm want to accept the order?
> When is the order actually a sale?
> Where is the order entered?
> When do the finished goods belong to the customer?
> How much is to be charged for finished goods and when?

Other questions of the same type must be asked relating to this area for effective systems design.

In Figure 7-10 (as well as Figure 7-6), orders are received from customers. Appropriate order forms are prepared and edited before the customer credit is

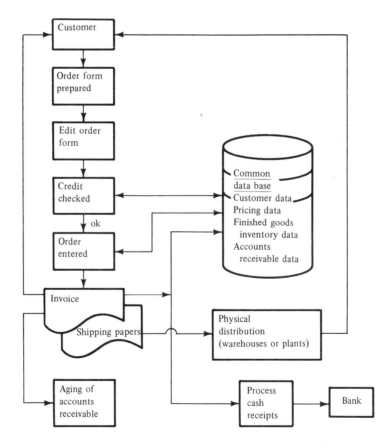

FIGURE 7-10.   Sales order processing—an essential part of the marketing subsystem (Consumer Products Corporation).

checked. If the order is not accepted because of poor credit, it is returned to the customer and the reason is noted. Generally, the order is approved for order entry whereby appropriate files (customer, pricing, and finished goods) are referenced for preparing shipping papers. Shipping papers are forwarded to the appropriate warehouses for regular shipment or to a particular plant for direct shipment.

At this point, other major subsystems interact with sales order processing (marketing subsystem). Shipping papers provide the basis for preparing customer invoices which are eventually utilized for aging accounts receivable and processing checks received from customers (accounting subsystem). In addition, they are used for assembling goods at the warehouse and plant levels. If items are available for shipment as noted by the perpetual finished goods file during the sales order processing phase, the file is changed from "finished goods on order" to "finished goods shipped" (physical distribution subsystem). Engineering also comes into contact with sales order processing through the receipt of special customer orders (engineering subsystem).

RESEARCH AND DEVELOPMENT SUBSYSTEM

Research and development (R & D) activities center around developing future products. Often, ideas are developed within the firm, while others originate from present and prospective customers. Regardless of the source, the essential modules of the research and development subsystem (Figure 7-6) are:

1. pure research
2. applied research (product development)

Each major R & D subsystem component is developed in Chapter Ten.

Owing to the nature of the firm, greater emphasis is placed on applied research versus pure research. Applied research is undertaken to anticipate future demand for new products. When integrated into a real-time MIS, this subsystem should be capable of assisting in answering the following questions:

> How much money should be spent on research and development?
> What research projects should be undertaken?
> How can R & D projects be controlled effectively?
> How and when should an R & D project be stopped (for some valid reason)?

The major function of the research and development subsystem, shown in Figure 7-11, is product development. Specifically, a prototype model is built and tested thoroughly before detailed engineering is initiated. As with other subsystems, R & D activities are integrated (with marketing and engineering subsystems). Although R & D may appear on the surface to be a somewhat isolated subsystem, it is not.

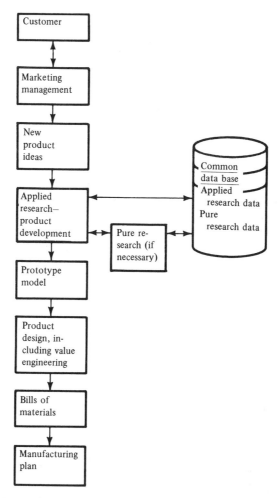

FIGURE 7-11. **Product development—the main function of the R & D and engineering subsystems (Consumer Products Corporation).**

ENGINEERING SUBSYSTEM

The engineering subsystem, as noted previously, is integrated with the marketing and R & D subsystems. A specific order request, initiated by the customer or the firm, must be engineered before manufacturing can commence. The important modules for the engineering subsystem (Figure 7-6) focus on:

1. product design (value engineering)
2. plant engineering (systems engineering)

The development of this engineering subsystem is found in Chapter Ten.

An important part of product design is value engineering, which considers whether the parts contained in the finished product perform the required function as efficiently and as inexpensively as possible. The sytems as designed should be helpful in answering these typical value engineering questions:

> Will the product give the customer an acceptable level of service?
> Will the service level cover the expected life of the product?
> Will internal manufacturing costs be low enough?
> Can the firm expect to meet its expected return on investment?

Once the prototype model has been developed as in Figure 7-11 (research and development subsystem), engineering draws the final prints that incorporate the essentials of value engineering. Bills of materials are also developed for the routing of parts and subassemblies through the manufacturing centers. These detailed drawings and bills of materials are forwarded to the production scheduling and control department for incorporation into future manufacturing plans (manufacturing subsystem).

MANUFACTURING SUBSYSTEM

The next important subsystem for getting regular or special production orders produced is manufacturing. Its essential modules for the illustrated firm are the following (Figure 7-6):

1. receiving
2. production scheduling and control
3. manufacturing operations:
   a. machine shop
   b. assembly—major and minor
   c. plant and machine maintenance
4. quality control and inspection
5. data collection system

An in-depth analysis of these components is presented in Chapter Eleven.

Common questions that must be handled by the management information system are:

> How much finished goods should be manufactured at one time?
> What raw materials are required where and when?
> What is the progress of job orders?
> How much work-in-process inventory is needed and where?
> What are the production schedules and how are they being met?
> Have the finished goods been finished and/or shipped?
> What are the manufacturing cost variances?

Generally, these typical questions can be answered with relative ease by a real-time MIS.

The manufacturing process is a continuation of prior subsystems for fore-casted finished goods. As shown in Figure 7-12 (reference can also be made to Figure 7-8), raw materials are ordered on a quarterly basis (purchasing subsystem) and, upon receipt, are placed under the supervision of stock control (inventory subsystem). They provide input for the manufacturing plan of the production scheduling and control section, whose job is to schedule, route, and dispatch orders through the various manufacturing work centers. The quality control section is responsible for making appropriate tests of manufactured and finished products before forwarding them to the warehouse or customer (physical distribution sub-system). As illustrated, there is an interplay between physical activities and data files for operations evaluation, allowing feedback of critical information where deemed necessary.

INVENTORY SUBSYSTEM

The inventory subsystem, although it might be considered a part of manufac-turing, is presented separately. It consists of these modules (Figure 7-6):

1. inventory:
   a. raw materials
   b. work in process
2. stock control

Each area is explored in Chapter Twelve.

These two basic components treat separate phases of inventory. Inventory is concerned with physical flow while stock control is directed toward information flow. From an informational flow viewpoint, questions can be raised, such as the following:

Are transfers of inventory made from one category to another as manufacturing progresses?

Are costs on items accumulated as they occur in the manufactur-ing process?

Is it possible to evaluate actual versus standard costs during the manufacturing cycle?

Are all inventories accounted for?

The answers to such questions can be designed as an integral part of a real-time management information system.

The inventory subsystem in Figure 7-12 is concerned basically with planned raw materials and nonforecasted raw materials acquisition and control. Nonfore-casted materials refer to items that are not forecasted on a quarterly basis, such as

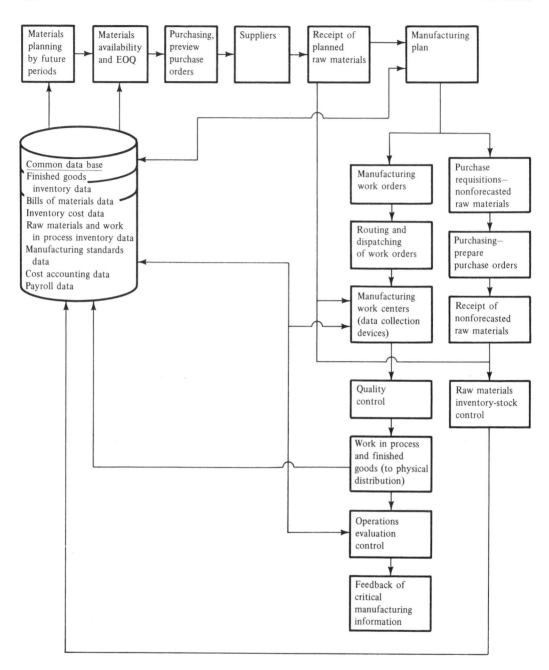

**FIGURE 7-12. Manufacture of work in process and finished goods—
important functions of the manufacturing, inventory,
and purchasing subsystems (Consumer Products Corporation).**

special production orders, experimental R & D projects, and plant maintenance supplies. Depending on the type of inventory, data files are updated before, during, and after their movement. With this approach, inventory data reflect current operations for the evaluation of actual versus standard costs. Likewise, raw materials and work-in-process data are available to other subsystems for ordering materials (purchasing subsystem) or requisitioning materials for production (manufacturing subsystem).

PURCHASING SUBSYSTEM

The purchasing subsystem, like inventory, could be considered a part of manufacturing for acquiring the necessary materials from outside suppliers. However, it will be treated as a separate subsystem, comprising the following modules (Figure 7-6):

1. buying, maintenance, and follow-up
2. vendor, buyer, and purchased-part performance

These areas comprise the subject matter for Chapter Thirteen.

Purchasing consists of more than buying materials at the lowest quoted price. In fact, this basis will probably not be an optimum one after the consideration of total procurement costs. To purchase manufacturing inputs in an efficient manner, the system should be capable of answering these basic questions:

What is the current status of orders?

Is an economic order quantity formula or an optimum number of orders per year formula being utilized?

Are other procurement costs being considered, such as clean-up costs before manufacturing, quality of materials, and delivery time?

Is past performance being analyzed before placing current orders with vendors?

Are the firm's buyers being analyzed as to their performance?

As explained in the purchasing subsystem chapter, the real-time MIS is capable of answering these questions.

The function of the purchasing subsystem, shown in Figure 7-12, is to procure planned raw materials on a quarterly basis as well as to purchase items as needs arise. Quarterly purchases represent the largest dollar amount of buying activities for the next cycle (manufacturing subsystem) of the Consumer Products Corporation. On the other hand, day-to-day purchases are applicable not only to manufacturing but also to most other subsystems because various types of forms, supplies, etc. are needed for operations. In addition to buying activities, vendor invoices must be approved by the buyer before being forwarded to the accounts-payable section (accounting subsystem).

PHYSICAL DISTRIBUTION SUBSYSTEM

The handling of finished goods after manufacturing is the responsibility of the physical distribution subsystem. Its modules (Figure 7-6) include:

1. shipping to customers and warehouses (outgoing traffic)
2. warehousing–finished goods
3. inventory–finished goods

These principal areas will be presented in Chapter Fourteen.

The manufacturing process culminates in having the finished goods transported from one of the three manufacturing plants to the customers directly (direct shipments) or to one or more of the twelve company-owned warehouses (nondirect shipments). In order to keep overall shipping costs for the firm at a minimum, the system designed must be capable of responding to these questions:

Can finished goods be allocated to warehouses such that customer orders can be filled promptly?

Can procedures be devised such that the appropriate quantity desired by customers are in the nearest warehouse to reduce shipping costs?

If goods are not available at the closest warehouse, are there procedures for locating goods at the next closest warehouse almost instantaneously?

Does the physical distribution system keep overall costs at a minimum?

These sample questions can be answered with a well-designed real-time MIS.

The shipment of finished goods, whether they be direct or nondirect, must be reflected in the company's data files. Likewise, certain file data on routing finished goods are utilized in effecting the lowest total costs. In addition, these files as shown in Figure 7-13 are referenced when finished goods are shipped to customers via order processing (marketing subsystem). As shown in Figure 7-10 previously, shipping papers, initiated by the physical distribution subsystem, start the customer billing and collection process (accounting subsystem).

ACCOUNTING SUBSYSTEM

The sales and cost factors generated by the previous subsystems are accounted for and reported by the accounting subsystem. They provide the required inputs for the accounting modules (Figure 7-6), which are:

1. receivables and payables
2. payroll
3. cost accounting
4. financial statements and tax returns

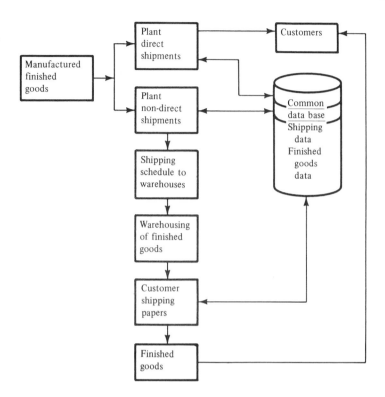

FIGURE 7-13. Distribution of finished goods from plants to warehouses and customers—the main function of the physical distribution subsystem (Consumer Products Corporation).

In Chapter Fifteen, these accounting components are discussed within the usual real-time MIS operating mode.

The accounting subsystem which involves keeping records, billing customers, arranging payments, and costing products, among others, is a myriad of details. For accounting information to assist other subsystems, it must focus on answers to these timely questions:

Can actual cost data be compared to standard data for the various manufacturing work centers?

Can information on the current status of customer accounts be obtained on a "now" basis?

Is all accounting data in a machine-processable form for compiling current financial statements?

Such an approach is found in real-time MIS for answering these typical accounting questions.

Generally, accounting activities, as set forth in Figure 7-14, center around those of recording and reporting sales and costs (expenses). Sales revenue and manufacturing cost data—raw materials, labor, and overhead—as well as marketing and general and administrative expenses, provide the necessary inputs per the general ledger for producing periodic—overall and detailed—income statements. Cash, receivables, payables, and other accounts are recorded in the general ledger for producing the balance sheet. These financial statements provide inputs for intermediate and long-range analysis (corporate planning subsystem). In a similar manner, detailed income analyses and cost(expense) analyses are helpful in determining future cash flow and capital budgets (finance subsystem).

FINANCE SUBSYSTEM

Accounting data become the needed input for the finance subsystem. By and large, this subsystem is directed toward obtaining funds for operational needs as well as evaluating projects that require funds. The essential modules of the finance subsystem (Figure 7-6) are:

1. capital budgeting
2. sources of capital
3. cash flow

These constitute the subject matter for Chapter Sixteen.

Like all other previous subsystems, common problems can be encountered. Expressed in the form of questions, typical ones are:

Are the required funds available where and when needed?
Are funds generated from the lowest cost capital source?
Are projects evaluated accurately in terms of cost factors?
Do projects go beyond just considering tangible benefits?

A real-time management information system, although it does not provide answers to this type of questions directly, does assist by generating instantaneous information to speed up the procurement of funds and evaluation of capital projects.

Sales—receivables and disbursements—payables information (accounting subsystem) as shown in Figure 7-15 are projected by the finance subsystem, providing cash flow for the next month and future periods. In order to undertake large capital projects, additional sources of capital may be necessary and may be obtained from outside sources—banks, financial institutions, bonds, debentures, and capital stock. Internal and external sources of funds should be committed only to those capital projects that meet an established return on investment (ROI). However, in some cases, tangible and intangible factors must be considered for a final decision, as in a real-time MIS project. As noted in the illustration, the capital projects and their sources of funds are integrated into the central subsystem around which all others focus (corporate planning subsystem).

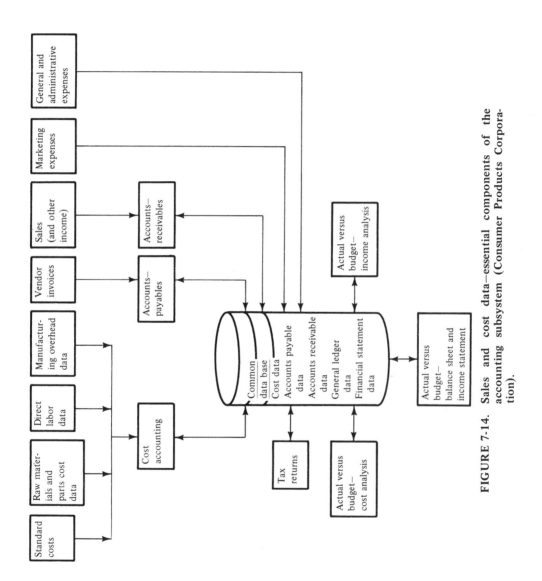

FIGURE 7-14. Sales and cost data—essential components of the accounting subsystem (Consumer Products Corporation).

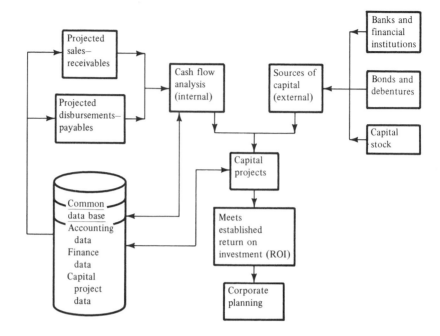

FIGURE 7-15. Financial sources for capital projects—an essential part of the finance subsystem (Consumer Products Corporation).

PERSONNEL SUBSYSTEM

Personnel, whose basic objective is to find "the right man for the right job," comes into contact with most other subsystems in fulfilling this stated purpose. To assist the personnel subsystem in this endeavor, certain modules (Figure 7-6) are necessary:

1. skills inventory
2. personnel selection and placement
3. training and education
4. wage and salary administration

Each area is detailed in Chapter Seventeen.

The recruitment of personnel for desired positions can be an extremely difficult task for any personnel department. Typical questions centering around recruitment are:

Can the position be better filled by someone within the firm?

Can the position be filled now as opposed to a later date by someone internally?

Has the best man been found for the job by exhausting internal and external recruiting procedures?

Many of these questions can be answered within a real-time MIS environment, especially those dealing with internal recruitment of present employees for new job openings.

The personnel subsystem, depicted in Figure 7-16, is designed to locate employees who have certain skills within the firm's operations by interrogating the skills-inventory data file. A listing of potential employees for job openings is scrutinized by the personnel department for immediate action. In addition, employee files can be utilized for paying employees (accounting subsystem) as well as providing a starting basis when negotiating with the firm's labor union. The personnel subsystem, then, is an integral part of the firm's subsystems when the focal point is the human element.

SUMMARY

Essentially, the chapter has focused on an overview of the Consumer Products Corporation in a real-time MIS environment. The various subsystems were treated on an integrated basis, indicating the direction taken in subsequent chapters. From this viewpoint, the feasibility of implementing an effective real-time management information system is validated.

Real-time MIS, as pointed out repeatedly in this chapter, represents the flow of information through the organization. It is structured such that information flows from one subsystem to another in order to provide the information when and where it is needed. In a real sense, real-time MIS represents the internal communications network of the business, providing the necessary intelligence to organize, direct, and control according to corporate plans. Stated another way, it is a reorientation of traditional information flow from a basic purpose of recording

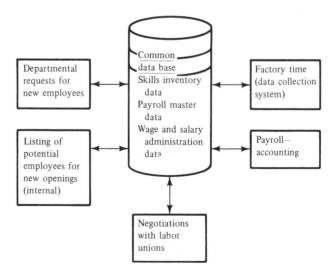

FIGURE 7-16. Essential personnel functions found in the personnel subsystem (Consumer Products Corporation).

what happened to a new purpose of telling not only what happened, but also how and why it happened, the amount of deviations from the plans, and the effect on the plans. A history-keeping orientation is replaced by a management planning and control orientation. Real-time MIS, then, utilizes plans, policies, methods, procedures, and control guidelines; mixes these with people; adds integrated operating information; and comes out with the organized use of data for better decisions.

In addition to the concept of integrated subsystems, a real-time MIS includes many other equally important characteristics. Among the more important ones to be emphasized in future chapters are

> on-line real-time processing—ability to make changes in time sufficient to control the environment
>
> forward-looking control system—ability to control current and future activities
>
> common data base—ability of all subsystems to reference the same data base elements
>
> I/O-oriented—ability to reference on-line data from remote I/O terminal devices
>
> timely and better reports—ability to practice exception reporting in order to control ongoing operations, especially at the lower and middle management levels
>
> operations research models—ability to control the operating environment through standard and custom-made OR techniques
>
> local and remote batch processing—ability to process small and large volumes of batch data from local (on-site) and remote locations.

With such desirable characteristics, the firm can start with market forecasts and control its operations in real time through timely and accurate decisions.

QUESTIONS

1. Suppose the Consumer Products Corporation was a much larger firm—would the data processing organization structure change in a real-time MIS environment?

2. a. Suggest alternative ways of setting up the data communications network for the Consumer Products Corporation in a real-time MIS operating mode.

b. Suggest an alternative way of setting up the hardware environment for the Consumer Products Corporation in a real-time MIS operating mode.

3. What problems are expected to be encountered by the Consumer Products Corporation when it changes from an integrated MIS to a real-time MIS?

4. What characteristics are found in a real-time MIS environment for the Consumer Products Corporation that are not present in integrated MIS?

5. What changes from an integrated MIS must be undertaken to design an effective real-time MIS for the Consumer Products Corporation?

6. How do the various subsystems and the component modules presented in the chapter differ in a real-time MIS from an integrated MIS for the Consumer Products Corporation?

7. Suggest additional modules for each of the subsystems presented in the chapter for the Consumer Products Corporation.

8. Can a real-time MIS be implemented for very large corporations, such as AT&T and General Motors?

REFERENCES

Barlow, G., "Development of Online Processing," *Computer Decisions,* May, 1974.

Bower, J. B., Schlosser, R. E., and Zlatkovich, C. T., *Financial Information Systems,* Boston, Mass.: Allyn and Bacon, Inc., 1969, Chap. 3.

Cassimus, P., "Design Considerations for Real/Time Systems," *Journal of Systems Management,* December, 1969.

Cornish, F. B., "Management Information Systems—Cause and Effect," *Managerial Planning,* January-February, 1971.

Couger, J. D., and Wergin, L. M., "Small Company MIS," *Infosystems,* October, 1974.

Farber, D. J., "Networks: An Introduction," *Datamation,* April, 1972.

Gildersleeve, T. R., "Organizing the Data Processing Function," *Datamation,* November, 1974.

Haavind, R., "Adding People to the MIS Loop," *Computer Decisions,* July, 1972.

Head, R. V., "Real-time Applications," *Journal of Systems Management,* September, 1974.

Hindman, W. R., "Integrated MIS: A Case Study," *Management Accounting* August, 1973.

Hodge, B., "The Computer in Management Information and Control System," *Data Management,* December, 1974.

Hopeman, R. J., *Systems Analysis and Operations Management.* Columbus, Ohio: Charles E. Merrill Publishing Co., 1969, Chap. 1.

Huhn, G. E., "The Data Base in a Critical On-Line Business Environment," *Datamation,* September, 1974.

Lowe, R. L., "The Corporate Datacenter: Getting It All Together," *Computer Decisions,* May, 1973.

Nolan, R. L., and Knutsen, K. E., "The Computerization of the ABC Widget Company," *Datamation,* April, 1974.

Prince, T. R., *Information Systems for Management Planning and Control.* Homewood, Ill.: Richard D. Irwin, Inc., 1970, Chap. 14.

Reside, K. D. and Seiter, T. J., "The Evolution of an Integrated Data Base," *Datamation,* September, 1974.

Sayer, W., "Galion: Blueprint for a Total Management System," *Modern Office Procedures,* February, 1970.

Seese, D. A., "Initiating a Total Information System," *Journal of Systems Management,* April, 1970.

Tersine, R. J., "Systems Theory in Modern Organizations," *Managerial Planning,* November/December, 1973.

Zani, W. M., "Blueprint for MIS," *Harvard Business Review,* November-December, 1970.

REAL-TIME MIS
CORPORATE PLANNING SUBSYSTEM

8

Corporate planning, the first of many subsystems to be examined in detail, is the focal point of any management information system. Its purpose is to decide what to do in terms of small-, medium-, and large-scale projects; how to implement projects in terms of men, materials, machines (including plant facilities), money, and management; and when to perform them in terms of short-, intermediate-, and long-range plans in order to accomplish company goals and objectives. There are important relationships and feedback found interacting among these three planning stages, but they are complicated; this fact plus revenue and cost factors make it extremely important that MIS management establish a highly systematic and analytic approach for corporate planning. The best approach for deciding what to do, how to do it, and when to do it is through systematic procedures in the corporate planning subsystem.

Like all succeeding chapters on the Consumer Products Corporation, the major elements of the prior system (integrated MIS) are explored before investigating essential design considerations for real-time MIS. Data base elements, OR models, and modules are examined for a corporate planning MIS subsystem, thereby providing a frame of reference for designing the following major components:

> long-range planning
> medium-range planning
> short-range planning

Basically, this subsystem is structured on these three important functions which, when performed effectively, allow information to flow upward and downward for effective corporate planning of the firm's many activities.

INTEGRATED MIS CORPORATE PLANNING SUBSYSTEM

The corporate planning subsystem for the Consumer Products Corporation operates in a much different manner than all other subsystems within an integrated MIS environment. Critical internal factors are received from the firm's subsystems for short-, medium-, and long-range planning as well as certain information is fed back to the appropriate subsystems where major deviations from plans occur. In like manner, feedback is utilized within the corporate planning subsystem itself to alter plans at the various levels. This overall internal data flow is depicted in Figure 8-1 along with the external factors that provide input for corporate planning. The center of all strategic planning activities for the firm's many subsystems, then, is the corporate planning function.

Corporate planning information is directed toward all management levels for planning, organizing, directing, and controlling the firm's activities. However, the greatest accent is on the management planning function. Planning information is of three basic types:

1. environmental—describes the social, political, and economic climate in which the firm operates now and in the future
2. competitive—explains the past performance, present programs, and upcoming programs of competing firms
3. internal—describes the firm's internal operations for evaluative purposes

In order to utilize this information (generated for the corporate planning subsystem) in an optimum manner, the Consumer Products Corporation created a staff group (consisting of two high-level employees) which is responsible for all corporate planning activities. This group is free from day-to-day activities and is charged with the responsibility of assisting the president. Among their most crucial functions are:

> To establish new and challenging standards of performance that are in conformity with the firm's goals, objectives, policies, and procedures
> To assure that growth plans on a one- to five-year basis are prepared

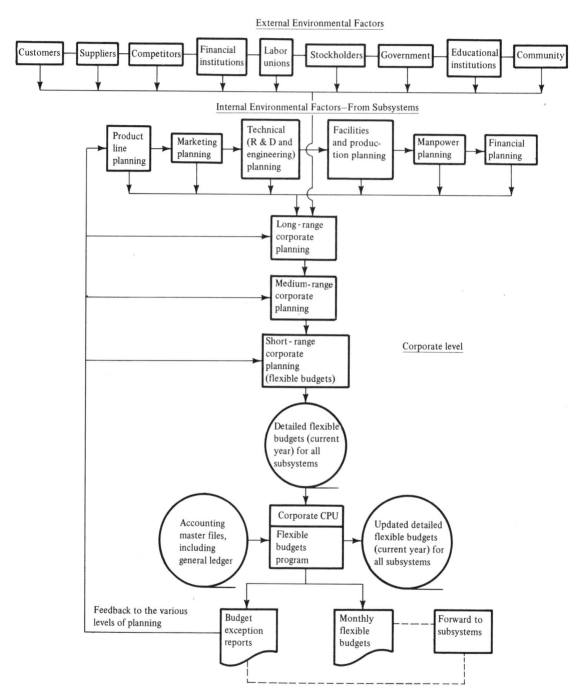

FIGURE 8-1. Corporate planning data flow for an integrated MIS
system.

To assist the various subsystems in the preparation of one- to five-year projections

To identify areas of product opportunity for corporate investment

To coordinate and monitor the preparation of a plan for longer than five years

To analyze the economic future of existing operations and to recommend programs of growth

To make analyses of business, economic, and social conditions bearing on existing or prospective areas of operations

After chief operating executives have reviewed the work of this high-level staff, evaluated the one- to five-year forecast, and are convinced that the financial figures are reasonable and feasible, the composite documents thereby gathered constitute the corporate plan for the stated period of years ahead. Sometimes these "working papers" are regarded as company goals, objectives, and plans. In other cases their significant elements are formalized into corporate goals and the various segments of the corporate plans for achievement are clearly spelled out in great detail. However, when the chief operating executives conclude that the anticipated results are not adequate, it becomes imperative that the planning staff create and construct a new or modified set of goals and a new plan to fulfill desired objectives.

LONG-RANGE CORPORATE PLANNING

Long-range planning starts with a realistic understanding of existing products, divisions, markets, margins, profits, return on investment, cash flow, availability of capital, research and development abilities, and skills and capacities of personnel, to name some of the more important areas. Analysis of present operations can be performed effectively by reviewing the past few years' performance as part of the evaluation of the current year's operating and capital budget forecasts. Significant aspects of current operations, evaluated in an orderly manner, are the basis for considering how well the goals and objectives are currently being met by the firm. In like manner, explicit plans for the next three to five years, based on current operations and existing plans for improving operations, become an essential part of a sound corporate planning program.

For the Consumer Products Corporation, an outline of a five-year strategic plan includes external and internal factors enumerated in Figure 8-1. The latter aspects, which are controllable by the firm, are summarized as follows:

1. *Product line planning*—aimed at expanding the present product lines and entering new product markets. Also includes expanding the present customer base by serving new market segments.
2. *Marketing planning*—increased use of selling outlets and/or distribution to sell the firm's products, changes in pricing policy and pricing practices to effect higher sales, and consideration of new advertising media for more effective penetration of the firm's markets.

3. *Technical (R & D and engineering) planning*—geared toward creating new or improved products for established markets and for those markets in which the firm does not participate or has such a small share as to be negligible.

4. *Facilities and production planning*—directed toward major facilities contemplated and improvements in processing efficiency. Also, includes the percent of capacity that is now and will be employed with present facilities and machinery as well as the steps that are being undertaken to utilize excess capacity where available.

5. *Manpower planning*—projected manpower requirements for key management personnel and production labor when considering turnover and future growth.

6. *Financial planning*—directed toward projected sales by product lines, gross profit (sales less manufacturing costs) by product lines, sales and general and administrative expenses, net profit by product lines, fixed and working capital needs, return on investment by product lines, and comparable financial analyses and ratios.

Although the firm has used past and present operations as a starting basis for projected long-range corporate plans, the planning staff has not employed the data bank of its integrated MIS to produce meaningful long-range information, except in the area of manufacturing. By and large, the planning group has been using the printed output of the many subsystems to finalize its three- to five-year programs. Probably the most important reason for not employing advanced data processing techniques is that the firm's managers must first be educated to the need for sound long-range plans. Then they must be taught to integrate all the elements of long-range planning with their programs. In this regard, a checklist of key elements might be extremely helpful to make certain that programs have been thoroughly analyzed. Generally, it would include:

> analyses—logical process of projecting the future
> potentials—skills as well as resources that are available and needed
> problems—apparent deficiencies
> establishment of best alternatives—suggested economic goals
> coordination, implementation, timing—expected results in both
> financial and nonfinancial terms

The foregoing listing enables managers to assess the reasonableness of their goals and objectives so as to come up with long-term policies that are realistic for integrating with other corporate goals and objectives as formulated by the planning group. In essence, the corporate planning group must impress upon managers an awareness of the importance of long-range planning as a vital part of their jobs.

Referring to integrated MIS for long-range manufacturing needs, input of proposed facilities (capacity available) and proposed products (time requirement and cost factors) is needed, as shown in Figure 8-2. These inputs, combined with the production scheduling data file which represents available capacity of present facilities plus time and cost factors of present products, are processed against a

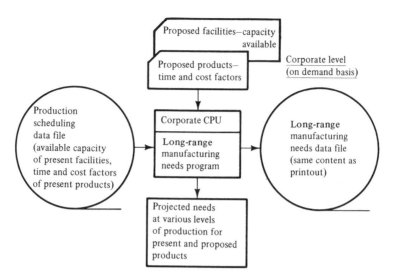

FIGURE 8-2. Long-range manufacturing needs as determined by an integrated MIS corporate planning subsystem.

linear programming program for printed output. Linear programming determines what products are to be manufactured in what plants, based on the new constraints and cost factors of the problem.

MEDIUM-RANGE CORPORATE PLANNING

Medium-range corporate planning, which centers around the second-year planning period, is a subset of long-range planning as shown in Figure 8-1. The five-year strategic plan that revolves around product line, marketing, technical, facilities and production, manpower, and financial planning is stated in more detail for this level.

The budgeting process for medium- (and short-) range corporate planning has several important aspects when utilized in conjunction with a computer system. First, certain assumptions as to what will happen by "passing" the transactions representing these assumptions through the budget system can be tested. Second, the firm can perceive what the financial effects will be—that is, whether they are favorable or unfavorable. Third, the budget system can determine whether or not some condition or constraint has been violated; for example, if working capital availability in the future has been violated. In reality, an integrated MIS approach to budgeting permits the firm to respond to the dynamics of the situation. It allows changes to medium- (and short-) range budgets whenever something significant happens to alter conditions. In addition, an integrated MIS provides an initial exposure to the fundamentals of financial modeling which will be helpful in a real-time MIS operating mode.

The more important budgets required for the second (and first year) are set forth in Figure 8-3. Initially, the areas of marketing and manufacturing are detailed before appropriate budgets are determined for selling, material purchases, labor, manufacturing overhead, and general and administrative expenses. All of the income and expense factors are expressed in terms of a cash budget. Finally, the results of the preceding budgets are expressed in a projected balance sheet and an income statement with supporting schedules and sources and applications of funds. It should be noted that throughout the budgeting analysis phase, certain constraints can be integrated in the budgeting process if and when deemed necessary by the planning group.

SHORT-RANGE CORPORATE PLANNING (FLEXIBLE BUDGETS)

Short-range planning, like medium-range planning, is an extension of long-range plans. The end result of all short-range planning activities focuses on flexible (variable) budgets which are developed for stated levels of possible production. In Figure 8-4, the overall budget for the Consumer Products Corporation is broken down further as is also shown in Figure 8-5 for the various possible levels of productive capacity, based on one of the firm's basic product groups. Other exhibits are also prepared—in particular, those by the major subsystems and manufacturing work centers. All of these budgets provide a basis for comparing projected to actual results.

Referring again to Figure 8-1, detailed, current-year flexible budgets for all subsystems and current month's accounting figures (both on magnetic tape) provide the necessary input for the computer's flexible budget program. Output is in the form of an updated magnetic tape and flexible budget reports which are forwarded to the appropriate subsystem. Similarly, budget exception reports are produced. Based upon the type and amount of deviations, information is fed back to specific management and planning levels. In this manner, adjustments can be made if conditions warrant.

REAL-TIME MIS DESIGN CONSIDERATIONS
FOR CORPORATE PLANNING SUBSYSTEM

As previously stated, the central point for design considerations in real-time MIS environment is the corporate planning subsystem; this subsystem is affected by external and internal factors which, in turn, have direct or indirect effects on the firm's other subsystems. For example, an overall change of one corporate objective, say customer service level, necessitates a change not only within the corporate planning subsystem, but also within those subsystems necessary to fulfill this desired objective. To take any other approach will generally not result in the most effective real-time MIS.

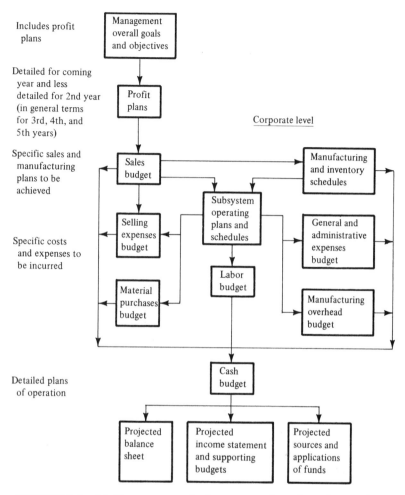

Includes profit
plans

Detailed for coming
year and less
detailed for 2nd year
(in general terms
for 3rd, 4th, and
5th years)

Specific sales and
manufacturing
plans to be
achieved

Specific costs
and expenses to
be incurred

Detailed plans
of operation

FIGURE 8-3.   Medium-range and short-range data flow for an integrated MIS corporate planning subsystem.

OVERVIEW OF CORPORATE PLANNING ENVIRONMENT

The major functions found in the corporate planning environment are the same for integrated and real-time MIS. As illustrated in Figure 8-6, they range from short- to long-range, planning. However, the structure of these functions is different owing to the computer's real-time capabilities. A certain amount of corporate planning data will be stored on the common data base and retrievable upon request by the corporate planning staff. Specifically, flexible budget data as well as current and past results of operations are capable of being extracted as input

By Basic Product Groups (values stated in thousands)

	1*	2	3	4	5	6	7	Totals
Sales	$4,120	$16,730	$14,150	$20,400	$15,940	$11,410	$11,800	$94,550
Variable Costs:								
Manufacturing	2,000	6,410	5,100	8,030	6,050	4,600	4,850	37,040
Marketing	200	2,340	2,200	2,520	2,290	1,070	1,080	11,700
Contribution to Fixed Costs and Profits	1,920	7,980	6,850	9,850	7,600	5,740	5,870	45,810
Fixed Costs:								
Manufacturing	410	2,640	2,420	2,900	2,600	2,180	2,200	15,350
Marketing	430	2,700	2,440	2,980	2,650	2,190	2,210	15,600
General & Admin.	280	590	280	670	430	110	120	2,480
Net Profit Before Federal Income Taxes	800	2,050	1,710	3,300	1,920	1,260	1,340	12,380
Federal Income Taxes	384	1,984	820	1,584	922	605	643	5,942
Net Profit After Federal Income Taxes	$ 416	$ 1,066	$ 890	$ 1,716	$ 998	$ 655	$ 697	$ 6,438

*Refer to Figure 8-5.

FIGURE 8-4. Budgeted income statement of the Consumer Products Corporation—computed at 80% of capacity for next year.

	Percent of Capacity (values stated in thousands)				
	70%	75%	80%	85%	90%
Sales	$3,718	$3,914	$4,120	$4,326	$4,542
Manufacturing variable costs					
Direct material	495	523	550	578	605
Direct labor	810	855	900	945	990
Indirect labor	71	76	80	84	88
Overtime	71	76	80	84	88
Fringe benefits	36	38	40	42	44
Supplies	90	95	100	105	110
Main. and repairs	18	19	20	21	22
Scrappage	45	47	50	53	55
Perishable tools	36	38	40	42	44
Utilities	72	76	80	84	88
Other manufacturing variable costs	54	57	60	64	66
Total	1,798	1,900	2,000	2,102	2,288
Marketing variable costs					
Commissions	108	114	120	126	132
Fringe benefits	13	14	15	16	17
Freight out	51	53	55	57	60
Other marketing variable costs	8	9	10	11	11
Total	180	190	200	210	220
Contribution to Fixed Costs and Profits	1,740	1,824	1,920	2,014	2,034
Manufacturing fixed costs					
Rent	40	40	40	40	40
Depreciation & amort.	200	200	200	200	200
Insurance	40	40	40	40	40
Taxes—real estate	30	30	30	30	30
Taxes—personal prop.	50	50	50	50	50
Other manufacturing fixed costs	20	20	20	20	20
Total	410	410	410	410	410
Marketing fixed costs					
Marketing salaries	150	150	150	150	150
Fringe benefits	25	25	25	25	25
Advertising	200	200	200	200	200
Travel & entertainment	25	25	25	25	25
Special promotions	25	25	25	25	25
Other marketing fixed costs	30	30	30	30	30
Total	430	430	430	430	430
General & administrative fixed costs					
Officer's salaries	110	110	110	110	110
Fringe benefits	20	20	20	20	20
Office salaries	100	100	100	100	100
Rent	10	10	10	10	10
Interest	10	10	10	10	10
Contributions	5	5	5	5	5
Bad debts	10	10	10	10	10
Insurance	10	10	10	10	10
Misc. taxes and other general & admin. costs	5	5	5	5	5
Total	280	280	280	280	280
Net Profit Before Federal Income Taxes	$ 620	$ 704	$ 800	$ 894	$ 914

FIGURE 8-5. Budgeted income statement of the Consumer Products Corporation—basic product group 1 for next year.

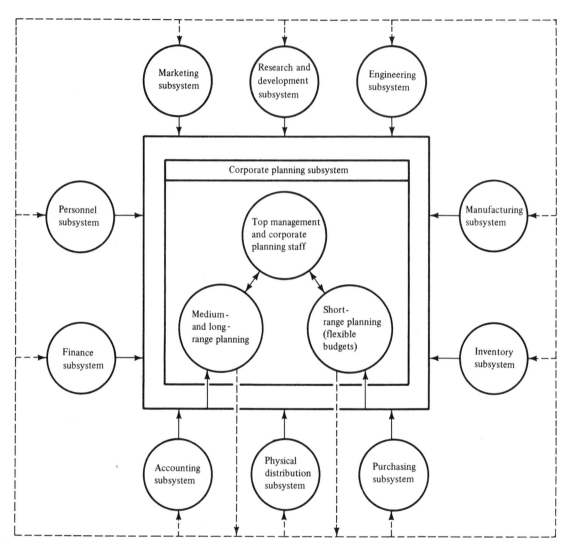

———— Information flow of current operations
— — — Feedback after analysis of current operations

FIGURE 8-6. Real-time MIS corporate planning subsystem flow to and from other subsystems.

for forecasting future sales, costs values, and similar information. Also, data on product lines, marketing, technical, facilities and production, manpower, and financial planning are retrievable from the common data base for corporate planning analysis.

Use of on-line data base elements, for example, could involve a series of values describing sales for a particular product over a period of years. Statistical treatment of this series would produce a forecast of future sales with a high degree of accuracy, including appropriate adjustments for seasonal trends and cyclical conditions. A statistical approach can also determine whether one cost account predicts the behavior of another or is dependent upon another and in what way. This leads to a series of observations about the character of the data. Or consider the situation where a statistical relationship between sales and several significant costs has been ascertained whereby an equation can be written to arrive at net income. Once the profit and loss environment has been modeled, this can be put to work by making assumptions about what is going to happen. The model has taken the form of a program which can interact with the common data base. Thus, the program can try certain assumptions and examine results on a real-time basis. By trial and error, certain assumptions can be examined, resulting in a better understanding of future operating conditions for improved corporate planning.

CORPORATE PLANNING DATA BASE

The corporate planning data bank (magnetic tape files for integrated MIS), consisting basically of flexible budgeting and production facilities data, must be converted to an on-line basis. These data, along with additional data as set forth in Figure 8-7, form the basis for the firm's corporate planning data base. The corporate planning data start with the long run, stated in general terms, followed by the short and intermediate runs in more specific terms. With this approach, corporate planning data can be structured in a logical manner, making programming and data retrieving a much easier job.

Structuring the corporate planning data base centers around the ability to move data from one level to another. Data generated and stored for long-range planning should be capable of providing input for medium-range planning—in particular, data for next year's financial budgets. These budgets, in turn, should be usable for preparing detailed budgets for the coming year. Of course, it is recognized that changes must be effected at all three planning levels. Changes can originate from many sources. External environmental factors can have a direct bearing on established plans, as can internal feedback from current and proposed operations. The employment of I/O terminal devices to make the required changes is an essential part of maintaining an up-to-date corporate planning data base. Thus, an orderly data base structure is an important design consideration for all corporate planning levels, particularly in relation to changes necessitated by external and internal factors.

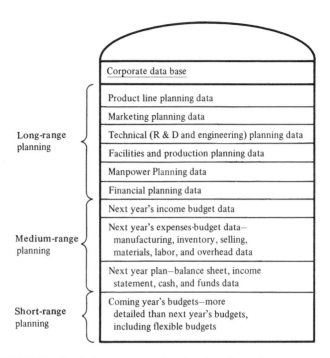

FIGURE 8-7. Typical corporate planning data base elements.

OR CORPORATE PLANNING MODELS

OR corporate planning models are capable of viewing the overall operations (macro) or a specific area (micro) of the firm. Generally, these models are concerned with the firm's finances and rely on simulation for their mathematical basis of analyses. Before presenting simulation—defined in Appendix A—on a macro and a micro level, key uses of corporate planning models are discussed.

The most obvious use of a corporate planning model is to assist in the development of long-range corporate plans. An appropriately designed model is capable, in theory, of projecting the financial results of a company for an unlimited number of years. As a practical matter, the user will usually be restrained by his diminishing confidence in the correctness of assumed conditions in distant years. To develop a plan, a variety of alternative courses of action should be investigated under different sets of assumed conditions whereby the most appropriate corporate plans can be selected. Whenever new information causes changes to be made, the corporate model can be used to evaluate the effect of a revised plan quickly and inexpensively.

The utilization of a corporate model for long- and medium-range planning provides other benefits to the planner; it forces him to state explicitly his assumptions. Assumed conditions can easily be made a regular part of a corporate model. Use of the computer also results in the employment of precise, reproducible, and documented methods. Discussion and analysis of the plans by the executives can then be based on an objective understanding of the underlying assumptions, conditions, and projection methods, thereby eliminating misunderstandings arising from ambiguous assumptions and unclear programs.

A second use of a corporate model is for short-range planning. The model can be designed to project results on a month-by-month or even week-by-week basis. It can be used to evaluate plans for the current year, taking into consideration year-to-date actual figures and the conditions expected to prevail throughout the remainder of the year. Such use would be particularly valuable for cash forecasting (cash management).

A third use of a corporate planning model is to undertake special studies which result from "what if" questions asked by top management. The timing of the requests for these special studies is often unpredictable and, when handled manually, can result in a scheduling crisis for the planning staff. This problem is minimized when a computerized model is used. Many "what if" questions arise from an unexpected change in the environment or a new insight on the part of management. For example, studies have been triggered by proposals for revising the tax laws. Management typically wants to know what effect these proposed changes will have on earnings, cash flow, future financing, and capital expenditure plans. A corporate planning model can provide information for answering such questions by comparing the projected results, using the existing tax regulations and then various proposed regulations.

Macrosimulation

Generally, the focus of a corporate planning model is on the entire firm. This approach emphasizes a global or overall management viewpoint in the analysis of problems and enhances the likelihood of capturing the full impact of proposed financial courses of action. A macro corporate planning model demands company-wide effort to take advantage of the knowledge and expertise in all subsystems of the firm. In order for the macro approach to be highly successful in evaluating the financial results of alternative courses of action, the model must contain appropriate subsystem details.

Simulating complex relationships on the macro level should both depict those of interacting subsystems and consider the time factor within these subsystems. Relationships frequently change as time passes. For example, expenditures for research (R & D subsystem) are not expected to produce revenue (marketing subsystem) in the immediate period because they are investments in future revenue. Administrative expenses may follow changes in revenue and, in other cases, lag. It is essential, then, that the time relationship of the model be representative of the firm's own processes. Similarly, the simulation model must be consistent with the financial practice of the firm in order to reflect policies and procedures of management. An overview of a corporate planning simulation model that considers these factors is illustrated in Figure 8-8 with sample inputs and outputs as well as the required submodels.

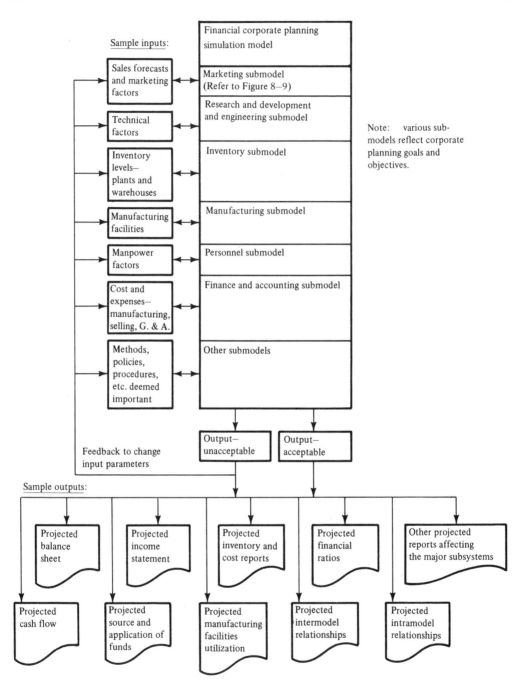

FIGURE 8-8. An overview of a financial corporate planning simulation model that depicts sample inputs and outputs.

Microsimulation

The overall or macro model llustrated in Figure 8-8 indicates that a series of submodels are required, resulting in a new simulation approach. Once the overview model has been validated, the next step is to diagram each submodel in more detail. Figure 8-9 illustrates how the marketing submodel, like the other submodels, would be structured for the Consumer Products Corporation. Basically, the marketing system is divided into six important parts:

1. The external environment model relates those forces in the environment that affect consumer demand.
2. The overall marketing decision model is tied in with its competitors' decision model. Also, it is related to other submodels (refer to Figure 8-8).
3. The detailed marketing decision models are associated with product lines, product prices, sales force, physical distribution and service, and advertising and sales promotion.
4. The physical distribution models center around direct and nondirect shipments using company-owned warehouses.
5. The customer behavior model shows the response of customers to the detailed marketing decision models, physical distribution models, and the external environment model.
6. The sales and costs models reflect the output of the previous models in the illustration, which then provide input for the firm's marketing decision model (see [2] above).

The level of detail for the marketing submodel should not end here; further refinements in terms of inputs and outputs are necessary for each box in Figure 8-9. For example, consider the firm's marketing decision model, which is set forth in Figure 8-10, for sample inputs and outputs. To obtain this information, marketing executives are asked to identify the major types of marketing decisions made in the firm and then list the various inputs and influences on these decisions. For the Consumer Products Corporation, they are:

> short- to long-range goals and objectives
> forecasted environmental factors
> competitive marketing factors

Each of their subparts is found in the illustration and can be elaborated further. Although this level of detail is not shown, it is necessary for a comprehensive marketing decision model. Thus, the attendant circumstances will dictate the level of detail necessary for each submodel of the financial corporate planning simulation model.

CORPORATE PLANNING MODULES

The major corporate planning modules and their submodules, set forth in Figure 8-11, are essential for the detailed design of this subsystem. As with most other subsystems, these modules must be coordinated with other modules.

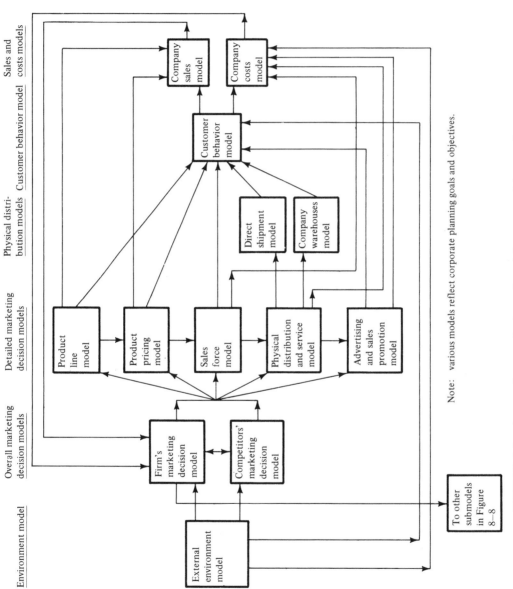

Environment model   Overall marketing   Detailed marketing   Physical distri-   Customer behavior model   Sales and
                    decision models   decision models   bution models   costs models

Note: various models reflect corporate planning goals and objectives.

FIGURE 8-9.   A complete marketing submodel, an essential part of a financial corporate planning simulation model.

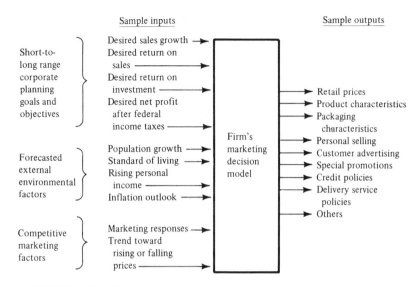

Sample inputs   Sample outputs

Short-to-long range corporate planning goals and objectives
- Desired sales growth →
- Desired return on sales →
- Desired return on investment →
- Desired net profit after federal income taxes →

Forecasted external environmental factors
- Population growth →
- Standard of living →
- Rising personal income →
- Inflation outlook →

Competitive marketing factors
- Marketing responses →
- Trend toward rising or falling prices →

Firm's marketing decision model

- Retail prices
- Product characteristics
- Packaging characteristics
- Personal selling
- Customer advertising
- Special promotions
- Credit policies
- Delivery service policies
- Others

FIGURE 8-10. Sample inputs and outputs of the firm's marketing decision model.

Basically, modules for the other major subsystems of the Consumer Products Corporation must be surveyed to insure compatibility in the system's final design. Otherwise, duplicated modules will abound in a real-time MIS environment.

A review of the corporate planning modules shown in Figure 8-11 indicates duplication. However, on closer examination, it will be found that submodules are for different time periods, thereby indicating a varying level of detail. For example, the long-range planning modules for projected cash flow, balance sheet, income statement, and source and application of funds are stated in general terms, while comparable values for medium-range planning are much more detailed. Similarly, values for short-range planning are even more detailed, making them feasible for controlling the firm's upcoming operations. Thus, the time period dictates the level of detail.

REAL-TIME MIS CORPORATE PLANNING SUBSYSTEM

The foregoing investigation of important corporate planning real-time MIS design considerations—namely, the data base, OR models, and modules—is helpful to systems personnel before undertaking the detailed design of this subsystem. The data base must be designed such that long-range plans can be eventually translated into medium-range plans, and finally, into short-range plans. This succession of longer-range plans to current plans calls for a structure of data elements that can be moved from one level to another with a minimum of difficulty. In essence, data base elements should be capable of meeting the needs of all planning levels rather than

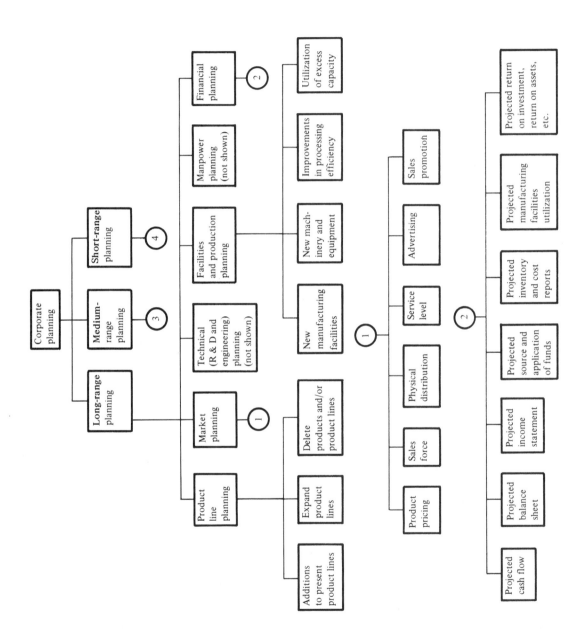

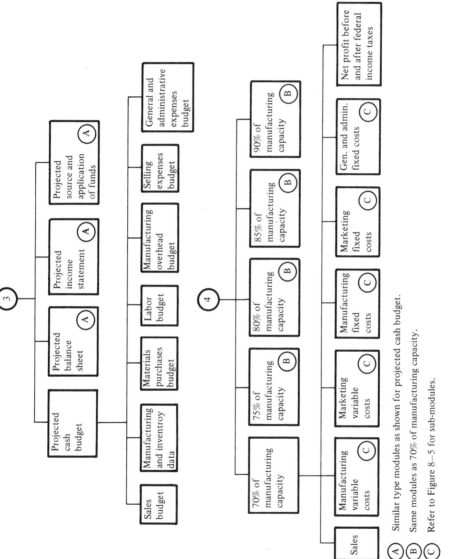

FIGURE 8-11. Corporate planning modules of the Consumer Products Corporation.

(A) Similar type modules as shown for projected cash budget.

(B) Same modules as 70% of manufacturing capacity.

(C) Refer to Figure 8–5 for sub-modules.

only selected ones. Otherwise, availability of storage will be a problem, not to mention the programming difficulties in such an environment. Thus, a thorough analysis of the data base and its requirements is a must if essential corporate planning data are to be forthcoming in a real-time MIS operating mode.

CORPORATE PLANNING SUBSYSTEM OVERVIEW

A corporate planning subsystem within a real-time MIS is linked directly with other subsystems through the internal environmental factors, as shown in Figure 8-12. In a similar manner, planning activities are related to external environmental factors through the firm's goals and objectives. Both internal and external factors form the basis for short- to long-range data base elements. These data elements, when used in conjunction with the appropriate program, provide the necessary corporate planning output for the various time levels. The ability to extract on-line data "now" makes this subsystem a forward-looking one. Information can be obtained in real time to answer "what if" questions about the future. From this viewpoint, the corporate planning subsystem utilizes advanced operations research techniques to answer tomorrow's questions in view of today's projections. The ability to extract answers for "what if" questions is a source of power that may make the difference between just meeting competition and beating it.

LONG-RANGE CORPORATE PLANNING MODULE

Long-range corporate planning in a real-time MIS environment can be accomplished effectively by utilizing the OR simulation model discussed previously. The financial corporate planning simulation model makes possible low-cost experimentation for long-range analysis and is also an efficient method for observing the dynamic behavior of a complex system under a wide variety of assumptions about the future. In a sense, this technique is like a laboratory experiment in which observations are made under carefully controlled conditions. Only one variable is altered so that its singular effect can be recorded. Then other variables can be changed in order to measure the interaction of various parts of the system.

Another reason for using the simulation model in long-range analysis is the predictive capabilities the method possesses. The model creates artificial time periods and thus, when provided with certain inputs, it can forecast desired outputs or whatever else it is designed to answer. Flexibility can be built into such models so that conditions under which the system is operating can be altered. This makes possible conditional forecasting or budgeting for the "what if" situations. Various projections can be obtained and the sensitivity of a company's financial performance to various conditions can be better understood.

A real-time MIS simulation model provides better answers to many of the problems confronting the Consumer Products Corporation. These include improved sales forecasting for the firm's basic product lines, optimum allocation of future advertising budgets, improved service to customers through more effective plant utilization and shipping schedules between plants and warehouses, improved vendor

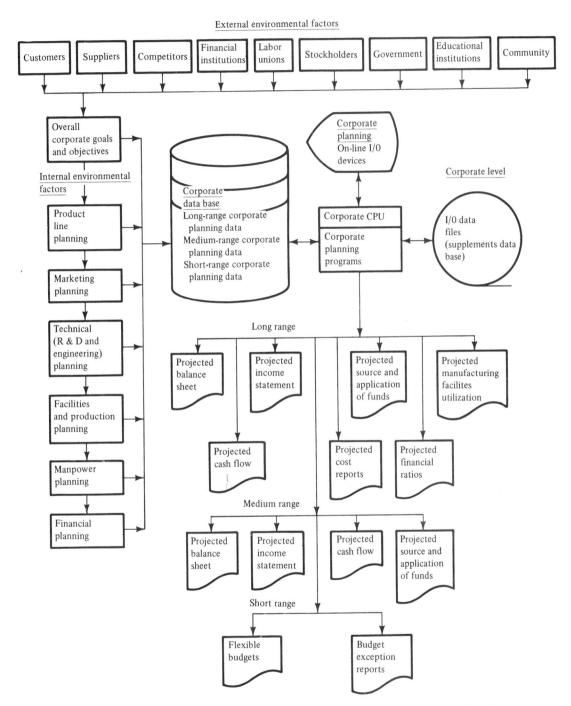

FIGURE 8-12. An overview of a real-time MIS corporate planning subsystem.

performance, and higher return on total assets. Other possible long-run outputs are evaluation of growth objectives, cash flow, financial and debt management, asset management, manpower planning, and profit maximization by product lines. In addition to providing management with desired long-range output, the simulation model actually improves the decision-making ability of managers. It points out inconsistent areas in decision making, allows the testing of independent decisions, and enforces planning discipline by having the manager specify formal relationships.

As shown in Figure 8-13, the financial corporate planning simulation model interacts with the data base elements and data files. The corporate computer is accessed through a remote I/O terminal. For example, management desires to develop, analyze, and evaluate the projected financial position of the company which will penetrate an uncertain market of five years and beyond. The financial model examines the investment decision. It operates on market projections and cost figures, and produces pro forma financial statements on a quarterly basis over the planning period of five years. It assumes that costs as provided by the finance and accounting departments and the revenues derived from the market are valid numbers. Uncertainties in the basic assumptions are not explicitly treated by the model. If the costs are exactly as stated, if the implementation plan and spending rate proceed as indicated by the inputs to the program, and if the market provides the revenue indicated, reliable financial information is produced by the model. Sensitivity tests show the importance of each basic assumption, develop important cost relationships, and show financial trends.

The corporate data base shown in Figure 8-13 is augmented by data files which are structured such that they are simple to maintain. Magnetic tape data files can be very readily updated on a permanent or temporary basis. A whole series of simulation runs can be stacked on one another as part of a continuous input, followed by a series of data files with a selected parameter or parameter set altered from run to run. The net effect of input stacking is that a series of sensitivity runs are produced to answer specific financial "what if" questions. The permanent file of the data base remains unaltered although its data base elements may be changed by the results of the simulation run. Similarly, the data file may change for each successive simulation run. In essence, the data base and data files come in contact with the simulation model to produce a series of successive runs to answer specific questions before pro forma financial statements are prepared as output.

MEDIUM-RANGE CORPORATE PLANNING MODULE

The six internal factors affecting long-range corporate planning—namely, product line, marketing, technical, facilities and production, manpower, and financial—provide the necessary input for medium-range planning or budgeting in a real-time MIS operating mode. Using a medium-range budget simulation model, long-range corporate planning data base elements are brought into play with medium-range income and expense data elements, shown in Figure 8-14. Output from the budget program is selected financial information—specifically, cash flow, source and application of funds, balance sheet, and income statement. As with long-range corporate planning, a remote I/O terminal can be utilized to simulate the

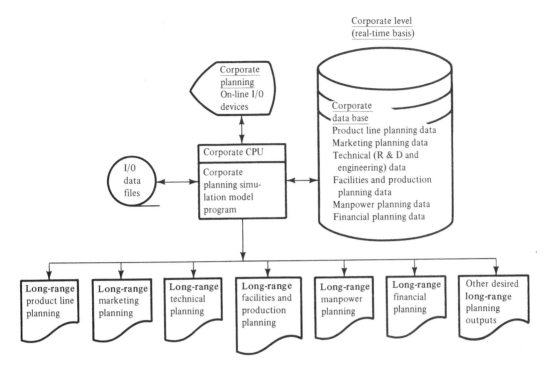

FIGURE 8-13. Long-range planning data flow for a real-time MIS corporate planning subsystem.

data to answer "what if" questions, store new information on the data base, or change existing data elements (Figure 8-15).

In developing a corporate budget model, several important factors are considered. First, the existing budgeting system must be an excellent analogue or measurable simulation of the firm. Its output mirrors the firm's physical activities. Of course, it should be recognized that there are some differences between the actual accounting/budgeting system and any model of it. One of these is the way in which the values of system variables (accounts) are derived. The actual system interacts with external parties and then processes these transactions by changing the balances in the appropriate accounts. In contrast, a simulation model does not have real transactions to make changes in the balances of various accounts. The user of such a model must create artificial transactions which have a high degree of similarity to the expected real-life version. The manner of processing these transactions is by formulating equations that define the values of the various accounts.

The second factor in constructing a budget model is to decide on the kind of output. Output options are illustrated by the following questions: (a) Do you want the model to tell you the level of sales that must be reached in order to achieve a predetermined profit or cash flow goal? or (b) Do you want to supply sales estimates and let the model work out the effects on the projected levels appearing on the financial statements? The second alternative is preferred because it utilizes the long- and medium-range corporate planning data elements. Regardless of the

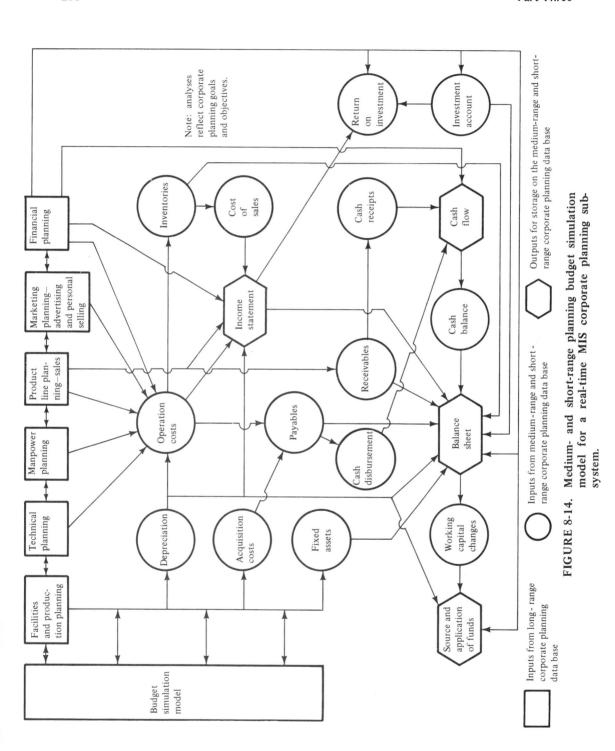

FIGURE 8-14. Medium- and short-range planning budget simulation model for a real-time MIS corporate planning subsystem.

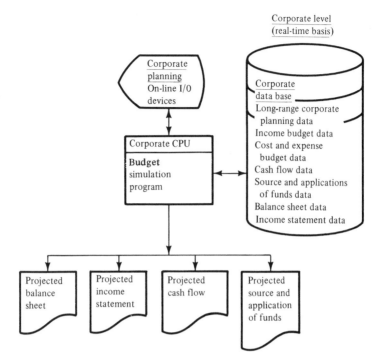

FIGURE 8-15. Medium-range planning data flow for a real-time MIS corporate planning subsystem.

approach, the conclusion to be drawn is that the desired output dictates the kind of input data that are required.

The third factor concerns the specifications of the model. These are the actual equations or formulas that define how the simulated account balances are derived. They are made up of variables and corresponding coefficients that represent a mathematical analogue of the account balances or budget variables that are being defined. These equations constitute the blueprint of the corporate budget model, and thereby, the essential part of the model.

The final factor in constructing the model is to make sure that it is valid. It must be a good approximation of reality. Here experience and intuition are indispensable. Seasoned judgment is the only way to decide finally whether or not the output of the model is reliable. Subtle relationships are discovered and new insights about the operation of the company are learned.

SHORT-RANGE CORPORATE PLANNING MODULE (FLEXIBLE BUDGETS)

The output from medium-range corporate planning does not end at that level, but provides input for short-range corporate planning. Budgets developed for next year are related to flexible budgets for this coming year so that compatibility is assured. The level of detail is expanded greatly for this year's figures. Basically, the same outputs for integrated MIS are applicable to real-time MIS. As shown in Figures 8-4 and 8-5, budgeted income statements are compiled by major product lines and percent of capacity, respectively. However, the method of compiling flexible budgets between integrated and real-time MIS differ.

Detailed balance sheet and income statement data for the coming year are fed into the corporate computer via an I/O terminal. The flexible budgeting program takes the values as set forth for this lowest level of expected plant capacity, say 70 percent, and develops corresponding figures for other levels of capacity—75, 80, 85, and 90 percent. Appropriate financial statements are developed and printed for these various levels of capacity. Flexible budgeting data are also written onto the corporate data base for comparison with actual figures as they occur month by month (refer to accounting subsystem). During this budgeting interaction phase in real time, budget exceptions are brought to the attention of the terminal operator. These are the result of comparing like values of the coming year and next year in accordance with the data base elements for medium-range planning. Where comparable values are deemed out of line by the computer program, exceptions are printed in order that they can be corrected. On-line processing for short-range corporate planning is illustrated in Figure 8-16.

SUMMARY

The corporate planning subsystem of the Consumer Products Corporation is the focal point of the entire real-time management information system. Long-range planning data are developed internally from the various subsystems, represented by product line, marketing, technical, facilities and production, manpower, and financial factors. In like manner, external data are evaluated in developing plans that are in conformity with company goals and objectives. Basically, the firm's long-range plans are employed in developing more specific financial plans for medium-range corporate planning. The output of this planning level serves as input for short-range corporate planning, resulting in flexible budgets for all levels of operations. Successive levels of planning provide for feedback whereby results may be analyzed objectively. This feedback process determines whether or not the system is doing the job for which it was designed, but more importantly, provides a basis for modifying plans at the various levels if warranted.

Within a real-time MIS corporate planning subsystem, a most important advantage is the ability to employ operations research techniques—in particular, financial simulation models. Corporate planning staff personnel can interact with the computer in a real-time operating mode and ask numerous "what if" questions, thereby determining their effect on short-, medium-, and long-range corporate plans. However, to design and develop such an environment is an extremely difficult and time-consuming task for any group of experienced systems designers.

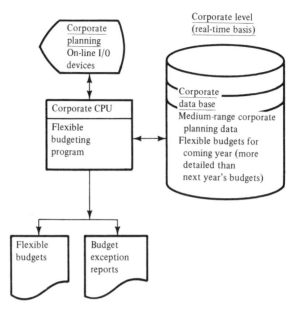

FIGURE 8-16. Short-range planning data flow for a real-time MIS corporate planning subsystem.

QUESTIONS

1. What advantages does the real-time MIS corporate planning subsystem have over the integrated MIS corporate planning subsystem?

2. Suggest additional OR techniques that can be employed for corporate planning time periods.

3. Take the long-range corporate planning data base elements in Figure 8-7 and define their detailed parts.

4. Referring to Figure 8-11, determine submodules for:
   a. technical (R & D and engineering) planning
   b. manpower planning

5. Referring to the section on long-range corporate planning, suggest system design changes that reflect an ideal real-time MIS operating environment.

6. What is the relationship of long-range corporate planning to medium-range corporate planning in a real-time MIS?

7. What is the relationship of flexible budgets to the accounting sub-system in a real-time MIS?

REFERENCES

Beehler, P. J., "EDP: Stimulating Systematic Corporate Planning," *Journal of Systems Management,* November, 1969.

Benson, L. A., "Predict Your Future With Simulation Models," *Computer Decisions,* July, 1971.

Boulden, J. B., and Buffa, E. S., "Corporate Models: On Line Real-Time Systems," *Harvard Business Review,* July-August, 1970.

Bucatinsky, J., "Ask Your Computer 'What If . . .'," *Financial Executive,* July, 1973.

Druger, L. N., "Computer Time-Sharing Aids in Forecasting," *Financial Executive,* August, 1972.

Eckstein, O., and McLagan, D. L., "National Economic Models Help Business to Focus on the Future," *Computer Decisions,* October, 1971.

Engberg, R. E., and Moore, R. L., "A Corporate Planning Model for a Construction Materials Producer," *Management Adviser,* January-February, 1974.

Gershefski, G. W., "Building a Corporate Financial Model," *Harvard Business Review,* July-August, 1969.

Hall, W. K., "Forecasting Techniques for Use in the Corporate Planning Process," *Managerial Planning,* November-December, 1972.

Hammond, J. S., "Do's & Don'ts of Computer Models for Planning," *Harvard Business Review,* March-April, 1974.

Kimball, W. L., "Planning with Mathematical Models," *Budgeting,* March/April, 1969.

Krueger, D. A., and Kohlmeier, J. M., "Financial Modeling and 'What If' Budgeting," *Management Accounting,* May, 1972.

LaCascio, V. R., "Financial Planning Models," *Financial Executive,* March, 1972.

McCarthy, D. J., and Morrissey, C. A., "Using the Systems Analyst in Preparing Corporate Financial Models," *Financial Executive,* June, 1972.

Most, K. S., "Wanted: A Planning Model of the Firm," *Managerial Planning,* July-August, 1973.

Pfeffer, J., Fogler, H. R., and Deeley, T., Jr., "A Computerized Planning Model That Management Will Use," *Managerial Planning,* November-December, 1970.

Pryor, L., "Simulation Budgeting for a 'What If . . .'," *The Journal of Accountancy,* November, 1970.

Seaberg, R. A., and Seaberg, C., "Computer Based Decision Systems in Xerox Corporate Planning," *Management Science,* December, Part II, 1973.

Sprague, R. H., "System Support for a Financial Planning Model," *Management Accounting,* June, 1972.

Thurston, P. H., "Make TF Serve Corporate Planning," *Harvard Business Review,* September-October, 1971.

Tryan, M. R., "A Computerized Decision Simulator Model," *Management Accounting,* March, 1971.

Weston, F. C., "Operations Research Techniques Relevant to Corporate Planning Function Practices: An Investigative Approach," *Academy of Management Journal,* September, 1973.

REAL-TIME MIS
MARKETING SUBSYSTEM

9

Marketing is a controversial subject when any type of data processing system is discussed. From one viewpoint, marketing is so dependent on human judgment, so involved with complex relationships, and so beset with imperfect knowledge that decisions are all too often made by sheer intuition rather than by computer analysis. In reality, behavioral phenomena are difficult to quantify and, hence, difficult to computerize as an essential part of a marketing subsystem. However, from another viewpoint, experience and intuition (or the behavioral aspects) are vital ingredients in marketing, but their value can be greatly enhanced by computer measurement that utilizes quantitative techniques. It is from this latter point of view that the major subparts of the marketing subsystem are developed in a real-time MIS operating environment.

Initially, the essential parts of an integrated MIS marketing subsystem are set forth before the important marketing design considerations are discussed for a real-time MIS. Representative data base elements, operations research techniques, and design modules are investigated from the viewpoint of the systems designer. This approach provides a logical framework for designing the major marketing components for the Consumer Products Corporation which are:

> forecasting and sales analysis
> sales order processing and customer service
> advertising and personal selling
> market research and pricing

INTEGRATED MIS MARKETING SUBSYSTEM

The basic input for the integrated MIS marketing subsystem of the Consumer Products Corporation is from the firm's customers. Not only are orders received from customers, but marketing efforts are also focused on them, as illustrated in Figure 9-1. The firm's marketing executives derive their information about customers and the marketplace through marketing intelligence, formal market research, and company accounting information. Marketing intelligence activity describes the continuous effort to keep informed about current developments among customers, competing products, and the marketing environment. In a similar manner, market research centers around a more formal approach to current developments—in particular, project-oriented research. The company accounting system generates sales and cost information in order to complement marketing intelligence and research.

The primary job of the marketing department is to contact potential customers and sell merchandise through advertising, personal selling, and special promotion. If products are sold, a multicopy *sales order* is originated by a salesman or the order section of the marketing department. Copies are distributed as follows: original copy to customer for acknowledging order, duplicate copies to the salesman and other departments as needed. The marketing department prepares other forms, such as *contracts, bids, back orders,* and *change orders*. No matter what form is involved, the marketing department starts the product information flow in the firm.

The basic procedures, devised in an integrated MIS environment for daily sales order processing and shown in Figure 9-1, indicate that processing orders include checking on the customer's credit as well as preparing computer outputs—customer shipment orders (printed output) as well as a sales order file (magnetic tape file). The latter output is used in preparing a daily sales analysis. In addition, processing procedures include warehouse shipment orders—shipping finished products from the three plants to the twelve warehouses. Thus, order processing procedures for the marketing subsystem focus on accepting or rejecting orders. If orders are accepted, they are forwarded to the physical distribution subsystem for further processing. Special orders are routed to the engineering subsystem during order processing.

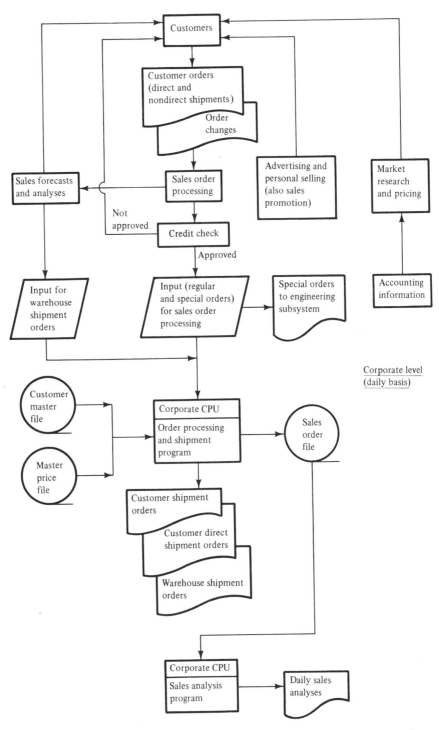

FIGURE 9-1. Marketing data flow on a daily basis for an integrated MIS system.

FORECASTING AND SALES ANALYSIS

Integrated MIS forecasting efforts of the Consumer Products Corporation center around projecting upcoming quarterly sales demand for seven basic product groups. Within each of these there are several specific products, resulting in over fifty products manufactured by the three plants. The present method employed to forecast quarterly sales is the "least-squares" method.

In projecting future marketing information based upon past and present data, there are many straight lines that can be constructed as possible trend lines, showing the movement and pattern of sales of the firm's products. A most useful trend line for each product is one that "best fits" the sales data under study. There is only one such line of best fit and it is called the "line of least squares," which can be defined as the trend line for which the sum of the squares of differences between the actual values (of the dependent variable) and the estimated values (for the dependent variable) is the least. In reality, we are trying to find an average line that minimizes errors between the trend line and the actual values.

The line of best fit or the line of least squares can be expressed by the following equation:

$$y = a + bx \qquad \text{Equation 9-1}$$

where y = the value of the dependent variable

a = the value of y where $x = 0$

b = slope of the line or $b = \dfrac{\Delta y}{\Delta x}$

x = the value of the independent variable

A systematic method for finding the line of least squares requires the solution of two normal equations to derive the value of the two unknown variables - (a) and (b). These two equations are:

$$\Sigma y = na + b\Sigma x \qquad \text{Equation 9-2}$$

$$\text{or} \quad a = \frac{\Sigma y}{n} - b\frac{\Sigma x}{n}$$

$$\Sigma xy = a\Sigma x + b\Sigma x^2 \qquad \text{Equation 9-3}$$

$$\text{or} \quad b = \frac{n(\Sigma xy) - (\Sigma x)(\Sigma y)}{n(\Sigma x^2) - (\Sigma x)^2}$$

where Σy = the sum of the values of the dependent variable

n = number of values

Σx = the sum of the values of the independent variable

Σxy = the sum of x times y

Σx^2 = the sum of the squared values of the independent variable

Equations 9-2 and 9-3 are used to forecast the firm's products on a quarterly basis. As shown in Figure 9-2, there is a printout of forecasted demand for each product

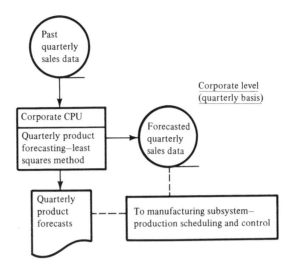

FIGURE 9-2. Quarterly product forecasting data flow for an integrated MIS marketing subsystem.

that is forwarded to the manufacturing manager and a tape containing demand that is forwarded to the manufacturing subsystem for producing the forecasted products.

After several years' experience with the least-squares method, the firm has found that conditions in the past do not always continue without change in the future. Thus, the least-squares or the trend-extension method, which looks to the trend factor, is not the only dominating factor in predicting demand; the seasonal factor is also important. For this reason, the firm has investigated other statistical methods and has decided to use exponential smoothing formulas (refer to OR Marketing Models section) when implementing the real-time MIS.

Before product forecasting of any kind can be undertaken, there is need for past sales analysis. As depicted in Figure 9-1, sales analyses are on a daily basis. From a longer viewpoint, the accounting subsystem supplies monthly and quarterly sales data as well as yearly information based on the firm's financial statements. Typical sales analyses include total sales (in dollars and units), sales by basic product groups, sales by customers and salesmen, and sales by geographical territory. Also, they encompass sales trends, market shares, and gross margins (contributions).

SALES ORDER PROCESSING AND CUSTOMER SERVICE

The activities performed by the forecasting system, as indicated above, trigger the generation of regular production orders on a quarterly basis. On the other hand, sales order processing initiates and provides the basis for control of daily activities that result in filling customer orders. It is of utmost importance that the information on the sales order form be complete and accurate. Otherwise, the sales order processing and warehouse shipment information, shown at the bottom of Figure 9-3, may be incorrect when forwarded to the firm's plants and warehouses.

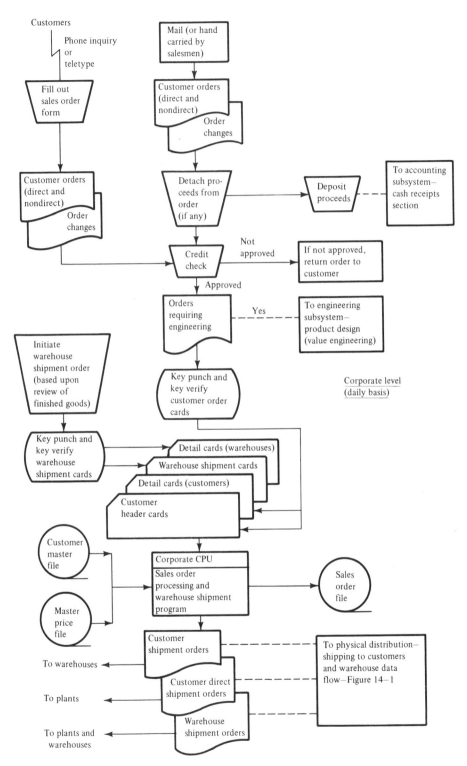

FIGURE 9-3. Sales order processing and warehouse shipment data flow on a daily basis for an integrated MIS marketing subsystem.

Once the sales order is received—by phone, teletype, mail, or hand-carried—the first major activity, aside from detaching proceeds on a few orders, is the credit check—that is, is the customer capable of paying the ordered amount? In those cases where the credit of the customer is in question according to the accounting department, the order is sent to marketing management for further checking and a decision. In most cases, credit clearance is obtained and the order proceeds to the next step in Figure 9-3, which is to see if there is need for product design (applies to special orders). If engineering is required, the order departs from the normal sales order processing flow; otherwise, the appropriate customer header card and detailed item cards are key-punched and key-verified. Also merged with customer order cards are warehouse shipment order cards, which represent the finished products to be shipped from the plants to warehouses or from one warehouse to another. These latter shipments are made to balance out inventories, thereby anticipating future customer shipments at the right warehouse.

The customer order and warehouse shipment cards are processed against the master name and address and price files, necessary for producing the three types of output shown in Figure 9-3. These outputs are forwarded to the respective plant or warehouse, depending on the type of order. Order processing stops here for the marketing subsystem at the corporate level and resumes at the plant or warehouse level through the physical distribution system for regular sales orders.

In conjunction with sales order processing, the level of customer service is considered. If the order can be filled from inventory or from current production, the order processing cycle continues with the development of shipping documentation and the scheduling of warehouse withdrawal and transportation. When the order cannot be filled from either source, the customer is notified through the marketing subsystem. Hopefully, the customer will allow the order to be back-ordered and filled at a later date. If not, he will probably use an alternative source of supply and his order at the Consumer Products Corporation will be canceled.

ADVERTISING AND PERSONAL SELLING

The selling function of the firm's integrated MIS focuses on three specific areas—advertising, personal selling, and sales promotion. Because the firm spends the most on the first two, these areas will be explored.

Selection of the best set of national magazines plus audio and visual media to communicate the firm's advertising message to present and potential customers is a many-faceted problem. The important variables influencing the media selection process are the availability of time or space in each media, the firm's advertising budget, whom the firm wishes to reach with a given message, the value of each repeat exposure, the quality of the advertising medium and the discounted cost of running a selected media. Consequently, it is not a simple task to formulate an effective advertising program by identifying the key variables and quantifying the relationship between them.

To solve the advertising media problem, the Consumer Products Corporation turned to linear programming. The linear programming advertising media model chooses the advertising mix that will maximize the number of effective exposures subject to the following constraints: the total advertising budget, specified minimum and maximum usage rates of various media, and specified exposure rates to the different market segments. The flowchart for this advertising approach on a quarterly basis is shown in Figure 9-4.

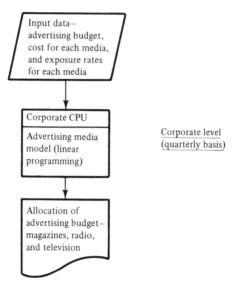

FIGURE 9-4. Advertising media model on a quarterly basis for an integrated MIS marketing subsystem.

After two years' experience with this approach the firm has found several shortcomings. The model assumes constant effects of repeated advertising exposures, which is, in fact, rarely true. Media costs are not always constant. In addition, there is no allowance for audience overlaps among media nor is there any indication of the best scheduling for the chosen media. Criticism of the linear programming approach focuses on the amount and kinds of simplifications of the real world needed to adapt the complex problem to the rigid form of the algorithm[1] and to keep the size of the problem small enough to fit the memory capacity of the firm's computer. As a result of these shortcomings, the firm has decided to use a simulation approach when the real-time system is installed.

Personal selling, another important method of selling, is unique in that the resources involved are people. The salesmen and their supervisors interact with customers, who respond to selling effort in a complex and variable manner. This makes it extremely difficult to computerize for effective control or to run controlled experiments and to shift salesmen around, except on a slow, evolutionary basis. As a result, using a computer-based mathematical approach can be both risky and expensive to simulate changes that may or may not result in a more effective

[1]Algorithm—a series of well-defined mathematical steps that are followed in order to obtain a desired result.

sales strategy. For best results, selling strategy decisions should be made within the constraints of the present organization and with changes in organizational resources taking place over long periods of time.

MARKET RESEARCH AND PRICING

Market research plays a major part in developing new profit opportunities in the form of new products. The rationale is that the rate of product innovation, the rate of new product failures, and the cost of bringing out new products are all extremely high and continue to rise. To survive in such dynamic markets, the Consumer Products Corporation must develop a sensitivity to changes in consumer behavior and in the conditions that influence behavior through effective market research. It is meaningless to talk of new products without considering, at the same time, the related marketing decisions that will have to be made. This consideration centers around the formulative role of research suggesting that market research is really a coordinating agent. Each marketing decision should be thought of as an input and research should be employed to coordinate these inputs before the actual product design begins.

Market research activities for the Consumer Products Corporation center around the systematic gathering, recording, and analyzing of data about problems relating to the marketing of goods. In order to carry out these research functions, current and past data must be fed into the batch-oriented computer and analyzed by an appropriate research program before meaningful output can be produced (Figure 9-5). Generally, one of the current techniques in market research is employed, such as multiple regression, multiple correlation, and sampling theory. As noted in Figure 9-5, these techniques are stored on magnetic tape for immediate referencing by the market research program being processed. Computer output can be in the form of potential market size, product pricing, and other factors deemed important for the product under study.

For many of the firm's research studies, large data files are rarely used as is. Generally, the research analyst first retrieves and summarizes information from computer-processable files before beginning an analysis. For example, if he wishes to estimate a stochastic[2] model of brand choice, he first retrieves the sequence of brands chosen by each household. Whether the ultimate analysis is the development of a stochastic model or another model, he develops a programming system to transform the edited data into a format appropriate for his statistical treatment. For models and statistical procedures used in marketing research, a system for retrieval and summary of data is developed in order to reduce the technological, time, and cost barriers to efficient market research.

In conjunction with developing needed market research data, exhaustive market research is undertaken with the possibility of attaining high unit volume as an objective. The selling of many units can bring both short- and long-run benefits to the firm. High unit volume can be sustained by many components of the market-

[2]Stochastic—ability, but not with absolute certainty, to know what will likely take place in the future.

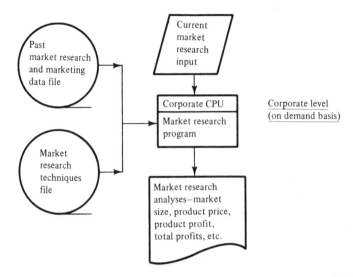

FIGURE 9-5. Market research data flow for an integrated MIS marketing subsystem.

ing mix. Good product design, attractive packaging, and effective selling and advertising play leading parts. But more importantly, price often exercises a powerful influence on unit volume and the ultimate success of the new product. Because of the prime importance given to price, a relationship between potential demand and varying prices is determined by the market research analyst. The combination of demand and price that yields the highest profits is generally the basis for price determination. Likewise, consideration is given to prices charged at the breakeven points at low and high volumes so as to indicate upper and lower price ranges corresponding to certain annual sales. Thus, marketing management is appraised of probable market volumes at various price levels for an overview of the proposed product.

REAL-TIME MIS DESIGN CONSIDERATIONS FOR MARKETING

Design considerations for the marketing subsystem are somewhat different from the firm's other subsystems. The marketing subsystem captures information about the external environment in terms of market forecasts and customer orders. It is the prime mover from which all other subsystems either directly or indirectly receive instructions on what must be accomplished. Its data base includes consumer sales forecasts, orders, shipments, product data, media data, advertising and promotion budgets, and other data, which must be designed carefully by the firm's systems analysts. An important part of their job focuses on the data base elements themselves—specifically, what they are, what the validity is for storing them on-line, how they can be stored for easy retrieval, how they can be combined with data from other subsystems, and what type of output they can produce for a real-time MIS operating mode.

In order to proceed with the design of the marketing subsystem (as well as any other subsystem), the systems designers must order their priorities in terms of what information and calculations are most valuable to management in a real-time environment. Ranking informational priorities, in particular, requires creative thinking and intuitive judgment of the highest order. Hard work is involved not only during the design phase but also in estimating the benefits of possible actions resulting from the new information. For effective results, there is an obvious need for systems personnel to interact with marketing personnel, especially marketing management, for concrete results. From these joint efforts, the most valuable informational opportunities can be pursued and developed to maturity for mutual benefit.

OVERVIEW OF MARKETING ENVIRONMENT

The marketing subsystem, the prime source of determining what must be accomplished presently, is controlled by the corporate planning subsystem. Its major functional subparts, shown in Figure 9-6, include the same ones as set forth for integrated MIS. They include forecasting and sales analysis, sales order processing and customer service, advertising and personal selling, and market research and pricing. However, their design will take on an added dimension because of the computer's real-time processing ability. Marketing data will be stored on the common data base, retrievable as is or manipulated depending on the user's needs. This added dimension to obtain current and exception marketing information via an I/O terminal device means information will be available much sooner. From this man/machine operating mode, corrective measures deemed necessary can be effected faster because of immediate feedback. Thus, real-time design requirements for such an environment are more stringent and difficult to coordinate than in a batch processing operating mode.

MARKETING DATA BASE

The marketing data bank (magnetic tape files), an essential part of the integrated MIS, must be converted to data stored on line in a real-time MIS operating mode. Data base elements should be structured by major categories, as demonstrated in Figure 9-7. This approach to the marketing data base assists the systems designer not only in effecting a logically structured design, but also in programming data for instantaneous display or printed output.

The real test of effectiveness for the marketing data base revolves around how well and, in some cases, how fast marketing information can be retrieved to explain the dynamics of the markets in which the firm is operating. If marketing data elements cannot be correlated and subjected to factual and statistical manipulations, they will be of little help to marketing personnel—in particular, management and market research. It is in the grouping of data in new and different ways that marketing management is likely to find new and better answers. Also, the use of exception reporting from the data base will relieve marketing of scanning masses

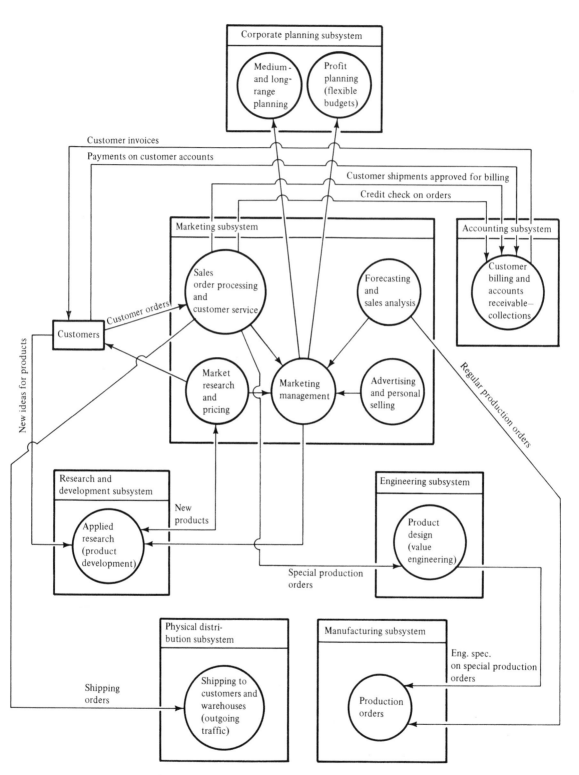

FIGURE 9-6. Real-time MIS marketing subsystem flow to and from other subsystems.

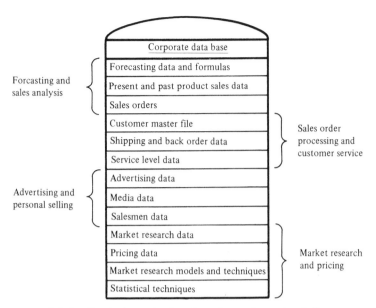

FIGURE 9-7. Typical marketing data base elements at the corporate level.

of numbers in the hope of finding meaningful ones. Thus, the systems designers must ascertain those combinations of marketing data and statistical manipulations which are the most valuable to the marketing subsystem.

Data as shown in Figure 9-7 for forecasting and sales analysis consist of such items as past forecasting amounts, forecasted data for the coming period, present and past sales data, and past and present sales orders. By and large, these data revolve around the dynamics of the marketplace—that is, present and future sales. The current sales orders are input to sales order processing, whose basic data elements consist of the customer master file, shipping data, back order data, and similar items. Essentially, the level of current orders is dependent on the advertising and salesmen efforts, the next group of data elements stored on line. All of the foregoing marketing data elements, in the long run, center on the developments of market research. Market research—which connotes product-oriented research that usually begins with a consumer need and ends with a product recommendation—must, by its very nature, have certain data elements in a retrievable mode. In other cases, large magnetic tape or disk files of past data may supplement on-line market research data. The foregoing major marketing elements, then, comprise the marketing data base needed in a real-time MIS environment for timely marketing information.

OR MARKETING MODELS

In the past, marketing managers of any firm, including the Consumer Products Corporation, have developed a natural suspicion about operations research models. There is no question that many facets of the marketing process will not submit to mathematical analysis, particularly those that rely heavily on creativity and human relations. However, there are other areas of marketing that respond well to systematic observation, analysis, and implementation of OR techniques. These areas offer an excellent opportunity for marketing executives willing to adopt an innovative attitude toward newer knowledge and technology.

Although mathematical models are relative latecomers in marketing, they have already paid off in such areas as new product development, product pricing, and advertising media selection. The first two areas are presented for the firm's real-time MIS. Initially, exponential smoothing—a technique for sales forecasting—is explored.

Exponential Smoothing

Exponential smoothing is a forecasting technique that is extremely accurate in predicting future market demand. The term *exponential* has a purely mathematical origin in that the repeated use of a smoothing constant tends to operate in a manner equivalent to an exponential multiplier. A computer program can be used such that period-to-period forecasts on many different products may be determined in a matter of minutes.

The exponential smoothing method develops a forecast of sales for the next period, say a quarter, by taking a weighted average of sales in the current period and a sales forecast made in the current period. The weighted values must total 1 (one). If the weight for actual current sales is set at .1, then the weight factor of the forecast made in the current period would have to be .9. The selection of the weighting factor is of utmost importance. If it is very large (close to 1), then any fluctuation of current sales will be strongly reflected in the forecast for the next period. On the other hand, if it is set close to zero, current sales will have relatively little impact on the next period's forecast. Experience has shown that setting the weighting factor somewhere between 1. and .2 leads to reasonably favorable results. This setting smoothes the extremes of current sales while allowing for definite fluctuations in sales trends. Obviously, management should experiment with various values.

The exponential smoothing formulas, both adjusted and unadjusted for seasonal and trend factors, are developed in Appendix B. For the Consumer Products Corporation, quarterly sales forecasts are adjusted to reflect both seasonal and trend factors because of the nature of the firm's markets. The selection of the weighting factors are based upon past experience. Although the development of the final exponential smoothing formulas may appear to be complex, it can be handled quite easily within a real-time MIS operating mode.

Venture Analysis

One of the most extensive and sophisticated marketing OR models is venture analysis. It is an investment planning system for analyzing new opportunities and encompasses such techniques as probability, decision theory, and the time value of money as well as mathematical modeling. Because it is a massive system of gathering, relating, appraising, and projecting all data pertinent to a complete business venture over its life cycle, this OR technique stores many kinds of information. All costs involved in the product project are developed. Manufacturing costs include raw material, direct labor, depreciation, and overhead. These data are modeled for each step of the production process. For the pricing and promotional effort, product prices are estimated at various desired levels in order to determine an optimum price. All promotional costs involved in marketing the product are broken down by media selected and projected. Research and development costs plus general and administrative costs are scheduled to make the data complete.

Because venture analysis is very comprehensive in nature, other members of the marketing chain—suppliers and retailers—are included in the model. In a similar manner, key decisions which would affect sales of the product, such as the introduction of similar products by competitors, are defined, related, and programmed. Also, the consumer's awareness and reaction are taken into account to make the model complete. All of the marketing factors, then, are modeled according to cause and effect. For any reaction on the part of a firm competing in the field, the firm estimates the reaction and effects on the other competitors. The total of all marketing interactions described above results in a sales forecast and a profitability picture. A computer simulation program provides for analyzing and summarizing in a logical manner all the available information about markets, investments, costs, customers, and competitors in venture analysis.

In summary, venture analysis that relies heavily on simulation directs management in judging a new product at the market research stage by presenting analyzed information within a logically structured framework. It considers both risk and gaming factors as well as indicating the expected economic impact of various possible decision routes. With this approach, management can reach a better decision under conditions of risk and uncertainty. In addition, the tendency of executives to delay decisions and commitments to new products will be lessened, because valuable information from a venture simulation method replaces intuition. Thus, venture analysis provides management with the means for better planning, forecasting, and decision making than would otherwise be possible.

Pricing Model (Using Differentiation)

Pricing is a very complex issue for many companies, including the Consumer Products Corporation. It is a problem when a new product is being introduced, when a price change is contemplated in the face of uncertain customer and competitor reactions, and when a company must react to a competitor who has just changed his price. Pricing is also a problem when sealed bids must be submitted. And it is a problem when the company's product line is characterized by substantial demand and cost interpendencies. In face of these problems, new product pricing at the market research stage can be best determined by applying differentiation (calculus) to proposed selling prices and estimated demand.

For sake of discussion, the firm has developed a prototype of a new consumer product that is much lower in price than the present basic products. Before differentiation can be applied to determine an optimum selling price that will maximize profits for the firm, the market research group developed important data, starting with the demand and price relationship for the product (Figure 9-8).

Price	Estimated Demand per Year Over Product's Life
$ 2	200,000
4	150,000
6	100,000
8	50,000
10	0

FIGURE 9-8. Demand and price relationship for proposed new product.

The firm's cost accounting section, in conjunction with the production control and scheduling department, has determined the annual fixed costs per year to be $300,000. Included in this figure is estimated straight-line depreciation on proposed new machinery and equipment to be acquired. This same group has calculated the variable costs at $.80 per unit.

Based on these data, mathematical equations can be developed that will express demand, total sales, total costs, and total profits. These are found in Appendix C, indicating an optimum selling price of $5.40. By substituting the calculated selling price into the profit equation (total sales function less total costs function), the firm can expect profits of $229,000 in the first year. Also, the number of units that can be sold annually—namely, 115,000 units—can be calculated.

An alternative method to this mathematical approach is the graphic solution, illustrated in Figure 9-9. This approach may be difficult to interpret for an accurate answer. Nevertheless, it can be used to check on the overall accuracy of the other approach.

MARKETING MODULES

Marketing modules, the prime movers of input for other subsystem modules, are depicted in Figure 9-10. The purpose of the breakdown in the figure is to aid in understanding the essential marketing functions and their detailed elements; it is also extremely helpful in designing the subsystem itself. Marketing modules must also be coordinated with submodules found in other subsystems so that compatibility of subsystems is assured. Under earlier approaches to detailed systems design, related subsystems were designed without giving thought to other areas. This resulted in duplicate stored data. Thus, it is of great importance that the systems designer consider the lowest-level marketing modules as they affect other subsystems and as they affect the overall marketing subsystem in a real-time MIS environment.

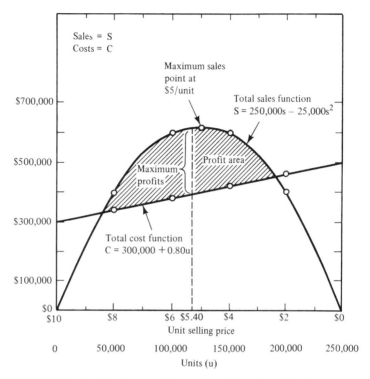

FIGURE 9-9. Total sales, total costs, and total profits for proposed new product.

REAL-TIME MIS MARKETING SUBSYSTEM

The foregoing background of the marketing data base, OR models, and modules assists the systems designer in understanding important real-time MIS design considerations. These analyses help the designer structure marketing data such that they can be retrieved from the common data base with a minimum of programming effort. Data elements are examined not only for what can be extracted from the marketing data base but also for duplication of data within and outside the system. In a similar manner, significant mathematical models that can be included in effecting marketing decisions are analyzed in terms of their basic concepts. In essence, a thorough analysis of important factors that are an integral part of a real-time MIS will help the systems designer in devising the marketing subsystem that will greatly enhance the managerial functions of planning, organizing, directing, and controlling.

MARKETING SUBSYSTEM OVERVIEW

An overview of the marketing subsystem in a real-time MIS environment is shown in Figure 9-11. Basically, inputs originate with the customer in the form of orders—regular and special, order changes, and other marketing information for

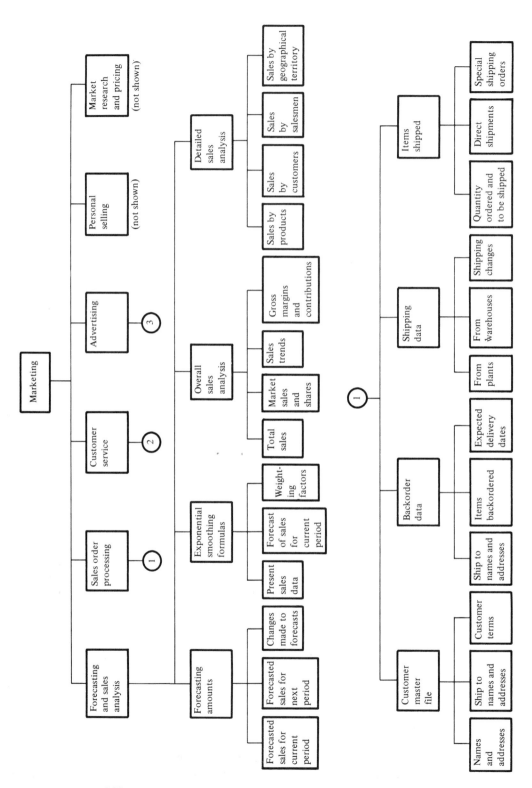

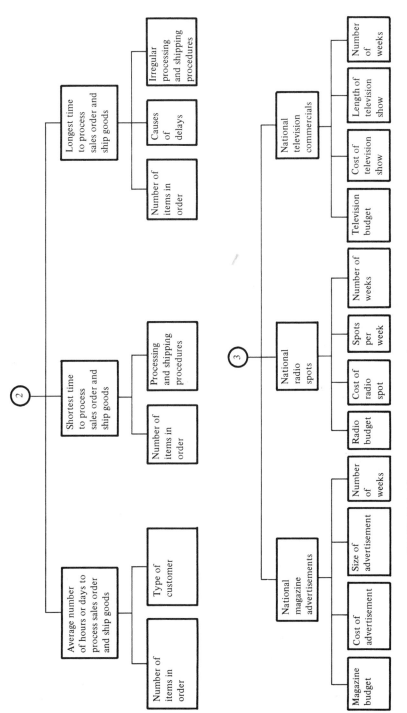

FIGURE 9-10. Marketing modules of the Consumer Products Corporation.

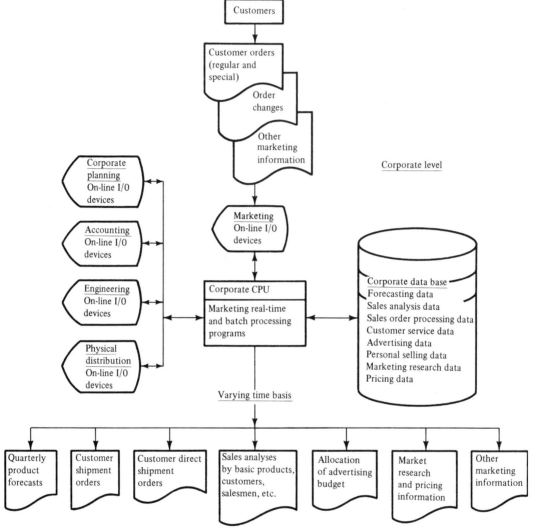

FIGURE 9-11. An overview of a real-time MIS marketing subsystem.

sales forecasting, market research, pricing, and like items. Processing of customer orders reaches a certain point in the marketing subsystem at which it is necessary to interrogate the accounting data base in order to determine the status of the customer's credit. After additional processing within marketing, orders that require product design and developmental work are forwarded to engineering while regular and direct shipment orders are sent on line to the closest warehouse or manufacturing plant, depending upon the type of the order. In addition to these activities, various outputs are produced as shown in Figure 9-11. Some of these are on a real-time, daily, weekly, or as needed basis. Thus, real-time MIS marketing activities, many and varied, are the subject matter for the remaining sections of this chapter.

FORECASTING AND SALES ANALYSIS MODULES

Sales forecasting for the Consumer Products Corporation in a real-time MIS environment, like integrated MIS, focuses on quarterly projections of the firm's products. Also, provision is made for interrogating the marketing data base at any time for utilizing the exponential formulas in conjunction with current sales data. As you will recall from the prior discussion, the basic concept of exponential smoothing is that next quarter's forecast should be adjusted by employing weighting factors for current sales and the current forecast. In a sense, the weighting factors update the upcoming forecast in light of what has happened most recently to actual demand. From this viewpoint, they are smoothing constants that are derived by examining past sales experience patterns. In addition, they allow seasonal and trend adjustments to be built into the forecasting formulas.

An I/O terminal, illustrated in Figure 9-12, is used to trigger on-line processing of exponential smoothing formulas quarterly in conjunction with the marketing data base. For real-time processing to begin, current sales, sales forecasts in the current period, and weighting factors for each product are read in from the data base and manipulated by the exponential smoothing equations. The resulting output from the Quarterly Product Forecasting-Exponential Smoothing Program is the printed quarterly product forecasts. But equally important in terms of output is the storing of these forecasts on the common data base.

Although it may appear that processing stops with a forecasted product printout and on-line storage of data, actually the forecasting program is just the beginning of a series of on-line real-time processing operations. Output of the Quarterly Product Forecasting-Exponential Smoothing Program is input for the Finished Goods-Production Schedule Program, which determines the number of

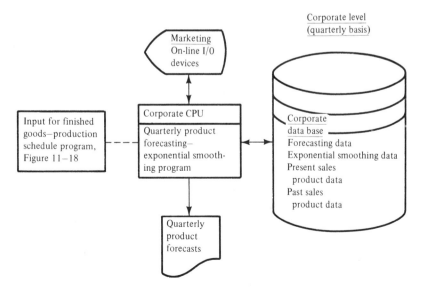

FIGURE 9-12. Quarterly product forecasting data flow for a real-time MIS marketing subsystem.

finished products to manufacture after considering goods on hand and on order. This output becomes input for the Linear Programming Program, one used to determine what products should be made at which plants. Based upon this allocation of finished products by plants, the next program—Materials Planning by Periods—explodes bills of materials for the finished product's component parts and determines to what planning periods the component parts apply in order to have them available at the proper time for manufacturing operations. The program on the next level—Materials Availability and EOQ (economic order quantity)—evaluates the component parts in terms of requirements by planning periods after considering what is on hand and on order. Generally, it will be necessary to buy large quantities of raw materials and parts from the outside as well as to place production orders for parts to be manufactured. In order to keep inventory costs at a minimum, orders from within and outside the firm are placed on an optimum basis by using EOQ formulas (refer to Chapter 12). Manufacturing orders are scheduled daily by plants using a Production Scheduling-Linear Programming Program. Thus, the sales forecasting program triggers a whole series of real-time programs which are the basis for daily manufacturing operations and buying from outside vendors.

The foregoing integrated programs do not end here in an on-line processing mode. Additional programs, such as plant attendance and recording of work in process for cost and factory payroll, are utilized. It should be noted that these latter programs are used for controlling activities as they occur in the manufacturing departments, while the sales forecasting through the economic ordering programs are processed at one time each quarter.

The forecasted sales stored on the common data base serve another purpose. They allow marketing management via an inquiry I/O terminal to compare projected product sales to actual sales activity (updated on a daily basis) for some specific time period. In order to make this information available to the proper marketing personnel, it is necessary to program different inquiry formats for maximum flexibility and ease of inquiry from the real-time system. For the Consumer Products Corporation, the systems designers have decided on a three-part division of inquiry formats:

1. total sales
2. detailed sales
3. exception sales

The highest level of marketing inquiry, or "total sales," is the overall performance summary that describes the month-to-date or current month, last month, year-to-date, last year-to-date, and other data pictured in Figure 9-13. A sample inquiry display for the firm's seven basic product groups is shown in Figure 9-14. A review of this illustration indicates that the function of this level is to provide further inquiry and analysis in an area that is over or under budget forecasts. If a given sales performance is deficient compared to the budget figures, control can then be transferred to successive levels of detailed reports relative to the area of interest.

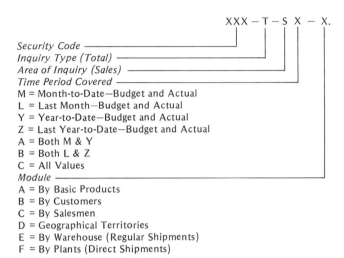

Security Code ──────────────────────────────────┐
Inquiry Type (Total) ────────────────────────┐ │
Area of Inquiry (Sales) ──────────────────┐ │ │
Time Period Covered ───────────────────┐ │ │ │
M = Month-to-Date—Budget and Actual
L = Last Month—Budget and Actual
Y = Year-to-Date—Budget and Actual
Z = Last Year-to-Date—Budget and Actual
A = Both M & Y
B = Both L & Z
C = All Values
Module ──────────────────────────────────────┘
A = By Basic Products
B = By Customers
C = By Salesmen
D = Geographical Territories
E = By Warehouse (Regular Shipments)
F = By Plants (Direct Shipments)

FIGURE 9-13.   Total sales inquiry format in a real-time MIS marketing subsystem.

Basic Products	MTD BUD	(000) ACT	LTD BUD	(000) ACT	YTD BUD	(000) ACT	ZTD BUD	(000) ACT
Group 1	412	400	394	410	1240	1195	1214	1275
Group 2	673	675	711	720	2103	2050	2202	2340
Group 3	1415	1450	1375	1379	4292	4095	4252	4242
Group 4	2040	2035	2100	2140	5954	5875	6010	5990
Group 5	1594	1505	1652	1695	4753	4852	4852	4950
Group 6	1141	1145	1133	1155	3502	3550	3493	3510
Group 7	1180	1195	1191	1193	3471	3480	3478	3495
Total	8455	8405	8556	8692	25315	25097	25501	25802

Question: What are the budget and actual month-to-date, last month-to-date, year-to-date, and last year-to-date total sales for the firm's seven basic product groups?

Code: XXX – T – S C – A. (based upon Figure 9-13)

FIGURE 9-14.   Total sales inquiry format example.

The second level of inquiry, or "detailed sales," contains many modules of optional levels of detail. Normally, the inquiries requested of this structure are triggered for further analysis by the total sales inquiry. As with the prior level, data are available for the same time periods and by the same sales categories at the detailed level. Also, this inquiry format is so programmed to enable the user to format his own report structures because marketing management might be interested in certain sales ratios or sales-to-expense ratios.

The last inquiry level, or "exception sales," is more complex and flexible than the prior two. The exception inquiry is structured to highlight a certain condition or conditions. A sample inquiry is: "Which products are above 110 percent of forecasted sales and below 90 percent of forecasted sales?" Another inquiry example is: "Which salesmen are below their sales quotas?" In essence, this inquiry level provides the user with the ability to ask basic questions about the efficiency or lack of it in terms of the firm's marketing effort. This area alone may justify the marketing subsystem because real-time information represents new knowledge to management for planning and controlling marketing activities.

SALES ORDER PROCESSING AND CUSTOMER SERVICE MODULES

Customer sales orders for the Consumer Products Corporation arrive via mail, telephone, and Teletype or are hand-carried by company salesmen. Where a check is attached, a memo is made on the order before forwarding it to the accounting cash-receipts section. These preliminary activities are illustrated in Figure 9-15. An I/O terminal is used in order processing that includes a credit check of the customer's order. Initially, the CRT terminal displays a request for customer identification. The customer number is entered unless the transaction is for a new customer, in which case the customer name, address, and other information are entered. If the customer number is unknown for an established customer, the name is entered and the system displays a list of "sound-alike" customers from which a selection is made.

The system then displays successive requests for the entry of the data pertaining to the order. Flashed on the CRT screen are a series of questions pertaining to the following:

> customer order number (the customer's purchase order)
> "ship to" number
> date of order
> mail, phone, or Teletype
> tax code (the customer's tax type)
> salesman number
> number of items ordered of each product and catalog number
> job control number

Questions are projected on the operator's screen in a list. New questions are flashed in a pagelike sequence, and can cover up to 30 items on a single order. Sets

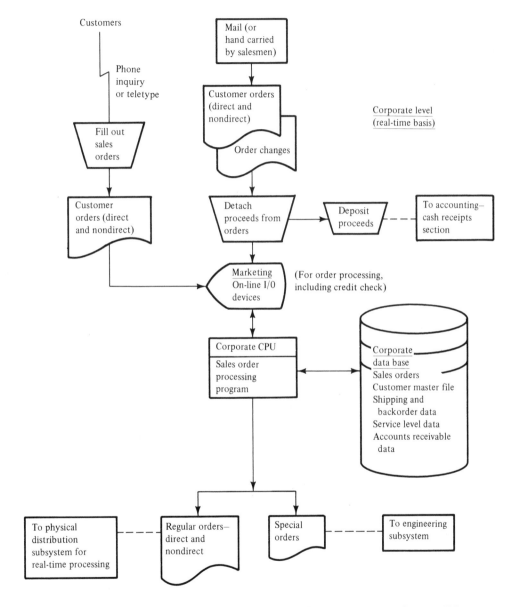

FIGURE 9-15. Sales order processing data flow for a real-time MIS marketing subsystem.

of questions continue until the operator enters an L for "last." Each keyed-in answer appears on the screen opposite the question. At that point the computer summarizes each series of answers and "plays back" the information for visual review. There is only one edit check for each item on order and the operator verifies that an entry is correct by keying in OK (okay) or NG (no good). After an NG, the operator redisplays the particular item in question and enters changes. An editing program stored in the computer checks the answers against preestablished facts, and question marks are flashed on the screen when the program finds an answer unacceptable. For instance, if the operator fails to include the number of items ordered, the program will flash a question mark. Or if the number of items ordered is present but the catalog number is not, another question mark will remind the operator that this information is missing. When all the questions on an order have been answered, the computer then checks the customer's credit and either approves the order for filling or, if there is a credit problem, holds it up and automatically prints out a warning message in the credit section of the accounting department on an I/O terminal unit.

Once the order has passed the credit check, the real-time sales order processing program accumulates finished goods requirements of the order for sales analysis and finished goods inventory. Finished goods items are not deducted from their on-line balances at this time, but are deducted by the physical distribution subsystem (Finished Goods Updating Program) later. Awaiting shipment by the PD (Physical Distribution) department, finished goods along with their order numbers are stored on-line. The rationale for this approach is two-fold. First, because there are discrepancies between what is physically on hand and the perpetual inventory on the common data base, the systems designers have found it better not to deduct amounts that could result in misleading balances on line. Second, at the end of the day, a computer program can be run to trigger all unposted finished goods of the prior day, indicating errors in orders not processed and billed. Thus, the sales order processing program makes a memorandum on the common data base concerning finished goods, which are checked against the actual items shipped before being deducted from the finished goods quantity.

As the above on-line sales order processing procedures are completed for each order at the corporate level, the order is processed in real time by the Shipping Schedule Program (see Chapter 14) for determining what warehouse(s) or plant(s) will ship the merchandise. Also, at this time a multiple-part customer order set is prepared at the corporate level. Likewise, a printout is teletyped to the appropriate warehouse(s) and/or plant(s) for shipping goods. The major aspects of the sales order processing procedures are complete with the actual shipment of the goods.

The order operations described above take about 15 to 25 minutes, depending on the complexity of the order from the time the operator starts with the customer order number until the information is received by the warehouse or plant. By and large, the time in which orders can be pulled after receiving them in a real-time processing mode ranges from one to several hours. When these two times are added together, the customer service level is very high, indicating that orders, in many cases, can be shipped the day they are received. However, owing to unforeseen operating conditions, it is possible for service time to be longer for orders, whether they are shipped from the warehouses or plants.

ADVERTISING AND PERSONAL SELLING MODULES

The OR method that has been used in the past to solve the advertising problem for the Consumer Products Corporation is linear programming. (As noted under integrated MIS, there are deficiencies in this approach.) The ideal goal of any advertising media model is to provide the optimum exposure in terms of potential consumers to be reached, frequency of exposure desired among various prospective consumer segments, and other relevant decision rules. The more promising approach, which comes closest to this goal and minimizes the deficiencies of linear programming, is a custom-made advertising simulation model that incorporates probability elements.

The need for probability factors enters into the model because of the time problem. For example, assume that a monthly magazine will be utilized, reaching the consumer directly. If the consumer was exposed (meaning that he noticed and read the advertisement) on the average of nine out of twelve issues, then the probability of exposure to the average issue would be .75; if the exposure was six out of twelve, the probability would be .50; and so forth. However, this approach fails to take into account the fact that the consumer's first exposure makes a greater impression than later exposures. The problem of how to treat additional exposures is solvable by ascertaining the effect of each additional exposure, given certain time intervals between exposures. Thus, the first month's exposure for a new product might be rated .9, the second month also .9 because of the newness of the product introduced, the third at .75, and so on.

The advertising simulation model, which evaluates alternative exposures to potential customers over time as submitted by the advertising manager, consists of procedures discussed below.

1. The use specifies the target customers by indicating their characteristics.
2. The media schedule to be evaluated is inserted—that is, each advertising medium and advertisements by time periods are listed. As noted above, the user inputs different weights for the first and successive exposures.
3. The time units (periods) to be used, say weekly or monthly, are stated.
4. The number of advertisements to be used during time period one, two, and succeeding periods are listed. This instructs the computer when to move from one time period to the next.
5. The program selects an individual from the target customers. The individual is asked if he was exposed to each of the specific media under consideration. Because it is not known which particular advertisements are seen by an individual, a random process is used to determine which advertisement he does see. For each advertising medium, a random number is generated. If the individual's probability for that particular

media is, for example, .75, and if the random number is less than .75, the program considers that he was exposed to that particular advertising message. If, on the other hand, the random number is greater than .75, the program considers that he did not see the advertising, and the next advertisements are analyzed in similar fashion with respect to the same individual.

6. The data score obtained in step (5) is recorded as part of the individual's record for first, second, and following exposures so that they can be appropriately weighted over the time period under study. The score consists of exposure multiplied by the value assigned to that particular exposure.

All further computer looping procedures are essentially the same process as in steps (4) through (6). All individuals selected are scanned with respect to their exposure to the time period for the advertising medium included in the model. The output consists of the individual's scores and a target audience exposure distribution.

The advertising simulation model in a real-time MIS environment can be employed at any time. As depicted in Figure 9-16, advertising personnel can utilize a remote I/O terminal for appropriate output. For example, the advertising manager can call the above program or a comparable media selection program. Depending on the program, he can type in information, such as the size of the advertising budget, the number and size of important market segments, media exposure and cost data, advertisement size and color data, sales seasonality, and other information. The computer will return a media schedule that is calculated to achieve maximum exposure and sales impact in the desired customer segment(s). Thus, advertising media models lend themselves to real-time responses.

Personal selling, like advertising, can benefit greatly from the real-time capabilities of the computer system. From the viewpoint of sales management, interactive models permit the manager via a remote I/O device to examine systematically the consequences of alternative selling strategies. By allowing the manager to work in a simulated environment, interactive models can provide important insights about "what would happen if . . ." without the difficulties inherent in experimenting with a real-world sales force. They do not make decisions for the manager per se, but provide a basis for analysis and decision. In a similar manner, programs for monitoring sales strategy and reporting potential marketing problems as soon as they begin to develop, on an "exception reporting" basis, are an integral part of a real-time management information system. For example, a sales manager can dial a sales redistricting program, type in data on the work load and/or sales potential of various geographical areas, their distances from each other, and the number of sales territories to be created. The computer will evaluate this information and assign various areas to make up new sales territories in such a way that (a) the sales territories are approximately equal in work load and/or sales potential and (b) they are compact in shape, thus cutting travel costs.

When personal selling is considered from the salesman's viewpoint in an interactive real-time mode, a salesman can enter the catalog number of a desired item through the terminal keyboard (followed by the character D for detailed). The

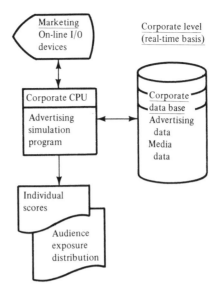

FIGURE 9-16. Advertising media model for a real-time MIS marketing subsystem.

CRT retrieves information from the inventory data base and flashes back a display, including description, availability for sale, in transit, and the quantity on order. Next to the description appears the name of the product and its catalog number. "Availability for sale" represents the most current inventory as calculated and stored on line by the system. "In transit" refers to the orders released to the warehouses and the plants. Finally, "quantity on order" refers to orders received but not as yet shipped. Current finished goods inventory data, then, can be retrieved by salesmen using either stationary (on the firm's premises) or portable (in the customer's office) I/O terminal devices.

MARKET RESEARCH AND PRICING MODULES

Throughout the development, introduction, and life of a product, the firm's marketing managers are faced with a number of decisions which require accurate market assessments. Frequently, substantial resources are committed for research and development, test marketing, and other related costs prior to the critical "go or no-go" decision. If the conclusion is to market the product, the marketing executive must decide on such matters as the amount of promotional expenditures, the allocation of these expenditures among different media, their allocation over a period of time, the amount of sales effort to be invested, and the duration of any special support for the product.

A chain reaction of other important decisions is initiated in other areas of the company, such as production and purchasing, because operations are geared to adjust to the new requirements. There may also be a substantial impact on research and development activities, because the potential success or failure of a new product could greatly affect the development of other similar or complementary products. In this regard, the success, or even the survival, of a business firm depends on the ability of the company's executives to anticipate the future (or at least to anticipate it better than the firm's competitors do).

Because of the complexity of the phenomena to be predicted, the need for greater accuracy, and the dependency of outcomes on so many different variables, marketing management of the Consumer Products Corporation has directed that its market research activities utilize venture analysis for the new product development phase only. This approach directs the systems designers to structure a marketing data base which will be conducive to employing this OR technique.

Of paramount importance for venture analysis is the definition and evaluation of the specific variables, assumptions, constraints, and like items to be considered for inclusion in the model. For example, in terms of variables, an itemization of all candidate variables based on the subjective judgments of marketing research and other marketing personnel is necessary. Knowledge of the marketing environment and the relative importance of various factors is imperative. Then a cursory review is made of the sources of needed historical information. It is necessary to build a data base of historical data covering not only this company's new products but also all new products introduced in the industry over the past few years for which adequate source data are available. It is from these data that the mathematical relationships subsequently expressed in the model are derived. Thus, it is apparent that considerable pertinent data are needed before a new product can be effectively evaluated.

Essentially, venture analysis measures the relationships among many factors expressed in mathematical terms for the purpose of predicting the future. The underlying rationale is that if (a) for all new products introduced over a substantial period of time there is a strong relationship between demand levels and the specific variables considered during the early period of a product's life, and if (b) this relationship persists, the probable market activity for future new products can be estimated from corresponding early-period variables. From these interacting relationships, reliable output can be generated which includes aggregate demand, levels of demand at various points in time, prices throughout the product's life cycle, upper and lower limits of profits that can be expected over its life, and comparable analysis as programmed into the model.

It should be noted that as time passes, the new product should be reevaluated periodically in light of new information and current market conditions. The marketing executive needs for decision-making purposes, during the critical first year after the product is introduced, include systematic reevaluation and possible revision of initial demand forecasts to reflect current knowledge. These analyses need to be generated at specific intervals after introduction.

Once the foregoing venture analysis program is operational, a market researcher can sit at an I/O device and call in the program (Figure 9-17). The researcher will then supply various estimates as they are called for by the computer, including the estimated size of the target group, recent product trial rates, repeat purchases, the promotional budget, size of investment, target rate of return,

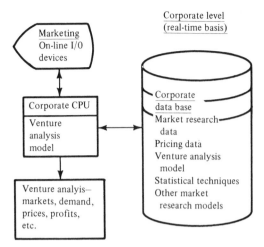

FIGURE 9-17. Market research model—venture analysis for a real-time MIS marketing subsystem.

product price, and gross profit margin. The computer will process this information and print out a forecast for the next few years of the total number of customers, company market share, price(s), period profits, and discounted cumulative profits. The market researcher can alter various input estimates and readily ascertain the effect of the altered data on sales and profits. Also, he can perform the analyses deemed necessary for the new product under study.

Included in the venture analysis model is a determination of prices at various stages during the life cycle of the product. Utilizing the pricing model (set forth earlier) within venture analysis, the program relates a myriad of price, advertising, personal selling, sales promotion combinations for the product under study, and pertinent facts about competing products. Heuristically, the venture analysis model must hypothesize about the degree to which competitors will react to a price change and in what form this reaction will occur. It "guesses" on the basis of a hypothesis what blend of marketing decisions will go best with a given price. In turn, it determines what effect the given price will have on the sales of other products in the product line. Thus, the pricing aspects of a new product are included in the venture analysis model.

SUMMARY

The marketing subsystem of the Consumer Products Corporation is the originating unit of real-time MIS order activities because it is the liaison between the firm and its customers' needs. Within this subsystem, forecasting centers around exponential smoothing formulas that combine past and current information in an objective manner, thereby providing a quantitative means to assist in making judgments about future sales levels to meet customer needs. Quarterly forecasts make "things happen" within the firm by triggering inputs to many of the other subsystems. In a similar manner, the customer order initiates action within and outside the marketing subsystem. Whether goods are produced based on a quarterly forecast or on special order, a prime concern of the marketing subsystem is fast and reliable customer service. Design considerations, then, for this type of environment represent a difficult undertaking.

The ability of the marketing subsystem to provide real-time responses applies not only to sales forecasting, sales analysis, and sales order processing but also to advertising, personal selling, and market research. Marketing personnel and their managers are capable of retrieving current data stored on the common data base and combining them with appropriate operations research techniques for evaluating new products over their life cycle, determining appropriate prices, selecting the best advertising medium in terms of exposures and constraints, and comparable information. In essence, marketing information can be retrieved and manipulated on a "now" basis. This enables the firm to be forward-looking in its many marketing modules that utilize real-time decisions.

QUESTIONS

1. In what ways is the real-time MIS marketing subsystem superior to the integrated MIS marketing subsystem?

2. Referring to Figure 9-7, define the detailed data base elements for:
   a. sales orders data
   b. advertising and media data
   c. salesmen data

3. Suggest additional operations research techniques that can be applied to the marketing subsystem.

4. Referring to Figure 9-10, determine submodules for:
   a. personal selling
   b. market research and pricing

5. Suggest an alternative OR method for forecasting the firm's sales each quarter.

6. Define in some detail the major modules of the sales order processing computer program.

7. How is the simulation advertising model superior to the linear programming model?

8. Referring to the section on market research, design an ideal real-time MIS operating environment for this marketing area.

REFERENCES

Berenson, C., "Marketing Information Systems," *Journal of Marketing,* October, 1969.

Brien, R. H., and Stafford, J. E., "Marketing Information Systems: A New Dimension for Marketing Research," *Journal of Marketing,* July, 1968.

Cardozo, R. N., Ross, I., and Rudelius, "New Product Decisions by Marketing Executives: A Computer-controlled Experiment," *Journal of Marketing,* January, 1972.

Chambers, J. C., Mullick, S. K., and Smith, D. D., "How to Choose the Right Forecasting Technique," *Harvard Business Review,* July-August, 1971.

Cravens, D. W., Woodruff, R. B., and Stamper, J. C., "An Analytical Approach for Evaluating Sales Territory Performance," *Journal of Marketing,* January, 1972.

Darden, B. R., "An Operational Approach to Product Pricing," *Journal of Marketing,* April, 1968.

Fogg, C. D., and Rokus, J. W., "A Quantitative Method for Structuring a Profitable Sales Force," *Journal of Marketing,* July, 1973.

Free, V. H., and Neman, T. E., "Market Research Matches Products to Consumers," *Computer Decisions,* May, 1972.

Haavind, R., "Computer Shape Products, Aids Sales Effort," *Computer Decisions,* January, 1972.

Hamburg, M., and Atkins, R. J., "Computer Model for New Product Demand," *Harvard Business Review,* March-April, 1967.

Kelly, J. P., *Computerized Management Information Systems.* New York: The MacMillan Co., 1970, Chap. 4.

King, W. R., "Methodological Simulation in Marketing," *Journal of Marketing,* April, 1970.

Kotler, P., "Corporate Models: Better Marketing Plans," *Harvard Business Review,* July-August, 1970.

——, "The Future of the Computer in Marketing," *Journal of Marketing,* January, 1970.

——, "Operations Research in Marketing," *Harvard Business Review,* January-February, 1967.

Lambin, J. J., "A Computer On-Line Marketing Mix Model," *Journal of Marketing Research,* May, 1972.

McNiven, M., and Hitton, B. D., "Reassessing Marketing Information Systems," *Journal of Advertising Research,* February, 1970.

Miller, D. W., and Starr, M. K., *Executive Decisions and Operations Research.* Englewood Cliffs, N.J.: Prentice-Hall, Inc., 1969, Chap. 11.

Montgomery, D. B., and Urban, G. L., *Management Science in Marketing.* Englewood Cliffs, N.J.: Prentice-Hall, Inc., 1969.

Montgomery, D. B., and Webster, F. E., "Application of Operations Research to Personal Selling Strategy," *Journal of Marketing,* January, 1968.

Moyer, M. S., "Management Science in Retailing," *Journal of Marketing,* January, 1972.

Poliski, I., "Ryerson Puts Its Salesmen On-Line," *Business Automation,* July, 1969.

Treason, R. V., Jr., "MARKAD: A Simulation Approach to Advertising Management," *Journal of Advertising Research,* Vol. 9, No. 1.

REAL-TIME MIS RESEARCH AND DEVELOPMENT SUBSYSTEM AND ENGINEERING SUBSYSTEM

10

The importance of research and development (R & D) to a company's growth cannot be understated. A productive research and development effort is a prime source of new products and processes crucial to the firm in the long run. Once new products have been developed to a certain stage, the engineering department takes over the detailed design and testing. This phase includes value engineering (value analysis) for controlling costs of the new product. Likewise, the engineering function is concerned with implementing manufacturing facilities that are capable of producing the product at the lowest cost. Thus, research and development, combined with engineering, provide the necessary thrust for meeting anticipated customer and market needs, now and in the future.

Initially, the chapter explores the essential elements of an integrated management information system for R & D and engineering before considering important design aspects for real-time MIS. For these two subsystems, data base elements, OR models, and submodules are discussed, thereby forming a basis for their detailed development and design. The design of R & D includes:

> pure research
> applied research (product development)

For engineering:

> product design (value engineering)
> plant engineering (systems engineering)

Essentially, research and development and engineering subsystems for the Consumer Products Corporation are structured on these functions.

INTEGRATED MIS RESEARCH AND DEVELOPMENT AND ENGINEERING SUBSYSTEMS

Input at the corporate level for the integrated MIS research and development subsystem of the Consumer Products Corporation generally originates with either the customer or the market research department, depending on the type of project. The marketing department may receive customer inquiries regarding a new product or a substantive modification to an existing product. A *research and development order* is then initiated for its development. Similarly, those in the market research section may have their own ideas on what new products should be developed. This, too, will result in an R & D order. Other times, one firm will want to utilize the talents and expertise of another firm in order to pool research talents such that a larger contract can be obtained. In the final analysis, research and development projects can originate from several sources.

Before physical operations for a new or revised product can commence, it is necessary to design the product from scratch, after which the engineering specifications are forwarded to the manufacturing department. The *engineering blueprints* form the basis for producing the parts, subassemblies, frames, and comparable items. The material requirements for the product to be manufactured are summarized on *bills of materials* and are the basis for determining the number of detailed items for the production order. With engineering specifications and appropriate bills of materials prepared, these data can be forwarded to the manufacturing subsystem.

Research and development and engineering subsystems, based upon the foregoing functions, do not operate alone, but rely on the output of a prior subsystem. As depicted in Figure 10-1, output from customers and market research play a vital role in R & D projects. Once research is completed for a specific project, the detailed design and testing is undertaken by the engineering subsystem. Once the

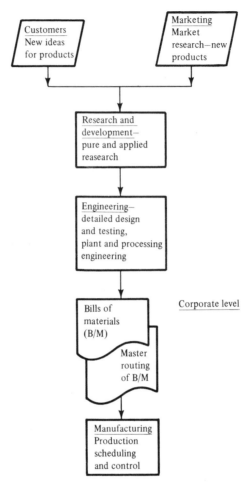

FIGURE 10-1. Research and development and engineering data flow
for an integrated MIS system.

prototype has been developed and is ready for regular production runs, the production scheduling and control department utilizes the bills of materials and master routing forms to integrate this new product into regular manufacturing operations. Thus, the efforts of R & D and engineering are integrated with the firm's other subsystems in order to achieve the desired objectives of providing the right product at the right time for the firm's customers.

PURE RESEARCH

Pure or basic research seeks new knowledge from which patterns of facts and ideas are developed that lead to a deeper understanding of man and his environment. The pure researcher uses all the knowledge that can be gathered from any source and exerts ingenuity in order to fulfill a certain need. Initially, there is no definite output expected in a pure research project. General ideas and concepts are set forth before specific ones are developed. At times, there may appear to be no overall direction to the project owing to the very nature of the research. A basic research area is pursued with the hope that it can be developed for business and/or industrial uses. In the final analysis, the primary aim of pure research is expansion of knowledge in a field without direct applications in mind.

The accent in pure research is on experimental theory and practice. From observation and careful study of phenomena or events, facts are obtained which may then be fitted together in an experimental pattern—that is, a working hypothesis. If the facts fit well into the hypothesis, new subjects for observation or new experiments from which come new facts are explored; and there is increasing confidence in the validity of the facts and the consistency of the theory. On the other hand, if the facts do not fit into a recognized pattern, further study of their validity must be undertaken to insure that they have not been vitiated by some error(s). At the same time, it may be necessary to reexamine the theory and, if necessary, to modify it in order to accommodate the new facts. The foregoing process is a cyclic one. Only when the facts and the experimental theory fit together can the R & D group be satisfied with final results. The product of this research is a pattern or general theory which enables the researcher to understand the phenomena or events under study.

Although the Consumer Products Corporation (like most other corporations) engages in very little pure research, it does explore possible consumer preferences in the long run, say ten years hence. In order to retrieve current literature on the subject, the R & D staff utilizes the batch processing computer approach, illustrated in Figure 10-2, which centers around a library search program. Basically, the subject matter search cards are key-punched and key-verified and run against the R & D master magnetic tape files. An output listing of appropriate sources for pure research is produced. The listing includes books, magazine articles, and special reports. Also, during this run, library R & D additions are added to the master files, resulting in new master files being written. The library search program, then, can not only retrieve research and development information on a demand basis, but can also produce updated R & D master files.

APPLIED RESEARCH (PRODUCT DEVELOPMENT)

Whereas pure research seemingly has no immediate payoff, it can be the fountainhead for new-product technology. The ideas and concepts gathered through its evolutionary process can give rise to a large number of products. Before the phenomenon can be turned to practical use, it must be understood and defined in practical terms. The endeavor to extend the understanding of basic phenomenon, determine its practical significance, and develop useful applications is called applied research. In some cases, a prototype product is developed. Other times, the principal effort of applied research is directed toward understanding the basic phenomenon being investigated in order to obtain sufficient information for use in the design of a prototype. Applied research will be used in the former sense and includes product development.

Applied research is an intermediate between the discovery of the basic phenomenon and the generation of a final product. It, like pure research, does not necessarily return immediate dividends. However, the possibility of attaining profits from this work is greater than with pure research. In many cases, applied research is performed by organizations that did not discover the basic idea(s) on which their R & D efforts are based. This is basically true for the Consumer Products Corporation because the firm is not financially able to spend much money or time on basic research.

The procedure set forth in Figure 10-2 for pure research is also applicable to applied research—that is, an output listing of applicable applied research information can be extracted from the R & D master magnetic tape files. In addition, the integrated MIS approach makes use of PERT/Time, which is a method of minimizing trouble spots by determining them before they occur so that various parts of the overall project can be coordinated. In effect, PERT usage on R & D projects keeps the research and development manager apprised of all critical factors and considerations that bear on his decisions. From this viewpoint, it can be a valuable managerial tool in R & D decision making.

When PERT is used for R & D projects, it is performed on a weekly basis, (see Figure 10-3). At that time, new R & D projects (if any) plus changes to current projects are key-punched and key-verified, thereby serving as input to the PERT/Time computer program as well as the previous week's R & D PERT magnetic tape file. Output of this processing run includes listings by activities and by slack time as well as the critical path. These PERT listings are scrutinized carefully by the R & D manager, who takes appropriate action deemed necessary.

PRODUCT DESIGN (VALUE ENGINEERING)

Once the prototype has been developed by the applied research group, the engineering department must determine the final design so that it can be manufactured in an efficient and economical manner. Engineers must determine the detailed specifications for the product. Not only must mechanical engineering detail be determined down to the lowest level, but electrical circuitry also must be designed by the firm's electrical engineers. The net result of these activities are drawings which are summarized by part numbers on a bills of materials (B/M) listing.

Before the product design can be finalized, there is need to apply *value engineering,* or *value analysis.* This concept requires that the engineer adopt a broader point of view and consider whether the parts contained in the finished product perform the required function both as efficiently and as inexpensively as possible. The appraisal focuses on the function which the part, or the larger assembly containing the part, performs. To illustrate, the product is dismantled and each part is mounted adjacent to its mating part on a table. The idea is to demon-

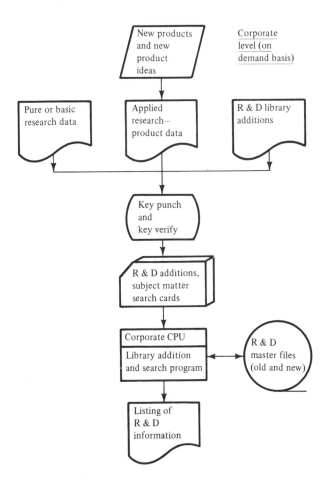

FIGURE 10-2. Pure research or applied research data flow for an integrated MIS research and development subsystem.

strate visually the functional relationships of the various parts. Each component is studied as it relates to the performance of the complete unit rather than as an isolated element. A value analysis checklist contains literally hundreds of questions and key ideas for reducing overall costs as well as maintaining the same level of product performance. Illustrative general questions found in the checklist (prepared by the National Association of Purchasing Management) are:

Can the part be eliminated?

If the part is not standard, can a standard part be used?

If it is a standard part, does it complement the finished product or is it a misfit?

Can the weight be reduced with lower-priced materials?

Are closer tolerances specified than are necessary?

Is unnecessary machining performed on the item?

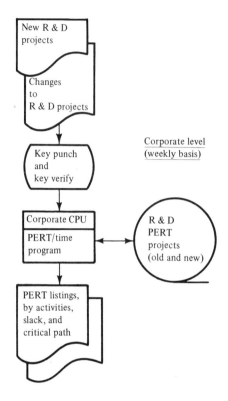

FIGURE 10-3. Applied research projects using PERT/Time in an integrated MIS research and development subsystem.

Are unnecessary finishes required?

Can you produce the part less expensively in your plant or should you buy from the outside?

Is the product properly classified for shipping purposes to obtain lowest transportation rates?

Can cost of packaging be reduced?

When using value engineering to appraise overall costs, possibilities for making component part design simplifications are frequently more apparent than is possible under the conventional design conditions. This in no way reflects unfavorably on the work done by the design engineer; the discovery of such potential improvements is the result of an analysis with a substantially broader orientation than that possessed by the original designer. A value analysis study undertaken by the Consumer Products Corporation utilizes the background and skills of several people because it is impossible to combine the multiplicity of skills and experiences in the person of a single designer. Resulting design changes often permit the substitution of standardized production operations for more expensive operations requiring special setup work. In other cases, an entirely different material or production process turns out to be more efficient than the one originally specified. In the final analysis, value engineering contributes to the profitability of new products.

The bills of materials, along with the master routing for manufacturing the product, are forwarded to the data processing section for key-punching and verifying (Figure 10-4). These cards and their respective changes, including the engineering master magnetic tape file, provide the input for producing a new engineering master file. While the foregoing processing occurs at the corporate level, these same data are transmitted to the appropriate plants to have their engineering master magnetic tape file updated. Likewise, printouts of bills of materials and master routings are produced at the plant or division level. With this direct tie-in of corporate headquarters with the division plants, data files on both levels are the same except for the time lag of one day's processing activities.

PLANT ENGINEERING (SYSTEMS ENGINEERING)

The engineering activities for a new product are not complete when product design and testing are completed. There is need for plant engineering, which determines the appropriate plant equipment and machinery for manufacturing the product. One of the essential requirements in any automation opportunity is to decide whether the possible automation plan really will accomplish what it should in terms of saving dollars and increasing the return on the firm's investment. This involves using systems engineering techniques to develop totally new concepts. Also, the Consumer Products Corporation's management can eliminate much of the guesswork about the eventual success or failure of any proposed automation program for one or more products by employing a thorough systems engineering analysis before making substantial capital expenditures. Because automation involves expensive capital equipment, it makes good sense to spend approximately 5 percent of the total equipment cost to determine (a) what should be purchased and (b) whether the ultimate total systems savings will be high enough to warrant replacing current nonautomated operations with automated equipment for one or more new products. The primary advantage of systems engineering, then, is that a competent planning job at a fraction of the overall cost will minimize the chances of a costly mistake in terms of equipment and machinery outlays.

Systems engineering is defined as an approach for finding the most profitable overall combination in choosing and using physical assets. The systems engineering method is the delineation of a clearly specified set of alternates, the formulation and use of a formal structure or model for comparing the merits of alternates according to some quantifiable objective, and the testing and probing of the chosen alternates to determine whether or not some new combination may be superior. Systems engineering techniques are an optimum blend of tried and true engineering economics plus the recent advances in the fields of optimization, operations research, and human factors engineering.

Automating a certain process might affect a number of operations before and after that process because of the changes in procedure or product flow brought

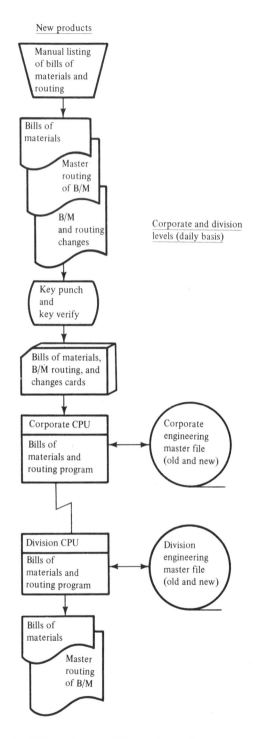

FIGURE 10-4. Bills of materials and routing data flow for an integrated MIS system.

about by automation. Systems engineering reduces the possibility of problems by spotlighting the various interactions between processes and also by defining how procedures in the entire manufacturing line should be upgraded to make automation work effectively. In reality, mistakes on automated machinery and equipment can be remedied through systems engineering.

Systems engineering, a concept new to the Consumer Products Corporation, has just begun to be implemented. By and large, the firm has not employed this concept for its integrated MIS; rather, it has used past experience, intuition, and judgment to determine the manufacturing process, the number of machines, and the number of plant personnel. However, in a real-time MIS environment, the system engineering concept will be utilized for installing plant engineering equipment and determining manufacturing processes.

REAL-TIME MIS DESIGN CONSIDERATIONS FOR RESEARCH & DEVELOPMENT AND ENGINEERING

Design considerations for R & D and engineering subsystems in a real-time MIS environment differ from those of an integrated MIS. However, the same input sources are employed—namely, customers for new-product ideas and the market research department for new products. A major difference between integrated and real-time MIS is the real-time processing capability of the latter, which allows R & D and engineering personnel the ability to retrieve data on a "now" basis. This capability allows highly paid company employees to be more productive in their respective departments, an important plus factor for keeping overhead under control. Thus, an effective design for real-time MIS R & D and engineering subsystems must concentrate on making professional and highly technical personnel more productive as well as integrating their activities with the firm's other subsystems.

OVERVIEW OF R & D AND ENGINEERING ENVIRONMENT

The major functions found in a R & D and engineering real-time MIS environment are depicted in Figure 10-5. Just as with integrated MIS, they include pure research, applied research, product design, and plant engineering. As indicated previously, the design of these subsystems will take on new dimensions because of the computer's real-time capabilities. Research and development and engineering data, being stored on the common data base, will be retrievable as is or capable of manipulation, depending on the user's needs. Also, within this operating mode, operations research models will be employed frequently. Simulation will become a common approach for answering questions relating to applied research, product design, and appropriate manufacturing processes.

As illustrated in Figure 10-5, sales order processing (which receives orders from customers) at the corporate level forwards regular production orders to the

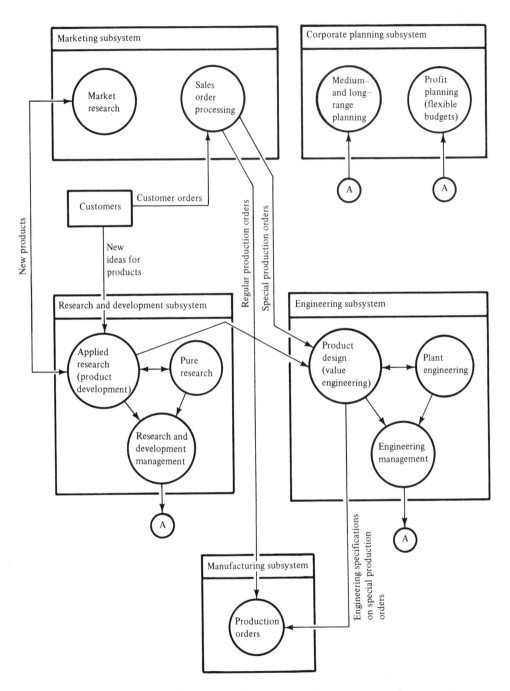

FIGURE 10-5. Real-time MIS research & development and engineering subsystems flow to and from other subsystems.

manufacturing subsystem on the division level. Special production orders, on the other hand, are forwarded to the product design section of the engineering subsystem. After design and value analysis of the new product, engineering specifications (blueprints), including bills of materials and master routing sheets, are sent to the manufacturing subsystem.

Although these procedures represent most activities for initiating production, the firm's customers as well as the market research department provide the impetus for innovation of new products. Eventually, some of these proposed products are developed to the prototype stage by R & D, after which they are designed by the engineering section. The processing flow thereafter follows the normal flow for special production orders.

R & D AND ENGINEERING DATA BASES

The research and development and engineering data bases as shown in Figure 10-6 should be structured by the type of data. Of equal importance is the ease of accessability to display or print critical information by a remote I/O terminal without extensive search of the data base and extensive manipulation. With these design considerations in mind, these two subsystems will be better able to meet the real-time demands placed on them. Also, this ordered, logical approach to data base design will result in lower system and day-to-day operating costs.

The common data base for R & D consists of time and cost data for current projects, literature reference to pure and applied research, and product development data. These elements, operating at the corporate level, are related to engineering. Common engineering data elements consist of engineering specifications for products, product design requirements, sample test values, bills of materials, master routing of parts through the plant for each product, plant engineering constraints, and process engineering specifications. As noted in Figure 10-6, bills of materials, master routing, and plant and process data are stored on the division data base. These data are needed for daily plant operations.

The cost data base elements of both subsystems are related to the corporate planning subsystem data elements. For example, the dollar amounts alloted to current R & D projects are an integral part of the corporate planning subsystem's flexible budgets. In a similar manner, engineering (when utilizing value analysis for new products) is given a stated percent of sales price for manufacturing costs which must not be exceeded. Otherwise, the firm's return on total assets and overall profits will start to decline. Hence, R & D and engineering must operate within the cost constraints placed on them.

OR R & D AND ENGINEERING MODELS

Numerous operations research models have been developed for the various modules of R & D and engineering. Specifically, these center around PERT and simulation techniques. PERT/Cost will be used for controlling research and development projects. Simulation, on the other hand, is an essential tool for analyzing

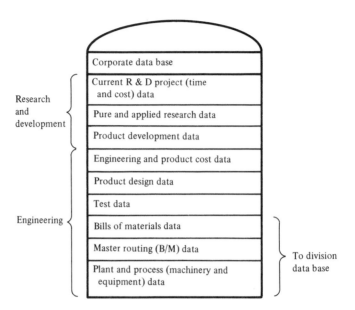

FIGURE 10-6. Typical R & D and engineering data base elements at the corporate level.

and evaluating applied research projects. In the engineering area, simulation has been employed to determine the amount of wear and tear on parts comprising the final product, the ability of the parts to withstand continued stress, and comparable analyses. Likewise, plant engineering has utilized simulation to determine the proper number of employees to work on a production line. PERT has been employed during the transition phases from development to prototype and add-on production. The transition phase can prove to be crucial because of such reasons as commitments to customers and the best utilization of factory facilities. In view of the emphasis on PERT/Cost and simulation techniques, each will be discussed.

PERT/Cost

PERT/Cost, an expansion of PERT/Time, integrates time data with cost data. It incorporates both time and cost into a network so that trade-offs of time and cost can be calculated. To understand the essentials of this OR technique, time and cost estimates must be indicated for each activity in the network. There is a normal time and cost estimate as well as a crash time and cost estimate. The *normal time estimate* is analogous to the expected time estimate using standards, and the *normal cost estimate* is the amount associated with finishing the product in the normal time. The *crash time estimate* is the time that would be required if no costs were spared in trying to reduce the project time. The project manager would do whatever was necessary to speed up the work. The *crash cost estimate* is the cost associated with finishing the project on a crash basis in order to minimize completion time.

The formula for *incremental cost* I_c (cost to crash an activity from the normal cost) is as follows:

$$I_c = \frac{C_c - N_c}{N_t - C_t}$$ Equation 10-1

where C_c = crash cost
N_c = normal cost
N_t = normal time
C_t = crash time

Employing this formula, incremental costs for each activity can be used to reduce the total project time at the least additional cost. A research and development project, such as in Figure 10-7, shows time and cost for each activity on a normal basis and a crash basis as well as incremental costs for each activity, calculated by Equation 10-1. It can be shown that the normal time is 23.5 weeks at a cost of $203,000. When the same project is crashed in terms of time and cost, the time is 19.5 weeks with a cost of $268,500. However, it may not be necessary to crash every activity in order to meet the time requirements of 19.5 weeks; this will be more apparent after the various activities are crashed week by week.

The PERT/Cost networks employing the values found in Figure 10-7 are located in Appendix D. The procedures center around crashing only critical activities. Based upon the final PERT network of 19.5 weeks, one of the two critical paths or 1-4-6-7 indicates that the network has been crashed as far as possible. Thus, all activities, 1-4, 4-6, and 6-7, have been crashed to the fullest extent. However, as indicated above, a question regarding the necessity to crash every activity in the project can be raised. Figure 10-8 will serve as a basis for answering this question.

Activity	Normal (or Expected) Time	Crash Time	Normal (or Expected) Cost	Crash Cost	Incremental Cost per Week
1-2	3.6	2.6	$ 8,000	$ 10,000	$ 2,000
1-3	5.0	3.0	15,000	20,000	2,500
1-4	4.6	3.6	25,000	32,500	7,500
2-5	2.4	1.4	4,000	6,000	2,000
3-5	3.6	2.6	6,000	7,500	1,500
3-6	8.0	6.0	30,000	40,000	5,000
4-6	9.4	8.4	45,000	60,000	15,000
5-7	8.8	6.8	35,000	50,000	7,500
6-7	9.5	7.5	35,000	42,500	3,750
			$203,000	$268,500	

FIGURE 10-7. Normal and crash estimates (time and cost) plus incremental cost per week for R & D project.

Project Time	Least Additional Cost	Project Cost
23 1/2 weeks (normal)	—	$203,000
22 1/2 weeks	$ 3,750	206,750
21 1/2 weeks	3,750	210,500
20 1/2 weeks	7,500	218,000
19 1/2 weeks (modified crash)	15,000 + 2,500	235,500
19 1/2 weeks (crash)	33,000	268,500

FIGURE 10-8. Project time and cost for PERT network.

The project cost of $235,500 (Figure 10-8) of 19½ weeks is called a modified crash program. Because the expenditure of an additional $33,000 does not further reduce the project completion time, there would be no logical reason for using the crash program costing $268,500. An examination of the original data reveals that it was not necessary to crash the following activities:

Activity	Number of Weeks	Cost
1-2	1	$ 2,000
1-3	1	2,500
2-5	1	2,000
3-5	1	1,500
3-6	2	10,000
5-7	2	15,000
		$33,000

Thus, instead of crashing every activity, only the critical activities need be crashed, resulting in a modified crash cost of $235,500 versus $268,500 (Figure 10-8) for crashing every activity.

Simulation

Simulation, as described in Chapter 8, is a quantitative technique for evaluating alternative courses of action based upon facts and assumptions with a computerized mathematical model in order to represent actual decision making under conditions of uncertainty. Although simulation methods are often employed as management decision-making tools, such as in working out production planning problems, they can also be applied to some types of engineering problems. For example, in a critical assembly involving an eccentric shaft supported by an eccentric mount, a question can be raised as to whether or not the assembly can be made because of highly demanding tolerance specifications. In such a case, the staff engineer has data concerning the part's dimensions and tolerances from past experience. He can feed these data into a computer and, in effect, instruct the computer to take randomly chosen samples of parts dimensions and combine them in accordance with trigonometric formulas to obtain the resulting assembly dimensions. The values obtained can be plotted automatically in the form of a frequency distribution pattern. If the results obtained are within the required assembly specifications, the engineer knows he can count on satisfactory production by using the equipment presently available.

R & D AND ENGINEERING MODULES

The major research and development module, like the major engineering module, can be expanded into its many submodules and their related parts. R & D can be subdivided into pure research and applied research and engineering can be broken down into product design and plant engineering which, in turn, can be divided further, as shown in Figures 10-9 and 10-10. These flowcharts of system modules allow the designer to visualize what components make up these areas. Also, they allow the pinpointing of duplicate functions within the module itself. Likewise, duplicate submodules can be related to other subsystems. It will be noted that the basic modules and their related submodules are basically the data base elements contained in Figure 10-6. The design of each major module, operating in a real-time MIS operating mode, is treated in subsequent sections of the chapter.

REAL-TIME MIS RESEARCH & DEVELOPMENT AND ENGINEERING SUBSYSTEMS

An examination of data base elements and OR models, as well as R & D and engineering modules, is extremely helpful to the system designer before he undertakes the detailed design. Generally, the design approach taken in the remainder of the chapter is not complex. However, as with other subsystems, there is need to recognize both input from other areas and output to integrated subsystems. In a similar manner, data base elements should be capable of serving user needs from other subsystems. Application of the foregoing items, then, is essential if the real-time R & D and engineering subsystems are to meet their objectives of timely information at a reasonable cost.

R & D AND ENGINEERING OVERVIEW

The research and development and engineering subsystems, as illustrated from an overview standpoint in Figure 10-11, are by necessity linked directly with other subsystems in a real-time MIS environment. The input from customers and market research provide R & D management with desired information that is used in developing new products. These outputs, in turn, form the basis for designing and testing new products. In addition, mechanical and electrical engineering drawings are summarized on bills of materials and master routing of parts are prepared. The information is stored on the corporate common data base, and is also forwarded to the three plants for exploding bills of materials and routing parts through the various manufacturing work centers. Thus, the outputs of R & D and engineering are the basis for planning and controlling manufacturing operations.

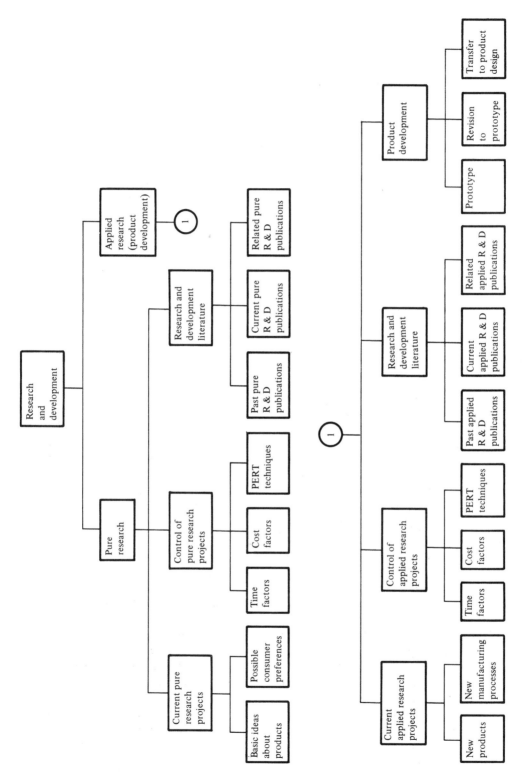

FIGURE 10-9. R & D modules of the Consumer Products Corporation.

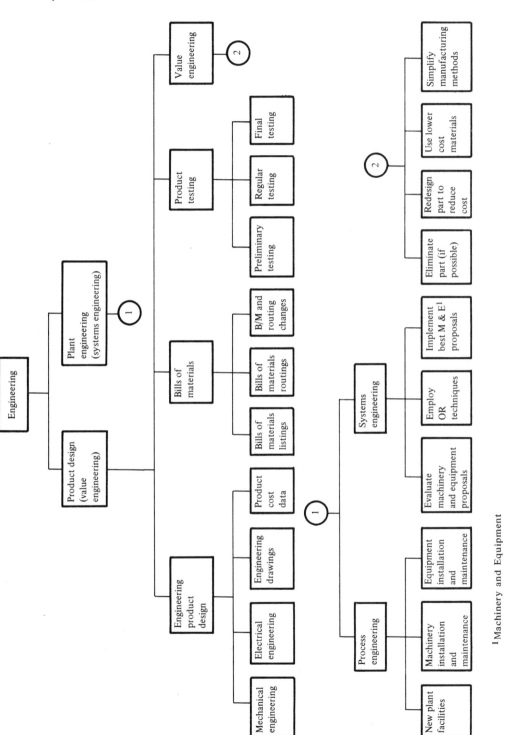

[1]Machinery and Equipment

FIGURE 10-10. Engineering modules of the Consumer Products Corporation.

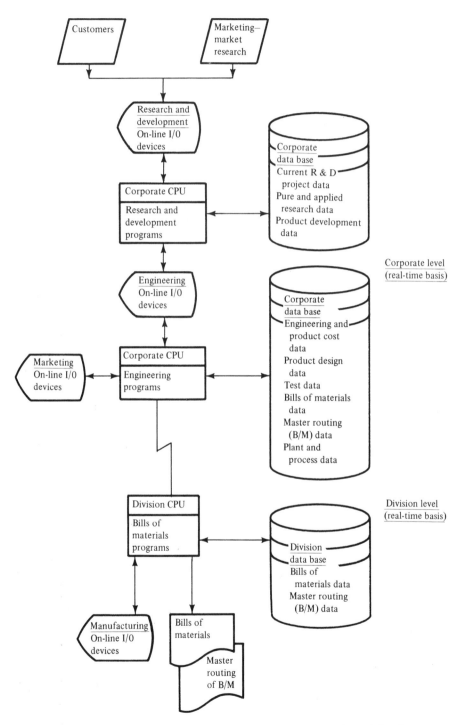

FIGURE 10-11. An overview of real-time MIS research and development and engineering subsystems.

PURE RESEARCH MODULE

The primary aim of pure or basic research for the Consumer Products Corporation, as stated earlier, is the expansion of knowledge without direct applications in mind. A basic difficulty the firm is experiencing with this type of research is that developmental problems are frequently ill-defined. Although the firm's involvement in basic research is limited, a considerable portion of its efforts is devoted to problems to which no formal problem-solving methods apply. In essence, there is a continuum that ranges from relatively well-defined problems to such undefined problems. Furthermore, the more abstract the project, the greater the uncertainty that surrounds the forecasting of success or failure.

In view of the foregoing difficulties in pure research (this also applies to applied research on a more limited basis), there is need to develop specific R & D guidelines. These include:

1. finding out what the firm's research people are doing and why
2. establishing a detailed schedule and planning system
3. setting criteria for satisfactory performance
4. controlling the selection of research projects

Initially, this calls for establishing a R & D control group, consisting of at least the R & D manager, one research specialist, and one independent management engineer.

Once the control group has been formed, its first task is segregating R & D employees into one of four categories: professional, semiprofessional, skilled, and semiskilled. Next, the present work activities can be broken down to see how much time professionals are spending on professional, semiprofessional, skilled, and semiskilled work as well as how much money they should be spending on each activity. Generally, the results are very revealing—higher-paid employees are often found to be doing work that could be easily accomplished by semiskilled R & D persons.

The second guideline—establishing a detailed schedule and planning system—is an integral part of the real-time MIS. Detailed step-by-step activities are developed for each R & D project using a PERT/Cost network, explained in a prior section of this chapter. As illustrated in Figure 10-12, current data about pure (and applied) research projects can be retrieved on a selected basis by those in charge, principally the R & D manager, the control group, and the corporate planning staff. For a more complete analysis of current R & D projects, PERT/Cost printouts can be obtained, indicating where the project is ahead or behind schedule as well as the cost status of each project. Likewise, the cost of crashing the project and a modified crash cost is retrievable from the common data base. Hence, this real-time approach provides close control over R & D schedules and their actual costs.

The third guideline, setting criteria for satisfactory performance, means segregating the defined activities and using tabulating methods to analyze them by employing an operations-methods matrix (operations are defined in the rows and methods are shown in the columns—their intersection is represented in weeks

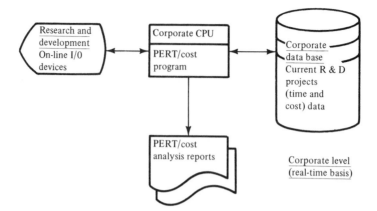

**FIGURE 10-12. Pure research (applied research) PERT/Cost data flow
for a real-time MIS research and development sub-
system.**

or percent of total project time). When the operations-methods matrix is properly
filled out, activities which consume large amounts of time can be examined closely
with the view of reducing time. To assist R & D personnel in researching current
research publications and thereby keeping overall project time to a minimum, I/O
devices are available for referencing the data base as shown in Figure 10-13. Current
research publications are displayed and the task of finding the research material is
relegated to a semiskilled researcher. Also, the I/O terminals located in the R & D
department can be used for simulating part or all of the project in order to obtain a
higher level of project performance.

The last guideline—controlling the selection of research projects—is integrated
with the corporate planning subsystem. Considerations center around the risks and
timing plus cash flow. Evaluation of R & D projects should provide a basis for
establishing priorities and projecting budgets. In addition, projects must be related
to long-range research planning and the company's objectives.

APPLIED RESEARCH MODULE (PRODUCT DEVELOPMENT)

Applied research, like pure research, utilizes the four guidelines set forth
above. However, because the very nature of applied research is oriented toward
new-product development, there is need to have a formalized product planning
committee. This group should meet on a prescribed basis and should include R & D,
marketing, and management personnel. Its task is to select the more promising
products for development to the prototype stage after going through a very careful
screening process of potential products.

Ideas from the group itself or company employees should be considered and
recognized. Recognition is particularly important when the company's own
employees are involved; often the best and least costly new product developmental
ideas are the ones generated in-house. Also, experience has shown that successful

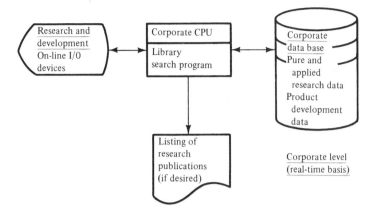

FIGURE 10-13. Pure research (applied research) search data flow for a
real-time MIS research and development subsystem.

new product ideas come from a systematic analysis of market needs, particularly
for long-range products.

Generally, many product ideas for new company marketing areas come
from external sources, such as universities, industrial research firms, product research
firms, large corporations who license some of their "offbeat" technology, trade journals, trade fairs and expositions, and company contractors and subcontractors. A variety of government sources of new-product ideas also exist. In addition, overseas
sources of new product ideas can be valuable. Almost invariably, a number of
approaches must be pursued vigorously and simultaneously to insure the likelihood
of a fruitful yield.

The major phases during the life of an applied research project are shown in
Figure 10-14. The first two steps are the responsibility of the product planning
committee described above. The corporate planning staff assigns the appropriate
funds, which are controlled by the PERT/Cost program; the degree of performance
in terms of time and cost are controlled via this OR technique. The product
planning committee evaluates the product's performance throughout its developmental stages and, as noted in the final decision shown in Figure 10-14, can
terminate the project if it does not meet its established criteria. Assuming that
progress is satisfactory and a successful prototype has been completed, the project
can then be forwarded to the engineering department for detailed product design
and extensive testing.

In addition to using the PERT/Cost technique (Figure 10-12) for planning
and controlling R & D projects, applied research, like pure research, relies upon the
ability to retrieve current published material on the product being developed
(Figure 10-13). But just as important to R & D activities is the utilization of
simulation models to develop the prototype itself. Likewise, simulation can be used
to test the proposed product under varying conditions. The real-time capabilities
for developing a new product, when used in conjunction with OR techniques, then

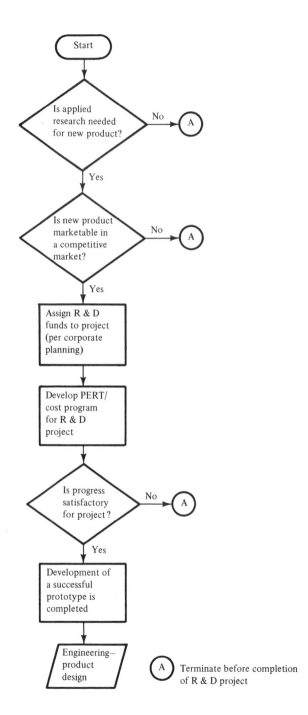

FIGURE 10-14. Phases is the life of an R & D project (applied research) in a real-time MIS environment.

can be employed extensively where there is need for man/machine interaction to solve the R & D project at hand. The ability to make additions and changes immediately can speed up the project and at the same time reduce the time and cost to complete applied research.

PRODUCT DESIGN MODULE (VALUE ENGINEERING)

Product design centers around the activities of mechanical and electrical engineering. The number of possible combinations for the design of complex parts is quite large. In such design situations, human experience and intuition, aided by a graphics display unit, plays an important role in their solution. The engineer displays on the screen curves interrelating the variables (Figure 10-15). The variables can be cross-plotted rapidly on the display screen. Using command-control techniques, he utilizes a light pen to identify a particular point, line, or character in the displayed image. The photo-detector associated with the pen, sensing light at that point, generates a signal for the program. The light pen can be used alone or in conjunction with a keyboard to rearrange or delete information, or to add lines from a base point already lighted by the CRT beam.

The use of computer-aided design techniques is an essential element of the detail drafting. For example, when the designer wishes to draw a two-dimensional mechanical assembly, the computer will be asked for a specific station cut or cross-section through the finished product. This view will be displayed on the graphics console. Using stored subroutines, the designer will "draw" the details of the assembly, consisting of straight lines, circular arcs, and various higher-order curves. In this manner, the computer will generate various geometric features such as a draftsman would make with a standard drawing instrument. When the designer wants to utilize a standard part, it will be called up by having its part number keyed in. He will build his assembly using a combination of standard parts and new construction. As he interacts with the graphics display unit, the computer is programmed to accumulate an up-to-date parts list on line as part of the engineering data base which automatically indicates the part number and the number of parts

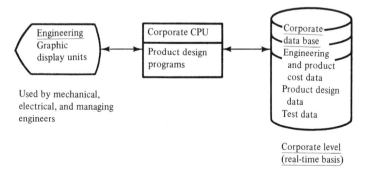

FIGURE 10-15. Product design data flow for a real-time MIS engineering subsystem.

used. When the design is complete, a printout can be requested of the bills of materials and master routing sheet. (More will be said about bills of materials and master routing data flow below.)

Once the new product has been designed and tested by the mechanical and electrical engineers, the product's component parts are subjected to value analysis, in the same manner described for the integrated MIS.

In using such a checklist, the value analysis group evaluates the component parts under investigation with respect to each item on the checklist. When a question is not answered to the satisfaction of the group, this becomes the starting point for a more detailed investigation. Thus, the checklist assists in focusing on those factors which past experience has proved to be potentially fruitful cost reduction areas.

Appropriate changes are made to the product's component parts based on value analysis before final bills of materials are prepared along with the final master routing of parts through the plant's manufacturing centers. They are input to the computer system, illustrated in Figure 10-16. As you will recall, data on new products have been stored on the corporate data base during the design phase. Input changes are used to update not only the corporate data base but also the division data base. Output at the division level is directed toward storing bills of materials and master routing about the product on the common data base as well as producing printouts of both, thereby providing each plant with essential information for manufacturing the finished product.

PLANT ENGINEERING MODULE (SYSTEMS ENGINEERING)

Engineering activities in a real-time MIS environment, as in integrated MIS, are not finished when product design and testing are completed. Automated equipment and machinery for manufacturing the new product must be engineered. Hardly any factory automation can be considered alone; what happens in one area has repercussions of some sort up and down the production line. In systems engineering analysis, each time a change is made at one point on the line, there is generally a corresponding increase or decrease in the costs incurred in another area.

In view of the difficulties and cost of setting up or modifying a production assembly line, simulation techniques enable plant engineers to get an "advance look" that can be obtained from different combinations of variable factors. The simulation approach taken in a real-time MIS varies, as indicated in Figure 10-17. For small simulation programs—that is, small in the sense of input and program data—real-time processing offers the faster approach. However, for programs requiring a large number of program steps and input data, batch processing is the better approach. It is much faster for the high-speed card reader to read input data than it is to enter data through the keyboard of an I/O device. The type of simulation study, then, determines the level of processing.

The introduction of a new product on the minor or major assembly lines generally calls for a simulation study because it is much easier and less costly to resolve bottlenecks and manufacturing problems on the computer than in the plant

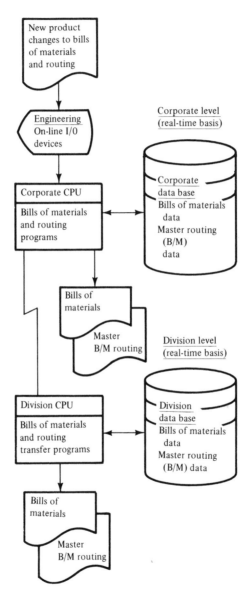

FIGURE 10-16. Bills of materials and routing data flow for a real-time MIS engineering subsystem.

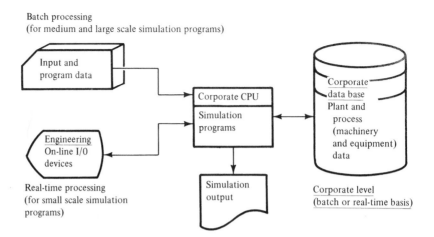

Batch processing
(for medium and large scale simulation programs)

Input and
program data

Corporate CPU

Simulation
programs

Corporate
data base
Plant and
process
(machinery
and equipment)
data

Engineering
On-line I/0
devices

Real-time processing
(for small scale simulation
programs)

Simulation
output

Corporate level
(batch or real-time basis)

**FIGURE 10-17.   Plant engineering simulation data flow in a real-time
MIS engineering subsystem.**

itself. In a similar manner, the question of making tool changes during the normal
two-shift operations or on a third shift at a very high cost is a task for simulation.
Referring to the latter problem, the first simulation run showed that operating
efficiency for the Los Angeles plant was quite low—about 45.6 percent—with tool
changes occurring during the regular two shifts. A second run was made using the
same assumptions as above, except that it was assumed that all tool changes would
be handled on the third shift, and therefore not effect downtime during working
hours. The results of this simulation run showed greatly improved efficiency—from
45.6 to 69.7 percent. The profit from the increase in output more than offset the
penalty paid for bringing workers in on the third shift to make the appropriate tool
changes. It should be noted that these two simulation runs represent only a small
portion of the variations that might be investigated.

SUMMARY

The research and development and engineering subsystems of the Consumer
Products Corporation, operating in a real-time MIS environment, are highly integrated with many of the firm's other subsystems. In particular, data are fed from
market research to R & D for product development, and are then forwarded to
engineering for detailed design. Engineering output in the form of drawings, bills of
materials, master routing, and comparable items are the basis for manufacturing
activities. All of these integrated activities are under the direction and control of
the corporate planning subsystem. Design considerations in this type of environment are a difficult undertaking, requiring the highest level of systems designing.

   An overview of R & D and engineering indicates that generalities in terms of a
new product become more exacting as it passes from pure research to applied
research and then to product design, testing, and plant engineering. Whereas pure

research has little interest in an end product per se, applied research is searching for a useful end result and product design is aimed at production from which potential profits can be substantial. Consequently, when applied researchers seek to obtain necessary funding from the corporate planning staff, they have an advantage over basic researchers. They are closer to the production phase in the product evaluation process and their work is subject to a somewhat smaller financial risk. Product design, still closer to the production phase, has even less difficulty in obtaining funds for the design and testing of the new product. Similarly, plant engineering generally experiences very little trouble in obtaining funds for new machinery and equipment if a favorable return on investment is forthcoming.

QUESTIONS

1. a. How is the real-time MIS research and development subsystem an improvement over an integrated MIS R & D subsystem?

b. How is the real-time MIS engineering subsystem an improvement over an integrated MIS engineering subsystem?

2. Distinguish between value engineering and systems engineering in a real-time MIS environment.

3. Refer to the engineering data base elements in Figure 10-6 and relate them to the corresponding engineering modules.

4. Suggest additional OR techniques that can be applied to R & D in a real-time MIS operating mode.

5. Refer to Figure 10-10 and determine submodules for:
   a. mechanical engineering
   b. electrical engineering
   c. product cost data

6. Referring to the section on applied research (product development), suggest changes that reflect an ideal real-time MIS operating system.

7. Referring to the section on product design (value engineering), suggest changes that reflect an ideal real-time MIS operating system.

8. How does the R & D subsystem complement the engineering subsystem in a real-time MIS?

REFERENCES

Bigosinski, J., "Risk Analysis for Project Identification, Evaluation, and Design," *Consulting Engineer,* November, 1970.

Bright, J. R., "Technology Forecasting—New Tools for an Old Responsibility," *Research Management*, July, 1972.

Clarke, C. V., and Manasse, F. C., "Put Your Research and Development Under a Microscope," *Business Management,* April, 1969.

Feigenbaum, D. S., "Systems Engineering and Management: Operating Framework of the Future," *Journal of Systems Management,* August, 1971.

Garver, D. P., and Srinivasan, V., "Allocating Resources Between Research and Development: A Macro Analysis," *Management Science,* May, 1972.

Gausch, J. P., "Value Engineering and Decision Making," *ASSE Journal,* May, 1974.

Hill, L. S., "Towards an Improved Basis of Estimating and Controlling R & D Tasks," *The Journal of Industrial Engineering,* August, 1967.

Ledly, R. S., Shaller, H. I., Rotolo, L. S., and Wilson, J. B., "Methodology to Aid Research Planning," *IEEE Transactions on Engineering Management,* June, 1967, Vol. EM-14, No. 2.

Libik, G., "The Economic Assessment of Research and Development," *Management Science,* September, 1969.

Lockett, A. G., and Gear, A. E., "Representation and Analysis of Multi-stage Problems in R & D," *Management Science,* April, 1973.

Magad, E. L., "Cooperative Manufacturing Research," *Industrial Engineering,* January, 1972.

Maker, P. M., and Rubenstein, A. H., "Factors Affecting Adoption of a Quantitative Method for R & D Project Selection," *Management Science,* October, 1974.

Moore, J. R., and Baker, N. R., "Computational Analysis of Scoring Models for R & D Project Selection," *Management Science,* December, 1969.

Plant, A. F., "Maximizing New Product Dollars," *Industrial Research,* January, 1971.

Russell, E. J., "R & D Evaluation—The Total Program Approach," *Financial Executive,* December, 1970.

Stults, F. C., "Management Engineering," *Journal of Systems Management,* March, 1970.

REAL-TIME MIS MANUFACTURING SUBSYSTEM

11

The manufacture of finished products involves many operations. Not only must plant, equipment, and tools be provided but appropriate personnel must also be hired and trained to utilize the manufacturing facilities. Raw materials and goods in process must be available when needed. Production must be planned, scheduled, routed, and controlled for output that meets specific deadlines. An effective management information system in this area, then, is a study unto itself.

Manufacturing informational needs vary from work center and production reports for operating management to specific operational machine data for in-plant line personnel. Pertinent information for these needs is extracted from common files and then is presented in a manner that permits timely and appropriate action. This chapter focuses on various methods of obtaining needed information from these on-line and off-line files. Also, it specifies the essential design components of a typical manufacturing subsystem in both an integrated and a real-time MIS operating mode.

353

Initially, the manufacturing subsystem for the Consumer Products Corporation, operating in an integrated MIS environment, is presented. After this brief review of present operations, real-time MIS design considerations are explored for this functional area. Specifically, the data base, operations research techniques, and manufacturing modules are discussed. This analytical approach provides a sound basis for the detailed design of important manufacturing modules which include:

> receiving
> production scheduling and control
> manufacturing operations
> > machine shop
> > assembly-minor and major
> > plant and machine maintenance
> quality control and inspection
> data collection system

Basically, these major functional modules are the structure upon which the manufacturing subsystem is built for the Consumer Products Corporation in a real-time MIS environment.

INTEGRATED MIS MANUFACTURING SUBSYSTEM

The firm's products can be produced in anticipation of demand, upon receipt of customers' orders, or some combination of the two. If goods are being produced to order, a sales order copy, in many cases, may be the *production order* (regular or special). The usual arrangement is to have the production scheduling and control department initiate action on the order, which is then distributed to stock control, shipping, and accounting departments. The original copy is kept in the manufacturing plant files.

Manufacturing materials can be obtained from outside or within the firm. If a *purchase requisition* is prepared, it is forwarded to the purchasing department; otherwise, a *materials requisition* is prepared. Other typical records and forms found within the manufacturing function are *periodic production reports, tool orders, material usage reports, material scrappage reports, inspection reports, labor analysis reports, cost analysis reports,* and *production progress reports.*

The central point of the integrated MIS manufacturing subsystem is a magnetic-tape-oriented data bank (Figure 11-1). Entries are made at different intervals depending on the type of data. Each manufacturing division (plant) employs punched card procedures in order to provide input for the data bank. The manufacturing divisions in Los Angeles, Minneapolis, and Philadelphia utilize a remote batch operation to send data to the corporate office. All period data are accumulated on interim magnetic tapes. At the end of a period, such as a week or a month, sort/merge program routines are employed to combine the latest data with past records. At that time, cumulative and exception manufacturing reports (and new magnetic tape files) are produced for division management. Summation reports

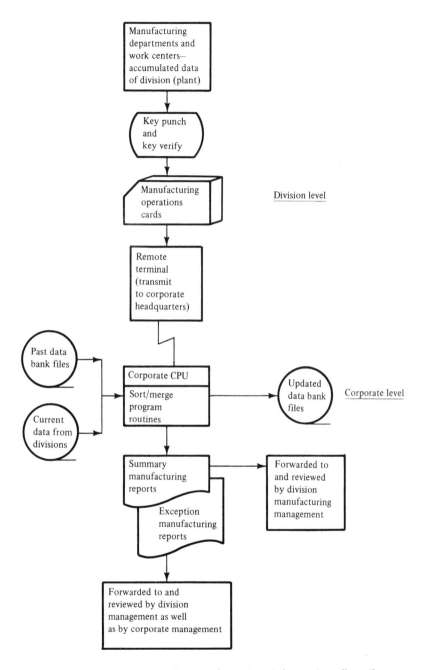

FIGURE 11-1. Overview of manufacturing information flow from divisions to corporate headquarters in an integrated MIS manufacturing subsystem.

are forwarded to the three manufacturing plants. Periodic summation and exception reports are reviewed by the plant managers and corporate management in terms of past activities. In essence, historical reports are produced in order to review the status of budgets, orders, production, and comparable manufacturing operating information.

RECEIVING

As soon as goods are received from suppliers, the receiving department checks the enclosed packing slip against a copy of the purchase order (Figure 11-2). Once the receiving clerk is satisfied that the goods correspond to those on the purchase order, he prepares receiving tickets, noting any discrepancies between the order and actual material received. Sometimes an inspection record may be prepared by the receiving department along with the receiving tickets. Copies of both are sent to data processing (for key-punching and key-verifying), purchasing, stock control, manufacturing, and accounting. A carbon copy is retained by the receiving department.

Goods are delivered by the receiving department to the stock control department or to any other department that has ordered them. Generally, the individual or department that physically takes possession of the materials acknowledges receipt by signing a copy of the receiving report. In this manner, the receiving department is relieved of responsibility for the acquired materials and supplies.

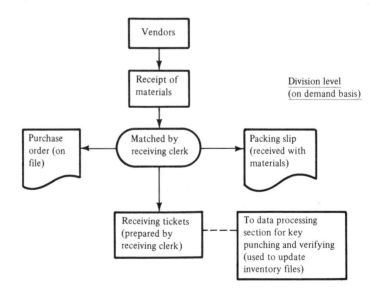

FIGURE 11-2. Receiving data flow for an integrated MIS manufacturing subsystem.

PRODUCTION SCHEDULING AND CONTROL

Production scheduling and control is predicated upon quarterly sales forecasts for the seven basic product groups (consisting of well over fifty individual products). As pointed out in a previous chapter on marketing, quarterly sales in an integrated MIS environment are forecasted by the "least-squares" method. These forecasts, in turn, are broken down by corporate manufacturing management as weekly production quotas for scheduling and control of each manufacturing plant.

The manufacturing operating function is based on a "production order" concept. Weekly, production quotas are sent to the production scheduling and control departments (three plants) by corporate manufacturing management and are the basis for the next week's production. Production scheduling and control issues production orders to the various manufacturing departments and work centers based upon exploded bills of materials (to be explored in a subsequent section), which are the basis for layup lists (detailed parts) which are sent to inventory stock control for parts procurement. The production order lists in sequence the departmental operations for each product to be produced. On completion in one work center, the parts are sent to the next work center in sequence. Expeditors and tracers follow the parts (Figure 11-3). Work center reports from production scheduling and control are issued weekly to corporate and division manufacturing management.

The present system leaves much to be desired, because manufacturing work centers receive operational information at least a week after the work has been completed. Exception reports are generated and distributed, but only after the critical time period has passed. The interaction of departmental delays is manually "guesstimated" and used to control the appropriate work centers. This approach leads to problems of human inefficiency—thus, an integrated MIS approach is not the most desirable one for controlling manufacturing operations.

MANUFACTURING OPERATIONS

All of the manufactured products for the Consumer Products Corporation must pass through three manufacturing departments—machine shop, minor assembly, and major assembly—as illustrated in Figure 11-3. However, there are a number of manufacturing work centers within each department. Depending on the product itself, it may have to be processed through more than one work center before manufacturing is completed for that department. In addition to the foregoing three manufacturing departments, a plant and machine maintenance department is maintained to service all work centers for more efficient production.

The machine shop is the first department to initiate a production order. Once an order is entered and scheduled, the parts layups are made. One layup proceeds immediately to the machine shop area, another goes to the minor assembly area, and a final one to major assembly. However, minor assembly cannot be started until

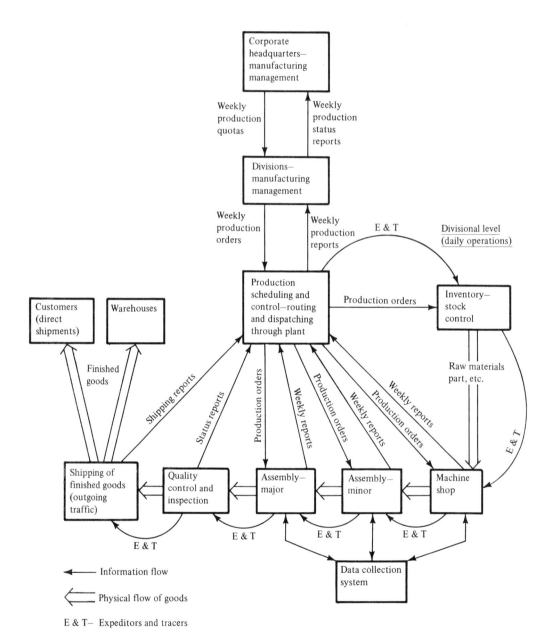

FIGURE 11-3. Manufacturing order processing flow in an integrated MIS environment under the direction of production scheduling and control.

the processed parts from the machine shop are received. The machine shop is the key to all assembly operations (Figure 11-3); completion dates from all succeeding departments depend on the availability of parts from the machine shop.

Before manufacturing activities of the various departments and work centers can begin, the weekly production order schedule (based on production quotas from corporate headquarters) must be key-punched and key-verified before being processed at the division level. Basically, the Bills of Materials Explosion Program (Figure 11-4) determines what quantities of materials and parts are to be withdrawn from inventory as well as the dates when they are needed. It should be noted that the proper level of inventory on hand to meet production requirements is a function of the inventory and purchasing subsystems, the subject matter for Chapters Twelve and Thirteen, respectively.

After exploded inventory requirements by periods have been prepared by the computer on a weekly basis, they are forwarded to departmental supervisors and work center foremen and are used to prepare material requisitions for layup lists. Completed materials requisitions are presented to the stockroom for forwarding of

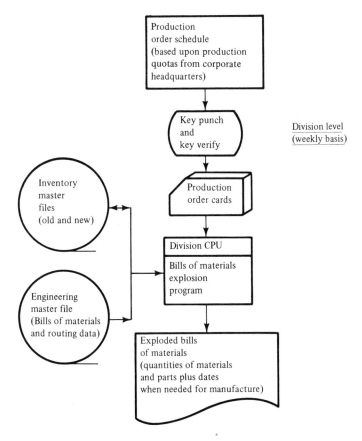

FIGURE 11-4. Exploded bills of materials data flow for an integrated MIS manufacturing subsystem.

the materials as required. As illustrated in Figure 11-5, the materials requisitions form the basis for cutting punched cards. Later, these cards, which represent issues to production, are input to update inventory files at the corporate level.

Operational procedures for handling plant and machinery maintenance are basically on a manual basis within an integrated MIS operating mode. Machine failures are reported by work center personnel to their respective foremen who, in turn, call for maintenance personnel to fix the required machine(s). (As will be seen in a real-time MIS environment, the real-time computer monitors machine functions and reports via I/O devices in the maintenance department the status of the machines. When failures are recognized by the on-line computer system, a typed output alerts personnel to the situation.)

QUALITY CONTROL AND INSPECTION

The quality control and inspection department is an important control point in the manufacturing subsystem. It can have a profound impact on the firm's profits. The detection here of a bad part costing only $2 can save hundreds of dollars in manufacturing troubleshooting and rework. Statistical analysis and control techniques are employed to aid this department in evaluating the quality of manufactured parts and finished products. Although their outputs take different routes, as seen in Figure 11-6, manufactured parts and finished products are nevertheless additions to their respective inventory files. Eventually, corporate inventory files are updated via remote batch processing.

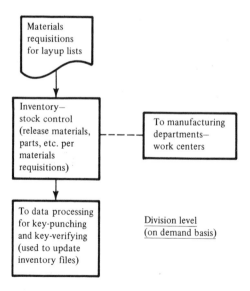

FIGURE 11-5. Materials requisitions data flow for an integrated MIS manufacturing subsystem.

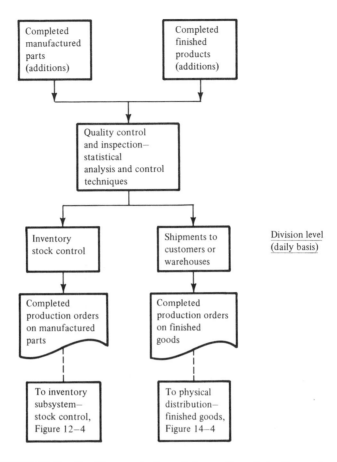

**FIGURE 11-6. Quality control and inspection data flow of manu-
factured parts and finished products for an integrated
MIS manufacturing subsystem.**

DATA COLLECTION SYSTEM

The data collection system at the division level for the three manufacturing
plants serves as a basis for paying plant employees as well as costing the firm's
products. In the first case, weekly employee time attendance cards are punched in
and out by employees on a time clock recorder. At the end of the week, these cards
are reviewed by the appropriate foremen before being forwarded to the data
processing section for key-punching and key-verifying. Immediately following this
punched card phase, these time cards are the initial input for computerized payroll
processing procedures found in the accounting subsystem. In the second case,
separate weekly employee production order cards are utilized to record time on the

various jobs. Plant employees ring in and out on a time recorder clock near their workplace. Weekly, the manufacturing work center foremen check these cards against the time attendance cards to insure that payroll records are compatible with cost records (Figure 11-7). Also at this time, production order cards are key-punched and key-verified before being merged on the divisional computer in order to produce a labor cost file. As will be seen in the chapter on the accounting subsystem, the labor cost file is employed to produce a weekly work center labor cost analysis report for division management.

REAL-TIME MIS DESIGN CONSIDERATIONS FOR MANUFACTURING SUBSYSTEM

Design considerations for a real-time MIS manufacturing subsystem are generally complex when viewed in terms of the data base. From this viewpoint, manufacturing activities are related to many other subsystems. To produce meaningful information from the data base for controlling manufacturing operations, OR models are often employed. Mathematical models which can access on-line data at any time allow manufacturing management and line personnel to control their activities on a "now" basis, quite unlike that available in an integrated MIS.

OVERVIEW OF MANUFACTURING ENVIRONMENT

The environment in which the manufacturing subsystem operates is illustrated in Figure 11-8. The information flow throughout the system is noted by a single arrow, while a double arrow denotes the physical flow of goods. Within this subsystem, management has the ultimate responsibility for coordinating manufacturing activities. However, the production scheduling and control section is the important coordinator of ongoing manufacturing operations. This group feeds back critical information based upon a programmed response to plant foremen or to higher levels of manufacturing management as deemed necessary.

MANUFACTURING DATA BASE

The data base elements of the Consumer Products Corporation which are needed for the manufacturing subsystem are related directly to many other subsystems. Important data base elements from other subsystems, as seen in Figure 11-9, are processed from on-line operations, stored, and retrieved by the manufacturing subsystem. The data base at the division level contains usable information for controlling current manufacturing operations. The real effectiveness of this data base approach is the fact that redundant manufacturing data are eliminated because all subsystems share the same manufacturing data elements.

In order for the manufacturing subsystem to operate effectively and efficiently, plant personnel utilize various I/O terminal devices for desired data base

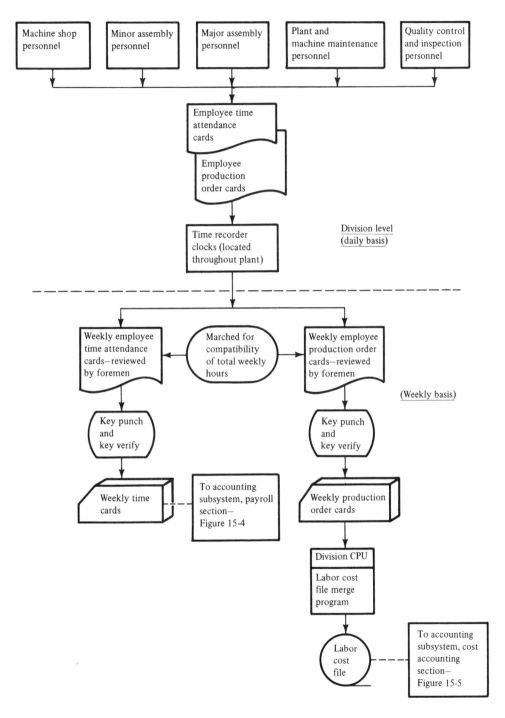

FIGURE 11-7. Data collection system for an integrated MIS manufacturing subsystem.

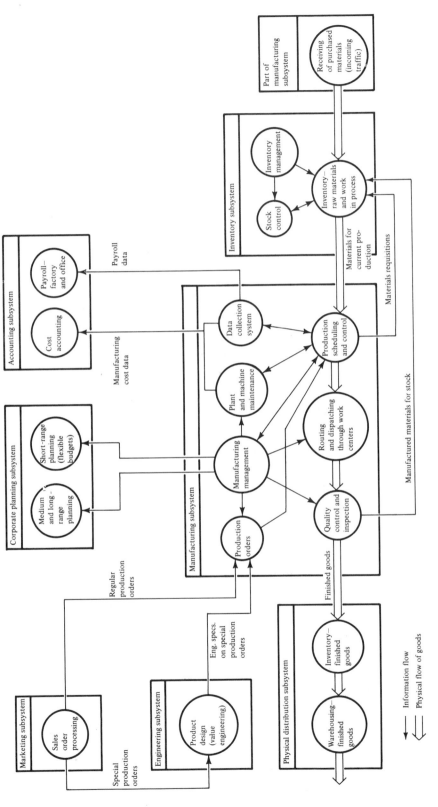

FIGURE 11-8. Real-time MIS manufacturing subsystem information and physical flow to and from other subsystems.

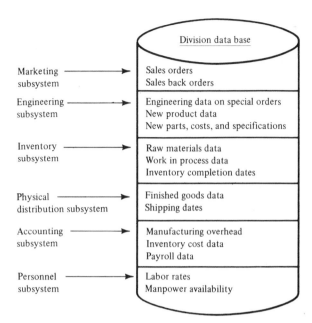

Marketing subsystem ────────▶

Engineering subsystem ────────▶

Inventory subsystem ────────▶

Physical distribution subsystem ────────▶

Accounting subsystem ────────▶

Personnel subsystem ────────▶

Division data base

Sales orders
Sales back orders

Engineering data on special orders
New product data
New parts, costs, and specifications

Raw materials data
Work in process data
Inventory completion dates

Finished goods data
Shipping dates

Manufacturing overhead
Inventory cost data
Payroll data

Labor rates
Manpower availability

FIGURE 11-9. Interrelated real-time MIS subsystem data base elements for manufacturing operations (division level).

responses. Data flows in and out of the data base according to the detailed design found in subsequent sections of this chapter. Before output responses can be operational, complex computer programs, many of which include OR models, are essential. Examples of OR program approaches are included in the next section and the remaining sections of the chapter.

By and large, divisional manufacturing management of the Consumer Products Corporation has need for a more detailed breakdown than that required for corporate manufacturing management. Whereas corporate management is concerned with flexible budgets, income statements, future production quotas, and summations and/or exceptions for all of its operations, division management is more concerned with day-to-day operations than with possible future operations. This division requirement lends itself to a separate and a more detailed data base than that for corporate headquarters. Typical manufacturing data base elements at the corporate and division levels are shown in Figure 11-10. Additional information regarding these two data bases will be given later in the chapter when each major manufacturing module is analyzed.

OR MANUFACTURING MODELS

Mathematical models of operations research, when used in conjunction with the firm's data base, provide an excellent way of controlling current and future manufacturing activities. Manufacturing management can plan, organize, direct, and

FIGURE 11-10. Typical manufacturing data base elements at the division and corporate levels.

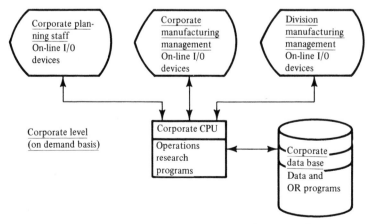

FIGURE 11-11. Real-time MIS operating environment between corporate headquarters and the three manufacturing plants.

control divisional production by real-time and daily computer output from remote I/O devices (Figure 11-11). Actual manufacturing times, capital equipment utilization, and comparable manufacturing information are sent to appropriate personnel as they occur. From this on-line accumulation of the data base, manufacturing management reports are produced on a timely basis.

An important responsibility of corporate manufacturing management is to determine the product loads for each manufacturing plant. From future sales forecasts, management can determine efficient manufacturing schedules. Drawing from the data base by an on-line I/O device, quarterly plant capacities can be utilized. In a similar manner, variable costs per product group and individual product can be calculated from the accounting subsystem data base. By utilizing the simplex method of linear programming, manufacturing quotas for the three manufacturing plants can be determined based upon the forecasted period sales.

Linear Programming (Simplex Method)

The approach illustrated for determining period production quotas of the Consumer Products Corporation is the simplex method of linear programming (Figure 11-12). Variable Costs and quarterly plant capacities necessary for this operations research technique are stored on the common data base and are as follows:

Basic Product Groups	1	2	3	4	5	6	7	Quarterly Plant Capacity
Plant (Los Angeles)	$ 6	$7	$5	$4	$8	$6	$5	700,000 units
Plant (Minneapolis)	10	5	4	5	4	3	2	400,000 units
Plant (Philadelphia)	9	5	3	6	5	9	4	1,000,000 units
								2,100,000 units

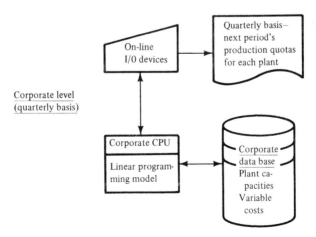

FIGURE 11-12. Data flow for determining production quotas for next period as found in a real-time MIS manufacturing subsystem.

The linear programming presentation will center around the seven basic product groups. However, the proper approach would be to include all of the cost factors and capacities for each of the firm's products (over fifty). In like manner, consideration should be given to the minimum number of products that must be manufactured by each plant in order that finished goods can be shipped to the nearest warehouse. This approach would keep overall shipping costs between manufacturing plants and warehouses at a minimum. Although these two factors should be an essential part of the linear programming model, space does not permit such a presentation.

Variations in the above quarterly plant capacities and product costs are due to differences in the number and the speed of machinery, regional wage contracts, and other manufacturing factors. Plant capacities are calculated from past data and represent average outputs per machine. The marketing department has forecasted next period's product group requirements (three months) to be:

Basic product group	
1	100,000 units
2	200,000 units
3	450,000 units
4	400,000 units
5	200,000 units
6	350,000 units
7	300,000 units
	2,000,000 units

It should be noted that the entire capacity of three plants (2,100,000 units) is not needed to meet next period's forecasted quotas (2,000,000 units). Thus, there is slack plant capacity of 100,000 units.

In order to express the problem mathematically, it is necessary to let a series of X's represent the quantities of the basic product groups that are to be manufactured by each plant. These are set forth as X_1 through X_{21} in Figure 11-13. In addition, plant capacities and next period's requirements are shown as well as the slack column, which represents the 100,000 units of unused capacity. In the final analysis, the optimum solution must satisfy the column requirements and the row requirements per Figure 11-13. With the addition of slack variables (X_{22} through X_{24}) and artificial variables (X_{25} through X_{31}), Figure 11-13 can be restated per Figure 11-14 for the simplex method of linear programming.

The optimum solution for the values set forth in Figure 11-14 are obtained by applying the iterative process of the simplex method, as found in Appendix E. Basically, matrix inversion is employed in determining the quantity variables. Based

Basic Product Groups	1	2	3	4	5	6	7	Slack	Plant Capacity
Plant— Los Angeles	X_1	X_2	X_3	X_4	X_5	X_6	X_7		700,000
Plant— Minneapolis	X_8	X_9	X_{10}	X_{11}	X_{12}	X_{13}	X_{14}		400,000
Plant— Philadelphia	X_{15}	X_{16}	X_{17}	X_{18}	X_{19}	X_{20}	X_{21}		1,000,000
Basic Product Group Requirements	100,000	200,000	450,000	400,000	200,000	350,000	300,000	100,000	2,100,000

FIGURE 11-13. Table for developing quantity variables in the initial linear programming tableau.

Basic Product Groups	1	2	3	4 Quantity Variables	5	6	7	Slack Variables	7	Plant Capacity
Plant— Los Angeles	X_1	X_2	X_3	X_4	X_5	X_6	X_7	X_{22}		700,000
Plant— Minneapolis	X_8	X_9	X_{10}	X_{11}	X_{12}	X_{13}	X_{14}	X_{23}		400,000
Plant— Philadelphia	X_{15}	X_{16}	X_{17}	X_{18}	X_{19}	X_{20}	X_{21}	X_{24}		1,000,000
Artificial Variables	X_{25}	X_{26}	X_{27}	X_{28}	X_{29}	X_{30}	X_{31}	—		—
Basic Product Group Requirements	100,000	200,000	450,000	400,000	200,000	350,000	300,000	100,000		2,100,000

FIGURE 11-14. Table for developing quantity, slack, and artificial variables in the initial linear programming tableau.

upon the final simplex tableau, the lowest cost production quotas by manufacturing plants for the next three months are as follows:

Factory—Los Angeles	Product Group 1 —	100,000 units
	Product Group 4 —	400,000 units
	Product Group 7 —	100,000 units
Factory—Minneapolis	Product Group 6 —	350,000 units
	Product Group 7 —	50,000 units
Factory—Philadelphia	Product Group 2 —	200,000 units
	Product Group 3 —	450,000 units
	Product Group 5 —	200,000 units
	Product Group 7 —	150,000 units
		2,000,000 units

As stated previously, the above solution should have included a listing of the firm's more than fifty products. This would have necessitated the addition of approximately fifty columns (equations) to the seven columns shown in Figure 11-14. Similarly, a minimum of units to be produced at each plant should have been included in our initial tableau (Figure 11-14). Hence, well over 100 columns should have been added to the illustrated problem in order to reflect the real world of the Consumer Products Corporation.

Once the master production quotas for all the firm's products during the next three months have been determined (via the linear programming model), division management at the three manufacturing plants are concerned with producing the assigned quotas in the most efficient manner. This means directing attention to manpower allocations, product costs, and smoothing out production requirements. It is the responsibility of division manufacturing management to determine daily production runs. Thus, each plant must determine optimum daily operation rates in view of the current status of manufacturing operations.

Factory loading can be inefficient and uneconomical because of bottlenecks, cumbersome work in process, and erratic labor utilization. Clearly, the iterative process of linear programming is needed to answer quickly the questions of production alternatives. The problems of the manufacturing manager can be shown as follows:

A. Production Quotas for coming period: *Quantity*
   1. Basic Product Group 1—product 1   10,000
   2. Basic Product Group 1—product 2   20,000
    .   .
    .   .
    .   .
   n. Basic Product Group 7—product 8   20,500
B. Manpower Availability   *Dollars Available*
   1. Marking $110,000
   2. Subassembly 15   180,200
    .   .
    .   .
    .   .
   n. Packing   120,300

C. Raw Material Resource   *Units Available*
   1. Metal Base   410,000
   2. Plastic Covers   380,500
   .   .
   .   .
   .   .
  n. Wood Crates   490,500

In addition to this information, there is cost data relating to each product stored on the data base. These data break down the bills of materials for each product into manufacturing work center categories. For example, the following variable costs necessary for a certain product might be:

   1. Marking $ .17
   2. Subassembly 15   1.32
   .   .
   o   .
   o   .
  n. Packing   .22

    Once the master production quotas are established, available manpower estimated, raw materials calculated, and variable costs of manufacturing determined, the job of the manufacturing manager reduces to that of a daily computational procedure utilizing simulation in conjunction with linear programming. Division manufacturing management accesses this OR model via a tele-typewriter unit for printed output. The OR program is run at the end of the daily shift because consideration must be given to current production bottlenecks and trouble spots as well as to where plant operations now stand—ahead or behind schedule. Thus, division management can obtain the optimum production schedule and routing from the Production Scheduling-Linear Programming Program, thereby coordinating this information with their understudies via the divisional data base (Figure 11-15). Once the plant's production schedule has been set for the next day, the manufacturing work centers can function under the supervision of the production scheduling and control group.

MANUFACTURING MODULES

    In addition to specifying the common data base and employing OR techniques, the detailed design of the manufacturing subsystem is difficult to specify without a manufacturing organization structure, such as found in Figure 11-16. Responsibilities must be defined and corresponding authority given for the various jobs. In a similar manner accountability for results are delineated.

    More importantly, from the systems analyst's viewpoint, is the breaking down of the manufacturing subsystem into its many subparts. Manufacturing modules applicable to the three manufacturing plants are depicted in Figure 11-17. These include receiving, production scheduling and control, manufacturing operations,

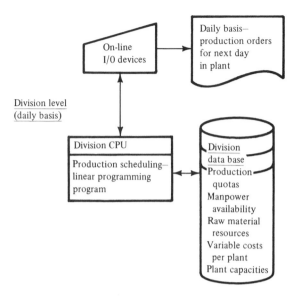

FIGURE 11-15. Daily scheduling operational flow for each division in a real-time MIS environment.

quality control and inspection, and data collection system. The design of each of these modules in a real-time MIS environment is treated in subsequent sections of this chapter. Inventory control, purchasing, and shipping, which are normally located within the manufacturing function, are treated separately in Chapters Twelve, Thirteen, and Fourteen, respectively.

REAL-TIME MIS MANUFACTURING SUBSYSTEM

The detailed design of the real-time MIS manufacturing subsystem for the Consumer Products Corporation can be specified now that certain important criteria have been defined. Design considerations included the data base (corporate and division levels), operations research models (linear programming), and manufacturing modules. From the preceding discussion, these areas are not only complex, but must be fully integrated for a timely response in a real-time operating mode. After an overview approach is presented, the important modules for the manufacturing subsystem are discussed in some detail.

MANUFACTURING SUBSYSTEM OVERVIEW

The procedure for determining next period's forecasts (three months hence) after adjusting for finished goods on order and on hand were set forth in Chapter Nine—Real-Time MIS Marketing Subsystem. Although these procedures will not be repeated again, you will recall that finished goods production requirements for the next three months provide the necessary input for the manufacturing function. The

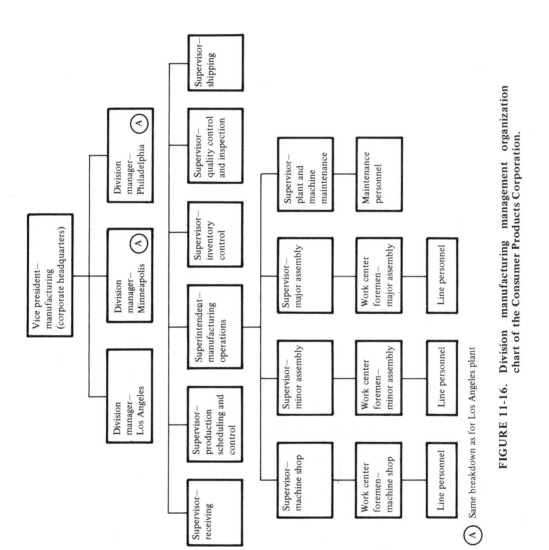

FIGURE 11-16. Division manufacturing management organization chart of the Consumer Products Corporation.

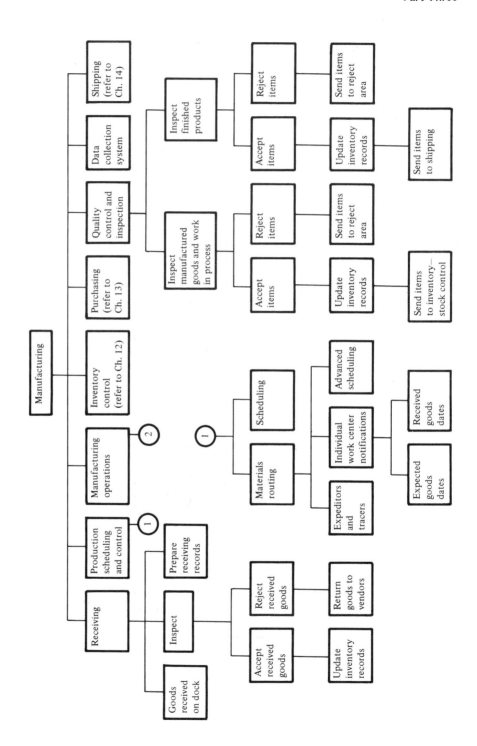

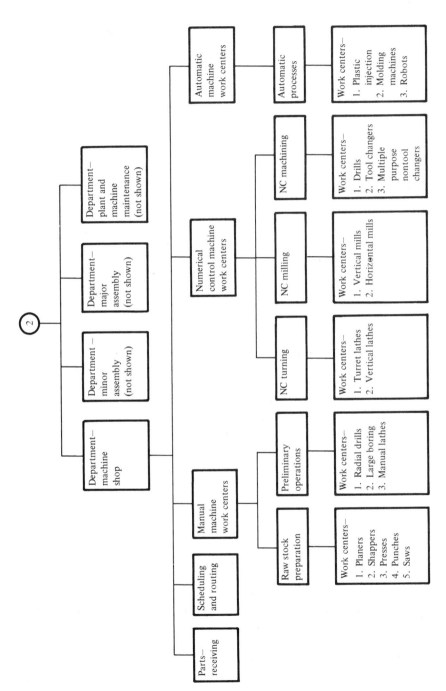

FIGURE 11-17. Division manufacturing modules of the Consumer Products Corporation.

OR technique—Linear Programming Program (Figure 11-12)—is utilized to determine what products will be produced in each of the three manufacturing plants. The relationship of sales forecasts, forecasted finished goods, finished goods production requirements are set forth in Figure 11-18.

Now that period requirement levels of on-line finished goods for each plant have been computed at the corporate level, the next phase is exploding bills of materials. The materials planning-by-periods program multiplies the quantity needed of each component times the number of final products that must be manufactured. Also, it places the component requirements in the appropriate planning period because some parts will be needed before others.

Continuing in a real-time processing mode, the output for the materials requirements by future planning periods can take two paths. One is the purchasing of raw materials and parts from outside vendors and the other is the manufacturing of parts within the plant. The outside raw materials provide the basic inputs for manufacturing specific parts used in the assembly of the finished product. Likewise, outside purchased parts are used in the assembly of the final product. Before materials are to be manufactured or purchased, it is necessary to determine if present inventory and materials on order are capable of meeting the firm's needs for future planning periods. At this point, it is important to note that perpetual inventories stored on line have been adjusted to reflect physical counts in order to produce accurate output for the materials availability and EOQ (economic ordering quantity) program.

The foregoing programs (Figure 11-18)—namely, (A) Quarterly Product Forecasting-Exponential Smoothing, (B) Finished Goods-Production Schedule, (C) Linear Programming, (D) Materials Planning-by-Periods, (E) Materials Availability and EOQ (includes price breaks and vendor evaluation)—have been handled by the corporate headquarters computer in a real-time MIS operating mode. By no means does the integrated operating mode stop here for the period under study. The planned daily requirements, determined by the (F) Production Scheduling-Linear Programming Program for all manufactured plant items, provide the means for scheduling production orders through the manufacturing work centers. Other (G) operational programs which are available to record and control daily activities include attendance, payroll, and work in process. The output of these programs provide operations evaluation reports on manufacturing activities.

Programs (A) through (E) shown in Figure 11-18 do not operate individually, but are integrated for real-time output. Sales forecasting serves as input for finished goods product requirements which, in turn, is input for next period's production schedule by plant. In a similar manner, this output is input for exploding bills of materials, forming the basis for material requirements by future planning periods. In turn, this information is employed for manufacturing orders within the firm's plants and placing orders with outside suppliers. This input/output approach provides a basis for day-to-day scheduling and dispatching of the various manufacturing facilities.

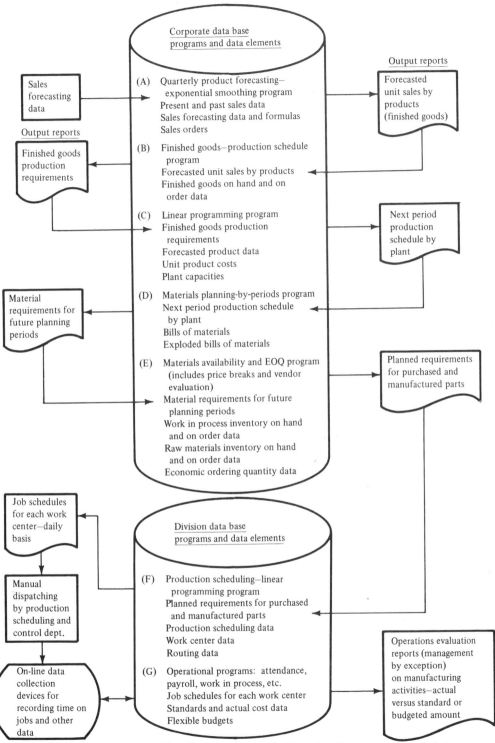

FIGURE 11-18. Corporate and division data base programs and data elements that control manufacturing activities in a real-time MIS environment.

RECEIVING MODULE

Receiving in real-time MIS is somewhat similar to that in integrated MIS. Upon receipt of materials from vendors, goods are checked and verified against the accompanying packing slip by the receiving clerk. In addition, the receiving clerk prepares receiving tickets, noting any apparent irregularities of materials received. However, before preparing receiving tickets, the clerk verifies on-line via an I/O terminal device the shipment with the purchase order to insure accuracy of incoming materials. Pertinent information is keyed in and the system responds. If the shipment is valid, the materials are accepted and the inventory data base at the division level is updated to include the shipment. Also, the system reduces the amount of goods on order in terms of outstanding purchase orders. On the other hand, if the system answers that the shipment is invalid and not due, the shipment is refused by the receiving clerk. The carrier returns the materials to the vendor. These procedures are illustrated in Figure 11-19.

Daily, the supervisor of receiving accesses the division's data base (Figure 11-19). Expected shipments of the day, along with prices, specifications, originator's name, and similar items, are shown. The receiving supervisor or receiving personnel can update the order file from an I/O device (as noted above). Date received and quantity information are entered. By special function keys on the I/O device, plant personnel can notify the inventory control subsystem that goods have been received and can be initiated for routing.

The key to an efficient real-time MIS in this area is the subordination to a set daily routine. If the receiving supervisor did not review expected receipts daily, the production floor could sit idle waiting for goods that are late. However, with I/O terminal capabilities, manufacturing departments can interrogate the data base and initiate requests to specific work centers for raw materials and purchased parts.

PRODUCTION SCHEDULING AND CONTROL MODULE

The production scheduling and control department is responsible for all traffic among manufacturing departments and within their respective work centers. This important department coordinates all activities concerning a production order from its initial recording, through inventory layup and manufacturing, to shipping from the plant. This module relies heavily upon the division's data base and its communications with all manufacturing work centers. But just as important for this department is the utilization of the Production Scheduling-Linear Programming Program (Figure 11-18), mentioned in a previous section.

In order to utilize the above production scheduling program, all production control and scheduling data must be entered as they occur, thereby permitting creation of an up-to-date division data base. Likewise, all production quotas for the present three-month period must be stored on line. It should be noted that periodically adjustments are made to period forecasts which are reflected on the data base. Before the start of each day (the program is actually run at the end of the prior day shift), the computerized scheduler first determines what products to

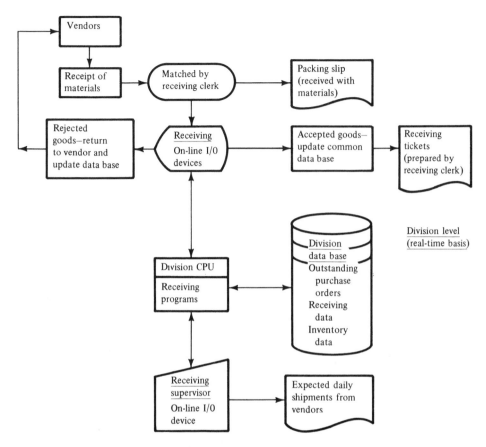

FIGURE 11-19. Receiving data flow for a real-time MIS manufacturing subsystem.

make for the day based upon the production quotas, stated on a daily basis, by
utilizing linear programming. Next, the scheduler considers where jobs are backed
up or behind schedule and where production bottlenecks are currently occurring.
Based on these basic inputs, the computerized on-line scheduler simulates the
activities of the plant for the coming day and determines what will happen as the
day begins, thereby alerting supervisors and foremen about critical areas that need
attention. Because all data affecting manufacturing activities are entered as they
occur, the scheduler feeds back information in real time—that is, information is fed
back in sufficient time to control upcoming manufacturing operations. The utilization of this computerized on-line scheduling program is illustrated in Figure 11-20.

Many on-line recording techniques can aid the production scheduling and
control department in its everyday operations. I/O devices, located in each manufacturing work center, enable the user to enter simple data regarding the name and
location of goods in process. These keyboard entries, monitored on line by the
division computer, enable the production scheduling and control department to

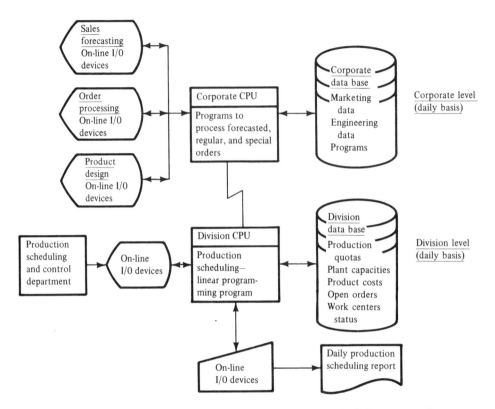

FIGURE 11-20. Utilization of the Production Scheduling-Linear Programming Program by the production scheduling and control department in a real-time MIS manufacturing subsystem.

know when goods enter and leave a work center. Exception reporting alerts the department when goods are overdue from a specific work center. Delay reasons can also be entered from the individual work center I/O devices. Prolonged delays, resulting in possible shipment delay, are brought to the attention of manufacturing managers, supervisors, and foremen through exception reports. Figure 11-21 shows the data flow interaction with the production scheduling and control department.

On-line monitoring of goods enables the production scheduling and control department to eliminate most expeditors and tracers. Partial orders can be processed through a work center and sent to another with the assurance that production control knows the status of all parts. Reasons for delayed orders can be numerically coded and entered into the data base from the remote I/O keyboard devices. Exception reports to the appropriate level will be converted from numeric codes to actual status reports.

The delay reports as entered onto the data base alert other manufacturing work centers about trouble areas. The work center(s) involved can enter "expected remedy" dates so that the rest of the line can make the necessary changes to the

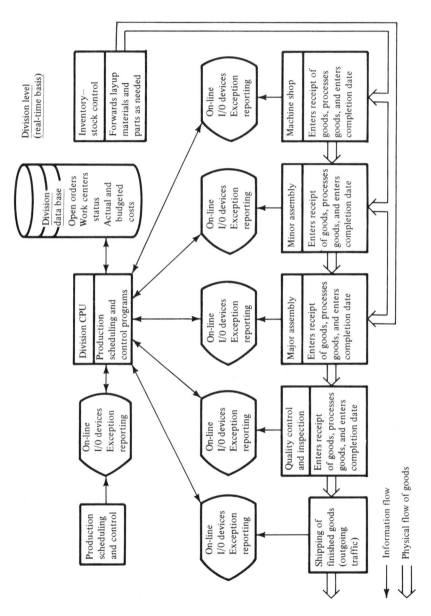

FIGURE 11-21. Production scheduling and control data flow within the real-time MIS manufacturing subsystem-emphasis on exception reporting.

production schedule. In this manner, if noncritical parts are missing, such as power cords, the majority of the work can be performed with the part added later. Or, if critical parts are missing, such as the assembly shell, the complete order can be deleted from the daily run sheet until the part becomes available.

Once again, the adherence to set procedures enables the plant to operate in an efficient manner. Each work center must enter parts status when new lots are received and must clear the parts from the record of the work center when they move on to another work center. Other data, such as delay reasons, can be requested of the computer system when the expected hours within a work center exceed the normal time.

MANUFACTURING OPERATIONS MODULES

The manufacturing operations of the Consumer Products Corporation comprises its physical manufacturing processes. Its major modules in a real-time MIS environment, like in integrated MIS, are as follows:

> machine shop
> assembly— minor and major
> plant and machine maintenance

In separate sections that follow, each module will be explored in terms of its detailed design.

Machine Shop

The machine shop, being the first department to start a production order in terms of the manufacturing process, requests parts from inventory-stock control. Completion dates from all other departments and work centers depend on the availability of parts from the machine shop. Scheduling of its operations follows the same path as through other manufacturing departments and work centers. The data base is updated when parts enter and leave the department and the master schedule shows expected work loads and dates. Typical data flowing in and out of the machine shop area are illustrated in Figure 11-22.

The Consumer Products Corporation utilizes many advanced manufacturing methods. Automated assembly lines, numerical control machine tools, and computer-monitored processes are typical ones. With the feedback mechanism of these advanced techniques, machine utilization reports are no problem. A minicomputer in the shop area monitors all processes and reports back to the division computer (Figure 11-23). Exception reports are made available on line by the minicomputer in order to assure immediate corrective action. When the storage capacities of the minicomputer are exceeded, this condition is reported to the division computer throughout the day. Daily summary reports are produced for the supervisor of the machine shop. Weekly summary reports are sent to the superintendent of manufacturing operations and the division manager. They are also transmitted to the corporate data base for future reference.

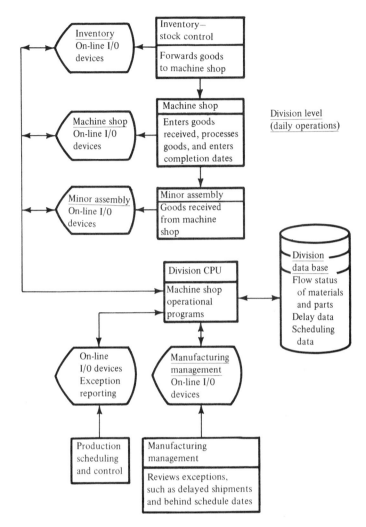

FIGURE 11-22. Machine shop (the first of the manufacturing operations modules) data flow in a real-time MIS manufacturing subsystem.

Because the machine shop is the heart of the manufacturing area, management has decided that it must know the status of all machines constantly. A "status board" has been installed in the supervisor's office under the control of the minicomputer. Through feedback lines attached to all plant machines, the computer knows if the machines are operating, idle, or in setup. Green, red, or yellow lights are illuminated respectively on the board for the proper condition (Figure 11-24). A manual key-in station, similar to the keyboards in the other departments, allows the machine operator to enter reasons for machine idle time.

The machine shop supervisor can monitor all machines. If a machine goes on "red" (idle) and no reason is received on the I/O device, attention can immediately

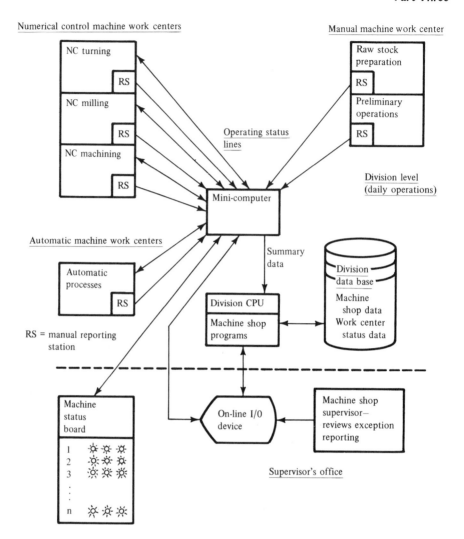

Numerical control machine work centers

Manual machine work center

FIGURE 11-23. Minicomputer control of machine shop data flow in a
real-time MIS manufacturing subsystem.

be called to the trouble area. Missing tools, operator sickness, and machine maintenance are typical reasons for the red light. If the supervisor foresees any prolonged delay, revised completion dates can be entered via his I/O device to the division data base. Other departments can then make their necessary adjustments.

The numerical control (NC) machine work centers have a great impact on the manufacturing subsystem. The advent of computer-controlled machine tools means the added efficiency of operations. Complete and accurate status reporting can be made without manual intervention and operator knowledge. This will eliminate "beat the game" tactics by operators and labor problems relating to "watchdog" activities.

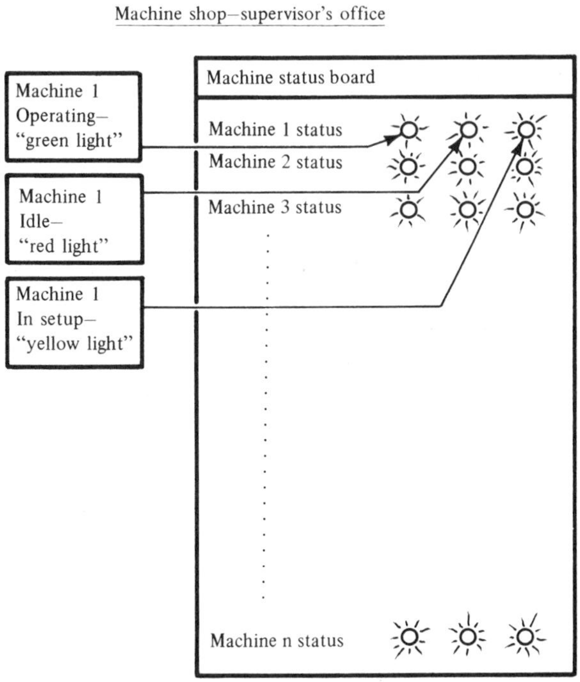

Machine shop—supervisor's office

FIGURE 11-24. Machine status board (refer to Figure 11-23) in the machine shop-supervisor's office.

The automatic processes in the machine shop consist of robot operations and fixed-cycle machine tools, such as plastic injection molding machines. Through past capital equipment utilization reports, the Consumer Products Corporation has justified the use of robot operations for constant, large lot size, monotonous jobs. Past history showed that manual operations are boring, thereby adding to scrap problems and health hazards. The robots do these jobs with ease. The mini-computer monitors the robots and produces exception reports to the machine shop's supervisor and the foremen when operations go out of tolerance.

Fixed-cycle machines are becoming more commonplace for this firm. They can do repeated operations without manual supervision. Parameters are input by dials on the machine and the process begins. The minicomputer again monitors the actions of these machines and outputs exception reports when tolerance limits are exceeded. The supervisor of the machine shop receives these exception reports in a real-time environment by use of the status board and I/O device (Figures 11-23 and 11-24). This enables the supervisor to take corrective action before a complete parts lot has to be scrapped. Also, the minicomputer contacts other responsible people for corrective action at the appropriate times. With I/O devices in the tool crib and in the plant and machine maintenance department, exception reporting schemes allow for real-time corrective action.

The routing of goods throughout the machine shop is handled by the mini in addition to the foregoing control activities of the minicomputer. The majority of parts require multiple operations and each machine operator keys in the date of arrival, exit, and amount of parts. The minicomputer keeps this information separate from the enter and exit dates for the total department so as not to invalidate the division's data base. The supervisor of the machine shop can use the I/O device to find out the exact status of each machine, including parts backlog, machine utilization rates, problem causes, and future loading status.

Various operations research techniques are applicable to the machine shop operation. Queuing theory, PERT/Cost, PERT/LOB (Line of Balance), and linear programming are logical candidates for the machine shop—in particular, for the loading of the machines, scheduling of operations, and the utilization of payback for capital investment opportunities. The application of linear programming, as demonstrated earlier, can be used to simplify this department's scheduling. The application of queuing theory to machine loading problems is similar to to those of the assembly area. For that reason, queuing will be discussed in the next section.

Assembly—Minor and Major

Even though the minor and major assembly departments constitute separate areas, they will be treated together because their data flow needs and applicable OR techniques are the same. Their data flow is shown in Figure 11-25. As in the machine shop, a minicomputer is used to monitor the automatic minor assembly and conveyor lines. Their status is reported on a "machine status board" in the supervisor's office. Exception reporting takes place via I/O terminals, as was illustrated for the machine shop.

OR techniques to assist management decisions concerning machine loading, systems operations, and comparable activities include queuing, linear programming, and PERT/Time. The locations of individual assembly areas can be implemented with the aid of PERT/Time charts. The sequence of operations can be determined by utilizing this technique. It is inefficient to place a thirty-minute assembly operation (activity G) in the middle of the network (Figure 11-26a), resulting in holdups down the line when the same operation can be performed toward the end of the sequence (Figure 11-26b). PERT/Time, then, is employed to highlight bottlenecks and dependent functions, thereby leading to improved manufacturing operations in the assembly areas.

The bottleneck problem can also be solved by using queuing theory, which permits the user to minimize costs of delays. Total assembly operations can be improved by careful analysis of existing procedures. For example, an operator has the job of keeping ten automatic assembly machines in operation. The machines periodically require attention, such as refilling an empty hopper, relieving a choke, or making adjustments. Because chokes and out-of-adjustment conditions occur at random, the servicing requirements cannot be scheduled. It has been determined,

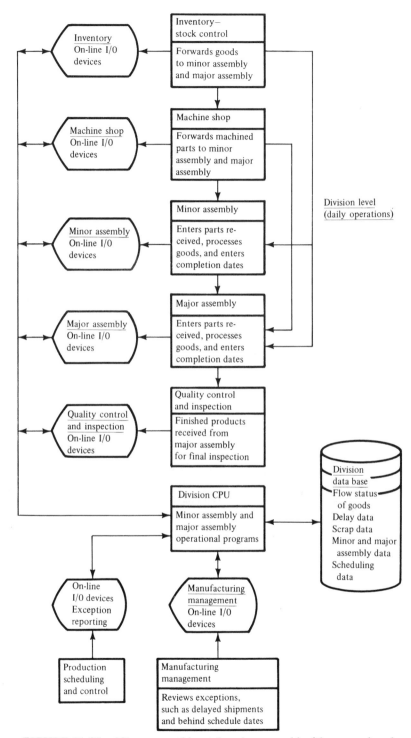

FIGURE 11-25. Minor assembly and major assembly (the second and third of the manufacturing operations modules) data flow in a real-time MIS manufacturing subsystem.

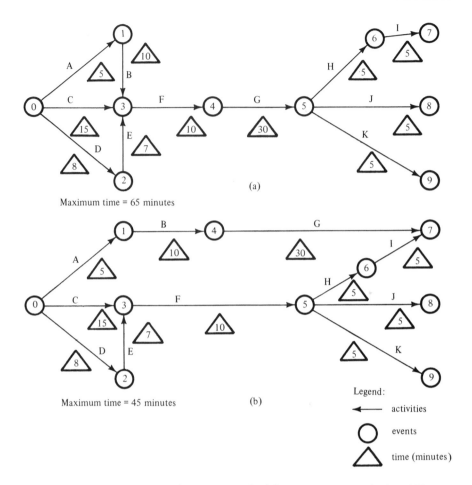

FIGURE 11-26. PERT/Time network—(a) nonoptimum solution (65 minutes) and (b) optimum solution (45 minutes).

however, that each machine requires an average of six minutes attention per hour by the operator, and that during this time, it is nonproductive. It is then assumed that:

$$\text{Downtime} = 100\% \times (6 \text{ min.}/60 \text{ min.}) = 10\%$$
$$\text{Efficiency} = 100\% - 10\% = 90\%$$

However, this assumption is not always correct, because one or more of the machines may be idle while another is being serviced. By using a table of queuing loss factors, it can be determined that if there are ten machines, the resulting queuing loss is 12.4 percent. Thus,

$$\text{Efficiency} = 90\% - 12.4\% = 77.6\% \text{ per machine}$$

By hiring another operator to help service the machines, the number of machines per operator becomes five. The comparable queuing loss factor from the table becomes 2.8 percent per machine.

Before manufacturing management can decide whether or not the hiring of another operator is justified, it must determine the new operator's cost. If it is assumed that the operator's wages plus fringe benefits are $160 per week, and that the contribution to fixed costs and profits from the output of the ten machines is $60 per hour, then the cost of an extra operator must be related to the reduction in queuing loss for hiring this operator. Thus,

$$12.4\% - 2.8\% = 9.6\% \text{ (approximately } 10\%)$$

Based on a forty-hour week and 10 percent gain in output as a result of the reduced queuing loss, there is an approximate gain of four hours per week. The increase in contribution is:

$$4 \text{ hours/week x } \$60/\text{hour contribution} = \$240$$

Therefore, the cost savings possible by using two operators is:

$$\$240.00 - \$160.00 = \$80.00/\text{week}$$

This example once again points out the necessity of an accurate data base. Efficiency rates, dollar costs, and times of manufacturing operations must be accumulated accurately.

Plant and Machine Maintenance

The manufacturing departments of the Consumer Products Corporation place a high priority on keeping their equipment operating. This is exemplified by the installation of the minicomputer in the machine shop and assembly areas. The computer monitors machine functions and reports via I/O devices in the maintenance department on the status of the machines. When failures occur, maintenance is immediately alerted to the problem machine or machines. In reality, corrective maintenance is an essential function of this manufacturing function.

But more importantly, there is preventive maintenance. As shown in Figure 11-27, the maintenance department requests maintenance schedule reports by work period from the corporate data base. These schedules are kept on the division's base but are divided into weekly schedules. Sufficient lead time for major maintenance activities is always given.

The structure of the data base information is as follows:

1. task number
2. task description
3. time period between performances
4. location of task
5. coded skill requirements
6. date of last performance
7. time required for performance
8. crisis factor—importance of performance

This type of data base allows for both "task" and "time" maintenance reporting. Task maintenance is that performed in regular time periods. Time maintenance is

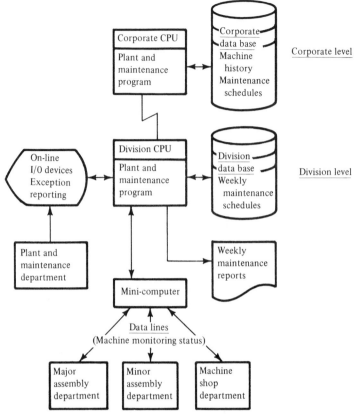

FIGURE 11-27. Plant and machine maintenance (the fourth of the manufacturing operations modules) scheduling data flow.

that performed after so many operating hours of the machine. The minicomputer monitoring the machine can keep accurate records of hours in operation. The daily records are transmitted to the corporate data base and, by means of a simple update program, the time records are adjusted.

Various simulation approaches can be employed to solve plant and machine maintenance problems. Mathematical models can define replacement times, payback periods, and expansion plans. Computer simulation of machine maintenance can be employed to predict failures. Also, it can be utilized for corrective maintenance so as to expedite location of problem areas and to suggest remedies.

QUALITY CONTROL AND INSPECTION MODULE

The quality control and inspection department is the most critical control point in a real-time MIS manufacturing subsystem. The internal workings of this department are illustrated in Figure 11-28 for completed manufactured parts and

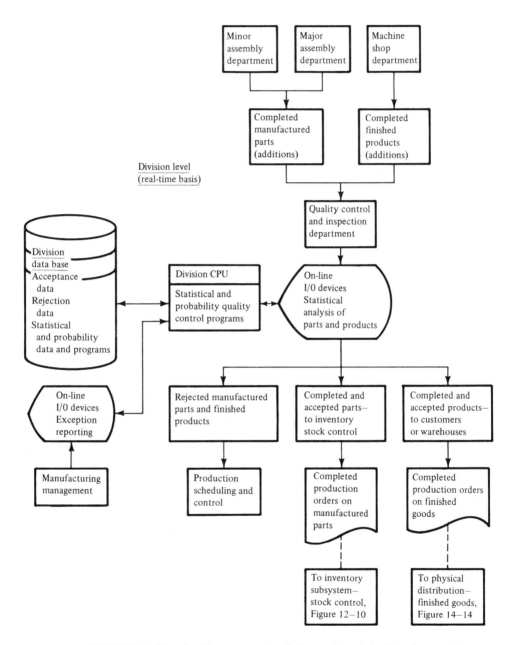

FIGURE 11-28. Quality control and inspection data flow in a real-time MIS manufacturing subsystem.

finished products. Mechanical methods are employed to test the completed output. Sophisticated equipment is used to accelerate accurate checkout. However, the deadline of customer shipments and available labor make 100 percent sampling of the firm's output impossible. For these reasons, tools of statistical analysis and probability theory come into play.

Probability theory, in terms of quality control, utilizes past product history to determine the acceptance or nonacceptance of completed manufactured parts and finished products. Because manufacturing is highly automated, the company can interrogate its product history files and determine the probabilities of producing good or bad parts and products. For example, if past history shows a certain manufactured part is acceptable 75 percent of the time, and that good lots have a probability of containing 90 percent good parts while bad lots contain 30 percent good parts, the quality control and inspection department can set standards as far as the number of pieces to inspect before classifying the delivery to customers or stock control as a "good lot." Let us say that the quality control group sets a standard of .95 for declaring a good lot. If one piece of a lot is inspected and is found to be good, what is the probability that the lot is good? First, it is necessary to calculate the probability of a good part for a good or bad lot, illustrated in Figure 11-29. This probability (.750) is the summation of joint probabilities—the probability of a good part given a good lot (.675) plus the probability of a good part given a bad lot (.075). To determine the revised probability that the lot is good, the formula for conditional probability under statistical dependence is used as follows:

$$P(A \mid B) = \frac{P(AB)}{P(B)}$$

or

$$P(\text{good lot} \mid \text{given one good part}) = \frac{P(\text{good lot and good part})}{P(\text{good part})}$$

$$= \frac{.675}{.750}$$

$$= .900$$

Event	P (B) Marginal P (Event)		P (A|B) Conditional P (1 good part | event)		P (AB) Joint P (1 good part, event)
Good Lot	.75	X	.90	=	.675
Bad Lot	.25	X	.30	=	.075
	1.00				.750

FIGURE 11-29.   Revised probability given one good part.

The probability that this is a good lot, given that one good part, is .90. This is lower than the quality control standards, thus another part is checked. If this part is good, a new probability can be calculated for acceptance of the lot. The new probabilities are illustrated in Figure 11-30. As before, the revised probability is calculated, using conditional probability under statistical dependence:

$$P(A \mid B) = \frac{P(AB)}{P(B)}$$

or

$$P(\text{good lot} \mid \text{given two good parts}) = \frac{.6075}{.6300} = .964$$

Two good parts give a revised probability of .964 (probability of a good lot), and thus the quality control and inspection department can accept the lot because it is greater than its .950 standard.

Event	*P (B)* *Marginal* *P (Event)*		*P (A ⏐ B)* *Conditional* *P (2 good parts ⏐ event)*		*P (AB)* *Joint* *P (2 good parts, event)*
Good Lot	.75	X	.9 X .9	=	.6075
Bad Lot	.25	X	.3 X .3	=	.0225
	1.00				.6300

FIGURE 11-30. Revised probability given two good parts.

In order to employ the above OR technique, an I/O device in the quality control and inspection department is hard-wired to the division computer (Figure 11-28). By keying in the proper codes and part numbers, the statistical analysis model comes on line and can direct the quality control section as to the number of parts to check, depending on the last part checked. The computer can relay the necessary information to the quality control and inspection department in order to make the decision on acceptance or rejection. This greatly relieves the manual burden of calculating the statistical probabilities by the quality control and inspection section.

DATA COLLECTION SYSTEM

A data collection system permits data to be fed directly into the real-time computer system via data collection devices which are located conveniently for all job production personnel (Figure 11-31). When a factory employee starts a job, he inserts his own plastic identification badge into a reader, which designates his work center and departmental number. He then places a punched card (a traveler card accompanies every production order as it progresses through the plant) into the same reader, which identifies the job being worked on. The data are transmitted to the division computer. Upon completion of the job, the above process is repeated, along with keying in the number of units produced. The data are automatically transmitted to the computer, where they are stored by job number for cost analysis, for paying the employees, making the necessary adjustments to production

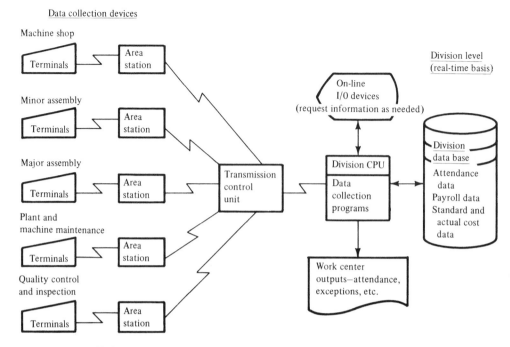

FIGURE 11-31. Data collection system informational flow for a real-time MIS manufacturing subsystem.

schedules and inventory balances, and so forth. Actually, the data collection system makes informational data available to many subsystems.

The data collection system has a great impact on cost performance because it compares the results of expended labor hours against standards. Potential problems can be identified, thereby eliminating excessive costs. In a similar manner, because pertinent manufacturing data are available for on-line retrieval, shop foremen, supervisors, and managers can track the status and performance of individual parts at various levels of manufacture and act whenever exceptional situations arise. Thus, the system cuts through time-consuming manual data preparation steps and delivers timely information that tells what is happening and not what has happened, as with prior systems. Captured data are usable after entry by plant personnel.

SUMMARY

The manufacturing subsystem in a real-time MIS environment has witnessed many exciting developments, such as numerical control machines and minicomputers. The automated factory, robots, and other new processes are appearing on the production floor. In addition to the utilization of advanced manufacturing methods and machines, OR techniques have helped to bring an entirely new approach to the manufacturing subsystem. Numerous operations research techniques are capable of producing fast and accurate results for management. Several of these techniques were discussed in the chapter, including linear programming, PERT/Time, queuing, revision of probabilities, and simulation.

In order for the foregoing hardware and technical advances to be operational in a real-time MIS manufacturing subsystem, a large common data base must be accessible by various I/O devices, especially those on or near the production floor. The manufacturing data base must be structured such that it meets the needs of those that require real-time responses, whether they be line personnel, operating management, or higher management. Only in this manner can the manufacturing subsystem operate in a real-time MIS environment, representing a considerable advancement over integrated MIS.

QUESTIONS

1. What are the essential differences between an integrated MIS manufacturing subsystem and a real-time MIS manufacturing subsystem?

2. a. Enumerate the manufacturing data that should be stored on the corporate data base for a real-time response.

b. Enumerate the manufacturing data that should be stored on the division data base for a real-time response.

3. State the various types of manufacturing information that can be and should be batch processed in a real-time MIS.

4. Referring to Figure 11-17, what submodules should be found under:
   a. minor assembly
   b. major assembly
   c. plant and machine maintenance

5. Prepare a system flowchart for a manufacturing subsystem that depicts the information flow and physical flow in a real-time MIS environment.

6. Referring to the section on the operations of the machine shop, recommend improvements that reflect an ideal real-time MIS operating mode.

7. Referring to the section on the operations of the major assembly area, recommend improvements that reflect an ideal real-time MIS operating mode.

8. How important is a data collection system for a real-time MIS manufacturing subsystem? Explain.

REFERENCES

Anderson, R. A., "Programmable Automation: The Bright Future of Computers in Manufacturing," *Datamation,* December, 1972.

Benedict, G. A., "Time Sharing Keeps Machine Shop Production on Time," *Computer Decisions,* February, 1970.

Birmingham, D. J., "Factory Data Systems Smooth Production Flow," *Computer Decisions,* March, 1972.

Buffa, E. S., *Modern Production Management.* New York: John Wiley & Sons, Inc., 1973.

Campbell, G. J., "Tapping Your Plant's Hidden Capacity," *Industry Week,* November 18, 1974.

Coupe, R. J., "Applying Data Base Management to Production Scheduling and Control," *Automation,* August, 1972.

Frankovic, E. J., "Integrated Data Base is Key to Production Control System," *Computers and Automation,* May, 1970.

Fryer, S. J., "Minicomputers Speed Automation on the Factory Floor," *Computer Decisions,* September, 1970.

Henry, B. B., and Jones, C. H., "Linear Programming for Production Allocation," *The Journal of Industrial Engineering,* July, 1967.

Johnson, N. E., "Real-Time Data Collection Systems," *Journal of Systems Management,* September, 1969.

Kelly, J. F., *Computerized Management Information Systems.* New York: The MacMillan Co., 1970, Chap. 4.

Kulerman, D., "Online in Real Time," *Tooling and Production,* June, 1973.

Lee, W. B., and Khumawala, B. M., "Simulation Testing of Aggregate Production Planning Models in an Implementation Methodology," *Management Science,* February, 1974.

Martin, J., *Design of Real-Time Computer Systems.* Englewood Cliffs, N.J.: Prentice-Hall, Inc., 1967, Chap. 18.

Miller, D. W., and Starr, M. K., *Executive Decisions and Operations Research.* Englewood Cliffs, N.J.: Prentice-Hall, Inc., 1969, Chap. 10.

Morris, R. G., and Cubbin, M. J., "Simulation of Material Handling Methods," *Industrial Engineering,* October, 1971.

Muther, R., "The Mag Count," *Modern Materials Handling,* February, 1974.

Peters, R. A. P., and Thumser, F., "On-Line Production Tracking Aids Integrated Management System," *Control Engineering,* January, 1970.

Post, C. B., Jr., "Updating a Quality Information Feedback System," *Automation,* August, 1972.

Prince, T. R., *Information Systems for Management Planning and Control.* Homewood, Ill.: Richard D. Irwin, Inc., 1970, Chap. 8.

Putnam, D. M., "MIS Sharpens Plant Maintenance," *Infosystems,* September, 1973.

Riggs, J. L., *Production Systems: Planning, Analysis, and Control.* New York: John Wiley & Sons, Inc., 1970.

Special Report, "Minicomputers That Run the Factory," *Business Week,* December 8, 1973.

Sundstram, J. F., "Simulation Tool for Solving Materials Handling Problems," *Automation,* December, 1969.

Wagner, H. M., "The Design of Production and Inventory Systems for Multifacility and Multiwarehouse Companies," *Operations Research,* March-April, 1974.

Williams, S. B., "Manufacturing Information and Control," *Data Management,* March, 1968.

REAL-TIME MIS INVENTORY SUBSYSTEM 12

Historically, the inventory function was one of the first to be incorporated into a computerized data processing system. The logic is that inventories are well-suited for computer application because there is a large number of items to be controlled. Also, computerized inventory control usually showed a market reduction in processing costs as well as a reduction in overall quantities on hand. However, in many cases, conversion to computer-controlled inventories did not solve the problem of stockouts because the computer's computational power was not utilized to its full potential.

In this chapter, present inventory applications found in an integrated MIS environment for the Consumer Products Corporation are followed by applications in a real-time MIS. The major areas discussed are:

   raw materials
   work in process
   finished goods (briefly noted)
   stock control

397

The control of finished goods is the responsibility of the physical distribution subsystem, working in conjunction with the marketing subsystem. For this reason, finished goods will be an integral part of Chapter Fourteen.

Real-time MIS inventory lends itself to the employment of operations research techniques. An OR approach provides a basis for structuring an efficient real-time MIS inventory subsystem. Great care must be used in applying OR models. Otherwise, their value will be negative because incorrect input can produce only erroneous output.

INTEGRATED MIS INVENTORY SUBSYSTEM

The main function of the integrated MIS inventory subsystem is to control materials needed for manufacturing operations. Inventory management must see that raw materials and work-in-process items are available at the right time and place. Specifically, they must plan to buy through the purchasing subsystem and provide the required materials to the manufacturing subsystem as needed.

The function of the stock control or the stores department is to store and protect all materials and supplies that are not required for current usage. The transfer of materials from an outside vendor to the stock control area is documented by the *receiving report*. The transfer of goods to the manufacturing work centers is authorized by the *materials requisition*. A most important source of information is the *inventory records* or *stock records*. Because the stock control department has all the necessary information for determining inventory levels, it is responsible for materials in and out of stock. Stock control, then, is an important source of data in keeping the basic business functions operating in a manner that is compatible with the firm's objectives.

The approach employed by the Consumer Products Corporation in controlling inventories is an EOQ (economic ordering quantity) calculation for each component part, whether it is purchased from outside vendors or manufactured within the plants. Basically, the EOQ formula equates ordering costs and carrying costs in order to obtain the lowest overall inventory costs. The EOQ formula is:

$$Q = \sqrt{\frac{2RS}{CI}} \qquad\qquad \text{Equation 12-1}$$

where $Q = EOQ$ in units or optimum number of finished products
$\quad R$ = annual requirements (units)
$\quad S$ = ordering costs or set-up costs
$\quad C$ = unit price
$\quad I$ = annual inventory carrying costs, expressed as a percentage of the value
$\qquad$ of average inventory

Although the basic EOQ formula does not consider inventory stockouts, consideration must be given to keeping a certain level of safety stock on hand to meet emergency inventory demand. Safety stock of the individual items to be carried are dictated by the firm's policy on desired service levels.

RAW MATERIALS INVENTORY

The raw materials inventory for the Consumer Products Corporation is controlled in much the same way as the finished goods. A separate forecast of raw materials is derived from exploding bills of materials and consideration is given to units on hand and on order. The EOQ formula is utilized. The level of safety stock (the extra inventory held as a protection against the possibility of a stockout) has been determined manually and is based upon past experience. This approach to safety stock has caused several out-of-stock conditions, resulting in manufacturing downtime.

The data flow for materials processing in the three plants is illustrated in Figure 12-1. The manufacturing department desiring raw materials prepares a materials requisition for each order from its production schedule. This requisition is presented to the personnel in the stock control area for release of necessary materials, supplies, and equipment needed to complete the order within that specific manufacturing department. At the completion of each shift, these requisitions are returned to the data processing department and converted to punched cards. The contents of these cards are transmitted to corporate headquarters in St. Louis, resulting in a remote batch processing approach. The raw materials inventory information is recorded on magnetic tape and used to update the perpetual inventory records—that is, to reduce inventories by the amount of materials removed from stock.

The raw material inventory levels are replenished from two sources: manufactured parts and outside vendors. The in-plant manufactured parts move from the quality control and inspection department into the stock control area. At this point, the personnel in stock control match the quantity of each item to the requirements of the production order. The materials are placed in the stock area and the production orders, with exceptions noted, are stored until the shift ends. Production orders are collected, sent to the data processing department, converted to punched cards, and processed via remote batch processing to corporate headquarters. The data are used to update inventory file as additions to stock.

The flow of materials from outside vendors is through the receiving dock to the stock control areas. Materials are accompanied by a packing slip showing the quantities and items shipped. The personnel on the dock match this slip to materials received and create their own receiving tickets. The materials flow into the stock control area and the receiving tickets are accumulated until the end of the shift. The tickets are then forwarded to the data processing section and converted to punched cards. This card file is processed via remote batch processing to corporate headquarters, where it is also used to update the inventory files. When all three

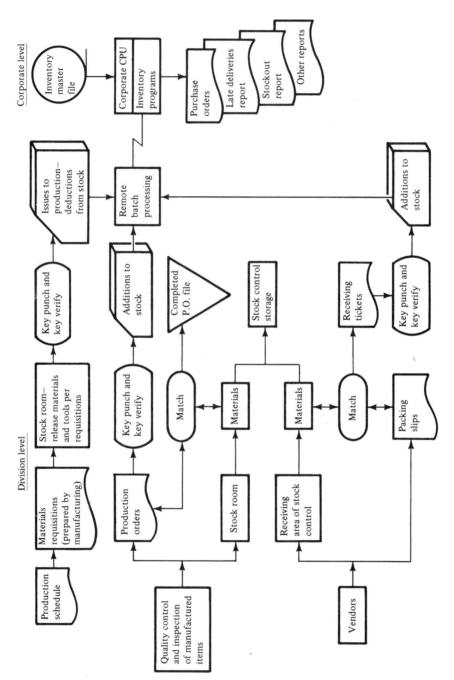

FIGURE 12-1. Materials inventory data flow for an integrated MIS manufacturing subsystem.

plants have transmitted their card files to the main data processing center at St. Louis, output reports, including new purchase orders, late deliveries, stockout reports, and year-to-date records, can be produced.

WORK-IN-PROCESS INVENTORY

Work-in-process inventories consist of those materials or subassemblies currently being manufactured or waiting to be worked on by production departments. In most manufacturing operations, the problems associated with this type of inventory is not so much the materials and parts being worked on, but the items that are waiting to enter a department. These create a backlog in the manufacturing sequence and may prohibit the smooth flow of materials through the plant. The level of work in process is also an indication of current production levels.

It is desirable to control work-in-process inventories for two reasons. First, these inventories have a dollar value associated with them and can represent a significant amount. Second, they have a direct affect on the manufacturing lead time.

In the present integrated MIS approach to work-in-process inventories, the Consumer Products Corporation employs a statistical method of analysis. For this method, a sample of the backlogs and the downtime in each department is taken. By extrapolating the results statistically, an improved level of work in process can be determined to ensure the smooth flow of material through the plant. This analysis is undertaken weekly in order to adjust the manufacturing flow for minor variations that have occurred.

An important part of this method is accumulating data for analysis. The firm has developed a policy of determining work in process at a fixed point in time— every Friday after the last shift. This level is not an actual physical count of units in an accounting sense, but rather it is determined by a count of paperwork associated in each department by the supervisor. Figure 12-2 shows the information flow of work in process and the relationship of this information to adjusting future production schedules. The departmental supervisors send their work-in-process reports to the inventory control department for analysis. The completed work-in-process adjustment report is forwarded to the production scheduling and control department. Here, the necessary adjustments are made to smooth the manufacturing work flow for the next week.

Work-in-process inventories are of prime concern to the accounting department for quarterly reports to management. The cost accounting section requires that a physical count of the work in process be taken by the manufacturing work centers at the end of each quarter. This information is forwarded to accounting, and a copy is also sent to the inventory control group in order that adjustments can be made to inventory records.

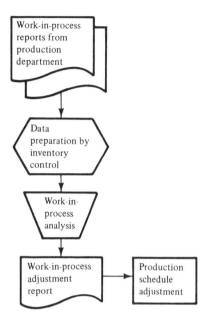

FIGURE 12-2. Information flow of work in process for an integrated MIS inventory subsystem.

FINISHED GOODS INVENTORY

The level of forecasted sales for the Consumer Products Corporation, determined by the marketing subsystem, is forwarded to the inventory subsystem as it becomes available. The projections are used to establish inventory levels for the finished items. Basically, the control of finished goods inventory is a function of the physical distribution subsystem.

STOCK CONTROL

The stock control area for each of the three plants is centrally located for convenient access by all manufacturing work centers. The space within this area is controlled by a random space storage system which allows items to be placed in any available empty space when they reach the stockroom. The system requires a method for keeping track of each item that is placed in the stockroom, hence the stock control clerk is responsible for a specific area and has a card record of each item kept within that area. Figure 12-3 shows an example of the inventory location card used by this subsystem. Whenever a receipt or withdrawal takes place, a particular inventory record and location is updated by the stock control clerk.

Data affecting stock control originate from one basic area—manufacturing. Manufacturing work centers can affect stock control by either removing or replenishing stock (Figure 12-4). If manufacturing removes materials from stock via

Inventory Record and Location Card											
Part # _____					Location						
Date	Received	Withdrawn	On Hand	Back Ordered	1	2	3	4	5	6	7

FIGURE 12-3. Inventory record and location card for an integrated MIS inventory subsystem.

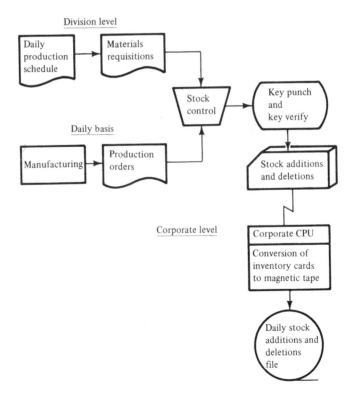

FIGURE 12-4. Data flow of stock control for an integrated MIS inventory subsystem.

materials requisitions, the stock control clerk must accumulate such requisitions each day and send them to data processing for conversion to punched cards in order to update raw material magnetic tape records maintained by corporate head-quarters. In addition, the clerk updates the inventory record(s) and location cards from these requisitions. If manufacturing is replacing stock, the clerk will receive a copy of the production order. These reports are accumulated and sent to data processing for use in updating inventories. Likewise, he updates his own files.

REAL-TIME MIS DESIGN CONSIDERATIONS FOR INVENTORY SUBSYSTEM

The inventory subsystem, as illustrated in the prior chapter, is an essential part of the manufacturing subsystem. Raw materials and, to a large degree, work-in-process inventories are the starting point of any manufacturing process. Without these inventories, there will be no finished products. For this reason, it is important to have close control over raw materials, intermediate goods, and final products. The lack of required manufacturing materials can cause idle personnel and production facilities, backlog of orders, higher costs, and comparable unfavorable conditions. Thus, consideration to these problems must be given during the design phase for an effective real-time MIS inventory subsystem.

OVERVIEW OF INVENTORY ENVIRONMENT

Within the inventory subsystem illustrated in Figure 12-5, there are two functions that make up the system—namely, stock control and inventory. They function on the operational level under the control of inventory management. The information flow begins when a receiving report is used to update the inventory data base. The purchased materials physically flow into the inventory area where the stock control clerk updates the data base via an I/O device.

Material requisitions flow into inventory from the production scheduling and control section. These forms are used to reduce the inventory levels of the in-ventory data base. Also, the flow of information to inventory control originates from the quality control and inspection section in the form of production reports. These reports represent manufactured materials for stock and are utilized to update the data base.

Other important functions are performed by the inventory subsystem and their personnel. These will be detailed in subsequent sections of the chapter.

INVENTORY DATA BASE

In designing an inventory subsystem, a prime consideration for the data bases at the corporate and division levels is a standard coding system for individual inventory items. The importance of a standard coding system is emphasized when

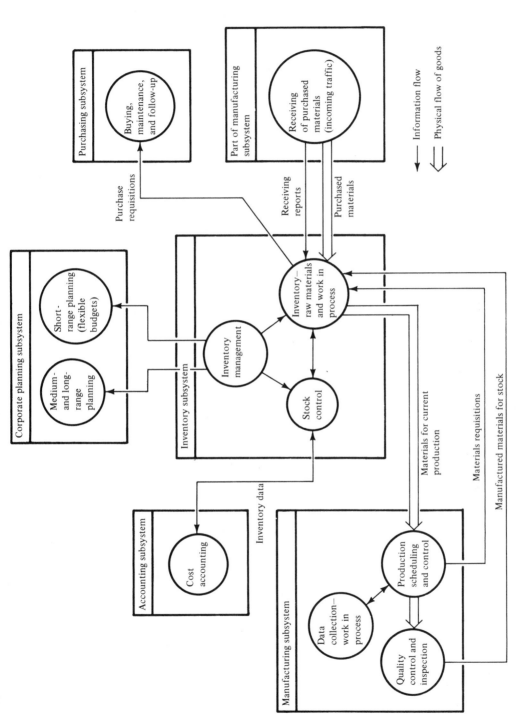

FIGURE 12-5. Real-time MIS inventory subsystem information and physical flow to and from other subsystems.

consideration is given to other subsystems that use inventory information. Other subsystems sharing common inventory data include marketing, engineering, manufacturing, purchasing, physical distribution, and accounting. Once a standard coding system is available, all other files contained in the inventory subsystem can be referenced by users.

In addition to using a common inventory coding system, the inventory data base should be built as an open-end structure—that is, it should have the ability to add inventory items without the need to reorganize the on-line files periodically. The use of open-end files makes it possible to add and delete old items as necessary.

The data base at the corporate level is directed toward overall inventory levels, while the division data base centers around detailed inventory levels. The division data base contains on-line inventory data which are usable by any subsystem and data which have meaning to the inventory subsystem only. A typical list of common data base elements, showing examples of each, is illustrated in Figure 12-6.

OR INVENTORY MODELS

For effective inventory control, there are several mathematical inventory techniques that are available to the systems designer. One is the fixed quantity-variable cycle inventory model, often called an "order-point system." This system calls for the use of the EOQ model with the addition of lead-time stock and safety stock.

Determination of the order point that is related to the lead-time stock and the safety stock is:

$$OP = (ADU \times LTD) + SS \qquad\qquad \text{Equation 12-2}$$

where OP = order point in units
ADU = average daily usage in units
LTD = lead time in days
SS = safety stock

When the inventory level falls to the order-point level, the system requires a purchase order to be prepared in the amount of the economic ordering quantity. If for some reason the demand exceeds the lead-time stock, the company is protected by the safety stock.

In order to determine the level of safety stock in Equation 12-2, the standard deviation for each inventory item must be calculated. However, because this is a time-consuming operation, the firm has resorted to the use of the mean average deviation (MAD) tables stored on line. MAD is a method in which the absolute deviation from the norm for each entry in a time series is averaged. The resulting MAD can be compared against the mean of the series to determine the amount of fluctuating demand. If the MAD is small, the item has a rather stable demand

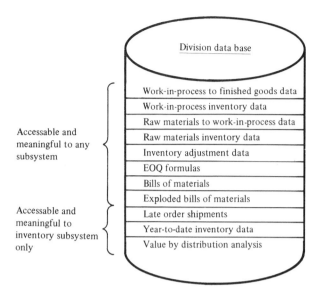

FIGURE 12-6. Typical inventory data base elements at the division level.

pattern. However, if it is large, this indicates that the item has an unstable demand pattern. The formula for MAD is as follows:

$$MAD = \frac{\sum\limits_{i=1}^{N} |Xi - \overline{X}|}{N}$$

Equation 12-3

where N = number of observations
Xi = individual observations
$\overline{X}$ = average for all observations

By using the MAD method instead of the standard deviation, confidence intervals can be established. One MAD added to the average will give a confidence interval of 78.81 percent; two MADs 94.52 percent; and three MADs 99.18 percent. Thus, Equation 12-2 can be written as:

$$OP = (ADU + LTD) + 3MAD$$

Equation 12-4

for a 99.18 percent assurance of not having a stockout throughout the year. In Figure 12-7, a typical order-point system depicts the inventory movement over time for all three elements—namely, lead-time stock, safety stock, and EOQ.

To understand Equation 12-3 for a 99.18 percent confidence level and its relationship to safety stock, the following inventory example is utilized. Ten periods

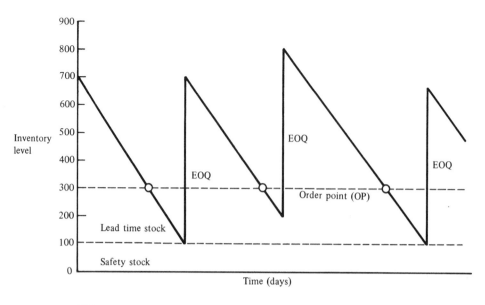

EOQ = 600 units

FIGURE 12-7. A typical order point (fixed quantity-variable cycle) system.

have been observed for actual usage, average usage, and absolute deviation, which are given as follows:

Period	Individual Actual Observations	Average of All Actual Observations	Absolute Deviations
1	611	603	8
2	629	603	26
3	617	603	14
4	580	603	23
5	573	603	30
6	625	603	22
7	623	603	20
8	578	603	25
9	582	603	21
10	612	603	9
Totals	6030		198

After computing the absolute deviations (individual actual observations less average of all actual observations), these values are summed for all observations and divided by the number of observations per Equation 12-3. Thus, for ten periods,

$$MAD = \frac{\sum\limits_{i=1}^{N} |X_i - \overline{X}|}{N} = \frac{198}{10} = 19.8 \text{ units}$$

A 99.18 percent confidence level of having stock requires a safety stock of approximately 60 (59.4) units, computed as follows:

$$\text{Safety Stock} = 19.8 \text{ units} \times 3 = 59.4 \text{ units}$$

In addition to employing the foregoing formulas, the Consumer Products Corporation makes use of value by distribution analysis or the ABC method of analysis. Basically, it is a systematic method of determining the inventory items which account for the largest dollar volume on a periodic basis. First, all inventory items along with both their usage and unit cost are listed. Next, the unit cost is multiplied by the usage to obtain some total cost estimate. The total costs are arranged in descending order. A close analysis of this inventory usage listing reveals that 80 to 90 percent of the total inventory cost of raw materials is associated with 15 to 20 percent of the total items. These items are then designated as "A" items. The next 60 percent of the items are called "B" items, and the remaining percentage, say 20 to 25 percent, are "C" items.

The A and B items are controlled by the order-point analysis system. However, the control differs in that A items have a 99 percent service level and the B items have a 95 percent service level. The order-point level for A and B items, then, is determined as follows:

A items:
$$OP = (ADU \times LTD) + 3MAD$$

B items:
$$OP = (ADU \times LTD) + 2MAD$$

Those items designated as C items are controlled by a visual review system or the two-bin concept. The inventory levels are set in terms of how many times a year to order an item and the space involved in storage. If an order is to be placed, say four times a year, a three-months' supply plus an extra bin for safety stock would be carried. The safety stock can be more or less, depending on the lead time. The logic behind such a system is to keep time controlling these items to a minimum and to keep an ample supply on hand to insure against stockouts.

Besides the foregoing inventory mathematical models, simulation and dynamic programming can be employed to solve complex inventory control problems on the computer. Simulation requires the formulation of an inventory model in a quantitative measure of performance and objectives. This means that the relationships existing within and outside the firm must be quantified. Once the model is complete, optimum results are obtained by changing those variables over which control is possible until the best solution is found. Dynamic programming can provide better results than the EOQ model when the demand for the item is unstable. This method is capable of reducing total inventory costs by producing a lower economic ordering quantity that is a more accurate solution. However, a preferred approach is to divide the task between the EOQ model and dynamic programming by using the former for stable demand and the latter for unstable demand.

INVENTORY MODULES

The detailed design of the inventory subsystem, as indicated previously, is dependent to a large part on the manufacturing subsystem. Thus, the systems designer must develop the manufacturing modules before determining the inventory modules. The manufacturing modules were discussed in the prior chapter and form the basis for the inventory submodules found in Figure 12-8. As illustrated, inventory—raw materials and work in process—and stock control are the major modules.

REAL-TIME MIS INVENTORY SUBSYSTEM

The detailed design of the real-time MIS inventory subsystem for the Consumer Products Corporation revolves basically around inventory storage and record keeping of raw materials and work in process. The inventory subsystem is actually a function of marketing, physical distribution, and manufacturing. The marketing subsystem provides the Consumer Products Corporation with the forecasted unit sales by products. From this output, the system generates the finished goods production requirements, which are used to explode the bills of materials for each finished goods item. Output results in the materials requirements for future planning periods by plants. As far as the inventory control system is concerned, this is where its activities begin.

INVENTORY SUBSYSTEM OVERVIEW

The output of the materials planning-by-periods program is the necessary input for the materials availability and EOQ program (specified as programs D and E, respectively, in Figure 11-18). The latter program compares the materials needed for the next planning period and deducts the on-hand and on-order data to obtain a net materials requirement by plants. By applying the economic ordering quantity formula to these requirements, the system generates purchase orders for raw materials and purchased parts as well as production orders of all manufactured subassemblies (Figure 12-9). It also computes these requirements by plants plus specifying vendors, ship-to dates, and appropriate routing. The EOQ model for the foregoing program is the same one as illustrated previously.

In addition, the materials availability and EOQ program take into account any price breaks which are allowed by the vendor. The price-break approach involves making a series of comparisons between the economic ordering quantities and the lowest quantity offered for sale at each price break. This approach allows the company to choose the optimum EOQ for each item and quantity.

The order-point analysis system (fixed quantity-variable cycle) supplements the materials availability and EOQ program throughout the three-month period. For those cases in which the economic ordering quantity does not cover the entire new planning period, the order-point analysis system automatically triggers the order to

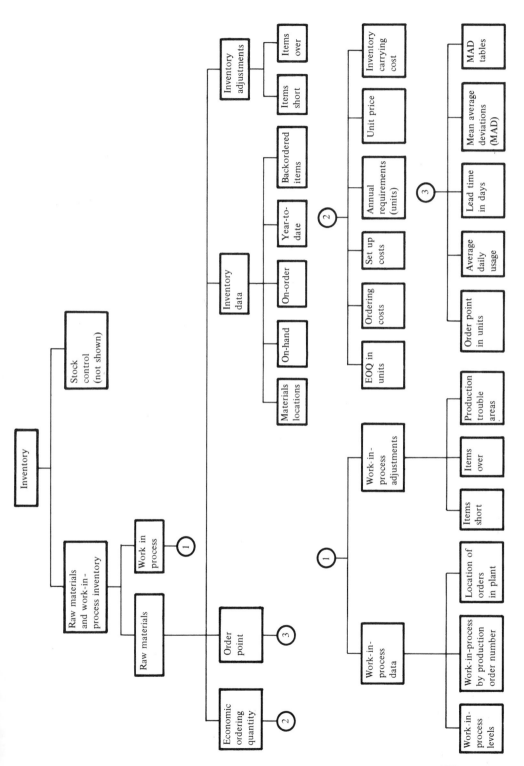

FIGURE 12-8. Inventory modules of the Consumer Products Corporation.

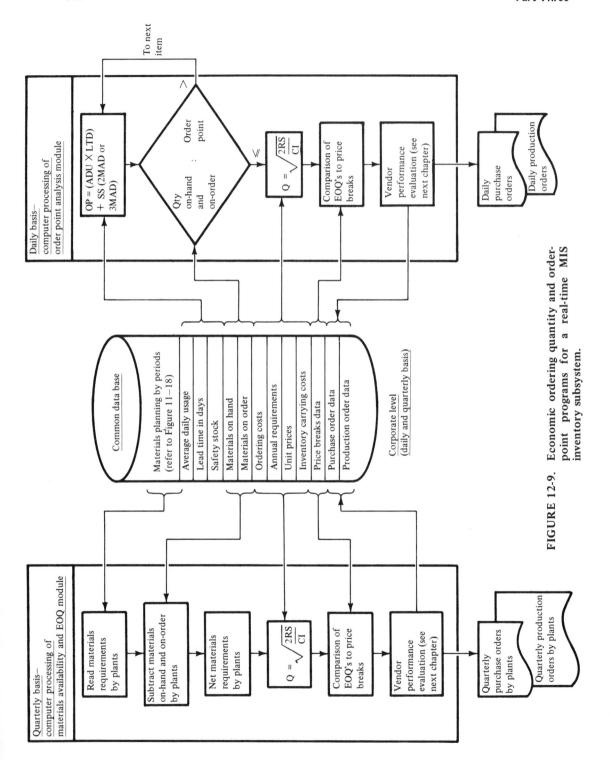

FIGURE 12-9. Economic ordering quantity and order-point programs for a real-time MIS inventory subsystem.

purchase or manufacture the materials (Figure 12-9). This approach permits the firm to keep inventory levels at a minimum. Instead of ordering two or more EOQ lots at the beginning of each period as required by the entire materials planning cycle, the order-point analysis system places an EOQ order when goods fall to the order level.

To illustrate the raw materials inventory system, the following values are stored on line in the data base for a specific part:

> 25,000 annual usage in units
> $5 per unit cost
> $20 setup cost
> 20% average annual inventory carrying cost
> 100 average-day demand in units
> 5 days lead time
> 75 units—MAD

The quantity for the materials availability and EOQ program as well as the reorder point quantity are determined as follows:

$$EOQ = \sqrt{\frac{2RS}{CI}} \qquad \text{Equation 12-5}$$

$$= \sqrt{\frac{2(25,000)\,(20)}{5 \times .20}}$$

$$= \sqrt{1,000,000}$$

$$= 1,000 \text{ units}$$

For a service level of 99 percent, the order point for this particular item is:

$$OP = (ADU \times LTD) + 3MAD \qquad \text{Equation 12-6}$$
$$= (100 \times 5) + (3 \times 75)$$
$$= 725 \text{ units}$$

Thus, whenever the inventory falls to 725 units, the real-time MIS inventory subsystem triggers an order for an EOQ of 1000 units.

In order to insure the proper placement of EOQ orders, the system runs a weekly check of all inventories as a safety margin for those cases in which the system somehow missed an order during the planning period. In a similar manner, the system keeps track of all purchase orders which are open and, if the order is past due, a daily check produces a listing of all late orders and ages them. The program also lists partial shipments and the quantities overdue.

Each plant of the Consumer Products Corporation has its own inventory subsystem. The three subsystems feed selected data to the corporate headquarters for the inventory master file, which acts as a data collection point for the materials availability and EOQ program. The operational level modules of inventory and stock control are handled at the division level by on-line I/O terminals with feedback to corporate headquarters. Plant data are transmitted at the time a transaction occurs instead of being held until the end of the shift. In the stock control area, some I/O devices are optical readers because all materials requisitions are in typed form. This frees the clerk from the time-consuming task of key entry.

The data flow which originates in stock control and receiving is depicted in Figure 12-10 for each plant. Materials taken from the stockroom are obtained by a materials requisition only. Data from these requisitions are fed via an on-line I/O device directly to the division CPU for storage on the data base. On-line inventory files are automatically updated to show the reduction in the particular stock levels.

RAW MATERIALS INVENTORY MODULE

The raw materials inventories, maintained at the three plants, contain all the materials and subassemblies necessary for the production of the firm's products. The data base elements consists of approximately 2000 items. There are many small component parts, such as nuts, bolts, gaskets, and screws, which are not stored on line. These (C) materials do not represent a significant inventory investment and, therefore, are not included in the materials planning forecast at the beginning of each three-month period.

C materials are controlled in the stockroom by the two-bin method. Under this system of inventory control, the clerk allocates one bin of materials for normal usage. When the first bin is empty and usage of the second bin begins, he places a new materials request with the inventory control system. The inventory subsystem, in conjunction with the purchasing subsystem, generates a purchase order for the part, stating quantity desired, price, vendor, and shipping instructions.

The complete flow of the raw materials module is set forth in Figure 12-10. The inventory levels of materials is controlled from two points in the plants. The stockroom supplies data concerning the withdrawal of stocks to the system; it also supplies the data on replenishment by the manufacturing process. All subassemblies manufactured for stock move directly into their respective storage areas along with the necessary paperwork covering the materials. The clerk checks the paperwork with the materials to insure that everything matches. If there are differences, the exceptions are noted and the data are transmitted in corrected form to the division CPU.

As shown in Figure 12-10, the receiving dock is another source of data for the inventory control subsystem. When a vendor ships materials, they are accompanied by a packing slip which is a carbon copy of the shipping notice listing all items and quantities. Upon arrival at the dock, the receiving clerk verifies the shipment with the purchase order to insure accuracy of shipped materials. He keys in pertinent information via an I/O device and the system responds. If the shipment is valid, the materials are accepted and the inventory data base at the division level is updated to include the shipment. However, if the system answers that the shipment is invalid and not due, it is refused by the receiving clerk and the carrier returns the materials to the vendor.

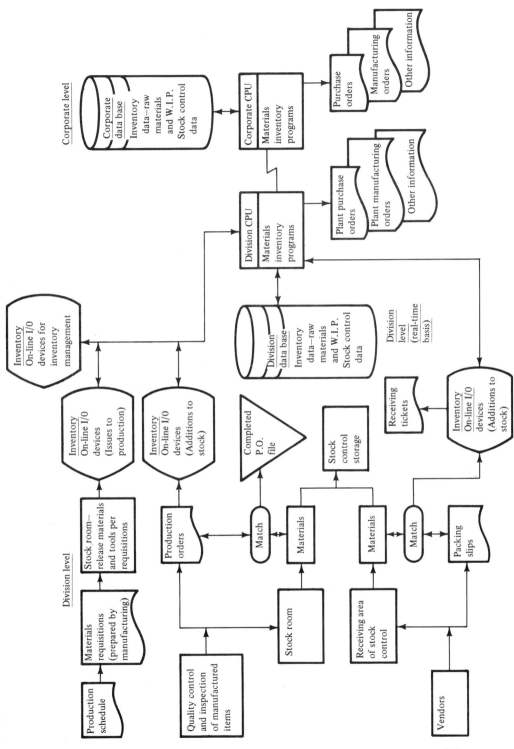

FIGURE 12-10. Materials inventory data flow for a real-time MIS inventory subsystem.

415

The system provides the flexibility of determining whether or not a particular shipment is short or over by a specified amount before rejecting the materials as invalid. At the time of inquiry and response, the system can be overridden. If the manager on the receiving dock feels the shipment should be accepted after contacting the appropriate purchasing agent, the system can be overridden to allow for the receipt of the materials in question.

WORK-IN-PROCESS INVENTORY MODULE

Work-in-process inventory for a real-time MIS takes on a more important role for the Consumer Products Corporation. This type of inventory is no longer controlled by an analysis of sample back orders and downtime. In the system's operations, work in process is controlled by a simulation model of the plant work flow. The model evaluates the relationship of downtime and the total work-in-process inventory levels.

The information flow of the work-in-process inventory is recorded by on-line data collection devices in each of the manufacturing work centers as shown in Figure 12-11. Personnel using these terminals are responsible for recording the time and labor involved in each manufacturing operation. The materials used for each manufacturing order are recorded by personnel via I/O terminals located in the stock control room. Between these sets of on-line terminals, a complete record of work in process is obtained on a "now" basis.

The work-in-process inventory gives management a complete and up-to-date picture of a plant's operations. The inventory system is of great value in maintaining customers' goodwill by quickly locating their orders in a plant by keying in the customer's order number from any of the on-line terminals. The user desiring the information receives back the location of the order in the plant along with an estimated shipment date.

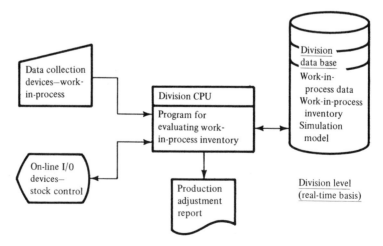

FIGURE 12-11. Work-in-process information flow for a real-time MIS inventory subsystem.

The value of the work-in-process simulation model mentioned above is its ability to adjust the production cycle when fluctuations unexpectedly appear. Even though the production cycle is normally a planned period, it is not able to cope with the small variations that occur during the production cycle. For example, if four or five personnel are missing from a key department, this leaves the next department with downtime owing to the lack of incoming work. The job of the inventory simulation model is to adjust the production flow and return the system to normal. As indicated previously, the work-in-process level in Figure 12-10 is created by data collection in manufacturing work centers and in the stockroom. Because the work-in-process levels are always up to date, the simulation model can be used at any time for determining the production adjustment. Generally, the simulation model is used once a day.

FINISHED GOODS INVENTORY MODULE

The marketing and physical distribution subsystems are responsible respectively for projecting the sales levels of finished goods and specifying the necessary inventory levels. Marketing controls the shipment priorities to customers and determines the best means of shipping in emergency situations. They also decide when to discontinue an item from stock. Physical distribution is responsible for keeping track of finished goods and adjusting the levels whenever necessary. In effect, this latter subsystem is concerned with record keeping of finished goods.

STOCK CONTROL MODULE

The physical storage of materials within the stockroom and manufacturing work centers are controlled by the stock control system. Each stockroom contains at least a CRT unit and an optical reader. The CRT unit is used for entering variable data from materials requisitions or production reports as well as for entering inventory adjustment data. The optical reader is used for the direct reading of typed materials requisitions and production reports. It frees the stock clerk from keying on-line data, allowing him more time to control the stockroom. The clerk can thus spend more time checking inventory levels for small items, keeping stock in its proper place, and similar inventory functions

The stock control system keeps track of storage. The division computer allocates empty space to incoming materials and gives instructions on where materials are to be moved for current manufacturing needs. The on-line terminal has the capability of producing hard copy for the stock clerks in order to avoid any memory problems with storing and moving materials.

The stock control system also feeds data to the cost accounting module of the accounting subsystem each time a transaction is transmitted to the division computer. Data are used by cost accounting to keep track of materials used during each accounting period. The system supplies data for work-in-process inventory in order to keep track of the flow of orders through the production facilities. The flow of data through stock control is depicted in Figure 12-12.

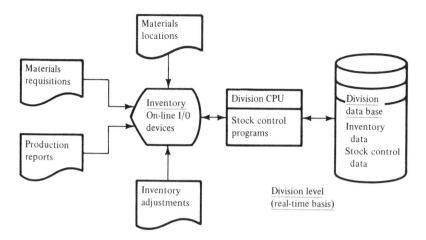

FIGURE 12-12. Data flow of stock control for a real-time MIS inventory subsystem.

All data entering the division CPU via I/O devices are used to update the data base. Each transaction, in turn, triggers a special program to update files not directly involved with inventory control, such as cost accounting and purchase order preparation.

SUMMARY

The real-time MIS inventory subsystem, being intimately related to the manufacturing subsystem, is basically one of record keeping for raw materials and work in process. The planning for materials usage is derived from a master forecast of finished goods which eliminates the task of determining how much materials to order and when to order them. By planning the materials usage, orders are developed prior to the required time and deliveries are scheduled to arrive as needed. This approach eliminates the competition between finished goods and raw materials in order to produce a smooth flow of operations.

The second inventory category is the on-line work-in-process module, which has the ability to adjust the production cycle for minor fluctuations. It is also a means of tracking customer orders through the production departments and locating a given order upon request. In summary, the real-time MIS inventory subsystem of stock control for work in process as well as raw materials is a sophisticated management tool, capable of controlling the firm's large current asset investment.

QUESTIONS

1. What are the essential differences between an integrated MIS inventory subsystem and a real-time MIS inventory subsystem?

2. Define the role of inventory management in a real-time MIS environment.

3. Enumerate the inventory data that should be stored at the division level and at the corporate level.

4. List OR models that are normally found in a typical real-time MIS inventory subsystem.

5. Referring to Figure 12-8, develop submodules for stock control.

6. How important is a data collection system for a real-time MIS inventory subsystem?

7. Referring to the section on raw materials inventory, recommend improvements that reflect an ideal real-time MIS operating mode.

8. Referring to the section on work-in-process inventory, recommend improvements that reflect an ideal real-time MIS operating mode.

REFERENCES

Barr, D. A., "GM's Parts Ordering System," *Datamqtion,* November, 1974.

Brown, R. G., "Information, Decision Rules and Policy for Inventory Management," IBM, *Production and Inventory Management,* 3rd Quarter, 1969.

Hopeman, R. J., *Systems Analysis and Operations Management.* Columbus, Ohio: Charles E. Merrill Publishing Co., 1969. Chaps. 7 and 9.

Kaimann, K. A., "Choosing Between E.O.Q. and Dynamic Programming for Purchasing," *Journal of Purchasing,* February, 1970.

Kaplan, R. S., "A Dynamic Inventory Model with Stochastic Lead Times," *Management Science,* March, 1970.

Landel, R. D., "Managing the Inventory Investment," *Journal of Systems Management,* July, 1971.

McMillan, C., and Gonzalez, R. F., *Systems Analysis, A Computer Approach to Decision Models.* Homewood, Ill.: Richard D. Irwin, Inc., 1973, Chaps. 5 and 6.

Parks, W. H., "Simplified Inventory Control for Computers," *Financial Executive,* May, 1968.

Pattinson, W. R., "Excess and Obsolete Inventory Control," *Management Accounting,* June, 1974.

Schmidt, J. W., and Taylor, R. E., *Simulation and Analysis of Industrial Systems.* Homewood, Ill.: Richard D. Irwin, Inc., 1970, Chaps. 4 and 9.

Thierauf, R. J., and Klekamp, R. C., *Decision Making Through Operations Research.* New York: John Wiley & Sons, Inc., 1975, Chap. 11.

Welch, J. L., and Starling, J. M., "An Introduction to Materials Management Simulation Model Building," *Journal of Purchasing,* May, 1974.

REAL-TIME MIS PURCHASING SUBSYSTEM 13

The basic function of purchasing, whether it be for an integrated or a real-time management information system, can be expressed as buying materials of the *right quality,* in the *right quantity,* at the *right time,* at the *right price,* and from the *right source* for delivery at the *right time and place.* Thus, there is considerably more to purchasing than just buying the lowest-price materials. The buyers for the Consumer Products Corporation must continually consult with research and development, engineering, and manufacturing personnel to know what they are planning to do and what can be done to lower overall costs of procuring materials. This approach is called "value analysis" or "value engineering."

Initially, the chapter examines the present method of handling the purchasing function operating in an integrated MIS environment for the Consumer Products Corporation. This brief review of current operations is followed by an investigation of the necessary real-time MIS design purchasing considerations—in particular, those relating to the data base, mathematical techniques, and their detailed modules.

420

Finally, the design of the purchasing subsystem in a real-time MIS operating mode is presented, centering around these functions:

> buying, maintenance, and follow-up
> vendor, buyer, and purchased-part performance

Essentially, the purchasing subsystem is structured on these two basic functions.

INTEGRATED MIS PURCHASING SUBSYSTEM

The purchasing function is concerned with procuring raw materials, parts, supplies, equipment, utilities, and other products and services required to meet the firm's operating needs. The procurement process begins with the completion of the purchase requisition, which is prepared in duplicate. One is forwarded to the purchasing department and one is retained by the originator. Basically, the purchasing department locates and determines the supplier(s) from whom the order is to be filled. If the desired information is not available, the buyer may send a *request for quotation* to prospective vendors. Once the outside supplier has been determined, a *purchase order* is typed and mailed to the vendor. It contains the items to be shipped, prices, specifications, terms, and shipping conditions. The original is forwarded to the vendor and duplicate copies are distributed to the purchasing, receiving, stock control, accounting, and originating departments.

By way of review, raw inventory levels in an integrated MIS operating environment are replenished from outside vendors. The flow of raw materials from outside vendors is through the receiving dock to the stock control area. Receiving tickets, which are accumulated until the end of the shift, are forwarded to the data processing section and converted to punched cards. These cards, in turn, are processed via remote batch processing to the corporate computer, where they are used to update the inventory files.

While the foregoing procedure handles the additions to stock, a comparable one is required for stock deductions. The various manufacturing departments, desiring specific raw materials, prepare materials requisitions for each order on its production schedule. These requisitions are presented to personnel in the stock control area for release of necessary materials. At the completion of each shift, these requisitions are converted to punched cards and transmitted to the corporate computer via remote batch processing for updating inventory files.

After all three manufacturing plants have transmitted their card files for additions and deductions to corporate headquarters, a new, updated inventory magnetic tape file is created. Also, during this computer pass, new inventory levels plus materials on order are added to determine whether or not an EOQ purchase order should be generated. Although purchasing of raw materials is placed on an optimum basis, purchase orders are reviewed before mailing by the respective purchasing agents. As will be illustrated later in the chapter, improved purchasing procedures are available with real-time MIS.

BUYING, MAINTENANCE, AND FOLLOW-UP

Regardless of the type of procedures employed, buying is a most comprehensive undertaking. A purchasing agent must spend considerable time consulting with company and outside personnel, assisting in developing better products, and procuring better sources of supply. Visiting salesmen must be interviewed for new processes, new types of products and materials, and lower prices relative to quality and delivery for the materials now purchased. While interviewing, searching, and analyzing, the purchasing agent continues to be responsible for processing requisitions that flow into the office and checking on undelivered goods. Furthermore, the purchasing agent should attempt to evaluate the quality of products and services supplied by vendors as a guide to future purchasing.

In an integrated MIS, the buyers for the Consumer Products Corporation maintain files showing alternative sources of supply for goods they might be called on to purchase. For goods purchased regularly, accurate records on current prices, quantity discounts, shipping terms, cash discounts, and comparable items are maintained on card files as well as on magnetic tape for purchasing on an optimum basis. Buyers also keep records on past prices and the timeliness of shipments based on periodic computer reports. As prices change, they update their records as well as forward these data for changing the magnetic tape files. Likewise, as major new suppliers become available, the buyers evaluate whether they might be used and have the necessary records inserted or updated. In essence, the firm's purchasing agents have a highly demanding job when attempting to keep overall costs at a minimum.

Buying within the purchasing subsystem, as depicted in Figures 13-1 and 13-2, centers around a daily (weekly) basis and a quarterly basis, respectively. On a daily basis, inventory additions and deductions are forwarded by the three plants at the end of the shift for updating the master inventory file (as indicated previously). In a similar manner, buyers prepare purchase requisitions for purchases, new vendor quotes, and other vendor changes which are forwarded to the keypunch section and converted to punched cards. The content of these cards is transmitted to corporate headquarters in St. Louis via remote batch processing.

At the corporate level, purchase orders are prepared daily on the computer by utilizing the EOQ approach presented in the prior chapter. Not only are purchase orders, purchase order changes, and stockout reports prepared by this purchase order EOQ program, but related files are updated—specifically, open purchase order, vendor master, and inventory master. Weekly, a purchase order follow-up program is processed at the corporate level to notify vendors and buyers as to late deliveries. Also, weekly purchase order follow-up files are created for evaluating vendor performance. This procedure will be covered in the next section.

The major files in Figures 13-1 and 13-2 include the following:

1. *Open purchase order*—contains vendor identification number, buyer code, quantity ordered, date due, prices, and closing date of the order.

2. *Vendor master*—encompasses vendor identification number, name, and address. Also includes the last shipment made by the vendor, price breaks, terms, summary of deliveries, rejections, and dollar amount of business over the last twelve months.

3. *Inventory master*—identifies raw materials and purchased parts, average daily usage, lead time, on-hand stock, on-order stock, ordering policy, cost, and planned purchases which can be utilized by purchasing. Also a history of the last four vendor quotations including price and terms, and the last four purchases of the item.

While the foregoing procedures focus on daily (weekly) procedures for purchases, buying centers around the bulk of the purchasing dollar volume in Figure 13-2. An economic order quantity magnetic tape file for the next quarter is utilized for placing orders with vendors. The placement of these large orders with the various vendors necessitates the updating of the open purchase, vendor master, and inventory master files. The procedure for follow-up on purchase orders is an integral part of the program illustrated in Figure 13-1. Both daily and quarterly purchase orders are analyzed weekly for appropriate action with the vendors as well as the buyers who placed the orders.

VENDOR PERFORMANCE

Purchasing activities for an integrated MIS do not stop with the placement and follow-up of the many purchase orders. They provide management with information regarding deviations from the purchasing plan, thereby enabling the purchasing department to concentrate on areas in which additional economies are feasible. For an efficient purchasing subsystem, vendor performance must be evaluated.

The starting point for vendor evaluation, illustrated in Figure 13-3, starts with a merger of the current week's and prior weeks' purchase order follow-up files. This merged file for the entire quarter's activities, along with the vendor master and the inventory magnetic tape files, provide the needed input for computer evaluation of vendors on the basis of price. In addition, buyer analyses and orders placed by value are obtainable on a quarterly basis. Although these foregoing analyses assist the buyers in performing their assigned functions, improvements are available in terms of timeliness and types of information with a real-time MIS.

REAL-TIME MIS DESIGN
CONSIDERATIONS FOR PURCHASING
SUBSYSTEM

The purchasing subsystem in a real-time MIS operating mode is dependent upon other subsystems—in particular, manufacturing and inventory. The materials planning-by-periods program provides the necessary input for the materials avail-

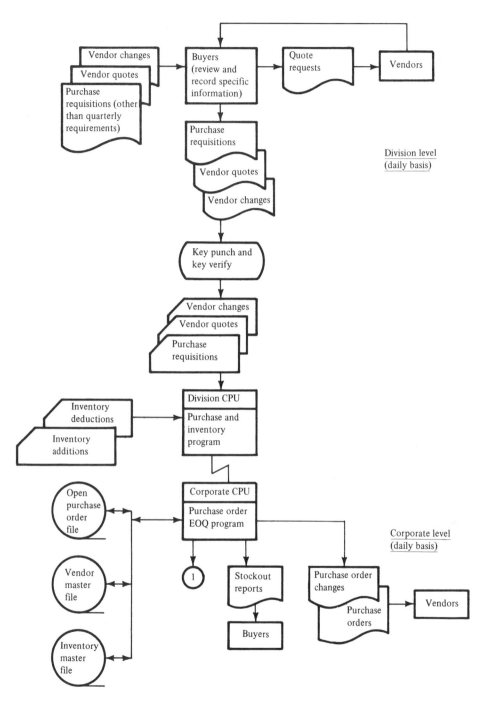

FIGURE 13-1. Buying, maintenance, and follow-up data flow for an integrated MIS purchasing subsystem.

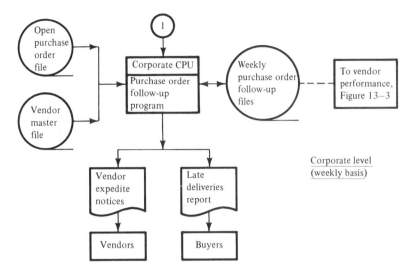

FIGURE 13-1.   (Cont.)

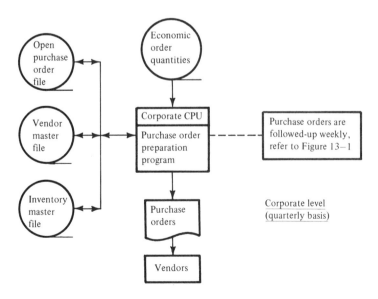

FIGURE 13-2.   Buying on a quarterly basis data flow for major purchases in an integrated MIS purchasing subsystem.

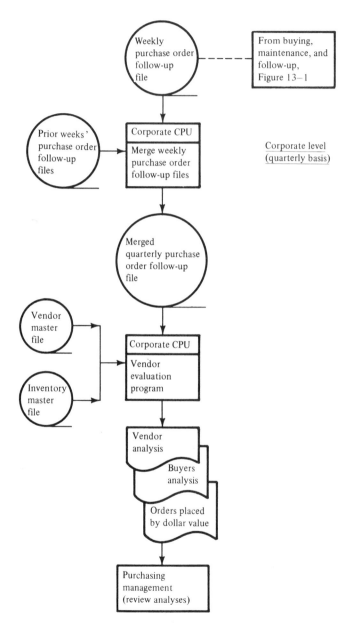

FIGURE 13-3. Vendor performance data flow for an integrated MIS purchasing subsystem.

ability and EOQ program. The output of this real-time inventory program provides the input for the production scheduling function and the purchasing function. The input information for the purchasing subsystem shows the quantity of a particular part needed and when it is needed. Although the purchasing process basically ended here for an integrated MIS approach, the same cannot be said for a real-time management information system.

Design considerations for the purchasing subsystem revolve around the proper placement of vendor orders that will minimize overall cost within the firm. This design approach goes beyond consideration of price. The quality of the materials and the reliability of delivery are also brought into play for the proper selection of vendor. It makes no sense to order at the lowest possible price if incoming materials must be reworked, cleaned, or rejected in part because of the low quality of the purchased items. By the same token, late deliveries can cause excessive downtime of manufacturing facilities or idle time of plant personnel. Thus, the combination of price, quality, and delivery factors must be an integral part of the purchasing susbsystem for an efficiently designed real-time MIS system.

OVERVIEW OF PURCHASING ENVIRONMENT

The purchase subsystem, depicted in Figure 13-4, comprises several basic functions—namely, buying, maintenance, and follow-up plus vendor, buyer, and purchased-part performance. Also, there is another functional area: reviewing vendor invoices before payment by the accounting section. All of these operational functions are under the supervision of purchasing management. As with the integrated MIS operating mode, the real-time MIS issues the bulk of its major purchase orders to vendors on a quarterly basis. However, a number of purchase orders for small amounts are issued daily.

The information flow for daily purchase orders begins when inventory personnel and personnel in other departments at the plant level express a need for specific materials and services. Purchase requisitions are forwarded to buyers who utilize an I/O terminal device to determine the status of the request—that is, whether or not the item or service is already on order at St. Louis. Obviously, there is no need to issue a purchase order if the item is on order currently. However, if a purchase order is warranted, the vendor past performance is extracted from the firm's data base before the computer system issues the order. Copies of the purchase order are distributed to the vendor, receiving, and accounts payable. Also, one copy is retained by the buyer or the individual who initiated the purchase order.

Quarterly purchases are handled exclusively by corporate headquarters, owing to the large cash requirements in the near future. The requirements for cash are projected by the finance department to insure that funds will be available when needed. Otherwise, the firm may find itself in an embarrassing situation when payment is due or it may not be able to take advantage of large cash discounts. Thus, the finance subsystem is an integral part of the purchasing subsystem for quarterly purchase commitments.

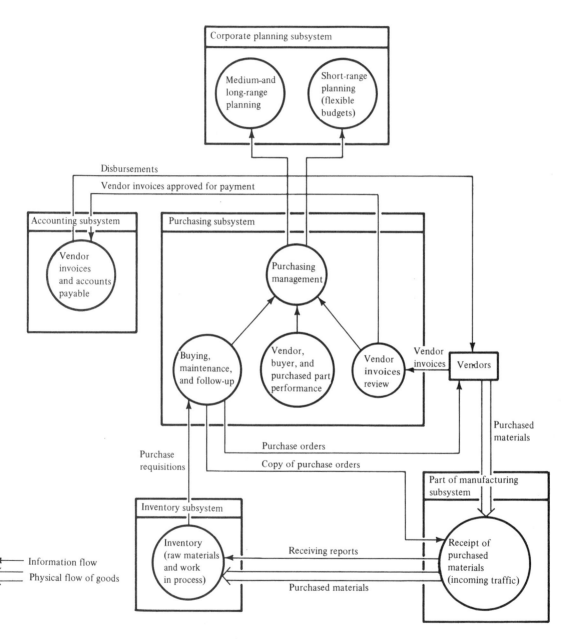

FIGURE 13-4. Real-time MIS purchasing subsystem information and
physical flow to and from other subsystems.

PURCHASING DATA BASE

The purchasing data base must be designed such that it is compatible with the standard coding system for individual inventory items. It must be an open-end structure that has the ability to add on-line purchase files and delete old ones as needed. The feasibility of such a data base at the corporate level allows for adding new products and deleting old products.

A typical list of purchasing data base elements is set forth in Figure 13-5. Basically, the corporate data base contains three major files—open purchase orders, vendor master, and inventory master. These files are comparable to those set forth previously for an integrated MIS. However, the inventory master file contains additional information needed to calculate price, quality, and delivery indices. The formulas for arriving at various indices are given in the next section.

MATHEMATICAL PURCHASING MODELS

Before meaningful purchasing reports and evaluation can be obtained for the Consumer Products Corporation, mathematical formulas that reference the firm's data base must be employed. These models are based on price, quality, and service, which are weighted according to their relative importance. The weights selected are judgments of the purchasing department, management in particular. No matter what weights are agreed upon, they form the basis for evaluating vendor and buyer performance.

Price

To measure the price variable, past costs provide the best available standard for the present. Current costs that are considerably above those of the previous period is a signal that the purchasing function might be performing poorly. Of course, it is possible that an increase in price is due to a general rise of prices in the economy. But such an all-encompassing movement would tend to affect all prices; in such situations, management should be able to filter out the impact of this general increase. More typically, variation of prices is due to a variety of causes. It is this type of variation that management wants isolated and remedied, if possible.

The price index formula for evaluating price changes for a single product is:

$$\text{price index} \atop \text{(for one product)} = \sqrt{\frac{P_o \times Q_o}{P_n \times Q_o} \times \frac{P_o \times Q_n}{P_n \times Q_n}} \times 100 \qquad \text{Equation 13-1}$$

where P_o = average old price (in base period)

P_n = new price

Q_o = old quantity (in base period)

Q_n = new quantity

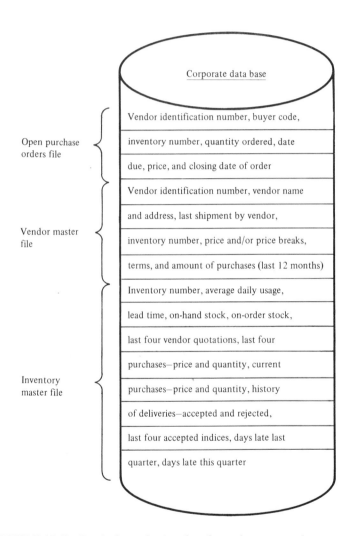

FIGURE 13-5. Typical purchasing data base elements at the corporate
                      level.

It compares the price and quantity purchased in the current period with the same data in the base period. (The square root symbol is needed because we are multiplying two like terms together to yield a "square" term.)

Before illustrating Equation 13-1, it is necessary to determine values for the last four purchases prior to the current one. For the data given below, the average price for the last four purchases prior to the current one is $2.30 for 11,000 units, whereas the current price is $2.50 for a quantity of 2000 units.

Last Four Purchases Prior to Current One

P_o	Q_o	$P_o \times Q_o$
$2.30	2,500	$ 5,750
2.15	4,000	8,600
2.50	1,500	3,750
2.40	3,000	7,200
	11,000	$25,300

$$P_o = \frac{\$25,300}{11,000} = \$2.30 \text{ average price of last four purchases prior to current one}$$

Based on the foregoing values, the price index for the purchased item is 92, computed as follows:

$$\text{price index} = \sqrt{\frac{P_o \times Q_o}{P_n \times Q_o} \times \frac{P_o \times Q_n}{P_n \times Q_n}} \times 100$$

$$= \sqrt{\frac{\$2.30 \,(11,000)}{\$2.50 \,(11,000)} \times \frac{\$2.30 \,(2,000)}{\$2.50 \,(2,000)}} \times 100$$

$$= \sqrt{\left(\frac{\$2.30}{\$2.50}\right)^2} \times 100$$

$$= \frac{\$2.30}{\$2.50} \times 100$$

$$= 92$$

The value of 92 means that there has been an unfavorable change in prices since the last period. If there has been no change, the price index would be 100. If the index value had been greater than 100, this would have been a favorable price change. In general, purchasing management would be pleased with rising indices and displeased with low or falling ones. A rising price index might be due to very effective purchasing, but it might also be due to declining price levels. Similarly, a falling index might indicate inefficiencies or might reflect a general price rise.

Often, it is useful to develop a measure showing how prices have changed for a group of products. In such cases, a formula similar to the above can be employed, except for summation signs (Σ). The price index formula for a series of products becomes:

$$\text{price index} = \sqrt{\frac{\Sigma(P_o \times Q_o)}{\Sigma(P_n \times Q_o)} \times \frac{\Sigma(P_o \times Q_n)}{\Sigma(P_n \times Q_n)}} \times 100 \qquad \text{Equation 13-2}$$

(for a series of products)

The end result is still an index that will vary up or down from 100. However, to reflect accurately how the total costs of all goods the company has purchased have fluctuated, it is necessary to weight each of the prices by their respective quantities.

Quality

Price is not the sole determinant of a "good buy." The firm must also consider the quality of goods it needs before it is possible to evaluate whether it really did get a good buy. The receiving department must examine the goods in order to determine whether or not incoming shipments contain defective items. Although the Consumer Products Corporation does not employ extensive statistical sampling of incoming parts and materials, many other firms have an extensive and organized inspection procedure. No matter what procedure is employed, a measure of the proportion of deliveries that actually are accepted is useful for measuring the effectiveness of purchasing.

The quality index formula, which depends upon a comparison of accepted to actual deliveries, is as follows:

$$\text{quality index} = \frac{\dfrac{\text{total accepted deliveries}}{\text{total deliveries}} \times 100}{\text{average of last four current acceptance indices}} \times 100 \qquad \text{Equation 13-3}$$

The quality index can be computed for one product or a group of products. All that is needed are data on accepted deliveries in relation to total deliveries for one or many products and the last four accepted indices for the product or products in question.

The calculation of the quality index can be illustrated for a group of products for which there have been 80 accepted deliveries out of 88 deliveries during the current quarter. If the average of the last four current accepted indices is 85, the quality index in this case is 107, computed as follows:

$$\text{quality index} = \frac{\frac{80}{88} \times 100}{85} \times 100$$

$$= \frac{.909 \times 100}{85} \times 100$$

$$= \frac{90.9}{85} \times 100$$

$$= 107$$

It should be noted that the illustrative index exceeds 100. As mentioned previously, this is a favorable sign—that is, the proportion of accepted deliveries has increased during the current period.

Delivery

Late deliveries, like poor-quality materials and purchased parts, can negate a seemingly good buy. At their worst, late deliveries may result in closing down a production line or even in the loss of future sales. From this viewpoint, it is easy to visualize why a measure of how well vendors meet their specified delivery dates is essential for evaluation purposes. Also, such a measure is useful in evaluating the delivery dependability of particular vendors and in evaluating the buyers who choose to purchase regularly from such vendors.

The delivery index is a comparison of the number of days late last period compared to this period. Specifically, the delivery index formula is:

Equation 13-4

$$\text{delivery index} = \frac{\text{total days late last period}}{\text{total days late this period}} \times 100$$

This index can be utilized for comparing the results for specific materials, vendors, or purchasing agents.

If the total number of days late last quarter for a particular vendor totaled 50 days, whereas the total days late this period totaled 40 days, then the delivery index for this particular vendor is 125.

$$\text{delivery index} = \frac{50}{40} \times 100$$

$$= 125$$

Again, note that this index is designed to be greater than 100 if conditions have improved. In the case under discussion, the total number of days late has declined during this period, resulting in an improvement of the delivery index.

Purchase Performance

The aggregate of the price, quality, and delivery indices is a purchase performance index, sometimes called PPI. The purchase performance index (a single value) summarizes the actual performance against expected performance, stated on a quarterly basis or some other time period. It is a composite index, requiring some kind of averaging or weighting process in order to combine these three indices into one. The weights depend upon purchasing management's judgment as to the relative importance of each index factor. Common weighting factors are to assign a weight of 50 to the price index, and 25 each to the quality and delivery indices. Such an assignment of weights indicates that the firm places twice the emphasis on price when compared to the remaining two factors.

The purchase performance index, based upon the foregoing weighting factors, is 104; its price, quality, and delivery indices are 92, 107, and 125, respectively.

Index	Index Value	Weight	Index Value × Weight
Price	92	50	4,600
Quality	107	25	2,675
Delivery	125	25	3,125
		100	10,400

$$PPI = \frac{10,400}{100} = 104$$

As with the preceding indices, a value over 100 represents an improvement over the prior period.

PURCHASING MODULES

The detailed design of the purchasing subsystem, which is quite dependent on the inventory subsystem, consists primarily of purchase order preparation, purchase order maintenance, and follow-up; purchase evaluation by vendor, buyer, and purchased part; and review of vendor invoices. Although these major purchasing modules have been set forth previously, the detailed modules for these purchasing activities are depicted in Figure 13-6. (These components are taken from the data base elements contained in Figure 13-5.) The design of each major module, except for vendor invoice review in a real-time MIS operating mode, is treated in subsequent sections of the chapter.

REAL-TIME MIS PURCHASING SUBSYSTEM

The detailed design of the real-time MIS purchasing subsystem for the Consumer Products Corporation centers around the same two basic functions found in an integrated management information system. An efficiently designed purchasing

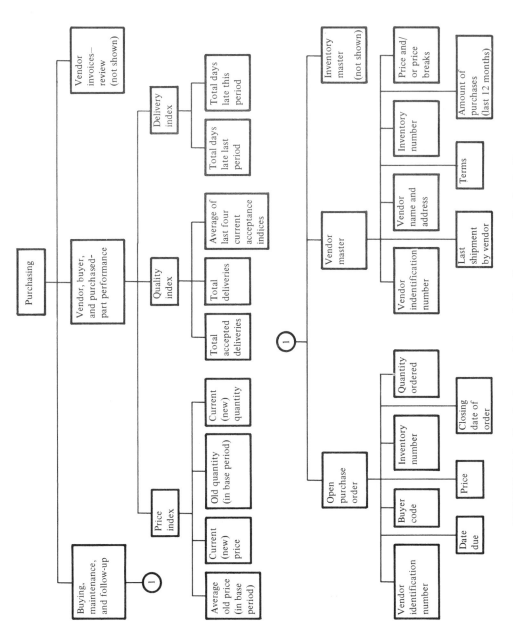

FIGURE 13-6. Purchasing modules of the Consumer Products Corporation.

subsystem can perform many of the necessary tasks that a purchasing agent must undertake. In particular, it can produce purchase orders after evaluating the best vendor for the purchase, it can produce required follow-up information, and it can evaluate overall performance factors deemed important to purchasing management. In addition, an expertly designed system can handle clerical and record-keeping activities as well as making simple calculations required in the purchasing department. All in all, a real-time MIS approach can lower procurement and overall purchasing costs of goods and services.

PURCHASING SUBSYSTEM OVERVIEW

The design of the purchasing subsystem is, to a large degree, dependent on the quarterly materials planning-by-periods program, which provides input for the quarterly materials availability and EOQ program (Chapter Eleven). Also, current order-point analysis supplies the needed input for the purchase order EOQ program (Chapter Twelve). These two basic outputs from the EOQ programs, as illustrated in Figure 13-7, form the basis for the purchase order and vendor performance evaluation program. Past vendor performance is employed to determine the feasibility of placing the order with the vendor who scores the highest of all potential vendors for the order under review. The output of this computer program is purchase orders, which are reviewed by the buyers before being mailed to the appropriate suppliers.

While the purchase order and vendor performance evaluation program, as well as the purchase order maintenance and update program, are geared to handle all plant orders on a daily (quarterly) basis, the purchase order follow-up program is employed weekly, as shown in Figure 13-7. However, purchasing personnel at all levels can access the common data base to retrieve follow-up information on any purchase order. In a similar manner, company executives can reference overall vendor, buyer, and purchased-part performance information immediately via an I/O terminal device even though these evaluation reports are issued quarterly.

BUYING, MAINTENANCE, AND FOLLOW-UP MODULES

The actual ordering phase of the purchasing subsystem, as stated previously, consists of these separate and distinct phases: buying or purchase order preparation, maintenance of purchase order file, and follow-up of purchase orders previously issued to vendors. In the purchasing overview illustration (Figure 13-7), only the purchase maintenance aspects are not depicted. However, all three areas will be discussed in the following sections.

Buying

An efficient purchasing operation in a real-time MIS operating mode goes beyond calculating an economic order quantity for a specific raw material or purchased part. It involves an evaluation of past vendor performance as a guide to future vendor performance. As illustrated in Figure 13-8, the EOQ is calculated, followed by a computation for price breaks, if applicable. The purchase performance index (PPI), which is a weighted composite of the price, quality, and delivery indices, is employed to select the appropriate vendor. The vendor having the highest PPI is selected for the order under consideration. All calculations are under the control of the purchase order and vendor performance evaluation program, as originally set forth in Figure 13-7 and further refined in Figure 13-8.

The purchase order and vendor performance evaluation program employs initially two of the three purchasing data base files—specifically, vendor master and inventory master. The output of the ordering and evaluation program is stored on the common data base. The purchase order data elements represent additions to the open purchase orders, one of the three on-line data files. Thus, the purchase order and vendor performance evaluation program uses all three major purchasing data base files.

Purchase Maintenance

Purchase maintenance involves the updating process of purchasing records. The open purchase orders, vendor master file, and inventory master file must be capable of being updated for the latest vendor additions and deletions, price and price break changes, revised vendor terms, and comparable items. In a similar manner, common data base elements which are stored incorrectly on line must be capable of being adjusted to the corrected amounts. In view of these many changes occurring outside and within the firm, approved changes and corrections via I/O terminals at the corporate and division levels can be made, as illustrated in Figure 13-9. This same type of adjusting and correcting process must be integrated not only in the purchasing subsystem but also in the other subsystems for a real-time management information system. Space does not warrant the inclusion of these flowcharts in prior and remaining chapters of this book.

Purchase Follow-Up

Purchase order follow-up, as was shown in Figure 13-7, keeps track of order progress. Prior-issued purchase orders are reviewed weekly by a computer program that references the open purchase orders and vendor master file. Exception reports are prepared for vendors and buyers. Vendor expedite notices are prepared by corporate headquarters and reviewed by the firm's buyers before mailing. Price changes, deliveries rejected, and late deliveries reports are issued to buyers along with copies of the vendor expedite notices. This approach gives buyers visual control over exceptions occurring in their areas.

Although the foregoing computer procedures center around weekly follow-up reports, the purchasing common data base can be referenced as needed to obtain critical information on a particular order. As depicted in Figure 13-7, I/O terminals are available on both the corporate and division levels for immediate response to important purchasing problems. An efficient purchasing system, then, provides managerial information regarding deviations from the purchasing plan, thereby

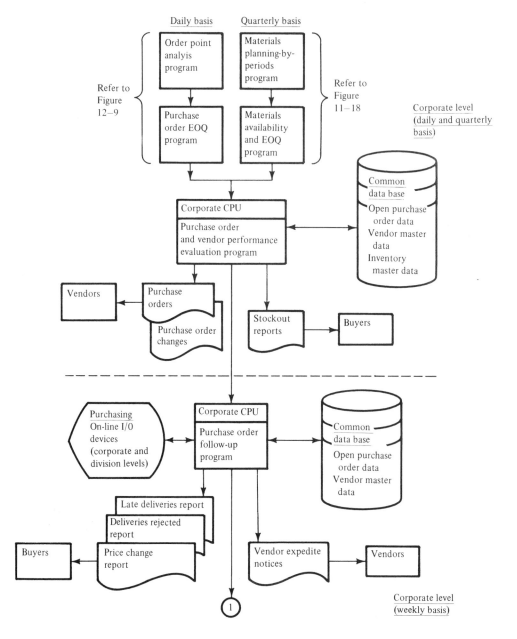

FIGURE 13-7. Common data base elements and programs for purchasing activities in a real-time MIS environment.

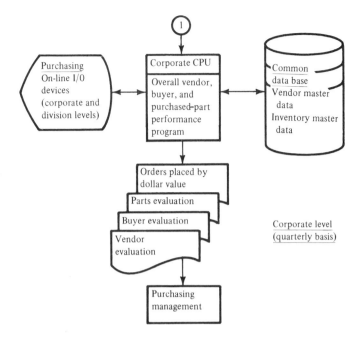

FIGURE 13-7. (Cont.)

enabling the organization to concentrate on areas in which additional economies are feasible. Also, there is a cost/quantity mix wherein certain purchasing activities are more worthy of management attention than others.

VENDOR, BUYER, AND PURCHASED-PART PERFORMANCE MODULES

The indices, explained in a prior section, provide a framework for evaluating the purchasing subsystem (Figure 13-7). Performance reports in this regard are calculations of the price, quality, delivery, and purchase performance indices for specific vendors, buyers, and purchased parts. They can be easily prepared by the real-time system because all appropriate data are stored on the common data base. Although the reports set forth below are stated on a quarterly basis, more frequent reports can be generated if the firm so desires.

Vendor

The vendor quarterly performance report, illustrated in Figure 13-10, is an evaluation of outside vendors who have supplied materials and parts to the Consumer Products Corporation. A comparison of the total amount purchased last quarter and this quarter gives an indication as to whether the company's buyers have been shifting business to or from certain vendors. Normally, it would be expected that vendors with indices below 100 would be used less currently than they had been in the past.

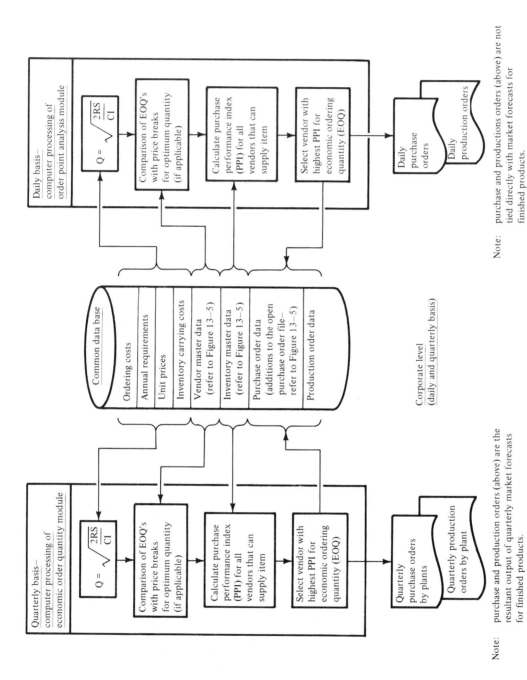

FIGURE 13-8. Purchase order and vendor performance evaluation program for a real-time MIS purchasing subsystem (continuation of Figure 13-7).

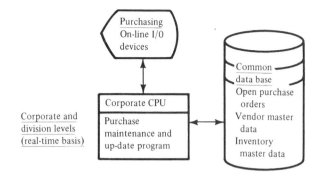

FIGURE 13-9. Purchase order maintenance for a real-time MIS purchasing subsystem.

		For quarter ending 6/30/7-			
Vendor Quarterly Performance Report		Date of report	7/2/7-		
Vendor Name	*Total Amount Purchased– Last Quarter*	*Price*	*Index*		*PPI*	*Total Amount Purchased– This Quarter*

Vendor Name	*Total Amount Purchased– Last Quarter*	*Price*	*Quality*	*Delivery*	*PPI*	*Total Amount Purchased– This Quarter*
A. A. Mfg. Co.	$42,000.50	98.25	105.20	115.15	104.21	$46.500.40
Aero Supply	18,000.00	108.15	102.25	95.45	103.50	19,000.00
Agham Corp.	61,000.80	100.50	88.75	100.20	97.49	55,000.50

FIGURE 13-10. Vendor quarterly performance report.

Buyer

Just as vendors can be evaluated, so can the firm's buyers. From a top-
management purchasing viewpoint, buyer quarterly performance reports have great
meaning. Management personnel have little direct control over vendors, but they
exercise considerable control over their buyers. By evaluating buyers on a
comparable basis, management can pinpoint the weaknesses of its buying staff.
Those buyers who are price-minded at the expense of quality materials and prompt
delivery will be highlighted. An example of this point is brought out in Figure
13-11, in which Mr. Robert Brown is shown as a buyer with a low PPI.

The above buyer performance report can be further refined for more detailed
analyses. Specifically, detailed analyses on price, quality, and delivery can be made
for buyers (this is also true for vendors and parts). To illustrate, Figure 13-12
depicts a detailed price analysis report for a specific buyer. Each line on the report
summarizes all purchases for a particular part from a specific vendor made by one
buyer. The most important part of this report is the last column. Quarterly percent
variances alert the firm's buyers to deteriorating price conditions, especially when
two or more suppliers are competing for the firm's business. As noted in the

Buyer Quarterly Performance Report

Buyer Name	Total Amount Purchased– Last Quarter	Price	Index Quality	Delivery	PPI	Total Amount Purchased– This Quarter
R. Breyer	$475,200.75	105.15	100.50	98.25	102.26	$481,275.75
R. Brown	445,988.22	120.25	75.15	78.15	98.45	450,978.12
J. Fox	501,675.67	99.50	102.50	105.15	101.66	471,981.68

FIGURE 13-11. Buyer quarterly performance report.

Buyer Name: R. Breyer

Inventory Part Number	Vendor Name	Quarterly Price Index	Unit Prices Standard Base Period	Actual Current Quarter	Quarterly Quantity Purchased	Quarterly Purchased Amount	Quarterly Percent Variance
10010	Ajax Mfg. Co.	97.78	2.20	2.25	8,000	20,000.00	102.27
10315	Argo Supply	96.77	3.00	3.10	4,200	13,020.00	103.33
10315	Link Supply	96.15	3.00	3.12	1,000	3,120.00	104.00
10907	Lodge Corp.	104.55	23.00	22.00	900	19,800.00	95.65
10920	Amco Steel	61.90	6.50	10.50	100	1,050.00	161.54
10920	Inco Steel	67.71	6.50	9.60	1,000	9,600.00	147.69

FIGURE 13-12. Buyer quarterly price analysis report.

illustration, two suppliers for part numbers 10315 and 10920, respectively, should be scrutinized to determine the status quo regarding prices. In this situation or any other, an extremely high (unfavorable) variance might show up for an item. Likewise, a much lower unfavorable variance might be associated with a much larger total expenditure. From an overall buying viewpoint, it would be more beneficial to the firm if the purchasing agents spent their time on these items, or at least started with these for critical appraisal.

Similar reports can be prepared for each buyer, showing the quality and delivery indices on his purchases of individual parts from specific vendors. Such reports are presented in Figure 13-13 and 13-14, respectively. The approach for these two reports is the same as above. The common data base elements are summarized if there has been more than one purchase of a specific part from a particular vendor. As above, quarterly percent variances are computed and printed in the extreme right-hand column for scrutiny by purchasing personnel.

Purchased Part

The quarterly purchased-part report, shown in Figure 13-15, centers on value analysis—that is, whether or not the firm is receiving value for parts purchased. If the price index is below 100, this might indicate that prices are rising, and

			Index		Current		
					For quarter ending 6/30/7-		
	Buyer Name: R. Breyer				Date of report	7/2/7-	

Inventory Part Number	Vendor Identification Number	Quarterly Quality Index	Index Base Period	Current Period	Current Shipments Accepted	Total	Quarterly Percent Variance
69744	4110	94.12	85.00	80.00	8	10	106.25
71407	9252	95.72	97.50	93.33	14	15	104.47
75509	4215	101.01	82.50	83.33	5	6	99.00

FIGURE 13-13. Buyer quarterly quality analysis report.

					For quarter ending 6/30/7-		
	Buyer Name: R. Breyer				Date of report	7/2/7-	

Inventory Part Number	Vendor Identification Number	Quarterly Delivery Index	Days Late Base Period	Current Period	Current Deliveries On Time	Total	Quarterly Percent Variance
10972	6207	120.00	18	15	10	12	83.33
27891	9201	104.55	23	22	14	15	95.65
29127	1705	91.67	11	12	7	8	109.09

FIGURE 13-14. Buyer quarterly delivery analysis report.

						For quarter ending 6/30/7-	
	Purchased-Part Quarterly Performance Report					Date of report	7/2/7-

Purchased Part Number	Total Amount Purchased— Last Quarter	Price	Index Quality	Delivery	PPI	Total Amount Purchased— This Quarter
10772	$18,950.78	98.02	103.50	107.25	101.70	$19,059.75
17020	4,975.25	105.78	98.25	96.54	101.59	6,205.95
19207	20,801.75	110.90	93.70	105.90	105.35	20,221.75

FIGURE 13-15. Purchased-part quarterly performance report.

consideration might be given to replacing this purchased raw material or part with another. The quality index might also be important if certain finished products are critical for the maintenance of the company's reputation, and especially if difficulty has been experienced in the past. In a similar manner, the delivery index might be critical in terms of meeting final customer shipment dates. The purchased-part quarterly performance report gives purchasing management an overview of what the buyers are procuring and how effective they are.

SUMMARY

The real-time MIS purchasing subsystem, which is associated closely with other subsystems, consists of two major modules—(1) buying, maintenance, and follow-up and (2) vendor, buyer, and purchased-part performance. The first module is concerned with buying (on a daily or a quarterly basis) the necessary raw materials, parts, and services at a price that will minimize overall cost to the firm. This means that price, quality, and delivery must be evaluated for an overall purchase performance index that will place all competing vendors for a specific order on a comparable basis. Also, the buying function is integrated with the maintenance of the purchasing common data base as well as the follow-up of all purchase orders—in particular, on an exception basis.

While the first module is oriented more toward current operations, the second major module is concerned with both current and periodic evaluations Current evaluations are those that are built into the system, resulting in self-correcting notices to other parts of the system or exception reports to management. Periodic evaluations, on the other hand, are designed to help purchasing management evaluate how effectively its buyers are performing their jobs in overall terms and in detail. In addition, management can evaluate vendors and purchased items for its manufacturing operations. By evaluating these purchasing reports, top management can better visualize where the firm is not meeting its objectives and what can be done to remedy this unfavorable condition.

QUESTIONS

1. What are the important differences between an integrated MIS purchasing subsystem and a real-time MIS purchasing subsystem?

2. What purchasing data base elements should be stored on the corporate level? Explain.

3. Why are mathematical formulas or indices used in periodic evaluation of the purchasing subsystem in a real-time MIS?

4. Referring to Figure 13-6, what submodules would be found under:
   a. vendor invoices—review
   b. inventory master

5. Define the role of periodic buyer and vendor evaluation in a real-time MIS environment.

6. a. What reasons can be given for incoming quality of purchased items being less than satisfactory?

b. State what quantitative measures could be developed to evaluate the quality of purchased items.

7. Referring to the section on buying follow-up, recommend improvements that reflect an ideal real-time MIS operating mode.

8. Referring to the section on purchased-part performance, recommend improvements that reflect an ideal real-time MIS operating mode.

REFERENCES

Ammer, D. S., "Purchasing Decisions Under Uncertainty," *National Association of Purchasing Guide,* Volume 1, 1972.

Dennis, "Coping with the Materials Crunch," *Factory,* August, 1974.

Duetsch, C. H., "EDP: Purchasing Bats .500," *Purchasing,* March 20, 1973.

Evans, R. A., "Centralization Versus Decentralization of the Materials Function," *Utility Purchasing and Stores,* June, 1973.

Gruber, A., "Purchase Intent and Purchase Probability," *Journal of Advertising Research,* February, 1970.

Hopeman, R. J., *Systems Analysis and Operations Management.* Columbus, Ohio: Charles E. Merrill Publishing Co., 1969, Chaps. 9 and 11.

Kelly, J. F., *Computerized Management Information Systems.* New York: The Macmillan Co., 1970, Chap. 4.

Lee, L., Jr., and Dobler, D. W., *Purchasing and Materials Management.* New York: McGraw-Hill Book Co., 1971.

Rinehard, J. R., "Economic Purchase Quantity Calculation," *Management Accounting,* September, 1970.

Zenz, G. J., "Systems Approach to Materials Management," *Journal of Systems Management,* May, 1971.

REAL-TIME MIS
PHYSICAL DISTRIBUTION SUBSYSTEM

14

The introduction of management information systems has brought about an increasing emphasis on the importance of an integrated physical distribution (PD) system. The term *integrated* in this context means grouping together of those activities which have an impact on customer order service into a single subsystem, separate and distinct from other subsystems. Normally, a physical distribution subsystem includes the functions of handling shipping orders from sales order processing, finished goods inventory control, outgoing traffic, shipping schedules to warehouses and customers, warehousing of finished goods, and other order-service-related activities. The physical distribution subsystem discussed in this chapter for integrated and real-time MIS centers around these activities—controlled from a central point.

The subject matter of the chapter focuses initially on an integrated MIS physical distribution subsystem in terms of its major functions. After an examination of the present system for the Consumer Products Corporation, real-time MIS design considerations for the physical distribution system are examined, specifically

446

those relating to data base elements, operations research models, and PD modules. The last part of the chapter presents the design of the physical distribution subsystem in a real-time MIS environment, focusing on these functions:

shipping to customers and warehouses (outgoing traffic)
warehousing—finished goods
inventory—finished goods

These functions form the essential parts of the physical distribution subsystem for the Consumer Products Corporation.

INTEGRATED MIS PHYSICAL DISTRIBUTION SUBSYSTEM

Once the goods for a customer order have been manufactured or the finished goods are available in the firm's warehouses, they are ready for shipment. The finished products must be packed, labeled, and transported to the customer. The *shipping order* which authorizes shipment is delivered with or in advance of the goods. If delivery is made directly to the customer, he will acknowledge receipt of goods by signing a copy of the shipping order, which is then filed in the shipping office. Shipments that are made via public carriers must be accompanied by a *bill of lading,* which is actually a contract between the consigner and the carrier. There is one copy each for the customer and the public carrier, and a third copy is filed by the physical distribution section as proof of shipment.

A physical distribution subsystem in an integrated MIS (or any other type system) focuses on inventories interconnected by a transportation network. A finished product, moving from a quality control and inspection point in the manufacturing process, passes through several storage points before reaching the customer. However, for direct shipments to customers, the physical movement of inventories is reduced to a large degree. Nevertheless, the desired goal of a PD subsystem is to find the lowest-cost method of providing movement and storage services that create time and place utilities for the firm's products. Or, to state it another way, the firm wants a physical distribution program that operates at the lowest possible cost consistent with satisfactory customer service.

In order to achieve the foregoing goal, certain basic questions can be asked. These include:

1. What customer service levels are desirable and at what cost?
2. Which products should be made at which plants and in what quantities?
3. Which markets should each warehouse serve?
4. How many warehouses should the firm use?
5. Should an additional plant be built to lower physical distribution costs?

Although these questions cannot be answered fully with an integrated MIS owing to the lack of readily available data and the need for advanced operations research models, a real-time MIS operating environment is better equipped to answer these basic questions. But before doing so, current physical distribution operations are presented.

SHIPPING TO CUSTOMERS AND WAREHOUSES (OUTGOING TRAFFIC)

The starting point for the PD system in an integrated MIS operating mode is found within the marketing subsystem. Customer shipments are initiated by this system at the corporate level—that is, customer shipment orders, including direct shipments, are forwarded to the appropriate warehouses and plants respectively. Also, warehouse shipment orders are forwarded to the plants by St. Louis. As illustrated in Figure 14-1, goods are packed at the warehouse and plant levels for shipment to customers and warehouses. All shipment orders are converted to punched cards, which contain sufficient information for billing the customer and making the proper adjustments to inventory. This informational data will be utilized in the section on Inventory—Finished Goods.

In order to route shipments to the appropriate destination, a visual card file with frequently used route and rate data for finished products is employed. A typical example of route, rate, and product information is shown in Figure 14-2. The sample card indicates that several products are distributed by two transportation modes plus appropriate weight breaks, among other factors. Routing information, then, is obtained manually after searching the applicable route, rate, and product information file.

WAREHOUSING—FINISHED GOODS

The major components for storing finished goods in the firm's warehouses are shown in Figure 14-3. In the receiving area of a typical warehouse, replenishment items arrive at the warehouse, usually via railroad or truck. The major functions performed in the receiving area are the unloading of the stock, verification of the unloaded quantities against the shipping invoice, inspection of the received materials for damage, and entering the received materials into the warehouse inventory. Typically, the handling required to move the received materials into the storage system involves the following functions: transfer to a palletizing area, palletizing the received stock, and transferring the pallet loads from the palletizing area into some relatively permanent location in the storage system. This movement into the storage system is accomplished by automatic conveyor.

The function of the storage area in Figure 14-3 is to hold the finished goods until they are needed for shipment. The layout of the storage area is fairly complex because items of differing shapes, sizes, and volumes are involved. Items which have the highest turnover have been located nearest the shipping area in order to minimize the amount of time expended in retrieving orders from the storage system. Thus, time required for handling between storage and shipping areas should be kept to a minimum.

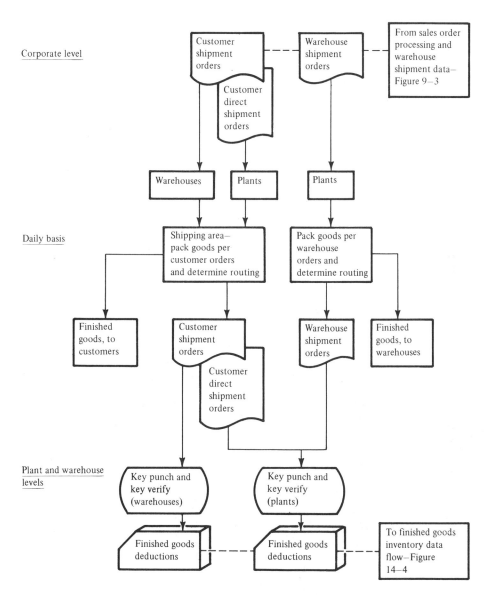

FIGURE 14-1. Shipping to customers and warehouses (outgoing traffic) data flow for an integrated MIS physical distribution subsystem.

RAIL R.B. 321									TRUCK R.B. 321		
		PRODUCT 1	PRODUCT 2	PRODUCT 3	PRODUCT 4	PRODUCT 5	PRODUCT 6	PRODUCT 7	PRODUCT 8	PRODUCT 9	PRODUCT 10	ROUTE NO.
RAIL	LCL	313	426	599	313	360						1
5m	VOL.	361	410	361	361	349						1
CL *24*	MR LBS.	174	333									3
CL *36*	M LBS.	51½										3
TRUCK UNDER *1*	M LBS.	386	475	667	386	386	520		452	475	400	5
1 2	M LBS.	372	453	630	372	372	495		432	453	384	5
5 M 2 LBS.	M LBS.	362	439	606	362	362	478		419	439	374	5
5 M LBS. & OVER		337	411	672	337	337	448		392	411	349	5
TL *20*	M LBS.				197		197					6
TL	M LBS.											
FORWARDER												

						MIN. CHG. 7.8G	FORWARDER
RAIL 1	*EL*			TRUCK 5	*H&S Motor Freight*	*7.8G*	9
2	*NYC*			6	*IPC Express*		10
3				7			11
4				8			12

EL Store door delivery 1.05¢ min, SDD $2.10

Atlanta, Ga.

FIGURE 14-2. Route, rate, and product information contained on outgoing traffic card.

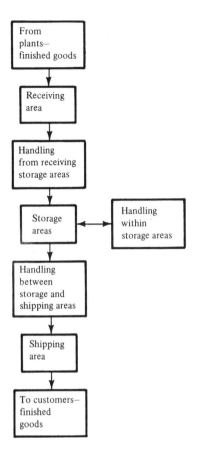

FIGURE 14-3. Physical flow of warehousing finished goods inventory in an integrated MIS physical distribution subsystem.

At the shipping area, customer shipment orders (refer to Figure 14-1) are received which demand retrieval of goods from the storage system. The handling component from storage to shipping has several functions associated with it. There is the removal of the pallet from its storage location and its transfer to a de-palletizing operation (unless full pallets are shipped). The depalletizing operation removes the required number of items from the pallet, deposits them onto a conveyor, and returns the partially unloaded pallet to the storage system. The depalletized items proceed directly either to the shipping area for loading or to an order consolidation area where an entire order is accumulated prior to movement into the shipping area.

The functions of the shipping area include checking off the quantities for each item as they are delivered from the storage system against the customer shipment order and inspecting the materials to be shipped for possible damage that may have occurred within the handling components of the warehouse. Also included is verification that the customer order has been properly loaded for rail or truck shipment.

INVENTORY—FINISHED GOODS

The finished goods deduction cards, prepared at the warehouse and plant levels, are forwarded via remote batch processing to the corporate headquarters at the end of the shift daily. On the other hand, finished goods additions are key-punched and key-verified by the data processing section from production orders completed, having been received from the quality control and inspection departments in the three manufacturing plants. These cards are forwarded via remote batch processing to the corporate headquarters daily. As illustrated in Figure 14-4, these finished goods inputs—additions and deductions—along with the customer master and finished goods inventory master files (magnetic tape) are utilized to update the finished goods inventory master file as well as produce a customer billing master file (magnetic tape) for preparing customer invoices daily.

The finished goods inventory master file provides input for preparing a weekly finished goods report. This printout is reviewed by physical distribution management in terms of what finished goods are stored at what warehouses. If there is an imbalance of stored products in one or more of the twelve warehouses, feedback is sent to those personnel in outgoing traffic at the plant level. Having been alerted to this condition, plant personnel alter the upcoming shipping schedules to rectify the specific warehouse overshipments made in the past. In this manner, too large as well as too small finished goods inventories at the various warehouses can be remedied.

REAL-TIME MIS DESIGN CONSIDERATIONS FOR PHYSICAL DISTRIBUTION SUBSYSTEM

Real-time MIS design considerations for PD must start outside this subsystem area. Specifically, they begin with the quality control and inspection function of the manufacturing subsystem, because this plant area checks finished goods before they are warehoused or shipped directly to the customer. For this reason, it is important to have close control over finished products before they leave the manufacturing subsystem. Otherwise, problems or incorrect data on finished goods at this control point will be forwarded to the physical distribution subsystem, thereby compounding further these difficulties.

OVERVIEW OF PHYSICAL DISTRIBUTION ENVIRONMENT

The physical distribution subsystem depicted in Figure 14-5 consists of three major functions as set forth previously and is under the supervision of PD management. The quality control and inspection department at the plant level forwards goods for shipment directly to customers or through company warehouses to customers. The information flow for the warehousing operations begins when a customer shipment order is received from the marketing subsystem, specifically

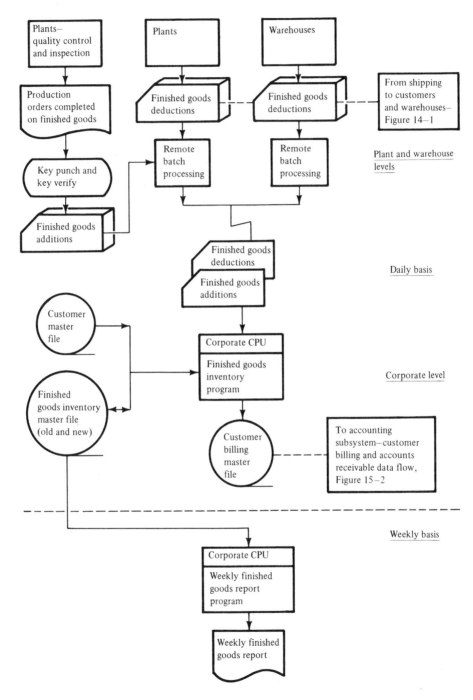

FIGURE 14-4. Finished goods inventory data flow for an integrated MIS physical distribution subsystem.

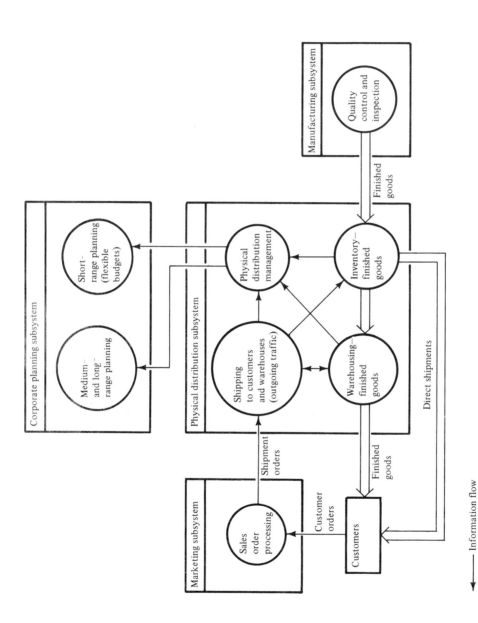

FIGURE 14-5. Real-time MIS physical distribution subsystem information and physical flow to and from other subsystems.

sales order processing. A clerk enters the data via an I/O device for storage on the common data base after checking and approving the customer's credit. The data are forwarded to the appropriate warehouse after checking for available finished goods.

Basically, the customer order is pulled and shipped. In those cases in which finished goods are not available because of inventory errors, incorrect entries, and other factors, the unavailable items are not back-ordered. But rather, the "next closest warehouse" routine (to be explained in a subsequent section) is employed by the shipping clerk at the warehouse filling the order. In this manner, the customer order can be filled as soon as possible rather than having to wait for a replenishment of stock from a manufacturing plant. This approach to finished goods speeds up the physical flow and improves service to customers.

PHYSICAL DISTRIBUTION DATA BASE

The design of a physical distribution subsystem, like the inventory subsystem, must have a standard coding system for finished goods inventory. This approach gives all other subsystems the ability to interact with finished goods inventory. For example, the sales order processing function must interrogate the common data base for appropriate data on goods available for shipment. In like manner, the quarterly marketing forecasts must be adjusted for finished goods on hand before determining product requirements. Thus, ready reference to finished goods data elements is extremely important to the operations of a real-time management information system.

Finished goods inventory must be structured on an open-end basis, as are the raw materials and work-in-process inventories. The utilization of open-end files makes it possible to add new finished goods inventory items as well as delete old items. This open-end approach is not only applicable to finished goods data elements but also is an integral part of other physical distribution data elements, shown in Figure 14-6. The opening or closing of a new warehouse, for example, establishes the need to add or deduct critical data within the corporate data base.

The physical distribution data base is constantly changing because of the type of data stored on line. This statement applies to more than just finished goods inventory. Shipping costs from plants to warehouses, freight costs from warehouses to customers, and warehousing costs, to name a few, are in a constant state of flux. Within this type of environment, the data base must be accessible via I/O devices for updating changes as they occur. Systems analysts must consider these factors in their design efforts.

OR PHYSICAL DISTRIBUTION MODELS

Several OR techniques, operating in conjunction with the common data base, lend themselves to a more efficient physical distribution subsystem. They include an adaptation of linear programming for a multistage distribution network and the next closest warehouse model. Although these areas will be explored below, other

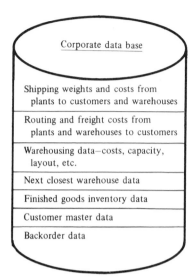

FIGURE 14-6. Typical physical distribution data base elements at the corporate level.

OR techniques, such as simulation, heuristic programming, and the facility location planner are frequently employed to resolve physical distribution problems. The objective of these models is to minimize overall distribution costs to the firm as opposed to minimizing costs for one selected part of the subsystem.

Multistage Distribution Model

The approach to physical distribution in the past, generally, has been to break down the distribution problem into two separate one-stage routes. As illustrated in Figure 14-7 for two plants, three warehouses, and four customers, the transportation from the plants to warehouses is considered as a problem in itself, while the shipment from warehouses to customers is treated as another problem. A more enlightened approach is illustrated in Figure 14-8, whereby the two one-stage problems are combined into a single multistage distribution problem.

The key to the multistage distribution approach is the fact that its mathematics are not concerned with the absolute identity of any single product item, but are directed toward moving x number of units of a product from a plant into a warehouse and out of the same warehouse to a customer, generally some retail outlet. In like manner, the OR analyst is concerned not with the fact that the actual physical shipments do not consist of the same individual articles but rather that the numbers are the sum of inbound and outbound shipments. Thus, in mathematical analysis, the warehouse can be treated as though it were nothing more than a stop along the transportation route.

In order to make the multistage distribution model a true representation of the real world, certain adjustments have been made in Figure 14-8 that are not found in Figure 14-7. A total of twenty-four routes (eighteen additional routes) have

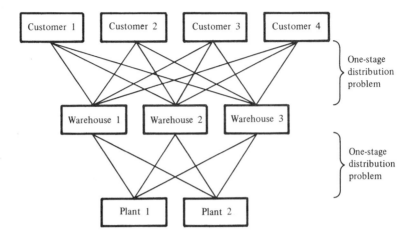

FIGURE 14-7.   Example of a two-stage distribution network which is solved one stage at a time.

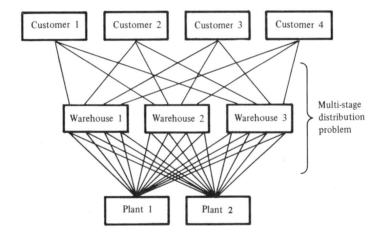

FIGURE 14-8.   Example of a two-stage distribution network which is solved as a multi-stage distribution problem.

been used to connect the plants with the warehouses. These additional routes allow the planner to trace one route from each plant to each customer through each warehouse. Because the per-unit costs over these routes are known, total shipping costs from the plants through warehouses to customers can be determined.

What has been accomplished with the foregoing approach is to transform the two-stage model into a one-stage model. For the twenty-four routes diagrammed in Figure 14-8, the plants serve as origins and the customers as destinations. This mathematical transformation of the two-stage model into a transportation model covering one stage permits the use of linear programming to solve the problem. In essence, an OR solution can be obtained without the inaccuracies caused by the stage-at-a-time treatment of the two-stage model.

Next Closest Warehouse Model

The purpose of the next closest warehouse model is to maximize customer service. For the company to lose a sale, because of a stockout at the warehouse getting the request, is not good business. The shipment of a small quantity from a neighboring warehouse is justifiable. In such cases, air freight is an acceptable means of shipment to prevent losing a customer to competition.

The basic OR model, set forth in Figure 14-9, locates materials in the next closest (least expensive) warehouse. It sets up a hierarchy of closest warehouses in terms of air freight costs. Warehouses are queried in sequence for the short item(s). When finished goods are located, they are shipped directly to the customer. If an item is not available from the closest warehouse, the order is automatically routed to the closest plant capable of producing the item. The order can take one of two paths: it can be cancelled by the customer if delivery will be too late or it can be manufactured by the selected factory. If manufactured, items are shipped directly to the customer. In either case, exception reports are generated to appraise management of the action taken.

PHYSICAL DISTRIBUTION MODULES

The detailed design of the PD subsystem includes the detailing of its three major modules, as set forth previously in the chapter The subparts of these modules are shown in Figure 14-10. Their design in a real-time MIS environment is treated in subsequent sections of this chapter. Although these minor modules appear to be independent of other subsystems, this is certainly not the case. For example, finished goods are an integral part of sales order processing, while many of the physical distribution cost factors are developed and maintained by the cost accounting section on the data base. Thus, physical distribution modules are common to many other subsystems.

REAL-TIME MIS PHYSICAL
DISTRIBUTION SUBSYSTEM

The important parts of the real-time MIS physical distribution subsystem for the Consumer Products Corporation can be detailed now that certain criteria—PD data base, OR models, and PD modules—have been specified. Although the design approach is somewhat complicated by the utilization of a computer to control warehousing operations, the physical distribution subsystem must be integrated with other subsystems for a real-time response. Specifically, marketing, manufacturing, and inventory must be designed with the physical distribution subsystem in mind. Likewise, PD must be designed in conjunction with the firm's other

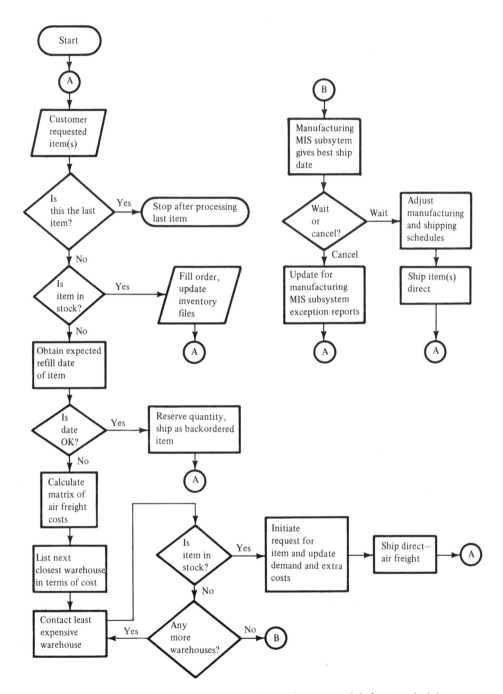

FIGURE 14-9. The next closest warehouse model for maximizing customer service.

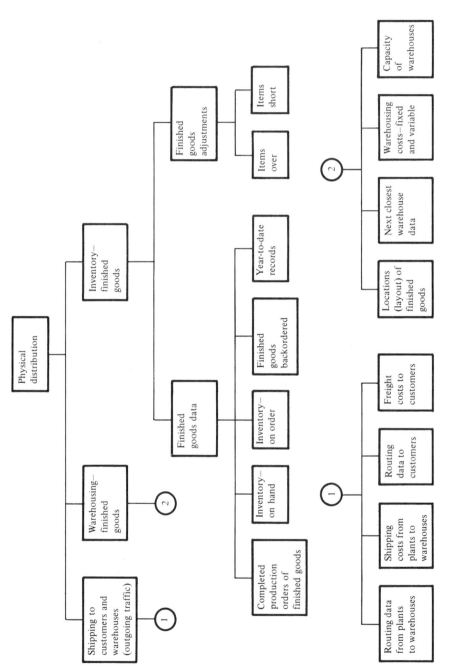

FIGURE 14-10. Physical distribution modules of the Consumer Products Corporation.

subsystems so that they will be logically related for real-time operations. The design of the major physical distribution functions (namely, shipping to customers and warehouses, warehousing–finished goods, and inventory–finished goods) is examined in the remaining sections of this chapter.

PHYSICAL DISTRIBUTION OVERVIEW

The overall framework for a real-time MIS physical distribution subsystem is illustrated in Figure 14-11. The interaction of the major subsystems with physical distribution provides PD management with real-time information for effecting improved customer service on orders. The marketing subsystem is capable of obtaining current information regarding shipment of goods because the common data base maintains up-to-date information on finished goods. The ability on the part of manufacturing to update the corporate data base on a real-time basis regarding completed production orders is a necessity for sales order processing to provide timely feedback on incoming orders. Thus, major subsystems have the capability to interact with the physical distribution computer programs in order to fulfill their information requirements as well as the timely demands of the PD system itself.

The output of physical distribution (Figure 14-11) is on a basis that is commensurate with its needs. Out-of-stock conditions, warehouse shipment orders, and production replenishment reports are on a real-time basis and back orders are issued at the end of the shift. On the other hand, the finished goods and exception report is issued weekly, as is the evaluation of warehouse shipping schedules. In reality, the foregoing PD reports are capable of meeting user demands to further the firm's objectives, and in particular, better service to customers.

SHIPPING TO CUSTOMERS AND WAREHOUSES MODULE
(OUTGOING TRAFFIC)

The shipment of finished goods is a multidimensional problem for the Consumer Products Corporation. As information is received in real time from sales order processing (marketing subsystem), finished products are shipped in one of the following ways:

> to warehouses from the plants for future sale
> to customers directly from the three manufacturing plants
based on regular or special orders
> to customers from warehouses based on regular customer orders

Going beyond a daily basis, these data can be analyzed weekly in order to determine an optimum method for stocking the firm's warehouses. Shipping on these two time bases is discussed below.

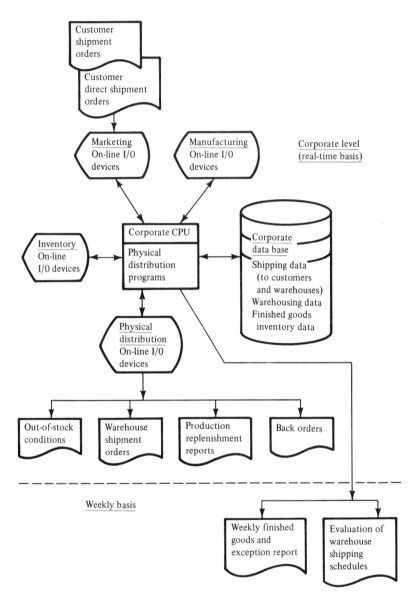

FIGURE 14-11. An overview of information flow for physical distribution in a real-time MIS environment.

Real-Time Basis

Shipments from plants to warehouses present special problems when consideration is given to keeping transportation costs between the two points at a minimum. The design analyst for the Consumer Products Corporation has devised an efficient method to keep costs as low as possible. Under this method, the corporate CPU triggers a warehouse shipment order when either of the following conditions take place:

1. sufficient product is accumulated to reach the programmed shipping quantity in terms of rails or trucks (weight)
2. the warehouse has reached the maximum allowable frequency delay (normally 2 days)

To handle this decision rule, the data base contains an optimum shipping weight for a factory to warehouse movement. As illustrated in Figure 14-12, there is no input needed to schedule shipments from plants to warehouses because this approach is under computer control.

Direct shipments to customers present no real problem to distribution management because the warehousing function is circumvented. Basically, the PD clerk interrogates the computer for instant shipping information. Rate, route, and carrier information is made available via an I/O terminal. The outgoing traffic clerk selects the appropriate means of transportation, which is stored on-line for billing the customer later. The customer shipment order is completed with this information and goods are shipped to the customer. The accounting subsystem takes care of customer billing.

The procedures for customer shipment orders are somewhat the same as for direct shipment orders, except that goods are shipped from one of the company's twelve warehouses rather than directly from one of the three plants. All outgoing traffic information is stored on line for instant retrieval by the PD department via an I/O terminal. The best routing method is selected to keep the firm's costs at a minimum. These data are also stored on the common data base—specifically, in the customer billing data file—for subsequent billing.

The second and last important difference between direct and nondirect shipments is the employment of the next closest warehouse model. In those cases in which finished products are not available at the closest warehouse, the next closest warehouse in terms of lowest shipping costs to the customer is queried for available finished goods. If goods are available from this alternate source, they are shipped. If not available, additional warehouses are interrogated for an answer. As was demonstrated previously (Figure 14-9), a factory order is initiated or the order is cancelled for the finished goods in question, depending upon the circumstances.

Weekly Basis

The daily procedures for shipping merchandise from warehouses to customers can operate best when goods are available at the right time and place for shipment. In order to be near this desired level, the multidistribution model is employed.

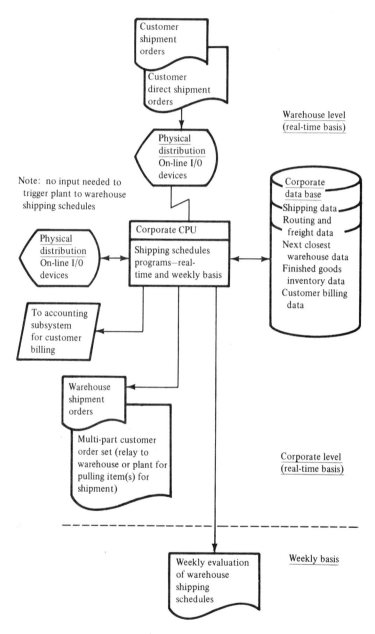

FIGURE 14-12. Shipment data flow at the corporate, warehouse, and plant levels within a real-time MIS physical distribution subsystem.

Weekly, this model reevaluates past shipping data, comparing actual shipping costs to the lowest possible costs as generated by the model. Not only is the comparison made, but it is also used to help schedule future shipments, because the firm has found a high correlation between actual customer shipments and projected customer shipments. The output of the three plants, then, is distributed on the basis of projected shipments for the twelve warehouses. Of course, current finished goods on hand are taken into account in the development of the forthcoming warehouse shipping schedules.

Before the foregoing shipping schedules can be developed, certain distribution factors must be determined and made available for computer usage. Among these are:

1. size of the market in terms of the units of each product that is serviced by a particular warehouse
2. location of alternative warehouse
3. transit times and costs from each alternative warehouse to each market
4. product mix in each market and products made in each plant
5. average weight and size for each product as well as the lbs. carried per rail car or truck
6. plant capacities for each plant and product class
7. unit manufacturing costs for each product of each plant
8. unit freight costs for less than carload lots (LCL), less than truckload lots (LTL), carload lots (CL), and truckload lots (TL).

In general, these data are stored on magnetic tape, because there is no need to keep them stored on the common data base.

Warehouse shipment data provide the necessary input for totaling actual weekly cost data. The multidistribution model relies on the foregoing listed file inputs plus rate and routing information from the originating plant through the warehouses and then to customers. In this way the output is an improved solution over the actual one, because it gives PD management precise knowledge about its efficiency.

WAREHOUSING—FINISHED GOODS MODULE

Warehousing of finished products in an advanced real-time MIS environment revolves around the utilization of the computer for three levels of control. The first level is computer scheduling control, which is concerned with the management of the warehouse as a whole. This includes scheduled ordering, perpetual inventory management, and shipping schedules. The second level is directed toward the flow of goods through the warehouse. Here, the computer is involved in the decisions concerning the flow of specific items through the materials handling equipment into and out of the various storage system areas (Figure 14-13). The third level involves the computer as the controlling device for all operations in the warehousing system. Every move that is made by the materials handling equipment is

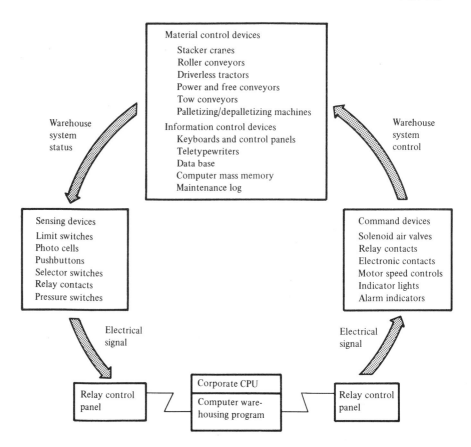

FIGURE 14-13. Control components of an automated warehouse for a real-time MIS physical distribution subsystem.

initiated by the computer. In reality, the computer program defines the sequence of operations that are to be undertaken by the materials handling equipment.

The major components of control for the Consumer Products Corporation and the role of the computer itself in directing materials handling control are depicted in Figure 14-13. Control components of an automated warehouse include materials control, information control, sensing devices, and command devices, as well as relay control panels and computer control. In such a system, the computer can simultaneously monitor many hundreds of limit switches, relays, and materials flow controls. Moreover, it contains within itself the definition of what constitutes a proper flow. It knows the sequence in which signals should be received in the relay control panels if they are to exercise proper control over materials flow.

Because the computer is monitoring individual relays and individual control points in the materials handling system, it prints a message when it diagnoses a failure within the system. The computer indicates to a maintenance man the particular relay or signal which led to the failure. In industrial applications of this concept of diagnostic monitoring, it has been found that trouble-shooting time for the vast majority of system failures has been virtually eliminated. Also, the failure recognition time has been considerably decreased; it cannot, however, be completely eliminated because it does not make economic sense to monitor each single relay in the entire warehouse. The relays that are considered essential to operation are the ones that are selected for monitoring. Accordingly, until one of the critical relays is found to be in error, a failure which may have occurred in the noncritical area will go unrecognized by the monitoring system.

Referring to the foregoing three levels of control, computer scheduling control (the first level) can be employed to great advantage in terms of dollar savings. The computer can be used to detect shifting patterns of demand. Management can be alerted for the purpose of evaluating whether or not the shifting is a temporary or long-range phenomenon.

Scheduling (the second level) can be integrated so as to take advantage in the area of scheduled maintenance. The computer is used to maintain equipment failure histories; on this basis it can derive statistics, such as mean time before failure, on specific components of the handling systems. In addition, the computer can more efficiently utilize the time of maintenance personnel in systematically checking portions of systems that are expected to cause trouble in the near future.

The direct computer control of materials handling equipment (the third level) is really a question of machine design and operation. The companies that manufacture and market these machines obviously have the most experience in designing reliable equipment. Refitting an existing handling machine to run under computer control is likely to be more expensive than purchasing new machinery specifically adapted or designed with computer control in mind. This last level of control, then, is critical to the entire warehousing operation and must be designed as expertly as possible.

INVENTORY—FINISHED GOODS MODULE

The objective of finished goods inventory is to have the right amount of inventory available when required by the customer. Too little finished goods inventory results in a condition of poor customer service, while too much inventory ties up excess funds, resulting in a lower return on the firm's total assets. The approach taken below for a real-time MIS considers these important factors whereby customer service and finished goods costs are placed in their proper perspective for optimizing overall PD objectives.

The finished goods inventory subsystem, depicted in Figure 14-14, is on a real-time basis for all finished goods inventory transactions. Generally, additions to inventory are the result of the completion of production orders at the plant level, having been forwarded from the quality control and inspection department to the division CPU and, in turn, to the corporate CPU for updating the corporate data base. Deductions from the finished goods data base are received via I/O terminals from the warehouses, representing shipments to customers. These data plus the

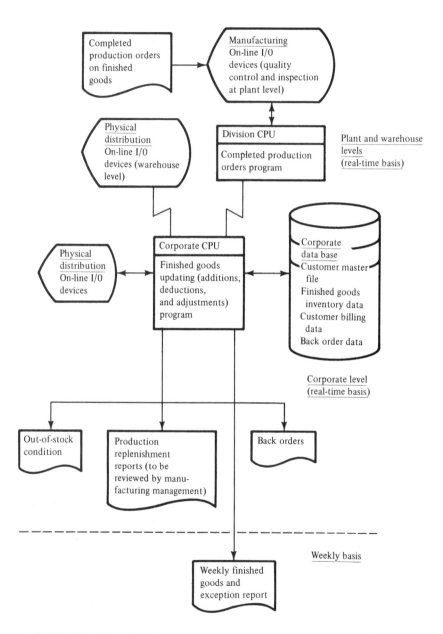

FIGURE 14-14. Finished goods inventory data flow for a real-time
MIS physical distribution subsystem.

customer master file are utilized by the accounting subsystem for customer billing. Also, all information concerning back orders are forwarded from the warehouses and stored on the common data base for billing and further on-line analysis and reporting. In addition to introducing plus and minus values at the plant and warehouse levels, adjustments can be made to correct shipments, inventory, and other errors that have come to the attention of warehouse and corporate headquarters. Thus, a real-time approach to finished goods keeps the corporate data base up to date at all times.

Two important finished goods reports are prepared for controlling this large financial investment. Those finished goods that are out of stock are reported immediately to physical distribution, inventory, and manufacturing management. Management may find it necessary to issue a production order if goods of this type are not on order. The weekly finished goods and exception report is not only a listing of items available for sale by warehouses; it also highlights out-of-stock conditions and what corrective action has been taken to remedy the situation. Those goods which are overstocked are starred for action by management. With such a summary and exception report, PD management can start corrective action, such as alerting marketing as to overstocked conditions of certain inventory items which can be candidates for special sales promotions. Likewise, finance managers can review the weekly finished goods and exception report to insure that neither too little nor too much is tied up in finished goods inventory. Their review is intended to insure that customer service in relation to the finished goods inventory is properly balanced. These reports and others, then, are designed to maximize the firm's investment in finished goods in order to meet the firm's overall PD objectives.

SUMMARY

The real-time MIS physical distribution subsystem is an improvement over the present integrated MIS subsystem. The ability to extract timely information allows the Consumer Products Corporation to provide better customer service throughout its major modules. In the area of outgoing traffic or shipping to customers and warehouses (first module), past information can be evaluated in order to improve current shipping schedules from the firm's three plants to the twelve warehouses. The utilization of computerized warehousing (second module) alerts management to shifting patterns of demand. Within the finished goods inventory function (third module), production replenishment reports are issued on a real-time basis for appropriate action by manufacturing management. In essence, PD management is supplied meaningful and, in some cases, instantaneous information for maintaining and improving service to the firm's customers

QUESTIONS

1. What is the rationale for placing the finished goods inventory module with the physical distribution subsystem rather than with the inventory subsystem?

2. What are the important differences between an integrated MIS physical distribution subsystem and a real-time MIS physical distribution subsystem?

3. Take the physical distribution data base elements in Figure 14-6 and define their detailed parts.

4. Suggest additional real-time MIS uses for the multistage distribution model.

5. Referring to Figure 14-10, list submodules for:
   a. location (layout) of finished goods
   b. next closest warehouse data
   c. warehousing costs—fixed and variable

6. Define in some detail the major subroutines of the daily shipping schedule program.

7. Referring to the section on warehousing of finished goods, suggest changes that reflect an ideal real-time MIS operating environment.

8. Define in some detail the major modules of the real-time finished goods updating program.

REFERENCES

Ackerman, K. B., "Physical Distribution—A New Business Revolution," *Business Horizons,* October, 1974.

Armstrong, R. E., "Pushbutton Handling of Small Parts," *Automation,* March, 1972.

Atkins, R. J., and Shriver, R. H., "New Approach to Facilities Location," *Harvard Business Review,* May-June, 1968.

Ballou, R. H., "Probabilities and Payoffs: Aids to Distribution Decision Making," *Transportation and Distribution Management,* August, 1969.

Bickerton, R. L., "The Many Faces of Automated Warehousing," *Transportation and Distribution Management,* February, 1971.

Bowersox, D. J., "Planning Physical Distribution Operations with Dynamic Simulation," *Journal of Marketing,* January, 1972.

Bowman, D., "It Takes One to Move One . . . Computers, That Is," *Production,* May, 1973.

Haavind, R., "Warehouse Without Men Acts as the Hub of a Production Information System," *Computer Decisions,* November, 1969.

Heskett, J. L., "Sweeping Changes in Distribution," *Harvard Business Review,* March-April, 1973.

Hopeman, R. J., *Systems Analysis and Operations Management.* Columbus, Ohio: Charles E. Merrill Publishing Co., 1970, Chap. 10.

Hoppe, C. W., "Using Simulation to Solve Transportation Problems," *Management Controls,* December, 1970.

Klahr, J. M., Newbourne, M. J., and Thomas, R. R., "Physical Distribution and the Mathematical Model," *Transportation and Distribution Management,* Part I—February, 1970, Part II—March, 1970, and Part III—April, 1970.

LaLonde, B. J., and Grashof, J. F., "Computer Oriented Information Systems Provide Effective P. D. Management," *Handling and Shipping,* October, 1969.

MMH Special Report, "How Computers Can Run Your Handling Systems," *Modern Materials Handling,* April, 1973.

Mueller, D. W., "Applying Computers to Warehousing," *Automation,* January, 1970.

Nugent, C. E., Vollmann, T. E., and Ruml, J., "An Experimental Comparison of Techniques for the Assignment of Facilities to Locations," *Operations Research,* January-February, 1968.

Rubal' Skiy, G. B., "On the Level of Supplies in a Warehouse with a Lag in Procurement," *Engineering Cybernetics,* January-February, 1972.

Smykay, E. W., "Anatomy of a Ready-Made PD Simulation Program," *Handling and Shipping,* February, 1968.

REAL-TIME MIS
ACCOUNTING SUBSYSTEM 15

The functions of accounting in a real-time MIS operating environment are no different from previous systems. Basically, they center around recording, classifying, and summarizing transactions and events that are, in part at least, of a financial character, and interpreting results thereof. Standard double entry is utilized to reflect the in- and out-flow of cash and non-cash transactions. Accounting data are stored either on tape, disk, drum, or some other machine-processable medium. Although original books of entry are not maintained per se for a real-time MIS, a general ledger can nevertheless be generated for visual output. But more importantly, a periodic balance sheet and income statement as well as comparable statements, can be prepared. The response depends upon the type of management information desired.

Within the chapter, the essential elements of an integrated MIS are explored before investigation of important design considerations for real-time MIS. Representative data base elements, OR models, and modules for accounting provide a basis for designing this area's major components, which include:

> receivables and payables
> payroll
> cost accounting
> financial statements and tax returns

Essentially, the accounting subsystem for the Consumer Products Corporation is structured on these four functions.

INTEGRATED MIS ACCOUNTING SUBSYSTEM

After the shipment of finished products, the accounting department prepares *customer invoices*. These not only serve as a record of charges but are also the basis on which the seller can legally claim payment for goods and services. Generally, the first two copies are sent to the customer and remaining copies are distributed to the marketing department, the salesman, and the accounting department's billing files. Depending on the terms of the invoice, payments are received from customers which are deposited in the firm's bank account. These payments are recorded in the *cash receipts journal* as documented evidence of their receipt by the firm. Periodically, *statements of accounts* are mailed to inform customers of the status of their accounts.

In addition to billing and collecting, the accounting department is concerned with disbursing funds, the major types being for payroll and for goods and services. *Time cards* are the originating source for paying salaries and wages. They may also be used for making labor distribution charges to various departments. *Payroll checks and earnings statements* are the output of payroll procedures.

The second type of disbursements involves checking the vendor's invoices against the purchase orders and receiving reports initially. Upon approval of payment by the purchasing department, *voucher-checks* are prepared. A voucher-check is a check with an attached voucher that contains sufficient space for date, purchase order number, vendor number, description, amount, discount, and net payment. The first copy is mailed to the payee on designated days of the month according to stated terms on the vendor's invoices, and duplicate copies are used for data processing. When processing is complete, they are filed.

The foregoing accounting functions are not complete until all legitimate governmental forms have been prepared and the proper voucher-checks drawn for the respective amounts due. Federal, state, and local governments require the preparation of specific tax forms, ranging from *federal income tax returns, reports on social security taxes withheld* (employer and employee), *federal and state unemployment compensation returns, state income tax returns, personal property tax returns,* and *city income tax returns.* Other governmental information returns that form the basis for statistical data on the United States are also required. In the final analysis, government requirements can place a substantial load over and beyond the normal data needed for the firm's internal operations.

The input for the integrated MIS accounting subsystem of the Consumer Products Corporation often originates in other subsystems. Marketing, manufacturing, inventory, purchasing, and physical distribution, to name the more important ones, forward data that are summarized onto magnetic tape for accounting. As illustrated in Figure 15-1, sales, payroll, receivables, payables, inventory, and cost data are direct inputs for the accounting subsystem. No matter what the sources are, these data are combined with existing accounting files for producing desired accounting output.

The four basic areas—receivables and payables, payroll, cost accounting, and financial statements and tax returns—provide the necessary input for computer processing at the corporate level. These detailed magnetic tape files, including accounting master files, are manipulated by the various processing programs whereby periodic general journals and trial balances are produced. The output of these runs results in updated master tape files which are the necessary input along with other required data for accounting information reporting programs per Figure 15-1. The net result of computer manipulation is output of the desired periodic and monthly reports. Basically, a balance sheet, an income statement, detailed product statements, and cost analysis reports are prepared on a monthly basis, supplemented by other period reports, such as data for preparing tax returns.

RECEIVABLES AND PAYABLES

The data processing flow for accounts receivable is an extension of the physical distribution subsystem—in particular, the finished goods inventory function (see Figure 14-4). The customer billing master magnetic tape file plus payment and adjustment cards provide the daily input for updating the accounts-receivable master magnetic tape file and producing customer invoices per Figure 15-2. Also, this program produces a sales-register and cash-receipts magnetic tape file that is used to print a daily-sales register and a cash-receipts register during two separate computer runs.

While the foregoing receivable activities center around daily operations, there are two other accounts-receivable computer processing runs on a monthly basis (Figure 15-2). These include aging of accounts receivable and printing customer statements. The first output breaks down the balances due by past time periods—that is, by 30, 60, 90, and over 90 days. The other output is an itemized statement of each customer's account, which is promptly mailed to expedite payments on accounts.

Accounts payables, the reverse of accounts receivables, are concerned with paying vendor invoices when they become due on the corporate level. Generally, vendor invoices are reviewed by the purchasing department for prices and quantities before they are forwarded to the accounting department. Those invoices which are found to be incorrect by the purchasing agent are reviewed with the appropriate vendor.

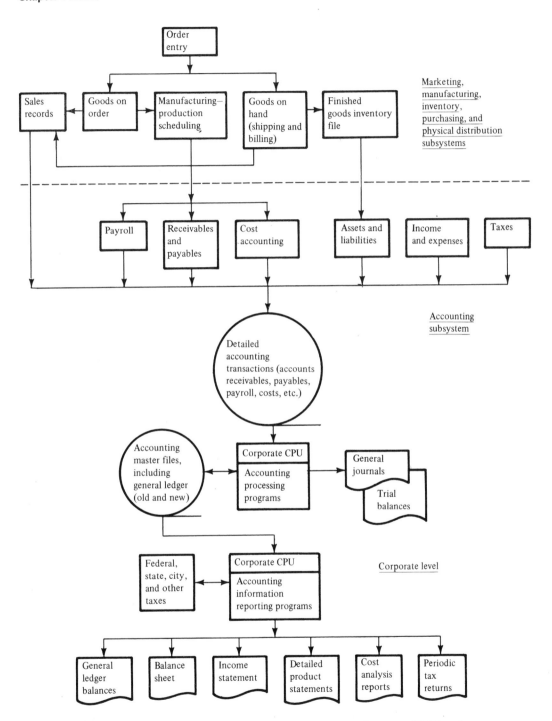

FIGURE 15-1. Accounting data flow for an integrated MIS system.

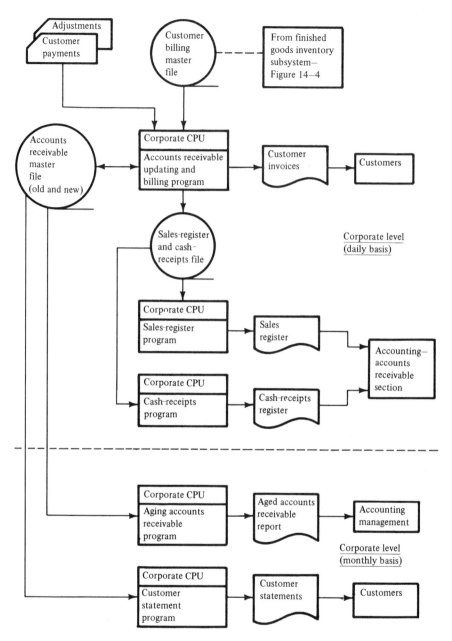

FIGURE 15-2. Customer billing and accounts-receivable data flow for an integrated MIS accounting subsystem.

Vendor invoice cards are prepared to update the accounts-payable master magnetic tape file twice a week. The output of the accounts-payable and voucher-register program is a new accounts-payable master file and a printed voucher regis-

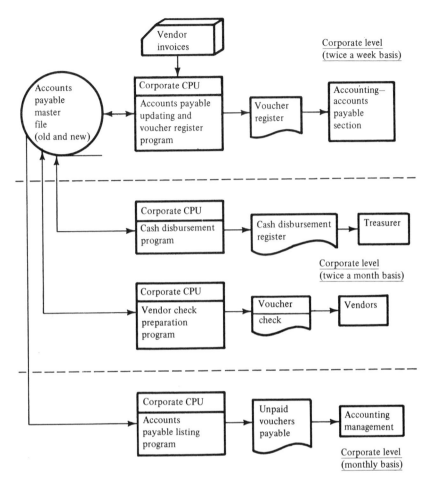

FIGURE 15-3. Accounts-payable and cash disbursements data flow for an integrated MIS accounting subsystem.

ter. As shown in Figure 15-3, on the 10th and 25th of each month, a cash-disbursements register is prepared initially on the computer, followed by the printing of the vendor checks, which are mailed to vendors. At the end of each month, a listing of unpaid invoices by vendors is prepared for analysis by the controller and treasurer.

PAYROLL

Payroll, like receivables and payables, must go through a series of preliminary steps before checks can be issued on the division level. As illustrated in Figure 15-4, weekly time cards are the input, along with the payroll master file for the gross pay and exception processing program. The output is the weekly time exception report,

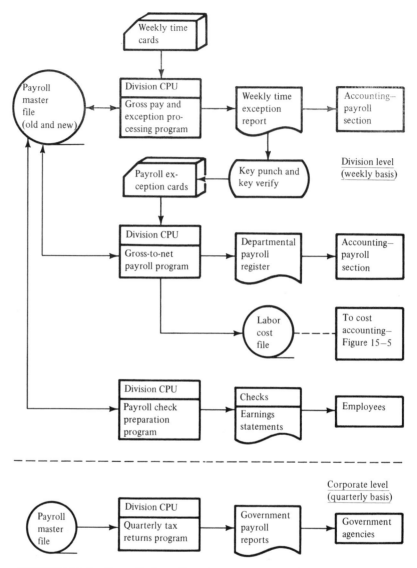

FIGURE 15-4. Payroll data flow for an integrated MIS accounting subsystem.

containing excessive hours worked by employees, missing weekly time cards, and comparable exception items. After all exceptions have been investigated by the accounting-payroll section, exception cards are prepared. The payroll master magnetic tape file, including these cards, are computer-processed for preparing the weekly payroll register and the labor cost file for cost accounting. The succeeding computer processing program produces the weekly payroll checks, which are then distributed to plant employees.

The preceding weekly processing steps are directed toward plant operations only. Comparable weekly payroll processing occurs at the corporate level for the firm's twelve warehouses and the corporate staff. Whether they are on the division or corporate level, governmental reports are prepared each quarter for reporting federal withholding and FICA taxes (required by law).

COST ACCOUNTING

Payroll and its distribution, like raw materials and work in process, are vital to cost accounting. A labor cost analysis processing run at the plant level, as shown in Figure 15-5, has as its output, a work center labor cost analysis. The report is reviewed by plant supervisors and foremen as well as by the cost accounting section. These data, per the labor cost file (magnetic tape), are forwarded via remote batch processing to corporate headquarters for producing overall cost analysis reports.

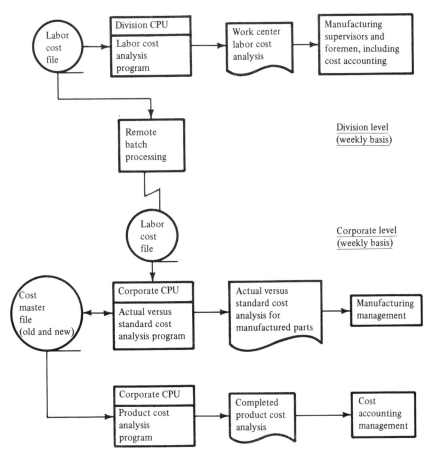

FIGURE 15-5. Cost accounting data flow for an integrated MIS accounting subsystem.

Cost analysis at St. Louis is concerned with taking management action where costs have exceeded standards by 5 percent. The first of the two cost reports is actual versus standard costs for manufactured costs. The second one is a completed product cost analysis. Both reports contain raw materials, direct labor, and manufacturing overhead for actual costs versus standard costs. Weekly, these reports are scrutinized by accounting management. Where unfavorable results are reported, the appropriate level of management is called upon to explain unfavorable deviations. Only in this manner can unfavorable operating conditions be corrected. However, as will be shown in subsequent sections on real-time MIS, an immediate response to unfavorable conditions is the key to reducing overall costs.

FINANCIAL STATEMENTS AND TAX RETURNS

The end result of all accounting activities is the preparation of financial statements, including tax returns. Before these outputs can be produced, detailed accounting transactions must have been compiled and accessible for computer processing. By and large, for this phase of accounting, these data will have been stored on magnetic tape, providing input as depicted in Figure 15-1. Also, accounting master magnetic tape files which include the general ledger will be an essential part of input for producing a general journal and a trial balance for the current month. The updated accounting master file is processed on line in order to produce the following:

> general ledger balances
> monthly balance sheet
> monthly income statement
> detailed product statements
> cost analysis reports

In like manner, periodic tax reports, also shown in Figure 15-1, are computer-prepared when the accounting master file and selected governmental tax cards are the source input. Thus, an integrated MIS does provide for a wide range of managerial reports. However, as is the case with many other functions, there is a time lag in receiving critical information needed to correct current operational deficiencies.

REAL-TIME MIS DESIGN CONSIDERATIONS FOR ACCOUNTING SUBSYSTEM

Design considerations for the accounting subsystem in a real-time MIS environment go beyond its own subsystem, as is the case for integrated MIS. Customer billing is initiated by marketing, while vendor invoices are received from purchasing. Payroll, whether it is factory or office, originates outside the accounting subsystem. Similarly, feedback of product cost data is forwarded from the manufacturing work centers and inventory. The only real accounting functions that are generated within

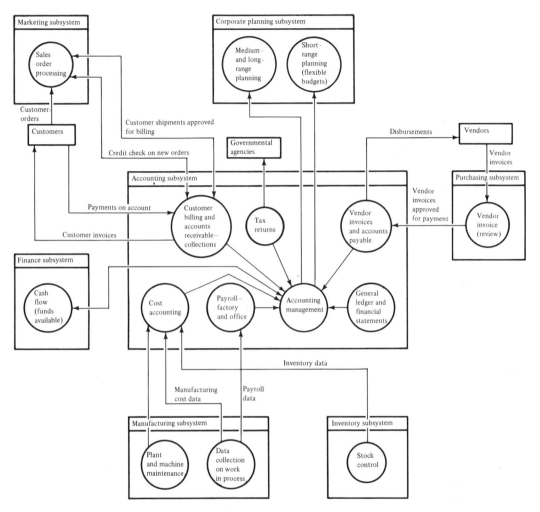

FIGURE 15-6.   Real-time MIS accounting subsystem flow to and from other subsystems.

their own module are financial statements and tax returns. The former are forwarded to all subsystems for management review as well as for appropriate corrective action. The latter, on the other hand, are mailed to the various federal, state, and local tax agencies. Thus, design considerations must take into account most other subsystems for developing an effective real-time MIS accounting subsystem.

OVERVIEW OF ACCOUNTING ENVIRONMENT

The major functions found in the accounting environment are shown in Figure 15-6. Just as with integrated MIS, they include receivables and payables, payroll, cost accounting, and financial statements and tax returns. However, the design of these functions will take on new dimensions because of the computer's real-time capabilities. Accounting data will be stored on the common data base, retrievable as is or capable of manipulation depending upon the user's needs. The real-time system will be capable of calculating accounting information on a current basis. Specifically, management will be able to retrieve current cost data, financial operating ratios, and cash balances. In fact, within this type of operating mode, current financial statements can be generated by utilizing a mathematical model that encompasses all of the firm's assets, liabilities, capital, income, and expenses. The maintenance of these data on an up-to-date basis is a necessary requirement for an accurate answer of the firm's financial condition at any time.

In conjunction with the preparation of financial statements by the accounting subsystem, other subsystems can benefit from this timely information. The finance subsystem can analyze the current cash position for determining short-time needs. Likewise, the corporate planning staff can evaluate current trends in profitability for last-minute budget changes. Also, inventory management can evaluate its investment in light of current operating conditions. Purchasing management can appraise its overall ability to keep raw materials cost at a minimum. The ability to extract current financial information via an I/O terminal can indicate changes to the user as they occur. From this viewpoint, corrective measures can be effected much sooner.

ACCOUNTING DATA BASE

The accounting data bank (magnetic tape files in an integrated MIS) must be converted to data stored on line in a real-time MIS operating mode. Accounting data should be structured by the type of data in the common data base, shown in Figure 15-7. But of equal importance, critical information should be easily accessible for instantaneous display or printing by a remote I/O terminal. Only in this manner will the accounting subsystem meet its real-time demands.

Data for accounts receivable and payable consist of such items as customer billing, accounts receivable, collection, vendor invoice, and accounts payable. Some of this information originates in other subsystems, while others are an integral part of the accounting subsystem. Ultimately, receivables and payables data elements are utilized in producing the firm's financial statements. In a similar fashion, payroll data base elements are received from the factory and office departments and are the basis for preparing weekly and monthly payrolls as well as periodic statements within the accounting subsystem.

Cost accounting relies heavily on data compiled by manufacturing, inventory, and payroll functions. Current input on operations are capable of being extracted and compared to standard cost data elements for meaningful analysis of operations. In addition, cost data are employed in the preparation of financial statements, the end result of all accounting activities.

The data base necessary to produce financial statements contains not only actual figures but also budgeted figures from the corporate planning subsystem—in particular, those for income and expenses on a flexible budgeting basis. Current tax rates for calculating estimated taxes are stored on the common data base for preparing periodic statements as well as for determining taxes due on the federal, state,

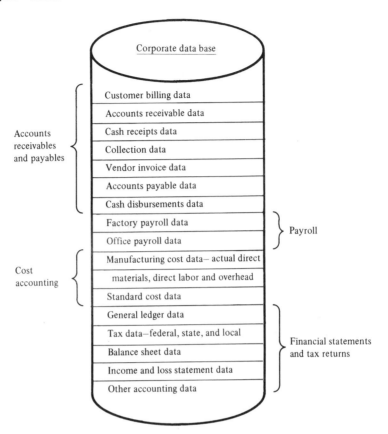

FIGURE 15-7.   Typical accounting data base elements at the corporate level.

and local government levels. Basically, these data elements comprise the accounting data base needed in a real-time MIS environment for timely accounting and finance information.

OR ACCOUNTING MODELS

Mathematical models have been developed for the major modules of accounting; however, there has been more concentration on the cost and financial statement modules. Numerous cost formulas have been developed to evaluate current manufacturing performance. Several mathematical cost models are presented below. Also, linear programming is discussed in order to evaluate overall performance as a supplement to the standard procedure of comparing actual to budgeted amounts.

Mathematical Cost Models

Manufacturing cost analysis, from an overall viewpoint, is directed toward its major components—material, labor, and overhead variances. Many more variances can be developed. Some are capable of a real-time response, while other variances are on a daily, weekly, monthly, or some other logical period-evaluation basis. The need for timeliness of data is the determinant of the reporting mode for the Consumer Products Corporation.

The materials-usage variance percent measures daily the deviation of materials used during the manufacturing process for a production order within a specific work center. The formula is:

$$\text{Work center materials-usage variance percent} = \frac{\Sigma AM}{(SM \times AU)} \times 100 \qquad \text{Equation 15-1}$$

where ΣAM = total cost of all actual materials used for a production order within a specific work center

SM = unit standard materials cost for a production order within a specific work center

AU = actual units for a production order within a specific work center

The summation (Σ) of all actual materials used to produce a manufacturing order within a particular work center are accumulated on the data base during manufacturing and compared to the total standard materials cost upon completion of the manufacturing process. It should be noted that the number of manufactured items are multiplied by the standard materials cost to arrive at total standard costs. As with many cost calculations, the resulting value must be multiplied by 100 to convert it to a percent.

The second important overall cost performance variance focuses on labor reporting by work center. All actual direct labor costs are accumulated by shift for each work center less standard time calculations in order to evaluate labor costs. This approach is represented by the following equation:

$$\text{Work center labor variance} = \Sigma ADL - (SH \times SLR) \qquad \text{Equation 15-2}$$

where ΣADL = total actual direct labor cost (includes fringe benefits) by a specific work center for a shift

SH = standard hours by a specific work center for a shift

SLR = standard labor cost rate (includes fringe benefits)

Equation 15-2 can be converted to a percent by dividing the first term of the equation by the terms in parentheses and multiplying by 100. Thus, the new equation is:

$$\text{Work center labor variance percent} = \frac{\Sigma ADL}{(SH \times SLR)} \times 100 \qquad \text{Equation 15-2 revised}$$

Overhead variances, like raw materials and labor, can take many directions in terms of reporting timely answers. One such variance is a weekly comparison of actual summarized overhead costs versus standard amounts. Actual overhead costs by a work center over actual hours times the standard overhead work center rate which, in turn, when multiplied by 100, are represented by the following formula:

$$\text{Overhead variance percent} = \frac{\Sigma AOC}{(AH \times SOR)} \times 100 \qquad \qquad \text{Equation 15-3}$$

where ΣAOC = total actual overhead costs by a specific work center
$\quad AH$ = actual hours worked by a specific work center
$\quad SOR$ = standard overhead cost rate by a specific work center

Numerous other variances can be developed for materials, labor, and overhead. Although these deviations highlight specific areas of manufacturing operations, equally important are variances that analyze overall operations, such as production and work centers. The production cost variance measures the accuracy of manufacturing plant reporting. Its mathematical equation is:

$$\text{Production cost variance} = (PR - PE) \times SC \qquad \qquad \text{Equation 15-4}$$

where PR = actual production reported
$\quad PE$ = production expected
$\quad SC$ = standard product cost

Actual production less expected production times the standard product cost gives the production cost variances for each completed production order. This weekly value tells whether or not the firm has held its production costs to a minimum.

Manufacturing operations can be further evaluated on the basis of work centers. The work center operation variance measures cost changes occurring due to alterations in production routing and lack of efficiency within the work center. Produced on a daily basis, its formula is:

$$\text{Work center operation variance} = (AVC - SVC) \times PR \qquad \qquad \text{Equation 15-5}$$

where AVC = actual unit variable cost of conversion for a specific work center
$\quad SVC$ = standard unit variable cost of conversion for a specific work center
$\quad PR$ = actual production reported for a specific work center

A plus variance indicates unfavorable work center operations, while a minus one indicates favorable or efficient operating conditions.

The prior two costs variances are supplemented by many others. These analyses are designed to measure some aspect of plant manufacturing efficiency. However, there are other formulas that are oriented to measuring how accurate standards are. A typical example centers around evaluating the direct labor standard rate whose formula is:

$$\text{Labor standard rate variance} = DL - (LE \times SL) \qquad \qquad \text{Equation 15-6}$$

where DL = actual weekly direct labor cost for a specific work center, including fringe benefits
$\quad LE$ = standard weekly labor hours earned by a specific work center
$\quad SL$ = standard labor rate for a specific work center, including fringe benefits

A continuous weekly plus value indicates that the standard labor rate (SL) may be too low and warrants an investigation. On the other hand, a large negative value over a long period of time may indicate that the standard is set too high. Thus, the cost department of the accounting subsystem needs to evaluate its standards and make appropriate adjustments that reflect current operating conditions.

Linear Programming Model

An interesting application of operations research is to structure the accounting subsystem on a linear programming model. This approach goes beyond a comparison of actual with flexible budgeted amounts. To be more specific, the differences between what the firm accomplished with its available resources for the month and what it should have accomplished with these same resources is calculated in terms of overall contribution. Thus, a true overall efficiency of operational variances can be determined using the linear programming model.

Basically, this approach requires the development of the objective function and constraint equations as found in any linear programming problem. Actual time available in the various manufacturing work centers for the month under study, manufacturing times for each product, contribution for each product, quantities that can be sold, and minimum sales requirements provide the necessary input to the OR model. The introduction of these variables for one plant means that well over a hundred equations with several hundred variables must be developed before computer processing can begin. Because most of these data are already stored on the common data base, the problem is simplified. The program would reference these data elements plus other data that can be entered via an I/O terminal device. In fact, the entire program can be handled via an I/O teletypewriter unit. There is no need to list all the intermediate tableaus in the problem—a printout of the first and last tableaus would be sufficient. It should be pointed out that an OR model of this magnitude takes considerable memory space and computation time. For this reason, it is advisable to perform these calculations during a nonoperating shift where there are little or no demands on the real-time computer system.

ACCOUNTING MODULES

The accounting subsystem, like finance, is under the control of the accounting and finance vice-president. The controller is in charge of the accounting functions and is assisted by several managers. Basically, these managers control the major modules of accounts receivable, accounts payable, payroll, cost accounting, financial statements, and tax returns. This simplified accounting approach to the organization permits efficiency of operations.

In Figure 15-8, the important modules and submodules essential for the design of the accounting subsystem are illustrated. However, before these are designed in detail, they must be coordinated with basic modules found in the manufacturing, inventory, purchasing, and other related subsystems. Only in this manner will compatibility of subsystems be assured. Too often in the past, subsystems were

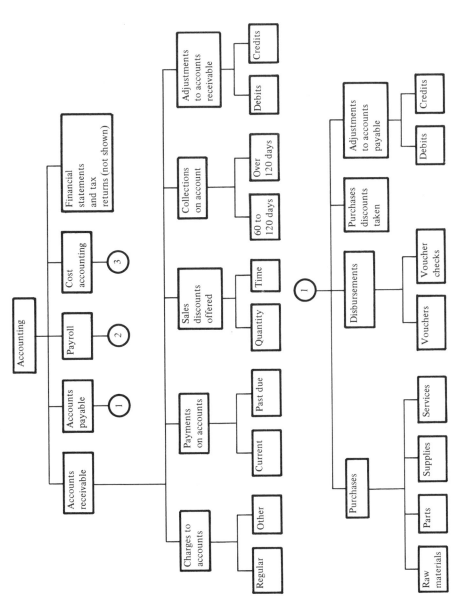

FIGURE 15-8. Accounting modules of the Consumer Products Corporation.

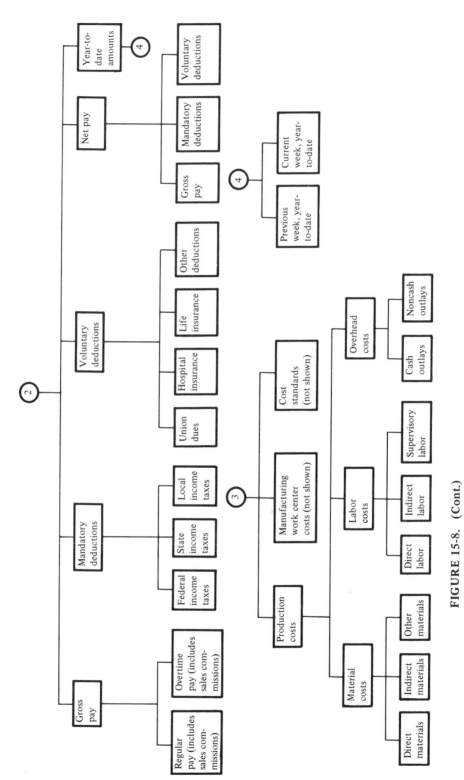

FIGURE 15-8. (Cont.)

designed without giving thought to other areas, thereby causing duplication of modules. It is of utmost importance that the systems designer consider the basic accounting modules as they affect other areas of the real-time MIS.

REAL-TIME MIS
ACCOUNTING SUBSYSTEM

A brief examination of the important design considerations (the data base, OR models, and accounting modules) for the real-time MIS accounting subsystem is extremely helpful before undertaking the detailed design. By and large, the design approach taken in the remainder of the chapter is not complex. However, there is great need to structure the accounting data such that information to be displayed or printed can be extracted from the data base with a minimum of effort. Likewise, data base elements should be capable of serving the needs of several subsystems. A thorough analysis of data base elements, then, is mandatory in the design of the real-time management information system.

ACCOUNTING SUBSYSTEM OVERVIEW

An accounting subsystem overview by necessity concerns many other subsystems. The input from these subsystems, along with the accounting subsystem as shown in Figure 15-9, provides accounting management with desired output. In addition, accounting exception reports are produced on a real-time basis if so needed. But just as important is the feedback of instantaneous information to operational levels that utilize accounting information for comparing actual operations to budgeted amounts or standards. From this viewpoint, the accounting subsystem is forward-looking in that deviations from current operations are detected and corrected in order to keep upcoming activities in line with planned performance. The major accounting modules in the remaining sections of this chapter are viewed from this perspective.

RECEIVABLES AND PAYABLES MODULES

The data flow for customer billing does not originate with the accounting function, but rather with the sales order processing function. By way of review, a sales order clerk enters the customer order via an I/O terminal. He checks the customer's credit, then interrogates the finished goods inventory file and/or enters the production order for the desired items not available from any of the firm's warehouses. Data are accumulated on the common data base regarding warehouse shipments and back orders. At the end of the day, a customer billing program is triggered and customer invoices are printed on the high-speed printer and mailed to customers. Likewise, a sales register is printed immediately following the customer billing run.

The foregoing procedures form the basis for charging the customer accounts, as

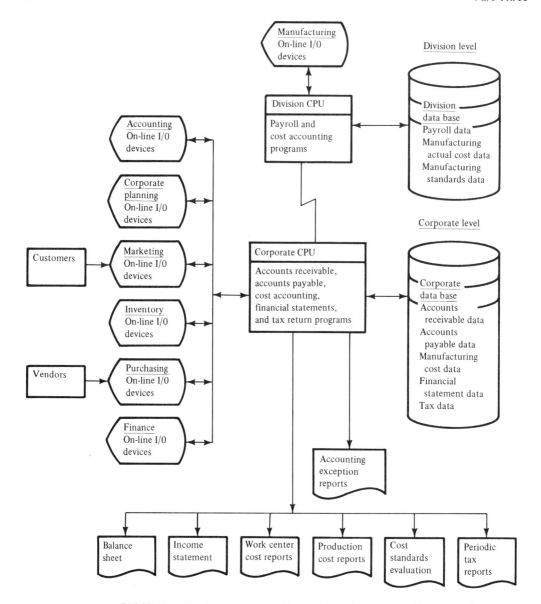

FIGURE 15-9. An overview of a real-time MIS accounting subsystem.

shown in Figure 15-10. The I/O terminal is also employed to post customer payments, only this time they are entered by the accounts-receivable section of the accounting subsystem. All legitimate complaints on customer accounts are handled as received and appropriate adjustments made to the common data base, thereby reflecting the correct (current) accounts receivable balances. Daily, a cash-receipts program is initiated after all customer payments have been posted, resulting in a

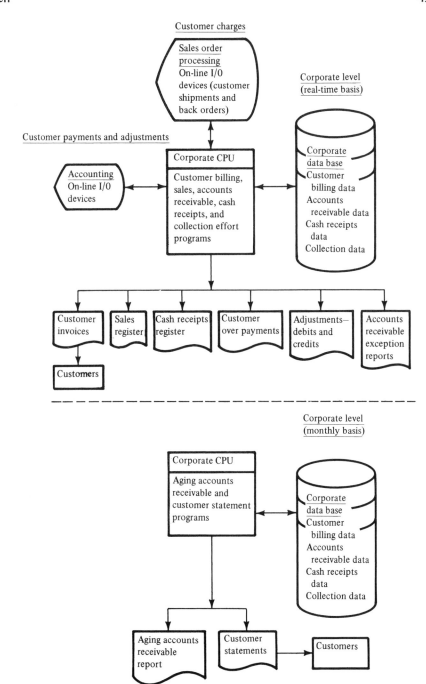

FIGURE 15-10. Customer billing and accounts-receivable data flow for a real-time MIS accounting subsystem.

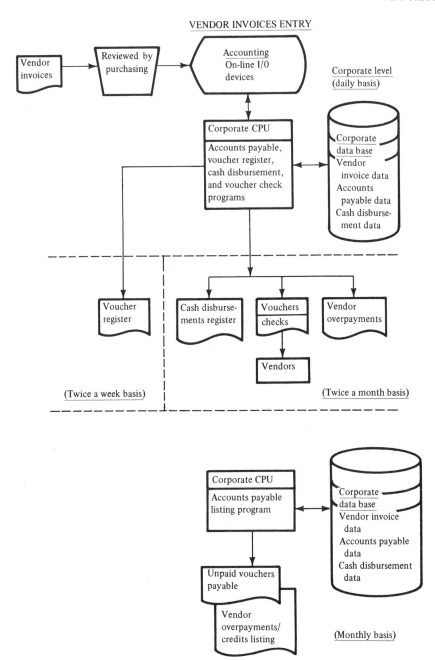

FIGURE 15-11.   Accounts-payable and cash-disbursements data flow
for a real-time MIS accounting subsystem.

cash-receipts register. In addition, daily exception reports are triggered at the end of the day, including customer overpayments and adjustments—debits and credits. Entries are automatically made to the general ledger stored on the common data base.

Just as with integrated MIS, reports are prepared on a monthly basis. These include aging of accounts receivable and the preparation of customer statements. Although an aging list is printed once a month, a terminal device can be used to retrieve information on accounts, thereby making customer account data available on a real-time basis.

Although the basic accounts-receivable functions are handled on a daily basis, the same time basis is not necessary for all accounts-payable activities. Basically, vendor invoices are entered by the accounts-payable section of the accounting department (Figure 15-11) after review by the purchasing subsystem. Daily entry is via an I/O terminal for storage on the common data base. Twice a week, a voucher register is prepared for invoices received since the preparation of the previous register.

The Consumer Products Corporation, which pays its bills on the 10th and 25th of the month, schedules cash disbursements and voucher-check runs on these days. The cash-disbursements register is a listing of checks to be paid and those which will take advantage of cash discounts offered. After a brief review by the accounts-payable section, voucher-checks are computer-prepared. At the end of the run is a listing of prior overpayments to specific vendors.

Monthly, a list of unpaid vouchers is prepared, as is the case for the integrated MIS. Also, a vendor overpayments/credits listing is printed for review by the accounts-payable manager. It should be noted that current accounts of individual vendors, like customers, can be interrogated for current information at any time from an I/O device.

PAYROLL MODULE

Payroll within a real-time MIS environment does not operate alone, but relies on input from other subsystems. Factory payroll is an essential part of the data collection system found within the manufacturing subsystem. When a factory employee enters his work center in the morning, he enters his plastic badge into a badge-reader remote terminal. As shown in Figure 15-12, such terminals are connected to an area station which, in turn, is connected to the division CPU through a transmission control unit. When it is time for the employee's shift to begin, his foreman activates the area station to receive a printout of work center attendance.

Depending on the employee's current work assignment, the job being worked on is entered via the remote terminal. The employee makes a setting on the terminal to indicate the type of transactions he is entering (work assignment). Next, he enters his employee badge number in the selector dial and inserts a prepunched job card in the card-reader slot. He presses the entry level and the data are recorded on the common data base. As the employee changes from one job to another, entry

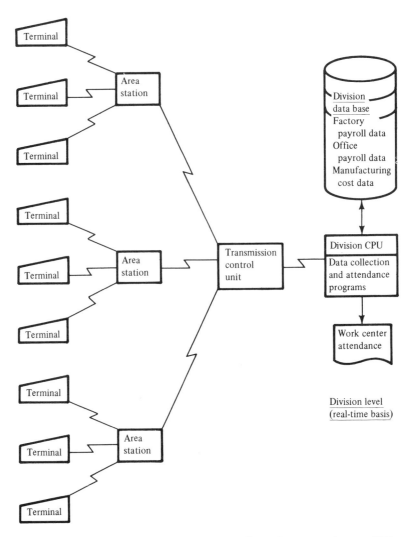

FIGURE 15-12. Factory payroll data flow for a real-time MIS accounting subsystem.

via the remote terminal is used to indicate the end of job. Likewise, the new production order to be worked on is also entered. In this manner, the common data base contains data for weekly payroll processing as well as for the costing of production orders.

Daily production-time data base elements are accumulated on a weekly basis and are summarized to produce a weekly time, gross pay, and exception report as shown in Figure 15-13. Approved payroll changes are made via an I/O terminal in accounting before final processing occurs. The payroll register and checks, including earnings statements, are then produced and distributed to factory employees.

Payroll activities do not end with weekly processing, but must be carried forward for monthly, quarterly, and yearly reports. Weekly figures are auto-

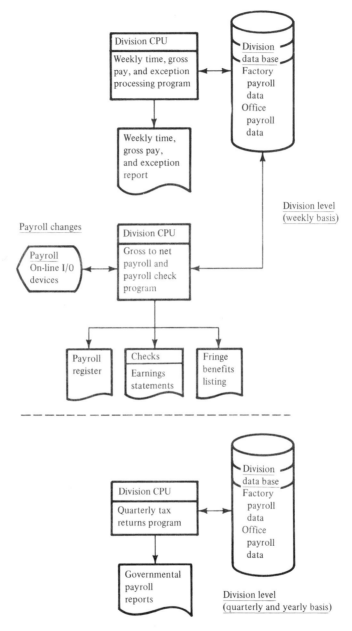

FIGURE 15-13. Overall payroll data flow for a real-time MIS accounting subsystem.

matically carried forward to the general ledger stored on line for producing
monthly statements. Quarter-to-date earnings are used in preparing quarterly
reports on federal income and FICA taxes withheld. Finally, year-to-date figures are
the basis for preparing W-2's.

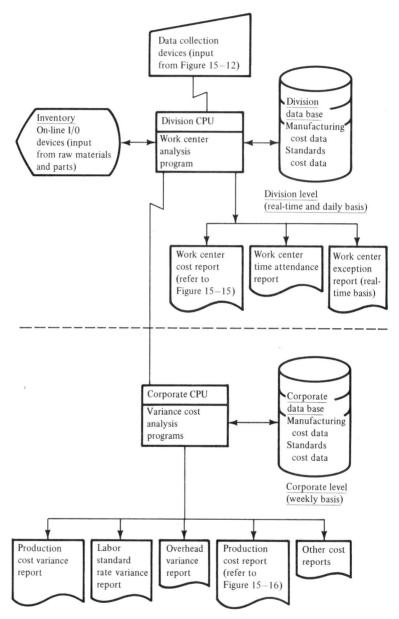

FIGURE 15-14. Cost accounting data flow for a real-time MIS accounting subsystem.

COST ACCOUNTING MODULE

Cost accounting in a real-time MIS operating mode depends upon data generated throughout the work day at the plant level by other subsystems. As indicated in Figure 15-14, usage of raw materials and parts is recorded by the inventory

Work Center No. 10   Date: 12/15/7-

Materials Usage Variance (Equation 15-1):

$$\frac{\text{Total cost of actual materials used}}{(\text{Unit standard materials cost} \times \text{actual units})} \times 100$$

$$\frac{\$3,150}{(\$3.09 \times 1000)} \times 100 = 102\% \text{ or } \$60.00 \text{ unfavorable variance}$$

Labor Variance (Equation 15-2):

$$\frac{\text{Total actual direct labor cost}}{(\text{Standard hours} \times \text{standard labor cost rate})} \times 100$$

$$\frac{\$1,410}{(220 \times \$6.00)} \times 100 = 107\% \text{ or } \$90.00 \text{ unfavorable variance}$$

Operation Variance (Equation 15-5):

(Actual unit variable costs − standard unit variable costs) × actual production

Product 11: ($2.95 − $3.00) × 1000 = $50 favorable variance
Product 40: ($2.90 − $2.85) ×   800 = $40 unfavorable variance

FIGURE 15-15. Daily work center cost report—analysis for work center 10 in a real-time MIS environment.

subsystem, capable of retrieval by cost accounting. In a similar manner, work center data collection devices within the manufacturing subsystem provide the input for costing analysis at the division and corporate levels. Basically, raw materials and labor data are compared to standards stored on the common data base.

An important daily report being generated at the plant level is the work center cost report, illustrated in Figure 15-15. Several daily variances are calculated—namely, materials usage (Equation 15-1), labor (Equation 15-2), and operation (Equation 15-5). Other reports, such as work center time attendance and exception reports, are generated daily and on a real-time basis respectively. In addition to the programs needed to produce these outputs, a program is triggered at the end of each day to transfer summary cost information from the division to corporate headquarters. These cost figures are used for longer-range analysis—in particular, to improve the operations of a specific plant as well as to compare one plant against another. Also, these analyses verify cost standard accuracy or lack thereof.

As shown in Figure 15-14, weekly costs analyses are processed at the corporate level. They include production cost variance (Equation 15-4), labor standard rate variance (Equation 15-6), and overhead variance (Equation 15-3). Of special interest is the weekly production cost report (Figure 15-16) that brings together information generated on other reports. This report is reviewed by manufacturing, inventory, and accounting management. Generally, the information contained in this report is the basis for weekly meetings and evaluation at the corporate and division levels.

Weekly Production Cost Report (Unit Basis)

Analysis of Product 15

Week Ending 5/8/7-

Work Center	Materials		Labor		Overhead		Total Manufactured Costs		Quantity
	Actual	Standard	Actual	Standard	Actual	Standard	Actual	Standard	
12 (machine shop)	$1.60	$1.55	$1.41	$1.35	$ .64	$ .60	$3.65	$3.50	1500
35 (minor assembly)	1.04	1.05	.60	.60	.45	.45	2.09	2.10	1500
54 (major assembly)	1.26	1.25	1.26	1.25	.76	.75	3.28	3.25	1500
72 (inspection)	-	-	.17	.15	.12	.10	.29	.25	1500
	$3.90	$3.85	$3.44	$3.35	$1.97	$1.90	$9.31	$9.10	

FIGURE 15-16. Weekly production cost report (unit basis)—analysis for product 15.

In addition to the above cost reports, other period analyses are generated. A monthly listing of materials, labor, and overhead costs to be absorbed by the financial statements is prepared. Also, a listing of raw materials, work in process, and finished goods is processed. On a quarterly basis, a cost analysis, similar to Figure 15-16, is run. Standard costs are evaluated in view of rising costs and are changed to reflect current operations.

FINANCIAL STATEMENTS AND TAX RETURNS MODULES

Financial statements, in a real-time MIS environment, can be prepared at most any time because the common data base contains immediately accessible general ledger data. Although this information originates mostly outside the accounting subsystem, this is no deterrent to producing periodic financial statements on-line because critical financial data are entered and recorded as they happen. The only problem with producing timely monthly statements is special one-time journal entries, which must be first determined and then entered on the common data base. Failure to include these special entries as a part of the general ledger data base could result in misstating financial statements.

The general ledger updating program, shown in Figure 15-17, is used through-

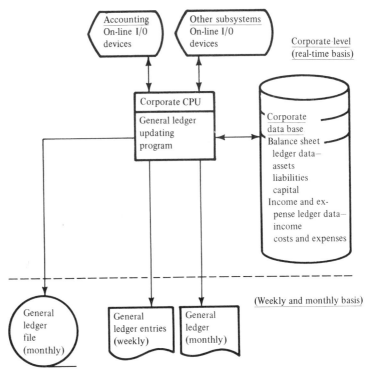

FIGURE 15-17. General ledger data flow for a real-time MIS accounting subsystem.

out the month to keep the data base updated. Data are fed from within and outside the accounting subsystem. At the end of the week, a listing of general ledger entries is produced by the computer to indicate the various debits and credits to specific accounts. In a similar manner, after all transactions have been processed for the last day of the month, general ledger balances and their detailed transactions are printed as well as written onto magnetic tape. The reason for this tape file is that general ledger items must be capable of being processed against the common data base the very next working day. Thus, the general ledger magnetic tape file can be changed at a later date to effect corrections and entry of special items. Of course, changes made to this file must also be made to the common data base for uniformity of accounting data.

For monthly financial statements, the magnetic tape file output per Figure 15-17 is computer-processed. Although the essential elements for these balance sheet items (on this tape) originate outside the accounting department as depicted in Figure 15-18, their physical flow is reflected in accounting entries, which are summarized for the month-end balance sheet. Similarly, income and expenses are the result of activities in other departments which flow into the common data base under program control, as general ledger entries. The resulting income and expenses are compared to budgeted values for meaningful analyses. (The responsibility for

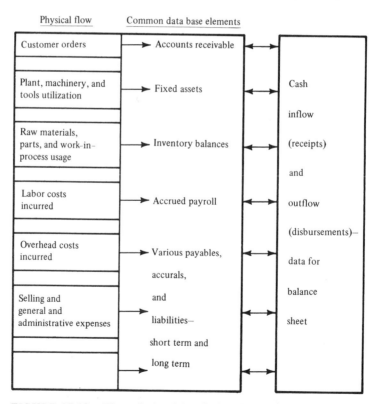

FIGURE 15-18. The relationship of the physical flow to the balance sheet in a real-time MIS environment.

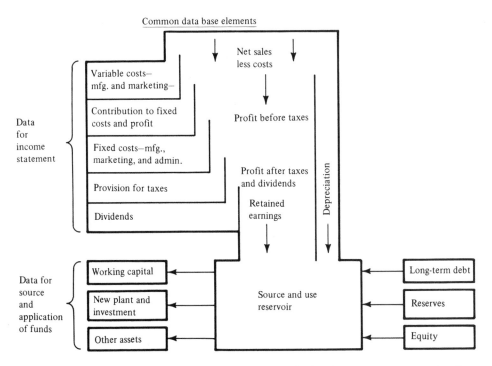

FIGURE 15-19. The relationship of the income statement to the
source and application of funds statement in a
real-time MIS environment.

maintaining budgeted data base elements belongs to the corporate planning subsystem.) The profit after taxes, in the form of retained earnings and depreciation
plus specific balance sheet items as shown in Figure 15-19, provides the source of
funds for the firm, which, in turn, are applied to financing specific projects.

From the foregoing presentation, the preparation of financial statements in a
real-time environment parallels that of an integrated MIS. However, financial
reports have been forwarded to the user on a timely basis. But equally important to
management is the provision for timely exception reports which highlight income
and expenses that fall outside predetermined limits. A real-time MIS can, for
example, compare actual sales against typical patterns and control limits, leading to
identification of *in-control* or *out-of-control* conditions as they occur. The same
approach can be applied to the firm's costs and expenses. Comparisons,
then, can be retrieved upon demand—enabling the capabilities of accounting
information in a real-time MIS operating mode to exceed those of its predecessor system.

The advanced design approaches outlined above for financial statements is
also applicable to the preparation of tax returns. By and large, data can be extracted from the data base as of a closing date and written onto magnetic tape. At a
later date, tax returns can be prepared in a batch processing mode. In this manner,
governmental reports and returns on the federal, state, and local levels present no
major obstacle for the firm.

SUMMARY

The accounting subsystem of the Consumer Products Corporation is an integral part of the marketing, purchasing, manufacturing, inventory, and physical distribution subsystems in a real-time MIS environment. Marketing is linked to accounts receivable, purchasing to accounts payable, manufacturing to payroll, and inventory and physical distribution to cost accounting. Despite this high degree of integration, there are numerous methods and procedures that operate within the accounting subsystem itself without reference to other subsystems. Thus, design considerations in this environment are extremely difficult.

A most important advantage of a real-time MIS approach over prior ones centers around timely accounting information. Accounting personnel and their managers are capable of retrieving current accounts-receivable data for checking customer credit, checking on the status of overpayments to or credits due from vendors, determining the accuracy of plant personnel attendance, analyzing actual versus standard costs, and retrieving current general ledger balances, among other things. In essence, information can be isolated and evaluated now about other subsystems and the accounting function itself, enabling the firm to be forward-looking in its approaches to decision making.

QUESTIONS

1. What advantages does the real-time MIS accounting subsystem have over the integrated MIS accounting subsystem?

2. Referring to the cost accounting data base elements in Figure 15-7, define their detailed parts.

3. Suggest additional cost accounting formulas that would be found in a real-time MIS environment.

4. Referring to Figure 15-8, determine submodules for:
   a. financial statements and tax returns
   b. manufacturing work center costs
   c. cost standards

5. Determine the major modules for the customer billing program.

6. Suggest changes to the payroll section in a real-time MIS environment that include the utilization of the division and corporate data bases.

7. Referring to the section on cost accounting, suggest changes that reflect an ideal real-time MIS operating mode.

8. What is the relationship of flexible budgets to the accounting subsystem in real-time MIS?

REFERENCES

Bower, J. B., Schlosser, R. E., and Zlatkovich, C. T., *Financial Information Systems* Boston, Mass.: Allyn & Bacon, Inc., 1969.

Cook, W. F., and Bost, W. J., "Standard Cost System: A Module of a Management Information System," *Journal of Systems Management,* March, 1969.

Davall, D. M., and Wilkinson, J. W., "Simulating an Accounting Information System Model," *Management Accounting*, January, 1971.

Demski, J. S., "An Accounting System Structured on a Linear Programming Model," *The Accounting Review*, October, 1967.

Enrick, N. L., "Be Mean About Management Reporting," *Computer Decisions*, September, 1970.

Hand, A. B. and Rives, W. L., "Constructing a Data Processing Cost Accounting System," *The Magazine of Bank Administration*, April, 1974.

Hartley, R. V., "Operations Research and Its Implications for the Accounting Profession," *The Accounting Review*, April, 1968.

Kelly, J. P., *Computerized Management Information Systems.* New York: The Macmillan Co., 1970, Chap. 4.

Moore, J. F., "Operations Research and the Modern Accounting System," *The Internal Auditor*, January-February, 1968.

Nichols, G. E., "Accounting and the Total Information System," *Management Accounting*, March, 1971.

O'Brien, J. J., *Management Information Systems.* New York: Van Nostrand Reinhold Co., 1971, Chap. 10.

Onsi, M., "Quantitative Models for Accounting Control," *The Accounting Review*, April, 1967.

Roy, H. J. H., "Credit Scoring: An Update," *Credit and Financial Management*, August, 1974.

Rupli, R. G., "How to Improve Profits Through Simulation," *Management Accounting*, November, 1973.

Sauls, E., "An On-Line System for Accounts Payable," *Journal of Systems Management*, May, 1973.

Theil, H., "On the Use of Information Theory Concept in the Analysis of Financial Statements," *Management Science*, May, 1969.

Thorne, J. F., "Real Time System in Accounting Applications," *Journal of Data Management*, January, 1970.

Wiener, H., "Putting Your Credit Line Online," *Computer Decisions*, September, 1973.

REAL-TIME MIS
FINANCE SUBSYSTEM 16

The finance function, like marketing and manufacturing, is essential to the operations of any manufacturing firm. Without the infusion of capital resources when needed, the firm cannot fulfill its goals and objectives. For this reason, the finance subsystem is related directly to the other subsystems. Although these relationships may not be seen visually, they are a viable force in the firm. In essence, the firm's finance subsystem plays an extremely important role in its efficient operation and its day-to-day profitability.

In this chapter, the finance sybsystem for the Consumer Products Corporation, operating in an integrated MIS environment, is explored initially. This review of present operations is followed by a discussion of design considerations for a real-time MIS finance subsystem and its actual detailed design. The entire chapter focuses on the major components of the finance subsystem, which are:

       capital budgeting
       sources of capital
       cash flow

504

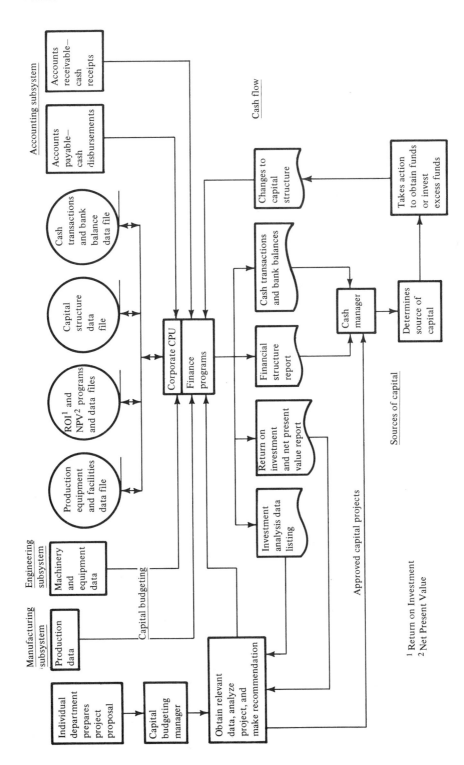

FIGURE 16-1. Financial data flow for an integrated MIS.

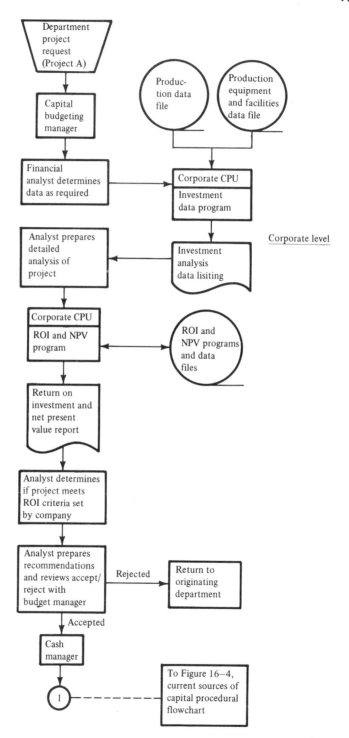

FIGURE 16-2. Capital investment analysis data flow for an integrated MIS finance subsystem.

Generally, these three major functions, along with financial ratios, provide the framework upon which the finance subsystem of the Consumer Products Corporation is built.

INTEGRATED MIS FINANCE SUBSYSTEM

The integrated MIS finance subsystem for the illustrated firm is an integral part of corporate activities. It is batch-processing-oriented, utilizing magnetic tape as storage for most of the finance data required by the system. As depicted in Figure 16-1, this subsystem consists of capital budgeting, sources of capital, and cash flow. The interworkings of these functions are presented in some detail in subsequent sections of the chapter.

The data bank for the finance subsystem is obtained from several sources. Production data (e.g., products produced, standard hours, scrappage, standard costs, and so forth) are input from the manufacturing subsystem. Machine capacity, machine utilization, accumulated depreciation, and data concerning other facilities are input from the facilities engineering section. Data pertaining to cash transactions are obtained through the accounts-receivable and accounts-payable departments daily, an essential part of the accounting subsystem. Finally, the cash manager keeps the capital structure data up to date by entering capital structure changes as they occur.

CAPITAL BUDGETING

Under the present system of analyzing capital investments, much time and effort are involved in gathering data relevant to each project proposed. In many instances after the data are gathered and organized into a meaningful form, they are out of date. Figure 16-2 portrays the procedure currently employed in evaluating capital investment projects.

To illustrate Figure 16-2, a proposed project, such as Project A, is initiated by an individual or group of individuals within a department and is approved by the department head. The proposal (Figure 16-3) describes what type of action is desired (e.g., the acquisition of a new machine to replace an old one). Also, it lists relevant information concerning the reason for the desired acquisition (e. g., the old machine is obsolete and inefficient) and specifies how the proposed acquisition can remedy the situation. In the example, Project A involves the replacement of an obsolete plastic molding machine with a new, more efficient model.

After the written proposal is forwarded to the capital budgeting manager at corporate headquarters, an analyst reviews the proposal and, after doing so, usually confers with the initiating department concerning questions about the proposal. The analyst also determines the data that will be required to properly evaluate Project A. For example, data concerning products produced on the old machine and products to be produced on the new machine, operating costs of the old versus the new machine, depreciation, salvage value of the old machine, and capacity and utilization factors for both the old and new machines must be obtained. As for the old machine, the analyst requests most of the required historical data from the

CAPITAL INVESTMENT PROPOSAL—PROJECT A

Department—Manufacturing Work Center #26
Plant—#3

Project Title—Project A; Plastic Molding Machine

Estimated Cost—$85,000
Estimated ROI—33% (after taxes)
Estimated Payback—3.7 years

Objective:
      To replace existing plastic molding machine #1624 with a new,
more efficient model.

Economic Justification:
      Machine #1624 is 17 years old, fully depreciated, and operating
at only 55% of its rated capacity. It is located in plant #3,
manufacturing work center #26. The quantity and quality of products
produced on this machine has resulted in a below-average contribution
to plant profits.
      The cost of the new machine is $85,000. Not only will the new
machine be more efficient, but it will consistently produce a
higher-quality product at a lower unit cost.

Initiator and Title: J. R. Smith, Production Supervisor   Date: 6/26/7-

Department Head Approval: R. D. Meade   Date: 6/26/7-

FIGURE 16-3. Typical project request for capital equipment—Project
              A.

computer department. The batch-oriented computer generates the required information from data stored on magnetic tape. The output is in the form of a listing
that is forwarded to the investment analyst. In the meantime, the analyst has
obtained the necessary data concerning the new machine from potential manufacturers, the department that initiated the project, and the facilities engineering section.

Once all relevant data have been obtained, the investment analyst prepares a
detailed analysis of the project. This includes a listing of the relevant costs and
savings associated with the acquisition of the new machine and disposal of the
existing one. Net cash flows are computed and sent to the computer department in
order that return on investment (ROI) and net present value (NPV) figures can be
generated by using standard program packages.

Now that all required information is complete, the analyst determines if
Project A meets the rate of return criteria established by company policy (e.g., to
be considered acceptable, the after-tax ROI must exceed 20 percent). Also, the
analyst compares Project A's initial investment, its return on investment, and other
pertinent information, such as the risk factor, to other proposed projects in order
to make a final recommendation and set project priorities. If the project is acceptable, it is necessary to determine the best method of financing. The project is
referred to the cash manager, whose task is to determine the best method of
financing.

SOURCES OF CAPITAL

The task of the cash manager is to decide on the optimal financing method
for each project or group of projects that requires substantial sums of funds for implementation. It is also the cash manager's job to control cash balances on a routine
basis.

After reviewing an analysis of the project, the cash manager requests financial
structure data, which is primarily of a long-term nature, from the computer
department (Figure 16-4). The computer retrieves the requested data stored on a
master magnetic tape file. A financial structure report, similar to the one in Figure
16-5, is generated and forwarded to the cash manager for review. He is now prepared to make a financing recommendation after considering the current debt-
equity ratio, current borrowing rates, interest charges for which the firm is
currently committed, current and projected sales, as well as other pertinent factors
in making the decision.

Once a decision, such as bank borrowing, has been made regarding financing,
the cash manager incorporates this information into the analysis of the project. The
formal report is prepared and then forwarded to the corporate planning staff. The
prescribed channels for endorsement and approval of large capital projects are the
vice-president of the department initiating the project, the vice-president of finance,
and the executive vice-president. When the project is finally approved, a copy of the
approval is forwarded to the cash manager, who takes the necessary steps to obtain

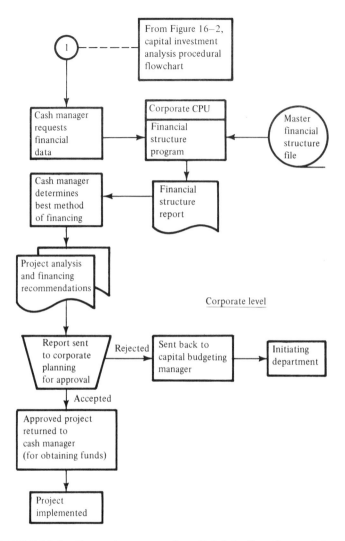

FIGURE 16-4. Current sources of capital data flow for an integrated MIS finance subsystem.

the funds for implementation. If the project is rejected, it is forwarded with the appropriate reasons to the capital budgeting manager who, in turn, contacts the initiating department and reviews the reasons for rejection.

CASH FLOW

Cash, the vital ingredient for sustaining the firm's day-to-day operations, must be available when needed. Because cash is an expensive commodity, it is important that it not be wasted and that any excess be employed in as profitable a manner as

FINANCIAL STRUCTURE REPORT

As of June 30, 197-

Long-term Debt:	
Loan payable (7 1/2%), due 198-	$ 4,500,000
6% Subordinated debentures, due 198-	10,000,000
7% Subordinated debentures, due 199-	8,000,000
Total Long-Term Debt	$22,500,000
Stockholders' Equity:	
Preferred stock, par value, $1 per share:	
1,500,000 shares authorized, none issued	
Common stock, stated value, $1 per share:	
1,000,000 shares authorized, 400,000 issued	$ 400,000
Capital in excess of par	12,000,000
Retained earnings	18,500,000
Total Stockholders' Equity	$30,900,000
Long-term debt due within one year	$ 500,000
Current Interest Charges (annual):	
Loan	$ 337,500
6% subordinated debentures	600,000
7% subordinated debentures	560,000
	$ 1,497,500

FIGURE 16-5. Financial structure report.

possible. The cash manager must keep the firm solvent while at the same time increasing profits through efficient cash management—that is, investing excess cash in treasury bills or in other short-term investments. Thus, it is important to be continually aware of changes in the firm's cash balance.

The present system of cash flow is portrayed in Figure 16-6. The accounts-payable and accounts-receivable departmental sections send copies of all daily transactions to the data processing department for input to the computer. The input transaction data are stored on magnetic tape. At the end of each week, two reports are generated by the computer which are forwarded to the cash manager. These reports—Cash Transactions Data and Summary and Bank Balances—are used in determining appropriate actions to take regarding the present cash condition. Duplicate copies of the first report are also forwarded to the accounts-payable and accounts-receivable sections.

The cash manager, with the assistance of a financial analyst, examines the reports and compares them to the original proforma cash flow statement. In addition, a determination is made regarding the adequacy of working capital. If it is determined that enough cash is not available for normal business operations in the period ahead, the cash manager informs the treasurer, who, in turn, takes the necessary action to insure that ample cash will be forthcoming. The treasurer might, for example, sell some treasury bills or borrow on a short-term basis from a bank. On the other hand, if it is found that too much cash is on hand, the cash manager will take action to invest it in some safe but profitable investment.

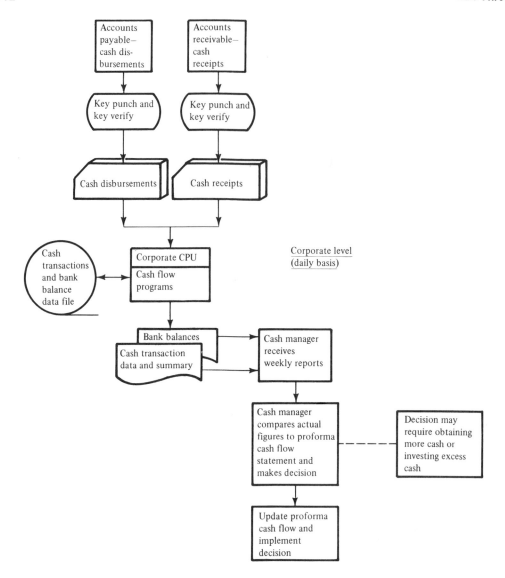

FIGURE 16-6. Present cash flow for an integrated MIS finance subsystem.

REAL-TIME MIS DESIGN CONSIDERATIONS FOR FINANCE SUBSYSTEM

The finance subsystem in a real-time MIS operating mode, like its integrated MIS counterpart, does not operate alone, but relies heavily upon the other subsystems—in particular, accounting and corporate planning. Without the accounting subsystem, there would be no financial information for determining the availability of funds. Also, there would be no cash receipts and disbursements figures for projecting future cash flow. Similarly, the corporate planning subsystem relies on capital budgeting and cash flow in formulating its plans for next year as well as several years hence. The finance subsystem interacts with outside firms, such as banks and financial institutions. Thus, considerations must be given to these interacting subsystems during the design phase for an effective real-time MIS finance subsystem.

OVERVIEW OF FINANCE ENVIRONMENT

The finance environment (Figure 16-7) encompasses three major functions—namely, capital budgeting, sources of capital, and cash flow. Although these are the same major functions employed on an integrated MIS basis, the design will be different because of the real-time capabilities of the computer system. The information flow generally begins with capital projects, which affect the level of cash requirements. Where cash is not sufficient to meet projected operational and capital project needs, outside sources of funds are secured on a short-term to long-term basis, depending upon the circumstances. On the other hand, if funds are sufficient for future needs, excess funds are either invested in internal capital project undertakings or placed with outside institutions for investing.

The finance subsystem is related not only to the accounting and corporate planning subsystems plus outside financial institutions but also to other subsystems, as shown in Figure 16-7. These subsystems are dependent on the availability of funds to lower their costs of operation. Without the necessary funds, many manual operations cannot be automated for lowering overall costs of finished goods to customers. Under these adverse conditions in the long run, the firm is in a vulnerable position. In reality, the availability or nonavailability of short-term to long-term capital for required projects can be the focal point for all operating subsystems.

FINANCE DATA BASE

In converting from an integrated to a real-time finance subsystem, consideration must be given to revising the data base. Revisions are necessitated by the desired type of output from the real-time system and the types of decisions that are to be made based upon the output. Also, data must be structured so as to be consistent and relevant for all who intend to use it. For example, data pertaining to disbursement of funds are needed not only by the accounting subsystem but also by the finance subsystem in performing the cash flow management function. It is important that these functional areas and others use consistent data.

Data for capital budgeting consists of such items as machine capacity and utilization, products produced on each machine, depreciation rates, original cost of machines, and maintenance costs. In addition, data concerning proposed acquisitions are obtained as each proposal is initiated. These data are input to the system in order to analyze the proposal.

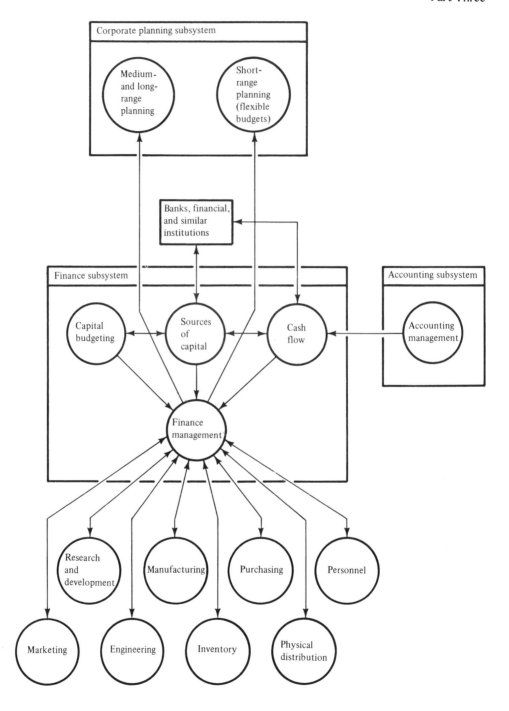

FIGURE 16-7. Real-time MIS finance subsystem flow to and from other subsystems.

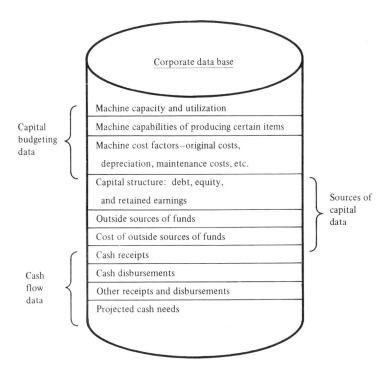

Corporate data base

Capital budgeting data
- Machine capacity and utilization
- Machine capabilities of producing certain items
- Machine cost factors—original costs, depreciation, maintenance costs, etc.

Sources of capital data
- Capital structure: debt, equity, and retained earnings
- Outside sources of funds
- Cost of outside sources of funds

Cash flow data
- Cash receipts
- Cash disbursements
- Other receipts and disbursements
- Projected cash needs

FIGURE 16-8. Typical finance data base elements at the corporate level.

Sources of capital require up-to-date data concerning the firm's capital structure—that is, existing debt, equity, and retained earnings. Data concerning outside sources of funds and the potential costs of these funds must be available, such as bank interest rate and common stock market prices. This outside information must be input to the system via an I/O terminal on a continuing basis.

Data for cash flow must be forthcoming from all other subsystems—that is, each subsystem enters expense data via an I/O device as they occur. It is also important that planned expenditures be input on a regular basis. The accounting subsystem enters data as they occur concerning receipts and disbursements of cash.

The foregoing major functional activities comprise the finance data base elements needed in a real-time MIS environment as shown in Figure 16-8. Input data, along with stored on-line data, are used to determine appropriate actions within the finance subsystem. By varying input data with available data base elements, output alternatives can be determined. An evaluation of these various alternatives can be employed for optimum results.

OR FINANCE MODELS

Operations research models can be applied to all three major modules of the real-time MIS subsystem. For capital budgeting, decision trees and Monte Carlo simulation are available. A decision tree is so named because it looks like a tree, although for convenience it is a horizontal one. The base of the tree is the beginning decision point. Its branches begin at the first chance event. Each chance event produces two or more possible effects, some of which lead to other events and subsequent decision points. Figures upon which the tree's values are based come from research data and the data base. This information provides probabilities for certain chance events and predicted payout or cash flow estimates of each possible outcome as influenced by various possible chance events.

The Monte Carlo method involves the simulation of transactions in the business environment by selecting outcomes of events at random. It is possible to generate a host of possible occurrences and note the frequency with which various end results occur. The relative frequency with which a specific result appears corresponds to the probability that it will occur in real life. Monte Carlo simulation is applied in developing a capital budgeting system later in the chapter.

Optimization, using such mathematical tools as differentiation, integration, partial differentiation, and the Lagrange multiplier, can be used in solving for sources of capital. For example, the Lagrange multiplier, capable of optimizing a function subject to certain constraints (in which it is not necessary to incorporate the constraints into the function to be optimized), can be used in arriving at the optimum arrangement of financing. Simulation can also be applied to determine the proposed source of capital.

Of the several operations research models that may be applied to cash flow, common approaches include the fixed-quantity inventory method and the fixed-interval inventory method as well as simulation which is applied to cash flow in the chapter. The fixed-quantity method involves obtaining cash in fixed amounts at various intervals. The fixed amount of cash may be determined by the use of the standard EOQ formula or on some other basis, depending upon the circumstances. The fixed-interval method involves more risk than the fixed-quantity method because it requires forecasting. The actual time interval between reviews of the cash position is determined by the circumstances involved—that is, size of firm, type of business, and type of products. This latter method results in obtaining varying amounts of cash at fixed intervals.

FINANCE MODULES

The important modules for the finance subsystem, which include capital budgeting, sources of funds, and cash flow, are presented in Figure 16-9. As noted previously, these finance modules affect the entire firm. The ability or lack thereof to acquire short-term to long-term funds has a decided impact on the firm's growth potential. Hence, the systems designers must consider this area in light of other major modules.

REAL-TIME MIS FINANCE SUBSYSTEM

The detailed design of the real-time MIS finance subsystem for the Consumer Products Corporation can be specified now that certain important criteria have

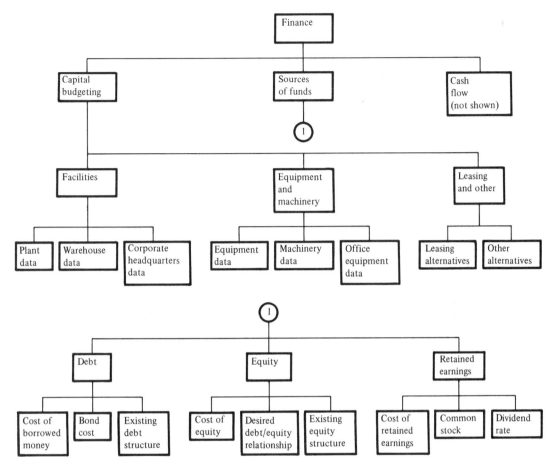

FIGURE 16-9. Finance modules of the Consumer Products Corporation.

been set forth—namely, the data base, operations research models, and finance modules. Although the design approach proposed is not complex, the finance subsystem must be integrated with other subsystems at the corporate level for a real-time response. The timeliness of finance information is of utmost importance for making critical decisions—in particular, those for investing short-term funds, taking advantage of purchase discounts, determining the proper allocation of funds for competing projects, and similar matters. All in all, real-time information can easily pay for itself if it is utilized properly.

FINANCE SUBSYSTEM OVERVIEW

An overview of a real-time MIS finance system is illustrated in Figure 16-10. The interaction of major subsystems with finance provides financial management with current analyses of capital investments, sources of capital, and cash flow. Although these important analyses can range from the short term to long term, the

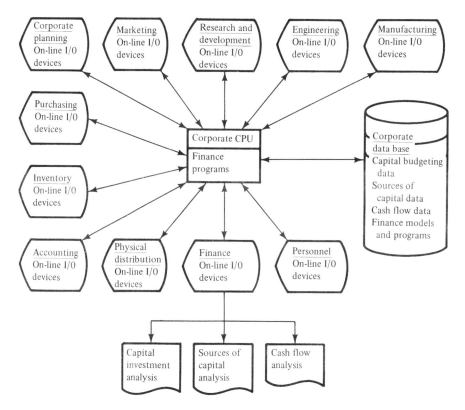

FIGURE 16-10. An overview of a real-time MIS finance subsystem.

short term is essential for optimizing current performance. However, the proper placement of funds in the long run can be just as critical as in the short run. No matter what performance standards are set by top management, they can be easily met with a forward-looking finance subsystem. The appropriate methods and procedures to produce the three analyses per Figure 16-10 are discussed below.

CAPITAL BUDGETING MODULE

In order to analyze projects in a real-time MIS operating mode, a Monte Carlo simulation model is used in conjunction with the common data base (Figure 16-11). Utilizing an I/O device, the financial analyst calls in the Monte Carlo simulation program and instructs it to read the specific data needed to analyze the project—the old machine's capacity, the old machine's utilization, products produced on the old machine, operating costs, depreciation, and comparable data. In addition, a complete data array concerning the proposed new machine acquisition, which has been obtained from the initiator of the project, the facilities engineering section, and the

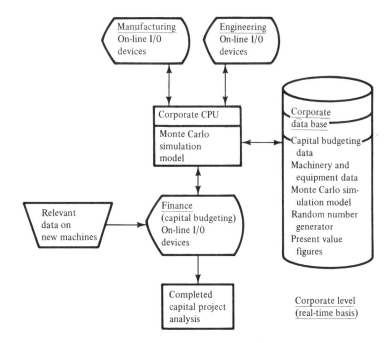

FIGURE 16-11. Capital budgeting data flow for a real-time MIS finance subsystem.

vendors (e.g., new machine's capacity; new machine's utilization; new machine's costs, both initial and operating; and others) is entered via the I/O terminal keyboard. This allows for considering differences between the old and new machines. Based upon the entry of the above data plus data concerning operating conditions, business conditions, existing products and planned products, and potential costs and sales, the capital project is simulated. The model simulates the savings and costs associated with the project and summarizes these detailed savings (Figure 16-12) and costs (Figure 16-13).

OPERATING SAVINGS		
Possible Operating Savings	Probability	Cumulative Probability
$20,000	.10	.10
30,000	.20	.30
40,000	.40	.70
50,000	.30	1.00

FIGURE 16-12. Operating savings, probability values, and cumulative probability values.

OPERATING COSTS		
Possible Operating Costs	Probability	Cumulative probability
$10,000	.10	.10
20,000	.70	.80
30,000	.20	1.00

FIGURE 16-13. Operating costs, probability values, and cumulative probability values.

In addition to the savings and costs tables, charts portraying the cumulative probabilities are generated by the computer (Figures 16-14 and 16-15, respectively) after probability values are entered. The illustrated tables and charts present values for one year only. It is necessary to generate as many years as required by the project. In the example, the expected life is ten years.

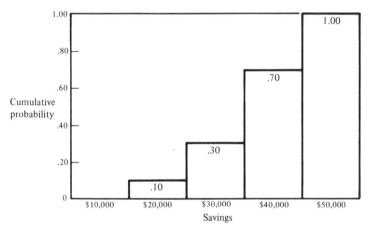

FIGURE 16-14. Cumulative probability distribution chart for operating savings.

Now that the cumulative probabilities have been determined, a random number generator is employed from the data base to simulate the expected savings and costs for the first year and each year thereafter up to and including ten. Only the calculations for the first year will be shown. Although several hundred random numbers should be drawn for a problem of this nature, twenty-five two-digit random numbers are used for the first year of this example (Figure 16-16). As each random number is generated, it is located on the cumulative probability charts (Figures 16-14 and 16-15) and the corresponding probability is determined. For example, a random number, 53, applied to the cumulative probability Figure 16-14, gives a $40,000 savings. This same approach is employed for costs (Figure 16-15).

The next step, after simulating savings, costs, and the resulting net savings

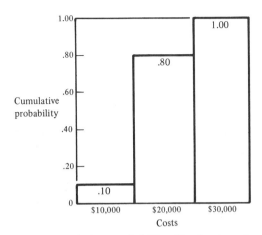

FIGURE 16-15. Cumulative probability distribution chart for operating costs.

using random numbers, is to summarize the net savings in a cumulative probability table, such as Figure 16-17. This table measures the frequency of the various net savings from Figure 16-16. From Figure 16-17, it can be seen that a net savings of $20,000 had a frequency of 9 and a probability of .36. The cumulative probability

Random Numbers	Savings ($10,000)	−	Random Numbers	Costs ($10,000)	=	Net Savings ($10,000)
53	4		19	2		2
28	3		08	1		2
10	2		05	1		1
97	5		13	2		3
07	2		59	2		0
99	5		27	2		3
69	4		81	3		1
75	5		93	3		2
42	4		33	2		2
65	4		51	2		2
16	3		54	2		1
68	4		29	2		2
61	4		25	2		2
98	5		07	1		4
43	4		83	3		1
80	5		04	1		4
76	5		33	2		3
03	2		64	2		0
29	3		68	2		1
29	3		26	2		1
95	5		97	3		2
34	4		39	2		2
61	4		83	3		1
33	4		01	1		3
84	5		02	1		4

FIGURE 16-16. Simulation of net savings based upon probabilistic values of savings and costs (first year only).

Frequencies of net savings and cumulative probabilities			
Net savings	Frequency	Probability	Cumulative probability
$ 0	2	.08	1.00
10,000	7	.28	.92
20,000	9	.36	.64
30,000	4	.16	.28
40,000	3	.12	.12
50,000	0	0	0

FIGURE 16-17. Frequency, probabilities, and cumulative probabilities of net savings for first year.

column indicates that there is a .64 probability that net savings will be as large or larger than $20,000 in the first year. The results of Figure 16-17 are graphed in Figure 16-18. The above procedure for determining net savings is repeated for each of the ten years.

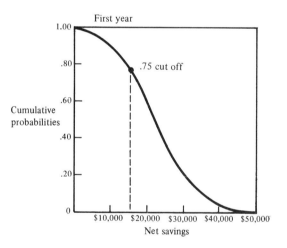

FIGURE 16-18. Cumulative probabilities graph of net savings for first year.

After the ten years of net savings (cash flows) have been developed by the computer Monte Carlo simulation program, the financial analyst must review the results in light of the firm's financial policies. A policy may, for example, require .75 cumulative probability cutoff in analyzing projects of similar risk. In such a case, the net savings for each of the ten years would be used in figuring the rate of return for the project. An illustration for a ten-year period of expected cash flows at the .75 cumulative probability cutoff is shown in Figure 16-19. It should be noted that this information is generated automatically by the simulation model. The first-year value of $16,000 is derived from Figure 16-18.

Year	1	2	3	4	5	6	7	8	9	10
Amount ($)	16,000	18,000	22,000	20,000	25,000	25,000	25,000	25,000	25,000	25,000

FIGURE 16-19. Expected net savings (cash flow) at .75 cumulative probability for ten years.

As for the project's rate of return, standard present value figures are stored on the data base for determining the internal rate of return. In the example, after the net savings values for ten years have been determined, a program for computing the rate of return is automatically activated and the rate of return (ROI) figure, calculated here to be 22 percent, is generated.

Once the rate of return figure is known for the capital project, it can be compared to the firm's after-tax cutoff rate of 20 percent to determine whether or not the project is acceptable. If the rate of return of the project is greater than the 20 percent cutoff rate, the project should be considered acceptable. However, prior to making a final decision, the project must be compared to other proposed projects. The degree of risk, amount of initial investment, payback period, priority, and comparable items must be evaluated in determining whether the project should be accepted, delayed, or possibly rejected. The analyst may even decide to use another means of analysis of one or more projects involving the calculation of net present value. This can be readily accomplished through the use of a financial on-line computer program. In any event, if the project is deemed acceptable, it is then necessary to determine the method of financing or the sources of capital for the project.

SOURCES OF CAPITAL MODULE

The proposed system of determining sources of funds is an extension of the present system. It entails the addition of certain elements to the common data base, reflecting vital data about the firm's capital structure and its cost of capital.

In order to determine the appropriate source of capital for the project under consideration, it is necessary to consider the average weighted cost of capital formula. The average weighted cost of capital is comprehensive in that all elements of the financial structure are considered. Also, it is not confined to a short-run view of only one element as a potential source of capital. Its formula is:

$$RA = (Xe)(Re) + (Xr)(Rr) + (Xd)(Rd) \qquad \text{Equation 16-1}$$

where RA = average weighted cost of capital

Xe = proportion of capital structure that represents equity

$Re = \dfrac{at}{1-b}$ (cost of capital)

Xr = proportion of capital structure that represents retained earnings

$Rr = at \dfrac{(1 - tp)}{(1 - tg)}$ (cost of retained earnings)

Xd = proportion of capital structure that represents debt

$Rd = at (1 - tc)$ (cost of debt)

at = capitalization rate ($\dfrac{\text{earnings per share of common stock}}{\text{current market price}}$)

b = brokerage charges

tp = personal tax rate (average)

tg = capital gains tax rate

tc = corporate tax rate

Application of Equation 16-1 is based upon the following given data:

Current year's earnings	$2,496,000
Common shares outstanding	400,000
Earnings per share	$6.24
Current market price	$52

capitalization rate (at)	.12
tp	35%
tg	17.5%
tc	50%
b	10%
$Xe = \dfrac{2,300,000}{6,200,000}$	.37
$Re = \dfrac{.12}{1 - .10}$	13.3%
$Xr = \dfrac{1,650,000}{6,200,000}$	.27
$Rr = (.12)\dfrac{(1 - .35)}{(1 - .175)}$	9.4%
$Xd = \dfrac{2,250,000}{6,200,000}$	.36
$Rd = (.12)(1 - .50)$	6.0%

The foregoing calculated values, when incorporated into Equation 16-1, result in an average weighted cost of capital of 9.6%, calculated as follows:

$$RA = (Xe)\ (Re) + (Xr)\ (Rr) + (Xd)\ (Rd)$$
$$RA = (.37)\ (.133) + (.27)\ (.094) + (.36)\ (.06)$$
$$RA = 9.6\%$$

The major activity of the sources of capital system is having the financial analyst determine the best method of financing through the utilization of a simulation model (Figure 16-20) that incorporates the average weighted cost of capital. Various data concerning the present and projected cost of borrowing money from commercial banks, the personal tax rate, capital gains tax rate, cost of underwriting a new stock issue, and factors effecting the capitalization rate are updated on line by the financial analyst if they are currently not available from the data base. These

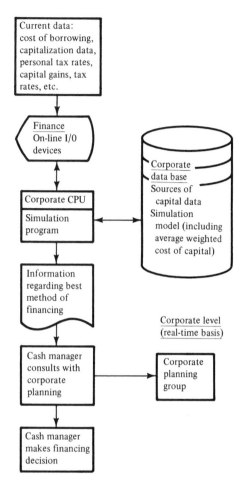

FIGURE 16-20. Sources of capital data flow for a real-time MIS finance subsystem.

input data to the on-line simulation model determine the best method or combination of financing (debt, equity, and/or retained earnings) for a desired amount of capital. The best method is generally one that produces the lowest average weighted cost of capital. However, if certain constraints, such as a desired debt-equity ratio of 35 percent, are introduced into the model, it may produce a somewhat higher weighted average cost of capital.

After simulating the method of financing for a particular project or group of projects, the financial analyst incorporates this information into his report and forwards the report to the corporate planning group for approval. Once final approval is forthcoming, the cash manager can then take action to obtain the desired funds in accordance with the method approved. For example, the simulation of the best financing method for several projects may result in the need to borrow funds at an interest rate of 8 percent from a commercial bank. If this is the case, the cash manager would contact the bank's lending officer and make the necessary arrangements to obtain the funds.

CASH FLOW MODULE

The cash flow system involves the use of another simulation model. This model is designed to provide cash flow information to the cash manager concerning the danger of insolvency. Insolvency, or the probability that the firm's cash balance will fall below zero at the end of each period or one week, is evaluated for the time period in question. Once the information has been provided, the cash manager is in a much better position to determine if it is necessary to obtain more funds for operations or if projected excess funds can be employed in some other manner. The cash management simulation model is:

$$CE = Cb + \widetilde{R} - \widetilde{V} - F - I - \widetilde{T} \qquad\qquad\qquad \text{Equation 16-2}$$

where CE = cash balance at end of period
  Cb = cash balance at beginning of period (initial cash balance of $350,000)
  R = collections on accounts receivable during the period
  V = total variable cash expenses during the period, excluding federal income taxes ($0.60 on $1 of sales)
  F = total fixed cash expenses during the period, excluding interest ($40,000 daily fixed cash expenses and $3,000 daily fixed noncash expenses)
  I = total interest payment during period (average rate of .017 per day) on a debt of $2,250,000 in its capital structure
  T = total federal income tax payments during period (50% tax rate)
  $\sim$ = used to distinguish random variables from constants

The above data base elements are input to the simulation model. The accounting subsystem maintains these data on a current basis, as depicted in Figure 16-21.

In order to employ the simulation model effectively, a probability distribution for sales and collections during the coming period must be generated, shown in Figures 16-22 and 16-23, respectively.

After the probability of distributions for sales and the increment in collections during the period have been established, a random number generator is employed to generate random observations on the level of period sales that is in accordance with the increment in collections during the period. Utilizing these random observations, repeated simulation runs using Equation 16-2 are made to determine the ending cash balance. The firm's risk of insolvency is the percentage of times when the value of the cash ending balance (CE) is below zero. For example, under conditions of the period being simulated, the result might show that there is a .03 probability that the firm will become insolvent.

An important feature of the simulation approach is that values can be changed to determine the effect on the ending cash balance. The initial cash balance can be raised or lowered to determine the resulting effect on the ending balance. The

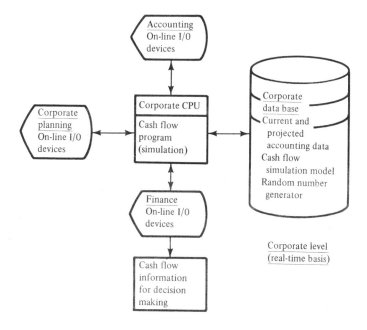

FIGURE 16-21.   Cash data flow for a real-time MIS finance subsystem.

Sales	Probability
$800,000	.1
700,000	.4
600,000	.4
500,000	.1

FIGURE 16-22.   Probability distribution of sales during coming period.

Increment in Collection Period	Probability			
	S $800,000	S $700,000	S $600,000	S $500,000
10 days	.5	.4	.1	.1
20 days	.2	.3	.2	.2
30 days	.2	.2	.3	.2
40 days	.1	.1	.4	.5

FIGURE 16-23.   Probability distribution of increment in collections during the period (S = daily sales during period).

same could be done for the ratio of cash variable expenses to sales. For example, planned advertising expenditures could be changed to determine the effect on cash flow. In another example, the cash manager may decide to decrease the initial cash balance because the probability that the firm will become insolvent during the coming period is very small, say .01. His decision might involve the reduction of the initial cash balance by $75,000 and the corresponding investing of these funds in treasury bills or certificates of deposit. This may be done realizing that even after reducing the cash balance by the above amount, the probability of insolvency is still very low, say .03.

FINANCIAL RATIOS

Although emphasis in the chapter has been focused on the design of capital budgeting, sources of funds, and cash flow modules, the real-time MIS finance subsystem for the Consumer Products Corporation is quite capable of producing important financial ratios. Overall operational ratios available on a "now" basis from I/O terminals are presented in Figure 16-24. These ratios are of great value for financial analysts as well as for the corporate planning group. Specifically, they can be used as the basis for financial management by exception when appropriate ranges are assigned to each ratio. For example, the ratio of current assets to current liabilities should be about two to one.

For this area to be an effectively designed module, additional ratios and performance criteria, apart from those in Figure 16-24, must be integrated into the system as control parameters. Examples, such as contribution analysis by product lines, selective expense evaluation, and salesmen analysis, enable the finance subsystem to render important management exception information.

Current assets to current liabilities
Net profit on sales
Net profit on tangible net worth
Net profit on net working capital
Return on tangible total assets
Net sales to tangible net worth
Net sales to net working capital
Average collection period in days
Net sales to inventory
Fixed assets to tangible net worth
Current liabilities to tangible net worth
Total liabilities to tangible net worth
Inventory turnover
Inventory to net working capital
Current liabilities to inventory
Funded debt to net working capital

**FIGURE 16-24. Important financial ratios available on a "now" basis
for a real-time MIS finance subsystem.**

SUMMARY

The real-time MIS finance subsystem is a desirable improvement over the present integrated MIS subsystem. The forward-looking design provides consistent, up-to-date data from which meaningful information can be generated. Output from the finance subsystem is extremely valuable to the corporate planning group.

Each component of the real-time MIS finance subsystem does not operate in a vacuum, but is integrated with its other components in a real-time environment. Capital budgeting interacts with the sources of funds, thereby providing a complete analysis of a project. In turn, the cash flow system is related to planned project expenditures as well as actual expenditures in order that effective decisions concerning the firm's cash position can be made by finance management. Thus, capital budgeting, sources of funds, and cash flow analysis are greatly integrated, specifically through the utilization of operations research models in a real-time MIS operating mode.

QUESTIONS

1. What advantages does the real-time MIS finance subsystem have over the integrated MIS finance subsystem?

2. Define the role of finance management in a real-time MIS environment.

3. What design considerations are involved in developing an on-line real-time finance subsystem within a manufacturing firm?

4. Referring to Figure 16-9, develop submodules for cash flow.

5. What OR models are frequently employed in a cash management system?

6. How could a data collection system be utilized for a real-time MIS finance subsystem?

7. Referring to the section on capital budgeting, recommend improvements that reflect an ideal real-time MIS operating mode.

REFERENCES

Beehler, P. J., "Cash Management,: Forecasting for Profit," *Management Adviser,* July-August, 1973.

Benson, L. A., "Simulating a Company's Finances and Capital Needs, *Computer Decisions,* September, 1971.

Berger, R., "Use Risk Analysis for Decision Making," *Computer Decisions,* March, 1972.

Bower, J. B., Schlosser, R. E., and Zlatkovich, C. T., *Financial Information Systems.* Boston, Mass.: Allyn & Bacon, Inc., 1969.

Brenner, V. C., "An Evaluation of Capital Budgeting Models," *Managerial Planning,* March/ April, 1972.

Bucatinsky, J., "Ask Your Computer 'What If . . .'," *Financial Executive,* July, 1973.

Garrison, R. H., "Linear Programming in Capital Budgeting," *Management Accounting,* April, 1971.

Haavind, R., "A New Breed of Financial Systems Is Coming," *Computer Decisions,* January, 1972.

Hertz, D. B., "Investment Policies That Pay Off," *Harvard Business Review,* January-February, 1968.

Hewitt, L. A., "An Inventory Technique Applied to Cash Management," *Management Services,* July-August, 1970.

Kelly, J. F., *Computerized Management Information Systems.* New York: The Macmillan Co., 1970, Chap. 4.

Krouse, C. G., "Optimal Financing and Capital Structure Programs for the Firm," *Journal of Finance,* August, 1972.

Lampe, J. C., "The Trend Toward Automated Capital Investment Decisions," *Management Accounting,* April, 1971.

Lee, S. M., and Keeling, J. F., "Decision Making Under Uncertainty: Utility Analysis Approach," *Managerial Planning,* November/December, 1969.

Makadak, S., "First Simulate That Capital Investment," *Mechanical Engineering,* January, 1968.

Miller, D. W., and Starr, M. K., *Executive Decisions and Operations Research.* Englewood Cliffs, N.J.: Prentice-Hall, Inc., 1969, Chap. 12.

Myers, S. C., and Pogue, G. A., "A Programming Approach to Corporate Financial Management," *Journal of Finance,* May, 1974.

Salazar, R. C., and Sen, S. K., "A Simulation Model of Capital Budgeting Under Uncertainty," *Management Science,* December, 1968.

Souder, W. E., "Management Science and Budgeting . . . Quo Vadis?" *Budgeting,* March/April, 1968.

Stern, J. M., "A Quantitative Approach to Financial Planning," *The Bankers Magazine,* Spring, 1969.

Tallent, W. J., "Cash Management: A Case Study," *Management Accounting,* July, 1974.

Weingartner, H. M., "What Lies Ahead in Management Science and Operations Research in Finance in the Seventies?" *Interfaces,* August, 1971.

Windal, F. W. and Dowell, C. D., "Linear Programming—A Tool for Investment Planning," *Managerial Planning,* May/June, 1974.

REAL-TIME MIS
PERSONNEL SUBSYSTEM 17

The personnel function, like many of its counterparts in a real-time management information system, does not operate alone, but rather is a most important part of each subsystem. Management wants a work force that is capable of handling the firm's current and future work volumes. Implied in this statement is the concept of flexibility—that is, a permanent work force is maintained for normal operations and is supplemented with an auxiliary force when there are peak work loads or emergency conditions to be met. In this manner, the firm can keep its personnel costs at a minimum while servicing the required business functions and subfunctions necessary to accomplish its objectives.

The same basic structure used in prior chapters will also be used to explore the personnel function. Specifically, the requirements for a personnel subsystem in an integrated MIS are discussed, followed by an explanation of the important design considerations for real-time MIS. Sample data base elements, OR models, and modules provide a framework for designing personnel's major components.

Basically, they are:

> skills inventory
> personnel selection and placement
> training and education
> wage and salary administration

The computerized aspects of the personnel subsystem for the Consumer Products Corporation are structured on these four functions.

INTEGRATED MIS PERSONNEL SUBSYSTEM

The input for the integrated MIS personnel subsystem of the Consumer Products Corporation originates partly in other subsystems—in particular, the payroll function of the accounting subsystem. However, as illustrated in Figure 17-1, skills inventory, personnel selection and placement, training and education, plus wage and salary administration originate within the personnel function. Regardless of the originating data, these input sources are combined with existing magnetic tape files—skills inventory, payroll master, and wage and salary master—to produce desired personnel reports. In addition, various personnel forms are maintained, such as *personnel history and promotion records* and *personnel requisition forms.*

Basically, the personnel functions that are batch-oriented center around determining new candidates for job openings at the plant level. While these efforts are directed toward regular and expanded operations, consideration must be given to printing appropriate reports for reducing overall operations. These two important outputs are depicted in Figure 17-1 at the division level. Also, appropriate updating of all magnetic tape files must be effected at the division and corporate levels before meaningful wage and salary administration reports can be produced at the higher level. Accurate personnel reports, then, are dependent upon the proper maintenance of magnetic tape files.

SKILLS INVENTORY

Providing technical talent for specialized manufacturing activities as well as recruiting appropriate personnel is an arduous task facing the Consumer Products Corporation. To aid each plant in this regard, a skills inventory subsystem is employed to assist the personnel department in placing the right man in the right job. Before recruiting personnel from outside the organization, the plant's internal records are searched. A detailed listing of employee interests and talents for the job under review is prepared for the personnel department. If qualified personnel are not available within the desired manufacturing plant after completing the review, the request is forwarded to the remaining two plants. All in all, this approach permits promotion from within, a more efficient way of utilizing the firm's talent, a fast means of locating vitally needed or unusual skills, and a good way to increase employee morale.

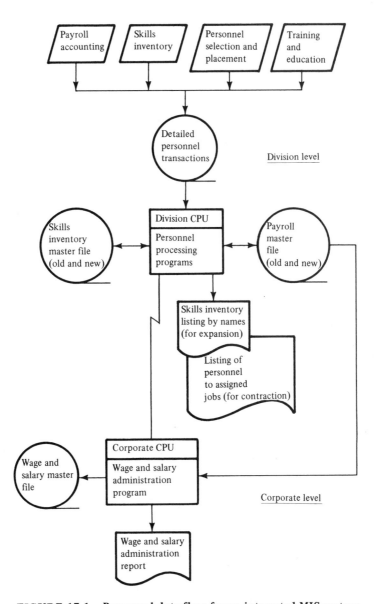

FIGURE 17-1. Personnel data flow for an integrated MIS system.

The initial step used in creating a skills inventory subsystem was to develop a human resources or skills inventory in the form of a master file, recording on magnetic tape the employee's name, age, address, education, training, skills, and experience. Once the master file has been created and is available for use, the computer takes over, because it can search magnetic tape files at fast speeds for a listing of appropriate names. As illustrated in Figure 17-2, changes in skills inventory accumulated since the last run are processed weekly. In like manner, personnel

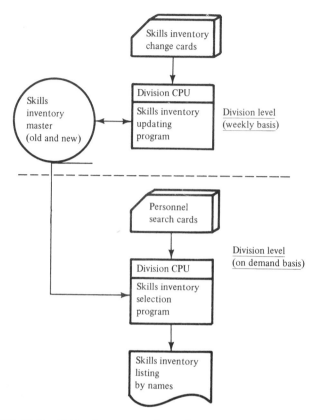

FIGURE 17-2. Skills inventory data flow for an integrated MIS personnel subsystem.

search cards, representing desired skills for present or upcoming vacant jobs, are processed as needed by the personnel department. The computer can produce a list of those qualified at the plant level within a few minutes. With manual methods, the search can take several days.

To standardize the entire process of retrieving the names of qualified candidates from the master file, a Skills Inventory Request Form is prepared. The requester completes this form by inserting the appropriate codes, representing the desired qualifications. For example, the first digit is used for level of education, 0 for high school diploma, 1 for college degree, etc. In the next two digits, 23 indicates accounting experience, 50 represents electrical engineering experience, etc. Other important qualities would be spelled out in a similar manner. In effect, the numerical coding represented on the punched personnel search card is the basis for selecting present plant personnel.

In addition to the output set forth in Figure 17-2—namely, skills inventory listing by names—other outputs can be produced by utilizing the skills inventory master file. Management summaries for long-range planning through timely data on retirement, age, service time, turnover, and educational level can be produced. A rundown of the concentration of talents necessary to maintain a well-balanced team within each plant can be undertaken. Also, special studies can be processed, such as the potential effects of possible wage increases and seniority on the firm. Thus, personnel data in such depth—normally unexplored because of cost and time factors—can be invaluable in making intelligent management decisions.

PERSONNEL SELECTION AND PLACEMENT

Personnel selection and placement within the Consumer Products Corporation is concerned with two important phases. First, it is concerned with forecasting personnel needs and skills and recruiting them at the proper time to meet organizational needs. Properly managed, the system will furnish information concerning skills required for current and upcoming company programs. An essential part of personnel selection is information centering around inventory of skills available in the firm, as set forth above.

Second, after personnel have been recruited from inside or outside the firm, the personnel system must match available personnel with current labor assignments in order to make effective use of available manpower. An effective integrated MIS personnel subsystem considers employee placement in light of expansion and contraction (Figure 17-3). Under contraction conditions, seniority rights are stored on the payroll master file for use at the time of a layoff.

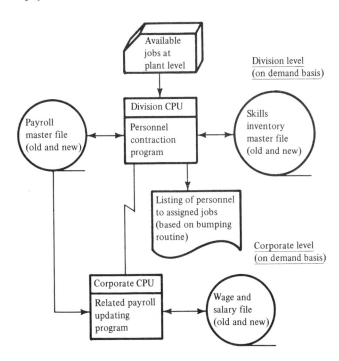

FIGURE 17-3. Personnel placement data flow for an integrated MIS personnel subsystem.

The personnel contraction bumps plant personnel based upon seniority. The basis for available jobs is data contained on card input. Thus, the personnel contraction program provides an automatic means of downgrading job positions and pay. Also, as noted in Figure 17-3, related files to the payroll master—namely, skills inventory and wage and salary magnetic tape files—must be updated to reflect current operating conditions.

TRAINING AND EDUCATION

As technology changes and demands for new skills accelerate, the Consumer Products Corporation, like most other firms, finds that it must develop much of its talent requirements from internal sources. Additionally, the firm must introduce new manufacturing techniques and developments to a large part of its work force over the years. This task is the function of training and education and includes a continuing skills inventory of company personnel matched against a forecast of current and estimated needs for improved skills.

Largely, the approach taken in an integrated management information system for training and education of plant operations is divorced from data processing operations. However, the same is not true for certain data processing operations in which computer-assisted instruction (CAI) is employed. The instrument for effecting CAI is an electronic communication station controlled by the batch processing computer. When programmed correctly, a CAI system is capable of accomplishing the following:

1. engage in a two-way communication with the trainee by means of natural-language messages
2. guide the individual through a program of tasks, helping him when difficulties arise, and accelerating the learning process when there is little challenge
3. simulate the operation of physical, mathematical, or environmental factors
4. analyze and summarize performance records and other behavioral records of individuals and also of groups

WAGE AND SALARY ADMINISTRATION

The last of the major personnel functions, wage and salary administration, involves working with selected data and ratios. A wage and salary analyst, for example, spends a great deal of his time at the corporate level determining salary and wage curves by job classifications and supplying comparative types of wage and salary information to higher management. The analyst's participation in salary surveys is usually a long and drawn-out job. Owing to the nature of wage and salary administration, data are maintained on magnetic tape, having been extracted monthly from the payroll master file.

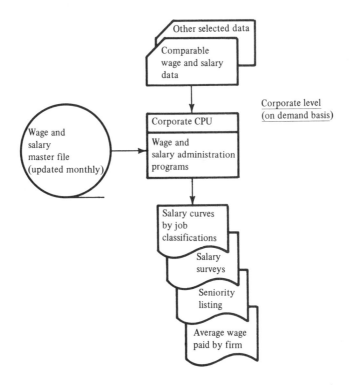

FIGURE 17-4. Wage and salary administration data flow for an integrated MIS personnel subsystem.

The approach taken in an integrated MIS environment is basically extracting wage and salary data as is or manipulating the data for desired results. The wage and salary master file used for input, and comparable wage and salary data plus other selected data are also needed to produce the reports illustrated in Figure 17-4. Note that the reports are produced as needed by management.

REAL-TIME MIS DESIGN CONSIDERATIONS FOR PERSONNEL SUBSYSTEM

Design considerations for the personnel subsystem in a real-time MIS operating mode go beyond its own basic structure. Specifically, payroll master data provide a starting point in terms of present personnel cost. Production scheduling and control centers around the proper placement of factory personnel to effect the highest output. Similarly, physical distribution considers the number of warehouse personnel to ship current customer orders. Thus, an effectively designed personnel subsystem must be related to most other subsystems in order to provide the necessary human resources for accomplishing organizational objectives.

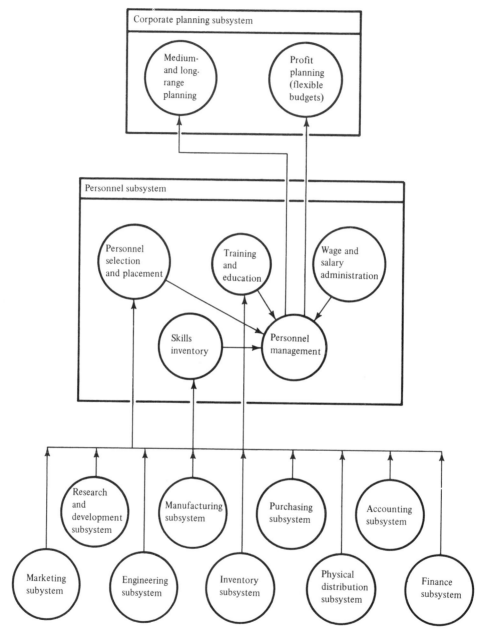

FIGURE 17-5. Real-time MIS personnel subsystem flow to and from other subsystems.

OVERVIEW OF PERSONNEL ENVIRONMENT

The personnel subsystem in a real-time MIS environment, as seen in Figure 17-5, interacts with other subsystems. These relationships can be viewed in three distinct but overlapping phases. Phase one covers the process of recruitment, screening, and selection with great emphasis on the skills inventory system. Phase two centers around the training and education of the employee during his period of employment. Phase three covers the obligation not only to the organization in the form of wage and salary administration but also to the individual for the accurate verification of employment when necessary.

Within these three basic phases, personnel have the ability to extract current personnel information via an I/O terminal. From this viewpoint, corrections and appropriate actions can be effected much sooner than without real-time capabilities. In fact, within this type of operating mode—a large on-line data base—more future personnel projections can be made with operations research models than with integrated MIS.

PERSONNEL DATA BASE

Conversion of personnel magnetic tape files (or data bank) within an integrated MIS is necessary for a real-time MIS operating mode. Personnel data are to be restructured according to the type of data in the common data base, illustrated in Figure 17-6. Although previous magnetic tape files have resulted in duplication, such as name and address in both the skills inventory and payroll master files, this problem must be avoided in the new system. Of prime importance for structuring data base elements is easy accessability for instantaneous display by a remote I/O

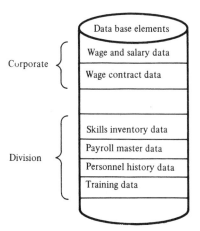

FIGURE 17-6. Typical personnel data base elements at the corporate and division levels.

terminal. Only in this manner can the personnel subsystem meet the real-time demands placed upon it.

Division data for skills inventory consists of employee number, educational background, on-the-job training, specific skills, and time at these skills. The payroll master file supplements these data base elements—specifically, the employee's name and address. Likewise, the personnel history and training data elements consist of additional detailed information that may be necessary to highlight the specific skills of a plant employee. Thus, on-line stored data elements are easily accessible to place the right man in the right job based upon expanding, normal, or contracting business conditions.

Moving up the corporate data base level, the design of the data base elements for personnel centers around wage and salary negotiations and cost studies. Wage and salary data are used to determine the labor costs for flexible budgets within the corporate planning subsystem. These data are also employed when management is negotiating with the union. The bargaining generally results in a compromise between management's initial offer and the union's initial demands. The offers made by management are not only wage improvements, but include changes in fringe benefits, work rules, and comparable items. Applications can be developed for company negotiators to test alternative proposals based upon data base elements stored on-line.

OR PERSONNEL MODELS

Operations research models developed for personnel have centered around predicting future personnel requirements, sometimes called manpower planning. Manpower planning involves specifying the kinds and numbers of qualified personnel an organization will need to accomplish its profit, growth, and service objectives. Two aspects of the forecasting task require attention: anticipating organizational demand for human talent of various types and anticipating available manpower supply within the organization. Personnel models simplify the forecasting components of manpower planning by manipulating available data by mathematical techniques. They provide a simplified and logical view of the levels and flows of personnel throughout an organizational system. They focus on variables considered by managers to be significant and consider assumptions or parameters underlying system behavior. Simulation techniques make it possible to evaluate the relative importance of the many factors that influence an organization's manpower needs and availability.

Techniques such as linear programming, regression analysis, and Markov analysis permit manipulation of important historical data for these variables. Specifically, modeling enables managers to explore aspects of systems that cannot be observed directly—for example; the movement patterns of employees among different jobs in an organization over time and reactions of personnel to changes in management policies and individual employment decisions. Within this section,

Markov analysis and simulation models are discussed to analyze future personnel requirements by job classifications.

Markov Analysis

Markov analysis is a way of analyzing the current movement of certain variables in an effort to forecast their future movement. When applied to projecting future personnel needs, this means analyzing current personnel skills—namely, professional, highly technical, technical, and semi-technical—with the view of predicting future personnel requirements. There is a need to know what the causes of gains and losses are as well as their percents or probabilities before future needs can be projected.

To illustrate this OR technique, certain concepts must be explained. The "hard-core component" describes those people who do not move from one job level to another. Personnel who switch from one level to another represent "gains" from the previous level. In a similar fashion, those who move to a lower-level job for one reason or another are represented as "losses." Retentions (hard-core component), gains, and losses are calculated in Figure 17-7 for an illustrative manufacturing plant. Note that zeros on the diagonals mean one group can incur neither gains nor losses from itself. Also, the losses columns represent transpositions of the gains in the rows.

Type of Personnel	Period One, No. of Personnel	Gains From				Losses To				Period Two (One Month Hence), No. of Personnel
		A	B	C	D	A	B	C	D	
A - Professional	220	0	40	0	10	0	20	10	15	225
B - Highly Technical	300	20	0	25	15	40	0	5	25	290
C - Technical	230	10	5	0	10	0	25	0	0	230
D - Semi-technical	250	15	25	0	0	10	15	10	0	255
	1000									1000

FIGURE 17-7. Retentions, gains, and losses of personnel in Markov analysis for one manufacturing plant.

From the data developed in Figure 17-7, the next step is to convert these data (retentions, gains, and losses) to matrix form. The problem is represented in this form per Figure 17-8 for ease of mathematical calculations. The rows in the matrix show the retention rate of personnel and the gain of technical and professional personnel, while the columns depict the retention rate of company personnel and the loss of personnel to a different positional level. In this figure, the first matrix is stated in terms of the actual number of personnel, whereas the second matrix is shown in terms of transition probabilities.

	Type of Personnel				Period Two (One Month Hence)			Type of Personnel			
	A	B	C	D	Number	Percent		A	B	C	D
A	175	40	0	10	225	22.5%	A	.796	.133	.000	.040
B	20	230	25	15	290	29.0%	B	.091	.767	.109	.060
C	10	5	205	10	230	23.0%	C	.046	.017	.891	.040
D	15	25	0	215	255	25.5%	D	.067	.083	.000	.860
Period One:											
Number	220	300	230	250	1000			1.000	1.000	1.000	1.000
Percent	22%	30%	23%	25%		100.0%					

FIGURE 17-8. Matrix of personnel transition probabilities.

Based on the present personnel distribution of 22, 30, 23, and 25 percent for categories A, B, C, and D, respectively, and data presented in Figure 17-8, the procedures for calculating equilibrium values (approximately one year hence) are found in Appendix F. Basically, these calculations center around developing equations for categories A, B, C, and D, and solving them by using simultaneous equations.

Comparison of equilibrium values to period one is illustrated in Figure 17-9. The results indicate that there is need to hire professional, technical, and semi-technical personnel versus highly technical personnel. Thus, Markov analysis is a method of analyzing movements of personnel from one group to another in order to determine where future recruiting efforts should be placed; this technique allows management to allocate and develop available talent within the firm by evening out future indicated surpluses and shortages of personnel.

Type of Personnel	Equilibrium	Period One	Difference Plus (Minus)
A - Professional	22.8%	22%	.8%
B - Highly technical	26.8%	30%	(3.2%)
C - Technical	23.7%	23%	.7%
D - Semi-technical	26.7%	25%	1.7%
	100.0%	100%	0.0%

FIGURE 17-9. Comparison of equilibrium and period one market shares.

Markov analysis should be used with discretion because probabilities employed are principally extensions of past experience, and past experience may not be representative of future trends.

Work Force Simulator

The Work Force Simulator, developed by IBM, is an example of a mathematical model used to evaluate manpower plans. The effect of new hiring, transferring, and retraining programs are tested against the data stored on line in a skills inventory system. Basically, the skills inventory system contains the following data:

1. employee profile—contains data about the employee, such as home address, marital status, and number of dependents
2. employment history—shows the positions the employee has held within the company, salary over the years, and appraisals
3. resumé and significant achievements, including previous employment
4. education data with major and minor fields of concentration
5. skills data, including on-the-job training and experience

These five blocks of skills inventory data provide regular reports to management in the areas of salary benefits analysis, education and training planning, placement resumés, and appraisal scheduling. Once a year, the basic data are printed for each employee in order to update records maintained about him. After review and appropriate corrections, the Work Force Simulator is employed to determine upcoming personnel requirements by major job classifications. In this manner, personnel with desired technical skills can be hired in conformance with the company's corporate plans.

PERSONNEL MODULES

The important modules and their related submodules, which are essential for the detailed design of the personnel subsystem, are set forth in Figure 17-10. However, before their design is finalized, they must be coordinated with basic modules found in other subsystems—in particular, the payroll module. This coordinated effort will assure compatibility of subsystems throughout the real-time MIS as well as eliminating duplicated information. In the final analysis, it is an important consideration that the systems designer determine the specific relationships of personnel modules to other areas of the real-time management information system.

REAL-TIME MIS
PERSONNEL SUBSYSTEM

An overview of the design considerations for the real-time MIS personnel subsystem will be helpful before determining the detailed design. Likewise, a review of other subsystems that are related directly or indirectly to personnel is beneficial. For example, the structure of payroll accounting data, when it is used in conjunction with personnel data, should be such that information to be displayed via I/O terminals or printed can be extracted from the data base without extensive manipulation. Otherwise, the common data base will not have sufficient space to house essential personnel data, nor will such a system be able to pay for itself.

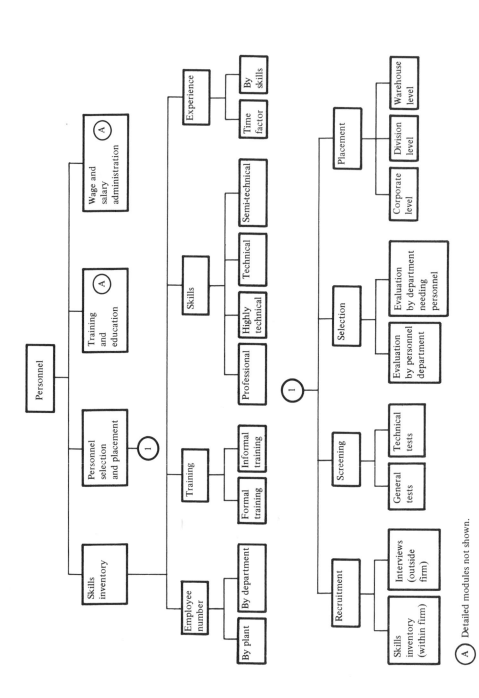

FIGURE 17-10. Personnel modules of the Consumer Products Corporation.

PERSONNEL SUBSYSTEM OVERVIEW

The personnel subsystem, as indicated several times previously, does not operate in a vacuum. As shown in Figure 17-11, it relies on inputs from other subsystems for its operations. These inputs at the division and corporate levels make it possible to retrieve vital personnel data on a real-time basis. For example, skills data regarding a specific employee can be retrieved instantaneously via a remote I/O device. In like manner, wage and salary data by departments and in total are retrievable immediately, making the personnel data base usable for negotiations with the firm's labor union. The ability to project higher labor costs via the

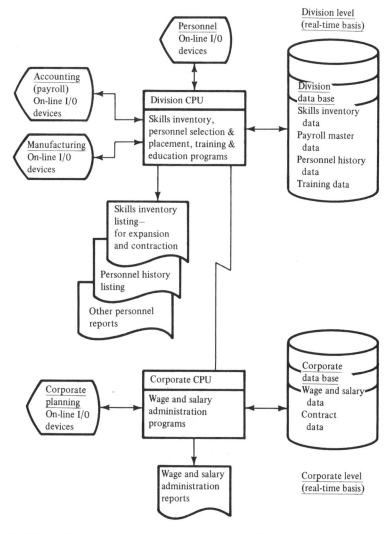

FIGURE 17-11. An overview of a real-time MIS personnel subsystem.

data base can demonstrate to management the effects of future labor contracts. In this way, a real-time approach gives an added dimension to personnel applications.

SKILLS INVENTORY MODULE

As a base for an automated skills inventory system, a library or thesaurus of "skill catalogs" must be developed in order to speed up the location of qualified employees for permanent jobs or special assignments. Such catalogs which must be determined for the various categories of skills should include:

> employee number (for basic reference)
> current occupation of employee
> fields of professional speciality and specific areas within that speciality
> type of products or services involved in the employee's current job
> various types of equipment on which the employee has experience
> past and current projects the employee has undertaken
> formal education level
> on-the-job training level
> what work the employee would like to do

After the library of skills has been written onto permanent disk storage, the same thesaurus is used to request data from storage. Requests of the on-line skills inventory system, as seen in Figure 17-12, are handled by a remote I/O device on the division level. The output listing from the system must be carefully evaluated because some personnel may be unavailable owing to prior project commitments. For those personnel who are likely candidates, biographical sketches are requested and are very helpful, say for a project leader, in determining the degree of contribution of each potential member. Permission to use selected names is then requested of the individual's respective department heads, because there is no commitment of availability implied in these lists.

Updating of the skills inventory system is relatively straightforward. New employees complete a checklist as part of their orientation procedure. Annually, a printout is prepared for each employee, indicating the capabilities previously checked for validation and updating. As individuals terminate employment, all skills data relating to their permanent numbers are dropped from disk storage. These simplified procedures assure timeliness of data printouts.

The output variations of such a computer-based skills inventory retrieval system are virtually limitless. Although the system described herein is designed to generate specific responses to the employer's needs, a cross-referenced printout in booklet form can be prepared periodically. Pie charts, discipline-project matrices,

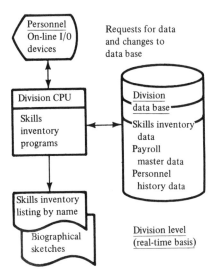

FIGURE 17-12. Skills inventory data flow for a real-time MIS personnel subsystem.

and employee-project matrices, to name a few, can be prepared from data stored on the common data base. Individual employee dossiers, which could serve as useful auxiliary documents for other personnel-related functions, can also be readily prepared from the basis data in computer storage.

PERSONNEL SELECTION AND PLACEMENT MODULE

Personnel management, in order to select and place the right employee at the right time in the firm, must continually review and evaluate alternative manpower plans. Included are such aspects as hiring, transferring, and retraining which may arise from changing work loads and/or technological advances. Decisions in this area should be quantitatively oriented in order that the people hired today can begin the kind of training necessary to fill new positions or vacancies as they occur. A Work Force Simulator, similar to that set forth in a previous section, can be employed for determining personnel information under varying conditions.

The Work Force Simulator, being a gross planning model, involves two basic concepts—namely, a phase approach and a matrix structure. In the phase approach, the interaction of different work-force factors are considered. A decision concerning a mandatory retirement age is stated. Also, an estimate of attrition due to reasons other than retirement is set forth. Factors for recruiting new personnel are added and provisions are made for internal transfers of employees because of promotion or retraining.

Type of Skill	One	Two	Years Three	Four	Five
Professional					
Job 1	①1	②2	③3	④4	⑤5
Job 2	⑥6	⑦7	⑧8	⑨9	⑩10
⋮	etc.				
Job *n*					
Highly technical					
Jobs 1 through *n*					
Technical					
Jobs 1 through *n*					
Semi-technical					
Jobs 1 through *n*					

FIGURE 17-13. Matrix structure of the Work Force Simulator—columns represent different time periods; rows represent different job levels.

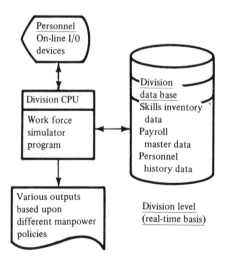

FIGURE 17-14. Personnel selection and placement data flow for a real-time MIS personnel subsystem.

In the matrix structure of the Work Force Simulator (Figure 17-13), consideration of job levels over a period of time is included. Each column of the matrix represents a different time period, such as a year or every five years. Each row of the matrix represents a different job level. At each intersection of rows and columns, one job level is represented by a certain time period.

The simulator is started by entering policy factors and data about the current plant level work force—age, experience, education level, and comparable data. By utilizing data about current employees from the division data base (Figure 17-14), the start of the simulation depicts the situation as it actually is. In the first phase of the model, the loss of manpower by retirement and attrition can be observed. In the next phase, future positions to be filled are determined under certain stated policies. The net effect of this Work Force Simulator is that it allows a hypothetical test of different manpower policies. This is an example of an imaginative use of the personnel subsystem in a real-time MIS environment that provides corporate planners with long-range information.

TRAINING AND EDUCATION MODULE

The repertoire of exercises in computer-assisted instruction permits the trainee to work on material commensurate with his or her ability. The logical power of the computer permits complex processing of the trainee's response in order to reveal individual deficiencies and to determine what assignment should be undertaken next.

Computer-assisted instruction can take many directions when operating in a real-time MIS environment. At the higher levels of management, it can be employed for operations gaming or management games in which the participants must make decisions based upon historical information. These decisions influence and create the environment under which subsequent decisions are made. Business game characteristics include sequential decisions, rapid feedback, and new responses. At the lower levels of the firm, CAI can be used to train office and key-punch operators who must operate key data systems that write data directly onto magnetic disk. In a similar manner, CAI can be employed where conventional methods are unable to approach ideal conditions for learning—for example, to simulate highly synchronized assembly operations.

Before CAI can become operational, the common data base must contain essential data which is linked to the appropriate training program. As shown in Figure 17-15, data are entered by the trainee and are evaluated by the training program working in conjunction with the common data base. Output to the trainee is in the form of feedback of how well or how poorly he has reacted to the area under study as well as what computer-assisted instructions should be undertaken next.

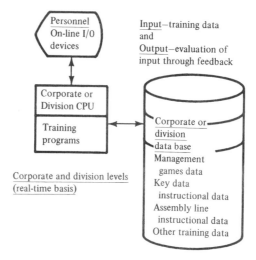

FIGURE 17-15. Training environment for a real-time MIS personnel subsystem.

WAGE AND SALARY ADMINISTRATION MODULE

In designing a wage and salary administration subsystem, the firm is confronted with two basic problems, the first of which is attempting to maintain "internal equity." This means developing a wage and salary structure in which employees perceive wage rates to be internally fair and consistent—positions calling for greater skills and responsibility pay more than lower level positions. Second, the firm must be concerned with the external problem of being competitive, salary- and wage-wise, in the labor market to avoid difficulties in hiring new employees and keeping present ones.

In order to handle internal and external problems, the wage and salary analyst should be capable of interacting with the real-time system for a response. The data flow depicted in Figure 17-16 indicates that he is able to draw upon the wage,

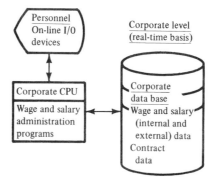

FIGURE 17-16. Wage and salary administration data flow for a real-time MIS personnel subsystem.

salary, and contract data stored on the data base and manipulate the data per the desired program in order to produce the desired output. For example, personnel on the assembly line in the Los Angeles plant are complaining that they are underpaid in relation to other plants. The wage and salary analyst, with the aid of the programming staff, can develop an operational program that plots a series of curves depicting their wage curve versus other curves for comparable skills. Thus, personnel data base elements can be extracted, manipulated, and printed to answer specific questions directed toward wage and salary administration.

SUMMARY

The personnel subsystem of the Consumer Products Corporation, like its counterparts in a real-time MIS environment, is related directly to other subsystems because all functional areas require the human factor to accomplish the firm's objectives. In terms of data generated, personnel relies heavily upon the payroll function of the accounting subsystem. However, despite this level of integration, many methods and procedures center around the personnel function with little or no reference to other subsystems. Designing a real-time MIS personnel subsystem is a difficult undertaking because a variety of design approaches can be developed to provide timely information. Specifically, the selected design should be capable of providing the right numbers and kinds of people to be at the right places at the right times in order to achieve organizational and personnel objectives.

Personnel functions center around skills inventory, personnel selection and placement, training and education, and wage and salary administration. A skills inventory system speeds up considerably the location of qualified employees for full-time special assignments. If in-house personnel cannot be located, the personnel selection and placement function takes over for hiring qualified personnel from outside the firm. Included in this function is personnel planning for the short, intermediate, and long run. Training and education of personnel must also be undertaken; and their pay must be indicative of their positions and skills required. The foregoing personnel functions can best be performed in the context of a real-time system.

QUESTIONS

1. What are the advantages of a real-time MIS personnel subsystem over an integrated MIS personnel subsystem?

2. Suggest additional OR techniques that can be employed by a real-time MIS personnel subsystem.

3. Suggest additional areas in personnel that could benefit from real-time processing.

4. Referring to Figure 17-10, determine submodules for:
    a. training and education
    b. wage and salary administration

5. Explain the relationship of skills inventory and personnel selection and placement in a real-time MIS environment.

6. Referring to the section on personnel selection and placement, suggest additional real-time MIS applications.

7. Referring to the section on wage and salary administration, suggest additional real-time MIS applications.

REFERENCES

Balinsky, W. and Reismon, A., "Some Manpower Planning Models Based on Levels of Educational Attainment," *Management Science,* August, 1972.

Blakely, R. T., "Markov Models and Manpower Planning," *Industrial Management Review,* Winter, 1970.

Bryant, D. R., Maggard, M. J., and Taylor, R. P., "Manpower Planning Models and Techniques, A Descriptive Survey," *Business Horizons,* April, 1973.

Cheek, L. M., "Cost Effectiveness Comes to the Personnel Function," *Harvard Business Review,* May-June, 1973.

Clarke, L. J., "Decision Models for Personnel Systems," *Personnel Administration,* July-August, 1970.

Cliff, S. H., and Hecht, R. M., "Job/Man Matching in the '70s," *Datamation,* February, 1971.

Connally, G. E., "Personnel Administration and the Computer," *Personnel Journal,* August, 1969.

Danner, J., "Management Information Systems: A Tool for Personnel Planning," *Personnel Journal,* July, 1971.

Doiron, R. C., "The Personnel Evaluation Process," *Journal of Systems Management,* July, 1970.

Fahnline, R. H., "The Skills Inventory Put On," *Journal of Systems Management,* May, 1974.

Fritton, P. F., "A Skills Inventory System," *Journal of Systems Management,* July, 1970.

Greenlaw, P. S., "Management Science and Personnel Management," *Personnel Journal,* November, 1973.

Greenslaw, R. S., and Smith, R. D., *Personnel Management: A Management Science Approach.* Scranton, Pa.: International Book Co., 1970.

Holt, C. C., and Huber, G. P., "A Computer-Aided Approach to Employment Service Placement and Counseling," *Management Science,* July, 1969.

Kahalas, H., and Key, R. A., "A Decisionally Oriented Manpower Model for Minority Group Hiring," *The Quarterly Review of Economics and Business,* Autumn, 1974.

Kelly, J. F., *Computerized Management Information Systems.* New York: The Macmillan Co., 1970, Chap. 4.

Robinson, D., "Two-Stage Replacement Strategies and Their Application to Manpower Planning," *Management Science,* October, 1974.

Sodan, S., and Auerbach, L. R., "A Stochastic Model for Human Resources Valuation," *California Management Review,* Summer, 1974.

Smith, R. D., "Models for Personnel Selection Decisions," *Personnel Journal,* August, 1973.

Teach, L., "Simulation in Recruitment Planning," *Personnel Journal,* April, 1969.

Tetz, T. F., "System for Managing Human Resources," *Journal of Systems Management,* October, 1974.

Todd, J. T., Thompson, P. H., and Dalton, G. W., "Management Control of Personnel," *Journal of Accountancy,* February, 1974.

Tomeski, E. A., and Lazarus, H., "Information Systems in Personnel," *Journal of Systems Management,* August, 1973.

Von der Embse, "Choosing a Management Development Program: A Division Model," *Personnel Journal,* October, 1973.

Walker, J. W., "Models in Manpower Planning," *Business Horizons,* April, 1971.

Weber, W. L., "Manpower Planning in Hierarchial Organizations: A Computer Simulation Approach," *Management Science,* November, 1971.

part four

THE FUTURE
OF
MANAGEMENT
INFORMATION
SYSTEMS

FUTURE MIS— DATA-MANAGED SYSTEMS 18

The preceding chapters have been directed toward the design of major subsystems and their modules which constitute a real-time management information system. Basically, a real-time MIS operating environment is a forward- and backward-looking control system whose output is directed mainly to lower and middle management for past, current, and future operations. Also, output is directed to top management in terms of historical financial reports. Although this MIS approach is considerably better than prior system approaches, there is still room for improvement.

The subject matter of this chapter focuses initially on the types of decisions that are made in the firm, followed by an investigation of the next important phase in continuing MIS developments. Specifically, the requirements for a data base

557

management information system, currently referred in the literature[1] and in this chapter as a "data-managed system," are discussed before defining it. Hardware, software, and computer systems are considered in light of this new systems design concept. Finally, continuing advancements for future MIS systems that extend beyond the firm, as well as the electronic money system, are treated.

INFORMATION IN A MIS ENVIRONMENT

In a real-time management information system, there is generally adequate information produced for the operational level. Not only are reports prepared on past operations, but they are also available on current and forthcoming activities. However, the question can be asked whether or not the firm's resources (men, money, materials, machines, and managers) at the lowest level are allocated in the most optimum manner in a real-time MIS environment. Depending upon the level of complexity involved and the competence of lower management, they may or may not be. Generally, they are not, because optimization of the firm must come from the top on down. In a real-time management information system, mathematical models basically are directed at one specific area or its related parts, but overall optimization of the firm is not employed. Hence, operational information is generally deficient from an overview standpoint.

The same question asked about operational information can also be asked about tactical information—that is, are the firm's resources at the middle organizational level allocated in the most optimum way for real-time MIS? The same answer can be given. Largely, they are not, because a real-time management information system does not employ comprehensive mathematical models from operation research whereby all of the firm's inputs and outputs are automatically coordinated. A real-time MIS provides most functional-level reports desired, but this information may not always produce optimum results.

Of greater importance is strategic information, which is paramount if a system is to optimize overall results. As has been discussed, a real-time MIS operating mode does not have the capability to provide top-level information that is capable of predicting tomorrow's results in view of today's operations and projected results. However, this limitation does not have to apply to future management information systems—a fact that will be made evident throughout the remainder of the chapter.

DISTINGUISHING CHARACTERISTICS OF
DATA-MANAGED SYSTEMS

Major deficiencies of real-time management information systems are remedied with data-managed systems, the next thrust in continuing MIS developments. However, before this next major systems approach can be initiated, considerable de-

---

[1]P. D. Walker and S. D. Catalano, "Where Do We Go from Here with MIS?" *Computer Decisions*, September, 1969, p. 36.

velopment work is required. In the past, *integrated MIS* has relied on a batch processing operating mode while presently, *real-time MIS* is geared to an on-line real-time response for important control information. Although the firm has hardware and software available to achieve the current phase of management information systems, the same is not completely true for the next important data processing phase. The problems associated with the *data-managed system* or *data base MIS* will become apparent in the following discussion of its distinguishing characteristics (Figure 18-1), especially that associated with the structure and management of the data base to serve all management personnel.

1. More forward-looking control system
2. Output and exception reports to all management levels
3. Large moving common data base
4. Greater use of complex OR models
5. Orientation toward visual output
6. Approximation of the total systems concept
7. Other essential characteristics (as found in real-time MIS)

FIGURE 18-1.   Distinguishing characteristics of a data-managed system (data base MIS).

1. MORE FORWARD-LOOKING CONTROL SYSTEM

A most distinguishing characteristic of the next phase in MIS is that it will be a more forward-looking control system. In addition to receiving a response from the system in time to satisfy their own real-time environmental requirements (as with real-time MIS), company personnel will be able to project the life cycles of products in developing strategic plans for the firm. This approach is extremely desirable in the increasingly complex business world. The environmental factors that affect success and failure are so dynamic that top management must be able to understand and react to them quickly and decisively. High operational costs provide another strong incentive for creating more forward-looking control systems.

The life cycle of a typical product, shown in Figure 18-2, helps to illustrate the corporate integration that management must accommodate. For operating and middle management to plan and schedule effectively, there must first be an awareness of the original product plan set forth by top management; there must be a continuous appraisal of actual performance and changes in the plan across the organization. Data-managed systems will be designed to process operational data so that organization-wide information requirements—in particular, those for strategic planning—can be satisfied.

2. OUTPUT AND EXCEPTION REPORTS TO ALL MANAGEMENT LEVELS

An essential difference between the real-time MIS and the data-managed system is their reporting function. Output and exception reports from a real-time

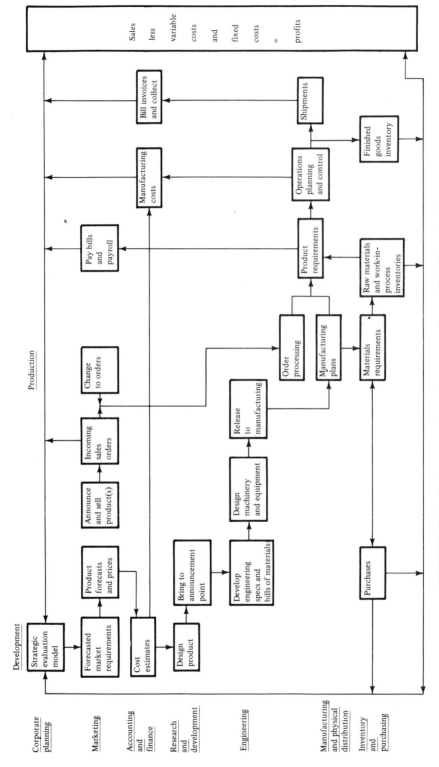

FIGURE 18-2. Data-managed system—more forward-looking in its consideration of the life cycle of products for developing long-range plans.

MIS are oriented mainly toward lower and middle management. Sample outputs focus on the following areas: accurate market forecasts, service to customers, marketing budgets, allocation of departmental manufacturing facilities, vendor performance, alternative investments of short-term assets, and negotiations with labor unions. On the other hand, reports from a data-managed system are designed to satisfy all management levels. Representative applications that apply to present and future conditions include:

> setting long-range plans and objectives for the entire firm that are fully integrated into the major subsystems and their related modules
>
> planning and evaluating new products over their life cycle (as discussed in the preceding section)
>
> determining manpower requirements and allocating company personnel so that the best man is placed in the appropriate job
>
> allocating available factory capacity in the most efficient manner for the entire firm
>
> determining materials requirements that reduce overall costs for the entire firm
>
> acquiring short-, intermediate-, and long-term capital funds as needed for the entire firm
>
> determining profit profiles of large alternative investment plans
>
> indicating improvements in operating revenues and costs

Data-managed systems, then, are quite different from their predecessors. While a real-time MIS environment is concerned with maximizing decisions for one major subsystem or one of its parts, a data-managed system cuts across the entire firm for optimal decisions. Thus, a new kind of business structure is needed to handle these difficult and complex conditions. At the heart of the structure must be an information processing system in which external and internal data interact with each other in countless variations. A data-managed system will allow all levels of management to be involved and will be dependent on a highly integrated, total corporate planning model that interacts with all of the firm's major subsystems and their related modules. A very large computer will become central to this type of management information system.

3. LARGE MOVING COMMON DATA BASE

The structure of a data-managed system will be both horizontal and vertical in nature (Figure 18-3), as is the case with real-time MIS. For this approach to become operational, the systems designer must determine how the data base elements form a common data base for the important needs of all management levels. He must ask questions regarding, for instance, whether or not current data being employed for lower management day-to-day decisions are valid when projected for the long run. Can the major business functions utilize the same inventory figures as those needed by top management for long-range planning? An even more important question concerns whether or not the requirements of top management are so

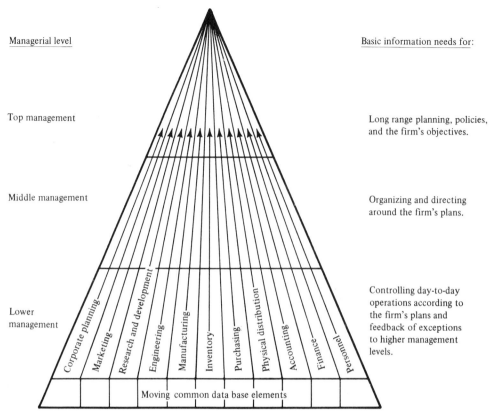

Managerial level

Basic information needs for:

Top management

Long range planning, policies, and the firm's objectives.

Middle management

Organizing and directing around the firm's plans.

Lower management

Controlling day-to-day operations according to the firm's plans and feedback of exceptions to higher management levels.

Corporate planning
Marketing
Research and development
Engineering
Manufacturing
Inventory
Purchasing
Physical distribution
Accounting
Finance
Personnel

Moving common data base elements

FIGURE 18-3. Horizontal and vertical structure of the common data base for the major subsystems and their modules in a data-managed system.

different as to be incompatible with lower and middle management needs. This type of question present a new challenge to the information system designer. Not only must a company data base be integrated that will serve all functions (subsystems and their related modules), but it must also be capable of servicing all management levels with their respective information needs. Thus, data sufficient to answer questions in the short or intermediate runs may not be adequate for the long run.

To accommodate the needs of all management levels for any time period, the common data base must be structured as illustrated in Figure 18-4. Basically, data must be classified according to its usage. Operational information pertaining to individual products or customers is needed for maintenance of the company's records and is of little interest to top management. Management control data consist of information on exception conditions triggered by the operational level systems. It involves summaries, recaps, and comparable information generally for use by middle management in controlling the firm's operations on a short-term basis. Planning information is intended for usage by top management in exercising its broad responsibilities for directing the long-range activities of the organization. In essence, operational data must be summarized for tactical or middle management needs which, in turn, must be summarized for strategic or top management requirements.

Although the foregoing approach to the hierarchial data base provides historical information about current operations, there is another type of information that is of more value and interest than, say, monthly operating statements and budget performance analyses. This is information that pertains to future operations, being predictive in nature since it augments the manager's own judgment about what performance is going to be like in the future. Here there is need for a wide array of quantitative and qualitative techniques for exploiting the information in the data base, ranging from simple extrapolations to the employment of complex OR models with the capability of manipulating numerous variables. Information techniques pertaining to probable future performance are more difficult to design and develop, and consequently, have not progressed as far as those techniques using historical information.

In order to produce meaningful future information, there is need to procure a certain amount of environmental or external information that is compatible with internal information contained in the common data base. This includes information about the industry in which the firm is competing as well as the pricing structure, advertising campaigns, and locations of its competing firms. Other external information not having to do directly with competition but still of great potential importance to management includes economic indicators, information about securities markets, and demographic data of many kinds. Acquisition and usage of such information is limited by the nature of the business, the difficulty of procuring the data, and its cost versus its value in management decision making.

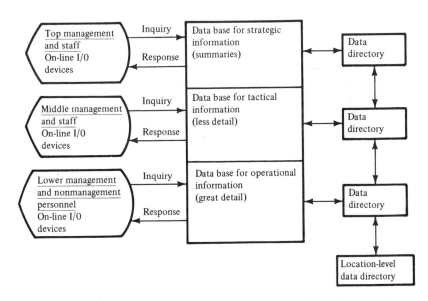

FIGURE 18-4. A dictionary/directory system used in a "moving data base" environment for a data-managed system.

It should be noted that environmental data need not necessarily be captured and stored in the data base on a continually recurring basis. Data may be obtained when needed to perform a particular type of analysis. For example, census data and other descriptive information might be stored on magnetic tape to assist in making an occasional determination of the best location for new manufacturing plants or sales offices.

A data base that is capable of handling the foregoing structural requirements must be built upon a "moving file" concept—that is, as operating data are received, appropriate adjustments will be made automatically through the system to the higher data levels. The "moving data base" reflects not only actual day-by-day operating activities but also the planned performance of these same activities at all levels. The lower-level operational data base feeds the next level, where data are summarized to reflect longer time periods which, in turn, are fed to the highest level of the data base for producing strategic information. This orderly arrangement of the firm's common data base allows the user to ask "what if" questions in order to determine if the firm's overall performance or some part of it can be improved or if plans should be modified. The dynamics of the moving file concept are very responsive to the changing environment in which all levels of management must plan, organize, direct, and control the business.

To handle the moving data base in an efficient manner, it is necessary to develop an organization-wide data element dictionary/directory which includes standard definitions, an index system, mathematical routines for deriving higher levels of data from the stored data base elements, and security rules for file access. Also, the dictionary/directory system is so designed that only critical data are referenced in memory or auxiliary storage devices, while less critical and more voluminous files are retrievable from magnetic tape or some other low-cost storage medium. As illustrated in Figure 18-4, the lowest level of the data base elements for operational information can be referenced by the data directory as well as the highest level of data for strategic information. This approach permits large on-line files to be handled on an interactive basis from the lowest to the highest level where data items can be sorted, manipulated, and chosen according to many criteria.

In the final analysis, a logical method must be selected as the optimum approach to organizing the data base after giving complete consideration to operational, tactical, and strategic information needed for various subsystems and their modules. Likewise, thought must be given to growth that can be anticipated in volume of records (data sets). In general, the insertion of additional or new records in the data base should not upset the file organization to the point that it will be necessary to reorganize them at frequent intervals. Thus, an approach to designing a large, moving data base in a data-managed system is a challenge for any group of systems analysts that may take years to solve.

4. GREATER USE OF COMPLEX OR MODELS

Even though present-level mathematical business models are adequate for the present state of real-time MIS, the same cannot be said for future MIS. The systems designer must be capable of understanding very complex mathematical models that encompass all the subsystems (of the firm) to create an effective and efficient overall mathematical model that relates the lower, middle, and top managerial needs in a logical manner. There must be a marriage of management information systems with operations research in order to utilize the forthcoming advancements in software and hardware. This combined effort is imperative. Although most OR activities presently are centered around solving well-structured problems for a specific area of a firm, the future trend is heading in two directions. First, many of the standard OR models are being combined into larger and more sophisticated models. Second, the large number of problems that are difficult to structure are getting increased attention from operations researchers.

In those cases in which poorly structured and unstructured problems do not lend themselves to mathematical modeling, typical problems encountered are: determining organization objectives; selecting, developing, and motivating employees; improving collective bargaining relations; humanizing the work environment; facilitating company relations with federal, state, and local governments; and learning to interact with the community that buys its wares and from which it draws both employees and public support. These aspects of the managerial job will rise in importance and will require broadly trained personnel who are sensitive to social, economic, political, and technical changes. The assistance of operations research, then, will allow the manager to relegate certain problem types to the data-managed system while time is spent on problems that are not logical candidates for OR solution.

5. ORIENTATION TOWARD VISUAL OUTPUT

In a real-time MIS environment, output is not restricted to printed output, but can be in a visual output form as well. Visual display screen devices include CRT units, picturephones, computer graphic devices, large-screen display systems, and management control centers (see Chapter 5). All of these devices will be employed even more in a data-managed system. Key managers will sit around a large display screen, and "what if"-type questions will be asked of the computer. The answers will be displayed on the screen and after discussions and iterations, a decision will be reached.

An example of "what if" questions would be the proposed introduction of a new product. A staff specialist (capable of mathematical programming and operations research), working with a marketing manager and using a CRT unit, might employ a mathematical model, such as venture analysis, that incorporates estimates of sales, costs, competitor reactions, and comparable data. To make a final decision on the proposed new product, the staff specialist would vary the inputs rather than entering only one estimate for each of the variables, constraints, and similar restrictions. For example, he might ask, "If I assumed sales to be X, *what* would happen *if* the sales value was set at some other value?" Or, ' "*What if* the various competitors did A rather than B or C?"

To answer "what if" questions, certain computer graphic devices that have been programmed to produce charts and graphs on the screen can be employed. By touching the screen with a light pen, the specialist can order the computer to calculate new values and redraw the graphs almost instantaneously. Thus, the manager and specialist team can test all or most possible feasible alternatives and can select the best one by analyzing quantitative data in a real-time, computer graphic environment.

6. APPROXIMATION OF THE TOTAL SYSTEMS CONCEPT

Data base MIS will be approximating the total systems concept which, though it tends to be utopian when carried to its highest level of achievement, is still an ultimate goal by and large for data-managed systems. Basically, this concept refers to the condition in which all of the firm's inputs—processing methods and procedures—and outputs are automatically coordinated to accomplish the firm's objectives.

In order to accomplish this Herculean feat, it is necessary to utilize mathematical models that cut across the entire firm. As has been discussed, these corporate models must coordinate the firm's resources in an optimum manner in order to achieve the firm's objectives. These models must not only be integrated and interacting on the highest level in the firm, but must also be related directly to the many subparts of the major subsystems. Only in this manner will overall optimization of the entire firm result.

To approximate the total systems concept, the ability to extract desired information from the multiple-level data base is essential. Because this type of data base will be structured on the moving file concept, it must be possible to retrieve the required information for most types of OR models. It should be pointed out that the present state of the art in OR modeling and data base designing has not reached this level of sophistication. Also, considerable advances must be made in MIS hardware and software before the next phase in MIS systems can approximate the total systems concept.

7. OTHER ESSENTIAL CHARACTERISTICS

The distinguishing characteristics that set the data-managed system apart from the real-time MIS have been discussed in the preceding sections. Other essential characteristics which parallel those found in a real-time MIS environment include integrated subsystems, input/output-oriented with many I/O terminals, and remote batch processing. A comparison of important characteristics for both systems is set forth in Figure 18-5, while an illustrative data-managed system is depicted in Figure 18-6.

A thorough examination of the characteristics of data-managed systems reveals more management and nonmanagement involvement, because this system will be the very heart of the business structure. More company personnel will interact with the computer via I/O terminal devices in order to obtain desired on-line

Important Characteristics of Management Information Systems	Real-Time Management Information System	Data-Managed System
Type of system	Forward-and backward-looking control system and integrated sub-systems	More forward-looking control system and integrated sub-systems
Reports prepared	Output reports directed mainly to lower and middle management for past, current, and future operations	Output reports directed to all levels of management for past, current, and future operations
Exception reporting	Current plans and objectives used for management exception reports	Current plans and objectives used for more management exception reports at all levels
Information orientation	Input/output-oriented with I/0 terminals	⟶
Processing mode	On-line real-time processing and remote batch processing	⟶
Data elements	Common data base	Enlarged common data base, including a moving data base concept
Modularity	Modular design approach	⟶
Type of files	Accent on random access on-line file storage	⟶
Mathematical models	Use of standard and some complex OR models for well-structured problems	Greater use of standard and complex OR models for well-structured and poorly structured problems
Type of output	Accent on written and visual output	Oriented toward visual output
Basic total systems concept	Contains elements of the total systems concept	Approximates the total systems concept

⟶ *Denotes continued use and development.*

FIGURE 18-5. **Comparison of important characteristics for real-time management information systems and data-managed systems.**

responses; man/machine interaction will evolve in a way that will facilitate more advanced applications than are possible in a real-time MIS environment. This increased interaction mode will lead to solving far more complex and qualitatively different high-level problems. A data-managed system will be an important link that allows company personnel to interact with tomorrow's dynamic environment.

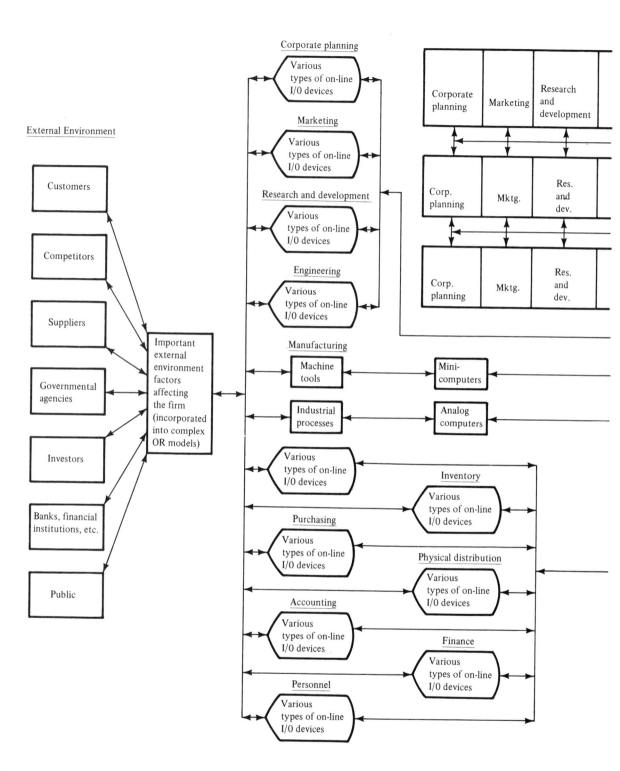

External Environment

568

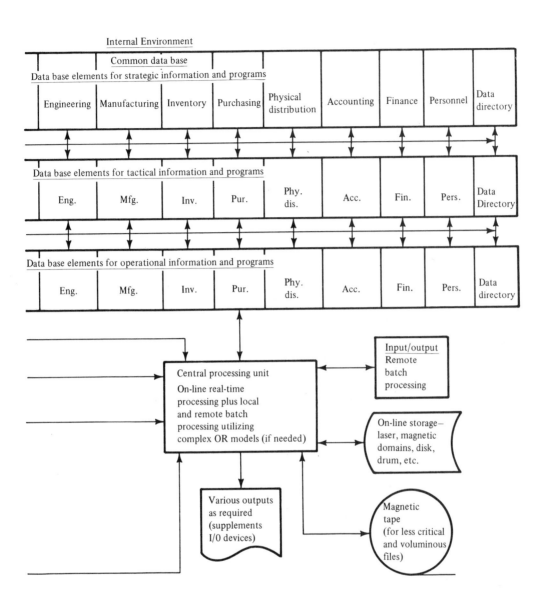

FIGURE 18-6. Data-managed system for a typical manufacturing firm—data base elements are summarized as they move up the hierarchial data base.

DATA-MANAGED SYSTEM DEFINED

An examination of the important characteristics within a data-managed system (Figure 18-5) provides a basis for defining it. Basically, the definition for a real-time MIS can be revised for defining a data-managed system. By way of review, a real-time management information system is "a group of integrated subsystems that is modularly structured on a forward- and backward-looking basis to accomplish company objectives wherein informational data are recorded, manipulated, and retrieved from a common data base via I/O terminals in order to plan, organize, direct, and control quantitative (and qualitative) managerial and operational activities in sufficient time to affect their respective operations."

Using this definition and the distinguishing characteristics set forth in Figure 18-5, a data-managed system can be defined as "a group of highly integrated subsystems that is modularly structured on a very forward- and backward-looking basis to accomplish overall and specific company objectives wherein informational data are recorded, manipulated, and retrieved from a large, moving data base via I/O terminals in order to plan, organize, direct, and control quantitative/qualitative managerial and operational activities in sufficient time to affect their operations on an immediate and a long-term basis." The use of the term *quantitative/qualitative* refers to the fact that operations research models will be employed to solve well-structured and poorly structured problems respectively—necessary for providing managerial and operational information. In the final analysis, the value of information to the firm is that it allows better decisions to be made.

One last comment about the foregoing definition is that it approximates the total systems concept more than does a real-time MIS. The rationale is that a data-managed system is highly integrated in terms of overall and detailed parts, resulting in a system that operates essentially as a whole unit. What happens in one area of the system is automatically coordinated with other related system modules. Basically, the firm's inputs and outputs are automatically coordinated through the firm's large, moving data base.

COMPUTER DEVELOPMENTS FOR DATA-MANAGED SYSTEMS

Current hardware, software, and operating costs which are indicative of the trend for future management information systems have been researched by many reputable consulting firms. A composite of these studies (average values) is found in Figure 18-7. The most costly aspect of an EDP installation is the software expense, which totals approximately 40 percent (24 percent for new applications plus 16 percent for current applications) versus about 36 percent for hardware or equipment rental and/or depreciation charges. The high cost of computer software, then, is evident.

With the trend toward the installation of sophisticated management information systems, software is becoming more complex and expensive and hardware costs are declining. Because of this, there is a marked tendency to acquire more advanced hardware. This is in opposition to spending great sums of money to create software

	Average (Approximate)
Hardware:	
Equipment rental and/or depreciation charges	36%
Software:	
Systems development—systems analysis, systems design, and programming of new applications	24%
Maintenance of current programs	16%
Operating Costs:	
Expenses for daily operations	24%
	100%

FIGURE 18-7. Classification of computer costs—based on several studies.

that will maximize the efficiency of the hardware. In effect, the cost factors of computer hardware affects the amount of software that will be required in installing a data-managed system.

Another reason for the trend to advanced hardware is that the equipment manufacturers have taken a different approach to marketing. In the past, they have sold both hardware and software systems that match existing or easily defined systems, such as basic accounting routines. This can be called "bottoms-up" marketing; it works well when the problem fits the system available or when the answer is a matter of trade practice or habit. However, future management information systems will demand a more tailored approach, or "top-down" marketing. For this approach, the first step is defining the problem the customer needs to solve, then designing the equipment to solve the problem, then integrating it into the user's established procedures. Thus, systems-level thinking by equipment manufacturers is the key to integrating all the pieces (hardware and software) so that they work in harmony.

HARDWARE

To accommodate real-time capabilities of the computer, there is and will continue to be a growing number of I/O terminals for each computer. By 1980, terminals will account for over half the total peripheral equipment market, reflecting a phenomenal growth in remote computing. This trend is illustrated in Figure 18-8. The cost of computer hardware will be highest for terminals (teletypewriter, CRT's, and similar devices), followed by perhipherals (input/output units, on-line files, and comparable units), and central processors (CPU's). By 1980, it is predicted that between 2.5 and 3 million terminals will be in operation. Approximately half of these will be visual display (CRT) devices.

Central Processors

Forecasts of computer costs (central processors and memories only) will decrease during the 1970's and thereafter. In Figure 18-9, three bands are shown: large computers, small but complete business computers, and the least expensive

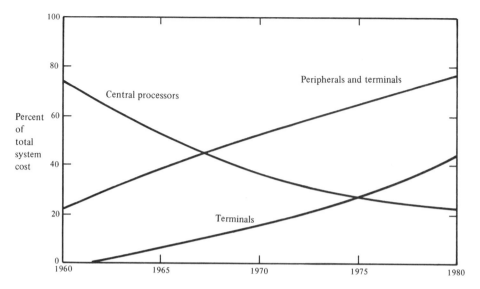

FIGURE 18-8. **Expenditures on terminals will exceed those of central processors by a wide margin. Terminals will account for over half the total peripheral and terminal market.**

minicomputers. The large computers of 1980 (and thereafter) should cost considerably less than comparable machines today, because of the extreme drop expected in the manufacturing cost of electronics for both logic and memory. However, much larger machines will exist, costing more than today, but their power will be so great that few users can be expected to need them. The smaller computers can also be expected to decline in cost, though less sharply. Late in the 1970's, low manufacturing costs for monolithic circuits will make possible memories cheaper than any today with higher performance.

Microelectronics

Microelectronics will play a major role in future hardware developments, as in the past, because it permits faster and more efficient hardware and enables manufacturers to reduce production costs. In particular, microelectronics will be employed in computer memories where the new technology permits smaller, faster, and cheaper storage of data. The current direction is associate memories. On the other hand, a host of new technologies are in development, including magneto- and electro-optical technologies, holographic approaches, lasers, and magnetic bubbles or domains. Some of these will be discussed below.

Associate Memories. For this hardware concept, data are addressed by association or on the basis of part of their contents, because all data are searched simultaneously to locate specific data. This is in contrast with a standard computer system, which requires that the specific location in memory be addressed for the

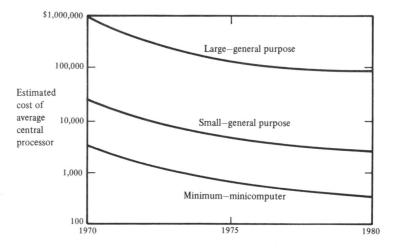

FIGURE 18-9. Central processor costs during the 1970's.

desired information. Likewise, the conventional system requires that the user keep track of the memory locations; with the associate memory, neither the programmer nor the machine need do this. Even though its costs are high, they are expected to decline in the future.

Lasers. A most promising hardware technique of the future is the laser, which has the capability of storing about one million bits per square inch on film. Laser-based computers, featuring many trillion bits of memory, will be common in the future. The basic principle of laser storage is the 0-bit and 1-bit combination of any binary system: it records a 1-bit by concentrating a very small beam of light for an extremely short period of time, which results in "burning the emulsion." The laser reads data by sensing the white and black spots (0 or 1).

Magnetic Bubbles or Domains. Equally promising in hardware development are the tiny magnetic "bubbles" or "domains" developed by Bell Telephone Laboratories. Like the transistor, the magnetic devices depend on basic solid-state physical phenomena. But while transistors use the electrical characteristics of semiconductor crystals to amplify and switch signals, the new technology takes advantage of the magnetic alignment properties of crystals grown from mixtures of iron or lead oxides and rare earth metals.

Compactness is only one of the advantages Bell Laboratories researchers have found in devices made from their magnetic materials. The devices have no moving parts to wear out, generate little heat, operate on very low power, and need very little wiring to interconnect them. Also, the manufacturing process will be much simpler than that used for making semiconductor devices. The potential is a vast reduction in the cost of storing and handling data.

These magnetic components have been nicknamed bubble devices because the technology is based on generating tiny magnetized areas known as magnetic domains in the thin crystalline slices. The domains—a fraction of a thousandth of an inch in diameter—move across the slices under the influence of electrical currents in printed conductors on the surface, or in response to changes in the magnetic fields surrounding the unit. Under polarized light, the domains are visible, and under a microscope they look like tiny bubbles. If the circuits are operated very slowly, it is possible to watch the bits of data move through the storage and logic patterns that are printed on the surface of the crystal to guide them. The bubbles blend into a blur as the speed of data transfer increases toward the present maximum of 3 million bits per second. Thin slices of these magnetizable crystals can store as many as a million bits of information per square inch. Stacks of slices might hold millions of words and numbers in a volume not much larger than a few cigarette packages. Currently, storing that much information takes units the size of clothes closets packed with precision machinery.

Mass Storage

Future management information systems will rely heavily on some type of mass storage. As illustrated in Figure 18-10 cost per bit is expected to drop significantly by 1980. Average access times are assumed to remain about the same. However, newer technology, such as laser, bubble, and optical mass storage, should produce faster access times.

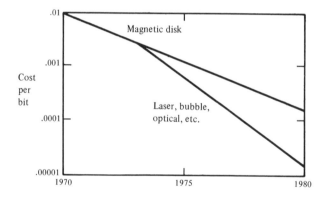

FIGURE 18-10. Mass storage during the 1970's.

SOFTWARE

The foregoing hardware developments are impressive when compared to earlier computer hardware; unfortunately, the same cannot be said for computer software. The promises of software designers have not lived up to expectations. Often the initial software specifications for a particular generation of computers are not obtained until another generation is announced to replace the existing one. Thus, another cycle of frustration with computer software begins because the next-generation software, when implemented, does not live up to its original expectations.

Programming Languages

General-purpose programming languages, such as COBOL and FORTRAN, have been widely used in the past and today. The trend has been and still seems to be toward some kind of combined programming language—one that utilizes English language words and statements plus mathematical formulas in a modular environment. This approach has been apparent in the modular or building block language PL/1, where there is an attempt to remedy the deficiencies of COBOL and FORTRAN.

Perhaps more important in programming language trends is machine independence of programming and operations. Procedure-oriented languages are already at the point where any program can be compiled and executed on a wide variety of machines. However, command languages—by which computer systems are directed in the operation of completed programs—are still in a primitive state. Manufacturers have become aware of the importance of command languages and are working hard on improving them. Command languages can become machine-independent when the system is capable of automatically scheduling itself and allocating its resources to meet the commands given it. A standard command language can then be applied to any system. A few computer systems already approach this capability, and most computer systems are expected to have it in the future.

Human Language Programming

Research is currently underway to ascertain the specific relationships between sentence structure and part of sentences used in normal speech and the ways in which the computer can handle them. This understanding will help equipment manufacturers in writing computer software languages that can better fit the human language. Hopefully, the ultimate of this research activity will allow the programmer to converse directly with the computer. Instead of being sent to a special programming course, the company's programmers will attend several sessions on how to instruct the computer for the most efficient program. Included in the training will be sessions on phonetics (conversing with the computer so that one is clearly understood) plus syntax and semantics (relating structure to the meaning of the language). Language research may prove to be the most effective and fastest means of increasing the efficiency of computer software.

The results of current research by Bell Telephone Laboratories is a system that converts input to synthetic speech. Words input through a Teletype are automatically produced as "nearly natural-sounding" synthetic speech. The experimental work takes advantage of an improved understanding of speech patterns. The computer is provided with mathematical approximations to the shapes and motions the human vocal tract assumes when uttering common sounds and sound sequences. It is also provided with a basic dictionary of word categories and definitions in digital form. Rules of timing, pitch, and stress which people use naturally in everyday conversation are also approximated.

When words are input, the system analyzes the sentence, assigns stress and timing to each word, and finds a phonetic description of each word in the dictionary. Mathematical descriptions of vocal tract motions are then computed, converted to signal, and generated as electrical speech signals which may be heard over a loudspeaker or telephone. Uses of this new technique include such things as the recitation of a page from a medical book for a doctor, information about inventory for a stock manager, or flight information for an airline clerk.

Although current and prospective software developments are headed toward more standardization, more efficient compilers, better firmware, and improved overall performance, software innovations have not taken advantage of hardware advancements. In fact, it may be quite a long time before software is on the same developmental level as its counterpart. The widening gap between hardware and software can be narrowed appreciably by an entirely different approach. This revolves around an effort to produce computers that will respond to the language of man, either directly or through a compiler.

COMPUTER SYSTEMS

Future large computer systems basically will operate with higher-level languages and will be capable of self-scheduling and self-organizing in terms of memory, file, and communications management. All stimuli presented to the system (run requests, inquiries, transactions for posting, program compilations, report requests) will be received by a conversational scheduler, which verifies the acceptability of the stimulus and schedules the required operation. The conversation with users will be conducted primarily in an improved command language, simpler and closer to English than the present command languages. New programs, report specifications, and the like will be stated by the users in improved versions of present programming languages.

File organization, memory allocation, linking, and all other internal system management functions will be conducted by automatic methods. The user will have no knowledge of the location of data or the detailed status of the system except through monitor programs. Although this will be inefficient, the use of hardware assists, such as virtual addressing, will improve the efficiency. Improvements in the price-performance of memories and processor electronics will help. Of course, the skilled user will have the opportunity to optimize the system's internal operation.

The system will be configured so that it cannot be incapacitated by the failure of any single element. Diagnostics will be run automatically to detect failures. Detection of a failure will cause automatic rescheduling so that operations on high-priority jobs can continue without pause at a reduced rate.

COMPUTER UTILITIES

Just as there are important trends in hardware and software, the same is true for computer systems, in particular those relating to computer utilities. Super computing ability is a must for the computer utility concept. A computer utility is a data processing service organization that provides a wide range of computer services through its large-scale computing power, large data banks, and vast data communication networks. In reality, the computer utility surpasses in capability what can be achieved with most in-house computer systems standing alone. Such firms as Control Data, through its network of national and international data centers (CYBERNET), are making sizable gains in implementing this enlarged concept of the traditional service bureau. Control Data's CYBERPAK allows customers to acquire the equivalent of from 1/16 to a complete CDC super-scale computer system with full support services and a wide range of proprietary software application packages. A computer utility, then, acts like any other utility, such as gas, electric, and water. It provides all the computer services that are needed for an automated data processing system.

Computer utilities will become more widespread because of the problems associated with operating an efficient data processing system for many firms. They will be capable of serving small, medium, and large firms with many remote I/O terminals connected to a computer system. The central processor in such a system shares a common memory that is quite large, highly efficient, and capable of handling many programs concurrently. Software that is basic to a large EDP system will be built into the hardware itself. The computer utility will integrate activities now undertaken on a separate basis. Systems development work, programming, time-sharing, optical character recognition processing, on-line processing, remote batch processing, financing, leasing, and the manufacture of peripheral hardware will be undertaken by one firm versus a series of firms, as presently.

In addition to external computer utilities, internal computer utilities will abound in the future. Large organizations will move away from manning and operating various sized computer centers. A massive central computer facility, coupled to all types of terminals at working areas all over the country or the world, will be operated to lower overall data processing costs. Low-cost computing power will be available to almost anyone who employs the computer utility concept.

DATA SYSTEMS THAT EXTEND BEYOND THE FIRM

The data-managed system is not the ultimate system despite its improvements over a real-time MIS. The next logical development to occur in very advanced future management information systems links the suppliers, manufacturer, distributors, and retailers in a comprehensive total system. This approach is the total systems concept carried beyond the limits of the firm. In such a system, the demand response of customers at the retail level will be relayed instantaneously back to the raw material suppliers, through a vast communications network (Figure 18-11). The desired raw materials and/or purchased parts will be forwarded to the manufacturer for producing finished goods which, in turn, will be shipped via the distribution channels to the retailers. Thus, sellers will have the right product available at the proper time and place for their customers in a minimum of time when an order is placed for immediate delivery.

Before such a system can be operational, there is need for hardware and

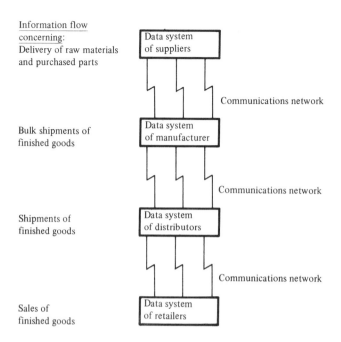

Information flow
concerning:
Delivery of raw materials
and purchased parts

Data system
of suppliers

Communications network

Bulk shipments of
finished goods

Data system
of manufacturer

Communications network

Shipments of
finished goods

Data system
of distributors

Communications network

Sales of
finished goods

Data system
of retailers

FIGURE 18-11. **A data system that extends beyond the firm—suppliers, manufacturer, distributors, and retailers are tied together by a sophisticated data communications network (manufacturer is the focal point of the data system).**

software to handle its complex relationships. Although data communication equipment is capable of handling computer-to-computer activities in a multiprocessing environment, the same cannot be said for operational intercompany programs. At this time, there are no master mathematical models that cross company boundaries for handling a supplier-manufacturer-distributor-retailer system whether it be order processing, production scheduling, or some other area. Considerable developmental work must be undertaken before this approach can become operational.

ELECTRONIC MONEY SYSTEM

Future computer developments in hardware, software, and systems make the feasibility of electronic money or the checkless society possible. The implementation of electronic money will drastically affect the banking industry. It will also have an effect on credit card companies, finance companies, oil companies, department stores, and mail-order houses, to name the major ones. Money transfers will be made instantaneously through electronic impulses and computers that utilize data communication channels. The present concept of money (passing paper from hand to hand and bank to bank) will become obsolete for the most part. However, paper money will be used to acquire small items and for those who will not accept

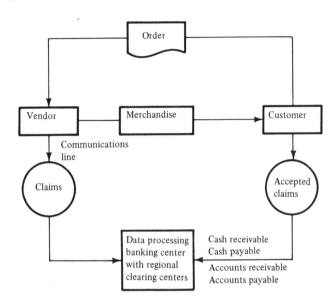

FIGURE 18-12. **Electronic money system utilizes a vast communications network.**

this new method of handling money.

An electronic money system would have all firms and institutions linked together in a massive data processing system. The entire system would be linked by a vast communications network (Figure 18-12). A data processing banking center would be employed to clear claims (equivalent to invoices) against accepted claims (equivalent to payments). Basically, the system would operate as follows. The vendor will submit invoices to one of the regional clearing centers. Similarly, the customer will submit a list of claims that he is willing to pay. Both the claims and the accepted claims will be transmitted to the data processing banking center in machine language. Payment could be made by means of a clearing operation. The net effect would be an elimination of checks.

An essential part of electronic money would be a firm's payroll check. Instead of the individual receiving his payroll check periodically, his salary less all legitimate deductions would be written electronically on tape. This tape from the company's office would be fed to a computer at the payee's bank and entered as a deposit. The computer at the individual's bank would automatically pay all his recurring bills (generally on a monthly basis), which include payments on a home, a car, insurance policies, department store accounts, and similar items. Likewise, the computer will transfer the excess bank balance to a savings account, mutual fund, stock account, or some other authorized account.

Under an electronic money system, the individual would handle daily transactions without physically utilizing paper money. This will be accomplished by having everyone carry a small plastic card that contains a voice pattern (Because a voice pattern is about as unique as one's fingerprints, the bank's computer will test for the correct one before accepting a charge for goods or services.) The seller will insert the plastic card in a reading device that will identify the customer at his bank via the computer. If sufficient cash is available in his account, the seller will ring up the sale, which will transfer the appropriate amount from the customer's account to the seller's account. If the customer has insufficient funds, the bank's computer can arrange a loan on the spot. On the other hand, if the customer prefers to let the bill run for a period of time, say to the end of the month (allowable by the seller), the transaction will be so recorded at the customer's bank. The seller will record the sale, but will not have the funds switched until the date agreed upon.

To determine the balance of one's account, the individual will slip his plastic card into a videophone terminal (installed in the home) and key in the appropriate code numbers. After a quick identity check of number and voice pattern, the computer will be ready for the request. The person will then enter a request to view his up-to-the-minute bank balance, which will be flashed on the viewing screen. The visual display unit will generally include: bank balance, savings account amount, mutual fund holdings, stock holdings, home mortgage balance, payments made in the last week, prearranged payments due in the next week, and projection of deposits from employer for payroll check. This current visual information would assist the individual in deciding whether or not additional large purchases would be made without jeopardizing his financial position.

Before this electronic money system can operate, there must be full acceptance of such a card by all banks of the country, which must be linked into one credit card system. This is necessary because a store that keeps its account at one bank must accept the card of a person who keeps his account at another. The use of an "Interbank Card" whereby all banks in the United States would honor each other's cards will be required. However, this problem is not as complex as trying to obtain public acceptance of this national system. For one thing, banks have been selling people on the idea of getting a receipt for everything they buy through cancelled checks. Now this concept must be undone. Generally, the psychological barriers are much greater than the technical problems. Perhaps in about twenty years all facets of the checkless society will have been assembled and operating in an efficient manner for most individuals in the United States.

CONCLUSION

Once real-time MIS has reached its height in the late 1970's and early 1980's, the next step in the evolving maturity of computer systems will be data-managed systems (data base management information systems). This approach requires a broader viewpoint of the organization structure because it is directed toward the higher level of the firm's management. Instead of being concerned primarily with the functional areas or the management of business functions at the divisional level, the accent will be on the management of the entire corporation at the corporate level. Standard data formats and procedures are needed to allow organization-wide use of shared data banks.

Newer MIS approaches are directed toward the total systems concept, the ultimate in automating data processing operations that are internal and external to the firm. Top management, with the aid of business systems analysts (well-versed in programming and operations research), will utilize game theory, Bayesian statistics, PERT networks, decision trees, and similar quantitative techniques to minimize the risk of doing business. Because the primary role of top management is to allocate scarce resources among the various factors of production, general managers, particularly in the future, must be able to recognize and assess alternative actions at the highest level in the firm. The dynamics of business, such as the complexity of a firm's mixes and the shifting of markets, dictate that top management must have the capability of assessing the effects of both internal plans and external business conditions on business objectives and operating performance. Top management's data-managed system, which utilizes complex and sophisticated OR models, must be capable of producing timely and accurate data on these critical issues.

The progression toward a data-managed system will not be accomplished in a short time, but rather over a long period. The development of this systems concept must be undertaken in a logical sequence. Basically, the approach must rely heavily upon the mathematical modeling concepts of operations research which result in overall optimization for the firm. The net result is that top management will be able to assess alternatives regarding the firm's future plans and select the optimum one. Considerable research and developmental work is required before this system can be implemented.

Going beyond the data-managed system, future system developments include data systems that extend beyond the firm, and an electronic money system. Even though there are presently many barriers to such systems, acceptance or rejection of these innovations revolve around the human element. To ignore the "people factor" in planning and implementing extremely advanced systems is completely unrealistic. System advancements do not operate in a vacuum, but are affected directly by the individuals who collectively form our society. In the final analysis, the key to successful newer and more complex systems is *people*.

QUESTIONS

1. What are the important differences between real-time MIS and data-managed systems?

2. How is a data-managed system more forward-looking than real-time MIS?

3. a. Explain what is meant by the "moving data base" concept.

   b. Is this concept the same as multiple data bases? Explain.

4. What type of mathematical models will be needed in a data-managed system environment?

5. Explain why the data-managed system approximates the total systems concept while a real-time MIS does not.

6. What affect will hardware developments have on data-managed systems?

7. What affect will software advancements have on data-managed systems?

8. A president of a leading computer manufacturer stated that he was "convinced that the future of electronic data processing lies in providing time-sharing services and selling computer terminals and software to specific industries to perform specific functions. By linking these terminals to its giant computer, [firm name] could make them available to small companies as well as to the big companies that now use them." Evaluate this point of view in terms of future management information systems.

9. Enumerate the essential characteristics of a data-managed system that crosses company boundaries.

10. Will our economy ever operate 100 percent with electronic money sometime in the future? Explain.

11. What affect will new system concepts have on the individual within the firm and on the firm itself? Explain thoroughly.

REFERENCES

Anderson, D. R., and Williams, T. A., "Viewing MIS from the Top," *Journal of Systems Management,* July, 1973.

Bruun, R. J., "When Will Core, Drum, and Disk Systems Be Just a Memory?" *Infosystems,* May, 1973.

Buckelew, D. P., and. Penniman, W. D., "The Outlook for Interactive Television," *Datamation,* August, 1974.

Carne, E. B., "Telecommunications: Its Impact on Business," *Harvard Business Review,* July-August, 1972.

Caruth, D. L., "How Will Total Systems Affect the Corporation?," *Journal of Systems Management,* February, 1969..

Cox, E. B., and Giese, P. E., "Now It's the 'Less-Check Society'," *Harvard Business Review,* November-December, 1972.

Haavind, R. C., "Adding People to the MIS Loop,"*Computer Decisions,* July, 1972.

———, "The Many Forces of Microprogramming," *Computer Decisions,* September, 1971.

Hopewell, L., "Trends in Data Communications," *Datamation,* August, 1973.

Houston, R., "Trillion Bit Memories," *Datamation,* October, 1973.

Kamman, A. B., "The Use of Display Terminals for Business Applications," *Computers and Automation,* May, 1970.

Kaufman, F., "Data Systems That Cross Company Boundaries," *Harvard Business Review,* January-February, 1966.

Lape, W. A., "The Home Office of the Future," *Journal of Systems Management,* April, 1972.

Lipis, A. H., "Electronic Funds Transfer Helps Banks Fight Check Deluge," *Computer Decisions,* November, 1972.

Mitroff, I. I., Nelson, J., and Mason, R. O., "On Management Myth Information Systems," *Management Science,* December, 1974.

Murdick, R. G., and Ross, J. E., *Information Systems for Modern Management.* Englewood Cliffs, N.J.: Prentice-Hall, Inc., 1971, Chap. 16.

———, "Future Management Information Systems," *Journal of Systems Management,* April, 1972.

O'Brien, J. J., *Management Information Systems.* New York: Van Nostrand Reinhold Co., 1971, Chap. 8.

Poliski, I., "The 'Dana Today' Show," *Business Automation,* August, 1971.

Ross, D. T., "Fourth-Generation Software: A Building-Block Science Replaces Hand-Crafted Art," *Computer Decisions,* April, 1970.

Walker, P. D., and Catalano, S. D., "Where Do We Go from Here With MIS?" *Computer Decisions,* September, 1969.

——, "Next in MIS: 'Data Managed' System Design," *Computer Decisions,* November, 1969.

Wineke, J. K., and Speigel, M., "Generation IV: The Shape of Systems to Come," *Computer Decisions,* October, 1970.

Withington, F. G., "The Next (and Last?) Generation," *Datamation,* May, 1972.

——, "Trends in MIS Technology," *Datamation,* February, 1970.

Zani, W. M., "The Computer Utility," *California Management Review,* Vol. XIII, No. 1.

——, "Beyond 1984: A Technology Forecast," *Datamation,* January, 1975.

APPENDICES

APPENDIX A

Simulation

Simulation is capable of evaluating overall operations (macro) or a specific subsystem or some part of it (micro).[1] It has been defined as the use of a system model that has the desired characteristics of reality in order to reproduce the essence of the actual operation. However, such a definition fails to include all of its fundamental characteristics—namely, the use of mathematical models, computers, statistics or stochastic processes, facts, assumptions, and alternative courses of action. A more inclusive definition of simulation is:

> A quantiative technique used for evaluating alternative courses of action based upon facts and assumptions with a computerized mathematical model in order to represent actual decision making under conditions of uncertainty.

[1]Refer to: Robert J. Thierauf and Robert C. Klekamp, *Decision Making Through Operations Research,* (New York: John Wiley & Sons, Inc., 1975), Chapter 14.

A macro-oriented financial corporate planning simulation model, for example, depicts the important relationships among the elements of a firm's financial structure. The total model consists of a set of submodels, one for each of the major subsystems that directly affects the firm's financial structure. Each of these subsystems has its output expressed mathematically. The overall model follows a logical sequence of financial operations—that is, the output of certain submodels forms the input for others. These input/output relationships reflect the cause and effect factors that exist within the firm. In defining cause and effect in the model, there are two important considerations—the intermodel relationship and the intramodel detail. The former refers to the factors that determine the ordering or relationships between the submodels; the latter refers to the level of detail essential in structuring one of the submodels. The significance of the intermodel relationship can be demonstrated by relating marketing to manufacturing. The marketing submodel must specifically describe the form in which marketing demands are translated into production requirements. Any decision made by the marketing subsystem which affects the demand rate will influence in varying degrees each of the manufacturing plants, even though the decision might affect only one product within a product line.

The level of detail necessary in this corporate planning model can be illustrated by tracing the impact of an input change. Suppose a change in the sales force for the firm's marketing efforts is to be evaluated. The demand forecast must be structured as a function of direct selling by salesmen. Also, for this change, the input of the demand change on equipment, service, revenue, cost of sales, and finished goods inventory must be evaluated. The change in demand, together with an inventory policy, permits the model to determine cost of sales and finished goods inventory. The same change in demand, together with an inventory policy, allows us to determine the resultant requirements of manufacturing, which is an input in calculating the in-process inventory. Determination of in-process inventories permits us to calculate the subassembly and parts requirements for manufacturing. These requirements are then related to variable and fixed costs of manufacturing, which affect the firm's ability to absorb burden. Marketing expenses, commissions, freight out, and similar items are brought into the analysis. The change in sales manpower will affect net profits, federal income taxes, accounts receivable, and the ability to pay off short-term and long-term debts. Likewise, it will ultimately determine dividends, a function of net profits after federal income taxes. Thus, the proposed marketing change is finally reflected in terms of the firm's cash flow. An overall flowchart that is capable of simulating the above changes is shown in Figure A-1.

APPENDIX B

Exponential Smoothing

The next period forecasts, unadjusted for seasonal and trend factors, are the starting point for exponential smoothing analysis.[1] The basic exponential smoothing formula is: new sales forecast for the coming period equals A times the actual

[1]Refer to Op. cit., Chapter 11, pp. 374-375.

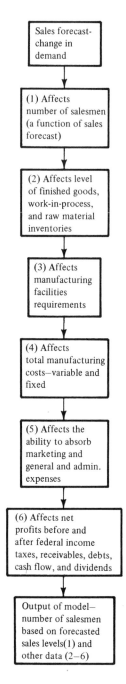

**FIGURE A-1.   A corporate planning flowchart that depicts the simula-
tion of a change in the firm's sales force.**

sales during the current period plus (1 -A) times the forecasted sales made in the current period. This formula is written as:

$$\bar{S}_t = AS_t + (1 - A)\bar{S}_{t-1} \qquad \text{Equation B-1}$$

where $0 \leqslant A \leqslant 1$

> $\bar{S}_t$ = new sales forecast (in units) for the coming period, made at the end of period t
>
> A = the weighting factor, some number between 0 and 1
>
> S_t = actual sales for period t (in units)
>
> $\bar{S}_{t-1}$ = sales forecast (in units) made in period $t - 1$ or in the previous period

Equation B-1 assumes that average sales over the year will be approximately constant or there will be no upward or downward trend and no seasonal influence. However, for the Consumer Products Corporation, the forecast method will be adjusted for both of these possibilities.

Seasonal factors where B is the seasonal smoothing parameter are included in the following formula:

$$F_t = B\left(\frac{S_t}{\bar{S}_t}\right) + (1 - B)F_{t-N} \qquad \text{Equation B-2}$$

where $0 \leqslant B \leqslant 1$

> F_t = seasonal factor for period t (ratio of actual sales to smoothed sales)
>
> B = seasonal smoothing factor, some number between 0 and 1
>
> S_t = actual sales for period t (in units)
>
> $\bar{S}_t$ = nonseasonal new sales forecast (in units) for the coming period, made at the end of period t
>
> N = number of periods for seasonal effect

Trend adjustment is applicable if forecasts for the whole economy or the firm suggests that sales prospects may steadily improve or decline. Adjustment for this trend can be made by adding a small amount to each forecast if there is a rising trend or subtracting a small amount if there is a declining trend. Experimentation with the weighting factor (C), used in trend extension, has shown that good results are obtained when it is in the neighborhood of A. The basic trend adjustment formula is:

$$R_t = C(\bar{S}_t - \bar{S}_{t-1}) + (1 - C)R_{t-1} \qquad \text{Equation B-3}$$

where $0 \leqslant C \leqslant 1$

> R_t = the trend adjustment (in units)
>
> C = trend weighting factor, some number between 0 and 1
>
> $\bar{S}_t$ = nontrend new sales forecast (in units) for the next period, made at the end of period t

$\bar{S}_{t-1}$ = nontrend sales forecast (in units) for period t made in period $t-1$ or in the previous period

R_{t-1} = trend adjustment (in units) for period t made in period $t-1$ or in the previous period

After solving for values $\bar{S}_t$, F_t, and R_t, the last step in forecasting sales for the firm's many products is to compute the revised forecast ($\bar{S}_t$ is adjusted for seasonal and trend adjustments) by using the formula:

$$\bar{\bar{S}}_{t,T} = (\bar{\bar{S}}_t + TR_t)F_{t-N+T} \qquad \text{Equation B-4}$$

where $T = 1, 2, ... N$.

Forecasts can now be produced on a quarterly basis.

APPENDIX C

Pricing Model (Differentiation)

The demand and selling price relationship (shown in Figure 9-8) can be expressed in terms of an equation, the first step in solving the pricing model (differentiation).[1] Plotting the data discloses in Figure C-1 that there is a linear demand function which can be expressed as:

$$y = a + bx \qquad \text{Equation C-1}$$

In the equation, y equals demand and x equals selling price, while a represents the intercept (the value of y when x equals zero) of the line and parameter b is the slope of the line. Substituting u and s for y and x, respectively, and 250,000 and $-25,000$ for a and b, respectively, in the foregoing equation, the resulting formula for demand and price is as follows:

$$u = 250,000 - 25,000s \qquad \text{Equation C-2}$$

The cost function per unit can be expressed as follows:

$$c = \frac{\$300,000}{u} + \$.80 \qquad \text{Equation C-3}$$

where c = cost per unit
u = total estimated demand per year in units

The next step is to determine an equation for total new-product costs—that is, a relationship between total fixed and total variable costs. This can be accomplished by converting Equation C-3 to a total cost equation (multiply both sides by the term u). The resulting equation is:

[1] Ibid., Chapter 10.

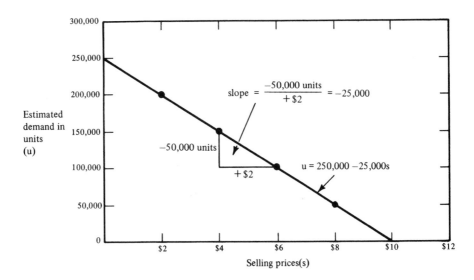

FIGURE C-1. Forecasted demand—selling price relationship.

$$C = \$300,000 + \$.80u$$

where C = total costs or $c \cdot u$

Substituting Equation C-2 (250,000 − 25,000s) for u in the above equation, the total cost equation becomes:

$$C = 500,000 - 20,000s \qquad\qquad \text{Equation C-4}$$

Now that the total cost (C) equation has been developed, we still need an expression for the firm's total sales (S). This can be readily developed:

$$S = u \cdot s \qquad\qquad \text{Equation C-5}$$

Equation C-5 defines total sales as the product of unit sales multiplied by unit price.

Combining Equations C-2 and C-5, the total sales (S) equation is as follows:

$$S = u \cdot s \qquad\qquad \text{Equation C-5}$$

$$u = 250,000 - 25,000s \qquad\qquad \text{Equation C-2}$$
$$S = (250,000 - 25,000s)s$$

$$S = 250,000 - 25,000s^2 \qquad\qquad \text{Equation C-6}$$

Equation C-6 represents a quadratic rather than a linear relation. Its curve is a parabola and symmetric with respect to the $5 per-unit selling price. This means as the unit price declines, the total sales amount will increase until a maximum point is reached, and will begin to decline thereafter.

Having developed Equations C-4 and C-6, we can construct a mathematical model for the optimum pricing policy that will maximize the firm's total profits. Maximum profits can be derived from the following expression:

$$P = S - C \qquad\qquad \text{Equation C-7}$$

where P = total profits
S = total sales
C = total costs

Now that all necessary equations have been developed, the final step is to substitute Equations C-4 and C-6 into Equation C-7. The profit equation that will determine an optimum selling price is:

$$P = S - C \qquad\qquad \text{Equation C-7}$$
$$P = (250{,}000s - 25{,}000s^2) - (500{,}000 - 20{,}000s)$$
$$P = 250{,}000s - 25{,}000s^2 - 500{,}000 + 20{,}000s$$
$$P = -25{,}000s^2 + 270{,}000s - 500{,}000$$

$$\frac{dP}{ds} = -50{,}000s + 270{,}000 = 0$$

$$50{,}000s = 270{,}000$$
$$s = \$5.40$$

In this solution, the basic concept of differential calculus is used—that is, we are concerned with the rate of change in the firm's profits (P) associated with a unit change in the firm's selling price (s). However, by making the rate of change equal to zero, we will be solving for the maximum profits with respect to an optimum pricing policy for the firm.

If the solution is not graphed (Figure 9-9), how can we be sure that the optimum selling price has been determined? Perhaps we have solved for a minimum selling price. This question can be resolved by utilizing a second derivative test as follows:

$$\frac{d^2 P}{d s^2} = -50{,}000 + 0$$

Because the second term becomes zero for its second derivative, the only remaining term is the first one. When the first term is differentiated for the second time, it becomes a - 50,000. A negative value, when evaluated from the results of the first derivative being set to zero, indicates that the slope has reached its maximum point and is declining. (This concept is in agreement with Figure 9-9.) Otherwise, if the sign were plus for the integer, it would have indicated an error in the calculations or we have solved for a minimum sales price. A positive answer in a second derivative test (evaluated for the result of the first derivative set equal to zero) indicates that the slope has reached its minimum point and is tending upward.

Having determined the optimum selling price mathematically, the total maximum profits can be calculated for the product by substituting the value for s ($5.40) in Equation C-7 (modified) as follows:

$$P = -25,000s^2 + 270,000s - 500,000$$
$$P = -25,000\,(5.40)^2 + 270,000\,(5.40) - 500,000$$
$$P = -729,000 + 1,458,000 - 500,000$$
$$P = \$229,000$$

Profit before federal income taxes based on sales and cost estimates is $229,000 the first year, a very favorable return on sales. In addition to profits, management might want to know the number of units that it could sell at a unit price of $5.40. This is calculated to be 115,000 units as follows:

$$u = 250,000 - 25,000s \qquad \text{Equation C-2}$$
$$u = 250,000 - 25,000(5.40)$$
$$u = 250,000 - 135,000$$
$$u = 115,000 \text{ units}$$

APPENDIX D

PERT/Cost

The normal and crash estimates (time and cost as seen in Figure 10-7) are necessary prerequisites before applying the procedures of PERT/Cost.[1] The network shown in Figure D-1 is a starting point for crashing the program one week at a time to 19.5 weeks. The beginning of the compression process is to determine the critical path, which is 1-4-6-7. In order to shorten the time factor by 1 week to 22.5 weeks, it is clear that one activity on the critical path must be shortened because it determines the total project time. Reviewing the incremental costs for the critical activities in Figure D-1, activity 6-7 has the lowest incremental cost of $3,750 versus $7,500 and $15,000 for activities 1-4 and 4-6, respectively. This is the selected activity to reduce the project time at the least additional cost. The revised PERT network is illustrated in Figure D-2, giving a total project cost of $206,750 ($203,000 + $3,750).

This procedure is repeated for subsequent PERT networks until the total project time has been reduced as far as possible (to 19 ½ weeks). The PERT network that reduces total project time to 21 ½ weeks crashes activity 6-7 again, thereby adding $3,750 to the prior cost ($206,750) for a total of $210,500. When crashing the network down to 20 ½ weeks, there is still the same critical path (1-4-6-7). This means that activity 1-4, costing $7,500, must be shortened. Total project costs at the 20 ½ weeks level is $218,000 ($210,500 + $7,500). The crashing process at this level now produces two critical paths or 1-4-6-7 and 1-3-6-7. For this condition, one activity on each critical path must be shortened—4-6 ($15,000) and 1-3 ($2,500), respectively. The total project cost is now $235,500 ($218,000 +

[1] Ibid., Chapter 5.

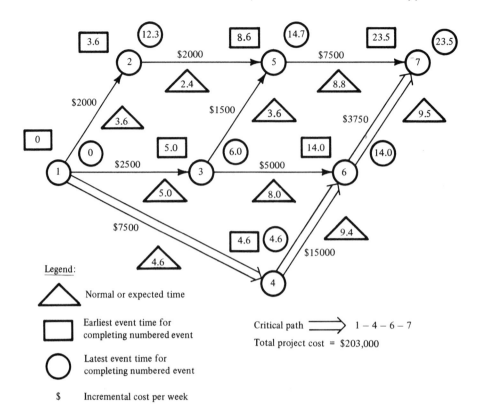

FIGURE D-1. Normal time-cost PERT network for 23½ weeks.

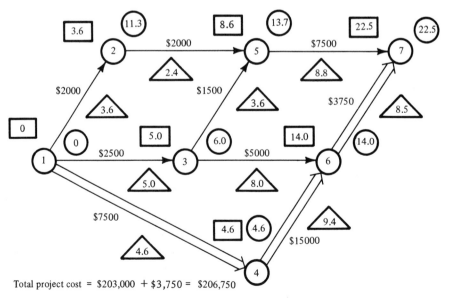

Total project cost = $203,000 + $3,750 = $206,750

FIGURE D-2. Time-cost PERT network for 22½ weeks.

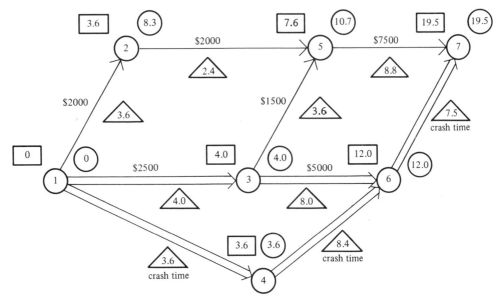

Total project cost = $235,500

FIGURE D-3.   Time-cost PERT network for 19½ weeks–modified crash program.

$15,000 + $2,500) and time is 19 ½ weeks, shown in Figure D-3. Inspection of activities on the critical path 1-4-6-7 indicates that we have crashed them as far as possible in terms of time. Thus, the crashing process is complete.

APPENDIX E

Linear Programming (Simplex Method)

The optimum solution to the linear programming problem (set forth in Figure 11-14) can be solved by applying the iterative procedures of the simplex method.[1] Initially, it is helpful to structure the problem, as in Figure E-1, such that the variables need not be rewritten each time. Instead, the coefficients of the variables are utilized in the procedures set forth below for succeeding tableaus.

The matrix inversion procedures for the first tableau (Figure E-1) and all succeeding tableaus of this minimization problem are as follows:

1. Determine the optimum column or the largest negative column value in the last row shown (X_{14} per Figure E-1).
2. Determine the replaced (old) row by dividing the quantity column by the intersectional or column elements for the column selected in step (1). Select the lowest quantity row (X_{31}) as the replaced row. Note: ignore all rows that are divided by zero because they are not feasible solutions.

[1] Ibid., Chapter 6

C_1	Product Mix	Quantity	$\$6$ X_1	$\$7$ X_2	$\$5$ X_3	$\$5$ X_4	$\$8$ X_5	$\$6$ X_6	$\$5$ X_7	$\$10$ X_8	$\$5$ X_9	$\$4$ X_{10}	$\$5$ X_{11}	$\$4$ X_{12}	$\$3$ X_{13}	$\$2$ X_{14}
$\$0$	X_{22}	700,000	1	1	1	1	1	1	1	0	0	0	0	0	0	0
$\$0$	X_{23}	400,000	0	0	0	0	0	0	0	1	1	1	1	1	1	1
$\$0$	X_{24}	1,000,000	0	0	0	0	0	0	0	0	0	0	0	0	0	0
$\$M$	X_{25}	100,000	1	0	0	0	0	0	0	1	0	0	0	0	0	0
$\$M$	X_{26}	200,000	0	1	0	0	0	0	0	0	1	0	0	0	0	0
$\$M$	X_{27}	450,000	0	0	1	0	0	0	0	0	0	1	0	0	0	0
$\$M$	X_{28}	400,000	0	0	0	1	0	0	0	0	0	0	1	0	0	0
$\$M$	X_{29}	200,000	0	0	0	0	1	0	0	0	0	0	0	1	0	0
$\$M$	X_{30}	350,000	0	0	0	0	0	1	0	0	0	0	0	0	1	0
$\$M$	X_{31}	300,000	0	0	0	0	0	0	1	0	0	0	0	0	0	1
	Z_j	2,000,000M	$\$M$	$\$M$	$\$M$	$\$M$	$\$M$	$\$M$	$\$M$	$\$M$	$\$M$	$\$M$	$\$M$	$\$M$	$\$M$	$\$M$
	$C_j - Z_j$		$\$6{-}M$	$\$7{-}M$	$\$5{-}M$	$\$5{-}M$	$\$8{-}M$	$\$6{-}M$	$\$5{-}M$	$\$10{-}M$	$\$5{-}M$	$\$4{-}M$	$\$5{-}M$	$\$4{-}M$	$\$3{-}M$	$\$2{-}M$

C_1	Product Mix	Quantity	$\$9$ X_{15}	$\$5$ X_{16}	$\$3$ X_{17}	$\$6$ X_{18}	$\$5$ X_{19}	$\$9$ X_{20}	$\$4$ X_{21}	$\$0$ X_{22}	$\$0$ X_{23}	$\$0$ X_{24}	$\$M$ X_{25}	$\$M$ X_{26}	$\$M$ X_{27}	$\$M$ X_{28}	$\$M$ X_{29}	$\$M$ X_{30}	$\$M$ X_{31}
$\$0$	X_{22}	700,000	0	0	0	0	0	0	0	1	0	0	0	0	0	0	0	0	0
$\$0$	X_{23}	400,000	0	0	0	0	0	0	0	0	1	0	0	0	0	0	0	0	0
$\$0$	X_{24}	1,000,000	1	1	1	1	1	1	1	0	0	1	0	0	0	0	0	0	0
$\$M$	X_{25}	100,000	1	0	0	0	0	0	0	0	0	0	1	0	0	0	0	0	0
$\$M$	X_{26}	200,000	0	1	0	0	0	0	0	0	0	0	0	1	0	0	0	0	0
$\$M$	X_{27}	450,000	0	0	1	0	0	0	0	0	0	0	0	0	1	0	0	0	0
$\$M$	X_{28}	400,000	0	0	0	1	0	0	0	0	0	0	0	0	0	1	0	0	0
$\$M$	X_{29}	200,000	0	0	0	0	1	0	0	0	0	0	0	0	0	0	1	0	0
$\$M$	X_{30}	350,000	0	0	0	0	0	1	0	0	0	0	0	0	0	0	0	1	0
$\$M$	X_{31}	300,000	0	0	0	0	0	0	1	0	0	0	0	0	0	0	0	0	1
	Z_j	2,000,000M	$\$M$	$\$M$	$\$M$	$\$M$	$\$M$	$\$M$	$\$M$	$\$0$	$\$0$	$\$0$	$\$M$	$\$M$	$\$M$	$\$M$	$\$M$	$\$M$	$\$M$
	$C_j - Z_j$		$\$9{-}M$	$\$5{-}M$	$\$3{-}M$	$\$6{-}M$	$\$5{-}M$	$\$9{-}M$	$\$4{-}M$	$\$0$	$\$0$	$\$0$	$\$0$	$\$0$	$\$0$	$\$0$	$\$0$	$\$0$	$\$0$

FIGURE E-1. First simplex tableau for linear programming problem (per Figure 11-14).

3. Determine the replacing (new) row values by dividing each value in the row (X_{31}) by the intersectional element (1). In this case, the row values remain unchanged because all values have been divided by the value one. However, the variable is changed from (X_{31} to X_{14}).

4. Determine new values for all remaining rows (X_{22} through X_{30}) by utilizing the following formula:

$$\begin{pmatrix} \text{Elements in the} \\ \text{old row} \end{pmatrix} - \left[\begin{pmatrix} \text{Intersectional} \\ \text{element of old} \\ \text{row} \end{pmatrix} \times \begin{pmatrix} \text{Corresponding} \\ \text{elements in} \\ \text{replacing row} \end{pmatrix} \right] = \begin{pmatrix} \text{New row} \end{pmatrix}$$

Those rows whose intersectional elements are zero have the same values in the next table.

In the second tableau, the above procedures are repeated:

1. Determine the optimum column (X_{13} or X_{17} because the other one will be used in the next tableau).
2. Determine the replaced row (X_{30}).
3. Determine the replacing row values (X_{13}).
4. Determine new values for remaining rows (X_{22} through X_{29} and X_{14}).

The above procedures are repeated for all remaining tableaus until all final row values are pluses and/or zeros.

Based upon the final simplex tableau utilizing the foregoing procedures, the lowest-cost production quotas by manufacturing plants for the next three months are as follows:

Factory - Los Angeles:

Product Group 1	100,000 units
Product Group 4	400,000 units
Product Group 7	100,000 units

Factory - Minneapolis:

Product Group 6	350,000 units
Product Group 7	50,000 units

Factory - Philadelphia:

Product Group 2	200,000 units
Product Group 3	450,000 units
Product Group 5	200,000 units
Product Group 7	150,000 units
	2,000,000 units

APPENDIX F

Markov Analysis

The starting point for Markov analysis of the first order is calculating the current rates of retentions, gains, and losses.[1] The calculations for the matrix of transition probabilities (per Figure 17-8) are as follows:

Type of Personnel

	A	*B*	*C*	*D*	*Period Two*
A	175/220 = .796	40/300 = .133	0/230 = 0	10/250 = .040	225
B	20/220 = .091	230/300 = .767	25/230 = .109	15/250 = .060	290
C	10/220 = .046	5/300 = .017	205/230 = .891	10/250 = .040	230
D	15/220 = .067	25/300 = .083	0/230 = 0	215/250 = .860	255
Period One	220	300	230	250	1000

For help in reading the rows: row 2 indicates that highly technical personnel are retained at a .767 rate while gaining .091 from professional personnel (caused by declining skills of older personnel) and .109 from technical personnel and .060 from semi-technical personnel. It should be noted that semi-technical personnel enter at their respective levels, but acquire more formal education and on-the-job training, enabling them to rise to a higher level. Reading down the second column, the retention rate of highly technical personnel is again .767, while .133, .017, and .083 of its employees are lost to professional, technical, and semi-technical positions, respectively. In effect, the basic gain and loss relationships can be observed.

The foregoing matrix calculations have focused on the changes from one period to the next period—that is, from one month to the next. What is needed from the above analysis is an equilibrium state that can be reached in the future. Specifically, what are the final or equilibrium personnel percents approximately one year hence? By utilizing the above matrix, the following equations are developed:

$$A = .796A + .133B + .000C + .040D$$
$$B = .091A + .767B + .109C + .060D$$
$$C = .046A + .017B + .891C + .040D$$
$$D = .067A + .083B + .000C + .860D$$
$$1.0 = A + B + C + D$$

The final equation is employed to show that the four personnel categories equal 1.0.

Because there are similar terms on both sides of the equation, the resulting equations which show the gains and losses for each personnel category are as follows:

$$0 = -.204A + .133B + .040D \qquad \text{Equation F-1}$$
$$0 = .091A - .233B + .109C + .060D \qquad \text{Equation F-2}$$

[1]Ibid., Chapter 9.

$$0 = .046A + .017B - .109C + .040D \qquad \text{Equation F-3}$$
$$0 = .067A + .083B - .140D \qquad \text{Equation F-4}$$
$$1.0 = A + B + C + D \qquad \text{Equation F-5}$$

Referring to these five equations in which there are four unknowns, it is necessary to drop one equation other than the last one in order to have a one to one ratio between the number of equations and the number of unknowns. The reason one equation can be dropped is that the equations are mathematically interrelated—that is, the sum of -.204A (Equation F-1), + .091A (Equation F-2), + .046A (Equation F-3), and + .067A (Equation F-4) equals zero. The ability to sum A values is also applicable to columns B, C, and D.

Solving for equilibrium (approximately one year hence) by simultaneous equations (or determinants) yields the following values:

A - Professional personnel	22.8%
B - Highly technical personnel	26.8%
C - Technical personnel	23.7%
D - Semi-technical personnel	26.7%
	100.0%

APPENDIX G BIBLIOGRAPHY

MANAGEMENT INFORMATION SYSTEMS

Blumenthal, Sherman C., *Management Information Systems.* Englewood Cliffs, N.J.: Prentice-Hall, 1969.

Boochino, William A., *Management Information Systems, Tools and Techniques.* Englewood Cliffs, N.J.: Prentice-Hall, 1972.

Boutel, Wayne S., *Computer Oriented Business Systems.* Englewood Cliffs, N. J.: Prentice-Hall, 1973.

Burch, John G. and Felix R. Strater, *Information Systems: Theory and Practice.* Santa Barbara: Hamilton, 1974.

Coleman, R. J., and M. J. Riley, *MIS: Management Dimensions.* San Francisco: Holden-Day, Inc., 1973.

Couger, Daniel J., *Computer-Based Management Information Systems.* New York: Wiley, 1968.

Cushing, Barry E., *Accounting Information Systems and Business Organizations.* Reading, Mass.: Addison-Wesley, 1974.

Davis, Gordon B., *Introduction to Management Information Systems: Conceptual Foundations, Structure and Development.* New York: McGraw-Hill, 1974.

Dearden, John, and F. Warren McFarlan, *Management Information Systems.* Homewood, Ill.: Irwin, 1966.

Eliason, Alan L., and Kent D., Kitts, *Business Computer Systems and Applications.* Chicago: SRA, 1974.

Enger, Norma L., *Putting MIS to Work: Managing the Management Information System.* New York: American Management Association, 1969.

Glans, Thomas B. et al., *Management Systems.* New York: Holt, Rinehart and Winston, 1968.

Hartman, W., H. Matthes, and A. Proeme, *Management Information Systems Handbook.* New York: McGraw-Hill, 1970.

Head, Robert V., *Manager's Guide to Management Information Systems.* Englewood Cliffs, N.J.: Prentice-Hall, 1972.

Johnson, Richard A., Fremont E. Kast, and James E. Rosenzweig, *The Theory and Management of Systems.* New York: McGraw-Hill, 1973.

Kelly, Joseph F., *Computerized Management Information Systems.* New York: Macmillan, 1970.

Krauss, Leonard I., *Computer-Based Management Information Systems.* New York: American Management Association, 1970.

Martino, R. L., *Management Information Systems.* New York: McGraw-Hill, 1969.

———, *MIS—Methodology.* New York: Mc-Graw-Hill, 1970.

Massey, L. Daniel, *Management Information Systems.* Braintree, Mass.: D. H. Mark, 1969.

Murdick, Robert G., and Joel E. Ross, *Information Systems for Modern Management.* Englewood Cliffs, N.J.: Prentice-Hall, 1975.

O'Brien, James J., *Management Information Systems.* New York: Van Nostrand, 1970.

Phillippakis, Andreas S., and Leonard J. Kazmier, *Information System Through COBOL,* New York: McGraw-Hill, 1974.

Prince, Thomas R., *Information Systems for Management Planning and Control.* Homewood, Ill.: Irwin, 1970.

Ross, Joel E., *Management by Information System.* Englewood Cliffs, N.J.: Prentice-Hall, 1970.

Schoderbek, Peter P., *Management Systems.* New York: Wiley, 1971.

Stimler, Saul, *Real-Time Data Processing Systems.* New York: McGraw-Hill, 1969.

Voich, Don, Homer J. Mottice, and William A. Shrode, *Information Systems for Operations and Management.* Cincinnati, Ohio: South-Western, 1975.

SYSTEMS ANALYSIS AND DESIGN

Alexander, M. J., *Information Systems Analysis: Theory and Applications.* Chicago: SRA, 1974.

Churchman, C. West, *The Systems Approach.* New York: Dell, 1968.

Cleland, David I., and William R. King, *Systems Analysis and Project Management.* New York: McGraw-Hill, 1968.

Clifton, H. D., *Data Processing Systems Design.* Princeton, N.J.: Auerbach, 1974.

Couger, J. Daniel, and Robert W. Knapp, *System Analysis Techniques.* New York: John Wiley, 1974.

Hare, Van Court, *Systems Analysis: A Diagnostic Approach.* New York: Harcourt, Brace & World, 1967.

Hopeman, Richard J., *Systems Analysis and Operations Management.* Columbus, Ohio: Merrill, 1969.

Joslin, Edward O., *Analysis, Design and Selection of Computer Systems.* Arlington, Va.: College Readings, 1971.

Lott, Richard W., *Systems Analysis.* San Francisco: Canfield Press, 1971.

Lyon, John K., *An Introduction to Data Base Design.* New York: Wiley 1972.

Martin, James, *Design of Real-Time Computer Systems.* Englewood Cliffs, N.J.: Prentice-Hall, 1972.

——, *Systems Analysis for Data Transmission.* Englewood Cliffs, N.J.: Prentice-Hall, 1972.

Matthews, Don Q., *The Design of the Management Information System.* Princeton, N.J.: Auerbach, 1971.

McMillan, Claude, and Richard F. Gonzales, *Systems Analysis: A Computer Approach to Decision Models.* Homewood, Ill.: Irwin, 1968.

Optner, Stanford L., *Systems Analysis for Business and Industrial Problem Solving.* Englewood Cliffs, N.J.: Prentice-Hall, 1968.

Rothstein, Michael F., *Guide to the Design of Real-Time Systems.* New York: Wiley, 1970.

Stone, Harold S., *Introduction to Computer Organization and Data Structures.* New York: McGraw-Hill, 1972.

Yourdon, Edward, *Real-Time Systems Design.* Cambridge, Mass.: Information Systems Institute, 1967.

——, *Design of On-Line Computer Systems.* Englewood Cliffs, N.J.: Prentice-Hall, 1972.

INDEX